THE MITZVOT
The Commandments and Their Rationale

THE MITZVOT

The Commandments and Their Rationale

by

Abraham Chill

BLOCH PUBLISHING COMPANY
New York

Published in the Western Hemisphere by
BLOCH PUBLISHING COMPANY
915 Broadway, New York, N.Y. 10010

ISBN 0-8197-0376-1
Library of Congress Catalog Card Number 74-14055

Set, printed and bound by Keterpress Enterprises, Jerusalem

Printed in Israel

TO LIBBIE

I remember you for the devotion of your youth,	זכרתי לך חסד נעוריך
the love of your bridal state,	אהבת כלולותיך
how you accompanied me. . . .	לכתך אחרי . . .
(Jeremiah 2:2)	(ירמי׳ ב״ב)

CONTENTS

FOREWORD

Judaism has always stressed the observance of the divine commandments as a prime discipline incumbent upon every Jew. The reasons for the observance were only secondary and, as such, the interpretation and meaning thereof may have assumed different aspects throughout the ages. The traditional commentators—biblical, rabbinic and kabbalistic—all sought meaning in the *mitzvot* in accord with the dictum: לא רצה הקב״ה אלא לזכות את ישראל לפיכך הרבה להם תורה ומצוות—"The Almighty sought to give merit to [or refine] Israel; hence He multiplied for them the Torah commandments." A clear understanding of this multiplicity and the manner in which the Sages gave meaning and value to the *mitzvot* is the essence of the present volume by Rabbi Abraham Chill. He has culled from many basic biblical exegetes, rabbinic commentators and codifiers, mystic-kabbalistic authors and Responsa authorities. His work presents in digest form each and every perspective of every one of the 613 divine commandments and, in clear style and comprehension, makes the reader part of the whole gamut of thinking in Oral Law perception. His magnum opus can well be used as a weekly study of the biblical portion, emphasizing each *mitzvah* therein, or in adult education classes as a text-book of the rationale of the divine commandments and the metamorphosis of their interpretation. It will serve as a revealing light to the inquisitive youth seeking to know the why's and wherefore's of the *mitzvot* and also for the general reader probing into the great treasures of Jewish interpretation of our daily lore and practice. Rabbi Chill's endeavor is to be highly commended and recommended.

Sidney B. Hoenig
Dean, Bernard Revel Graduate School
Yeshiva University

PREFACE

No author works in splendid isolation. Whatever he may achieve he owes to the influences, direct and indirect, which have acted upon him and accompanied him throughout his life.

In this spirit I wish to acknowledge my debt of gratitude first of all to my parents, Moshe Hayim and Rose Chill of blessed memory, the inspiring teachers and guides of my youth, who first taught me the value of Torah and *mitzvot* and whose meticulously Jewish lives and noble example have been an inspiration to me throughout the years. Whatever I have achieved or may achieve, I owe first and foremost to them.

Next I wish to record my deepest appreciation of my dear wife, Libbie, who has been a tower of strength and an unfailing source of encouragement and without whom this work would never have been completed. She has given abundantly of her patience, energy, and talent throughout the latter stages in the preparation of this book. I must thank also my devoted children, who have not only given me moral support but have also been a valuable stimulus to pursue this work.

To Rabbi David Cohen I wish to express my abiding gratitude for his devoted, invaluable, and most erudite counsel. Thanks go to Rabbi Dr. S. M. Lehrman, formerly of London and now of Jerusalem, for his most helpful editorial advice. Nor should I omit a word of acknowledgment to Mr. E. J. Frank and Rabbi Dr. Aaron Rothkoff who have rendered editorial assistance in the final stages.

"How great is the reward to them who perform generous acts"
(*Yalkut Shimoni,* Ruth)

INTRODUCTION

What is a *mitzvah* and what is its fundamental intent? It would be simple and uncomplicated if we could define the *mitzvot* merely as "commandments." We could even go a step further and add the word "God"—God's commandments. This oversimplification is unacceptable as much more is involved in the definition of a *mitzvah*. The Psalmist put it eloquently when he said: "From the depths of my being, I hold communion with Thee, O God." The proper performance of a *mitzvah* is a soul-stirring experience which raises the Jew to unprecedented spiritual heights in his urge to seek out and communicate with God. Judah Halevi maintained that the *mitzvot* elevate a person to the sublime crest of prophecy.[1]

Naḥmanides saw in the *mitzvah* a purging-agent that cleanses the Jew of his frivolous and vicious vagaries and caprices.[2] Maimonides, on the other hand, approached the subject from the opposite viewpoint. To him, the *mitzvot* are a source of joy and great spiritual satisfaction.[3] Because it is a fathomless fountain of joy, the *mitzvah* must be performed in a state of ecstasy. The *mitzvah,* according to Maimonides, acts as a prophylactic against the onslaughts of the *yetzer ha-ra*—"man's evil inclination."[4] Ḥasdai Crescas, confronted by the bold and aggressive challenge of Christianity, viewed the *mitzvot* as instruments designed to bind the Jew to his God and foster the love and the fear of Him. This is the central theme of his classic *Or Ha-Shem*. Joseph Albo[5] and Eliezer of Mainz[6] concurred with Crescas.

[1] *Sefer ha-Kuzari*, Chap. 1, Sec. 109.
[2] Commentary on the Torah, Deuteronomy 22:6.
[3] Yad, *Hilkhot Lulav*, Chap. 8, Sec. 15.
[4] Yad, *Hilkhot Temurah,* Chap. 4, Sec. 13.
[5] Introduction to *Sefer ha-Ikkarim*.
[6] Introduction to *Sefer Yere'im*.

Some of our intellectual giants[7] addressed themselves to the question: What value or purpose is there in the practical observance or the intellectual analysis of those *mitzvot* that seem to be outdated, such as those concerned with the Temple sacrifices and the rituals of purification? If they are no longer applicable, how can they then serve as a fountain of joy? One authority[8] is of the opinion that there are two separate duties which the Jew must perform. First, he must obey the commandments of God as they stand. Secondly, there is the separate and distinct duty to study the *mitzvot*. Hence, even if there are some commandments which are not observed today, we are nevertheless morally bound to study all the *mitzvot*. Another authority[9] asserts that there is educational and religious value even in the mere recollection of those *mitzvot* which once played an important role in Jewish life and which will be brought back and revived in a Messianic era. Another viewpoint, expressed by Abraham Samuel Benjamin Sofer,[10] was that the first obligation of the Jew is to observe the *mitzvot* without questioning, doubting, or rationalizing. When the Jews received the Torah at Mount Sinai, he points out, they proclaimed *"na'aseh ve-nishma"*—first we will obey God's instructions; later we may try to understand and fathom their full meaning.

A concomitant question that arises is: How many *mitzvot,* in fact, are there? A cursory study of the Torah would lead one to the conclusion that there are perhaps several thousand. A remark dropped casually in passing by one of the Sages in the Talmud has caused an intellectual tempest, particularly among the early rabbinic authorities of the Middle Ages. Rabbi Simlai stated[11] that 613 *mitzvot* were given to Moses on Mount Sinai. These comprise 248 positive commandments, corresponding to the number of component parts of the body, and 365 negative commandments, which correspond to the number of days

[7] As, for example, Introduction to *Sefer Mitzvot Gadol.*

[8] *Ibid.*

[9] Introduction to *Sefer Mitzvot Katan.*

[10] *Ketav Sofer* on the Torah, beginning of Sidra *Ekev*, Deuteronomy 7:12.

[11] B. Makkot 23b. See explanation of Maharsha.

in the year. Each part of his body urges man to do good; every day of the year he is warned against committing sin.

If, as we said above, the number of commandments in the Torah is far greater than this, the question then arises: Which 613 commandments did Rabbi Simlai have in mind? It was the lack of specification and detail on the part of Rabbi Simlai that created the sharp differences of opinions between the great luminaries in rabbinic literature. This is clearly brought out by Baruch Heilprin,[12] who bemoans the glaring discrepancies among the outstanding early scholars in their individualistic classifications of the 613 *mitzvot*. He deplores the apparent confusion and cries out: "To whom shall we turn amongst these saintly scholars?"

Nevertheless, it becomes clear that most enumerations are in accordance with the calculation of Maimonides. In his *Sefer ha-Mitzvot,* he lays down general rules for his summation of the 613 *mitzvot*. He does not include, for example, those *mitzvot* that the Rabbis of the Talmud instituted on the strength of the authority vested in them from the Bible, such as Ḥanukkah, Megillah, etc.,[13] nor does he count those *mitzvot* that were derived by way of the thirteen rules for expounding the law, such as respect for a Sage.[14] Furthermore, he does not accept among the 613 *mitzvot* those that were not of an everlasting character, such as the directives concerning the Tabernacle and hallowed food during the wanderings of the Jews in the desert.[15] This position taken by Maimonides was particularly intended to counter that of a few great authorities, such as the Ba'al Halakhot Gedolot, whose approach to the count was entirely different.

Rashi[16] notes that in the "*Azharot*" of Saadiah Gaon, the latter classifies all the 613 *mitzvot* in the framework of the Ten Commandments. For example, all the laws pertaining to marriage would come under the classification of "You shall not commit

[12] Introduction to *Mitzvot Ha-Shem.*
[13] *Sefer ha-Mitzvot,* Shoresh 1.
[14] *Ibid.*, Shoresh 2.
[15] *Ibid.*, Shoresh 3.
[16] Commentary on the Torah, Exodus 24:12.

adultery." As if further to complicate the maze of computations, we find a remarkable statement in the Talmud.[17] Rabbi Simeon ben Lakish said: "There are many verses which, to all appearances, ought to be burned but are really essential elements in the Torah." In other words, what may seem to us to be inconsequential is really basic and of great importance. Whatever approach and from whatever vantage-point the great scholars dealt with the *mitzvot*, the number 613 remained intact. They differed only in the choice of which *mitzvot* would be selected for inclusion.

If in the area of enumerating the acceptable *mitzvot* we meet with great confusion, we become even more disconcerted by the great labyrinth of conflicting opinions as to whether it is altogether necessary or even permissible to find reasons for the *mitzvot*. Is it actually necessary to determine reasons and motivations behind the *mitzvot*? Is it not more commendable to accept God's word as it is? Interestingly, most of the early authorities favored delving and searching for a rationale of the *mitzvot*, while many of the later authorities were content with the basic status quo of the *mitzvah* and left it at that. The Torah itself, with very few exceptions,[18] avoids giving reasons for the *mitzvot*.[19] In the Scriptures, the central theme is *"Va-yomer Ha-Shem"*—"So spoke God." While the Rabbis of the Talmud ventured a little into the field of rationalization, they still fell far short of the mark in propounding an elaborate and systematized study of the reasons behind the commandments. To them, the cardinal rule was that the *mitzvot* were presented *"le-tzaref et ha-beriyyot"*—"to refine the character of man."[20] It never occurred to the Rabbis that the reason for circumcision, as Maimonides would have it, is to reduce the sex-passions of

[17] B. Ḥullin, 60b.

[18] These exceptions include Passover, *matzah*, *sukkah*, Sabbath, honoring parents, sending away the mother-bird.

[19] See Heinemann, *Ta'amei ha-Mitzvot be-Sifrut Yisrael,* Vol. I, p. 17.

[20] This is the opinion of Heinemann. Natan Ẓevi Friedman speculates whether the Rabbis made incursions into the *ta'amei ha-mitzvot*. See *Darkhei Noam be-Halakhah, Shanah be-Shanah* 5733, p. 156. See Rashba, *Ein Ya'akov* to Sukkah 28a, Chap. 2, No. 6, on the subject of "Hillel had 80 disciples."

a man. Their guidepost was invariably *"Asher kiddeshanu be-mitzvotav"* ("Who has sanctified us through His commandments") —the *mitzvot* were intended to sanctify. It is also possible that the Rabbis were so preoccupied with the fundamental clarification of the Torah that their thoughts did not turn often to the advisability of proposing reasons.

Saadiah Gaon differentiated between two categories of *mitzvot: sikhliyyot:* the *mitzvot* that man's intellect would readily accept; and *shimiyyot:* those that must be accepted for no reason other than that they were proclaimed by God. This early theologian advanced the viewpoint that in both categories a serious effort should be made to seek out intelligible motives for the *mitzvot*.

Even the most enthusiastic subscribers to the values of establishing reasons for the *mitzvot* warn not to rely solely upon our own intellectual prowess and analytical capacities in determining the true essence of the *ta'am ha-mitzvah* (i.e., the reason for the commandment). Baḥya ibn Paquda makes a strong plea along these lines,[21] although he is definitely in favor of seeking out reasons.[22]

Judah Halevi advocated the *ta'amei ha-mitzvot* because he was afraid that, without a full, rationally-convincing theory of the *mitzvot,* the Jew would be performing them mechanically and by rote,[23] whereas an intellectual perception of the *mitzvot* would generate enthusiasm and spontaneity in the fulfillment of God's law.

Maimonides was probably the first to enter the "lion's den" unabashed and undeterred. In the face of the severest criticism, he embarked on a methodical approach to the rationalization of the *mitzvot*. He agreed that there are grounds for questioning the validity of seeking out a rationale of the *mitzvot*.[24] He lent some credence to the talmudic premise that the underlying reason for the Torah's not revealing the reasons for the *mitzvot* was that King Solomon, the wisest of all men, himself went astray

[21] *Ḥovot ha-Levavot,* Sha'ar 1, *Sha'ar ha-Yiḥud,* Chap. 3.

[22] *Ibid.,* Sha'ar 5, *Sha'ar Yiḥud Ha-Shem,* Chap. 1.

[23] Heinemann, *op. cit.,* Vol. I, p. 64.

[24] *Guide of the Perplexed,* Part 3, Chap. 26.

because he presumed to know the motives behind the *mitzvot,* although he actually lacked the knowledge of their true purpose.[25] All the same, he exhorted the scholars to emulate him and to make every effort to rationalize.[26]

To Levi ben Gershom, the purpose of the *mitzvot* was to guide the Jew to spiritual perfection. This is a sine qua non. He did not hesitate to associate a number of *mitzvot* with hygienic and sociological factors. To illustrate his point, he contended that circumcision has a prophylactic value against disease and that all the laws pertaining to forbidden foods are of inestimable hygienic value. In a like manner, the commandments pertaining to the seven-year cycle have sociological and economic merits. While Abrabanel, at times, also speculated along those lines, most of the exegetes rejected this approach.[27]

Thus we run the gamut ranging from those who are unafraid to face the consequences of lacking a legitimate rationale for the *mitzvot* to those who are deeply concerned about diluting the impact of "Thus saith the Lord," i.e., the commandments are to be obeyed simply because they are God-given. Even in the *Sefer ha-Ḥinnukh,* we discover that the author, perhaps the foremost advocate ever of the *ta'amei ha-mitzvot,* was not quite certain whether his premises were adequately substantiated. He begged for the reader's indulgence if some of his reasoning was not as logical as it should have been.[28]

While we have directed our attention to the proposition that we must seek a motive to the *mitzvot*, we must not overlook the fact that there were those who strongly believed that not only was there no reason to search for a purpose, but that there was no rationale at all. This is brought to light in the debate between Rabbi Judah and Rabbi Simeon[29] as to *"darshinan ta'amei di-kera"*—whether we have a right to expound a reason for the

[25] *Ibid.,* cf. *Sefer ha-Mitzvot,* Shoresh 5.

[26] Yad, *Hilkhot Temurah,* Chap. 4, Sec. 13 and *Hilkhot Me'ilah,* Chap. 8, Sec. 8. See *Perishah, Tur Yoreh De'ah,* Chap. 181, Sec. 1, where Maimonides is castigated for his attempts at formulating *ta'amei ha-mitzvot.*

[27] See Introduction to *Sefer Me'ah She'arim* by Recanati.

[28] See end of his introduction, and cf. *Mitzvot* 397 and 598.

[29] B. Bava Metzia 115a.

mitzvot. Even among our intellectual giants there were those who joined only cautiously and with reserve in the search for *ta'amei ha-mitzvot*. Their hesitation revolved around the theological axis of the rational and the irrational aspects of the *mitzvot*—in other words, whether there is a reason for the commandments depends on those whose position we intend to justify. If our purpose is to discover the reasons why the *Metzavveh* (God) gave the *mitzvot*, then the commandments become irrational. Man could never fathom God's purpose and motives. There simply is no basis for the reasoning behind the *mitzvot*. Man was never meant to seek the answers. On the other hand, if we are concerned about the *metzuveh* (man)[30] there could be some validity and wisdom in searching for possible reasons. In fact, a foremost modern authority[31] contends that a *mitzvah* is not dependent upon the rationale for its justification; on the other hand, once the *mitzvah* has been established and confirmed, it is permissible to seek the reasons for it.

It remains for us to ask: What actually prompted great scholars, particularly those of the Middle Ages, to steadfastly explore the vast riches of the *ta'amei ha-mitzvot*? What stirred them to rummage for that to which their predecessors were reluctant to put their inquiring minds? Heinemann[32] suggests that one cause may have been apologetic. Some rabbinic leaders were confronted with vicious anti-Semitic onslaughts and they felt that an intelligent reply would reduce the weight of the calumny. We are not convinced that any of the propounders of the *ta'amei ha-mitzvot* were prompted by anti-Semitic attacks to the extent that they felt it necessary to resort to apologetics.

He offers two other lines of thinking that are more plausible. First, if man has progressed to the point where he attempts to fathom the mysteries of the universe and the wonders of God, why should he not probe into the reasons of the religion of God? Secondly, the educational aspects of the *ta'amei ha-mitzvot* are

[30] See Yad, *Hilkhot Me'ilah*, Chap. 8, Sec. 8; also Introduction to *Sefer Me'ah She'arim* by Recanati.

[31] *Beit ha-Levi* by J. B. Soloveitchik, Shemot, Sidrah *Bo*, p. 18.

[32] *Op. cit.*, Vol. I, p. 12.

of inestimable value. We may also add that these early probers into the *ta'amei ha-mitzvot* were not satisfied with the attitude implied in *"Lama yomru ha-Goyim"*—concern with the attitudes of non-Jews toward Jews and Judaism. They saw and recognized the dynamic power of *"ko amar Ha-Shem."* What Heinemann or the present writer may surmise is of little consequence. It is more important that we listen to the words of some of the shining lights who dealt with the *ta'amei ha-mitzvot*.

Moshe Ḥagiz[33] and Shabbetai Cohen[34] showed acute sensitivity to the almost prophetic statement in the Talmud:[35] *"Atidah Torah she-tishtakaḥ mi-Yisrael"*—the Torah is destined to be forgotten in Israel. They were apprehensive that this calamity might occur in their day. This could have been the unacknowledged but ever-present suspicion in the minds of many other spiritual luminaries throughout the centuries. The rank and file of the people were so preoccupied with eking out a meager livelihood and also confronted with a savage and hostile world, which could find no better argument against their way of life than repeated pogroms, that these harried and persecuted people were in no state of mind to study the law with any degree of profundity. *Am ha-aratzut* (ignorance of Jewish learning) was rampant. In order, therefore, to call a halt to this accumulation of ignorance, various Rabbis in different periods devoted themselves to the vital task of writing basic comments on the *mitzvot*. These were a most welcome aid for the unlearned layman in understanding and grasping the fundamentals of Judaism.

Today, a different situation has arisen. A unique problem has appeared on the Jewish horizon which nevertheless demands the same approach as that of years gone by. Intellectuals by the score, who during most of their lives were estranged and far removed from the mainstream of Judaism, have suddenly found themselves drifting back gradually to their spiritual origins. They are not content, however, with merely drifting either with or against the

[33] Introduction to *Eleh ha-Mitzvot*.
[34] Introduction to *Po'el Tzedek*.
[35] B. Shabbat, 138b.

stream. They are ravenously hungry to learn; their appetite for knowledge and understanding is insatiable. Because of their high intelligence and scholastic background, we can no longer just tell them: "This is it; do not ask questions." If we are not to abandon this soul-searching, truth-seeking generation, we must be ready to give them answers to their questions which will be palatable and intellectually acceptable.

It is in this spirit that I make this very modest contribution to Jewish learning in the hope that both the scholar and the average layman will find in it something to enhance and widen their knowledge of Judaism.[36]

Along the lines of the rabbinic giants who preceded me and whose greatness completely overshadows the meager stature of my inadequate erudition, I wish to reemphasize their warning: that if in these *ta'amei ha-mitzvot* there may be a rationale that is unappealing, then the reader should not arrogantly assume to himself the monopoly of wisdom and reject that rationale. Humility is an indispensable characteristic of the true student and scholar. What may appear to us irrational today, may become clear, lucid, and thoroughly acceptable tomorrow.

I shall be well satisfied if I can convince the reader that beneath the surface of the *mitzvot* lie depths of meaning to exercise the mind of the thinking Jew.

Erev Shabbat Ha-Gadol 5734
April 5, 1974

[36] The form and style of this work are a fusion of those employed mainly by the *Sefer ha-Ḥinnukh,* the *Sefer Mitzvot Ha-Shem,* and the Encyclopedia of the *Taryag Mitzvot* by Haim Itzhak Lipkin. It was felt that, for the purpose of this work, the individual styles of these authors and others would not suffice, but in keeping with their precis of the *mitzvot* we, too, adhere to the *Yad ha-Ḥazakah* of Maimonides.
The *mitzvot* are presented in the order in which they appear in the Torah.

ANNOTATED LIST OF AUTHORS

Abrabanel (Abarbanel, Abravanel), Isaac ben Judah. Abrabanel was born in Lisbon in 1437 and died in Venice in 1508. Endowed with great intellectual qualities, he was an astute politician, brilliant commentator on the Torah, and profound religious philosopher. Despite his popularity at the court of King Ferdinand and Queen Isabella, being Minister of Finance at the time of the Expulsion of Jews from Spain, he was unable to avert the calamity which befell his coreligionists on the Ninth of Av, 1492.

Abrabanel followed his brethren into exile. After brief sojourns in Naples, Corfu, and Venice, he died in 1508. While in exile he wrote his commentary on the Bible, as well as a popular explanation of the Passover *Haggadah* and a commentary on *Pirkei Avot* and the *Guide of the Perplexed* of Maimonides. In his Biblical exegesis, he cited historical parallels, even referring occasionally to non-Jewish exegetes. As a philosopher, he endeavored to reconcile the rationalistic philosophy of Maimonides with his own firm faith.

Alshekh, Moses. Born in Adrianople in the 16th century, Alshekh studied in Salonika and emigrated to Eretz Israel, settling in Safed where he gained prominence as a halakhic authority, a teacher in two talmudic academies, and a preacher.

He reworked his sermons into commentaries to most of the books of the Bible. His commentaries, which are permeated with religious-ethical and religious-philosophical ideas supported by ample quotations from talmudic and midrashic sources, became very popular and have often been reprinted.

Avi Ezer (Solomon ben Eliezer ha-Kohen). Solomon ben Eliezer lived in Posen at the end of the 18th and beginning of the 19th century. He was a *shoḥet* (ritual slaughterer) and made a careful study of Ibn Ezra's commentary on the Bible, on which he wrote a supercommentary, the *Avi Ezer,* published in 1802.

Ba'al Halakhot Gedolot (i.e., the author of Halakhot Gedolot). The precise identity of the author of this classic halakhic work has aroused divergence of opinion. Whereas some scholars are of the opinion that he was Simeon Kayyara, who lived in the eighth century C.E., others maintian that its real author was Yehudai Gaon, who also lived in the eighth century. Many scholars hold that there are actually two different works by the same name, with Simeon Kayyara being the author of one, and Yehudai Gaon authoring the other.

The work was printed in Venice in 1548. Previously it had been copied in manuscripts and frequently studied and quoted by scholars.

Ba'al ha-Turim (Jacob ben Asher). Jacob ben Asher, son of Asher ben Jehiel, lived in the last half of the 13th and the first half of the 14th century. In 1303 he accompanied his father from Germany to Toledo, where he lived in great poverty, devoting himself to study. In his learning he avoided prolixity and casuistry. Typical of his style is his first halakhic work, *Sefer ha-Remazim*.

His enduring fame rests upon his major work, the *Arba'ah Turim*, hence he is commonly referred to as "Ba'al ha-Turim" (i.e., the author of the "Turim"—"rows"). The work embraces all the laws and customs incumbent upon the individual and the community. The arrangement of the book, its simple style, and its wealth of content made it a basic work in Hebrew law and opened a new era in the realm of halakhic codification.

Jacob also wrote a comprehensive commentary on the Pentateuch (published in Zolkiew, 1806) containing the best expositions of the *peshat* (literal meaning) by earlier Bible commentators, such as Saadiah, Rashi, Ibn Ezra, and others, in particular abstracting the straightforward explanations from the commentary of Naḥmanides and disregarding the kabbalistic ones.

A late tradition mentions that Jacob set out for Eretz Israel but died on the journey.

Baḥya ben Asher. Baḥya was one of the shining stars of the Jewish "Golden Age" in Spain where he was a renowned disciple of the famous Solomon ben Adret. He died in Saragossa, in 1340. Though his biblical commentary favors the midrashic approach, he seldom wanders from the literal meaning *(peshat)* of the text, or from the logical implications of the *mitzvot*. His approach is also colored, at times, by kabbalistic nuances such as appear in the works of Naḥmanides.

He completed his commentary in 1291. He also wrote the *Kad ha-Kemaḥ,* comprising 160 sermons on various themes and arranged in the alphabetical order of the ethical subjects discussed. His commentary on Job *(Sova Semaḥot)* and his book on the Dietary Laws *(Shulḥan*

Arba), as well as his philosophical treatise *Ha-Emunah ve-ha-Bitaḥon,* in which he quotes Arabic, Spanish, and French works, have deservedly earned for him a foremost niche in the gallery of biblical experts.

Da'at Zekenim (Ba'alei ha-Tosafot). This collection of reflections on the biblical portion of the week partakes of the nature of the *Tosafot* comments on Rashi's explanation of the Torah. It is replete with literal explanations, both midrashic and halakhic, hints and fantasies, and many questions and answers.

Ḥinnukh, Sefer ha- (Aaron Ha-Levi). A native of Barcelona in the 14th century, Aaron Ha-Levi is said to be the author of *Sefer ha-Ḥinnukh,* a monumental work, intended primarily for the instruction of the youth. It speedily became a classic used by young and old and has been translated into Latin and Spanish, and in abridged form also into French. In this book are listed all the 613 *mitzvot* as they occur in the weekly scriptural portions *(sidrot),* which the author elucidates in a scholarly and comprehensive manner.

Ḥizzekuni (Hezekiah ben Manoah). Little is known about this French exegete who lived in the 13th century. Tradition relates that in memory of his father, who lost his right hand because of his loyalty to his ancestral faith, Hezekiah wrote (about 1240) a commentary on the Pentateuch which he called *Ḥizzekuni* ("Strengthen Me"), printed in 1524.

This work is based principally on the work of Rashi, but it is clear that the author consulted at least 20 other commentaries.

Ibn Ezra, Abraham. In his 75 years (1092–1167), Abraham ibn Ezra displayed great versatility as a biblical commentator, scholarly grammarian, and profound philosopher. Born in Toledo, he was a roaming scholar all his days, carrying his vast knowledge with him from his native Spain to Africa, Egypt, Eretz Israel, Babylon, Italy, France, and England.

Despite, or perhaps because of, the poverty which persistently dogged his footsteps, he won renown as a philosopher of distinction. No sphere of knowledge seemed alien to him, for he shone as a brilliant mathematician and astronomer, as well as a most able Hebrew grammarian and biblical commentator.

Apart from his own original works, he also translated classical Arabic works into Hebrew, so that Jews might be cognizant with the thought of Moslem culture. He was also a zealous defender of Saadiah Gaon in his polemics against the Karaites (a sect which accepted only Scripture as authoritative), who were making bitter attacks against rabbinic traditions. Most important, however, is his biblical commentary on the entire Bible, which displays to the full his masterly knowledge of the Hebrew language and his ingenuity in clarifying obscure passages.

In the introduction to his commentary, he cited the opinion of his critics, often criticizing them in turn for introducing unnecessary material. His main thesis was that tradition was indispensable to correct interpretation. He charged many biblical commentators with reading into the text allegory and fantasy, making opaque and ambiguous that which was clear. In avoiding these mistakes, he aimed at clarifying the text in a simple, logical manner almost in the style Rashi had written 50 years earlier except that the latter had woven in midrashic interpretations.

Keli Yakar (Ephraim Solomon of Luntshitz). Known chiefly by his commentary on the Torah, the *Keli Yakar,* Ephraim of Luntshitz, who died in 1619, won great acclaim during his stay in Lemberg (Lvov) and Prague as a gifted and inspiring preacher. He produced a commentary on Rashi and elucidated many rabbinic utterances in the course of his great commentary. He was a disciple of the famous talmudist, Solomon Luria (the Maharshal). In 1604, he was called to Prague where he served as rabbi and head of the *yeshivah.*

His sermons are aggadic and ethical in nature, their main aim being to bring the hearts of his listeners nearer to God. His books became immensely popular among all sections of his community and the many editions printed were widely sold. Apart from his main work, the *Keli Yakar,* he also wrote *Ir Gibborim,* another volume of sermons on the weekly *sidra; Olelot Ephraim, Oraḥ le-Ḥayyim, Siftei Da'at,* and *Ammudei Shesh,* all of which reflect his great learning and his humane, ethical approach when teaching the Torah to the masses.

Maimonides (Rambam, Moses ben Maimon). Born in Cordoba in 1135, Maimonides died in Fostat (Egypt) in 1204, leaving behind a literary legacy which age has not withered. He received his training in *halakhah* (Jewish Law) from his father; his scientific and metaphysical knowledge from Jewish and Arabic channels. He was a physician by profession.

Forced to leave Spain in 1148, owing to the fanatical Almohadic persecutions, his family first settled in Fez in 1160, and five years later made their home in Fostat (Old Cairo). Maimonides became court physician in 1194; he was a master of scientific subjects, and wrote on medicine and astronomy.

Apart from his authoritative commentary on the Mishnah, which he wrote in Arabic, but in Hebrew characters, as he did his philosophical work, the *Guide of the Perplexed (Moreh Nevukhim),* his fame as a codifier rests on his *Yad ha-Ḥazakah,* a monumental presentation of the halakhic contents of both the Jerusalem and Babylonian Talmuds. This work—the only one of his books written originally in Hebrew, is divided into 14 Books (the numerical value of the Hebrew *"Yad"*). In it he cited the final decisions arrived at by the talmudic sages after what were, sometimes, interminable discussions and covered the whole, vast field of Jewish Law without mentioning the sources; in this way, one is able to see the forest, as well as the trees.

Next to this work on *halakhah* must be placed his philosophical masterpiece, the *Guide of the Perplexed.* To quote his own words: "The aim of the book was to promote true understanding of the real spirit of the Law; to guide religious persons who, adhering to the Torah, have studied philosophy but who are embarrassed by the seeming contradictions between the teachings of philosophy and the literal sense of the Torah." In this work he opposed Aristotle's theory of the eternity of matter and demonstrated the possibility and the necessity of the Jewish traditional idea of creation. He firmly believed that the biblical doctrine of *creatio ex nihilo* ("creation from nothing") was truer than Aristotle's theory of the eternity of matter and the universe. He also taught that Judaism requires that one walk in the "Middle Path," the "Golden Mean" which is equidistant from the extremes of too much or too little.

Since his death in 1204, he has been the central figure in the world of *halakhah* and Jewish philosophy, exerting vast influence not only on Jewish philosophers but also on great non-Jewish thinkers.

Naḥmanides (Ramban, Moses ben Naḥman). The Ramban, the name by which he was mostly known, was born in Gerona (Spain) in 1194 and died in Acre, in about 1270. He acquired an illustrious reputation as a talmudist and kabbalist; in both fields he was a great authority. Like his great predecessor, Maimonides, he also studied medicine. He wrote many exegetical works on the Talmud and was often quoted and interpreted by his disciples, as well as scholars of all ages.

He was strongly attracted to Kabbalah. In his work *Torat ha-Adam,* dealing with mourning rites, he treated the functions of the super-soul in a highly mystical fashion. After a complete victory in his public disputation with the apostate Pablo Christiani, in which he was compelled to engage by King James of Aragon, he left Spain and settled in Acre where he revived Jewish learning in the Holy Land. There he composed his best-known work, his commentary on the Pentateuch, which was very significant in showing how a purely rationalistic approach could be combined with a search for hidden meanings and the use of Kabbalah. More than anyone else, he directed the attention of Jewish intelligentsia to the Kabbalah as an alternative to philosophy.

Or ha-Ḥayyim (Ḥayyim ben Moses Attar). Born in Morocco in 1696, Attar died in Jerusalem in 1743, where he had settled only a year or so earlier. His chief claim to fame is as a talmudist and kabbalist, and legend has glorified him as a saint and worker of miracles.

His many literary works are composed of halakhic and kabbalistic treatises and he wrote an exegetical work on the Pentateuch, familiarly known as *Or ha-Ḥayyim.* Among his disciples and contemporaries he was always referred to as *Ha-Kadosh,* "The Holy One."

Radak (David ben Joseph Kimḥi). This noted biblical commentator and grammarian was born in Narbonne in 1160 and died in 1235. One of his chief claims to scholarly fame is his *Mikhlol,* a grammatical work whose excellence time has not dimmed or outmoded. A second part to this standard work soon followed, which he called *Sefer ha-Shorashim* ("The Book of Roots"), a dictionary of biblical Hebrew.

Not less important, and perhaps even more popular, is his commentary on the Prophets and Psalms, in which he expressed his easy mastery of biblical scholarship in an elegant and lucid style. His work was frequently translated into Latin and exercised great influence on the translators of the Hebrew Bible into various languages.

Mention should be made of Kimḥi's polemics against Christianity, originally inserted in his commentary on the Psalms, which he called *Teshuvot la-Notzrim.*

Radbaz (David ben Zimra). David ben Zimra was born in Spain in 1479 and died in Safed in 1573. When only 13, he was exiled with all other Spanish Jews in 1492, and settled with his family in Safed. In 1512, he went to Egypt where he was recognized as its spiritual leader for over 40 years, during which he wrought many improvements for the Jews in that country.

In 1569, he went back to the Holy Land and settled again in Safed. Among the many who honored him there was none other than Joseph Caro, the compiler of the *Shulḥan Arukh* and *Beit Yosef.* The Responsa *(She'elot u-teshuvot)* he left behind are numerous. In consonance with the kabbalistic spirit which then prevailed in Safed, the Radbaz composed his *Magen David,* a mystic work on the shape and secret of the letters of the alphabet, his *Metzudat David* on the literal and exegetical meaning of each of the 613 *mitzvot,* as well as a commentary on the Song of Songs approached from the kabbalistic angle.

Ralbag (Levi ben Gershom, Gersonides). Ralbag lived in France in 1288–1344. Little is known about his life beyond the fact that he maintained relations with important Christian persons. He had very broad intellectual interests and contributed to many areas of learning, including mathematics, astronomy, philosophy, and biblical exegesis.

He wrote commentaries on Job (1325), Song of Songs (1325 or 1326), Ecclesiastes (1328), Ruth (1329), Esther (1329), the Pentateuch (1329–38), the Former Prophets, Proverbs, Daniel, Nehemiah, and Chronicles (1338). All of these were published, some in several editions.

These biblical commentaries are the work of an exegete and philosopher. Diverse questions of a philosophical or theological nature are discussed, such as the problem of providence, miracles, and the Messiah. In his voluminous commentary to the Pentateuch, Ralbag attempts to reconstitute the *halakhah* rationally, condemning allegorical interpretations.

Rashbam (Samuel ben Meir). Samuel b. Meir was born in about 1085 near Troyes in France. Besides finishing the commentary on tractate *Bava Batra* (from p. 29 to the end of p. 176) of his grandfather Rashi, uncompleted before the latter's death, Rashbam also wrote commentaries on the Scriptures, stressing the *peshat* (literal meaning) rather than its homiletical nuance *(derash)*. His younger brother was Jacob Tam, the recognized talmudic authority of his age. Both deprecated extreme casuistry which was then coming into vogue. Samuel ben Meir opposed idle conjectures, resting on personal opinion and unsupported by any talmudic source and fanciful flights of homiletical explanations. He died in about 1174. He was one of the Tosafist school of which his younger brother was the leading figure.

Rashi (Solomon ben Isaac). The leading commentator on the Bible and Talmud, Rashi was born in Troyes in 1040 and died in 1104. Little is known about his early life. After his initial education in Troyes, Rashi was attracted to the great academies of Mainz and Worms where he studied after his marriage. At about the age of 25 he returned to Troyes where he founded a school which attracted many outstanding pupils.

Rashi's last years were aggrieved by the massacres committed at the outset of the First Crusade (1095–96), in which he lost relatives and friends. There is a legend that during this period he transferred his school to Worms. His burial place is not known.

Rashi commented on most, if not all, the books of the Bible. The main distinguishing characteristic of his commentary is a compromise between the literal and the midrashic interpretations. At least three-quarters of his comments are based on rabbinic sources. The few that are original are mainly philosophical explanations.

Another characteristic aspect is the manner in which Rashi formulated his comments. In many instances he did not quote a Midrash literally but either augmented or abridged it, or even altered its wording, his aim being to make for easier understanding and to adapt the language of the Midrash to that of the text.

Rashi's commentaries are centered on meticulous analysis of the language of the text. He was both philologist and linguist and derived his grammatical principles from rabbinic literature and the Hebrew works of Spanish grammarians. His language is concise and straightforward and he explains many difficult problems with a word or a mere hint.

Rashi's commentary on the Bible, and particularly that on the Pentateuch, enjoyed an enormous circulation. More than 200 supercommentaries were written on his Pentateuch commentary. An English translation of it was made by M. Rosenbaum and A. M. Silbermann (5 volumes, London, 1929–34).

Recanati, Menahem ben Benjamin. Recanati was the only Italian Rabbi of his period (the 13th century) to take up the study of the Kabbalah. He seems to have been immersed in kabbalistic ideas which he quoted with august respect.

His *Perush* was translated into Latin by the Christian humanist Pico della Mirandola and was republished with a commentary by Mordecai Jaffe in Lublin in 1595. Besides this work, he wrote a *Perush ha-Tefillot* and *Ta'amei ha-Mitzvot*. Like his commentary on the Torah, these two works are tinged with mysticism. Recanati frequently quotes Judah He-Ḥasid of Regensburg and Eleazar of Worms (Rokeaḥ), and also the Spanish kabbalists, including Naḥmanides.

Saadiah ben Joseph (Saadiah Gaon). This celebrated scholar was born in 882 and died in 942. He was one of the first Jews who combined Jewish with Arabic scholarship, but he always remained a staunch upholder of rabbinic authority and at an early age set himself to combat Karaism and other heresies. He competed with the Karaites in their own special fields of literary activities, such as Hebrew philology and the interpretation of the Bible.

At the age of 20, he compiled a Hebrew dictionary, called *Agron,* and some years later produced an Arabic translation of and commentary on nearly the whole of the Bible, which exercised a profound influence on Arabic-speaking Jews. Its particular merit is in its literary and logical treatment. He eventually settled in Babylon, where his great services to Jewish learning were crowned by his appointment in 928 as head of the Academy of Sura, one of the three cradles of the Babylonian Talmud (the others being Pumbedita and Nehardea). He gave new life to the Academy.

Having incurred the displeasure of the Exilarch, he fled to Baghdad. There he wrote his masterpiece *Emunot ve-De'ot,* one of the standard works of Jewish religious philosophy which exercised a great influence on Jewish thought.

Sefer Mitzvot Gadol (Semag, Moses ben Jacob of Coucy). Moses of Coucy lived in the first half of the 13th century, at the time of the holocaust at Paris, when the Talmud was burnt in 1240. In 1250 he arranged the religious laws of the Talmud in the order of the Pentateuchal commandments and called the work *Sefer Mitzvot Gadol (Semag)*. He was followed by Isaac, son of Joseph of Corbeil, with *Sefer Mitzvot Katan (Semak)*.

His *Semag* proved to be a very popular codification of the Law and was of tremendous help in acquainting Jews with the precepts and customs of Judaism. It deals with each of the 613 *mitzvot* and is written in a very lucid style. Its importance also consists in the fact that he quoted many previous sources. It was first printed in 1488.

Sforno, Obadiah ben Jacob. This renowned exegete, philosopher, and physician was born in Italy in about 1475 and died in Bologna in 1550. He founded a *yeshivah* in Bologna. His chief claim to fame rests, however, on his erudite and illuminating commentaries to most books of the Bible.

About 1525, he left Rome and led the life of a poor wanderer for some time before he settled for the rest of his life in Bologna. Sforno, as he is generally called, was very active in the field of biblical exegesis, his characteristic feature being a respect for *peshat* (literal explanation) and a reluctance for mystical interpretations. He displays great judgment in his quotations from Rashi, interpretations which reflect an extensive knowledge of grammar and philology. In addition to his *Kavvanot ha-Torah,* he also wrote commentaries on most books of the Bible.

Besides being a noted physician, he also reigned supreme in the domain of religious philosophy. He challenged the views of Aristotle and in his *Or Ammim* he expressed surprise that even so great a man as Maimonides had agreed with Aristotle in many of his theories. His commentary on *Pirkei Avot* also reflects his religious philosophy. Some of his works still await publication.

GLOSSARY

Amidah, main prayer recited at all services; also known as *Shemoneh Esreh.*

B., Babylonian Talmud (abbreviation).

Bar Mitzvah, ceremony marking a boy's initiation into the religious community at the age of 13.

Bet Din, rabbinic court of law.

Eglah arufah, an expiatory ceremony prescribed in the Bible for an untraceable murder in which the elders of the nearest settlement broke a heifer's neck to profess their innocence of the bloodshed.

Eruv, technical term for rabbinic provision permitting the alleviation of certain restrictions.

Haggadah, ritual recited in the home on Passover eve at the *Seder* table.

Halakhah, an accepted decision in Jewish law.

Ḥametz, "fermented dough;" leaven prohibited on Passover.

Ḥaroset, paste made of fruit, spices, wine which forms part of the *Seder* rite.

Havdalah, ceremony marking the end of the Sabbath.

Ḥol ha-mo'ed, intermediate days of the Festivals of Passover and Tabernacles.

J., Jerusalem (Palestinian) Talmud (abbreviation).

Karaites, Jewish sect which rejected rabbinic Judaism and accepted only Scripture as authoritative.

Karet, "extirpation;" divine punishment in the form of premature death.

Kasher, ritually permissible.

Kashrut, Jewish dietary laws.

Kiddush, blessing over wine on the Sabbath and Festivals.

Kohen, Priest, Jew of priestly (Aaronide) descent.

Korban, sacrifice, offering.

Matzah, unleavened bread.

Menorah, candelabrum; seven-branched oil lamp used in the Tabernacle and Temple.

Mikveh, ritual bath.

Minyan, quorum of ten adult male Jews, the minimum required for communal prayer.

Mitzvah, commandment; biblical or rabbinic injunction.

Mohel, one who performs circumcision.

Nevelah, the flesh of an animal or fowl that died of natural causes or was not slaughtered by *sheḥitah.*

Noahide Laws, seven laws considered by rabbinic tradition as the minimal moral duties enjoined by the Bible on all men.

Omer, forty-nine days counted from the time that the first of the barley harvest was offered in the Temple (second day of Passover) until Shavuot.

Pesaḥ, Festival of Passover.

Peshat, literal (or plain) meaning of the text.

Responsa, written opinions given to questions on aspects of Jewish law by qualified authorities.

Rosh Ha-Shanah, 1st of Tishri (Sept.–Oct.); Jewish New Year's festival observed for two days.

Rosh Ḥodesh, New Moon; first of the Hebrew month.

Seder, ceremony of the first night of Passover (in the Diaspora first two nights), when the *Haggadah* is recited.

Sefer Torah, manuscript scroll of the Pentateuch.

Sekhakh, covering of the *sukkah.*

Shavuot, Pentecost, or Feast of Weeks, pilgrim festival and agricultural festival on the anniversary of the giving of the Torah at Mount Sinai, celebrated for one day in Israel, two in the Diaspora, in Sivan (May–June).

Sheḥitah, ritual slaughtering of animals.

Shemini Atzeret, final festal day of Sukkot.

Shemittah, Sabbatical Year.

Shofar, ram's horn sounded for memorial blowing on Rosh Ha-Shanah and other occasions.

Shoḥet, ritual slaughterer.

Simḥat Torah, holiday marking the completion of the annual cycle of reading the Pentateuch in the Synagogue.

Soferim, "scribes;" scholars active during the period of Persian rule, after the return from Babylonian exile.

Sukkah, booth or tabernacle erected for Sukkot.

Sukkot, Tabernacles, festival beginning on 15th of Tishri (Sept.–Oct.).

Ta'amei ha-mitzvot, rationale of the commandments.

Tefillin, phylacteries, worn by male Jews during weekday morning service.

Terefah, the flesh of an animal or fowl that was killed by a predatory animal or had physical defects or injuries rendering it not *kasher.*

Torah, Pentateuch; the entire body of traditional Jewish teaching and literature.

Tosafot, glosses to talmudic commentary of Rashi.

Yeshivah, Jewish traditional academy devoted primarily to the study of the Talmud and rabbinic literature.

Yom Kippur, Day of Atonement, 10th of Tishri (Sept.–Oct.); most solemn day of the Jewish religious calendar.

THE MITZVOT

GENESIS

PROCREATION

Be fruitful and multiply, and fill the earth, and subdue it (Genesis 1:28)

1. When a man reaches the age of 18 he becomes subject to the *mitzvah* to marry and to have children.

2. The *mitzvah* of procreation is incumbent only upon the male, not the female.

3. To fulfill this *mitzvah* adequately, a man must beget at least one son and one daughter who, in turn, must be physically capable of begetting children of their own. In other words, one has not fulfilled the *mitzvah* of procreation if, for example, he begets a son who is sexually impotent or a daughter who is barren.

4. Thus, a man should not marry an elderly woman or a young woman if he knows beforehand that she cannot have children. However, should he have already had children by a previous wife, he may enter into such a marriage.

5. A convert to Judaism to whom children were born prior to his conversion is considered to have fulfilled the *mitzvah* of procreation, provided that these children also convert.

6. If he had children who died and left children of their own, he is also considered to have fulfilled the *mitzvah*.

7. Even if a man has reached the age when he can no longer beget children, it is his duty to marry so that he will not spend time in sexual diversions. Although a woman is not obligated so to do by Jewish law, she should marry even after her child-bearing days are over so that no one will suspect her of indulging in immoral practices.

COMMENTATORS

Ḥinnukh, Baḥya ben Asher: Contrary to the common belief that the purpose of procreation is to populate the world and enjoy what it has to offer, the object of this *mitzvah* is to make possible the fulfillment of the word of God. God, who created the world, has laid down a plan to guide it. This plan consists of the Torah and the *mitzvot,* and obviously there must be people to carry out these *mitzvot*. Besides, it is necessary for man to reproduce so that the Omnipresence of the *Shekhinah* (Divine Presence) in the world may be perpetuated.

Recanati: He questions whether the sex act, necessary though it is for procreation, should not be looked upon as something repulsive or despicable. The answer he offers is that it becomes holy and pure by virtue of the fact that it is founded on holiness and purity. Accordingly, the Talmud teaches that when the act is performed in the spirit of holiness, God Himself is present. Only if the act is not performed in this spirit does it become contemptible.

Abrabanel: Since there is no other way of begetting children except through sexual relations, why was it necessary for the Torah to specify that man should join with woman in order to be fruitful? A person might think that, since he was created in the image of God, he should not perform the act, even for the purpose of begetting children for, after all, man is expected to live in a state of Godliness. It was in order to correct this attitude that God warned man not to neglect his physical duties. On the other hand, if man can procreate only through the sex act, what makes him superior to lower animals, who also reproduce by means of mating? Abrabanel answers that, even when he performs this earthly physical function, man must elevate himself so that he will not act like an animal. When he understands that man should perform the sex act to fulfill the will of God, he rises above all the other living things on earth.

Alshekh: He contrasts those who have faith in God and those who lack this faith. Those who have faith believe that the world is meant to serve man and provide for his needs, and to this end it is permissible for man to exploit nature. Those who lack faith become slaves to the laws of nature. [As an example of this idea we can take the problem of "population explosion." A person who has faith will not abandon hope by refusing to bring children into the world, but will look for ways to make the earth and the sea provide sufficient sustenance for all. The person who lacks faith, on the other hand, will be afraid to beget children because he will blindly accept the "scientific theory" which cannot provide for an ever-growing population.]

Or ha-Ḥayyim: Areas which are allowed to remain unpopulated and desolate are breeding places for phenomena that are harmful to human existence. Man must, therefore, see to it that the world's population should grow.

References:

B. Yevamot 61b, 62, 63, 65b; Yad, Hilkhot Ishut, 15; Sefer ha-Mitzvot (Aseh) 212; B. Berakhot 16a; B. Gittin 41b; Sefer Mitzvot Gadol (Aseh) 49; Sefer Mitzvot Katan 284; Tur, Even ha-Ezer; Shulḥan Arukh, Even ha-Ezer, Chap. 1; B. Kiddushin 29b; J. Ketubbot, Chap. 5; Midrash Rabbah, *Bereshit,* 17; B. Pesaḥim 49a.

CIRCUMCISION

Every male among you shall be circumcised (Genesis 17:10)

1. It is incumbent on the father to circumcise his son. If the father cannot perform this act himself, he may appoint a *mohel* as his agent to perform the *mitzvah* for him. If for some reason the father fails to have his son circumcised, it becomes incumbent on the *Bet Din* of the community to see that the circumcision is performed. If the *Bet Din* too fails to perform this obligation, it becomes the responsibility of the uncircumcised male himself to fulfill this *mitzvah* when he is older.

2. Circumcision must take place as early as possible on the eighth day after the infant's birth.

3. If the child is physically unfit for circumcision, the ceremony must be postponed until the child is in good health.

4. When the circumcision is performed on schedule, i.e., on the eighth day, it may even take place on the holiest days of the year, including Yom Kippur. A postponed circumcision, on the other hand, must not be performed at night, on the Sabbath, or on holidays.

5. A convert to Judaism who was circumcised before his conversion, or a baby who was born without a foreskin, must undergo a symbolic circumcision. This is done by drawing one drop of blood from the place where circumcision is ordinarily performed.

6. If possible, the circumcision should be performed in the presence of a *minyan,* a quorum of ten adult males.

COMMENTATORS

Maimonides: When an incision is made on any part of the human body, that area remains defective and weakened to some degree, even after the wound has healed. Accordingly, circumcision has been prescribed in order to weaken the sex drive of man, so that he will not be excessively stimulated.

Ḥinnukh: Just as the Jew is spiritually different from the Gentile, so God desired that he should also be physically different. Why was the sex organ chosen as the place where this sign of differentiation should be set? Because it is the organ of procreation. This implies that the uniqueness of the Jew should be apparent in every new generation that is born. Also, an uncircumcised male organ is considered imperfect. Circumcision brings man's body closer to perfection. If the presence of the foreskin implies imperfection, why did God not have all male children born without a foreskin? To show to man that he must not expect perfection to come to him ready-made. He must exert an effort on his own to achieve perfection of body and mind.

Abrabanel: Circumcision is an atonement for the original sin of Adam and its sexual implications. Furthermore, if this organ, which is the source of physical pleasure, is sanctified through circumcision, then the children whom he will eventually beget will be conceived in holiness.

Or ha-Ḥayyim: If the ritual of circumcision is an atonement for the original sin, why was not some atonement required also of the woman? Or ha-Ḥayyim answers that the first man sinned merely because he was misled; he was therefore granted a means of atonement. The woman, on the other hand, who had listened to the serpent, was the initiator of the original sin and so she could not be granted pardon as easily as the man. She was, therefore, subjected to menstrual periods to recall the role she played in the original sin.

Keli Yakar: The removal of the physical obstruction (i.e., the foreskin) through circumcision is symbolic of the removal of the spiritual barrier that may separate the heart of man from his God.

Naḥmanides: According to the Torah, circumcision is a "covenant." But, contrary to popular opinion, the covenant is not intended to remind the Jew to think of God, but rather to remind God to remember the Jew. Naḥmanides cites the rabbinic interpretation according to which the act of circumcision is considered as the offering of a sacrifice. As in the case of the animal sacrifices that were performed in the Temples, the blood from the circumcision is meant to atone for sins. Similarly, even as the sacrificed animal must be at least eight days old, so, too, the male child must have reached the age of at least eight days before being circumcised. As a matter of fact, circumcision is an act of true sacrifice even more than the symbolic animal offering, because it is performed not with an animal but upon the body of a human being.

References:
B. Shabbat 137a, 132a, 135a, 108a; B. Kiddushin 29a; B. Yevamot 47b, 72a; Tosefot Yom Tov, Shabbat, Chap. 19, Mishnah 2; Pirkei de-Rabbi Eliezer, Chap. 29; Sefer ha-Mitzvot (Aseh) 215; Sefer Mitzvot Gadol 28; Sefer Mitzvot Katan 157–9; Shulḥan Arukh, Yoreh De'ah, 260–266; J. Kiddushin, Chap. 1, Halakhah 7; J. Shabbat, Chap. 19, Halakhah 1; Sefer ha-Ḥinnukh, Mitzvah 2.

THE PROHIBITION OF EATING THE THIGH MUSCLE

Therefore the children of Israel are not to eat the thigh muscle on the hip socket (Genesis 32:33)

1. Because an angel in the guise of a man wrestled with the patriarch Jacob and dislocated his hip, we are forbidden to eat any part of the thigh muscle, both of the right and left hind-legs, of an animal. There are two tendons extending from the hip to the thigh, an inner tendon and an outer tendon. Even he who eats an amount of the inner tendon no bigger in size than an olive violates a biblical injunction. Eating the outside tendon is a violation of rabbinic law.

2. The thigh muscle includes the "sirloin" area.

3. This prohibition is applicable also to the thigh muscle of a fowl, if its hip is shaped and constructed like that of cattle.

4. As a rule, we are not permitted to benefit in any manner from food that we are forbidden to eat. Among the few exceptions to this rule is the thigh muscle, which may be given as a gift to a non-Jew.

COMMENTATORS

Sforno: The symbolic significance of this *mitzvah* is to show that a Jew must not allow a physical handicap to discourage him in his fight for survival.

Ḥinnukh: This *mitzvah* is a symbol of Israel's survival. Just as Jacob faced a dangerous foe and emerged victorious, so, too, Jews throughout the ages should have faith that they will survive even the most devastating onslaughts of their enemies. The author stresses that the Jew must not despair, because help will be forthcoming. According to other commentators, a Jew must not only keep up his spirits in the face of a physical defect; he must compensate for his handicap by cultivating his spiritual potential.

Maimonides: Maimonides rejects the belief that this, or any other *mitzvah,* was meant to recall events in the lives of the patriarchs. To cite an example: It is sometimes believed that we practice circumcision because Abraham circumcised himself and we are his descendants. According to Maimonides, this is a mistaken concept. We practice circumcision because God instructed us at Sinai to do so. Similarly, we refrain from eating the thigh muscle not because we are descendants of Jacob, whose thigh muscle was hurt, but because God commanded us at Sinai not to eat that part of an animal.

Ḥizzekuni: The Torah relates that on the night before his confrontation with Esau, in which his thigh was injured, Jacob was left by himself. He was alone when he encountered the angel who engaged him in a struggle. How could his sons and the rest of his entourage have allowed him to remain alone all that night? In memory of this incident, we refrain from eating the thigh muscle to remind us that we must never permit a fellow Jew to feel that he is alone in the world.

Alshekh: There is a rabbinic interpretation that Jacob was stricken with lameness as a punishment for having married two sisters, although the law forbidding a man to marry two sisters* had not yet been given to the children of Israel. We are therefore forbidden to eat the thigh muscle in order to remind us that not even the saintly Jacob was immune from sin. Accordingly, we should mend our ways and keep far from evil.

References:

B. Ḥullin 89b, 96b; Yad, Ma'akhalot Asurot, Chap. 8; Sefer ha-Mitzvot (Lo Ta'aseh) 183; Sefer Mitzvot Gadol (Lav) 139; Sefer Mitzvot Katan 203; Shulḥan Arukh, Yoreh De'ah 65; Perush ha-Mishnayyot of Maimonides on Ḥullin, Chap. 7; B. Krittot 21a; Sefer ha-Ḥinnukh, Mitzvah 3.

EXODUS

THE SANCTIFICATION OF THE NEW MOON

This month shall be unto you the beginning of months; it shall be unto you the first month of the year (Exodus 12:2)

1. Except for leap years (see below), the lunar year has 354 days. Some lunar months have 29 days, others 30. The exact length of the lunar month is 29 days, 12 hours, and 793 parts.

2. The solar year has 365 days, 5 hours, 96 parts, and 48 subdivisions. Each day is divided into 1,080 parts, each of which in turn is divided into 76 subdivisions.

3. Although the Jewish calendar is based on the lunar year, we must guide ourselves by the sun in the celebration of our holidays. Passover must be celebrated during the spring season and Sukkot must be observed in the fall, at harvest-time. Since the lunar year is shorter than the solar year the difference in length between the lunar and solar years must be adjusted periodically, or else

* According to Jewish law, a man is permitted to marry the sister of his deceased wife, but in the days when men were still allowed to have more than one wife at a time, it was forbidden to marry one's wife's sister while the wife was still living.

we would find ourselves one year observing Passover in the fall and Sukkot in the spring. The adjustment is made by intercalating an additional month after the month of Adar every third, sixth, eighth, eleventh, fourteenth and seventeenth year of each nineteen-year cycle.

4. The biggest problem was the correct determination of the lunar months. In talmudic days, the *Bet Din* would assemble on the 30th of each month to await the testimony of two reliable witnesses that they had just seen the new moon. If the *Bet Din* was thoroughly convinced that the witnesses had given correct testimony, they proclaimed that day to be the day of the New Moon—the first of the month. If the moon's crescent was not seen on the 30th day, the new moon was automatically celebrated on the 31st day.

5. The announcement of the new moon was signaled by burning beacons from mountain to mountain throughout the land of Israel and in parts of the Diaspora. Later the word was spread by messengers. Since these messengers could not reach the outlying communities in time, they always celebrated the 30th day as the new moon. If they were informed of postponement to the the 31st day, they would celebrate that day as well.

COMMENTATORS

Naḥmanides: Immediately after commanding this *mitzvah,* the Torah speaks of Passover (see Exodus 12:6–51), indicating that this month, (i.e., the month of Nisan), as well as all the other months of the year, are to be associated with the Exodus from Egypt. The year begins with Tishri. However, Nisan is called the "first month" of the year, because the Exodus took place in that month. Just as in the case of the days of the week, which are numbered in relation to the Sabbath, so is each month connected with Nisan and the Exodus from Egypt. Thus we find that in the Torah the months are not named but numbered (i.e., the first month after the Exodus, the second month after the Exodus, etc.). It was only in Babylon that the months first became known by identified names (Nisan, Iyyar, Sivan, etc.).

Ibn Ezra: If Nisan is the first month of the year, why do we refer to Tishri and not to Nisan as "Rosh Ha-Shanah," the "beginning of the year"? Ibn Ezra answers that the various phenomena of life require different time-tables. The New Year for produce, which involves the first fruits, tithes, and heave offerings, is different from the national New Year that is connected with the Exodus from Egypt.

Ḥinnukh: Why is it necessary to add a month to the calendar at stated intervals? Because the Torah commands us: "Observe the month of spring and make a Passover to the Lord." This means that Passover must come during the spring season. The same applies to the Feast of Tabernacles, which must occur at harvest time because it is written: "When you gather your produce from the field."

Recanati: Why does the Jewish calendar follow the lunar system? Because the moon is the only heavenly body that renews itself each month. This indicates that, if God can renew the moon each month, it was certainly He who created the world in the first place. This serves as a lesson in faith. Recanati further observes that the slightly darkened hue of the moon is a sign that it is grieving over the plight of the Children of Israel in exile. Another reason why the Jewish calendar is guided by the moon is that the moon, unlike the sun, can be seen both by day and by night. Non-Jews reckon their years by the sun, which symbolizes only one aspect of life—the existence of man on earth. Jews, on the other hand, look to both worlds—this world and the world to come.

Abrabanel: Every nation bases its calendar on some historic event in its existence. Thus, at one time the Romans began their year with the coronation of Augustus Caesar; the Greeks with the battle of Alexander the Great; and the Muslims with the flight of Mohammed. The Jews began their national calendar with the Exodus from Egypt. If this is the case, asks Abrabanel, why does the Jew also accept Tishri as Rosh Ha-Shanah, the beginning of the year? Because there are two beginnings of the year, and Tishri, which commemorates the beginning of Creation, reminds us of the growing things which we need for our sustenance. In a national sense, however, it was ordained that we begin the year with the month of the Exodus from Egypt.

References:

B. Rosh ha-Shanah 7a, 18a, 20a, 22a; B. Sanhedrin 11a, 42a; B. Ketubbot 21b; B. Berakhot 10b, 63a; J. Berakhot, Chap. 9; Yad, Kiddush ha-Ḥodesh, 1, 4, 5; Sefer ha-Mitzvot (Aseh) 153 (See Naḥmanides' sharp differences with Maimonides. Also, see Naḥmanides' comments toward the end of Shoresh 1 in Sefer ha-Mitzvot. Also, commentary Megillat Esther); Sefer Mitzvot Gadol (Aseh) 46, 47; Midrash Rabbah, Pesikta Rabbati on Exodus 12:2; B. Menaḥot 29a; B. Megillah 22; Sefer ha-Ḥinnukh, Mitzvah 4.

THE PREPARATION OF THE PASCHAL LAMB

Then the whole assembly of the congregation of Israel shall slaughter [the lamb] at dusk (Exodus 12:6)
You shall not offer the blood of My meal-offering with leavened bread, neither shall the fat of My meal-offering remain overnight until the morning (Exodus 23:18)

1. The Passover festivities began when the Jew brought his Paschal lamb to the Temple on the afternoon of the fourteenth day of the month of Nisan. This sacrifice was either a male lamb or a he-goat in its first year, without blemish.

2. Any Jew who deliberately failed to perform the Passover sacrifice without a legitimate reason, e.g., because he happened to be ritually impure or on a journey far from home, was punishable by *karet*.*

3. In the days of the Temple, the Paschal lamb would be sacrificed after the regular evening sacrifice which signaled the end of the day's offerings. In this manner, the Paschal offering was clearly set apart from the many other sacrifices that had been offered during the day.

* *Karet* is a punishment usually explained as "being cut off from the people of Israel." There is a difference of opinion among the Rabbis as to what form this punishment takes:
1. Death of the sinner without any surviving descendants.
2. Death of the sinner at an early age—50 or sometimes before he reaches the age of 60.
3. According to Maimonides, *karet* involves the destruction of the soul. Naḥmanides disagrees: he holds that, since the soul must live to answer for the sinner's misdeed, the soul can never be destroyed.

4. Each householder would approach the Temple and wait for his turn to enter the courtyard to start processing the sacrifice.

5. The Priest slaughtered the animal, the blood was sprinkled upon the base of the altar, and the entrails and fat were placed on a pyre to be consumed by the flames. The celebrant then returned to his home with the remainder of the carcass to partake of the repast with his family and friends.

6. It was not permitted to leave the entrails of the Paschal lamb to smolder unattended. They had to be burned as quickly as possible.

7. If either the host or any one of the guests he had invited to share the Passover feast with him had retained possession of leavened bread in any form, the entire offering and the Passover celebration were considered invalid.

COMMENTATORS

Ḥinnukh: The stringent nature of these laws was intended to remind the Jew of the great miracles that had been performed for him by God during the Exodus from Egypt. Each phase of the celebration has its own singular significance that should be individually emphasized. Thus, if the Paschal lamb is to be significant, all leaven must be totally removed from the surroundings. This is also the reason why the residue of the Paschal sacrifice could not remain overnight.

Ḥizzekuni: Why did the entire community, through its emissary, participate in the sacrifice of the lamb? The reply is: In order that it be a united project; for should a crisis arise, then no one could deny his own participation in the act.

Alshekh: This commandment is a symbol of total, all-embracing holiness which cannot be achieved by one individual alone. Only unified participation can succeed in receiving this gift of freedom from God. This effort can only be achieved through the conglomerate virtues of the entire community; for one may possess what the other lacks.

References:

B. Pesaḥim 58a, 64a, 63b (see Tosafot), 66a, 71a (see Tosafot); J. Pesaḥim, Chap. 5, Halakhah 4; B. Sukkah 42b (see Tosafot); Mekhilta (Sidrah *Bo*); Yad,

Hilkhot Korban Pesaḥ, Chap. 1, 4, 10; Sefer ha-Mitzvot (Aseh) 55, (Lo Ta'aseh) 115, 116; Sefer Mitzvot Gadol (Aseh) 223, (Lav) 347, 348; B. Kiddushin 41b; Sefer ha-Ḥinnukh, Mitzvot 5, 89, 90.

PARTICIPATION IN THE PASCHAL FEAST

And they shall eat the flesh in that night (Exodus 12:11)
Ye may not eat of it raw, nor boiled in water (Exodus 12:9)
With unleavened bread and bitter herbs shall they eat it (Exodus 12:8)

1. Every Jew had to partake of the meat of the Paschal lamb on the night of the 15th of Nisan. If he ate any of the meat during the daylight hours of the 14th, he was punished by flogging.

2. The Paschal lamb could be eaten at any time during the night of the 15th of Nisan. However, the Rabbis set the deadline at midnight to insure that the sacrifice would be completely consumed by daybreak.

3. The Paschal lamb had to be eaten together with *matzah* (unleavened bread) and bitter herbs. But if, for some reason, *matzah* or bitter herbs were not available, eating the meat alone satisfied the requirement.

4. The Paschal lamb had to be broiled. If it was only slightly roasted or boiled in water, it was disqualified and anyone who partook of it was punished by flogging. "Slightly roasted" was understood to mean meat at which the flames had just begun to lick. "Boiled in water" was understood to mean meat cooked in any liquid whatsoever.

5. The Paschal lamb was to be eaten after the meal to show that this was part of a ritual and not part of a meal to satisfy one's hunger. Other sacrifices were brought on the festival, such as the *shalmei ḥagigah*—offerings in honor of the festival. These had to be eaten before the meat of the Paschal lamb so that the participants could taste the unique flavor of the Paschal lamb and would no longer be so hungry as to feel they must break the bones of the lamb to suck out the last bits of marrow.

COMMENTATORS

Rashbam: The rituals entailed in the preparation and eating of the Paschal lamb were designed to connote haste, reminiscent of the haste in which the children of Israel went forth from Egypt.

Ḥizzekuni, Abrabanel: The commandment to eat the Paschal lamb in roasted form had nothing to do with haste. It was simply an act of defiance on the part of the Children of Israel against their Egyptian taskmasters who worshiped the lamb as an idol, and to whom, therefore, the sight and the smell of lambs being roasted was the ultimate insult.

Ḥinnukh: The Paschal lamb had to be eaten roasted because a roast lamb was a royal dish of which slaves were not permitted to partake. Now that the Jews were free, they were, in fact, commanded to partake of this dish to mark their new freedom.

Ibn Ezra: In discussing the reason for eating bitter herbs, Ibn Ezra quotes an unnamed Spanish sage to the effect that sharp foods, such as radish and mustard, were eaten in Egypt to guard against illnesses resulting from the humidity in the Nile region. Ibn Ezra, however, does not agree with this interpretation; he insists that the bitter herbs were meant to serve as a reminder of the "bitterness" of the life of the Children of Israel as slaves in Egypt.

References:

B. Pesaḥim 41a, 76b, 85a, 89b, 93a, 96a, 115a, 120; B. Zevaḥim 11b; B. Megillah 21a; B. Berakhot 9a; B. Ḥullin 32b (see Tosafot); Mekhilta (Sidrah *Bo*); Midrash Rabbah (*Shemot* 11–23); Yad, Hilkhot Korban Pesaḥ, Chap. 5, 6, 8; Yad, Hilkhot Sanhedrin, Chap. 18, Par. 3; Yad, Hilkhot Bikkurim, Chap. 9, Par. 22; Sefer ha-Mitzvot (Aseh) 56, 58, (Lo Ta'aseh) 119, 122, 125; Sefer ha-Mitzvot, Shoresh 9 (See difference between Maimonides and Naḥmanides on whether one or two commandments are involved in the case of raw or sodden Paschal lamb.); Sefer Mitzvot Gadol (Aseh) 224, 225, 227, (Lav) 350, 351, 357, 358, 359; Shulḥan Arukh, Oraḥ Ḥayyim, 475 (see Turei Zahav); Tosefta Pesaḥim 9; J. Yevamot, Chap. 8, Halakhah 1; Sefer ha-Ḥinnukh, Mitzvot 6, 7, 381.

THE PROHIBITION OF LEFTOVERS FROM THE PASCHAL LAMB

And ye shall let nothing of it remain until the morning (Exodus 12:10)
They shall leave none of it until the morning (Numbers 9:12)
And nothing of the flesh shall remain all night until the morning (Deuteronomy 16:4)

1. In addition to the Paschal lamb, the Jews were commanded to bring a festival offering *(korban ḥagigah)* on the 14th day of Nisan to insure an abundance of food at the Passover feast. The feast was to be celebrated with such enthusiasm that no part of the sacrifice would be left over for the next day. Accordingly, the law specifies that no part of the meat must remain until the morning of the first day of Passover.

2. The meat of the festival offering, on the other hand, could be consumed as late as two days after it had been offered (but no later).

COMMENTATORS

Ḥizzekuni: The prohibition against leaving any part of the lamb for the next day is a symbolic reminder of the Exodus. A person about to make a long journey usually eats a good, hearty meal before he starts out. He will not want to save part of the food for a meal to be eaten at some later date. Another reason for the prohibition is that it would be sacrilegious to leave part of the Paschal lamb behind and take the chance that the leftovers would be eaten by stray animals.

References:
Mekhilta (Sidrah *Bo*); B. Pesaḥim 70b, 71a; Guide of the Perplexed, Part 3, Sec. 46; Yad, Hilkhot Korban Pesaḥ, Chap. 10, Halakhah 11 (See Kesef Mishneh and Mishneh le-Melekh, who challenge the premise of Maimonides.); Yad, Hilkhot Pesulei ha-Mikdashim, Chap. 18, Halakhah 9; Sefer ha-Mitzvot (Lo Ta'aseh) 117, 119; Sefer Mitzvot Gadol (Lav) 349, 358; Sefer ha-Ḥinnukh, Mitzvot 8, 382, 486.

THOSE FORBIDDEN TO PARTAKE OF THE PASCHAL LAMB

No alien shall eat thereof (Exodus 12:43)
A sojourner and a hired servant may not eat thereof (Exodus 12:45)
No uncircumcised person shall eat thereof (Exodus 12:48)

1. Anyone seeking to partake of the Paschal lamb during the Passover celebration had to qualify as a Jew in the fullest sense of the term, physically and spiritually.

2. An apostate was not eligible to partake of the lamb. Some authorities go so far as to say that this prohibition applied also in the case of an individual who had remained Jewish but had rejected all, or part (no matter how little), of Jewish religious law.

3. A "sojourner" is a non-Jew who only accepted the discipline of the "Seven Noahide Laws."

4. He who desires to partake of the Paschal lamb must not only be spiritually committed to Judaism but must also bear the physical mark of Jewishness; that is, he must have been circumcised. Consequently, no uncircumcised male was permitted to partake of the Paschal lamb, including even a male who was exempt from circumcision under Jewish law because two of his older brothers had died as a result of complications arising from the operation.

COMMENTATORS

Ḥinnukh: An uncircumcised male is not a complete Jew in the physical sense of the term. Circumcision is a token of the submission by the Jew of his own will to the will of God. According to Jewish tradition a Jew who does not bear this physical token of submission on his body has not fulfilled all the requirements entailed in the *mitzvot,* even if this omission is due to no fault of his own. He therefore is not capable of experiencing the true joy that the real Jew feels. As a consequence, he is disqualified from partaking of the Paschal lamb.

References:
B. Pesaḥim 3b, 96a; B. Yevamot 71a; Yad, Hilkhot Korban Pesaḥ, Chaps. 5, 9 (Maimonides' position is that the injunction against the sojourner applies to a Jew who permits the sojourner to partake of the Paschal lamb. Others contend that it applies to the sojourner himself who is forbidden to eat thereof.); Exodus Rabbah, *Bo;* Sefer ha-Mitzvot (Lo Ta'aseh) 126, 127, 128; Sefer Mitzvot Gadol (Lav) 353, 354, 355; Mekhilta *Bo;* Sefer ha-Ḥinnukh, Mitzvot 13, 14, 17.

NOT TO BREAK THE BONES OF THE PASCHAL LAMB

And no bone shall you break [of the lamb] (Exodus 12:46)
And no bone shall they break of the lamb (Numbers 9:12)

1. Most authorities explain this prohibition as deriving from the fact that on Passover, the Festival of Freedom, the Jew becomes a king, and royalty is expected to show decent table manners and to refrain from such primitive eating practices as breaking the bones of the animal and sucking out the marrow.

2. This prohibition applies to the lamb both of the normal Passover in Nisan and to the lamb of the Second Passover held in Iyyar for those who were prevented from celebrating the First. The penalty for this violation was flogging.

3. The only instances that warranted this penalty were if the bone was attached to the meat which was at least the size of an olive, or if the bone had marrow in it. Even if he broke a shattered bone, he would be subject to the same penalty.

COMMENTATORS

Maimonides: This prohibition recalls the fact that at the time of the Exodus the Paschal lamb had to be eaten in haste. When a meal is eaten in haste, one does not take time to "play" with the bones of the "meat course."

Radbaz: Breaking the bones and sucking out the marrow shows an overpowering desire to destroy, literally to the last bone, one of the creatures of God. At the time when the Children of Israel celebrate their own freedom, they must not appear before the world as destroyers of God's creatures. Here, as in all other things, Judaism counsels dignity and moderation.

Ḥizzekuni: If one breaks the bone of the lamb to suck out the marrow, this is an indication that he is eating the meat to satisfy his hunger, but this was not the purpose of the Paschal lamb.

References:

B. Pesaḥim 84a, 89a, 96a; J. Pesaḥim, Chap. 7, Halakhah 2; B. Zevaḥim 97b; Yad, Hilkhot Korban Pesaḥ, Chap. 5, 6, 10; Sefer ha-Mitzvot (Lo Ta'aseh) 121, 122; Sefer Mitzvot Gadol (Lav) 351; Sefer ha-Ḥinnukh, Mitzvot 16, 383.

WHERE TO EAT THE PASCHAL LAMB

You may not carry forth any of the flesh away from the house (Exodus 12:46)

1. The Feast of Passover was to be celebrated in the midst of one's family and close friends to symbolize the close links that bound together the entire "family" of the Jewish people. Going off by oneself to eat the Paschal lamb would therefore signify an act of isolation contrary to the spirit of Passover, and of Judaism.

2. The moment that the group sat down to partake of the Paschal lamb, no individual member could leave this group and join another. Nor was he permitted to take any part of the Paschal lamb out of the house, even a piece as small as an olive. A violation of this law was punishable by flogging.

COMMENTATORS

Ḥizzekuni: The entire Paschal lamb had to be eaten informally at home, and in one sitting to indicate haste.
Abrabanel: Sinners who joined with the righteous to celebrate the Feast of Passover would obtain Divine forgiveness for their sins.
Ḥinnukh: When the kings of ancient Egypt arranged banquets, they honored some of their "lower friends," who were not eligible for an invitation to the palace, by sending them some of the food. Not so the Jew who became "king" by virtue of his newly-won freedom. He invites all his friends to share the feast with him at his home.
Baḥya ben Asher: The practice of eating the Paschal lamb in company with others is motivated by simple economy. It is less expensive to celebrate a feast with others than to celebrate it alone.

References:
B. Pesaḥim 85b, 86a; J. Pesaḥim, Chap. 7, Halakhah 12; Mekhilta *Bo;* Yad, Hilkhot Korban Pesaḥ, Chap. 9; Sefer ha-Mitzvot (Lo Ta'aseh) 123; Sefer Mitzvot Gadol (Lav) 352; Sefer ha-Ḥinnukh, Mitzvah 15.

THE BAN ON LEAVEN DURING PASSOVER

Even the first day you shall put away leaven out of your houses (Exodus 12:15)
In the first month, on the fourteenth day of the month, in the evening, you shall eat unleavened bread (Exodus 12:18)
Seven days shall there be no leaven found in your houses (Exodus 12:19)
And no leavened bread shall be seen (Exodus 12:17)
Whatsoever contains leaven shall ye not eat (Exodus 12:20)
No leavened bread shall be eaten (Exodus 13:3)
You shall eat no leavened bread with it (Deuteronomy 16:3)

1. The preparations for Passover and the celebration of the festival itself are distinguished by fundamental activities: the removal of all leaven, and the eating of unleavened bread. Both these acts are commandments specified in the Bible.

2. Talmudic law requires that every trace of leaven *(ḥametz)* must be removed from the home on the 14th day of the month of Nisan, even before the biblical injunction against *ḥametz* actually takes effect.

3. *Ḥametz* includes any food derived from wheat, barley, spelt, rye, or oats. Originally vegetables of the pea family were permitted on Passover. Later, peas and rice were prohibited, though they are still permitted in Sephardi communities. The prohibition of these foods on Passover is because of the particles of wheat which are frequently found mixed in with them and which could cause fermentation ("leavening") when the vegetable is cooked, or because of doubts as to whether they might be classified as grain.

4. We must also "annul" in our minds any *ḥametz* which remains in our possession and consider it "as the dust of the earth." Nevertheless the Rabbis insisted that we also make a physical search to remove all *ḥametz* even from property that is not part of our actual dwelling, for if we merely "annulled" the *ḥametz* in our minds, economic considerations might inhibit us from removing it physically from our homes. Also, we may forget and partake of the *ḥametz*.

5. To make sure that no Jew would have *ḥametz* in his possession during Passover, the Rabbis instituted the custom of *mekhirat ḥametz,* the "sale of *ḥametz*" to a non-Jew for the duration of the festival. In this way a Jew who has large quantities of *ḥametz* can legally divest himself of ownership during Passover without a great economic loss.

6. One who deliberately has contact with *ḥametz* during Passover commits a twofold violation of Jewish law. He disobeys the law that *ḥametz* must neither be "seen" nor "found" on one's premises.

7. Anyone who partakes of *ḥametz,* from the night of the 15th of Nisan until the close of the festival, will be punished by *karet* (see above p. 12).

8. Not only is it forbidden to eat *ḥametz* on Passover; but the law also prohibits us from deriving any benefit from *ḥametz* during the holiday. The Rabbis specified that one could not at any time in the future derive any benefit whatsoever from *ḥametz* which he had kept in his possession during Passover.

9. One is enjoined to eat *matzah* on Passover. The Torah stresses: "You shall watch the *matzah*" (Exodus 12:17; hence the phrase *matzah shemurah*). There is a distinct difference of opinion between Maimonides, who argues that the "watching" of the *matzah* must begin with the *ketzirah* (the cutting of the wheat), and Naḥmanides, who contends that the "watching" does not start until the kneading of the dough.

10. Every Jew—man, woman, and child—is obliged to eat *matzah* on the first night of Passover. During the rest of the holiday, one need not eat *matzah;* it goes without saying, however, that the prohibition against *ḥametz* applies to the entire holiday week.

COMMENTATORS

Ḥinnukh: The laws pertaining to *ḥametz* and unleavened bread serve as a reminder of the Exodus from Egypt, when the Children of Israel left in such haste that they could not wait for the dough to rise.

Abrabanel: He accepts the relationship of the *matzot* with the redemption from slavery but asks: "Why must we also refrain even from possessing any leaven during the seven days of Passover?"

Two reasons are offered: First, that if we have leaven in our house we may be tempted to eat of it.

The other reason is symbolic: Leaven is interpreted as denoting the evil inclination. Spring, the season at which Passover is celebrated, is compared to youth. When the nation of Israel was first established (spring), it was free of the evil inclination *(ḥametz)*. If we can make sure that the *ḥametz* of evil will not take possession of our youth today, we may hope that it will remain absent from our young people for the rest of their lives.

Sforno: God's decision to redeem the Children of Israel was made in an instant. Therefore, when we celebrate this event, there is no place for leaven which, slow to rise, symbolizes slowness and deliberation.

Baḥya ben Asher: Leaven is to be compared to stern judgment, for just as leaven spreads out and does not retreat, so judgment too, does not retreat. Accordingly, we must have no leaven around us when we celebrate our festival of freedom, to teach us that life cannot be based solely upon the attribute of judgment. Mercy and compassion are indispensable to life.

References:
B. Pesaḥim 5a, 5b, 21b (see Tosafot), 28b, 120a; J. Pesaḥim, Chap. 1, Halakhah 2; B. Betzah 7b; Exodus Rabbah, *Bo;* Yad, Hilkhot Ḥametz, Chaps. 2, 4; Sefer ha-Mitzvot (Aseh) 156, 158, (Lo Ta'aseh) 197, 198, 199, 201 (See dispute between Maimonides and Naḥmanides and the Ravad regarding the eating of *ḥametz* after midday, prior to the start of Passover that evening. According to Maimonides, the penalty is lashes. According to the others, there is no penalty. See Ravad in Yad, Chap. 4); Mekhilta *Bo;* Sefer Mitzvot Gadol (Aseh) 39–40, (Lav) 76, 77, 78, 79; Sefer Mitzvot Katan 34, 35, 36, 98, 219, 222; Shulḥan Arukh, Oraḥ Ḥayyim, 431–440, 443, 446, 471; Sefer ha-Ḥinnukh, Mitzvot 9, 10, 11, 12, 19, 20, 485.

SANCTIFICATION OF FIRST-BORN HUMAN AND ANIMALS

Sanctify unto Me all the first-born, whatsoever openeth the womb (Exodus 13:2)
The first-born of man you shall surely redeem (Numbers 18:15)
But the firstling of an ox, or the firstling of a sheep, or the firstling of a goat, you shall not redeem (Numbers 18:17)
You may not eat within your gates the tithe of thy corn, or of thy wine, or of thine oil, or the firstlings of your herd or of your flock (Deuteronomy 12:17)
You shall do no work with the firstling of your ox, nor shear the firstling of your flock (Deuteronomy 15:19)

1. Man is expected to express his profound gratitude to God for the first samples of His beneficence. Hence, the first male child born to him and also the first offspring of any ritually clean animal born in his household should be presented to the Priest.

2. All first-born animals, whether physically perfect or defective, must be presented to the Priest. If the animal is without blemish, the Priest must offer it as a sacrifice and may eat what is left over afterward. If the animal is not perfect, the Priest may dispose of it in whatever way he chooses; he may sell it or use it for food.

3. Laymen (ordinary Jews not in the priestly class) must not derive any benefit from their first-born animals, except in cases when the law explicitly specifies that they may do so. A first-born animal is consecrated even before it is born, consequently no one may use the animal for work or shear its fleece. Anyone who unwillingly violates this rule must bring a *korban me'ilah*, an offering of atonement for his misappropriation of a sacred object.

4. Since the ass is an "unclean" animal (i.e., one of the animals whose flesh Jews may not eat) first-born asses cannot be offered as sacrifices upon the altar. For this reason first-born asses must be "redeemed" by presenting a lamb or sheep to the Priest in the Temple as a sacrifice in the place of the ass (see below, p. 27).

5. In the case of a human, the father is duty-bound to "redeem" his first-born son 30 days after his birth by presenting the Priest with five pieces of silver, or an object of equal value. Notes, real property, or slaves cannot be used for this purpose.

6. "First-born" means the first male child born to its mother through natural birth. This definition exempts children who are born by Caesarean section.

7. The first-born children of Priests and Levites, or of daughters of Priests or Levites, need not be "redeemed."

8. If a father neglected to "redeem" his first-born son, that son must perform the act for himself as soon as he is in a position to do so.

COMMENTATORS

Ḥinnukh: One reason for this *mitzvah* is that man can be easily led astray by the misconception that he has unchallenged rights over all his possessions. The laws pertaining to the first-born are to teach us that, in reality, everything that we possess belongs to God. Another reason is that we must never forget how God dealt with the first-born of our foes, the Egyptians. It is sacrilegious to enjoy any benefit from a first-born animal.
Baḥya ben Asher: He cites two comments which he attributes to his mentor, Rabbi Solomon ibn Adret, on the subject of the first-born son of his mother Leah, so there must be no question that the Children of Israel are the "first-born" people to God. And just as we are sure that a natural mother would not exchange her own son for the son of another woman, so, too, God would not exchange His people for another nation.
Sforno: Why must first-born sons be "redeemed"? Because all our first-born are dedicated to God and therefore, by right, would not be permitted to engage in any profane activity. But since an ordinary human being cannot be expected to lead such a life of complete dedication, we may claim our first-born as our own, so that they may lead normal lives.

References:

B. Bekhorot 4a, 46a, 48a; B. Zevaḥim 37b, 56b, 75b; B. Temurah 5b, 21a; B. Arakhin 28a; B. Berakhot 4a, 4b, 9b, 10b, 12a, 13a, 19a, 37b, 47a, 51b, 53a; B. Niddah 21a; B. Kiddushin 29a; B. Shabbat 135b; B. Ḥullin 130a, 132a; B. Bava Kamma 11b (see Tosafot); Yad, Hilkhot Bikkurim, Chap. 11; Yad, Hilkhot Me'ilah, Chap. 1; B. Me'ilah 18a; B. Bava Metzia 54a; Yalkut Shimoni, *Va-Yikra;* Exodus Rabbah, *Bo;* Sifre *Koraḥ;* Mekhilta *Bo;* Pesikta Zutrata *Bo;* Sefer ha-Mitzvot (Aseh) 79 (See dispute between Maimonides, who maintains that these laws are applicable only in the Homeland, whereas the Ravad, Naḥmanides, Rashba (Responsa 337), and others maintain that they are effective outside the Homeland, too.), 80, 118, (Lo Ta'aseh) 108, 113, 114; Sefer Mitzvot Gadol (Lav) 340, 341, 343, (Aseh) 144, 210; Sefer Mitzvot Katan 102, 244; Shulḥan Arukh, Yoreh De'ah, 305, 310, 321; Sefer ha-Ḥinnukh, Mitzvot 18, 127, 392, 393, 446, 483, 484.

RELATING THE STORY OF EXODUS TO ONE'S CHILD

And you shall tell your son on that day (Exodus 13:8)

1. Since the Exodus from Egypt was the most important event in the history of the Jews, the master of the house is duty-bound to tell the story of the Exodus to his children on the night of the *Seder*. Why particularly on that night? Because on that night the *matzah* and the bitter herbs—both symbols of the story of Passover—are on the table as visual reminders of the Exodus.

2. It is not enough merely to tell the story of the Exodus. It must be told in such a manner as to be understood by the youngster. When the child is still very young, he should be told the story in simple terms. An older child, or a child of above-average intelligence, may be told the story in greater detail and in a more sophisticated manner. If there is no child in the family, the wife should take the role of the child at the *Seder* table. If a man has neither children nor wife, and celebrates the *Seder* by himself, he should ask the questions and then answer them himself.

3. The specific visual features of the *Seder* are:

a. The *matzah,* reminding us of the unleavened bread which our ancestors baked when they left Egypt for the Promised Land.

b. The *four cups of wine,* representing the four expressions of redemption which God used in his promise. Even the poor who depend on charity for their sustenance must drink these four cups of wine.

c. *Ḥaroset*—which was an innovation by the *Soferim*—symbolizes the mortar with which the ancient Hebrews built the cities of Pharaoh.

d. *Maror* (bitter herbs), which the Bible (Numbers 9:11) commands us to eat together with the *matzah* and the Paschal lamb. After the destruction of the Temple, the Rabbis decided that an amount of *maror* equivalent to the size of an olive should be eaten without any other food, as a sign of mourning for the Temple.

e. The *afikoman.* This piece of *matzah* takes the place of the

Paschal lamb. The Paschal lamb had to be eaten at the end of the meal to show that it was intended as a ceremonial feast and not as food to appease one's hunger. Therefore the *afikoman* is also eaten at the conclusion of the *Seder*-meal.

COMMENTATORS

Or ha-Ḥayyim: What happens if a man has no children to whom to tell the story of Exodus? According to Maimonides, he must then relate the story to himself. The *Or ha-Ḥayyim* states that, if a childless man relates the story to himself, he will eventually be found worthy of having a son to whom to tell it at future *Sedarim*.

Ḥinnukh: The Torah only specifies that one must tell the story of the Exodus to one's son. Why, then, should a man who has no son have to tell the story to himself? Because reciting the story aloud, even to oneself when no one else is listening, is likely to have a much greater emotional impact on a person than if he merely "thinks" about the miracle of the Exodus.

Recanati: The importance of relating the story of the Exodus lies in the fact that a person who is convinced that these miraculous events really came to pass will retell the story for his own benefit and for the benefit of others; he and his listeners will become increasingly convinced that God will also deliver His people from future perils.

References:

B. Pesaḥim 116b; Mekhilta *Bo;* Yad, Hilkhot Ḥametz, Chap. 7; Sefer Mitzvot Gadol (Aseh) 41; Sefer Mitzvot Katan 144; Sefer ha-Ḥinnukh, Mitzvah 21.

REDEMPTION OF THE FIRST-BORN OF ASSES

And every firstling of an ass you shall redeem with a lamb. If you do not redeem it, then you shall break its neck (Exodus 13:13)

1. As has already been noted (see p. 24), the ass is the only "unclean" animal to which the laws concerning the redemption of the first-born are applicable.

2. The Torah enjoins the owner of the first-born ass to "redeem" it by giving to the Priest a lamb, or the ass's value in money. If he will not redeem the animal, he must kill it by breaking its neck.

3. No benefit may be derived from a first-born ass prior to its "redemption." If it is sold, the money must not be used. If it died, or if its neck was broken before it was redeemed, the ass must be buried.

4. The redemption of a first-born ass must take place some time during the first 30 days of the animal's life.

5. The first-born ass of a Priest or Levite is exempt from redemption.

6. If the owner of the ass cannot afford to buy a lamb for the redemption of the ass, he may redeem it with a sum of money somewhat less than the value of a lamb.

7. If a Jew and a non-Jew own a first-born ass in partnership, the ass need not be redeemed.

COMMENTATORS

Ḥinnukh: This *mitzvah* was instituted to recall to the Jew the slaying of all the first-born in Egypt at the time of the Exodus.
Baḥya ben Asher: "Why was the donkey made subject to the laws of redemption of the first-born although he is an unclean animal?" To answer this question, Baḥya cites (1) the talmudic passage in which the Egyptian people are compared to an ass, and (2) the talmudic story that every Israelite left Egypt with at least 90 asses laden with gold and silver.
Maimonides, Abrabanel: "Why does the Torah specify, as an alternative to 'redemption,' the cruel practice of breaking the ass's neck with a hatchet?" The reply is that this alternative was offered because most people, rather than go through with such a brutal act, would prefer instead to redeem the first-born ass with a lamb. The performance of this *mitzvah* also brings something good to the Priest—he is permitted to eat the lamb.

References:
B. Kiddushin 37a; Tosefta Bekhorot, Chap. 1; Guide of the Perplexed, Part 3, Sec. 39; B. Bekhorot 9a, 13a; Yad, Hilkhot Bikkurim, Chap. 12 (See dispute between Maimonides and the Ravad on the subject of breaking the ass's neck. According to Maimonides, the redemption of the animal is a *mitzvah* by itself and the breaking of the animal's neck is a *mitzvah* by itself. According to the Ravad, however, the breaking of the animal's neck is considered a sin and deprives the Priest of a source of income. Radbaz takes issue with the Ravad and questions his terminology. How can the Torah instruct us to commit a sin? Furthermore, in breaking the animal's neck a definite good is performed, since the Jew can carry out a *mitzvah* appropriately.); Sefer ha-Mitzvot (Aseh) 81; Sefer Mitzvot Gadol (Aseh) 145–146, Shulḥan Arukh, Yoreh De'ah, 321; Sefer ha-Ḥinnukh, Mitzvot 22–23.

THE BELIEF IN ONE GOD

I am the Lord, your God, who brought you out of the land of Egypt, out of the house of bondage. You shall have no other gods before Me (Exodus 20:2–3)

1. The basic premise of Judaism is the uncompromising commitment to One God: omniscient, omnipresent, and omnipotent, the Prime Cause of all things. A person who refuses to accept this premise thereby rejects all of Judaism.

2. We must hold this total commitment to monotheism throughout our lives.

3. No concept of any other deities may so much as enter one's mind at any time.

4. It is forbidden even to utter a word that may be interpreted by others as an indication that other deities may exist.

5. One must not accept any other thing as a "deity," even if refusal to acknowledge the existence of other gods would mean certain death.

COMMENTATORS

Naḥmanides: He explains why God prefaced His commandments with the first commandment. He compares God to a king who tells his subjects that before he gives them his laws and ordinances they must first accept him as their ruler and believe in him. Belief in one God is a prerequisite for all the other *mitzvot*.

Why are the Ten Commandments addressed to the individual in the second person singular? To imply that every individual is responsible for any violation of these commandments and that the argument that "everyone else is also doing the same thing, so why should not I?" is not a valid excuse.

Naḥmanides further asks: What is the relationship between "I am the Lord, your God" and the words, "Who brought you out of the land of Egypt?" This is to teach us that nothing, not even the Exodus, can take place unless God so wills it.

Ibn Ezra: Why did God introduce Himself as the Power who brought the Children of Israel out of Egypt, rather than as the Creator of the universe? Was not the creation of the world a much greater miracle than the Exodus? Ibn Ezra answers the question by explaining that unlike creation, which no one ever witnessed and no one could truly understand, the Exodus was an event which an entire generation had experienced in its own lifetime. People who do not believe in a personal God will identify God with a blind force that takes no hand in human affairs. But anyone who has witnessed the historical fact of the Exodus would be so overwhelmed by the miracle he saw before his own eyes that he will be forced, as it were, to believe in a personal God who guides the destinies of man. Accordingly, one should not give charity simply to impress other people, because that would indicate that he does not care about how he impresses God.

An atheist, one might say, is worse in this respect than a pagan, because the pagan, at least, recognizes the existence of some almighty power, whereas the atheist regards man as the supreme force.

References:

B. Shabbat 88b; B. Makkot 24a; B. Sanhedrin 99a; J. Berakhot, Chap. 1; J. Sukkah, Chap. 4; B. Kiddushin 31a; Song of Songs Rabbah, Chap. 1, Sec. 45; Pesikta Rabbati 21; Yad, Hilkhot Yesodei Torah, Chap. 1; Sefer ha-Mitzvot (Aseh) 1, (Lo Ta'aseh) 1; Sefer Mitzvot Gadol (Aseh) 1, (Lav) 1; Shulḥan Arukh, Oraḥ Ḥayyim, Chap. 61; Ḥovot ha-Levavot, Beginning of Sha'ar ha-Yiḥud; Sefer ha-Ḥinnukh, Mitzvot 25, 26.

PROHIBITION OF IDOL WORSHIP

You shall have no other God before Me. You shall not make unto you a graven image, nor any manner of likeness (Exodus 20:4)
You shall not prostrate yourself unto them, nor serve them (Exodus 20:5)
Make no other mention of the name of other gods (Exodus 23:13)
Nor make to yourselves molten gods (Leviticus 19:4)

1. To make idols oneself, or even to instruct someone else to make an idol, is a sin subject to flogging.

2. One who worships an idol knowingly and deliberately is subject to capital punishment—death by stoning.

3. The belief in One God demands that a Jew must lay down his life rather than worship idols.

4. A Jew must never even appear as if he were worshiping an idol. Thus, if one sees a coin on the ground in front of an idol, one is forbidden to stoop to pick it up because that would look like bowing to the idol.

5. A Jew must not even pretend in jest to be worshiping an idol.

6. A Jew must not perform any act which, though it is not idol worship, is a kind of lip-service to pagan deities. Hence he is forbidden to take an oath in the name of such a deity or even to demand such an oath from a heathen.

7. It is not permitted to utter the name of a pagan deity except for deities that are no longer worshiped (e.g., the gods of ancient Greece and Rome).

COMMENTATORS

Or ha-Ḥayyim: Why was it necessary for the Torah to state, "You shall not make unto you a graven image?" Does not the first commandment already declare, "I am the Lord, your God"? The answer: The second commandment makes it plain that "The Lord, your God" is not just one deity, nor even a supreme deity among many other gods, but that He is the One and Only God and there is no god beside Him. A man may innocently reason that he acknowledges the complete supremacy of the true God and that this idol (*pesel,* derived from the word *pesolet,* "trash") cannot be considered a deity. Continuing with his reasoning, he feels that he is inadequate to pray before the Supreme Being and that he requires an intermediary, even if it is mere "trash" compared to the true God. Thus, the worshiper regards the idol as closer to the level of God and invests in it the power to plead for him. Even this minimal homage to an intermediary is forbidden.

Naḥmanides: There are three types of idol worship. The most primitive of these is the worship of human beings who are regarded as heroes. The second type of idol worship is the adoration of celestial bodies or the adoration of any individual "born under a lucky star." The third is necromancy or the art of foretelling the future by supposed communication with the dead.

Baḥya ben Asher: It is even forbidden to make a "graven image" symbolizing an event in the history of the Jewish people, such as commemorating *sukkot, matzot,* etc.

Recanati: The second commandment was given to disabuse men of the notion that God may be working through intermediaries who are gods in themselves and may be worshiped.

References:

B. Sanhedrin 60b, 61a, 62b, 63a, 63b; B. Avodah Zarah 43b, 54a; J. Sanhedrin Chap. 7, Halakhah 11; B. Ketubbot 33b (see Tosafot); B. Shabbat 149a; B. Rosh ha-Shanah 24b; Yad, Hilkhot Avodah Zarah, Chaps. 2, 3, 5. (Maimonides takes the stand that if a second party created the graven image for someone, the latter is punished. See the famous rebuttal of Leḥem Mishneh *(ibid.),* that this is a negative commandment that involved no action, and in these circumstances there should be no penalty.); Sefer ha-Mitzvot (Lo Ta'aseh) 2, 5, 6, 10, 14; Sefer Mitzvot Gadol (Lav) 14, 17, 18, 19; Sefer Mitzvot Katan (Lav) 63, 64; Shulḥan Arukh, Yoreh De'ah, 139–152; Guide of the Perplexed, Part 1, Sec. 36; Sefer ha-Ḥinnukh, Mitzvot 27, 28, 29, 86, 214.

PROHIBITION AGAINST MAKING IMAGES OF SILVER AND GOLD

Ye shall not make with Me gods of silver and gods of gold (Exodus 20:23)

1.According to rabbinic interpretation, this *mitzvah* is intended to apply to the molding of three-dimensional images (i.e., sculptures, statues, etc.) of human figures.

2. Two-dimensional images of human figures (as in photography, tapestries, or stained-glass windows) are permissible because they do not project.

COMMENTATORS

Ḥinnukh: This commandment means that, just as we are not permitted to portray God in a human form, so we are not allowed to portray man in sculpture, since man was created in the image of God. When we are told that God created man "in His image," this refers to intellectual and spiritual qualities, not features. Furthermore, three-dimensional figures of a man may be a temptation to idol worship.

Ibn Ezra: He interprets this injunction to mean that, since the Jews were the only people to whom God spoke directly, they needed no intermediary to worship Him.

Or ha-Ḥayyim: What happens when one worships an intermediary, not because he believes in him, but because he is paid to do so? This is also forbidden, and the prohibition is implied in the concluding words of the commandment, "you shall not make for yourselves [i.e., for any benefit you may derive from it] . . . ." Even when a person himself does not believe in the idol, but worships it for the reward of gold and silver, he is a transgressor.

Baḥya ben Asher: It is not possible for a monotheistic people to worship God through an intermediary. He therefore interprets the commandment to mean that, if one thinks of gold and silver during his prayers, he is regarded as if he actually worships gods of gold and silver.

References:

B. Avodah Zarah 43b, 46a; B. Sanhedrin 7b; B. Rosh ha-Shanah 24a; Mekhilta

(Yitro); Yad, Hilkhot Avodah Zarah, Chap. 3; Yad, Hilkhot Beit ha-Beḥirah, Chap. 7; Sefer ha-Mitzvot (Lo Ta'aseh) 4; Sefer Mitzvot Gadol (Lav) 22; Sefer Mitzvot Katan 162; Shulḥan Arukh, Yoreh De'ah, 141; Sefer ha-Ḥinnukh, Mitzvah 39.

TAKING THE NAME OF THE LORD IN VAIN

You shall not take the name of the Lord your God in vain (Exodus 20:7)

And you shall not swear by My Name falsely (Leviticus 19:12)

1. To "take the name of the Lord" means swearing in the name of God.

2. There are four types of oaths that are considered as examples of "taking the name of the Lord in vain": *shevu'at bittui, shevu'at shav, shevu'at ha-pikadon* and *shevu'at ha-edut.*

a. *Shevu'at bittui* or *shevu'at sheker.* This is simple perjury.

b. *Shevu'at shav* is a superfluous oath using the name of God. A "superfluous" oath involves making a vow which one knows in advance one is unable to fulfill or swearing to a fact that is obvious (e.g., "I swear that this stone is a stone").

c. *Shevu'at ha-pikadon* was an oath to the effect that one does not have in his possession an object that rightfully belongs to someone else, when, in fact, the object is in his possession. If he had taken the false oath intentionally, he had to pay to the rightful owner the full original value of the object, plus one-fifth of the value. In addition, he had to bring an offering of young doves. However, if he had not been aware that he had sworn falsely, he was not considered guilty.

d. *Shevu'at ha-edut,* a false oath which a potential witness takes to the effect that he knows nothing about the litigation and, therefore, can offer no testimony, when in fact he could testify. If the witness took this false oath willfully, he had to bring a *korban oleh ve-yored*—an "adjustable" offering (i.e., according to his financial means: if he was able to do so, he brought a lamb as an offering; if he was less affluent, he brought doves; if he was poor, it was sufficient if he brought a meal offering.) However, if at the time he took the oath he had indeed forgotten all the facts of the case, but remembered them again after he had sworn the oath, the witness was not considered guilty.

COMMENTATORS

Ḥinnukh: Man is transitory whereas God is everlasting. When a man uses the name of God in a vow, he is swearing by that which is eternal; he thus declares that nothing on earth can keep him from carrying out his pledge. After all, man is subject to external forces that may keep him from fulfilling his promise. If something happens to keep him from doing as he has vowed, he will have taken the name of the Lord in vain. But under ordinary circumstances, one cannot be released from a vow made with the name of God.

Rashbam: The prohibition of taking the name of the Lord in vain is followed by the *mitzvah* to observe the Sabbath. The observance of both these commandments is an expression of respect for God. The fifth commandment, to honor one's father and mother, concerns the respect which is due both to God and to one's parents.

Keli Yakar: When one takes the name of the Lord in vain, one is, in fact, upsetting the equilibrium of all nature, because every living thing has a part of God in him. A person who has taken the name of the Lord in vain is comparable to one who shakes the trunk of a tree, for when he shakes the trunk, the branches and the leaves of the tree will also begin to shake.

Ibn Ezra: Many people consider taking God's name in vain as a minor sin, especially as compared to murder, adultery, and stealing. However, Ibn Ezra holds that the transgression of this *mitzvah* is, in fact, a more serious sin than the violation of any of the commandments that follow. Why is this so? Because one does not normally make a habit of murder, theft, or adultery. In the case of these three transgressions, one must wait for an opportunity to sin; besides, one is usually afraid of being caught each time one commits these crimes. Swearing in the name of God, however, can become a habit to such an extent that one may even swear that he did not take an oath in the name of God. Furthermore, murder, adultery, and theft are acts from which the sinner derives some satisfaction; accordingly, one might conceivably find some mitigating circumstances in passing judgment over such a transgression. Taking the name of the Lord in vain does not, on the other hand, even afford satisfaction to the transgressor. It is stupid, inexcusable sin and hence subject to particularly stringent penalties.

Naḥmanides: This *mitzvah* is linked with the two preceding commandments, "I am the Lord, your God," and "You shall have no other God." Naḥmanides holds that the punishment for him who transgresses the first three commandments is the same: "God will not hold him guiltless" and "will remember the sins of the fathers upon their children." This indicates that the present *mitzvah,* like the first two, involves a transgression against the essence of God. People who make vows in God's name and take them lightly should be aware that the punishment for this sin is as stringent as the punishment for disobeying the first two commandments.

References:

B. Shevu'ot 21a, 25b, 39a; B. Berakhot 33a; B. Shabbat 120a; B. Nedarim 8b, 18a; J. Nedarim, Chap. 3, Halakhah 4; Pirkei de-Rabbi Eliezer, Chap. 38; Midrash Tanḥuma, *Va-Yeshev,* 2; Sifre *Matot,* 103; Sefer ha-Mitzvot (Lo Ta'aseh) 61, 62; Sefer Mitzvot Gadol (Lav) 238, 239; Sefer Mitzvot Katan (Lav) 129; Shulḥan Arukh, Yoreh De'ah, 236.

REMEMBERING THE SABBATH

Remember the seventh day to keep it holy (Exodus 20:8)
You shall not do any work (Exodus 20:10)
And on the seventh day, you shall rest (Exodus 23:12)
Keep the Sabbath day to sanctify it (Deuteronomy 5:12)

1. God created the heavens and the earth and all that is therein in six days and on the seventh day He rested. Man, too, was ordered to work six days and to rest on the seventh. He must not fear that he will suffer socially or economically by observing the Sabbath because God has shown him, by His own example, how one should arrange one's life. By following God's own plan of working six days and resting on the seventh, he manifests his faith in God's ways. Conversely, one who openly desecrates the Sabbath is considered no better than an atheist or idol-worshiper.

2. The Rabbis teach that the observance of the Sabbath involves (1) the fulfillment of the commandments relating to the Sabbath and (2) refraining from work. By "remembering" the Sabbath we mean sanctifying it from beginning to end. This sanctification is performed by the *kiddush* on Friday night and the *havdalah* at the end of the Sabbath. The Rabbis added that both these ceremonies must be performed over a cup of wine. The prophet Isaiah (58:13) teaches us that the Sabbath is to be a day of joy and delight. Accordingly, one must honor it by putting on one's best clothing and enjoying food and drink. At least three meals should be eaten during the Sabbath day. All tension must be avoided, because this would be contrary to the spirit of the Sabbath. Thus the Sabbath is not a proper time for discussing business matters. *Melakhah,* the term for "work" which the Torah uses in connection with the Sabbath, does not necessarily imply work causing physical or mental fatigue. The biblical concept of *melakhah* applies to work involving the production, creation, or transformation of an object. One may spend the entire Sabbath opening and closing books until one drops with exhaustion and yet not violate the Sabbath. On the other hand, the mere striking of a match, just once, is a desecration of the Sabbath because it involves creation.

3. There are 39 major categories of *melakhah* with hundreds of subcategories. These categories are based on the operations that were involved in the building of the Tabernacle in the wilderness: sowing, plowing, reaping, binding, threshing, winnowing, selecting, grinding, sifting, kneading, baking, shearing, bleaching, carding, dyeing, spinning, making two loops, threading needles, weaving, separating, tying, untying, sewing, tearing, hunting, slaughtering, flaying, salting, treatment of skins, scraping, cutting, writing, erasing, building, demolishing, carrying, kindling or extinguishing fire, and putting the finishing touches to a piece of work already begun before the Sabbath.

4. For an activity to be considered as work forbidden on the Sabbath, it must come under the category of *melekhet maḥshevet,* i.e., a task performed consciously and on purpose. Thus, it is permissible to move a chair from one place to another, although there is a chance that this will leave a mark in the ground; or one may walk upon grass, although there is a chance that some of the grass will be crushed under his feet, and it is forbidden to make a rut in the ground or to cut blades of grass. If, however, the original intention was solely to move the chair or to walk on the grass, he has not thereby violated the Sabbath. On the other hand, tasks which are in themselves permitted on the Sabbath but which always result in a violation of the Sabbath are forbidden. Thus, it is forbidden to wash oneself on a lawn, because it is inevitable that he will thereby water the grass, and the watering of plants or grass is one of the forbidden categories of work.

5. In view of the above, the Rabbis forbade various types of work which, though in themselves not constituting violation of the Sabbath, might lead indirectly to the performance of one of the 39 main categories *(avot)* or subcategories *(toledot)* of work that are forbidden. A rabbinic law of this type is known as a *shevot* (colloquially called *shevut*).

6. However, it is self-understood that all these regulations are suspended in cases involving questions of life and death even if there is only a slight chance that such danger to life may be involved.

COMMENTATORS

Ibn Ezra: "To remember" the Sabbath means that one should not only think of the significance of the Sabbath as a day of rest, but also spend the day in meditation on the sovereignty of God and the study of the Torah. Ibn Ezra draws an analogy between the Sabbath and *Shemittah*, the seventh or Sabbatical year on which the soil, too, was allowed to rest. At the beginning of each *Shemittah* year, all the people of Israel were assembled to hear the Torah read to them "in order that they listen and learn." This is also one of the purposes of the Sabbath.

Naḥmanides: Why was the injunction to "keep" the Sabbath not included in the fourth commandment but mentioned only subsequently, in Deuteronomy 5:12? Naḥmanides answers: The injunction to "remember" was chosen in preference over "keep" to show that "remembering" the Sabbath in a spirit of love and reverence is preferable to "keeping" the letter of the law out of no motive other than fear.

Naḥmanides, Or ha-Ḥayyim: We must remember the Sabbath on every single day of the week, because in so doing we will remember the six days of creation which, in turn, should remind us daily of the greatness of God. The Jew counts his weekdays in relation to the Sabbath: e.g., "Today is the first day of the Sabbath"; "Today is the second day of the Sabbath," etc. In this way, we remember the Sabbath, the six days of creation, and the greatness of God every day of the week and every week of the year.

Naḥmanides, Sforno: On the Sabbath we must not engage in any activities that are ordinarily identified with the workday week, even though these acts in themselves may involve no violation of the Sabbath. The Sabbath should be devoted to spiritual and religious activities.

Ḥinnukh: The *Mekhilta* says that *zakhor* means to "remember" (the Sabbath) with a cup of wine. The author explains that a small quantity of wine stimulates the mind and the senses, so that one can better appreciate the joy of the occasion.

Abrabanel: The cycle of weekdays and Sabbath indicates the cycle of life as a whole. We work all our lives until the day we go to our eternal rest.

Recanati: By remembering the Sabbath we start a chain-reaction; for remembering the Sabbath leads to the recognition of the sovereignty of God, which in turn makes us realize that we are of no significance on earth unless we acknowledge the sovereignty of God and submit to His will all the days of our lives.

References:

B. Shabbat 10b, 33b, 49b, 86b, 105a (see Tosafot), 113b, 117b, 118b, 154a; J. Shabbat, Chap. 15, Halakhah 3; Chap. 2, Halakhah 1 (see Torah Temimah to Exodus 20:10.); B. Rosh ha-Shanah 16b; B. Nedarim 49b; B. Yevamot 5b (Note the disagreement between Rashi and Tosafot); Avot, Chap. 5, Mishnah 8; B. Berakhot 20b; B. Pesaḥim 48a, 106a, 117b; B. Betzah 15b; B. Shevu'ot 20b;

B. Krittot 2a; B. Sanhedrin 66a; Midrash Tanḥuma, *Ki Tissa,* 33; Avot de-Rabbi Nathan, Chap. 11; Yad, Hilkhot Shabbat, Chap. 1, 29, 30; Sefer ha-Mitzvot (Aseh) 154, 155, (Lo Ta'aseh) 320; Sefer Mitzvot Gadol (Aseh) 29, 30, (Lav) 65; Shulḥan Arukh, Oraḥ Ḥayyim, 242, 246, 260, 262, 271, 280, 289, 300, 301, 305; Sefer ha-Ḥinnukh, Mitzvot 31, 32, 85.

GOING FORTH FROM ONE'S PLACE ON THE SABBATH

Let no man go out of his place on the seventh day (Exodus 16:29)

1. A Jew must not travel more than 2,000 cubits from any point of the city limits, unless he deposits an *eruv* at that point. (An *eruv* is a symbol consisting of food which symbolically changes the status of a place or time.) It is understood, of course, that "traveling" in this instance means walking on foot. Travel by a vehicle (wagon, train, automobile) is not permitted on the Sabbath, even within the city limits.

2. If one travels more than 2,000 cubits beyond the city limits for the purpose of saving a human life, he may travel an additional 2,000 cubits from the place where he performs the act of rescue.

3. The concept of *eruv teḥumim* was instituted only for the purpose of allowing an individual to fulfill a *mitzvah* that required some traveling. Therefore, to deposit an *eruv* simply so that one can go on an extended hike beyond the city limits would be a violation of the Sabbath spirit.
The following *eruvin* are used:

a. *Eruv teḥumim:* A quantity of food deposited some time before the Sabbath at a place 2,000 cubits outside of the city limits. In view of the fact that a person has placed a quasi-meal there, he has turned the place outside the city into a "dwelling place" from which he may travel another 2,000 cubits in either direction.

b. *Eruv ḥatzerot:* Carrying in a public domain is forbidden on the Sabbath. Therefore, one would not be allowed to carry any object from one house to another. But if, for example, in a large courtyard, all the tenants contribute food to be placed at a central point some time before the Sabbath, the courtyard is transformed from a series of individual dwellings into one common dwelling belonging to all. This legal device was traditionally instituted by King Solomon.

c. *Eruv Tavshilin:* It is forbidden to prepare meals on holidays for the next day even if the next day is a Sabbath. However, if one sets aside a platter of cooked food and a baked item before the holiday begins, the housewife may cook on the holiday for the Sabbath. Two explanations for this kind of *eruv* are given. One, that by not preparing food for the next day unless there is an *eruv* one realizes the stringent rules of the holiday and will not think of cooking on the holiday for the week to come. Also, the *eruv* serves as a reminder that we must not eat all our food on the holiday but should leave over some food for the Sabbath.

COMMENTATORS

Ibn Ezra: Taken literally, the injunction that no one should go forth from his place on the Sabbath implies also that one should not make plans on the Sabbath for a project involving work forbidden on the Sabbath.

Ḥinnukh: The importance of the spirit in which the Sabbath is observed should be stressed. God labored for six days to create the world and on the seventh day He rested. We are therefore told not to use the Sabbath for going on journeys associated with weekday activities. We may only go on leisurely strolls that will enhance enjoyment of the day of rest.

References:

B. Sanhedrin 66a; B. Eruvin 17b, 48a, 49a, 51a; J. Eruvin, Chap. 3; B. Yevamot 47b; B. Shabbat 34a, 69a–70b (see Rashi); Yad, Hilkhot Shabbat, Chap. 27 (Note the inconsistency between the opinion of Maimonides in the Yad, where he establishes the boundary as three miles and his contention in the Sefer ha-

Mitzvot, where he sets the boundary at 2,000 ells. Also see Naḥmanides' dispute with Maimonides in the Sefer ha-Mitzvot (Lo Ta'aseh 321). According to Maimonides, the specific boundaries are of biblical origin. Naḥmanides, however, is of the opinion that they are of rabbinic legislation.); Sefer Mitzvot Gadol (Lav) 66; Mekhilta *Bo*; Shulḥan Arukh, Oraḥ Ḥayyim, 398; Sefer ha-Ḥinnukh, Mitzvah 24.

THE HONOR DUE ONE'S PARENTS

Honor your father and your mother, that your days may be long upon the land which the Lord, your God, gives you (Exodus 20:12)
You shall fear, everyone, his mother and his father (Leviticus 19:3)

1. The importance of this *mitzvah* is shown by the fact that this is one of the only two biblical *mitzvot* for which we are promised the reward of long life, and that the Rabbis equated it with the fear of God.

2. In Leviticus 19:3 the Torah stresses "fear" of our mothers and in Exodus 20:12 "honor" for our fathers. One should "fear" (i.e, stand in awe) of his mother just as much as one does of his father, even though the mother inspires tenderness rather than awe. By the same token, one should "honor" (i.e., revere) his father, even though the father may inspire "fear" rather than affectionate reverence.

3. To "fear" one's parents means not to sit in the seat reserved for him at the table, not to contradict him, not to call him by his first name, etc.

4. To "honor" a parent means to provide him with food, clothing, and shelter.

5. To what lengths must one go to honor his parents? Even if the parent were to throw the son's purposeful gold coins into the sea so that it is lost forever, the son must not reproach his parent for this act, either in word or in deed.

6. To what extent must one show "fear" of his parents? If the son sat at a communal gathering in the seat of honor, dressed in beautiful garments, and the parents were to go up to him, tear off these garments, beat him and spit upon him in full view of the audience, the son must remain calm and not react to this humiliation.

7. The only instance in which a son or daughter may, and indeed must, disobey a parent is when the parent asks him or her to disobey a precept of the Torah.

8. When the father and the mother each make a request of the son or daughter, the father's request takes precedence over that of the mother, because both the child and the mother are duty bound to honor the father.

9. "Honoring" one's father includes showing respect for one's stepmother or one's stepfather, but only as long as the natural parent to whom they are married is alive.

10. In addition to one's parents, one must also honor one's eldest brother. Some authorities say that one must honor all one's older brothers.

11. In instances when the father specifically renounces the privilege of being honored by his children, the son is exempt from the *mitzvah*.

12. A married woman is also obliged to honor her parents. However, if her husband objects to this, she must do as he tells her.

COMMENTATORS

Ba'al ha-Turim: Why was the commandment to honor one's parents placed immediately after the commandment to observe the Sabbath? To show that even as a person must honor the Sabbath, because in doing so he will recall God and His wondrous works, so must he honor his parents, because in so doing he will be reminded of another aspect of the greatness of God, namely God's partnership with the parents in the creation of each child.

Keli Yakar: Why should one stress God's participation in the begetting of a child? Is not the hand of God evident in all that we do? Because in this aspect of life, God is an active partner. The parents provide the child's body and God provides the soul. Therefore God and the parents each play a vital part in the creation of the human personality. Hence we owe equal respect to God and to our parents.

Ḥinnukh: We should honor our parents out of gratitude to them for having begotten us, and for having sustained and cared for us in our youth. If we take this attitude, we will see even more clearly the debt of gratitude we owe to God, because it was He who gave our parents the means to sustain us, and who gave us a soul which elevates men above the animals. In other words, respect for one's parents must lead to respect for God.

Saadiah: Why does the Torah promise long life as a reward for honoring one's parents? If a child honors his parents and cherishes them in their old age when they can no longer care for themselves, his own children will be inspired by this example, and he will have the privilege of enjoying a long life and a blessed old age surrounded by the tender care of his own sons and daughters.

Abrabanel: There are two reasons why we should honor our parents. First, because they have endowed us with talents and capacities which we can use to enhance our own lives. Second, by honoring our parents, we set an example for our own children to respect us. The benefit we derive as a reward for our attentiveness to our parents will help us in our own daily lives.

Naḥmanides: Why does the Torah specify a reward, i.e., "that you may live long upon the land the Lord your God gives you"? In the previous commandments no reward is specified. Naḥmanides argues that this promise of a reward actually means to emphasize the very opposite, namely, that when it comes to honoring our parents one must do so not for the sake of a reward (such as an inheritance) but as he honors God—without questioning.

References:

B. Kiddushin 30b, 31a (see Tosafot); B. Sanhedrin 50a; B. Ketubbot 103a; B. Bava Metzia 32a; B. Yevamot 6a; J. Pe'ah, Chap. 1, Sec. 1; J. Kiddushin, Chap. 1; Yad, Hilkhot Mamrim, Chap. 6, Halakhah 7; Sefer ha-Mitzvot (Aseh) 210, 211; Sefer Mitzvot Gadol (Aseh) 112, 113; Sefer Mitzvot Katan 7, 50; Tanna de-Vei Eliyahu, Chap. 26; Shulḥan Arukh, Yoreh De'ah, 240; Sefer ha-Ḥinnukh, Mitzvot 33, 212.

THE PROHIBITION OF MURDER

You shall not murder (Exodus 20:13)
That the manslayer die not, until he stands before the congregation for judgment (Numbers 35:12)
Moreover, you shall take no ransom for the life of a murderer (Numbers 35:31)

1. Both the body and the soul of man are the handiwork of God. Hence, when one murders his fellow man, he has committed a cardinal sin.

2. Since willful murder is punishable by death, everything must be done to make sure that the suspect is really guilty before he is executed. The Rabbis said that a court of justice that administered capital punishment even only once in seventy years was to be considered a "brutal" court.

3. No one, except the immediate survivors of the murder victim, is allowed to lay a hand upon a murderer, even if he was a witness to the actual crime. A murderer may be put to death only after he has been duly tried and convicted by the court of justice. Anyone, even a witness to the actual crime, who takes the law into his own hands, is considered guilty of murder and subject to the death penalty.

4. In order to be subject to the death penalty, a murderer must have committed the crime with his own hands. If he has merely hired someone else to commit the murder, or tied the victim's hands and feet and a wild animal later killed him, the murderer is not subject to execution. He will eventually die by Divine punishment.

5. During the era of the First Commonwealth, when the Land of Israel was ruled by kings, a murder suspect could be executed by royal decree even on the strength of circumstantial evidence, which was not sufficient basis for a death sentence by a court of justice. However, in emergencies, a court of justice also could issue a death sentence even on the basis of circumstantial evidence.

6. Murder, by definition, includes any act that may hasten the demise of a person, even if that person is already close to death.

7. The family of a murder victim does not have the right to waive murder charges in return for compensation paid them by the murderer, for the body and soul of the victim did not belong to his family but to God.

COMMENTATORS

Naḥmanides: Why does the prohibition of murder immediately follow the commandment to honor one's parents? The logic is as follows: God is the partner of the father and mother. It is obviously a crime to destroy that which was created by such a sacred partnership.

Alshekh: In the eyes of God every man is a light unto the world and no one has a right to extinguish this light.

Keli Yakar: Man was created in the image of God, being endowed with such Divine attributes as mercy and compassion. When one man kills another, he thereby denies the Godliness in his fellow man. The same is applicable to cases of suicide; a man who takes his own life thereby denies the Godliness inherent in his own person.

Abrabanel: Murder does not only refer to the immediate physical destruction of one's fellow man, but also includes acts creating situations that will eventually lead to physical or psychological destruction. For example, the Rabbis say that one who withholds charity from the poor or one who humiliates another person in public is, in fact, guilty of murder.

Ḥinnukh: God created the world so that man should dwell and be fruitful therein. Therefore, when a person commits a murder, he is interfering with God's plan. But if causing the death of a fellow man is against God's purpose in creating man, how do we justify the capital punishment to which a murderer is subject under Jewish law? Obviously, those who committed crimes subject to capital punishment are not the sort of people who are worthy to dwell in the world and want to make it a better place in which to live. They are set upon destroying themselves and the world, and since they thereby frustrate God's design it is necessary that they should be removed from the world.

References:

B. Makkot 6b, 12a; B. Ketubbot 37b; B. Bava Kamma 83b; B. Sanhedrin 72b,

76b; Yad, Hilkhot Rotze'aḥ, Chap. 1; Sefer ha-Mitzvot (Lo Ta'aseh) 289, 292, 295, 296; Sefer Mitzvot Gadol (Lav) 160–163; Sefer Mitzvot Katan 82; Shulḥan Arukh, Ḥoshen Mishpat, 425; Sefer ha-Ḥinnukh, Mitzvot 34, 409, 413.

THE PROHIBITION OF THEFT

You shall not steal (Exodus 20:13)
If a man steals an ox or a sheep. . . he shall pay five oxen for an ox and four sheep for a sheep (Exodus 21:37)
You shall not steal (Leviticus 19:11)

1. Theft is a serious sin. This is true whether one steals as a joke or even with the intention of making restitution immediately.

2. If witnesses testify that a man committed a theft, the accused must make restitution in an amount double the value of the property he has stolen.

3. In some instances, restitution must amount to four or five times the value of the item stolen. If a man stole a lamb and then sold or slaughtered it, he has to pay the owner an amount four times the value of the animal. If he stole an ox and then sold or slaughtered it, he has to pay the owner an amount five times the value of the animal.

4. If a thief is financially unable to make restitution for the stolen article, the courts have a right to sell him as a slave and then repay the victim of the theft from the proceeds of the sale. This covers only the basic cost of the stolen object, not the additional fine imposed. A woman guilty of theft cannot be sold into slavery.

5. A thief who repented, and who confessed to the court of his own free will that he had committed a theft, needs merely to repay the basic value of the object. He need not make double restitution.

6. It is forbidden to buy or accept stolen property, even if the property is not recognized as such. One must therefore not buy a goat from a shepherd, because the shepherd is probably making the sale without the knowledge of his employer and intends to keep the money.

7. The penalty for kidnapping—the "theft" of a human being—which this commandment implies, is death by strangulation. The law explicitly states, however, that mere abduction is not subject to capital punishment; the death penalty applies only if the kidnapper "humiliated" his victim; i.e., if he forced him to work for him, or if he sold him into slavery.

COMMENTATORS

Maimonides: The assessment of restitution in the amount of twice, or four times, or five times the original value of the stolen property is made dependent on the risk the thief runs in committing his crime. The less his risk of being apprehended, the greater his punishment. If he commits his theft in a "crowd situation" he runs a high risk of apprehension; hence, he need make restitution in an amount of only twice that of the value of the stolen property. The risk is somewhat less if he steals sheep in the open field because the shepherd cannot watch over the flock all the time; hence, if the thief is caught, he must make "four-fold" restitution. If he steals an ox which is in the habit of straying from the herd, the risk of apprehension is even less because it is difficult for the cowherd to watch over the oxen in his care; hence, if the thief is caught, he has to make "five-fold" restitution.
Keli Yakar: Why does a thief have to make restitution in the amount of double the value of the property he has stolen? Because he may already have had some possessions of his own, hence his sin involved not only theft but also the unjust coveting of the possessions of another.
Abrabanel: A thief must make "two-fold" restitution because he must be punished also for the discomfiture suffered by his victim. If, for example, he has stolen a chair, he has thereby deprived the victim not only of his property but of his comfort; hence, the thief must not only return the chair he has stolen, but also deprive himself of a chair, even as he deprived his victim of it. He therefore must give his victim an additional chair, or the monetary value of one.

Why does one who stole an animal have to make "four-fold" and "five-fold" restitution? Abrabanel explains that each step involved in the theft represents a separate act of theft for which restitution must be made. Aside from the theft itself, therefore, the thief is liable to punishment also for the separate acts of tying down the animal, placing it into position, and slaughtering it.

Abrabanel contends that these penalties were intended to counteract some of the punishments meted out to thieves in some barbaric societies of the time, which would execute a thief or mutilate him physically. Jewish law viewed such punishments as cruel and unnecessary. Aside from the monetary penalty which the thief had to pay, the humiliation he experienced at being caught and sentenced was considered sufficient punishment.

Where in the Torah do we find mentioned a case of kidnapping which was considered tantamount to theft? In the account of how Joseph was kidnapped by his brothers. The biblical account of the anguish suffered by the victim's father shows the justification for making such a crime liable to the same severe punishment as theft.

Recanati: Of what crime is a thief actually guilty when he commits a theft? He is guilty of thwarting the plan of God, who intended that the victim should have in his possession the object which he, the thief, has stolen from him.

References:

B. Bava Metzia 61b, 112a; B. Bava Kamma 57b, 62b, 67b, 79b; B. Yoma 85a; B. Sanhedrin 72b, 86a; Yad, Hilkhot Genevah, Chap. 1, 3, 9; Sefer ha-Mitzvot (Lo Ta'aseh) 243, 244, (Aseh) 239; Sefer Mitzvot Gadol (Lav) 154, 155, (Aseh) 71; Sefer Mitzvot Katan 263; Shulḥan Arukh, Ḥoshen Mishpat, 348, 359; J. Sanhedrin, Chap. 8, Sec. 3; Sefer ha-Ḥinnukh, Mitzvot 36, 54, 224.

BEARING FALSE WITNESS

You shall not bear false witness against your neighbor (Exodus 20:13)
Then shall you do unto him, as he had planned to do unto his brother (Deuteronomy 19:19)

1. One who bears false witness destroys the whole order of society, therefore one should be extremely cautious in giving testimony against one's neighbor. Even if the greatest saint and scholar told him that his neighbor had committed a crime, he should not testify unless he himself actually witnessed the crime.

2. The court of justice is duty bound to put each witness through careful questioning to ascertain whether the witness is reliable.

3. One who hires others to give false testimony will eventually be punished by God.

4. When a group of several witnesses (i.e., at least two) are found to have perjured themselves by bearing false witness against a defendant in court, they are to be given the same punishment that they would have brought upon the defendant if he had been pronounced guilty on the basis of their false testimony. Thus, if, by their testimony they would have caused an innocent person to be stoned to death, the witnesses themselves must be stoned to death. If their testimony, if accepted, would have caused only monetary loss to the defendant, they are to join in paying to the defendant the total amount of money that he would have had to pay had he been found guilty on the basis of their testimony.

5. There are two different instances when the testimony of one or more witnesses is invalidated because of conflicting testimony:

a. *Hakhḥashah:* The court has four witnesses who are willing to testify. Two of the witnesses testify in court that A owes B money. The other two witnesses then attack the substance of testimony of the first witness by testifying that A does not owe B any money. In such an instance the defendant cannot be punished because there is no way of finding out the truth.

b. *Hazamah:* Again, the court has four witnesses willing to testify. Two of the witnesses testify that A owes B money because they actually saw A borrowing the money from B. The two other witnesses, however, testify that the first two witnesses were in another city at the time of the alleged loan and thus could not have seen the transaction take place. In this case, Jewish law accepts the testimony of the last two witnesses, and the first two witnesses, who perjured themselves by their testimony, must pay the penalty.

6. The rule that a false witness receives the same punishment that would have been given the defendant if he had been found guilty on the basis of the false testimony is applicable only where such punishment is feasible. For example: Two witnesses testify that a certain *Kohen* (Priest) is the offspring of a marriage between a *Kohen* and a divorced woman. If this allegation is true, the man is permanently disqualified from performing priestly functions because the child of a *Kohen* and a divorcee is a *ḥallal* i.e., a non-*Kohen*. But if the witnesses lied, they cannot be given the "penalty" that would have been meted out to the "defendant" since the "penalty" could not be exacted if the witnesses were not *Kohanim*. In this and similar cases the false witnesses are punished by flogging.

If the witnesses happened to be *Kohanim* themselves, of course, they would receive that punishment: i.e., to be permanently disqualified from priestly functions. Their offspring, too, would then be disqualified because the defendant's offspring, too, would have been disqualified also had the defendant been found guilty.

COMMENTATORS

Ḥinnukh, Ralbag: When there are two groups of witnesses, with one group contradicting the other, why do we accept the testimony of the second group and not that of the first? In the absence of any explanation from Maimonides, the *Ḥinnukh* accepts the reasoning of Naḥmanides. Example: Group A testifies that Reuben killed someone. Group B testifies that Group A was not at the scene of the murder but was in the company of Group B at the time the murder was allegedly committed.

The testimony of Group B therefore casts a doubt on the testimony of Group A. As a result, Group A now becomes the accused, with Group B acting as witnesses against Group A. Group A cannot testify in its own behalf because its testimony has been rendered suspect. Accordingly, the testimony of Group B is accepted as against Group A.

Abrabanel: He cites Rabbenu Nissim who reasons that, under the circumstances, there is no reason to fear that the testimony of Group B, rather than that of Group A, could be false. For argument's sake, assume that Group B, motivated by the wish to protect Reuben, had given false testimony. Under the circumstances, Group B would hardly have testified that Group A had been in their company at the time of the murder because if this testimony were not true, it could be proven false easily enough. Group B would therefore have been more likely to attempt to discredit the A testimony on other grounds, such as that Group A were unacceptable as witnesses because they had violated the Sabbath. If, therefore, Group B was not afraid to make this allegation regarding the whereabouts of Group A, it behooves us to accept the testimony of Group B as discrediting that of Group A.

Naḥmanides, Abrabanel, Baḥya ben Asher: If Reuben was executed for murder because of the testimony of Group A, but it should subsequently turn out that the testimony of Group A had been false, no penal action may be taken against Group A. What are the reasons for this ruling?

First: God has made the court of justice His personal emissary in dispensing justice. Since God is perfect, the judgments of the courts must therefore also be perfect. Hence, although Reuben was executed for the wrong reason, namely, on the basis of the false testimony of Group A, it must be assumed that the defendant was undoubtedly deserving of death for some other crimes unknown to the court at the time. Had he been completely innocent, God would not have permitted him to be executed. This reasoning may be one answer to the question of how a judge can appease his conscience when he finds out that he has condemned a man on the basis of false testimony.

Second: The court did what it thought best under the circumstances and there was sufficient evidence to send Reuben to his death. If the death penalty were to be inflicted on Group A because an innocent man had died through their false testimony, the reason for the death of Group A would have to be announced in public and the people would then lose their faith in the courts. Thus, to save the dignity and credibility of the courts, Group A is not given the death penalty.

References:
B. Makkot 2b, 4b, 5a, 5b; B. Ḥullin 11b; B. Ketubbot 20a, 33a; B. Bava Kamma 5a, 72b, 88a; B. Sanhedrin 37a, 90a; J. Sanhedrin, Chap. 11, Halakhah 8; J. Makkot, Chap. 1, Halakhah 1; J. Nedarim, Chap. 3, Halakhah 2; Yad, Hilkhot Edut, Chap. 17, 18; Sefer ha-Mitzvot (Lo Ta'aseh) 285, (Aseh) 180; Sefer Mitzvot Gadol (Lav) 216, (Aseh) 110; Mekhilta *Yitro*; Shulḥan Arukh, Ḥoshen Mishpat, 28, 38; Sefer Mitzvot Katan 236; Sefer ha-Ḥinnukh, Mitzvot 37, 524.

YOU SHALL NOT COVET

You shall not covet (Exodus 20:14)
And you shall not covet (Deuteronomy 5:18)

1. Covetousness can take one of the following two forms:

A man casts a covetous eye upon the possessions (wife, home, etc.) of another individual but his envy does not go beyond daydreaming. This too, is forbidden, but such feelings are not subject to penalty because they represent a *Lav she-en bo ma'aseh*, a violation of Jewish law in thought but not in deed.

Next, there is the envy that leads to action. Here, the coveting involves not only a desire for the possessions of another, but scheming and crafty attempts to talk the other person into giving up his possessions. The covetous man may even exercise undue pressure upon his victim to persuade him to sell the coveted property to him. This action is, in fact, a violation of two commandments, because the individual is guilty of envy both in thought and in deed.

2. If covetousness leads one to steal the possessions of another, he has violated three commandments—envy in thought, envy in deed, and theft.

COMMENTATORS

Maimonides: Simple envy often leads to desire that overrides all other

considerations, with serious consequences. Thus, according to Maimonides, mere envy is a sin in itself, but one who is seized by desires that override all other considerations is guilty of not only one, but two sins.
Ibn Ezra: How can man avoid being covetous, seeing that envy seems to be a normal human attribute? If a man sees that his neighbor has a beautiful wife or a magnificent home, he should realize that it was God's will that these should belong to his neighbor and not to him. He must therefore understand that his neighbor's possessions are beyond his reach. As an example, Ibn Ezra cites the case of someone who has a beautiful mother. It would not even occur to him to desire her, because he has been taught from earliest childhood that she belongs to his father and can never become his. This should be his attitude also with regard to any other possession that belongs not to him but to someone else.
Sforno: If one should find himself coveting an object belonging to his neighbor, he must train himself to pretend that the object does not exist at all. Only in this manner can a man become immune to the inevitable chain reaction in which envy begets lust, lust begets theft, and theft begets murder.
Ḥinnukh: It may be said that the commandment not to covet was included by implication in the seven commandments given to Noah, which were intended for all men on earth to observe (Genesis 9), for although these commandments do not mention envy, they include the prohibition against murder and murder is one of the results of envy.
Alshekh: What is the underlying psychological motivation of a man's lust for someone else's wife? Could it stem from obedience to God's pronouncement that "it is not good for man to be alone" and that he should have a helpmate? It is man's God-given desire and drive that impels him to seek out the opposite sex. But how can a woman who is already married in the eyes of God and the law agree to become the helpmate of another? We see then that a man's desire for a woman who is already the wife of another cannot be interpreted as a sincere attempt on his part to seek out a helpmate in accordance with the will of God. This is pure lust.

References:

B. Sotah 9a, 9b; B. Sanhedrin 25b, 75a; B. Bava Batra 21a; Pirkei Avot, Chap. 4; B. Bava Metzia 5b; Yad, Hilkhot Gezelah, Chap. 1, Sec. 9; Sefer ha-Mitzvot (Lo Ta'aseh) 265, 266; Sefer Mitzvot Gadol (Lav) 158; Sefer Mitzvot Katan 19; Shulḥan Arukh, Ḥoshen Mishpat, 359; Sefer ha-Ḥinnukh, Mitzvah 38.

THE PROHIBITION OF ADULTERY

You shall not commit adultery (Exodus 20:14)

1. The purity and honor of a family are the basis of a stable and strong society. Licentiousness and loose morals cause the disintegration of society and thus contribute to the downfall of civilization.

2. If a man and the wife of another man were found guilty of an adulterous relationship, both were liable to death by strangulation. However, this penalty applied only if both parties had been previously warned that their behavior was immoral. If the parties had been given no such warning, the penalty was Divine punishment; if the parties did not know that their behavior was immoral, they had to bring a sin-offering.

3. The daughter of a *Kohen* who voluntarily engaged in an illicit affair was liable to death by fire, which is considered more severe than strangulation. The man involved was executed by strangulation.

4. When a man had an illicit relationship with a virgin who was betrothed to another man, both parties in the act had to be stoned to death.

5. If the virgin was still below the age of puberty when the crime was committed, the man involved was stoned to death, but the little girl, of course, was not liable to punishment.

COMMENTATORS

Ibn Ezra: There are three reasons why a male wants to engage in sex: his desire to reproduce, his desire to satisfy his physical needs, and the animal instinct of conquering and mastering a woman. The first two motives are legitimate; the third is not. If a man had relations with a woman not his wife, and claimed that he was driven not so much by his urge for conquest as by his desire to reproduce, this does not excuse his behavior, because the woman was not his wife.

Keli Yakar: The right side of the Tablets of the Law bore the five commandments dealing with the relationship between man and God, while the left tablet bore the five commandments concerning the relationship between man and his neighbor. The prohibition of adultery (the seventh commandment) thus appeared opposite the prohibition of idolatry (the second commandment). This was meant to show some of the reasons why adultery was forbidden; namely that it could lead to idol worship.

Ḥinnukh: There are four reasons why adultery was forbidden:

1. God intended that sexual relationships should be stable. Accordingly, man and woman each must have only one spouse.
2. If men and women engage in promiscuous relationships, a child produced by such a union may never know who his father is, and so be unable to fulfill the commandment to honor his father. Worse, he may marry a woman without knowing that she is his sister, and so become guilty of incest.
3. Adultery is a form of theft in that the man steals the woman's affection from her husband.
4. Adultery can lead to murder because the jealous husband may kill his wife's lover.

Ḥizzekuni: Some misguided patriots or politicians might try to persuade the public that it is the duty of each male to impregnate as many females as possible to increase the population of the country, and that for him to do so is not a sin, but a patriotic act. The Torah, however, insists that this is sinful behavior, calculated not to improve the world, but to destroy it.

References:

B. Shevu'ot 47b; B. Niddah 13b (see Rashi and Tosafot); B. Pesaḥim 113b; B. Nedarim 20a; B. Ketubbot 44a, 45a, 48b; B. Sanhedrin 52b, 84b; B. Kiddushin 21b (see Tosafot); Midrash Rabbah, *Ba-Midbar,* Chap. 9, Sec. 6; Yad, Hilkhot Issurei Bi'ah, Chap. 1, 3; Sefer ha-Mitzvot (Lo Ta'aseh) 347; Sefer Mitzvot Gadol (Lav) 97; Shulhan Arukh, Even ha-Ezer, 17, 20, 26; Sefer ha-Ḥinnukh, Mitzvah 35.

THE BUILDING OF THE TEMPLE

And if you make Me an altar of stone, you shall not build it of hewn stones; for if you lift up your tool upon it, you have profaned it (Exodus 20:25)

1. Since the Temple was God's dwelling place, where man made peace with God, it was not permissible to use in its construction any tool made of iron, because iron is also used for making weapons of war.

2. Any stone touched by an iron implement was ruled unfit for use in the Temple. If it was part of the altar, the entire altar was unfit for use until the stone had been replaced by one untouched by tools of iron.

3. Stones used for the altar had to be perfectly smooth. If, as in the case of a *shoḥet* examining his knife, a stone was found (by the test of a finger-nail) to be notched, it was disqualified and had to be put into a *Genizah* (archive for sacred books and ritual articles).

COMMENTATORS

Keli Yakar: The use of a sword or similar iron implement to shape a stone connotes arrogance. This is why the Torah forbade the use of iron tools in the building of the altar; to indicate the attitude of humility with which one must enter the Temple.

Ibn Ezra: There is another reason for the ban on iron tools for the hewing of stones for the Temple: A block of stone taken out of the quarry for use in the building of the Temple becomes holy. If an iron tool is used to shape this stone, it is inevitable that chips would fall from it. If these chips were ever to be lost and land with some refuse, that would be an act of desecration because the chips, like the stones from which they fell, were holy.

Maimonides: If stonecutters were permitted to use fine iron tools, they might be tempted to carve designs into the stone, and this would be contrary to Jewish practice.

Abrabanel: *Ḥerev*, "sword," is related to *ḥurban*, the Hebrew for "destruction." In other words, by applying a tool of iron to the stones to be used in the building of the Temple, one "destroys" the original simplicity and beauty of the stone.

Rashbam: If a stonecutter were permitted to use tools of iron in his work, he might turn the stones into works of art, and the worshipers who came to the Temple might be so spellbound by the art that they might forget the purpose for which they had originally come, namely, to worship God.

Naḥmanides: He opposes Maimonides and Ibn Ezra by pointing out that, while the use of iron tools was forbidden, it was permissible to shape the stones with tools of other metals such as silver, or by applying to them the *shamir,* a worm that could bite through stone. He therefore insists that iron was forbidden simply because it is the metal associated with the making of swords, in other words, potential weapons of destruction. The sword is mentioned in the blessing that Isaac gave to Esau, the enemy of Israel. This is an undesirable association with regard to the Temple.

References:

B. Zevaḥim 54b, 61b; J. Middot, Chap. 3; B. Sanhedrin 76b; B. Avodah Zarah 52b; Mekhilta *Mishpatim*; Guide of the Perplexed, Part 3, Sec. 45; Yad, Hilkhot Bet ha-Beḥirah, Chap. 1; Sefer ha-Mitzvot (Lo Ta'aseh) 79; Sefer Mitzvot Gadol (Lav) 290; Sefer ha-Ḥinnukh, Mitzvah 40.

APPROACHING THE ALTAR WITH DIGNITY

Neither shall you go up by steps unto Mine altar, that your nakedness be not uncovered (Exodus 20:26)

Although the Priests wore trousers, there was always the possibility that their private parts might be exposed beneath their garments as they ascended the steps. Modesty demanded that not even the bare stones of the Temple steps should "see" the private parts of the Priests. To eliminate this possibility, the Priests ascended to the altar not by way of steps but by way of a ramp. Even then, they were commanded to walk slowly and with short steps, on pain of flogging.

COMMENTATORS

Sforno: *Ervatkha* ("nakedness") means levity. In Sforno's view, this text implies that this precaution against the exposure of the Priest's private parts is not enough; anyone serving in the Temple must be careful not to indulge in any form of levity no matter how seemingly inconsequential.
Rashbam: The ramp was made of rocks and sprinkled with salt to prevent the Priests from slipping and falling.
Keli Yakar: Why were stairs forbidden? Because the act of walking in a stately manner up a stairway gives an impression of pomp and arrogance, an attitude which in turn might lead to immodesty and immorality.
Ibn Ezra: Ben Zuta, the Karaite, interprets the word *be-ma'alot* ("steps") as being derived from *ma'al* ("to trespass"). In other words, Ben Zuta said this meant: Do not approach My altar with the attitude of a trespasser of the word of God. By "trespassers" Ben Zuta, of course, meant the Rabbis who followed the Oral Tradition. In order to destroy the Karaite argument Ibn Ezra explains that Ben Zuta is wrong even from the viewpoint of etymology. *Be-ma'alot* can be derived only from *aleh* ("to go up").
Ḥinnukh: The Priest must not allow his private parts to be exposed even to the stones upon which he treads when approaching the altar. Of course, stones cannot really "see" his private parts or become the object of disrespect, but by remembering the precepts of modesty even in the presence of the stones, the Priest will be reminded of the attitude of modesty and reverence he must show when he is in the Temple.

References:
B. Nazir 45a; J. Berakhot, Chap. 1, Halakhah 1; Mekhilta *Mishpatim;* Yad, Hilkhot Bet ha-Beḥirah, Chap. 1; Sefer ha-Mitzvot (Lo Ta'aseh) 80; B. Sotah 48b; Sefer Mitzvot Gadol (Lav) 291; Sefer ha-Ḥinnukh, Mitzvah 41.

CONSIDERATION TOWARD THE HEBREW SLAVE

If you buy a Hebrew servant (Exodus 21:2)
You shall not force him to serve as a slave (Leviticus 25:39)
For they are My servants. . . They shall not be sold as bondsmen (Leviticus 25:42)
He shall not dominate with harshness over him in your sight (Leviticus 25:53)

1. When one became so poor that he had no money or personal possessions left with which to pay his debts, he could sell himself as a slave. It was considered preferable that he should sell himself to a fellow Jew. If he sold himself to a non-Jew, it was incumbent upon the family of the slave, and in fact upon the entire Jewish community, to "buy him back" from the non-Jew. A slave sold to a Jewish master had to serve his master only for six years, even if the amount of money the master had paid for him was greater than the value of the services which the slave had rendered. If, during those six years, the master died and left no son to inherit him, the slave went free. The slave could also "redeem" himself, or be redeemed by others, and then the master had no right to keep him against his will. If a Jewish master caused his non-Jewish slave to lose a limb, the slave automatically went free. If the slave was a Jew the master had to pay him an indemnity in addition to releasing him.

2. A Jewish slave had to be treated with respect for his dignity. The master could not expect his slave to perform duties that were debasing or humiliating, nor could he behave toward him with the arrogance of a "lord and master." He was not permitted to say to him: "Work this field until I return," but rather: "Please work this field until a certain hour, and then stop and rest." He could not command him: "Tie my shoes" or "Bring my linens into the bathhouse," because these were considered menial duties violating the personal dignity of the slave.

3. A Jewish slave could not be sold on an auction-block, or in an alley; the transaction had to be made quietly and with dignity.

4. A Jewish slave, male or female, was to be regarded as part of the master's family. The slave had to get the same food and drink as the master. On the other hand, the slave had to conduct himself not as an equal with the master but show him proper deference with regard to the work he had to do.

5. One sold as a slave by the *Bet Din* because he could not make restitution for, say, a robbery he committed, had to serve six years from the day of purchase. At the start of the seventh year, he went free. But when the seventh, or *Shemittah* year occurred during these six years of servitude he had to go on serving until he had completed the six years. On the other hand, if the Jubilee year fell during his period of servitude, he had to be set free even if he had not completed his term. One who sold himself to a non-Jew and was not ransomed by his family or community, had to serve until the Jubilee year. Any Jewish slave could "redeem" himself by paying his master an amount of money computed as follows: if he sold himself for 400 coins of silver, to serve over a period of ten years, each year of service was worth 40 pieces of silver. Hence, he could redeem himself at the end of five years by paying his master 200 pieces of silver.

6. While the slave was in his service, the master was obliged to support the family of the slave, but was not permitted to derive any gain from any income earned by the children of the slave. In biblical times it was customary for masters to force their male slaves to beget children by female slaves, so that the children, too, could serve in the master's household. Since the conscience of Judaism would rather have seen such practices abolished, it was obvious that one could not abrogate overnight a custom that had become entrenched so firmly in the society of the time. The Bible set about regulating the circumstances under which a Jewish slave could be asked to beget children with a heathen maidservant of the household. Thus, probably in order to prevent intermarriage between Jews and heathens, the Bible ordained that a master could make this request only of a slave who was already married to another woman and thus had a stable family life.

7. If at the end of his six years a Jewish slave had come to like his life of servitude and expressed a desire to continue serving his master, his master had to bring him to the court of justice where the master pierced the slave's earlobe. After that the slave could continue in servitude until the Jubilee year, when he was obliged by law to accept his freedom. It is interesting to note that if the Jewish slave was a *Kohen* he was not permitted to have his earlobe pierced because a *Kohen* with a physical blemish or defect could no longer perform his functions in the Temple. The law pertaining to the slave who refused to go free after six years was not applicable to a female slave.

COMMENTATORS

Most of the commentaries apparently acknowledge the fact that in certain ancient societies, slavery was a social and economic necessity. However, they were outspoken in their condemnation of cruelty to slaves.

Naḥmanides: He stresses the injustice of slavery in the light of the first of the Ten Commandments: "I am the Lord your God who brought you out of Egypt." He interprets this to imply that "if I the Lord freed you from slavery, you have no right to enslave others."

Or ha-Ḥayyim: He deals with the economic considerations of slavery. For example, he considers buying a non-Jewish slave (who did not have to be freed) preferable to having a Jewish slave who had to be released after six years. However, he had little respect for individuals who sold themselves into slavery out of their own free will. A man would not permit himself to be a slave, he says, unless he had so divested himself of his human dignity that being a slave no longer holds any embarrassment for him. Also, one who permits himself to be sold into slavery is an individual who always had a "slave mentality."

Naḥmanides: One who was sold into slavery against his will had to be accorded treatment that would make him feel eventually as if he had become a slave from his own choice. He had to be given adequate food and clothing.

Ibn Ezra: A master could expect service from his slave, but he could not employ cruel means of coercion.

Ḥinnukh: There are two reasons why a master had to treat his slave with kindness and compassion. First, one must not forget that the fortunes of man are subject to change. The master may have to become a slave himself some day and may be in a position where he himself must seek compassion. Second, kindness to one's servants is merely another exercise in the effort to perfect oneself in the qualities of kindness and compassion.

Abrabanel: Why were Jews obligated to "redeem" a fellow-Jew who had been sold into slavery to a non-Jew? Because a Jew's first obligation is to his God. "Do not rule with vigor" meant that the master was not permitted to keep the slave from doing his duty to God. Even as a slave, the Jew was expected to observe all the *mitzvot,* for they represented his duty to his real master.

References:

B. Arakhin 18b, 29a; B. Bava Metzia 65a, 71a; B. Ketubbot 43a; B. Bava Kamma 116b; B. Kiddushin 14b, 15a, 15b, 16a, 17a, 21b, 22a, 22b; B. Makkot 13a; B. Sanhedrin 86a; J. Kiddushin, Chap. 1, Halakhah 2; Sifra *Behar;* Mekhilta *Mishpatim;* Sifre *Re'eh;* Yad, Hilkhot Avadim, Chap. 1–4; Sefer ha-Mitzvot (Aseh) 232, (Lo Ta'aseh) 257, 258, 259, 260; Sefer Mitzvot Gadol (Aseh) 83, (Lav) 175, 176, 177; Sefer Mitzvot Katan 265; Sefer ha-Ḥinnukh, Mitzvot 42, 344, 345, 346, 348.

LAWS APPLYING TO THE JEWISH MAIDSERVANT

If she does not please her master, who espoused her to himself, he shall let her be redeemed. He shall have no power to sell her to a foreign people, since he has dealt deceitfully with her (Exodus 21:8)

1. Jewish Law deals with women on the basis of three phases in their physical development:

a. *Ketanah:* one below the age of twelve.

b. *Na'arah:* a girl between the age of twelve years and one day, and twelve years and six months, who has already entered puberty.

c. *Bogeret:* a girl who has passed the age of twelve years, six months, and one day, when she is regarded as a mature woman.

2. The biblical references to a maidservant apply to a *ketanah* who was sold into slavery by her father because of the family's extreme poverty. A *na'arah* and *bogeret* could not be sold, nor could they sell themselves into servitude. As a matter of fact, if a *ketanah* developed the symptoms of *na'arut* the day after she was sold into slavery she had the right to go free, and her master was not entitled to any compensation. Ordinarily, a *ketanah* served the standard six-year period and then went free.

3. The Torah was very sensitive to the social position into which a young girl was placed when she was sold into slavery. Jewish law required the master, or his son, to make the child his bride so that she might attain a social position of honor and respect. This *mitzvah* of betrothal took priority over the *mitzvah* of redemption. The girl then had to be treated not as a servant, but as a prospective member of the master's family—as his wife or his daughter-in-law.

4. However, such betrothal presupposed the girl's consent. If she refused to become engaged to the master, or to his son, she was permitted to obtain her freedom through outright cancellation of her sale by cash or notes, or by serving the full six years, or by financial arrangements taking into consideration her years of servitude. She could also be set free if the Jubilee year occurred during her term of servitude, or if the master died, or if she developed signs of puberty. Her master was not permitted to sell her to anyone else.

COMMENTATORS

Naḥmanides, Sforno, Or ha-Ḥayyim, Ḥinnukh, Abrabanel: A Jewish maidservant did not belong to her master body and soul. He had a right only to her services as a worker. The fact that her own father had to sell her into slavery because the family was in dire want was sufficiently humiliating for the girl. Therefore, in order to offset this stigma, the master, or his son, was required to marry her and thus accord her an honorable position in society.

Naḥmanides: He quotes the ninth-century Gaon, Simeon Kayyara, who contends that if the maidservant was not treated well by her master, both the master and her father who sold her into slavery were punishable for violating the commandment in Exodus 21:7: "She shall not go out as the menservants do." Everything had to be done not to humiliate this maidservant but rather to raise her status in the eyes of the community.

References:

B. Kiddushin 14b, 16a, 18b, 19a; B. Bekhorot 13a; Mekhilta *Mishpatim;* Yad, Hilkhot Avadim, Chap. 4; Sefer ha-Mitzvot (Aseh) 233, 234, (Lo Ta'aseh) 261; Sefer Mitzvot Gadol (Aseh) 85, 86, (Lav) 179; Sefer ha-Ḥinnukh, Mitzvah 43.

THE RIGHTS OF A WIFE

He may not diminish his wife's allowance, her clothes, or her conjugal rights (Exodus 21:10)

1. When a man marries, he pledges himself to fulfill ten specific obligations toward his wife. Three of these are imposed by the Torah; the rest, by the Rabbis.

2. The husband's three biblical obligations are: a) to supply his wife with food, b) to clothe her, and c) to have sexual relations with her.

3. The husband's seven rabbinic obligations are:

a. To make provisions for the fulfillment of the terms of the *ketubbah* (marriage contract), under which he makes a settlement on his wife if he should divorce her or if he should predecease her.

b. To pay for her medical treatment.

c. To ransom her if she is captured.

d. To give her a dignified burial if she should predecease him.

e. To make provisions for her support from his assets if he should predecease her.

f. To make provisions for the support of her unmarried daughters after his death, such support to continue until they marry.

g. To make provisions that, if his wife should predecease him, the sons she bore him will inherit any property she brought with her as her marriage portion. Her sons are to inherit this property in addition to the share they will receive from the father's inheritance along with any sons their father has from a previous marriage.

4. On the other hand, rabbinic law specifies that a husband has certain legal claims on his wife's possessions.

a. Her earnings belong to him.

b. Any valuables she finds belong to him.

c. Any dividends paid on her assets belong to him.

d. He inherits her property if she predeceases him.

COMMENTATORS

Rashbam: He stands almost alone in his opinion that *onah* (a term usually rendered as "the conjugal rights") should be interpreted instead as "home" because it is derived from *maon,* the Hebrew term for "home." In other words, a man must provide a respectable home for his wife. Although the Rashbam does not explicitly state this, his contention may stem from the consideration that man would hardly need a commandment to remind him of a duty toward which he is so strongly impelled by his own physical drives.

However, almost every other classical commentator insists that the reference is not to the home but to conjugal relations. Their thinking stems from the premise that a wife will consider the assurance of her husband's love much more important to her than a nice home.

References:

B. Ketubbot 47b, 48a, 59b, 61a, 66b; B. Bava Metzia 59a; B. Ḥullin 84a; B. Yevamot 62b; B. Shabbat 25b, 118b; Tanna de-Vei Eliyahu 9; B. Nedarim 15b; Yad, Hilkhot Ishut, Chap. 12–25; Sefer ha-Mitzvot (Lo Ta'aseh) 262 (See the opinion of Sefer Mitzvot Katan who considers conjugal rights as a separate *mitzvah,* contrary to all other commentaries, in 277, 278.); Sefer Mitzvot Gadol (Lav) 81; Shulḥan Arukh, Even ha-Ezer, 70, 73, 76; Sefer ha-Ḥinnukh, Mitzvah 46.

CAPITAL PUNISHMENT

And he that strikes a man so that he dies shall surely be put to death (Exodus 21:12)

If a man smites his bondsman . . . and he dies . . . he shall surely be avenged (Exodus 21:20)

If a man takes with his wife also her mother . . . they shall be burned with fire (Leviticus 20:14)

If a betrothed virgin cohabits with a man . . . you shall stone them with stones (Deuteronomy 22:23–24)

1. Under Jewish law capital punishment was imposed only when the Temple was still in existence, when the offerings were still brought on the altar, and when the Sanhedrin still sat in the *Lishkat ha-Gazit*, the Chamber of Hewn Stones.

2. As has already been noted elsewhere, the death sentence was imposed only after much investigation and deliberation on the part of the court of justice. The judges made every effort to avoid imposing capital punishment. Circumstantial evidence was not accepted in trials for a capital offense and once the defendant in such a case had been acquitted, he could not be brought to trial again for the same offense, even if direct evidence had turned up in the meantime to prove his guilt.

3. Individuals who were executed were not buried in the communal burial ground. Two separate cemeteries were reserved for them—one for individuals that had been stoned or burned, and one for those executed by the sword or by strangulation. After a time the remains of such individuals could be exhumed and reinterred in the communal burial ground.

There were four types of capital punishment—death by strangulation, death by the sword, death by fire, and death by stoning.

The following six crimes were punishable by strangulation:

a. Sexual relations with the wife of another man.

b. Kidnapping another Jew.

c. Inflicting an injury on one's parents.

d. Defection by an elder of the people from God and the Torah.

e. False prophecy.

f. Prophecy in the name of false gods.

Death by the sword was the penalty for murderers and for the people of a city who had permitted themselves to be misled so that they became idol worshipers.

Individuals guilty of the following ten crimes were punishable with "death by fire" (this did not involve "burning at the stake" but the pouring of hot, molten lead into his body):

a. Adultery by the daughter of a *Kohen*.
b. Sex relations with one's own daughter.
c. Sex relations with one's daughter's daughter.
d. Sex relations with one's son's daughter.
e. Sex relations with one's stepdaughter.
f. Sex relations with the daughter of one's stepson.
g. Sex relations with the daughter of one's stepdaughter.
h. Sex relations with one's mother-in-law.
i. Sex relations with the mother of one's mother-in-law.
j. Sex relations with the mother of one's father-in-law.

The following crimes were punishable with death by stoning:

a. Idol worship.
b. Working on the Sabbath.
c. Sexual relations between a man and a virgin betrothed to another. (Both partners were subject to the penalty.)
d. Cursing the name of God with another appellation customarily used to denote Him.
e. Inciting an entire community to worship idols.
f. Incest with one's mother.
g. Sex relations with one's daughter-in-law.
h. The sacrifice of children on the altar of Moloch.
i. Incest with one's stepmother.
j. Sodomy with an animal.
k. Sodomy with another male.
l. Sexual relations between a woman and an animal.
m. Conduct described in the biblical characterization of "the wayward son," who gorges himself with food and drink to the point where he may eventually commit murder.
n. Spiritualism.
o. Witchcraft.

p. Cursing one's mother or father, using the name of God.
q. Inciting an individual to worship idols.
r. Sorcery.

COMMENTATORS

The exegetes make no comment on the reasoning behind the four distinctive methods of capital punishment. They do cite, however, the famous dispute between Maimonides and Naḥmanides. According to Maimonides, it was of cardinal importance to know which penalty was relevant to a particular crime. In his view, each individual procedure in capital punishment was a *mitzvah* by itself. Naḥmanides, on the other hand, asserted that punishment was merely a detail related to the crime and not a *mitzvah* in itself.

References:
B. Sanhedrin 43b, 44a, 45a, 46a, 49b, 52b; B. Ketubbot 30a; B. Makkot 10b; Yad, Hilkhot Sanhedrin, Chap. 14, 15; Sefer ha-Mitzvot (Aseh) 226, 227, 228, 229 (See the dispute between Maimonides and Naḥmanides in Shoresh 14.); Sefer Mitzvot Gadol (Aseh) 99, 100, 101, 102; Sefer ha-Ḥinnukh, Mitzvot 47, 50, 261, 555.

CURSING OR STRIKING ONE'S PARENTS

One who strikes his father or his mother shall be put to death (Exodus 21:15)
One who curses his father or his mother shall be put to death (Exodus 21:17)
Everyone that curses his father or his mother shall be put to death (Leviticus 20:9)

1. Anyone who cursed his parents by using the name of God was stoned to death. Anyone who struck his parents was strangled to death.

2. Cursing one's parents was punishable regardless of whether or not the parents were alive at the time. However, capital punishment was mandatory only if the son had used the name of God in cursing his parents. If he merely reviled his parents but did not use the name of God, he was subject only to flogging.

3. Striking a parent meant injuring a parent so that he let blood, even if the parent lost no more than a drop. One who struck his parent without causing the parent to lose blood was punished by flogging.

4. The question has been asked whether a surgeon may operate on his parents, since surgery, too, would cause loss of blood. The rabbinic ruling is that the son should not perform the surgery, if another surgeon is available. But if no other surgeon is available, he is permitted to perform the operation himself.

5. A man employed by the court of justice to administer floggings was not permitted to administer that punishment to his father. If his father was sentenced to flogging, the son had to ask the court to find another man to administer the punishment in his place.

COMMENTATORS

Naḥmanides: He gives two reasons why the misdemeanors of cursing one's parents and striking them were not liable to the same punishment. Why was stoning ordained in the case of the former and strangulation in the case of the latter? He points out that stoning was a more severe punishment than strangulation. Since children are more likely to curse their parents than to attack them physically, cursing one's parents was made subject to the severer punishment to deter others from this sin. Besides, a child who uses the name of God in cursing his parents thereby also curses God; he therefore is guilty of two sins—cursing his parents and using the name of the Lord in vain. From either viewpoint, therefore, a child who curses his parents is deserving of more severe punishment than one who strikes his father or mother.

Da'at Zekenim: God is an equal partner with the mother and the father in the birth of each child. Accordingly, a child who curses his parents thereby also curses God. On the other hand, striking one's parents is not tantamount to striking God, because it is not possible to inflict physical injury on God. Hence, the one who strikes his parents has sinned only against his parents. This is the reason why a child who cursed his parents was liable to more severe punishment than one who struck his father or mother.

References:
B. Kiddushin 30b; B. Shevu'ot 36a; B. Ḥullin 11b; B. Sanhedrin 53a, 66a, 84b, 85b; Mekhilta *Mishpatim;* Yad, Hilkhot Mamrim, Chap. 5; Sefer ha-Mitzvot (Lo Ta'aseh) 318, 319 (See the difference of opinion between Maimonides and Naḥmanides. Maimonides states that cursing and smiting are two separate injunctions, because their penalties are different. Naḥmanides looks upon them as one injunction, because the biblical warning is the same for both.); Sefer Mitzvot Gadol (Lav) 219; Shulḥan Arukh, Yoreh De'ah, 241; Sefer ha-Ḥinnukh, Mitzvot 48, 260.

CAUSING INJURY TO A FELLOW MAN

And if men quarrel and one strikes the other [the guilty party must pay for the loss of his time and for his cure] (Exodus 21:18)

1. *Adam mu'ad le-olam,* "A man is held responsible for any damage that he inflicts upon others," whether intentionally or unintentionally, consciously or unconsciously.

2. According to the literal interpretation of the scriptural law, "An eye for an eye" etc. (Exodus 21:24), one who injures another should have had the same injuries inflicted upon him; the Oral Tradition, however, interprets this commandment to mean merely that the victim was entitled to monetary compensation for his injury.

3. The injured is entitled to compensation for the permanent physical disability, the pain, the medical treatment, the loss of earning power resulting from his injury, and also for the indignity inflicted upon him.

4. The following considerations enter into the assessment of proper compensation:

a. *Nezek* (Permanent physical disability). If the injury resulted in loss of limb to the injured party, the compensation amounted to the difference between the financial value of the individual's service when he still had the limb and the value of his services without the limb.

b. *Tza'ar* (Pain). Here compensation amounted to the difference between the amount of money the individual would have demanded for having a limb amputated under anaesthesia and the amount of money he would ask for having the limb amputated without anaesthesia.

c. *Rippui* (Medical treatment). All doctor's bills must be paid for the injured until he has fully recovered.

d. *Shevet* (Loss of earning power). The calculation of this compensation depends upon the nature of the injury. If the injury results in no more than, say, a swollen arm, the victim must be paid for every day he must remain away from his work, that is to say, how much a person would ask to compensate for loss of income in his particular field of work. If, on the other hand, the injury makes it necessary for the arm to be amputated, the injured party is to be paid for lost working hours on the basis of the salary customarily paid a watchman for watching over a vegetable patch. Since he is already receiving compensation for permanent physical disability, he is to be paid for lost time not on the basis of the income he would have received in his original field of work but only on the basis of the wages which he could receive from such work as can be performed by a person in his present physical condition.

e. *Boshet* (Indignity). The compensation due to the injured party for this aspect of his injury depends on who inflicted the injury and on the status of the injured party. There is a difference between being subjected to indignity by an important personage and being insulted by a mere child.

5. It is not only forbidden to injure others, but also to inflict an injury upon oneself.

6. The Rabbis went so far as to use the adjective "wicked" to refer to any person who so much as raises his hand with the intent of inflicting injury upon another person.

7. It is not enough that the injured be compensated, in full, for every aspect of his injury. The one who inflicted the injury upon him must also seek the forgiveness of the victim.

8. Judaism holds that the lives of all living things are sacred; therefore, if someone has been killed or injured, those nearby are commanded under Jewish law to cover up the blood of the victim *(kissui ha-dam)*. This law applies even to beasts and fowls, the blood of which must be covered by the *shoḥet* after slaughter. At one time this *mitzvah* was taken so seriously that if another person on the scene hastened to perform it, thus depriving the *shoḥet* of the opportunity to do so himself, with the appropriate blessing to be recited on such occasions, the *shoḥet* was entitled to compensation in the amount of ten golden coins.

COMMENTATORS

Ibn Ezra: The Rabbis interpret the law of "an eye for an eye" to mean that one who caused another person to lose an eye had to pay the injured party a monetary compensation for the value of the eye. What led them to interpret the law in this manner, rather than literally?

Ibn Ezra and others cite a dialogue on this issue between Saadiah Gaon and Ben Zuta, a member of the Karaite sect which rejects the Oral Tradition and believes in the literal interpretation of every word of the Bible. Saadiah Gaon defends the interpretation given in the Oral Tradition. He points out that justice would not necessarily be served by simply gouging out the eye of one who caused another to lose an eye. The injured party might be in excellent health so that he would survive the injury, while the guilty party might be sickly and might not survive the loss of his eye. Hence, the value of the eye of the injured party and that of the eye of the guilty party cannot be regarded as identical. Besides, even partial loss of vision is not the same in the case of any two people who have suffered the loss of an eye. Even if the injury resulted in no more than a bruise, how can one make sure that the bruise inflicted on the guilty party will be no more severe than the one he inflicted on the victim?

In view of these considerations, the only just punishment for one who inflicts an injury on another is to have him give a monetary compensation to the party he has injured. In this manner, the offender has to pay a fine as it were, for the physical "punishment" he has inflicted on his victim. And, at the same time, the victim is thus helped toward his recovery or rehabilitation.

References:

B. Bava Kamma 83b, 84a, 85a, 90b, 91a, 92a; B. Sanhedrin 58b; Yad, Hilkhot Ḥovel u-Mazik, Chap. 1; Yad, Hilkhot Sanhedrin, Chap. 5, Sec. 10; Mekhilta *Mishpatim;* Sefer ha-Mitzvot (Aseh) 236; Sefer Mitzvot Gadol (Aseh) 70; Shulḥan Arukh, Ḥoshen Mishpat, 1, 420; Sefer ha-Ḥinnukh, Mitzvah 49.

DAMAGE CAUSED BY ANIMALS: THE GORING OX

And if an ox gores a man or a woman so that they die, the ox must must be stoned and its flesh may not be eaten (Exodus 21:28)

1. Men are responsible for the animals in their possession. The owner of an animal must see to it that it should cause no damage to persons or to property. If the animal causes any damage to another party, the owner is liable for the damage.

2. "Destructive animals" are classed into two categories:

a. *Tam* ("unconfirmed"). An animal that causes damage in a manner not usually expected. For instance, a young ox is likely to cause damage by trampling property or by eating it. He is not expected to use his horns to gore a person or object. Accordingly, if the ox causes damage with his horns, the owner is liable only for half of the damage, and this amount must not exceed the value of the ox that did the damage.

b. *Mu'ad* ("Confirmed killer"). An animal that causes damage in a manner that may usually be expected if it is not kept under control. The owner of such an animal is liable for the full amount of the damage caused by the animal. If an animal classed as *tam* inflicts the same damage on three different occasions after the owner has been warned for three consecutive days, it, too, is considered a *mu'ad,* and the owner is liable for the full amount of whatever damage it causes.

3. Any ox that has killed a man must be stoned to death. This rule is applicable to both *tam* and *mu'ad.* The owner of a *mu'ad,* in addition to losing his animal, must pay "redemption money" *(kofer)* to the family of the individual killed by the animal. The owner of a *tam* need not make this payment.

4. An animal that has been stoned to death by order of the court becomes ritually unclean. Its flesh may not be eaten by Jews; it may not ever be sold to non-Jews or fed to dogs. The carcass must be buried.

COMMENTATORS

Baḥya ben Asher: Even as the serpent in the Garden of Eden was instinctively conscious of the harm it inflicted on Eve, so too, an animal that is classed as a "confirmed killer" of men is somehow aware of the evil it is doing. This is the reason why one must neither eat the flesh of such an animal nor derive any benefit from it even after it has died.
Ḥinnukh: The law is intended to serve as a lesson to man. If even an animal that disturbed the peace of the community is shunned by both God and man, even after its death, how much more severe must be the punishment for an intelligent human who disturbs the peace or ruins the morals of his fellow men!

References:
B. Bava Kamma, Chap. 1, 2, 3, 4, 5; B. Kiddushin 56b; B. Pesaḥim 22b, 112b; J. Avodah Zarah, Chap. 5, Halakhah 12; Mekhilta *Mishpatim;* Yad, Hilkhot Nizkei Mamon, Chap. 1, Sec. 4; Sefer ha-Mitzvot (Aseh) 237, (Lo Ta'aseh) 188; Sefer Mitzvot Gadol (Aseh) 66, (Lav) 135; Shulḥan Arukh, Ḥoshen Mishpat, 389–400; Sefer ha-Ḥinnukh, Mitzvah 51.

DAMAGE CAUSED BY NEGLIGENCE

If it is a goring ox, one that had already gored yesterday and the day before, [the ox must be stoned, and its owner also put to death] (Exodus 21:29)

If a man shall open a pit [and an ox or ass shall fall into it] (Exodus 21:33)

If a man shall cause a field or a vineyard to be eaten [by an animal in his possession] (Exodus 22:4)

If a fire breaks out [so that the fields of another man are destroyed] (Exodus 22:5)

1. The Rabbis deduced from scriptural law four major areas *(Avot Nezikin)*, as well as ancillary types *(Toledot)*, of damage caused by negligence.

a. *Shor* (Ox). According to some, this term refers to the "goring ox" described in the previous *mitzvah*. Others maintain that this refers to damage done by an animal goring, trampling, or eating an object.

b. *Bor* (Pit). This term refers to the case of one who dug a large hole in a public domain, or one who uncovers an existing pit and leaves it uncovered, thus creating a danger to men and animals. If an accident happens as a result, and the pit is at least ten hands' breadths deep, the wrongdoer is liable to all the damages. If an animal falls into such a pit and is killed, full compensation for the animal must be made. By contrast, if a man falls in and dies, there is no penalty. However, if the victim suffers an injury and survives, he must be given compensation. If the pit is less than ten hands' breadths deep, and either a man or an animal falls in and is killed, full compensation need not be paid even for the animal. But if the man or animal suffers an injury and survives, compensation is due just as if it would be in the case of the deeper pit. The *Toledah* (ancillary) to this type of damage caused by negligence is the placing of any kind of impediment in a public domain where it can cause harm.

c. *Maveh* (Bodily damage). According to some, this *Av Nezikin* refers to an animal which tramples or eats objects within the domain of the one who suffered the damage. Two ancillaries of this damage resulting from negligence are damages an animal causes with its flanks or with the yoke on its neck, and the collapse of a wall caused by an animal rubbing or pushing against it. In each of these instances, the owner is liable for full damages.

d. *Esh* (Fire). One who lights a fire in the field of another person, causing destruction of property, is liable in full for any damages that result. If he starts a fire in his own backyard, he must be sure that it will not spread to his neighbor's property. An example of an ancillary of this negligence is the placing of a stone or a knife on a roof from where they can be blown off by an ordinary light wind and cause injury to a passerby.

COMMENTATORS

Maimonides: In *The Guide of the Perplexed* he states that it is incumbent upon everyone to make sure that neither his property nor the product of his work should cause harm to others. If we acknowledge the fact that most people value their possessions almost as much as they value their lives, we will understand why the law is so explicit about the compensation to be paid for damage to property. A person who is warned that he must pay from his own assets for any damage caused to another person through his own negligence will be doubly careful to make sure that such damage will not occur through any fault of his.

References:

Mekhilta *Mishpatim;* B. Sanhedrin 15b; B. Gittin 48b, 49b; B. Bava Kamma 2b, 3a, 3b, 17b, 23a, 23b, 28b, 30a, 39a, 50b, 51a, 55b, 60a, 61b; J. Bava Kamma, Chap. 1, Halakhah 2, Chap. 5, Halakhah 6; Yad, Hilkhot Nizkei Mamon, Chap. 1, 3, 12, 13, 14; Sefer ha-Mitzvot (Aseh) 237, 238, 240, 241; Sefer Mitzvot Gadol (Aseh) 66, 67, 68, 69; Shulḥan Arukh, Ḥoshen Mishpat, 389–400, 410, 418; Sefer ha-Ḥinnukh, Mitzvot 51, 53, 55, 56.

LAWS PERTAINING TO THE LOAN, HIRING, AND SAFEKEEPING OF PROPERTY

If a man shall give his neighbor money or articles to be looked after (Exodus 22:6)
For every matter of trespass, whether it be for ox, for sheep, for ass, for raiment, or for any manner of lost thing, whereof one says: "this is it," the cause of both parties shall come before the judges. He whom the judges condemn shall pay double unto his neighbor (Exodus 22:8)
If a man deliver unto his neighbor an ass, or an ox, or a sheep, or any beast to be looked after (Exodus 22:9)
And if a man borrow aught from a neighbor (Exodus 22:13)

1. Good faith, honesty, and integrity are the indispensable ingredients for a stable society.

2. There are four ways in which one man may entrust his property to another:

a. *Shomer ḥinam*—Safekeeping without remuneration.
b. *Shomer sakhar* or *nose sakhar*—Safekeeping for payment.
c. *Sokher*—Hiring the property of another.
d. *Sho'el*—Borrowing property.

3. A *Shomer ḥinam,* onc who has received the property of another for safekeeping even without receiving money for it, is obligated by law to see to it that the object entrusted to him will not be stolen or lost. If the object is lost or stolen, he must be able to state under oath that he had no hand in the disappearance of the object. In such a case, the courts will ask him to take an additional oath *(gilgul shevu'ah)* that he was not derelict in his duties as "guardian" of the object. One who is entrusted with money for safekeeping is duty bound to guard it in a manner which is considered as adequate protection against loss or theft. If a man was given for safekeeping a rare object which he could not readily buy with his own money, and the object disappeared, and then the man offered to pay for the object without taking the oath required under the law, in these cases, we have reason to suspect him of wrongdoing; he may have had a hand in the disappearance of the object, or he may have been careless about guarding it, and he may even have stolen the money which he has so readily offered in payment for this expensive object.

4. The laws for *shomer sakhar* (one who is paid to safeguard the property of another) and for *sokher* (one who hires the property of another) are the same. If the object is stolen or lost, he must reimburse the original owner in full. On the other hand, if the loss came as the result of armed robbery, he must state under oath the cause of the loss and he is then exempt from paying restitution. This would be the case if someone took a cow for safekeeping or hire and then had the cow stolen from him by highway robbers. These laws apply only to movable goods, not real property.

5. The *sho'el* (the borrower) is responsible for almost any misfortune that befalls the object he has borrowed. He has to pay for it not only if it is stolen but also if an accident happens to it. If he borrows an ox, and the animal accidentally falls off a cliff and is killed, he must pay the owner for it. On the other hand, if the animal died while plowing the field of the one who borrowed it, the man is exempt from paying restitution to the owner. This is so because if someone borrows an ox, it is obvious that he will use the animal to plow the fields, and if the animal dies out in the field it probably would also have died working the field of its owner.

6. As a general rule, any plaintiff can summon a defendant to court and the court must grant a hearing. In the absence of witnesses, the plaintiff cannot collect unless the defendant either confesses to the debt, or partially accepts the claims of the plaintiff (*modeh be-miktzat* or "partial admission"). In the latter case, the defendant pays the stipulated sum and swears that he does not owe the plaintiff any more money. However, there must be agreement between the parties as to the specific object and values involved. For example: if the plaintiff demands money for 20 barrels of grapes which he says he lent to the defendant, but the defendant admits to having borrowed only ten barrels of wheat, there is no case on which the court can pass judgment.

COMMENTATORS

Maimonides: According to most commentators the reasons for the aboved-mentioned laws of safekeeping are as follows:

1. *Safekeeping without remuneration.* If A accepts from B a small item for safekeeping free of charge, A is acting out of the kindness of his heart and B receives all the benefit because he can attend to his other affairs without having to worry about his property. Hence, if anything happens to the object, A is not held liable because only B has benefited in any way from the arrangement.

2. *Safekeeping for pay, or hiring of property.* In these cases, A and B both benefit. A benefits, either because he is being paid for watching the animal of B, or because he uses it to good advantage while paying for its hire. B also benefits, because he can go about his business and not worry about the safety of his property, or because he receives money for hiring out his animal to A. Since both A and B benefit, they both share responsibility. In case the property is stolen, A is held responsible. If the property's disappearance is due to an accident such as armed robbery, B must bear the loss.

3. *Borrowed property.* A borrows an animal from B free of charge. Hence, A has all the benefit, while B is acting out of the kindness of his heart. Accordingly, A is held fully responsible for any mishap that may befall the animal he has borrowed.

References:

B. Bava Metzia 41, 42a, 57b, 93a, 94a, 95a, 95b; B. Bava Kamma 63a, 93a, 107b; B. Shevu'ot 42a, 45a; J. Shevu'ot, Chap. 8, Halakhah 1; Mekhilta *Mishpatim;* Yad, Hilkhot She'elah u-Pikadon, Chap. 4, 6; Yad, Hilkhot To'en ve-Nitan; Yad, Hilkhot Sekhirut, Chap. 1; Sefer ha-Mitzvot (Aseh) 242, 243, 244, 246; Sefer Mitzvot Gadol (Aseh) 88, 89, 92, 95; Shulḥan Arukh, Ḥoshen Mishpat, 87, 291, 293, 303, 306; Guide of the Perplexed, Part 3, Sec. 42; Sefer ha-Ḥinnukh, Mitzvot 57, 58, 59, 60.

SEDUCTION OF A VIRGIN

And if a man seduces a maid that is not betrothed, and lies with her, he shall surely pay the price of a virgin's worth to her (Exodus 22:15)

1. Judaism has always attached great importance to the morals of young people, for only a nation of strong moral fiber can grow and prosper.

2. Under Jewish law, when a man uses his power of persuasion upon a girl and blinds her sense of propriety, he is compelled to marry her, if she is willing, and is not permitted to divorce her. In addition, biblical law required him to pay the girl's father for the disgrace and injury he caused the girl *(boshet u-pegam)*. If he did not care to marry her, or the father or the girl herself refused to consent to the marriage, the man had to make the following payments to the girl's father: (1) Fifty shekels as a fine for having talked a virgin into having sexual intercourse with him. (2) An additional amount for the shame and disgrace suffered by the girl *(boshet)*, and (3) for the physical injury done to the girl *(pegam)*.

3. All these laws were applicable only in the case of a *ketanah*, a girl older than three years, who had not yet attained puberty. If the girl was a *na'arah* or a *bogeret* (a maiden showing the physical signs of womanhood) the man only had to compensate her for the shame and injury caused her.

4. To be classed as "seduction" rather than rape, the act had to have been committed within the limits of a city where the girl could have screamed and attracted the attention of passersby.

5. As stated above (p. 68), if the girl was already betrothed to another man, the act was a crime much more serious than mere seduction. Both the seducer and the girl were subject to the penalty of death by stoning.

COMMENTATORS

Naḥmanides: He disagrees with Rashi in his explanation of *pittui* ("seduction"), and with Maimonides' interpretation of *mohar* ("marriage settlement"). They all agree that in cases of seduction, as distinct from rape, the penalty imposed on the seducer is less severe because seduction implies a measure of sinfulness also on the part of the girl. They differ, however, on what should be considered as "seduction." According to Rashi, seduction has occurred when the girl submits to the man in return for the promise of a gift. Naḥmanides, however, holds that "seduction" involves deceit and betrayal on the part of the seducer. For example: A young man promises a virgin that he will eventually marry her if she will have sex relations with him now. Naḥmanides holds that the boy never intended to marry the girl but lied to her. The girl allowed herself to be deceived, because she may be insecure or ambitious and was willing to submit to a man of higher social station who promised her marriage, even though she herself should have realized the unlikeliness of the fulfillment of the promise.

Naḥmanides also disagreed with Rashi and the *Targumim* on the meaning of *mohar* ("marriage settlement"). Rashi contends that it implies "marriage" and the handing of a *kettubah* (marriage contract) by the man to the woman. But since the *kettubah* was not a biblical instrument but only a rabbinic innovation, Naḥmanides claims that the word *mohar* as used in the Torah means "to hasten," and that the verse (Exodus 22:15) tells the man who has seduced a virgin to "hasten" to court her and take her for his wife.

References:

B. Ketubbot 10a, 29b, 38a 39b, 40a, 46a, 54a; J. Ketubbot, Chap. 1, Halakhah 1; Yad, Hilkhot Na'arah Betulah, Chap. 1; Sefer ha-Mitzvot (Aseh) 220; Sefer Mitzvot Gadol (Aseh) 53; Shulḥan Arukh, Even ha-Ezer, 177; Sefer ha-Ḥinnukh, Mitzvah 61.

PROHIBITION OF WITCHCRAFT

You shall not allow a witch to live (Exodus 22:17)

1. It is a cardinal sin to mislead people with various kinds of witchcraft. While intelligent people will not believe in witchcraft, simple folk can easily be exploited by practitioners of the black art.

2. Anyone who practiced witchcraft was liable to the death penalty because such a person could divert others from belief in God to reliance on sorcerers.

COMMENTATORS

Maimonides, Naḥmanides: Sorcery is not a form of idol worship or a primitive, misguided cult based on belief in God. It is simply a way of exploiting the illiterate and the gullible by confusing their minds. In view of the fact that sorcerers take advantage of simple, naive folk for their own selfish ends, Jewish law imposed the death penalty on sorcerers.
Ḥinnukh: Witchcraft is not a simple fraud, but a potent, dangerous force which can bring about some happenings that run counter to the course of nature. He, therefore, equates witchcraft with *sha'atnez,* the forbidden mixture of wool and linen fibers and the forbidden interbreeding of two different animal species. Like these forbidden mixtures, witchcraft, too, represents an interference in the patterns of the universe established by God, an act of defiance against the Lord of the universe. Man has no right to tamper with the supernatural.

References:
B. Sanhedrin 56b, 67a, 67b; Yad, Hilkhot Avodat Kokhavim, Chap. 11; Yad, Hilkhot Sanhedrin, Chap. 15, Sec. 10; Guide of the Perplexed, Part 3, Sec. 37; Mekhilta *Mishpatim;* Sefer ha-Mitzvot (Lo Ta'aseh) 310; Sefer Mitzvot Gadol (Lav) 198; Sefer ha-Ḥinnukh, Mitzvah 62.

CONSIDERATION TOWARD STRANGERS, WIDOWS, AND ORPHANS

A stranger shall you not wrong, nor oppress; for you were strangers in the land of Egypt (Exodus 22:20)
You shall not afflict any widow or orphan (Exodus 22:21)

1. Judaism rejects "the law of the jungle." It does not permit the rich and the powerful to oppress the poor and the weak.

2. When a Jew taunts a proselyte, who is termed a *ger,* "stranger," by reminding him of his former idolatry, he is "wrongdoing a stranger." A Jew who violates this commandment is guilty not only of oppressing a coreligionist (since a proselyte is a full Jew) but, even worse, of hurting a man who once was "a stranger" to the Jewish people.

3. It is forbidden to wrong a stranger, a widow, or an orphan either financially or by the spoken word.

4. The Rabbis warned that we must be particularly careful not to upset widows and orphans.

5. However, we are permitted to be harsh with an orphan if this is necessary to guide his life in the right path, as by giving him an education and teaching him a trade or profession.

COMMENTATORS

Rashi: Do not oppress the stranger in your land, for if you do so, he will retaliate by reminding you of your own origin. Our ancestors, too, were strangers in a foreign land: "For you were strangers in the land of Egypt."
Ibn Ezra: He approaches this prohibition from an ethical point of view. Do not treat a stranger unjustly, because you have more power than he has in the Jewish society in which you both live, and it would not be right for you to exploit the advantage you have over him. By the same token, it is not fair to be cruel to a widow or an orphan just because your position is more secure than theirs. Remember that our ancestors were also politically and economically insecure in Egypt. Did they appreciate or enjoy being exploited?
Naḥmanides: One who abuses a widow and her orphan child at the same

time is guilty on two counts—afflicting a widow, and afflicting an orphan. Strangers, widows, and orphans [are vulnerable because they] have no one to defend them or to whom they can turn for aid. Because God is merciful, He swiftly answers the cries of those who are victims of social injustice. Remember how our ancestors were oppressed in Egypt and how God saved them. He did this not necessarily because they had deserved it by virtue of their good deeds, but because He always hears the cries of the oppressed.

Or ha-Ḥayyim: Everyone stems from the same Divine source. No one, therefore, has the right to sit in judgment over his fellow man and decide that the other—the stranger, the widow, or the orphan—is not as worthy of respect as he is himself.

Rashbam: "Oppress" means assigning menial tasks to strangers, widows, and orphans. Since these people have no defender, they are likely to become the victims of exploitation even as our forefathers were in Egypt.

References:

B. Bava Metzia 58b, 59a, 59b; B. Ketubbot 50a; B. Ta'anit 24a; Mekhilta *Mishpatim;* Yad, Hilkhot De'ot, Chap. 6, Halakhah 10; Yad, Hilkhot Mekhirah, Chap. 14, Halakhah 15; Sefer ha-Mitzvot (Lo Ta'aseh) 152, 153, 256 (See the difference between Maimonides and Naḥmanides over the detail of widow and orphan: according to the former, they are considered as one injunction; according to the latter, they are considered as two separate injunctions.); Sefer Mitzvot Gadol (Lav) 8, 172, 173; Sefer Mitzvot Katan 86, 87, 88; Shulḥan Arukh, Ḥoshen Mishpat, 228; Sefer ha-Ḥinnukh, Mitzvot 63, 64, 65.

LENDING MONEY TO THE NEEDY

If you lend money to any of My people (Exodus 22:24)
You shall not be to him as a demanding creditor (Exodus 22:24)
At the end of every three years, you shall bring forth all the tithe of your increase and shall lay it up within your gates (Deuteronomy 14:28)
Of a foreigner you may exact payment (Deuteronomy 15:3)

1. Jewish law deems the granting of an interest-free loan *(gemilut ḥasadim)* a better way of helping the poor than outright charity.

In fact, the Torah makes it obligatory to lend money, without interest, to anyone in financial need.

2. According to Jewish law, the lender must not embarrass the borrower in words or action. He must not ask him to repay the loan, nor even hint at it, if he knows that the borrower is poor and is in no position to repay.

3. On the other hand, the borrower must not take advantage of the lender's generosity. He must not squander the money, nor may he tell the lender to "come back some other time" when, in fact, he could repay the loan on demand. If the borrower fails to repay the loan, and it turns out that the borrower is not destitute, the court may order him to repay most of the loan at once, retaining only that amount which the court will find necessary for his immediate financial needs.

4. The Rabbis caution that loans of money should not be transacted without witnesses.

COMMENTATORS

Ibn Ezra, Naḥmanides: If you are in a position to lend money to another, it is only because God helped you attain that position. Accordingly, it is improper for the lender to humiliate the borrower or to feel superior to him, because he owes his own good fortune not to his own power, but to God.

Ḥinnukh: Instead of giving outright charity to a poor man, it is better to give him a loan so that he can reestablish his solvency and not be forced to accept charity or to undergo the humiliation of bankruptcy. It is the will of God that man should always practice mercy and compassion, because it is only to the good and compassionate that God will send His blessings.

Or ha-Ḥayyim: God makes some people wealthy and others poor because poverty is frequently a form of punishment for sin. But God does not want to abandon the sinner completely. He therefore allows some people to become wealthy so that they may help the poor. This is, in fact, part of the sinner's punishment; instead of receiving his sustenance from God, he must go to his fellow man to beg him for help.

Recanati: In the universe, the survival of each galaxy is dependent on the divinely-ordained interaction between all the galaxies of space. So, too, the survival of man and of human society requires that men do not live in isolation from one another, but interact for each other's welfare. This implies that we must help supply each other's needs by lending and borrowing.

Keli Yakar: The lender actually derives a greater benefit from his generosity than the borrower does from the loan. The borrower is helped only in this world, but the lender receives a reward in the world to come for having helped the poor on earth.

References:

Mekhilta *Mishpatim;* B. Shabbat 63a; B. Bava Batra 10a; B. Yevamot 63a; B. Ketubbot 67b; B. Bava Metzia 71a, 75b; Pirkei Avot, Chap. 2; Midrash Rabbah, *Shemot* 31, Sec. 3, 5, 16; Yalkut Shimoni, Psalms, 37; Midrash Tanḥuma, *Mishpatim,* 15; Sefer ha-Mitzvot (Aseh) 142, 197, (Lo Ta'aseh) 234; Sefer Mitzvot Gadol (Aseh) 93, (Lav) 191–193; Sefer Mitzvot Katan 249; Yad, Hilkhot Milveh, Chap. 1, 4; Shulḥan Arukh, Ḥoshen Mishpat, 97; Sefer ha-Ḥinnukh, Mitzvot 66, 67, 476.

PROHIBITION AGAINST CURSING

You shall not curse a judge, and a ruler of your people shall you not revile (Exodus 22:27)

You shall not curse a deaf man (Leviticus 19:14)

1. Cursing is one of the basest expressions of human anger and frustration. Man must use the gift of speech to uplift and not to degrade himself and others.

2. In Hebrew literature, the term *Elohim* is employed to refer to God (which pious Jews pronounce *Elokim,* in order not to utter God's name in vain) in his attribute of the Supreme Judge, and also to judges who issue decisions according to the word of God. This appellation must be used with proper reverence. It may not be employed in a curse.

3. Under biblical law, one who uses the Tetragrammaton, the Ineffable Name of God, for blasphemy, was subject to execution by stoning. One who used the name of God to curse a judge was liable to a double flogging; one for having cursed a judge and another because cursing a judge also meant to curse a fellow Jew.

4. One who cursed a *nasi,* the ruler of the Jewish people or the head of the Sanhedrin, was given a triple flogging: one for having cursed a *nasi;* another, because cursing a *nasi* also meant to curse a judge; and a third, because cursing a *nasi* or a judge also meant cursing a fellow Jew.

5. One who hears another man cursing God, should be so shaken at the thought that he is obliged to rend his clothes from sheer grief.

6. The above-mentioned penalties for cursing God, or a *nasi,* or a judge, or even oneself, were applicable only if the individual actually used the name of God in the curse, and if he had been forewarned of the gravity of this sin and its consequences.

7. The prohibition against cursing a fellow Jew is derived from the biblical verse: "You shall not curse a deaf man." The reasoning of the Rabbis was that if one was not even permitted to curse a man who could not hear it, it was certainly forbidden to curse a man who was able to hear what was said of him.

COMMENTATORS

Ibn Ezra: Exodus 22:27 (above) follows the passage pertaining to the proper behavior of the wealthy creditor to his needy debtor. The Bible linked these two passages to show that where there is much poverty, the government, especially the judiciary, will come under attack from the suffering populace.

Sforno: A litigant who has lost his case is likely to curse the judge because he often refuses to admit that he was in the wrong.

Naḥmanides: According to the Rabbis the word *"Elohim,"* one of the Hebrew terms for God, refers also to a judge, a priest, or any elected leader, such as a king, who is in a position of authority. This implies that we owe respect both to God, the Heavenly Judge, and judges and rulers on earth who see to it that the will of God is carried out.

Rashbam: Since it is normal for the loser in a law case to resent the judge who ruled against him, the decision of the court must be implemented at the earliest possible moment. Too long a delay in the execution of the sentence will give the guilty party too much time in which to build up resentment, which can lead him to additional transgressions, namely, to curse his judge.

Ḥinnukh: It is forbidden to defy the decision of judges, because, as their designation *Elohim* implies, they are acting in the name of God. A defendant must not say that he will disregard the court decision because he will gladly pay the fine or undergo the punishment for his contempt of court. For by this act he does not defy only the judges but also God Himself, who cannot be appeased by the mere payment of a fine or other punishment devised by judges on earth.

Recanati: Recanati discounts the theory that a curse in itself can harm the victim. Why, then, is he so concerned about the effect of a curse on an individual, such as a judge? He explains that, while a curse in itself has no power, it may cause the victim mental anguish and thus indirectly affect his future. For instance, a judge who is cursed by a defendant whom he has committed may decide that judgeship is a thankless task and, as a result, he may resign from his office, to the detriment of the entire community. This may happen even if he has not heard the curse with his own ears but was informed of it by a third party.

Maimonides: Also not believing that a curse in itself can harm the victim, he holds that cursing was prohibited not because of what it can do to the victim, but because of its effect on the individual who pronounces it. Jewish law seeks to keep the individual from acquiring the habit of venting his anger and frustration on others.

Ralbag: Man must be aware at all times that God placed man on a higher intellectual level than all other living things on earth. If, therefore, a man curses God, he misuses his God-given intellect and thus acts counter to God's plans for the world. Moreover, every creature of God, animal and vegetable alike, attests to the glory of its Creator. Therefore, when a man, instead of proclaiming the glory of God in all that he does, sinks so low as to curse God, he thereby makes himself lower than even a humble blade of grass.

Radbaz: Blasphemy is the only instance where, before the guilty party is executed, the witnesses and the judges place their hands on the head of the criminal and solemnly proclaim: "Your blood be on your head!

You have brought this upon yourself." This is to emphasize that his transgression was not only a sin but also an act of gross stupidity, for while other transgressions, such as theft, rape, or murder, may be explained as having been committed in hopes of personal gain, there can be no such rationalization for blasphemy.

References:

B. Shevu'ot 35b, 36a; B. Yevamot 22b; B. Sanhedrin 56b, 66a, 85a; Midrash Rabbah, *Shemot, Mishpatim,* Chap. 31, Sec. 8, 17; Yad, Hilkhot Avodah Zarah, Chap. 2; Yad, Hilkhot Sanhedrin, Chap. 26; Sefer ha-Mitzvot (Lo Ta'aseh) 315, 316, 317; Sefer Mitzvot Gadol (Lav) 16, 209, 210, 211, 212; Sefer Mitzvot Katan 125, 127 (Note that he considers the cursing of a *nasi* and a judge as two separate injunctions); Shulḥan Arukh, Ḥoshen Mishpat, 27. Sefer ha-Ḥinnukh, Mitzvot 69, 71, 231.

THE PROPER PAYMENT OF TITHES AND OTHER IMPOSTS

You shall not delay to offer of the fullness of your harvest and of the flow of your presses. The first-born of your sons you shall give to Me (Exodus 22:28)

1. The Torah insists that all its laws must be carried out in the proper order, in strict accord with the rules it has laid down, and not according to the whims of the individual. In the case of tithing, the proper order for each year was as follows:

a. *Bikkurim*, the "first fruits," which had to be presented to the Priest in the Temple.

b. Next, *Terumah Gedolah,* approximately two percent of the harvest, to be presented to the Priest in the Temple.

c. *Ma'aser Rishon,* "the first tithe" of the harvest had to be presented to the Levite, who in turn gave one-tenth of his receipts to the Priest *(Terumat Ma'aser).*

d. *Ma'aser Sheni,* "the second tithe," one-tenth of what remained of the harvest after the deductions mentioned above, had to be taken to Jerusalem, where the farmer himself had to eat it or to sell it. This procedure had to be followed in the first, second, fourth, and fifth years of the seven-year agricultural cycle. In the third and sixth years, the *Ma'aser Sheni* was not brought to Jerusalem, but was set aside as *Ma'aser Ani*—a tithe for the poor.

2. It should be pointed out, however, that the Torah did not consider minor or incidental changes in this order as sins warranting severe punishment.

COMMENTATORS

Ḥinnukh: The *Ḥinnukh* translates the word *"te'aḥer"* ("delay") as meaning "to disarrange," so that the *mitzvah* would read, "You shall not disarrange the offering of the fullness of your harvest . . ." In other words, the proper order of tithing as specified in the law must not be changed, because this would alter the total percentage of the harvest offered up by the farmer.

Alshekh, Ḥizzekuni: These authors explain why the reference to tithing and the reference to the redemption of the first-born were put side by side in the same verse. The juxtaposition implies that even the poor farmer must be conscientious in giving his tithe; he must not be deterred by the fact that his tithe will amount to very little, because God will reward him for it by blessing him with many children.

References:

B. Temurah 4; Mishnayyot, Terumot, Chap. 3, Mishnah 6; B. Shabbat 127b (see Tosafot); Yad, Hilkhot Terumot, Chap. 3; Sefer ha-Mitzvot (Lo Ta'aseh) 154; Sefer Mitzvot Gadol (Lav) 253; Shulḥan Arukh, Yoreh De'ah, 331; Sefer ha-Ḥinnukh, Mitzvah 72.

PROHIBITION OF THE FLESH OF A "TORN ANIMAL"

You shall not eat any flesh that is torn by beasts in the field, you shall cast it to the dogs (Exodus 22:30)

1. Animals and fowl that may not be eaten (aside from "unclean" animals) are divided into two classifications: *Nevelah* (carcass) and *terefah* ("torn"). *Nevelah* refers to the flesh of an animal or fowl that died of natural causes or was not slaughtered by *sheḥitah;* i.e., in accordance with Jewish law. *Terefah* refers to the flesh of an animal or fowl that was killed by a predatory animal or one that had physical defects or injuries with which it could not have survived for twelve months. The flesh of an animal with such physical defects is forbidden food, even if the animal was ritually slaughtered. The general rule is that any injury with which the animal cannot survive renders it *terefah* or unfit for consumption under Jewish law.

2. Any of the following eight defects discovered on examination following ritual slaughter renders an animal *terefah:*

a. *Derusah:* An animal or fowl whose flesh was torn by a bird of prey or a wild beast.

b. *Nekubah:* An animal or fowl with a perforated vital organ; e.g., a perforated heart.

c. *Ḥisurah:* An animal or fowl with an underdeveloped or atrophied organ; e.g., a lung of less than normal size.

d. *Netulah:* An animal or fowl that is found to have, for example, no liver.

e. *Pesukah:* An animal or fowl with a cut windpipe.

f. *Keru'ah:* An animal or fowl with a torn membrane, such as that of the stomach.

g. *Nefulah* (lit. "a fallen animal"): An animal or fowl whose "limbs were loosened from one another" as the result of a fall from a high place.

h. *Shevurah* (lit. "a broken animal"): An animal with most of its ribs fractured.

3. An animal with these defects is *terefah,* regardless of whether they were inflicted on the animal by accident, by other animals, or by a man (e.g., a hunter).

4. During the era of the Temple, any meat from a major sacrifice that had been removed from the Temple courtyard, any meat from a "minor" sacrifice (the classifications of "major" or "minor" sacrifices are based on the procedure followed when these sacrifices were offered in the Temple) that had been taken beyond the walls of Jerusalem, or any meat from a Paschal lamb that had been taken away from the place where the family had gathered to eat it, were also considered *terefah.*

COMMENTATORS

Ḥinnukh: An animal that has been mauled by a wild beast falls prey to infection and disease even if the direct cause of the animal's death was *sheḥitah.* The meat of such an animal is detrimental to man's health. *Ḥinnukh* adds that whatever food is bad for a man's body will also be bad for his soul.

Abrabanel: This, too, was the reason why hunting is forbidden. However, although we are forbidden to eat the meat of animals killed by a hunter, we may derive other benefits from such meat; e.g., it may be given to one's dogs.

Ibn Ezra, Da'at Zekenim: Why does the Torah mention no other means of disposing of *terefah* meat than to feed it to dogs? Because dogs act as the guardians of flocks of sheep and herds of cattle. Should one of the herd, nevertheless, become prey to a wild beast, the dogs should be given the meat of the dead animal and should be rewarded for their efforts to protect these animals.

References:

B. Ḥullin 37a, 47b, 68a, 73b, 102b; B. Makkot 18a; B. Zevaḥim 82b; J. Nazir, Chap. 6, Halakhah 1; J. Terumot, Chap. 8, Halakhah 3; Mekhilta *Mishpatim;* Yad, Hilkhot Ma'akhalot Assurot, Chap. 4, Halakhah 6; Yad, Hilkhot Sheḥitah, Chap. 5; Yad, Hilkhot Ma'aseh ha-Korbanot, Chap. 11, Halakhah 6; Yad, Hilkhot Korban Pesaḥ, Chap. 9, Halakhah 2; Sefer ha-Mitzvot (Lo Ta'aseh) 181; Sefer Mitzvot Gadol (Lav) 134; Sefer Mitzvot Katan (See detailed analysis of this *mitzvah,* p. 204.); Shulḥan Arukh, Yoreh De'ah, 29; Sefer ha-Ḥinnukh, Mitzvah 73.

JUSTICE UNDER THE LAW

And even to a man who has become impoverished you shall not give preference by showing him honor in his lawsuit (Exodus 23:3)
You shall not incline justice toward the poor in his lawsuit (Exodus 23:6)
And show no preferential honor to the great (Leviticus 19:15)
Your eye shall not pity him (Deuteronomy 19:13)

1. The early codifiers summarized many of the commandments as *mitzvot sikhliyyot*—commandments that are based on good common sense. The *mitzvah* referred to in the four verses cited above is an example of such a commandment.

2. It is obvious that showing leniency to a poor man in a civil case for no other reason but his poverty is a perversion of justice. A court should make every effort to aid the poor, but not at the expense of the other party in the lawsuit.

3. It is also unjust for a court to favor the more "important" of the two parties in a lawsuit. True, it is commendable that the judges should want to show respect to an important person, but then they must give equal attention to the less "important" party.

4. The court must not allow its decisions to be influenced by preconceived notions as to the effect of its ruling on the welfare of the community. Thus, the court may not refrain from imposing the mandatory death penalty on a murderer because it happens to feel that the death of the murderer "will not solve the problem."

COMMENTATORS

Ḥinnukh: Without a just system of law, society cannot endure. A judge must not allow his decision to be influenced by the past criminal record of the defendant. The defendant must be judged for the crime for which he is now being tried, and not for his past transgressions. Only God may judge all the actions of men—past and present.

References:
B. Ḥullin 134a; B. Sanhedrin 36b; Mekhilta *Mishpatim;* Sifra *Kedoshim;* Midrash Tehillim, Chap. 82; Yad, Hilkhot Sanhedrin, Chap. 20, Halakhah 4; Sefer ha-Mitzvot (Lo Ta'aseh) 275, 277, 278, 279; Sefer Mitzvot Gadol (Lav) 202, 203, 204; Sefer Mitzvot Katan 229, 230, 232; Shulḥan Arukh, Ḥoshen Mishpat, 17; Sefer ha-Ḥinnukh, Mitzvot 79, 81, 234, 521.

PROTECTING THE INNOCENT FROM MISCARRIAGES OF JUSTICE

An innocent or an acquitted man shall you not slay (Exodus 23:7)

1. Since man was created in the image of God, a judge must make sure that the man he has condemned to death is not, in fact, innocent of the crime for which he has been tried and sentenced. It is better that a guilty person should go free than that an innocent man should be condemned to death.

2. Circumstantial evidence is not admissible under Jewish law. The only admissible testimony is that of witnesses who actually saw the crime committed. If two witnesses saw a man pursuing another with the intent to murder and warned the man against committing the crime, but then their attention was distracted and by the time they turned back to the scene the crime had already been committed, their testimony will be dismissed as circumstantial evidence, even if they both saw the blood dripping from the victim and from the sword of the pursuer.

3. The law goes even further than that. If two witnesses appeared before the court to condemn a man to die for idol worship, but one of the two testified that the accused worshiped the moon while the other testified that the accused worshiped the sun, the accused goes free because in cases involving capital punishment identical testimony from two witnesses is necessary to convict the accused.

4. The same rule applies if one of the two witnesses says he saw the crime committed as he looked out from one window, while the other testifies that he saw the crime committed as he looked out from another and the two witnesses did not see each other; under these circumstances, the accused goes free.

COMMENTATORS

Ibn Ezra: Who would think that a court should want to take the life of an innocent man? The Torah felt it necessary to set down this *mitzvah* for the protection of individuals who were found innocent of the crime for which they were tried, but who might be condemned to death nevertheless because of their previous criminal record. The commandment means to stress that a judge must not be influenced by a man's past record, but may judge him only on the basis of the charge for which he stands trial at the moment.

Maimonides, Ḥinnukh: If circumstantial evidence is unacceptable in courts of justice, will not many criminals go unpunished and continue committing crimes? They define circumstantial evidence as evidence that is close to, but not identical with, the actual facts in the case. If such testimony were accepted, there would be the danger that an innocent man might be condemned to death. The Torah would rather have many guilty men go free than even one innocent man condemned to death on the basis of circumstantial evidence.

References:

B. Sanhedrin 33b, 37b; J. Sanhedrin, Chap. 4, Halakhah 3; Mekhilta *Mishpatim;* Yad, Hilkhot Sanhedrin, Chap. 20, 24; Sefer ha-Mitzvot (Lo Ta'aseh) 290; Sefer Mitzvot Gadol (Lav) 200; Sefer ha-Ḥinnukh, Mitzvah 82.

BRIBERY

You shall accept no bribes (Exodus 23:8)

1. Even a child knows that it is a crime to bribe a judge. A judge must not accept any gift from a litigant even if he intends to base his decision on a fair and just trial.

2. Even as it is a crime for a judge to accept a bribe, so it is forbidden for a litigant or his friend to offer a bribe to a judge.

3. Even acts involving no actual gift may be considered as bribes. For example, the Talmud tells of a judge who found out that the man who helped him out of a boat was scheduled to appear before him in a law case. The judge promptly disqualified himself because he felt that the man's act of courtesy constituted a bribe of sorts.

COMMENTATORS

Ḥinnukh: If a judge accepts gifts from the parties in a lawsuit it is bound to influence him on behalf of the giver, even if he is convinced that this cannot happen. However, a judge who is not paid by the community for his services, but makes his living from some other occupation to which he cannot attend while he holds court, may accept a fee paid in equal shares by both the parties involved in the litigation. This sum is not considered a bribe but is just compensation due him for the time which he spent on the trial and which he could have spent on the work by which he earns his livelihood.

References:
B. Ketubbot 105a; Mishnayyot, Pe'ah, Chap. 8, Mishnah 9; Mekhilta *Mishpatim;* Midrash Tanḥuma, *Mishpatim;* Yad, Hilkhot Sanhedrin, Chap. 23; Sefer ha-Mitzvot (Lo Ta'aseh) 274; Sefer Mitzvot Gadol (Lav) 208; Sefer Mitzvot Katan 231; Shulḥan Arukh, Ḥoshen Mishpat, 9; Sefer ha-Ḥinnukh, Mitzvah 83.

USURY

Neither shall you lay upon him any usury (Exodus 22:24)
Take no interest of him or increase (Leviticus 25:37)
You shall not lend to your brother upon interest (provided it is done by mutual agreement—Rashi and Sforno) (Deuteronomy 23:20)
You may lend upon interest to a foreigner (Deuteronomy 23:21)

1. The Torah does not permit a man to arrange his life so that he becomes completely dependent on the mercy of another; conversely, it does not allow a man to come into a position of complete control over his fellow man. Some people may be more successful than others, but wealth must not make it possible for an individual to have complete power over the life of another person, or to disregard another person's personal dignity.

2. In cases of usury, the burden of guilt rests not only upon the one who lends out money at interest, but also upon the borrower who accepts such terms. The law even condemns individuals such as witnesses, scribes, or brokers, who are only indirectly involved in the transaction.

3. The Hebrew term used in the Torah for "interest" is *neshekh,* literally, "bite." This is to show that usury is like the bite of a scorpion, in that it may jeopardize the borrower's economic survival.

4. *Ribbit ketzutzah* is the rabbinic term for the "increase" (i.e., additional goods and services demanded and received by the lender in return for a loan) that is forbidden by biblical law. The following agreements are examples of *ribbit ketzutzah:* "If you will lend me $100.00, I will repay the loan in six months' time, plus $50.00, making a total of $150.00," or conversely, "I will lend you $100.00 providing that you will permit me to live in your house rent-free." In each of these cases, the lender received some additional goods or services for the original loan he made, and this is forbidden. The law goes so far as to state that, if the borrower was not in the habit of greeting the lender in the past, he should not greet him now that he is indebted to him, because this, too, could be construed as "additional goods or services" received by the lender in return for the loan.

5. *Avak ribbit,* literally, "the dust of usury," is a form of interest that appears legitimate because it does not involve outright "increase" but it is, nevertheless, forbidden by Jewish law. If a lender says, "I will lend you $1,000.00 providing I receive a share in the profits from the enterprise for which you have taken the loan," the agreement may seem legitimate because the borrower is not obligated to pay a specific amount in goods or services, and if he makes no profit at all no payment whatsoever is due. Nevertheless even such terms constitute a violation of the law because of the implication that the lender might be entitled to goods or services in return for the loan.

6. *Ribbit ketzutzah* must be returned to the borrower if the court so rules; on the other hand, the court cannot enforce the return of *avak ribbit* to a borrower.

7. As the economy came to depend increasingly on money transactions, the Rabbis devised a legal instrument called a *hetter iskah,* literally, "permission to do business," which in fact made it possible for the lender to receive some return for his loan. When a loan is transacted with a *shetar iskah* (business permit), the lender becomes a partner or a shareholder in the borrower's business ventures, and thus the interest he receives is not really considered interest on a loan but a dividend due the lender for his investment.

COMMENTATORS

Ḥinnukh: The payment of interest on a loan may be compared to a progressive wasting disease. It begins with a very slight loss but rapidly progresses to a point where the unfortunate borrower loses all he has.
Ibn Ezra: Obtaining interest on a loan does not only mean demanding additional revenue above the original borrowed sum. It may also mean demanding a favor from the borrower because of the loan he has been granted.
Keli Yakar: A businessman who invests in an enterprise does not know

whether he will make a profit or incur a loss. He can only hope and pray to God that the enterprise will succeed. One who lends money on interest, on the other hand, shows lack of faith in God, because by charging interest he insists on a guarantee of profit for himself, regardless of whether the enterprise will succeed or not. The borrower is equally guilty, because by accepting such terms he enables the lender to enter into business ventures without demonstrating his willingness to entrust the enterprise to the care of God.

Alshekh: Everything that man possesses is a gift from God. Therefore, to demand interest is an effrontery against God Himself, because the lender is taking a gift from God and using it to exploit the poor. The argument that the lender demands interest not in order to take advantage of the borrower, but only to impress upon him that he has an obligation to repay his loan is not considered admissible under Jewish law, because such an arrangement is bound to create ill-will.

Abrabanel: The ready acceptance of interest from Gentiles does not apply to Christians and Moslems, because some of their beliefs stem from Judaism and they are not considered totally foreign to Jewry and Judaism.

Radak: In connection with the law making it permissible to lend money to Gentiles at interest, he hastens to point out that a non-Jew who has shown consideration for Jews is entitled to equal consideration from his Jewish creditor.

Naḥmanides: If the exacting of interest is frowned upon, then why is it permitted in the case of Gentiles? Why is usury not looked upon as stealing, which is forbidden to Jews and Gentiles alike? Logically, if the borrower and lender both agree to terms, there should be no reason why interest should be forbidden. The Torah, however, implored the lender to have compassion on his less fortunate coreligionist. This does not necessarily have to be his policy concerning hostile Gentiles. Stealing, on the other hand, cannot be classified as a business deal and applies, therefore, to Jew and Gentile alike.

References:

B. Bava Metzia 60b, 61a, 69b, 71a, 75b; B. Makkot 24a; Sifre *Ki Tetze;* Midrash Rabbah, *Shemot* 31; Midrash Rabbah, *Vayikra* 3; Midrash Tanḥuma, *Mishpatim;* Sifra *Behar;* Yad, Hilkhot Malveh ve-Loveh, Chap. 3, 5; Sefer ha-Mitzvot (Aseh)198, (Lo Ta'aseh) 235, 236, 237; Sefer Mitzvot Gadol (Lav) 191, 192, 193; Shulḥan Arukh, Yoreh De'ah, 160; Sefer ha-Ḥinnukh, Mitzvot 68, 343, 572, 573.

TO PURSUE TRUTH IN JUSTICE

You shall not utter a false report (Exodus 23:1)
You shall not stand in awe of the face of any man (Deuteronomy 1:17)

1. If a person seeks the office of judge or allows himself to be appointed as a judge, he must have a zeal for fairness and the courage to stand by his decisions.

2. A judge must not listen to the arguments of one litigant when the other party is not present and therefore is not able to offer a rebuttal.

3. When the judge senses that a litigant has difficulty in expressing himself with the testimony that will bring out the true facts, the judge may, cautiously and diplomatically, assist him in his thinking and articulation.

4. The commandment "You shall not utter a false report" is a warning against slander. The Rabbis included this injunction in the laws concerning fairness in court, because slander is a form of unfair behavior toward a victim who may be in no position to defend himself.

5. If for any reasons a judge wishes to disqualify himself, he may do so at any time before the testimony has been completed and before he senses the direction which his decision will take. But once the presentation of the case is finished and he senses what direction his decision is likely to take, he can no longer withdraw from the case, no matter what his reason for wishing to do so.

6. In justice, there is no place for fear or intimidation. Thus, when a disciple feels that his master is about to commit a miscarriage of justice, he must not hesitate to bring it to his attention at once. He must not remain silent and wait to discuss the matter with his teacher after the latter has handed down his decision.

7. It is commendable for a court to seek to settle a case by compromise rather than decide strictly on the basis of law. In a compromise, both litigants can be satisfied. In a pure lawsuit, one side will definitely feel that he has been treated unfairly.

COMMENTATORS

Ḥinnukh: The central theme involved in these two laws is that man must emulate the virtues of God. Thus, since God represents truth, we, too, are expected to champion the cause of truth. We must not shrink from this responsibility. Thus, a person should not be afraid to accept the office of judge because of all the worry and anxiety it will bring to him. He must love truth so much that he will allow no consideration to inhibit him from furthering its cause.

Naḥmanides: God's laws are the quintessence of justice. It is His wish that justice, in its purest sense, be dispensed among mankind. A judge who sits in judgment over a fellow man is dispensing God's law. He should allow nothing to impede him in the administration of justice, nor should he have any fears about carrying out his duties as a judge. If he has such fears, it is an indication that he lacks faith in God and belief in the validity of God's law.

References:

B. Pesaḥim 118a; B. Sanhedrin 6b, 7a, 7b; B. Shevu'ot 31a; Mekhilta *Mishpatim;* Sifre *Devarim;* Yad, Hilkhot Sanhedrin, Chap. 21, 22; Sefer ha-Mitzvot (Lo Ta'aseh) 276, 281; Sefer Mitzvot Gadol (Lav) 10, 207; Sefer Mitzvot Katan 233; Shulḥan Arukh, Ḥoshen Mishpat, 12, 17; Sefer ha-Ḥinnukh, Mitzvot 74, 415.

NOT TO FOLLOW IN THE PATHS OF THE WICKED

Put not your hand with the wicked to be an unrighteous witness (Exodus 23:1)

Fathers shall not be put to death for the [sin of their] children (Deuteronomy 24:16)

1. Testimony given in court must be clear, spontaneous, and decisive. When there is a cloud of suspicion over a witness or his testimony, the court must not accept the testimony of that witness. Suspicion includes not only doubts concerning the character of the witness but also misgivings about his conduct, his reputation, and his accuracy in relating facts.

2. Ten types of witnesses were disqualified under biblical law:

a. Women, because they tend to allow their emotions to rule their judgment.

b. Slaves, because they have not acquired the habit of thinking independently.

c. Minors, because of their mental immaturity.

d. Imbeciles, because they cannot think at all.

e. Deaf-mutes, because they can neither hear the questions nor answer them clearly.

f. The blind, because they could not have been "eyewitnesses" to any act or event.

g. Relatives of the parties involved in the case, because their testimony would be biased.

h. Those personally involved in the case, because their testimony would naturally be slanted in their own favor.

i. A shameless person (the example is given of one who eats and drinks in the streets because of an uncontrollable lust for food). Such an insensitive individual cannot be expected to grasp the importance of telling the truth before a court of justice.

j. A wicked person (one who is defiant, undisciplined, and not committed to religious observance). Thus, a compulsive gambler, a thief, or usurer is not fit to testify in court. Even one guilty of a sin subject to a penalty no more severe than lashing must not testify. (However, if this man should repent of his sin, his testimony is acceptable.) Some would even disqualify a Jew who is not conversant in Torah and Mishnah, for in the eyes of the Sages, there was no excuse for ignorance. Anyone who went through life as an ignoramus was considered a wicked man.

COMMENTATORS

Ḥinnukh: Is it not possible that even a flagrant sinner could tell the truth? The answer is that it is indeed possible, but that one should not be inclined to believe him because any man who is indifferent to his own moral welfare will surely be indifferent also to the welfare of others. The cause of justice can best be served only through objective, unbiased testimony. Testimony from relatives of the accused is also unacceptable.

Ibn Ezra: He reconciles what seems to be a contradiction between these two biblical statements, "Fathers shall not be put to death for the children" (Deuteronomy 24:16) and that God insists "the sin of the fathers upon the children" (Exodus 20:5). Ibn Ezra explains that the former verse applies to a death penalty imposed by society, society being duty-bound to dispense truth and justice. The latter verse applies to Divine retribution for children who follow in the wicked ways of their elders.

References:

B. Bava Kamma 72b, 88a; B. Sanhedrin 25b, 26a, 27a, 27b; B. Berakhot 7a; Mekhilta *Mishpatim;* Sifre *Mishpatim, Ki Tetze;* Yad, Hilkhot Edut, Chap. 10, 13; Sefer ha-Mitzvot (Lo Ta'aseh) 286, 287; Sefer Mitzvot Gadol (Lav) 214, 215; Sefer Mitzvot Katan 235, 237; Shulḥan Arukh, Ḥoshen Mishpat, 33, 34; Sefer ha-Ḥinnukh, Mitzvot 75, 589.

THE RULE OF THE MAJORITY

You shall not follow the majority to do evil; neither shall you bear witness in a cause to incline after a multitude to pervert justice (Exodus 23:2)

1. Following the majority of even one may be the most expedient way of carrying out justice. However, in Jewish jurisprudence, majority rule is not always applicable. In cases punishable by capital punishment, a majority of one in a court of twenty-three judges is not sufficient to convict the accused. There must be at least a majority of two.

2. A judge must realize that he is accountable only to God and his conscience. Society expects him to exercise his independent thinking. He must not look upon the decisions of the more learned members of the court and veer his thinking to coincide with theirs. His own analysis of the case may be superior to those of the more erudite members of the court.

3. In cases punishable by capital punishment, the first judges to speak are the junior or less learned justices, followed by the senior members. The reason for this is that, if the elders speak first, the juniors may hesitate to contradict them even if it is necessary to do so. In civil cases, a judge may express himself in any manner he chooses and at any time.

4. Always aware of the sanctity of man, the court should first explore every avenue to freedom for the accused. The court must realize that, if a mistake is made and the criminal is killed, there is no way to rectify its error. In fact, if one of the disciples sitting before the court gives grounds for exoneration of the accused, he is elevated to become a member of the court.

5. As has already been noted, in cases where the penalty could be capital punishment, the accused may never be returned for retrial once he has been exonerated. This holds true even if new evidence is presented. There is one exception, however, in the case of an instigator toward idol worship. In that case, even if he is exonerated, the instigator can be returned for retrial with the presentation of new evidence.

COMMENTATORS

Ḥinnukh: In the case of a possible death sentence, why should there be a difference that a majority of two is necessary for an indictment and a majority of one needed for an aquittal? He replies thus: Since, in the case of capital punishment, we are dealing with a situation where, if the court is wrong, the mistake cannot be rectified, we are requested to take every possible measure in order to obtain acquittal. After all, God in His relationship with the sinner has also shown him justice tempered by mercy.

It is vital, nevertheless, that each judge should search the law meticulously before reaching a decision. He must not subscribe to the thinking of another judge, although reputed to be an outstanding jurist, and join in his decision without having independently arrived at the same conclusion. The reason for this is that there is the danger that only one man's opinion may eventually dominate the court's decision, whereas the Torah is said to have seventy faces, that is, many approaches.

Or ha-Ḥayyim: It is forbidden for a judge to employ subtle machinations to achieve his desired goal, albeit with the purest intentions. For example: A judge may be convinced that the prosecuted is innocent and should be set free. This judge is, however, aware that he is alone in his thinking. If he casts his vote for an acquittal, he is afraid that the majority will rule and the prisoner will die. He contrives therefore to cast his vote for the decision "guilty" because in Jewish law when a court unanimously finds an accused guilty, he is set free. By voting contrary to his convictions, the judge will have gained his point. This is forbidden. The judge must realize that he is required to give an honest, forthright opinion. Actually, it is not he who is sentencing the condemned to die, but it is the Heavenly Court that has issued the sentence. If it were God's wish that the accused be acquitted, He would have placed that thought in the minds of the majority of the members of the court and the suspect would have been set free.

References:

B. Sanhedrin 3b, 18b, 33b, 34a, 36a; B. Bava Kamma 46b; B. Ḥullin 11a (see Tosafot); J. Sanhedrin, Chap. 4, Halakhah 8; Tosefta Sanhedrin, Chap. 3; Mekhilta *Mishpatim;* Yad, Hilkhot Sanhedrin, Chap. 8, 10; Sefer ha-Mitzvot (Lo Ta'aseh) 282, 283, (Aseh) 175; Sefer Mitzvot Gadol (Lav) 195, 196, (Aseh) 98: Sefer Mitzvot Katan 226; Shulḥan Arukh, Ḥoshen Mishpat, 18; Sefer ha-Ḥinnukh, Mitzvot 76, 77, 78.

HELPING ONE'S FELLOW MAN AND HIS ANIMAL

You shall surely release it with him (Exodus 23:5)
You shall not see your brother's ass or his ox fallen down by the way and withdraw yourself from them. You shall surely help him to lift them up again (Deuteronomy 22:4)

1. When a passerby sees an overburdened ass lying on the ground and unable to rise, he must help the owner unload the ass and relieve its distress. One is obliged to do this whether the ass is owned by a friend or a foe, and whether or not there be compensation for his efforts.

2. Furthermore, he must not leave the owner and his ass helpless, but he must assist in reloading the animal and escorting it a measurable distance. In the case of reloading however, the passerby is entitled to renumeration in addition to the spiritual benefits derived from the *mitzvah.*

3. The rule by which one should guide himself is to put himself in the place of the troubled owner. What would he do if the animal were his? For example: When an old and weak man approaches the owner of the ass and his animal in distress, he is not expected to fulfill this *mitzvah*. Or, if a *Kohen* observes from the distance this troubled scene taking place in a cemetery, he is not expected to defile himself by entering the precincts of the burial ground.

4. When a passerby comes upon such an incident, and the owner asks him to unload and reload the ass, claiming that it is a *mitzvah* for the passerby to do so but not for himself, it is illogical for the passerby to help the owner.

5. When one encounters two such incidents simultaneously—one calling for unloading and the other for reloading—he should first assist the unloading to relieve the distressed animal. Should a passerby meet two similar situations, the animal in one belonging to a friend, the other belonging to a foe, he must first assist the foe so that he does not fall prey to his baser feelings.

COMMENTATORS

Keli Yakar: A man who is in difficulty should first try to help himself and then seek assistance from others. This is for the sake of his own dignity and honor. Thus, *imo,* "with him," means that he should be helped together with his own efforts. *Keli Yakar* denounces poor people who would rather resort to charity than go to work to support their families and thus preserve their own self-respect.
Ḥinnukh: The purpose of these laws is to instill within us a spirit of compassion and mercy to the extent that we will be gravely concerned and rush to the assistance of our fellow man, enemy as well as friend. This *mitzvah* includes helping people who are in financial as well as physical difficulties.

References:
B. Bava Kamma 54b; B. Bava Metzia 30b, 31a, 32a; Mekhilta *Mishpatim;* Sifre *Ki Tetze;* Yad, Hilkhot Rotze'aḥ, Chap. 13; Sefer ha-Mitzvot (Aseh) 202, 203, (Lo Ta'aseh) 270; Sefer Mitzvot Gadol (Aseh) 80, 81, (Lav) 169; Sefer Mitzvot Katan 77; Shulḥan Arukh, Ḥoshen Mishpat, 272; Sefer ha-Ḥinnukh, Mitzvot 80, 540, 541.

THE SABBATICAL YEAR (SHEMITTAH): LEAVING THE FIELDS FALLOW

But during the seventh year you shall let [your land] rest and lie fallow (Exodus 23:11)
And the land shall keep a Sabbath unto God (Leviticus 25:2)
You shall not sow your field, nor prune your vineyard (Leviticus 25:4)
You shall not reap the aftergrowth of your harvest (Leviticus 25:5)
And you shall not gather the grapes of your undressed vine (Leviticus 25:5)

1. The Law of the Sabbatical year was given to the Jew in order that he might learn to trust God to provide him with all the sustenance he needs, and also that he might emulate God, who rested on the seventh day after six days of creation. For six years the Jew was to work his soil and to prune his trees, but in the seventh year he was to cease completely from all work upon his land. The soil was left to lie fallow, except that it was permitted to water a tract of land which would become unfit for cultivation if it were left unwatered for an entire year.

2. Any fruits or vegetations that grew by themselves during the Sabbatical year became *hefker,* i.e., public property, free for consumption by man and beast alike.

3. The owner of a field was not permitted to store up in his home large amounts of produce, because this would deprive the poor of their sustenance. He was permitted to retain only enough fruits and vegetables for his own normal needs.

4. The owner of a field was permitted to eat of his produce in his home only so long as there was produce available also in his field for the animals. If there was no more produce left in his field, he was obliged to remove his produce from his larder and make it *hefker* for all.

5. During the Sabbatical year it was forbidden to do any work that could be construed as a preparation of the land for cultivation the following year or as a preparation of trees to improve their fruit yield during the year to come.

6. It was forbidden during the Sabbatical year to do anything to alter the physical character of fruit or produce. For example, produce that was normally eaten raw during the six preceding years could not be eaten cooked during the Sabbatical year. It was also forbidden to make commercial use of any product of the soil during the Sabbatical year.

7. The laws of the Sabbatical year became operative thirty days before the beginning of the year. From that time on, all agricultural work was forbidden for the entire year. (For the remission of debts during the Sabbatical year, see below, p. 413.)

COMMENTATORS

Ibn Ezra: The seven-year agricultural cycle parallels the Divine plan of Creation. God completed His work of Creation in six days and each day comprised a cycle of morning and evening, light and darkness. On the seventh day, He rested. So, too, the Jew is asked to work his soil. Each year parallels one day of Creation, and the seasons of spring, summer, fall, and winter parallel the day's morning and evening hours. The seventh year is equivalent to the seventh day of Creation; accordingly, the Jew must not work his fields during that year.

Naḥmanides: He cites Ibn Ezra, adding that since the seven-year agricultural cycle parallels the seven days of Creation, anyone who violates the Sabbatical year thereby actually denies the existence and omnipotence of God.

Keli Yakar: *Keli Yakar* rejects Maimonides' explanation of the *Shemittah* laws; i.e., that the farmer was bidden to let his field lie fallow every seventh year so that the soil could yield a more abundant crop during the six years to come. If this were so, *Keli Yakar* argues, the penalty for tilling the soil during the seventh year might be a poor harvest. But in fact, the biblical penalty is exile from the land. Hence, Maimonides' interpretation is not sufficient explanation for the law.

Keli Yakar also rejects the thesis that the seven-year agricultural cycle is meant to recall the seven days of creation, because we already have the weekly Sabbath for this purpose. The author concludes that the purpose of the law is to teach us not to regard man as absolute lord over the yield of the soil. Also, it is to teach us to trust that God will provide us with adequate crops during the sixth year so that we will be able to subsist on them also during the seventh year when we do not till our soil. In other words, the laws of *Shemittah* are intended as an exercise in faith and self-discipline.

Abrabanel: During the six-day week of work, man is constantly under stress and in a state of fatigue. When the Sabbath arrives, he declares that he has had enough of the chase after material gains. On this seventh day, he is resolved to rest his weary body and devote himself to the development of his moral and religious potential. This is also the purpose of the *Shemittah* (the seventh year) and the Jubilee year in the human life-span. During his productive years—adolescence and maturity—man must work diligently for his livelihood, if he is to survive. But there comes a time when he must think in terms of loftier ideals, when he must cease pursuing material gain and earthly pleasures and must turn to the fulfillment of his innate yearning for sanctity and Godliness.

References:
B. Rosh ha-Shanah 8b, 31a; B. Mo'ed Katan 3a; B. Sanhedrin 39a; B. Bava Metzia 39a; B. Nedarim 42b; B. Sukkah 40a; J. Pe'ah, Chap. 6, Halakhah 1; J. Shevi'it, Chap. 4, Halakhah 3; J. Orlah, Chap. 1, Halakhah 2; B. Shabbat 33a; Pirkei Avot, Chap. 5, Mishnah 9; Mekhilta *Mishpatim;* Sifra *Behar;* Midrash Tanḥuma, *Behar;* J. Pe'ah, Chap. 7, Halakhah 7; Midrash Tehillim, Psalm 85; Yad, Hilkhot Shemittah, Chap. 1, 4; Sefer ha-Mitzvot (Lo Ta'aseh) 220, 221, 222, 223, (Aseh) 134, 135; Sefer Mitzvot Gadol (Aseh) 147, 148, (Lav) 266, 267, 268, 269; Sefer ha-Ḥinnukh, Mitzvot 84, 112, 326, 327, 328, 329.

OFFERING OF THE FIRST FRUITS

You shall bring the choicest first fruits of your land into the House of the Lord, your God (Exodus 23:19)
You may not eat within your gates the tithe of your corn, or of your wine, or of your oil, or the firstlings of your herd, or of your flock; nor any of your vows which you vow, nor your free-will offerings, nor the offering of your hand (Deuteronomy 12:17)
I declare this day unto the Lord, your God that I have come to the land which the Lord swore to our fathers to give us (Deuteronomy 26:3)

1. Every year, when the Jew went out into his fields and saw that his wheat, barley, grape vines, fig trees, pomegranates, olives, and dates were beginning to ripen, he would mark his "first fruits" by tying a straw around them. When they had ripened completely, he would bring them to the Temple in Jerusalem and present them to the Priests any time between Shavuot and Sukkot. These offerings–including oil from his olives and wine from his vineyard–were known as *bikkurim.*

2. The offering of the first fruits was a festive occasion accompanied by good cheer and rejoicing. Hence an *onan* (i.e., one in deep mourning between the time of the death and the burial of a close relative) was not permitted to participate in this *mitzvah.*

There is some difference of opinion as to whether women were obliged to perform this *mitzvah* since this is one of the commandments that had to be fulfilled at a specific time *(mitzvah she-ha-zeman geramah)* and such commandments as a rule are not obligatory for women.

3. The procedure for the offering of the first fruits was as follows: The farmer bringing the offering would take an amount equal to at least one-sixtieth of his first fruits and place it into an attractive basket for presentation at the Temple. If he used a wicker basket, the Priest kept the basket; if the basket was of gold, the Priest returned it to him after taking out the offering. The farmer also took with him seven doves: some of these served as ornaments for the offering and others he carried separately. Those that served as ornaments were sacrificed as burnt offerings; the others were given as a gift to the Priests. When he reached the outskirts of Jerusalem, the farmer was given a joyous welcome by the inhabitants of the city. When he entered the courtyard of the Temple, the Levites would chant psalms. He would then approach the Priest on duty and, still holding the basket upon his shoulder, would recite the biblical declaration: "I declare this day unto the Lord our God that I have come into the land which the Lord swore to our fathers to give us" (Deuteronomy 26:3). He would then lower the basket and hold it in his hands by its rim, and the Priest would place his hands beneath it and lift it. The farmer would then recite the prescribed biblical passage summarizing the history of the people of Israel and proclaiming his gratitude for the land that God had given to him and his people (Deuteronomy 26:5–10). After that, he would place his offering near the southwest corner of the altar, bow, and leave the Temple. He would spend the night in Jerusalem, returning to his home the next day.

COMMENTATORS

Ibn Ezra, Naḥmanides, Sforno, Rashbam: The purpose of the offering of the first fruits was to express gratitude to God (not only for the harvest but) for having kept His promise to the Children of Israel to give them the land He had "sworn to our fathers to give us."

Maimonides, Or ha-Ḥayyim, Alshekh, Keli Yakar: The declaration of thanksgiving was meant to be an expression of gratitude for the bounty of the soil and an acknowledgment that the fruits of the earth are the work of God and not of man.

References:

B. Ḥullin 136a; B. Yevamot 73b; B. Makkot 17a; B. Kiddushin 66b; Mishnayyot Bikkurim; B. Ta'anit 28a; B. Pesaḥim 36b; Midrash Tanḥuma, *Ki Tavo,* Chap. 1; Guide of the Perplexed, Part 3, Sec. 39; Yad, Hilkhot Bikkurim, Chap. 1, 2, 3, 4; Sefer ha-Mitzvot (Aseh) 125, 132, (Lo Ta'aseh) 149; Sefer Mitzvot Gadol (Aseh) 139, 140, (Lav) 265; Sefer ha-Ḥinnukh, Mitzvot 91, 449, 606.

THE PROHIBITION AGAINST MIXING MILK AND MEAT

You shall not seethe a kid in its mother's milk (Exodus 23:19)
You shall not seethe a kid in its mother's milk (Exodus 34:26)
You shall not seethe a kid in its mother's milk (Deuteronomy 14:21)

1. The fact that the prohibition against mixing meat and milk is repeated in three different biblical passages implies a threefold ban: namely, that (1) milk and meat must not be eaten together, (2) they must not be cooked together, and (3) it is forbidden to derive any benefit from food containing a mixture of milk and meat. Violations of this law were subject to a penalty of flogging.

2. It is permissible, however, to cook the meat of a kosher animal in the milk of a non-kosher animal, or the meat of a non-kosher animal or fowl in the milk of a kosher animal, as long as one does not eat the mixture but merely derives some other benefit from it; e.g., by giving it as a gift to a non-Jew.

3. The Rabbis designated a waiting period between eating meat and milk products. It is customary for a six–hour waiting period between meat and milk; some wait three hours, while others wait for one hour. According to some commentaries, the reason for the rabbinic prohibition is because of the taste remaining in the palate after eating meat. Others explain that it is due to the meat particles which are caught between the teeth. The mixing of meat and milk products, albeit not cooked together, would make a person indifferent to the prohibition and he might eventually come to actually cook the milk in the meat products. It is similarly prohibited to eat meat within six (or three, or one) hours after eating "hard" cheese.

4. While the Torah speaks only of the meat of an animal which gives milk, i.e., mammals, the Rabbis included the meat of fowl as well.

COMMENTATORS

Ibn Ezra: There is no specific explanation for the prohibition against mixing milk and meat except that "seething a kid in its mother's milk" implies extreme barbarism. He places this *mitzvah* in the same category as that of *shiluaḥ ha-ken,* sending away the mother-bird before taking the young from her nest (Deuteronomy 22:6). In both instances the quality of humanism is stressed.

Rashbam: He points out that the word "kid" was specified in the prohibition because in biblical times goat's milk was in abundant supply and therefore frequently used in the cooking of meat. He, too, considers the practice of "seething a kid in its mother's milk" as denoting gross insensitivity and cruelty.

Keli Yakar: A calf in the embryonic stage, like a human being, is conceived and develops through the nourishment of its mother's blood. Milk, another product of the animal, is also a derivative of its mother's blood. This *mitzvah* is mentioned (Deuteronomy 14:21) immediately before the commandments to tithe all one's first fruits in order to stress that, even as the first fruits must not be mixed with the later fruits of the same tree in the process of tithing, so the "kid" must not be cooked in milk, although both are the products of the bloodstream of the dam.

Ḥinnukh: He regards the mixing of milk and meat as an interference with the laws of nature, because he considers the "kid" and the "milk of its mother" to symbolize two distinct aspects of the animal's life cycle. He disagrees with the explanation offered by Maimonides for the prohibition: namely, that mixing meat and milk was a pagan custom and therefore an improper practice for Jews.

References:
B. Ḥullin 105a, 113b, 114a, 115b; B. Shabbat 130a; B. Sanhedrin 4b; B. Pesaḥim 24b; Mekhilta *Mishpatim;* Guide of the Perplexed, Part 3, Sec. 48; Yad, Hilkhot Ma'akhalot Assurot, Chap. 9; Sefer ha-Mitzvot (Lo Ta'aseh) 186, 187 (Maimonides holds that although there is a third reference to this injunction in Numbers 14:21, which should be applied to the ban on any sort of benefit from mixing milk and meat, this is not taken into consideration, because cooking and eating cover all types of benefit.); Sefer Mitzvot Gadol (Lav) 140, 141; Sefer Mitzvot Katan 176; Shulḥan Arukh, Yoreh De'ah, 87; Sefer ha-Ḥinnukh, Mitzvot 92, 113.

THE TREATMENT OF IDOLATORS

You shall make no covenant with them nor with their gods (Exodus 23:32)
They shall not dwell in your land, lest they cause you to sin against Me (Exodus 23:33)
Nor show mercy toward them (Deuteronomy 7:2)
You shall not leave any soul alive (Deuteronomy 20:16)

The Children of Israel left Egypt and entered the Promised Land not merely to secure freedom and a homeland for themselves, but also in order to bring the message of One God to all the peoples of the earth. When they came to the Promised Land, they found there seven nations—the Hittites, the Amorites, the Perizzites, the Hivites, the Jebusites, the Girgashites, and the Canaanites—which not only practiced idolatry but refused to permit the Israelites to spread the basic teachings of monotheism. These nations were not only an obstacle to Israel's purpose on earth—the dissemination of the belief in one God—but also a threat to Israel's own moral integrity because they even refused to observe the Noahide commandments incumbent on all civilized human beings. For this reason the Children of Israel were forbidden to have any traffic with them or to show them mercy.

While this law still applies to the descendants of these seven nations, Maimonides believes that such descendants probably no longer exist.

COMMENTATORS

Naḥmanides: He cites Rashi's view that the seven pagan nations that inhabited the land of Canaan posed a threat to the Jews because of the possibility that through them the Jews might be led astray from the Godly way of life. Naḥmanides does not consider Rashi's statement strong enough; in his opinion it was not only possible, but inevitable, that these heathen nations, if left alive, would have corrupted the Children of Israel.

Ḥinnukh: Why were the Children of Israel commanded to be uncompromising in their effort to uproot the idolatrous nations of Canaan? Because there could be no coexistence between the ideals of monotheism and the pagan mentality.

If these seven pagan nations were meant to be destroyed, then why did God create them in the first place? Like all other men and nations, these too had been born with the gift of free will to choose between right and wrong. Had they chosen the right path, it would not have been necessary to destroy them. Besides, if any of these nations produced so much as one individual who made a worthwhile contribution to the welfare of mankind, this alone would have made the creation of that man worthwhile.

Maimonides: Why should one still regard the destruction of pagan nations as a commandment when, in fact, most of the pagan nations had been destroyed and their descendants absorbed by other civilizations? There can be no statute of limitations when it comes to uprooting the sources of evil.

References:
B. Avodah Zarah 20a, 21a, 26b; J. Avodah Zarah, Chap. 1, Halakhah 9; B. Sanhedrin 67a; B. Gittin 45a; Sifre *Shofetim;* Tosefot B. Yevamot, 23a; Yad, Hilkhot Avodah Zarah, Chap. 7, 10; Yad, Hilkhot Melakhim, Chap. 6; Sefer ha-Mitzvot (Lo Ta'aseh) 48, 49, 50, 51 (See the conflicting opinions on whether these injunctions apply to all hostile nations, or only to the seven original peoples who lived in Canaan.); Sefer Mitzvot Gadol (Lav) 47, 48, 49, 225; Shulḥan Arukh, Yoreh De'ah, 151; Sefer Mitzvot Katan 135; Sefer ha-Ḥinnukh, Mitzvot 93, 94, 426, 528.

THE BUILDING OF THE SANCTUARY

Then you shall make a Sanctuary for Me (Exodus 25:8)

1. During their journey through the wilderness, the Children of Israel prepared a mobile Sanctuary from wood and cloth which could be set up and dismantled as they proceeded on their way. After entering the Promised Land, they erected a Tabernacle in Gilgal which was in existence for 14 years. The next Sanctuary was the one at Shiloh, a structure built partly of stone, which remained in use for a period of 369 years. From Shiloh, the Ark was moved first to Nob, and then to Gibeon. After 57 years of this temporary arrangement, the Israelites erected a permanent Temple on Mount Zion in Jerusalem.

2. The outstanding features of the Temple were: the western side which consisted of the *Heikhal*—the Spiritual Palace. The *Heikhal* comprised the Holy of Holies, the Holy, and the *Ulam*—the Hall, a foyer in front of the Holy. A curtain separated the Holy of Holies from the Holy.

In the Holy of Holies stood the Ark, encasing the Tablets. The Golden Altar, upon which the incense was burned, stood in the center of the Holy Section. The Golden Candelabrum stood southwest of the altar. Northwest of the altar stood the Table upon which was placed the shewbread. A partition separated the *Ulam* from the Holy Section. Opposite this partition were steps that led down to the *Ḥatzer,* the courtyard. This was also known as the *Azarah.* In the *Azarah* stood the altar for sacrifices. From this altar was a ramp leading to its top. Between the altar and the steps leading into the *Ulam,* on the southwest side, was located the Washbasin and its stand.

COMMENTATORS

Ḥinnukh: God does not require a specific place where His glory may reside. The Sanctuary was not intended as a dwelling place for God but as a setting where man might receive the spiritual inspiration conducive to the proper worship of God.
Alshekh: God desires that we should have a Sanctuary on earth to parallel His own Sanctuary in heaven and to give us an opportunity to cultivate His spiritual potential. However, He will not build this Sanctuary for us; rather, He requires of us to lead lives of holiness so that we ourselves may be spiritually fit to establish our Sanctuary on earth.

References:
B. Sanhedrin 16b, 20b; B. Temurah 31a; B. Shevu'ot 15a, 16b; J. Yoma, Chap. 1, Halakhah 1; B. Menaḥot 110a; Avot de-Rabbi Natan, Chap. 11; Midrash Rabbah, *Bereshit,* Chap. 2, 3, 13, 15, 22, 38, 98, 99; Midrash Tanḥuma, Sidrah *Shemot,* Sidrah *Va-Yikra;* Yad, Hilkhot Bet ha-Beḥirah, Chap. 1; Sefer ha-Mitzvot (Aseh) 20 (Note the difference of opinion between Maimonides, who reasons that the construction of the utensils is to be included in the *mitzvah* of the construction of the Sanctuary, and Naḥmanides, who reasons that the construction of the utensils was a *mitzvah* in itself.); Sefer Mitzvot Gadol (Aseh) 163; Sefer ha-Ḥinnukh, Mitzvah 95.

THE SHEWBREAD IN THE SANCTUARY

And you shall set upon the Table shewbread before Me continuously (Exodus 25:30)

1. The shewbread that was placed on the golden Table consisted of 12 loaves, corresponding to the Twelve Tribes of Israel. The 12 loaves were arranged upon the Table in two rows of six each. The loaves were placed on shelves in such a manner that a space was left above and below each loaf, permitting the air to circulate between the loaves so the bread would not become moldy.

2. On either side of each row there was a censer of frankincense.

3. The shewbreads were replaced once each week, on the Sabbath, in a ceremony carried out as follows: eight Priests would go up to the Table. Two of them carried the 12 loaves (one carried six and the other the remaining six) and two others carried one censer each. The other four Priests had their hands free. While two of these last four Priests slid out the old loaves from the shelves, the two Priests bearing the new loaves eased in their loaves so that the Table was not bare for even one moment. Then two Priests who had their hands free removed the two old censers and the two Priests bearing the new censers fitted these into their proper places.

4. Afterwards, all the eight Priests proceeded to a golden table in the *Ulam* upon which they placed the 12 loaves. The frankincense in the censers was burned as an incense offering. The Priests then removed the loaves from the Table and distributed to the Priests who were about to go on duty. The High Priest took six loaves; the remaining loaves were divided among the other Priests.

COMMENTATORS

Ḥinnukh: There are certain essentials without which man cannot survive. One of these essentials is bread. Because bread is vital to his continued existence, he must demonstrate his awareness that it is a gift from God.

With this in mind, the Children of Israel were commanded to heap 12 loaves of shewbread on the Table in the Temple, symbolizing the hope that the tables in their homes, too, would be laden with bread at all times.
Baḥya ben Asher: The Table on which the shewbread was placed was considered as an altar of sorts because the shewbread was regarded as offerings brought on behalf of sinners. In our own day, we still regard the ordinary tables at which we eat as altars and the food upon them as offerings. Now that we no longer have the Temple, our offerings consist of the food we are prepared to offer to the poor.
Abrabanel: The arrangement of the shewbread in two rows of six loaves each was intended to recall the manna which fell from heaven to feed the Children of Israel in the wilderness—one portion for each person in the morning, and another in the evening—twice six (for six days each week). In recalling this manna to us, the shewbread was intended to remind the Jew to place his trust in the Lord who will surely send sustenance to His people without fail, even as He did in the wilderness.

References:
B. Menaḥot 94a, 96b, 97a; B. Ḥagigah 26b; J. Ḥagigah, Chap. 3, Halakhah 8; J. Shekalim, Chap. 6, Halakhah 3; Yad, Hilkhot Temidim, Chap. 4, 5; Sefer ha-Mitzvot (Aseh) 27; Sefer Mitzvot Gadol (Aseh) 196; Sefer ha-Ḥinnukh, Mitzvah 97.

TO KINDLE THE LAMP (MENORAH) IN THE SANCTUARY

Aaron and his sons shall tend [the lamp] (Exodus 27:21)

1. The Priests were obliged to tend the lights of the seven-branched *Menorah* every morning and every evening. There is some difference of opinion among various commentators as to whether the lights in the Lamp were actually rekindled twice a day, or only in the evening. In any event, this *mitzvah* also included discarding old wicks, cleaning the oil cups, and refilling them with sufficient oil to burn through the night.

2. If the Priest found that one of the lights in the *Menorah* had gone out, he immediately replaced the wick and the oil, and rekindled the light not with a new fire, but with the fire from one of the other lights of the *Menorah.* The light in the center of the *Menorah,* however, was rekindled with fire from the outer altar.

3. The procedure followed by the Priest on duty for tending the lights of the *Menorah* was to check (and, if necessary, rekindle) five of the seven lights, then attend to some other task that had to be performed in the Temple, and then return to attend to the remaining two lights.

4. The lights of the *Menorah* had to be kindled even on the Sabbath, just as burnt offerings were brought on that day, too, although kindling of other fire is forbidden on the Sabbath.

COMMENTATORS

Sforno: The Priest in charge of the *Menorah* had to kindle the seven wicks in the following order: Working up from the last light on the right hand side toward the center, and then working from the last light on the left hand side toward the center. This was intended to convey the idea of the central point of unity to which all Jews, no matter what their position—to the right or to the left—must rally. The concept of the basic unity of the people of Israel was also stressed by the fact that the entire seven-branched *Menorah* was fashioned from one single block of gold.

Keli Yakar: The *Menorah* symbolized the radiance that enters the life of one who commits himself to God and Torah.

Ḥinnukh: The purpose of the *Menorah* and the reason for the care with which its lights were tended was the enhancement of the beauty of God's Sanctuary.

Baḥya ben Asher: The *Menorah* was situated on the south side of the Sanctuary. The Table was situated directly opposite. Since the lights of the *Menorah* symbolized the soul, and the Table the body of man, this arrangement betokened the "opposites" represented by the concepts of "soul" and "body." At the same time, by virtue of this arrangement, the Priest attending to the lights of the *Menorah* had to stand somewhere between the *Menorah* and the Table, symbolic indication that man must provide also for the needs of his body if his spirit is to survive.

References:
B. Menaḥot 88b, 89a, 98b; B. Shabbat 21a, 22b; B. Pesaḥim 59a; B. Yoma 14b, 33b; Midrash Rabbah, *Shemot,* Chap. 36; J. Sukkah, Chap. 5, Halakhah 3; Yad, Hilkhot Temidim, Chap. 3; Sefer ha-Mitzvot (Aseh) 25 (The position of Maimonides, as opposed to most other commentaries, is that the preparation of the wicks and their kindling is one and the same.); Sefer Mitzvot Gadol (Aseh) 193; Sefer ha-Ḥinnukh, Mitzvah 98.

THE PRIESTLY VESTMENTS

And you shall make holy garments [for Aaron] (Exodus 28:2)
And they shall bind the breastplate...to the rings of the ephod...so that the breastplate does not move from the ephod (Exodus 28:28)
[The robe of the ephod]...shall have a binding of woven work around the hole...so that it should not be torn (Exodus 28:32)

1. There were three types of priestly vestments worn by the Priests during their service in the Temple:

a. The vestments of the "Ordinary Priests" consisted of a coat, breeches, a hat, and a girdle. These garments were made of white linen, except for the girdle which was embroidered in wool.

b. The basic vestments of the High Priest consisted of the four garments worn by the Ordinary Priest, except that the High Priest did not wear a hat but a miter. In addition, he wore a breastplate with the Ineffable Name of God placed somewhere within it, and the ephod, an apron worn in the back and attached by suspenders to the breastplate; he also wore a woolen robe *(me'il),* and a golden diadem *(tzitz)* on which were inscribed the words "Holy unto the Lord."

c. The vestments worn by the High Priest on Yom Kippur

consisted of the four white garments of the Ordinary Priest along with two additional shirts, one to be worn during the morning sacrifices, and the other during the afternoon service.

2. All priestly garments had to be attractive, in good condition, and made in the proper size for the Priest who wore them.

3. When the vestments of Ordinary Priests became soiled, they were not laundered but were torn and the cloth was used to make wicks for the candelabra. The soiled vestments of the High Priest could not be destroyed but had to be stored. The vestments worn by the High Priest on Yom Kippur could only be worn once, even if they were not soiled.

4. The robe of the High Priest was slipped on over the head.

5. If a Priest failed to put on all the garments prescribed by the Torah, or if he put on garments in addition to those specified, his service was invalidated and he was subject to punishment from God. A Priest who disregarded the biblical instructions concerning his robes was considered like a stranger who was forbidden to perform priestly duties at the altar.

COMMENTATORS

Ibn Ezra: There was nothing intrinsically holy about the priestly garments themselves. Their sanctity derived from the fact that they were used during the divine service in the Temple.

Sforno: The splendor of the priestly garments was intended to inspire the worshipers who beheld them.

Naḥmanides: The priestly vestments were similar to the robes worn by royalty at the time. Since the Temple was a spiritual palace, it was only fitting that the Priests serving there should be dressed in royal robes. The workers who prepared these garments had to keep in mind the holy purpose for which they were intended.

Ḥinnukh: The special garments worn by the Priest were intended to remind him of the sacred character of the functions he had to perform in the Temple. This was the reason why the law was so explicit in its instructions as to the care to be taken of the vestments and as to the manner in which they should be worn, for if a Priest were to allow his garments to tear, or if he were to be careless in putting them on, the purpose for which the garments had been intended would be lost.

Abrabanel: The priestly vestments consisted of four basic garments, each with a symbolic meaning.

a. The *shirt:* This garment was worn next to the body to remind the wearer that every act he performed with his body had to be pure and wholesome, and directed to a higher purpose.

b. The *breeches* were intended to cover up the private parts. (In the days of the Temple, most men wore no breeches under their robes.)

c. The *girdle* held up the breeches. At the same time it was to remind the wearer of his duty to "gird" or to do battle against the evil and the temptations to do evil which he encountered at every turn.

d. The *hat* worn upon the head was to remind the wearer to direct his thoughts at all times within the framework of God's commandments.

The four additional vestments worn by the High Priest also have special purposes.

a. The *ephod* with two shoulder straps, encrusted with two onyx stones, of which each bore the name of six of the Twelve Tribes of Israel. It was intended to symbolize the unity of the people of Israel of whom the High Priest was the spiritual leader.

b. The outer robe *(me'il)* had golden bells around its hem to remind the wearer that there is a God above who hears everything.

c. & d. The *diadem* and the *breastplate* with the Ineffable Name of God proclaimed the spirit of truth that was unique to Judaism.

References:

B. Arakhin 16a; B. Sotah 48b; B. Yoma 25a, 72b, 73b; B. Zevaḥim 19a, 88b, 95a; B. Shabbat 139b; J. Yoma, Chap. 7, Halakhah 3; Midrash Rabbah, *Tetzaveh;* B. Sanhedrin 83b Tosafot; Midrash Tanḥuma, *Tetzaveh;* Yad, Hilkhot Kelei ha-Mikdash, Chap. 8, 10; Sefer ha-Mitzvot (Aseh) 33, (Lo Ta'aseh) 87, 88; Sefer Mitzvot Gadol (Aseh) 173, (Lav) 298, 299; Sefer ha-Ḥinnukh, Mitzvot 99, 100, 101.

THE PRIESTS AND THE OFFERING OF SACRIFICES

And they shall eat those things with which atonement had been made (Exodus 29:33)
You may not eat within your gates the tithe of your corn, or of your wine, or of your flock (Deuteronomy 12:17)
Nor of your free-will offerings, nor the heave offering of your hand (Deuteronomy 12:17)

1. The sacrifices offered in the Temple may be classified under two main categories:

a. *Kodshei Kodeshim:* The "most holy" of the offerings, in-including guilt-offerings and sin-offerings. The individual who brought these animal sacrifices turned them over to the Priest on duty in the Temple, who had to perform the sacrifice and to eat the flesh of the animal within specified time limits, and within the Temple courtyard *(azarah)*.

b. *Kodeshim Kalim:* The sacrifices of "lesser holiness." These included the offerings of thanksgiving, the peace-offering, the Paschal lamb, etc. These sacrifices, too, had to be offered at a specified place (the altar) and partaken within specified time limits soon after the offering had been completed. As distinct from meat of the *Kodshei Kodeshim,* meat from a sacrifice of "lesser holiness" could be eaten by the Priests anywhere within the walls of Jerusalem, and the Priest was permitted to distribute it to members of his household.

2. Before anyone could partake of the meat of the sacrificial animal, the blood of the animal had to be sprinkled upon the sacrificial altar (for explanation of this practice, see Ḥinnukh below).

COMMENTATORS

Ḥinnukh: Priests had to exercise the utmost care and punctiliousness in dealing with guilt-offerings or sin-offerings, because they were brought by someone who had sinned and was seeking forgiveness. Accordingly, the Priest dealing with these offerings had to eat the meat of the animal at the prescribed time and place in the Temple. It was forbidden for him simply to dispose of the meat in a haphazard fashion, giving it to his servants or animals, or allowing it to putrefy. He also had to be sure to sprinkle the blood of the animal upon the altar before partaking of the meat. This was to emphasize that the needs of the soul have priority over the needs of the body. If the individual knew that the Priest had taken care of his offering in full accordance with all the pertinent laws and precepts, he was able to return to his house confident that the sin for which he had made the offering would be forgiven.

References:
B. Pesaḥim 59b; B. Makkot 17a; B. Yoma 68b; Sifre *Re'eh;* Yad, Hilkhot Ma'aseh ha-Korbanot, Chap. 10, 11; Sefer ha-Mitzvot (Aseh) 89, (Lo Ta'aseh) 145, 147; Sefer Mitzvot Gadol (Aseh) 184, 185 (Lav) 324, 325; Sefer ha-Ḥinnukh, Mitzvot 102, 446, 448.

THE BURNING OF INCENSE IN THE TEMPLE

And Aaron shall burn thereon incense of sweet spices, every morning when he dresses the lamps, shall he burn it (Exodus 30:7)
You shall offer no strange incense on the altar, nor burned offering, nor meal offering; and you shall pour no drink offering upon it (Exodus 30:9)
And the incense which you shall make for yourselves; it shall be for you holy unto the Lord (Exodus 30:37)

1. As has already been noted, the altar of gold in the area of the *Heikhal* was used for the burning of incense. This was done twice daily–once in the morning and once in the evening. Maimonides counts this ritual as one *mitzvah* but Naḥmanides looks upon it as representing two separate *mitzvot,* because it had to be performed at two distinct times each day. The Priests were not permitted to approach the altar, or to use it for any other purpose than for the daily incense burning, and for sprinkling the blood from sin offerings or from the High Priest's Yom Kippur sacrifice.

2. The incense was compounded by a Priest from eleven ingredients, and was divided into separate portions, by weight for each day of the year. The formula called for the preparation of 368 *manim*–each *maneh* weighing 50 *shekalim*. One *maneh* was allocated per day, one half in the morning and one half in the evening. This accounted for 365 days of the year. The remaining three portions were burnt by the High Priest during his rituals on Yom Kippur.

3. During the burning of the incense, the area of the *Heikhal* was cleared of all persons except the one Priest who performed the ritual. The Priest stepped up to the golden altar upon which another priest had previously placed hot coals from the outer altar, and gently sprinkled the incense upon the glowing coals. After he had completed his task, he bowed before the altar and left the hall.

4. The incense made with the prescribed formula could be prepared only for use in the Temple. Anyone who prepared it for any other purpose was subject to the penalty of *karet* (being cut off from his people).

COMMENTATORS

Ḥinnukh: What was the purpose of the incense in the Temple? The scent of the incense was conducive to noble thoughts and the proper inspiration for worship.

Keli Yakar: What was the purpose of the sacrifices and of the incense? Both were intended as means by which men could make atonement for their sins. Sinners are deserving of death, but by the grace of God they were given an opportunity to substitute an animal for their own bodies. Just as the body was defiled by the sin, so was the soul defiled. The soul, too, was in need of an atonement. The intangible scent of the incense which rose heavenward atoned for the intangible soul of man that stemmed from God.

Why was the incense offering made in the morning and in the evening?

Because morning represents the birth of man and evening represents his death. This is to insure, symbolically, that man is born free of guilt and should be free of guilt when his soul returns to God.

Or ha-Ḥayyim: It was forbidden for both Priests and ordinary individuals to use the Temple formula to prepare incense for non-religious purposes. Even the act of preparing incense for such purposes was considered an act of desecration.

Abrabanel: According to tradition, the Priest who pounded together the eleven ingredients for the incense did so to the rhythm of a special chant. Doing the work in rhythm to music, it was felt, would result in a better and more evenly united compound.

Radbaz: The reason why the Priests were required to burn incense was to prevent them from tarrying in the area of the altar unnecessarily. Casual gazing and loitering was forbidden even for the Priests. The preparation of the candles caused a blinding smoke and choking odor. This ensured that the Priest finished his work and left the area quickly.

References:

B. Menaḥot 49b, 50a, 50b; B. Yoma 26a, 33b, 44a; B. Pesaḥim 59a; B. Krittot 5a, 6a; Guide of the Perplexed, Part 3, Sec. 45; Midrash Rabbah, *Bamidbar,* Chap. 4, Sec. 21; Chap. 18, Sec. 7; Zohar, *Behar,* 109a; Yad, Hilkhot Temidim, Chap. 3, Halakhah 4; Yad, Hilkhot Kelei ha-Mikdash, Chap. 2, Halakhah 11; Sefer ha-Mitzvot (Aseh) 28, (Lo Ta'aseh) 81, 85; Sefer Mitzvot Gadol (Aseh) 167, (Lav) 294, 295; Shulḥan Arukh, Yoreh De'ah, 265, Sec. 11; Sefer ha-Ḥinnukh, Mitzvot 103, 104, 110.

TO OFFER HALF A SHEKEL TO THE LORD

This shall they give, everyone that passes among these who are numbered, half a shekel . . . for an offering to the Lord (Exodus 30:13)

1. National interests are the responsibility of every citizen. No one has a right to claim exemption, if these national projects are to be carried out successfully. During the Temple days, some of the offerings were brought on behalf of all Israel, as contrasted to those brought by individuals. Who was to pay for these offerings?

Every year, during the month of Adar, every Jew was required to donate half a shekel to pay for the daily sacrifices *(temidim)* brought not by individuals, but by the Priests on behalf of the entire people of Israel. Even to the present day we read the portion of the Torah dealing with the half a shekel on the Sabbath preceeding the month of Adar. This is called *Shabbat Parshat Shekalim.* This contribution was mandatory upon every Jew, and had to be paid at one time, in full, even if it was necessary for an individual to sell one of his garments in order to be able to do so.

2. Priests and Levites, too, were required to make this contribution, putting their coins into the large baskets prepared at the Temple for this purpose. Women, children, and slaves were exempt, but could make the half-shekel donation if they so desired.

COMMENTATORS

Baḥya ben Asher: He translates the term *shekel ha-kodesh* (shekel of the sanctuary; Exodus 30:13) as "shekel of holiness" and questions the Torah's use of the term to describe the shekel. What, indeed, he asks, was "holy?" He then proceeds to explain the sacred significance. This coin was pure unalloyed silver. This implies that even *mitzvot* involving monetary donations, such as the half shekel and the redemption of the first-born, are as important as any other *mitzvah,* and must be performed. Furthermore, he observes that when the shekel was halved, the two parts resembled the two parts of man, body and soul. Neither body nor soul can be treated exactly as half a man's makeup. Precisely because of this reason, God deliberately asked the Jew to donate just half a shekel and not a whole shekel, to imply that even this half must be considered as a complete unit. In other words, the body of man cannot act as an independent half of man, but in its own sphere of activities it must be in complete harmony with the other half, the soul. The same is true of the soul's relationship to the body.

Da'at Zekenim: Why were the wealthy not required or even permitted to donate more than half a shekel? Because when it comes to involvement in sacred causes, no one should be in a position where he can say that he had a greater share in the cause than others in a less fortunate financial position.

Abrabanel: The purpose of the commandment that no one could contribute more—or less—than half a shekel was to avoid embarrassment for the poor and undue acclaim for the wealthy. If everyone had been permitted to give according to his financial position, a poor man would have suffered the embarrassment of having his plight become widely known because of his small contributions. On the other hand, one who used to be poor and suddenly became wealthy might have made a larger donation for no other reason but in order to receive the acclaim of his community.

Keli Yakar: He makes the following three comments:

1. The half-shekel donation was intended as an offering of atonement for the worship of the Golden Calf, of which all the Children of Israel had been found guilty. The "half" a shekel was meant to recall how Moses, in his anger at seeing what the people had done, had broken the Tablets of the Law (Exodus 32:19).
2. Since this shekel was an offering of atonement, the same amount had to be contributed by rich and poor alike, so that no one could deem himself morally superior to another because he had made a greater donation to gain forgiveness for his sin.
3. What was it that led the Children of Israel to turn away from God and make a golden calf as a new "god" for themselves? It was greed for riches and the satisfaction of physical desires. Accordingly, God instructed the Children of Israel to offer, for their atonement, half a shekel to teach them that even if a person had much more money and could have given more, he was considered no better in the eyes of God than one who could give only half a shekel.

References:

Mishnayyot Shekalim; B. Megillah 13b, 29b; J. Shekalim, Chap. 1, 2, 3, 6; Midrash Tanḥuma, *Ki Tissah;* Pesikta de-Rav Kahana, Chap. 2; Yad, Hilkhot Shekalim, Chap. 1; Sefer ha-Mitzvot (Aseh) 171; Sefer Mitzvot Gadol (Aseh) 45; Sefer ha-Ḥinnukh, Mitzvah 105.

THE WASHING OF THE HANDS AND FEET OF THE PRIEST

And Aaron and his sons shall wash their hands and their feet at the laver (Exodus 30: 19)

1. The washing of the hands and feet was a symbolic act of purification which all the Priests had to perform every morning before entering the Sanctuary to worship God.

2. This ritual had to be performed by the Priest only once each day unless he took a nap, relieved himself, or left the confines of the Temple any time during the day, or if he was diverted from his tasks by thoughts other than those relating to his priestly function. If any of these things occurred, he had to perform the ritual over again. A Priest who performed the Divine service without having washed his hands and feet was considered subject to the extreme penalty of *mitah bi-ydei shamayyim,* "death by the hand of God."

COMMENTATORS

Ḥinnukh: The washing of the hands and feet was an act of sanctification which every Priest had to perform before starting on his duties in the Temple. It symbolized the spiritual purification which the Priest had to undergo before performing his priestly acts.

Maimonides: This ritual of washing was incumbent upon Priests the moment they entered the area of the *Heikhal,* irrespective of whether or not they would actually have any duties to perform there.

Naḥmanides: The Priests were not required to wash their hands and feet if they entered the Temple grounds without having any specific priestly duties to perform. Naḥmanides pointed out that, in addition to being a symbolic act of purification, the washing of the hands and feet had the practical purpose of removing dust and dirt from the hands and feet of the Priests before they entered the Sanctuary to perform the Divine service.

The priestly ritual of washing hands and feet has survived into the present day practice of washing one's hands in the morning before reciting one's morning prayers.

References:

B. Sanhedrin 83b; B. Ḥullin 106b; B. Zevaḥim 15a, 15b, 19b, 21a, 22a; B. Yoma 28a, 32b; B. Ṡukkah 50a (see Tosafot); B. Sanhedrin 83a; J. Yevamot, Chap. 12, Halakhah 1; Yad, Hilkhot Bi'at Mikdash, Chap. 5; Sefer ha-Mitzvot (Aseh) 24; Sefer Mitzvot Gadol (Aseh) 175; Sefer ha-Ḥinnukh, Mitzvah 106; Tanna de-Vei Eliyahu, Chap. 15.

TO PREPARE THE OIL OF ANOINTMENT

And you shall make it an oil for holy anointment (Exodus 30:25)
It shall not be poured upon the flesh of man [i.e., on a non-priest] (Exodus 30:32)
And according to its composition, you shall not make any other like it; it is holy and it shall be holy for you. Whosoever compounds anything like it, or whosoever puts any of it upon a stranger, shall be cut off from his people (Exodus 30:32,33)

1. The religious and secular leaders of the people of Israel were inducted into office by the ritual of anointment with a specially consecrated oil, which was also used for the consecration of the holy vessels in the Tabernacle.

2. A supply of the oil used for this purpose *(shemen ha-mishḥah)* had to be on hand at all times. In the anointment of High Priests the oil was poured over their heads and spread over their eyes in the form of an X. In the anointment of a king the oil was spread on his head in the shape of a crown. The ritual of anointment had to be performed for every new High Priest, but not for kings who succeeded their fathers on the throne, unless there had been opposition to their assuming the throne.

3. The anointing oil was prepared from a mixture of myrrh, sweet cinnamon, sweet calamus, and cassia. Olive oil was then poured over the mixture which was boiled until the water evaporated, leaving the oil with the fragrance of the spices.

4. Only the holy vessels in the Tabernacle were "anointed." The vessels used in the Temple in Jerusalem were consecrated by the very act of being put into service.

5. Anyone who prepared oil according to the formula for anointing oil, but for a purpose other than that of ritual anointment or consecration, was subject to the penalty of "being cut off from his people."

COMMENTATORS

Naḥmanides: The stipulation that the oil must not be found "upon the flesh of man" does not only mean that the oil must not be used by non-priests. It implies that even a Priest or king who is anointed may not use the oil upon his whole body but only upon his head during the ritual of anointment.

Ibn Ezra: The ritual of anointment could not be performed on anyone who was not a direct descendant of Aaron. He then asks the obvious question why King Solomon, who was not a descendant of Aaron, was anointed with the *shemen ha-mishḥah*. He answers that this was an exception, a *hora'at sha'ah*.

Ḥinnukh: The use of rich and fragrant oils in ancient times was reserved exclusively for kings and princes. The ritual of anointment for the descendants of Aaron implied that the Priests in Israel were to be considered as royalty among their people. Since this oil was considered sacred, it was forbidden to prepare it for any other purpose.

References:

B. Krittot 3a, 5a, 6a, 6b, 7a; B. Horayot 11b; B. Yoma 73a; Yad, Hilkhot Kelei ha-Mikdash, Chap. 1; Sefer ha-Mitzvot (Aseh) 35, (Lo Ta'aseh) 83, 84; Sefer Mitzvot Gadol (Aseh) 166, (Lav) 292, 293; Sefer ha-Ḥinnukh, Mitzvot 107, 108, 109.

THE PROHIBITION OF SOCIAL CONTACT WITH PAGANS

Take heed to yourself, that you do not make a covenant with the inhabitants of the land (Exodus 34:12)

1. The scriptural passage above and Deuteronomy 32:38 ("Who did eat the fat of their sacrifices and drank the wine of their drink offering?") teaches us that Jews were forbidden to eat the food or drink the wine that were brought to pagan temples as offerings to the idols of the heathen world.

2. Biblical law forbids the drinking of *yayin nesekh* (wine that was used for idol worship) or its use for any other purpose from which Jews might benefit. *Setam yeinam* is the ordinary Gentile wine, even when it was not known that it was used for non-Jewish worship. Under rabbinic law this wine is subject to the prohibition of *yayin nesekh*. Even wine that was prepared by a Jew but had been touched or handled by a non-Jew was forbidden.

3. The purpose of these prohibitions was to avoid social contacts that might lead to intermarriage between Jews and pagans.

4. All who violated these laws were subject to the penalty of lashes.

COMMENTATORS

Ibn Ezra: "Entering into a covenant" with pagans is tantamount to entering into a covenant with their idols.

Or ha-Ḥayyim: Even if these pagan inhabitants of the land should willingly sign a covenant and vow not to worship idols and promise to observe all the Noahide laws, they should not be trusted because they will eventually return to idol worship.

Sforno: One who forms bonds with idol worshipers will eventually come to worship idols, because one or both of the following situations is bound to occur:

1. He will join their religious festivities and this will lead him to join in their worship.

2. Social contacts may lead to intimate relations which in turn will result in intermarriage. Intermarriage will eventuate in religious deviations.

Naḥmanides: Alliances with idol worshipers will result in dire consequences. But even if no such consequences ensue, the Torah makes it clear that it is forbidden in itself to join idol worshipers in eating food or drinking wine set aside as offerings for pagan idols.

Ḥinnukh: The *Ḥinnukh* stresses that even food and beverages that are only indirectly associated with pagan worship are forbidden. This applies especially to wine. Both the special sacramental wine which is poured upon the pagan sacrifices and the ordinary wine of pagans which may or may not have been used for idol worship were forbidden to Jews by the biblical verse (Deuteronomy 32:38) which implies that Jews should not participate in idolatrous sacrifices.

References:

B. Avodah Zarah 8a, 29b; B. Bava Kamma 80b (see Tosafot); Yad, Hilkhot Ma'akhalot Assurot, Chap. 11; Yad, Hilkhot Avodah Zarah, Chap. 9, Halakhah 15; Sefer ha-Mitzvot (Lo Ta'aseh) 194 (Note that while Naḥmanides derives the injunction from the above verse, Maimonides derives it from Deuteronomy 32:38.); Sefer Mitzvot Gadol (Lav) 148; Shulḥan Arukh, Yoreh De'ah, 133, 152; Sefer ha-Ḥinnukh, Mitzvah 111.

THE PROHIBITION OF FIRE ON THE SABBATH

You shall kindle no fire throughout your habitations on the Sabbath day (Exodus 35:3)

1. In addition to the general prohibition of all manner of work on the Sabbath, of which the Torah enumerates 39 primary activities which are forbidden, there is a specific prohibition against the kindling of fire on the Sabbath, and the Talmud discusses the reason for this specific mention. It includes everything which appertains to the kindling of light even if no actual work is involved, e.g., the striking of a match or the switching on of electric light. Such light, however, as has been kindled before the Sabbath (e.g., the Sabbath candles, a stove for cooking, a burner for heating water) is permitted.

2. In addition, the rabbis interpret this law to include not only the prohibition of executing a condemned criminal by burning on the Sabbath, but extend its provisions by analogy to include even the infliction of lesser punishments such as flogging on this day.

COMMENTATORS

Ba'al ha-Turim: One might be justified in saying that, since the use of fire is essential to human welfare, it should not be interrupted even for the Sabbath. However this contention is refuted by the statement that God does not stoke the fires of Gehinnom (Gehenna) on the Sabbath day.

Sforno: Most of the work forbidden on the Sabbath is associated with creative endeavors. While it is true that fire, for the most part, is associated with destruction rather than creation, the lighting of fire on the Sabbath is nevertheless prohibited because fire is used also for such creative work as the forging of metal.

Naḥmanides: This specific *mitzvah,* rather than some other prohibition, was singled out for inclusion in this verse for the following reason: While menial work is forbidden on the three "Pilgrim Festivals" (Passover, Shavuot, and Sukkot), it is permitted on these holidays to cook and bake the food needed for that particular day. The prohibition against kindling fires on the Sabbath is specified here to point out that, as distinct from the holidays, cooking and baking are not permitted on the Sabbath.

Naḥmanides cites the *Midrash de-Rabbi Nathan,* according to which the prohibition against making a fire for the purposes of cooking, baking, or similar labors is underscored so that no one should rationalize that these labors should be permitted to enhance our personal pleasure and comfort: e.g., lighting a torch so that it will not be dark or firing a furnace in order to have hot water for a bath.

Keli Yakar: He views the word "habitations" as expressly excluding the Temple, where, of course, fires were kindled for the offering of the sacrifices on the Sabbath. Furthermore, since the various types of labor that are forbidden on the Sabbath day are inferred from the 39 forms of labor associated with the building of the Temple, we might justifiably assume that the type of work permitted in the Temple, such as the kindling of fire, should also be permitted to us. This *mitzvah* rules out this contention.

Da'at Zekenim: Why was this particular prohibition singled out for inclusion here? In order to disabuse us of the notion that it would be permissible to light a fire on the Sabbath for work to be done some time after the Sabbath.

Ḥinnukh: The prohibition against lighting a fire on the Sabbath is already implicit in the fourth commandment. The purpose of stressing this prohibition again here is to teach us that courts of justice should recess for the Sabbath. The reasoning here is as follows: If judges were to continue their deliberations on the Sabbath, they might come into a situation where they have to pass a death sentence on the Sabbath, in a crime calling for death by fire. Since the law decrees that sentences passed by a court of justice must be carried out at the earliest possible moment, this would mean that the fire for executing such a death sentence would have to be kindled on the Sabbath. This would be a violation of the Sabbath. Moreover it would be a violation of the commandment that the Sabbath was to be a day of rest even for those accused of crimes. In order to avoid these breaches of the Sabbath law, courts of justice should close for the Sabbath.

References:

B. Shabbat 20a, 70a; B. Yevamot 6b; B. Sanhedrin 35b, 46a; B. Betzah 36b (see Tosafot); J. Betzah, Chap. 5, Sec. 2; Mekhilta *Va-Yakhel;* Yad, Hilkhot Shabbat, Chap. 24; Sefer ha-Mitzvot (Lo Ta'aseh) 322; Sefer Mitzvot Gadol (Lav) 67; Shulḥan Arukh, Oraḥ Ḥayyim, 339; Sefer ha-Ḥinnukh, Mitzvah 114.

LEVITICUS

SOME PREFATORY REMARKS CONCERNING THE BOOK OF LEVITICUS

1. Some of the greatest thinkers in Jewish history have deliberately, and perhaps prudently, avoided the attempt to rationalize the sacrifices. Others of equal stature have made efforts in that direction. The sharp difference between Maimonides and Naḥmanides is a case in point. Maimonides contends that sacrifices were necessary because in the days of pagan worship sacrifices were brought to all kinds of gods. Our order of sacrifices was intended to offset the worship of the pagans. Abrabanel, in his defense of the position of Maimonides, argues that the Jewish people, in their early history, would have understood no other type of worship. Naḥmanides argues that the purpose of the animal sacrifices was to bring home to the sinner that by committing his sin he had, if strict justice were applied, forfeited his life. Through the grace of God, however, he was allowed to substitute the life of an animal for his own. According to the *Sefer ha-Ḥinnukh,* an animal sacrifice symbolized the thought that man's selfish and sensual desires, which so easily led him to sin, must be made subservient to God's will. The sight of a living creature being destroyed was a vivid image of the destruction of a sinful soul which failed to save itself by repentance. Furthermore, sin is due to the animal nature of man, and the destruction of his possessions symbolized the destructive power of sin.

There is some authoritative thinking on the purpose of sacrifices. In fact, they should be called "offerings." The Hebrew word in this context is *korban,* which derives from the root meaning "to draw near." In other words, through these rituals, we offer ourselves—body and soul—to the will of God and strive to approach Him and thus commune more readily with Him.

2. To generalize, the offerings stemmed from four different sources.

The first to be brought were the community-offerings. These were presented, on behalf of the entire people, on the Sabbath and the first of the month, as well as on all festivals. The second kind were those brought by individuals, either as a free-will gesture or as a way of atonement for sins and misdeeds committed, accompanied by a request for forgiveness. Some of the occasions of individual-offerings were as follows: if a man said or did something evil; at his purification, or after being cured of leprosy; on the occasion when a convert was finally accepted into the Jewish fold; when a man brought his first-born animal as a gift to the Temple; when he came to the Temple to celebrate the three major Pilgrim Festivals. The third source of offerings was that of the courts that erred in their interpretation of a biblical law thus misleading the entire people by permitting something that the Torah expressly forbids. Lastly, there was the Paschal lamb which heads of families sacrificed. While it was the offering of the individual, it nevertheless was similar to a community offering; for, like the latter, it was not affected by the laws of the Sabbath.

3. All offerings were grouped into four categories: the burnt-offering; the sin-offering; the guilt-offering; and the thanksgiving offering. The burnt-offering was completely consumed by fire, except for the hide. Man's misdeeds are initiated in his mind. His thoughts wander off in the wrong direction. This offering was brought as a symbol of his acknowledgment that his head, his limbs, and his inwards were misled by the corrupt thinking of his mind. The sin-offering was brought by one who was spiritually mature, to the extent that he acknowledged his violation of the law, though it was unintentional. The guilt-offering was brought by one who was in doubt whether he had committed a wrong. Instead of seeking pretexts and excuses to exonerate himself, he condemned himself for not being more cautious with the law, so that doubts of his sins of commission or omission would not exist. Both in the case of the guilt-offering and the sin-offering, part of the animal was consumed by fire and part eaten by the Priest. The thanksgiving offering was brought by one who had either been the recipient of some extraordinary blessing in the past, or hoped for some special Divine gift in the future. In case of these offerings, part of the animal was burned, part went to the Priest, and part belonged to the donor. A meal-offering was brought either to accompany an animal sacrifice or, most often, as a substitute for an animal owed by an individual who lacked the means to provide one.

4. Generally speaking, the offerings were brought from animals, fowl, or vegetation. In the category of animals were included the domestic kind of the larger animal such as an ox, lamb, or goat. In the category of fowl were doves and turtledoves. Vegetation included the products of wheat, olives, and vines. The three types of animals were commemorative of the three Patriarchs. The doves and the turtledoves were chosen because of the modesty in their intimate behavior. The fruits of the soil were a symbol of the gifts that an agricultural people brought to their king.

5. The thought that is central to the whole concept of offerings is that the Jew should feel that with his sinning, the world did not come to an end. He would sense that with this type of worship, zealously and reverently carried out, he made his peace with God and that he was being given another opportunity to be righteous and God-fearing.

6. At the time of the offering, the Priest had to concentrate on six matters: the animal was to be brought as an offering; it had to be brought in the name of the specific owner; it was brought as an offering to God; only the meat had to be roasted in the fire, and the roasting to be done for the purpose of its fragrance; that it would be pleasurable before God that His will be done. In the case of a sin-offering, it was brought for a specific sin.

BURNT-OFFERINGS

If his offering be a burnt-offering of the herd (Leviticus 1:3)

1. The burnt-offering or *Korban Olah* was brought by one who had been guilty of sinful talk or thoughts.

2. This type of offering could be made with cattle, or lambs, or fowl. If it was a lamb, a goat, or cattle, it had to be a male animal. It had to be slaughtered in accordance with the rules of *sheḥitah* (ritual slaughter of meat); its blood was sprinkled on the altar and its skin presented to the Priest. The rest of the carcass (except for the thigh sinew) was then placed upon the altar to be consumed by fire. In addition, a meal-offering of flour, oil, and frankincense along with a wine libation had to be presented to the Priest on duty in the Temple. If the burnt-offering chosen was a fowl, i.e., a dove or a turtledove, its neck was snapped and its blood was sprinkled on the altar. The inner organs were removed; the rest of the carcass was placed upon the altar to be consumed by fire. If the burnt-offering was a fowl, no meal-offering was required.

3. Anyone partaking of the meat of a burnt-offering either before or after the blood had been sprinkled on the altar was subject to the penalty of flogging.

COMMENTATORS

Naḥmanides, Keli Yakar: Both accept the rabbinic premise that the burnt-offering was brought not for sinful acts but for sinful thoughts. But they offer two separate explanations for the commandment that the offering had to be consumed by fire. According to Naḥmanides, the act of burning the entire carcass (except for certain specified parts) is intended to symbolize man's awareness that there is no act or thought which he could conceal from God. *Keli Yakar* notes that the flames of the offering, as they leap heavenward, should remind man to direct his spiritual endeavors toward heaven, from where his soul originally came forth.

References:
B. Menaḥot 5b; B. Bava Kamma 66b; B. Arakhin 21a; B. Makkot 16b, 17a, 19b; B. Ḥullin 68b; B. Krittot 4b; B. Sanhedrin 43b; B. Zevaḥim 53b; Zohar *Va-Yikra,* 8b; Sifre *Re'eh;* Sifra *Va-Yikra;* Midrash Rabbah, *Va-Yikra,* Chap. 2, Sec. 8; Midrash Tanḥuma, *Tzav;* Yad, Hilkhot Ma'aseh ha-Korbanot, Chap. 6; Yad, Hilkhot Bekhorot, Chap. 1; Sefer ha-Mitzvot (Lo Ta'aseh) 144, (Aseh) 63; Sefer Mitzvot Gadol (Lav) 342, (Aseh) 180; Sefer ha-Ḥinnukh, Mitzvot 115, 447.

MEAL-OFFERINGS

And when a person brings a meal-offering (Leviticus 2:1)
But if his means are not sufficient for two turtle doves . . . he shall put no oil upon it (Leviticus 5:11)
Neither shall he put away any frankincense thereon (Leviticus 5:11)
And Aaron and his sons shall eat that which is left of it (Leviticus 6:9)
It shall not be baked with leaven (Leviticus 6:10)
Every meal-offering of the Priest shall be entirely burned; it shall not be eaten (Leviticus 6:16)

1. Meal-offerings were brought not as additions to other major offerings, but rather as separate and individual offerings and were of two distinct types: communal meal-offerings, and the meal-offerings of individuals, such as a poor man who could not afford to offer an animal or a fowl.

2. Communal meal-offerings were brought on the following three occasions: Passover (i.e., the *Omer*), Shavuot (the two loaves of bread), the Sabbath (the twelve loaves of shewbread). The Book of Leviticus enumerates nine occasions for individual meal-offerings. Most of these applied to poor people who could not afford to offer an animal.

3. With two exceptions, all meal-offerings included flour, oil, and frankincense.

4. The Torah specifies the exact amount in which these three ingredients were to be used in preparing the offering. The Priest would remove a portion of flour with the index, middle, and ring fingers of his hand for burning upon the altar. The remainder of the flour was left for the personal use of the Priest.

COMMENTATORS

Keli Yakar: Why was a wealthy man required to bring an animal as a sin offering, while a small amount of flour was considered sufficient for a poor man? Because of his exaggerated self-image, a wealthy man tends to be defiant and arrogant. By contrast, a poor man who sins is likely to be sufficiently humble to repent of his sins almost immediately. He, therefore, was not required to bring as great a sacrifice as his rich brother in order to attain atonement for his error.

Alshekh: The very fact that he is not in a position, nor even required, to bring as lavish a sin-offering as his wealthy brother should be sufficient humiliation for a poor mán to make him contrite and turn to God for forgiveness for his sins. When a man is so poor that he cannot even offer a fowl but must make do with an offering of flour, this in itself constitutes not only humiliation but an actual punishment for his sin.

Ḥinnukh: There are two reasons for the prohibition against adding frankincense and oil to the meal-offering.

1. Oil nearly always rises to the top when mixed with other liquids; it therefore suggests haughtiness rather than the spirit of humility which the meal-offering was intended to foster in the sinner.
2. A man who was so poor that he could afford to bring no more than a little flour as a sin-offering could not very well be expected to pay the additional cost of fine oil and frankincense.

Maimonides: When a layman brought a meal-offering, the Priest received a part of it; but when a Priest brought a meal-offering, the entire offering was burned; neither he, nor any other Priest, was permitted to partake of it. What is the reason for this discrepancy in the law? To make sure that the Priest would feel the shame of his transgression. Had he been permitted to offer up his own flour, and then to bake it and eat it himself, or to give it to one of his fellow Priests to eat, it would not be conducive to feelings of contrition and remorse and the whole purpose of the offering by the Priest would be defeated.

References:

B. Sotah 23b; B. Menaḥot 4a, 11a, 19b, 51b, 56b, 59b, 60a, 74b, 104b, 106b; Sifra *Va-Yikra;* Sifra *Emor;* Midrash Rabbah, *Va-Yikra,* Chap. 3, Sec. 5; Yad, Hilkhot Ma'aseh ha-Korbanot, Chap. 10, 12, 13; Sefer ha-Mitzvot (Aseh) 67, 88, (Lo Ta'aseh) 102, 103, 104, 138; Sefer Mitzvot Gadol (Aseh) 185, 186, (Lav) 322, 328, 329, 330; Sefer ha-Ḥinnukh, Mitzvot 116, 125, 126, 134, 135, 137; Guide of the Perplexed, Part 3, Sec. 46.

THE PROHIBITION AGAINST LEAVEN AND HONEY ON THE ALTAR

For you shall burn no leaven nor any honey, in an offering made by fire unto the Lord (Leviticus 2:11)

1. Leaven and honey symbolized sweet and pleasant thoughts which scarcely befitted an occasion when man stood before God, who knew even his innermost thinking and who required him not to spare himself in his confrontation with his spiritual shortcomings.

2. This prohibition applied only to honey or leaven intended as part of the actual offering, but not if these ingredients were used only as fuel for the fire.

3. Maimonides and Naḥmanides differ on the number of lashes to which a Priest was subject if he brought both leaven and honey with the sacrifice. According to Maimonides, he violated only one law. In the eyes of Naḥmanides, on the other hand, the offering of leaven and honey represented the violation of two separate laws and was therefore subject to double the number of lashes decreed as punishment for the violation of a single law.

COMMENTATORS

Ḥinnukh: He concedes that he can find no cogent basis for rationalization of this *mitzvah,* but since he stated at the outset of his own work that his purpose was to find reasons for every *mitzvah,* he suggests two possible reasons for the prohibition of leaven and honey on the altar.

1. Both leaven and honey symbolize concepts that run counter to the alacrity with which man should hasten to do the will of God. Leaven symbolizes procrastination; for, unlike unleavened bread, it takes a considerable time to rise. Honey denotes the "sweet" things in life which must be used in moderation lest they distract man from the fulfillment of the word of God.
2. By its "swelling" leaven symbolizes haughtiness. Honey is a food which is said to excite the passions. Accordingly, neither leaven nor honey has a place in God's holy Temple.

Maimonides: These two ingredients were prohibited for use on the altar because they were customarily employed by the pagans in their idolatrous rites.

Ba'al ha-Turim: Leaven and honey are related to the evil impulses of man. The evil impulses multiply just as leaven causes the dough to swell and eventually they become a temptation as sweet as honey.

Baḥya ben Asher: In keeping with the logic of the Ba'al ha-Turim, Baḥya reasons that, if it were not for the evil impulse, man would never have cause to bring a sin-offering. Leaven and honey must therefore be kept out of the offerings to remind man of his duty to remove the causes of sin from his heart and mind.

References:

B. Menaḥot 58b (see Tosafot); Sifra *Va-Yikra;* Guide of the Perplexed, Part 3, Sec. 46; Yad, Hilkhot Issurei Mizbe'aḥ, Chap. 5; Sefer ha-Mitzvot (Lo Ta'aseh) 98; Sefer Mitzvot Gadol (Lav) 318, 319; Sefer ha-Ḥinnukh, Mitzvah 117.

THE SALTING OF OFFERINGS

And do not allow the salt of the covenant of your God to be lacking from your meal-offerings. With all your offerings, you shall offer salt (Leviticus 2:13)

1. All offerings and the ingredients associated with them had to be salted thoroughly before being placed upon the altar, except for the following: any wine that was part of the offering, the blood from the offering that was sprinkled upon the altar, and the logs that were used in the fire to burn the offering. Wine brought as a separate offering had to be salted. A Priest who did not follow the rules for salting the offerings was punished by flogging.

2. Our present-day custom of sprinkling a little salt on our bread before reciting the blessing over it stems from the rabbinic concept that equates our homes with the holy Temple, our table with the altar, and our food with the offerings that were brought in the Temple.

COMMENTATORS

Maimonides: The Jews were commanded to place salt on their offerings in order to stress their difference from the pagans who deliberately refrained from salting the meat of their animal sacrifices because salt absorbs blood and they wanted to retain every drop of blood for their deity.

Abrabanel, Baḥya ben Asher, Ḥinnukh: The Jews were commanded to place salt on their offerings because meat is considered a complete dish only after it has been seasoned with salt, and our offerings to God, too, must be "complete" in order to be acceptable.

Da'at Zekenim: Salt is a preservative. Hence, the use of salt in our offerings teaches us that the sacrificial ritual will be "preserved" forever as a means of securing forgiveness from God.

Keli Yakar: Salt embodies two opposing concepts—the cool water from which it is derived and its ability to burn the food or objects in which it is placed. In this manner it reminds us of the two distinct, apparently antithetical aspects of God's nature—the gentle quality of mercy and the stark harshness of justice.

References:

B. Menaḥot 19b, 20a, 20b, 21a, 21b; Sifra *Va-Yikra;* Yad, Hilkhot Issurei Mizbe'aḥ, Chap. 5; Guide of the Perplexed, Part 3, Sec. 46; Sefer ha-Mitzvot (Aseh) 62, (Lo Ta'aseh) 99; Sefer Mitzvot Gadol (Aseh) 179, (Lav) 320; Shulḥan Arukh, Yoreh De'ah, 69; Sefer ha-Ḥinnukh, Mitzvot 118, 119.

WHEN THE SANHEDRIN ERRS

And if the whole Congregation of Israel shall err (Leviticus 4: 13)

1. The Sanhedrin was a High Court composed of 71 of Israel's greatest scholars of the Law. It served as the guide for the entire people of Israel in matters of religious law. Accordingly, when the Sanhedrin erred (unintentionally), permitting an act which, in fact, was a violation of law that required a sin-offering, the entire Sanhedrin had to bring such an offering. The people who committed the error on the strength of the Sanhedrin's decision were considered innocent and did not have to bring such an offering.

2. The questionable decision of the Sanhedrin had to be only partly contradictory to the Oral Law of the Torah. For example: a Sanhedrin which taught that one was permitted to carry objects from one domain to the other on the Sabbath, or that one was permitted to bow to idols (which is specifically forbidden in the Scriptures) is not liable to bring a sacrifice, and those people that relied upon their ruling must bring individual sin-offerings. However, if the Sanhedrin ruled that one may not carry but may throw from one domain to the other, or if they taught that one of the acts constituting work on the Sabbath which is not specifically mentioned in Scripture is permissible, then they are liable to bring this offering, called the *Par Helem Davar*.

3. If most of the Twelve Tribes sinned, even if they did not comprise a majority of the people of Israel, or if a majority of the people sinned, even if they were but a minority of the tribes, the Sanhedrin must bring an ox *(Par Helem Davar)* for each tribe, i.e., twelve oxen.

COMMENTATORS

Ḥinnukh: Even such an august body as the Sanhedrin is no different from the individual when it comes to sin. When a Sanhedrin errs, it must bring a sacrifice to atone for its mistake like any individual who has erred. Because their error in judgment is due to a weakness in reasoning, it is fitting that they offer a sacrifice in the Temple, the seat of all ultimate knowledge.

Sforno: If the Sanhedrin sinned because of an error in a decision, why does the Torah (Leviticus 4:21) call this sin-offering "the offering of the people" and not of the Sanhedrin? The answer is, because mistaken decisions of the Sanhedrin reflect a lack of proper judgment by the people of the nation. The people should have been alert and should have brought this mistake to the Sanhedrin's attention. Because they failed to do so, they are held accountable for the sin.

Or ha-Ḥayyim: If the Sanhedrin erred, why should it be made to bear the full brunt of the resulting sin? Because the Sanhedrin sinned in that it did not take sufficient care in keeping the people on the path of righteousness.

Keli Yakar: Why should the Sanhedrin be subject to such severe public censure if it has erred? Because when a body of sages such as the Sanhedrin has misled the populace, even the sincere repentance of the members of the Sanhedrin will not undo the damage by their mistaken decision.

References:

B. Zevaḥim 41b; B. Horayot 3b, 5a, 5b, 7b, 8b; Yad, Hilkhot Shegagot, Chap. 12; Sefer ha-Mitzvot (Aseh) 68; Sefer Mitzvot Gadol (Aseh) 217; Sefer ha-Ḥinnukh, Mitzvah 120; Sifra *Va-Yikra*.

OFFERINGS FOR UNINTENTIONAL SINS

And if the common people sin through error (Leviticus 4:27)

1. Most people do not deliberately go out of their way to commit transgressions. Those guilty of unintentional sin could obtain atonement by bringing a *ḥatat kavua*—an established sin-offering, one which was applicable to Jews of all ranks.

2. This offering could be brought only for an unintentional sin which would be subject to the penalty of *karet* (being cut off from the people of Israel) had it been committed intentionally.

3. The sin had to be the violation of a negative commandment: it had to involve an actual deed (not merely thoughts or words) and it had to have been completely unintentional. One example of a sin of this type would be the consumption of non-kosher fat in the belief that it was, in fact, kosher, or in unawareness that the consumption of non-kosher fat was forbidden by the Torah.

4. Jewish law lists 43 specific transgressions which, if committed unintentionally, could be atoned for by the *ḥatat kavua*. Many of these transgressions involve violations of the prohibition against marrying close relatives.

5. If the *ḥatat kavua* was to fulfill its purpose, it was essential that the thoughts of the person making the offering should be directed to his desire for atonement. If the sinner's only thought was: "How could this offering possibly erase my sin?" his offering was considered ineffective.

COMMENTATORS

Alshekh: Too many people are under the impression that they should not be penalized if they sin unintentionally. After all, one can commit a sin without having meant to do so purposely. Alshekh holds that, in fact, no sin is ever commited completely without intention. A person cannot sin unless there is within him a physical or mental tendency to sin. Thus we have no right to state categorically that a given individual committed a given sin in complete innocence of what he has done.

References:

B. Horayot 2a, 8a, 11a; B. Shabbat 73a, 93a; Midrash Rabbah, *Va-Yikra;* Chap. 4, Sec. 5; Sifra *Va-Yikra;* Yad, Hilkhot Shegagot, Chap. 1, 6, 7, 15; Sefer ha-Mitzvot (Aseh) 69; Sefer Mitzvot Gadol (Aseh) 213; Sefer ha-Ḥinnukh, Mitzvah 121.

THE DUTY TO GIVE TESTIMONY

And if a person sins and hears the voice of adjuration, he being a witness, whether he has seen or known of it, if he does not utter it, then he shall bear his iniquity (Leviticus 5:1)
Then you shall inquire, and make search, and ask diligently (Deuteronomy 13:15)

1. Since justice is the foundation of society, anyone who deliberately impedes justice is thereby guilty of perpetrating an act of injustice. If one could give testimony that would help a court of justice come to a decision, but he fails to do so, he has committed a sin.

2. As a rule, courts of justice under Jewish law require the testimony of two witnesses to establish a fact. In litigation involving money, one need not volunteer to give evidence, but if he is called upon to do so by one of the litigants, or by the court, he is duty-bound to testify. In trials involving capital punishment, anyone who actually saw one person murder another is obliged to present his evidence without delay.

3. When witnesses present themselves, the court is duty-bound to examine them in the greatest detail possible: e.g., "At what hour, and on what day, week, month, or year were you witness to this act?" or "You say that this person worshiped an idol. Well, what sort of idol was it and exactly how did he worship it?" or "You contend that he ate on Yom Kippur. Well, exactly what kind of food did he eat and precisely how much of it did he eat?" There must be no "leading" questions; all questioning had to be direct and straightforward.

4. If a person swore that he had no knowledge of any evidence, and it was later established that he had knowledge of certain facts but had concealed them, he was required to bring an offering.

COMMENTATORS

Baḥya ben Asher: When one withholds testimony, he is obstructing justice and thereby denying the power of God's influence on the course of world events. In other words, a person may assume that this is but an insignificant transgression and one that may easily be ignored. In truth, however, this must not be ignored. Today's slight error, if ignored, might lead to tomorrow's major transgressions.

Ḥinnukh: Why is the *Bet Din* explicitly commanded to cross-examine its witnesses with great diligence? Because the testimony these witnesses may give and the decision which the court may make on the basis of their evidence may have much wider repercussions than might be believed at a superficial glance. For instance, because of the lack of legitimate witnesses, or authentic evidence, a court awards a sum of money to A, when in fact, it was his opponent B who deserved this money. If A goes out to do business with this money, which was awarded to him by mistake, then any person who enters into a business relationship with A becomes involved—albeit unwittingly—in transactions with stolen merchandise.

References:

B. Shevu'ot 30a, 32a, 33b, 35a; B. Bava Kamma 55b, 56a; B. Pesaḥim 113b; B. Sanhedrin 30a, 30b, 40a; B. Krittot 9a; B. Arakhin 18a; B. Yoma 74a; B. Gittin 71a; B. Ketubbot 18b; J. Sanhedrin, Chap. 3, Halakhah 9; Tosefta Shevu'ot, Chap. 3; Midrash Tanḥuma, *Va-Yikra,* Chap. 7; Sifre *Re'eh;* Yad, Hilkhot Edut, Chap. 1; Yad, Hilkhot Shevu'ot, Chap. 1, 9; Yad, Hilkhot Shegagot, Chap. 10, Halakhah 4; Sefer ha-Mitzvot (Aseh) 178, 179; Sefer Mitzvot Gadol (Aseh) 108, 109; Sefer Mitzvot Katan 239 (Note that the commentary considers this to be a negative *mitzvah,* instead of a positive one.); Shulḥan Arukh, Ḥoshen Mishpat, 28, 30; Sefer ha-Ḥinnukh, Mitzvot 122, 463.

ALTERNATIVE SIN-OFFERINGS

And if his means are not sufficient for a lamb, he shall bring for that wherein he hath sinned, two turtledoves or two young pigeons, to the Lord (Leviticus 5:7)

1. There were six categories of sinners who were only required to bring "alternative" offerings *(korban oleh ve-yored)* according to their means, to make atonement for their sins (the offering could be an animal, a fowl, or a meal-offering):

a. One who took an oath that he had no testimony to give, but later realized that he had sworn falsely, and repented for it.

b. One who took an oath to do a certain thing and failed to do so.

c. An unclean person who unintentionally partook of sacred food forbidden to the unclean.

d. An unclean person who unintentionally entered the precincts of the Temple.

e. The mother of a newborn baby, who, during her labor pains, vowed that she would never again have intercourse with her husband.

f. One who was stricken with leprosy (because he had slandered a fellow man).

2. The choice of the *korban oleh ve-yored* depended upon the financial position of the sinner at the time he was about to bring his offering. This meant that, if he was poor at the time he set aside his meal-offering but had come into money by the time he was ready to bring the offering, he was obliged to bring an animal sacrifice in place of the meal-offering.

COMMENTATORS

Da'at Zekenim: Why was the privilege of bringing an atonement offering according to his financial means reserved exclusively to individuals guilty of the above-named categories of sin? Because these were sins from which the transgressor had no personal gain. One whose sin brought him personal gain (e.g., one who ate on the Day of Atonement or one who worked on the Sabbath) is not entitled to the privilege of making atonement with alternative offerings.

Naḥmanides: A Priest may sin while performing his priestly duties and yet not be aware of it until told about it later. The reason that the privilege of offering an alternative sacrifice was extended to him is because he was in the process of performing a *mitzvah* when the wrong was committed.

Ḥinnukh: Persons guilty of one of these six categories of sin were given the privilege of making atonement with alternative offerings because these are sins to which man is susceptible by nature. For example: A person is always in danger of uttering slander or gossip because he constantly has occasion to talk. Or, a man might easily enter the precincts of the Temple while in an unclean state because his urge to worship God is so strong that he may temporarily forget that he is unclean, or that he should not enter the Temple when he is unclean. Or, a man may easily swear falsely because he is often tempted in the stress of daily life to insist that something is true (or false), or to give testimony that is exaggerated or not entirely accurate. While the Torah certainly does not condone sins such as these it seeks to facilitate the act of repentance on the part of persons guilty of them. The important element is that the individual who has committed a sin in this category genuinely regrets what he has done.

References:
B. Krittot 10b, 27b; B. Arakhin 30b; B. Horayot 9a; Yad, Hilkhot Shegagot, Chap. 10; Sefer ha-Mitzvot (Aseh) 72; Sefer Mitzvot Gadol (Aseh) 216; Sefer ha-Ḥinnukh, Mitzvah 123.

OFFERINGS OF "DOUBTFUL" AND "CERTAIN" GUILT

And if anyone should sin. . . though he does not know it, he is still guilty and shall bear his iniquity (Leviticus 5:17)
And he shall bring his trespass to the Lord (Leviticus 5:25)
And this is the law of the guilt-offering (Leviticus 7:1)

1. There were two types of guilt-offerings: (1) The *asham talui* or "offering of doubtful guilt" and (2) the *asham vadai* or "offering of certain guilt." The *asham talui* was required when a person admitted having had contact with something unlawful but was in doubt as to whether he had actually committed a violation of the law. One example: A man had seen two pieces of fat before him, and had eaten one of them. He later learned that one of the two pieces of fat he had seen had been non-kosher but he had no way of finding out whether the piece he had eaten had been the kosher or the non-kosher one. As long as he had no possibility of knowing, he had to bring an "offering of doubtful guilt." If, and when, he found out beyond doubt that the piece he had eaten had been non-kosher, he had to bring a sin-offering. The second type of guilt-offering, the *asham vadai,* was brought by individuals guilty of any one of the four following transgressions:

a) carnal knowledge of an handmaiden who had already been married to a Jewish slave;

b) swearing falsely that one was not in possession of an object which, in fact, he had stolen or borrowed;

c) unintentional appropriation for one's own use, or benefit from, an object that was the property of the Temple or of the Priest;

d) a Nazirite who had contact with a corpse. This offering also had to be brought by a leper at the time of his purification.

2. In each of these cases, the sinner had to place his hands on the sacrifice he was about to offer and openly confess his sin. If he brought the offering without this confession, his offering was disqualified.

COMMENTATORS

Ḥinnukh: The "offering of doubtful guilt" was brought by the sinner to atone for his lack of discretion in not knowing whether or not he had actually committed a sin. Failure to know whether or not one had violated the law was in itself considered a sin of sorts.

The "offering of certain guilt" given by individuals guilty of unintentional theft was intended to teach us that, in addition to returning the stolen property to its rightful owner, the thief also must pay his debt to God, because a sin committed against a fellow man is also a sin against God.

Baḥya ben Asher: Why was the "offering of doubtful guilt" more costly than the "offering of certain guilt"? When a person knows for certain that he has sinned, he will feel guilty and it will be natural for him to repent for his sin. One who is in doubt whether he has sinned or not, on the other hand, is less likely to have feelings of guilt or remorse. The Torah held that, if he were required to bring a costly offering to atone for the possibility that he may have done wrong, he would in the future exercise greater care in making sure that he would remain far away even from the chance of sin.

Radbaz: A person who is not sure whether he has sinned or not had to bring an "offering of doubtful guilt" against the chance that he may have sinned in actual fact, since the pangs of doubt surely must have some basis in fact. The offering was in the form of a ram which symbolized the grace which God had bestowed upon Abraham when Abraham was about to sacrifice Isaac. The offering symbolized the hope that even as He had mercy upon Abraham, God would have mercy also upon him who might have committed a sin unintentionally, without his own knowledge.

References:
B. Krittot 17b, 19b, 22b; B. Zevaḥim 24b; B. Menaḥot 110a; B. Kiddushin 81b; B. Horayot 8b; B. Nazir 23a; Sifre *Va-Yikra, Tzav;* Yad, Hilkhot Shegagot, Chap. 8, 9; Yad, Hilkhot Ma'aseh ha-Korbanot, Chap. 9; Sefer ha-Mitzvot (Aseh) 65, 70, 71; Sefer Mitzvot Gadol (Aseh) 182, 214, 215; Sefer ha-Ḥinnukh, Mitzvot 128, 129, 140.

REMOVAL OF THE ASHES OF THE OFFERINGS

[The law of the burnt-offering] . . . [the Priest] shall take up the ashes to which the fire has consumed the burnt-offering (Leviticus 6:3)

1. *Terumat ha-deshen,* the "removal of the ashes" left from burnt-offerings, was a duty very much sought after by the Priests in the Temple. According to the law, ashes from the burnt-offerings of the previous day had to be removed from the altar every morning. The ashes were taken to a place beyond the walls of Jerusalem where they were buried so that they would not be scattered by the wind or disturbed by animals.

2. The ritual was performed every morning with the appearance of the morning star. On festivals and other special occasions, it was performed during the second third of the dark hours of the night. On Yom Kippur, it was done at midnight.

3. When a Priest was assigned to perform this ritual he would wear vestments less costly than those which he wore when performing his other Temple functions.

4. A Priest suffering from a physical defect that disqualified him from performing the sacrificial rites was also not permitted to perform the function of removing the ashes left from the sacrifices.

COMMENTATORS

Ḥinnukh: Although, on the face of it, the removal of the ashes from the previous day's sacrifices appeared to be a very insignificant feature of the sacrificial procedure, it was, nevertheless, one of the many acts carried out for the purpose of preserving the dignity, decorum, and beauty of the Temple.

Baḥya ben Asher: Even for the performance of this seemingly unimportant ritual, the Priest was required to wear special garments. This was intended to teach us that no duty toward God or toward one's fellow man may ever be regarded as inconsequential.

References:

B. Yoma 22a, 24a; B. Zevaḥim 83b; B. Me'ilah 9a; B. Pesaḥim 26a; Mishnayyot Tamid, Chap. 1; J. Yoma, Chap. 2, Halakhah 1; Sifra *Tzav,* Chap. 2, Sec. 11; J. Shabbat, Chap. 10, Halakhah 3; Yad, Hilkhot Temidim, Chap. 1; Sefer ha-Mitzvot (Aseh) 30; Sefer Mitzvot Gadol (Aseh) 192; Sefer ha-Ḥinnukh, Mitzvah 131.

THE FIRE UPON THE ALTAR

Fire shall be kept burning continually upon the altar. It shall not go out (Leviticus 6:6)

1. Although there was already a heavenly fire in the Tabernacle, the Torah instructed the Priests of the Temple to kindle a fire and keep it burning all day.

2. On the altar, there were three stacks of firewood, of three different sizes, each of them intended for use in lighting a separate fire. The largest fire was used for the burnt-offerings. The smaller fire served as the source from which the Priest took the embers to light frankincense on the golden altar. The smallest fire was maintained merely in fulfillment of the *mitzah,* namely to have a fire burning on the altar all the time.

3. A Priest who extinguished even as much as one ember of the fire was subject to the penalty of flogging. However, if this happened accidentally while the Priest took fire from the altar in order to perform another *mitzvah,* such as lighting the candelabra, it was not counted as a transgression.

COMMENTATORS

Baḥya ben Asher: The altar was not in constant use. Why, then, was it necessary to have a fire burn there at all times? In order to demonstrate to the people the miracle that they were to associate with the altar. Here, before them stood an altar of wood and copper, with a fire burning upon it at all times, yet the wood of which the altar was made did not catch fire, nor did the copper melt.

Ḥinnukh: Man's gifts from God are commensurate with his specific service to God. The temperature of one's body is of vital importance; a high temperature may indicate a severe infection and a below-normal temperature may indicate some physical disorder. Proper body temperature is essential to good health. We must, therefore, serve God by keeping an even flame on His altar. The flame had to be kept burning evenly; it was not permitted to flare up into a roaring blaze at some times and to die down into a faint glow at others. If we obey this commandment God will reward us by keeping us the desired normal body temperature at all times.

References:

B. Zevaḥim 91b; B. Yoma 21a, 45b, 46a, 46b; J. Yoma, Chap. 4, Halakhah 6; Yad, Hilkhot Temidim, Chap. 2; Sefer ha-Mitzvot (Aseh) 29, (Lo Ta'aseh) 81; Sefer Mitzvot Gadol (Lav) 334, (Aseh) 191; Sifra *Tzav;* Sefer ha-Ḥinnukh, Mitzvot 132, 133.

MINḤAT PITTIM—THE OFFERING OF THE PRIEST

This is the offering of Aaron and of his sons, which they shall offer to the Lord on the day when he is anointed (Leviticus 6:13)

1. In addition to the regular daily offering *(korban tamid),* it was the duty of the High Priest to bring a daily offering known as *minḥat pittim*—meal-offering of cakes offered up in broken pieces. Ordinary Priests had to bring this offering only once, on the day when they were installed into their service at the Temple.

2. The High Priest prepared *minḥat pittim* as follows: He took a tenth of an *ephah* of fine flour, and divided this measure of flour into two parts. Three *logs* of oil were mixed with the flour. Each half of the flour was used for making six cakes, the total of twelve cakes corresponding to the twelve tribes of Israel. The mixture was kneaded, baked, and then fried lightly in oil. He would then break each of the twelve cakes into two parts, placing each half over the other. Twelve halves were taken together, with a half of a handful *(kometz)* of frankincense and burned on the altar in the morning. The other twelve halves, also with half a handful of frankincense added, were burned at the altar in the evening.

3. If this was not made by a High Priest but by an Ordinary Priest, all the twelve cakes were offered whole and at one time, with one handful of frankincense.

COMMENTATORS

Abrabanel: He makes several interesting comments on the purpose of the *minḥat pittim.*

a. Before a man can take the liberty of criticizing his fellow man, he must be sure that his own affairs are in order. By his own offering the High Priest demonstrated symbolically that, asking his people to bring their sacrifices, he himself had taken stock of his conduct and had brought an offering to atone for his own transgressions.

b. The people will understand that if even so exalted a personage as the High Priest felt it necessary to examine his conscience, they, too, must not hesitate to look into their own hearts.

c. Why was the High Priest's offering so modest? So that the poor among the people would not feel ashamed of their own modest offerings.

d. Another reason for the modest character of the High Priest was to show that the Jew was expected to approach religious worship in a spirit of humility and contrition.

e. Why was it required that the *minḥat pittim* should be burned in its entirety upon the altar? In order to impress the people that the basic purpose of a sacrifice was not to provide food for the Priests but to symbolize the desire to carry out the will of God.

f. The *minḥat pittim* was an offering of thanksgiving brought by the Priests to demonstrate their gratitude to God for the sustenance they were receiving from the Israelites in accordance with the Divine command.

g. Another reason why the *minḥat pittim* was burned in its entirety rather than set aside as food for the Priest was to make up for the possible carelessness on the part of Ordinary Priests in that the latter sometimes did not draw off a sufficient amount of flour from the meal-offerings brought by the people and could thereby invalidate the act.

h. The *minḥat pittim* was brought together with the lamb that was offered daily—one in the morning and one in the evening—on behalf of the entire nation.

i. One of the purposes of the offering brought by the High Priest was to recall, and atone for, the sin committed by his ancestor, Aaron, when he allowed the Children of Israel to make the Golden Calf as their god in the wilderness. The fact that the personal offering was brought together with the lamb that was offered on behalf of the entire People of Israel reminded the people that their ancestors in the wilderness had been guilty along with Aaron, the first High Priest, in the making of the Golden Calf.

References:

B. Mo'ed Katan 15b, 16a; B. Menaḥot 51b, 78a; Sifra *Tzav;* Midrash Rabbah *Tzav,* Chap. 8, Sec. 3; Yad, Hilkhot Temidim, Chap. 3; Sefer ha-Mitzvot (Aseh) 40; Sefer Mitzvot Gadol (Aseh) 195; Sefer ha-Ḥinnukh, Mitzvah 136.

THE SIN-OFFERINGS

This is the law of the sin-offering (Leviticus 6: 18)
And no sin-offering, whereof any of the blood is brought into the Tent of Meeting for making atonement in the holy place, shall be eaten; it shall be burnt with fire (Leviticus 6:23)
[If the offering is a fowl, the Priest shall] pinch off its head close by the neck but shall not break it apart (Leviticus 5:8)

1. The sin-offering referred to in these commandments could be brought only to atone for transgressions that had been committed unintentionally. Had these transgressions been committed knowingly and on purpose, the transgressor would have been liable to severe punishment. There were two types of sin-offerings—animal and fowl. The animal offering could be made by an individual on his own behalf, or on behalf of the entire community. The poor, who could not afford the price of an animal, were permitted to offer up pigeons instead.

2. An individual who offered an animal on his own behalf would take his offering to the northern section of the Temple Court. There he would place both his hands upon the head of the animal, confess his sin, and ask for Divine forgiveness. The animal was then slaughtered and its blood transferred to a receptacle left for that purpose on the altar. The priest then dipped his right forefinger into the blood and sprinkled a few drops upon the upper sections of the four corners of the altar. He then dressed the animal and burned its inner organs. The rest of the carcass was divided among all the Priests, who were obliged to eat the meat within a day and a night following the offering.

3. If the animal was offered on behalf of an entire community, as in a case where a whole community had unintentionally sinned, no one was permitted to partake of the meat of the animal. Following the ritual at the altar, the carcass was cut into quarters, taken outside the city walls, and burned in a place designated for that purpose.

4. If the sacrifice took the form of turtledoves or pigeons the Priest would kill the bird by breaking its neck and nipping either the gullet or the windpipe with his fingernail. He then sprinkled some of its blood upon the lower part of the altar. This quick and simple procedure, used in place of the more complicated and time-consuming *sheḥitah,* was intended as an act of consideration for the transgressor who obviously was a poor man; had he not been poor, he would have been able to bring an animal sacrifice. The idea of the shortened ritual was to enable the transgressor to leave the Temple and to return to his work at the earliest possible moment.

5. If the Priest accidentally sprinkled some of the blood of the sacrifice on his garments, the garments had to be washed in the Temple courtyard.

COMMENTATORS

Alshekh, Keli Yakar: Why does the Torah emphasize the sacred character of the sin-offering? Because the transgressor is worthy of praise for having the courage to admit that he has sinned, and for demonstrating in public his desire to return to the path of righteousness.

Ḥinnukh: Why does the Priest who receives pigeons as a poor man's sin-offering, break the pigeons' necks instead of using a knife to kill them? Because the Torah wanted to emphasize that when a poor man calls for help, there must be no delay whatsoever. Thus he does not take the time to select the proper knife and examine its blade but, instead, he quickly and efficiently snaps the bird's neck.

References:

B. Sotah 32b; B. Zevaḥim 53a, 64b, 65a, 90a, 92a; B. Menaḥot 110a; B. Pesaḥim 24a; B. Ḥullin 21a; J. Yevamot, Chap. 8, Halakhah 3; Sifra *Tzav;* Midrash Tanḥuma, *Va-Yikra;* Chap. 6; Yad, Hilkhot Ma'aseh ha-Korbanot, Chap. 1, 5, 7, 8, 11; Yad, Hilkhot Pesulei ha-Mikdashim, Chap. 2, Halakhah 4; Sefer ha-Mitzvot (Lo Ta'aseh) 112, 139, (Aseh) 64; Sefer Mitzvot Gadol (Aseh) 181, (Lav) 324, 327; Sefer ha-Ḥinnukh, Mitzvot 124, 138, 139.

THE PEACE-OFFERINGS

And this is the law of the sacrifice of peace-offerings (Leviticus 7:11)
He shall not leave any of the flesh until the morning (Leviticus 7:15)

1. Peace-offerings were brought on five different occasions. They were classed as follows:

a. The peace-offering brought on Shavuot on behalf of the entire community.

b. The peace-offering brought by individuals on their own behalf on the three major festivals.

c. The offering of thanksgiving, brought in gratitude for recovery after serious illness or for deliverance from other perils, such as imprisonment. This offering was accompanied by an additional offering of bread. Today the place of this offering has been taken by *Birkat ha-Gomel,* the prayer recited publicly in the synagogue by one who has recovered from a serious illness or has come safely through some other dangerous experience.

d. An offering in fulfillment of a vow made at a time of stress, or a free-will offering which could be made at any time a person desired to do so.

e. The offering brought by a Nazirite (see Numbers, Chap. 6) upon the completion of his period of self-denial. This offering, like the offering of thanksgiving, was accompanied by an additional gift of bread.

2. Peace-offerings were made with cattle, goats, lambs of either sex, but never with fowl of any kind. One part of the carcass was burned upon the altar, another part was eaten by the Priest on duty at the altar, and the third part was eaten by the donor himself.

COMMENTATORS

Da'at Zekenim: Why were the offerings described above called "peace-offerings"? These offerings symbolize the feelings of the donor after having experienced the goodness of God, i.e., the peace between himself and his Master.

Rashbam: The author of *Da'at Zekenim* regards offerings as peace-offerings because he interprets *shelemim,* the Hebrew term for these offerings, as a derivative of *shalom,* "peace." Rashbam, on the other hand, holds that *shelemim* is derived from the word *shalem,* a verb meaning "to pay." In other words, this type of offering is to be considered as the "payment" for a vow taken by the donor.

Keli Yakar: Why was an offering of bread added to the offering of thanksgiving? In order that the donor might be able to share this, the tangible demonstration of his gratitude to God, with as many of his friends and neighbors as possible. No chances were taken that there would be a shortage of bread while this group was partaking of the meat of the offering.

References:

B. Menaḥot 77b, 79b, 80b; B. Zevaḥim 50a, 55a, 120b; Sifra *Tzav;* Midrash Tanḥuma, *Tzav,* Chap. 14; Yad, Hilkhot Ma'aseh ha-Korbanot, Chap. 9; Yad, Hilkhot Pesulei ha-Mikdashim, Chap. 18, Halakhah 9; Sefer ha-Mitzvot (Aseh) 66, (Lo Ta'aseh) 120; Sefer Mitzvot Gadol (Aseh) 183, (Lav) 336; Sefer ha-Ḥinnukh, Mitzvot 141, 142.

SACRIFICES INVALIDATED BECAUSE OF FAILURE TO OBEY INSTRUCTIONS

And if any part whatsoever of the flesh of the sacrifice of his peace-offering should be eaten on the third day, it shall not be accepted, neither shall it be credited to him who offers it; it shall be an abomination (Leviticus 7:18)

You shall not eat any abominable thing (Deuteronomy 14:3)

1. In order for a sin-offering to be regarded as acceptable for purposes of atonement, the donor had to make it in a spirit of humility and in strict accordance with the relevant instructions given in the law. In this manner he demonstrated his total submission to the will of God. Accordingly, failure to follow the ritual even in its minutest details as prescribed by the law was considered sufficient to invalidate the entire offering.

2. Sacrifices were even considered invalid if they were offered with any of the following mental reservations:

a. *Maḥashevet ha-zeman.* If the donor or the Priest in charge of the offering, took it into his mind to sprinkle the blood of the sacrifice upon the altar at a time other than that specified in the Torah, in such a case the entire sacrifice was considered *piggul,* an "abomination," and one who deliberately ate of the meat of this offering was subject to the penalty of *karet,* or being cut off from his people.

b. *Maḥashevet ha-makom.* If the donor, or the Priest in charge of the offering, took it into his mind at the initial point in the ritual to sprinkle the blood of the offering upon a spot other than the one designated by the law, in that case the offering was also considered invalid, but it was not considered as an "abomination." One who deliberately ate of the meat of the offering was therefore subject only to the penalty of flogging.

c. *Maḥashevet shinui ha-shem.* If the offering was a sin-offering or a Passover offering, and the Priest, or donor (during the time he slaughtered the animal) made it with the intention of bringing it for a purpose other than the one for which it was originally intended, the offering was considered unacceptable.

In the case of other offerings, such a change of purpose was also forbidden; however, these offerings were not disqualified, providing the donor brought an additional sacrifice.

d. *Maḥashevet shinui.* If the donor or the Priest in charge, during the service had in his mind to offer it as an atonement for a transgressor other than the donor, the offer was not disqualified, but the Priest or donor who made the offer with the mental reservation was subject to the penalty of flogging.

COMMENTATORS

Ḥinnukh: Most of the classic commentators construe the injunction in the Book of Deuteronomy, "You shall not eat any abominable thing," as referring to foods prohibited because they were part of the pagan's diet and that the food was also forbidden for health reasons. The *Ḥinnukh* and Maimonides, on the other hand, interpret this verse as referring to Leviticus 7:18 which describes certain disqualified sacrifices as "abominations." The *Ḥinnukh* interprets this repetition of the injunction as stressing the fact that a sacrifice can be considered acceptable only if it is offered in the proper spirit and without mental reservations. The mere act of bringing an offering does not fulfill the requirements of the Torah with regard to sacrifices.

References:

B. Menaḥot 17b; B. Avodah Zarah 66a; B. Zevaḥim 13a, 13b, 27a, 28b, 29a, 29b; Yad, Hilkhot Pesulei ha-Mikdashim, Chap. 13–18; Sefer ha-Mitzvot (Lo Ta'aseh) 132, 140; Sefer Mitzvot Gadol (Lav) 337; Sifre, Sidrah *Re'eh*; Sefer ha-Ḥinnukh, Mitzvot 144, 469.

SACRIFICES INVALIDATED BECAUSE OF DEFILEMENT BY CONTACT

But that which remains from the flesh of the sacrifice on the third day shall be burned with fire (Leviticus 7:17)
And the flesh that touches any unclean thing shall not be eaten; it shall be burned with fire (Leviticus 7:19)
A woman who bears a male child shall be unclean for seven days, and she shall continue in the blood of purification for 33 days. No hallowed thing shall she touch until the days of her purification are fulfilled (Leviticus 12:4)

1. A ritually pure person who partook of an offering that had been ritually disqualified was subject to the penalty of flogging. When one who was ritually unclean (and thus subject to the penalty of *karet* if he entered the Temple grounds) partook of a sanctified offering inside the Temple or anywhere else, he was liable to the penalty of *karet*.

2. All offerings that were disqualified because they had been defiled had to be burned. Liquids that were part of such an offering had to be buried.

COMMENTATORS

Ḥinnukh: Only people who were pure of mind and clean of body were permitted to enter the Sanctuary and participate in so sacred a ritual as the sacrificial service. Accordingly, if an unclean person touched the meat of an animal set aside as an offering, the meat thereby became defiled and had to be burned at once. Why did the law insist that the meat had to be destroyed by fire, and without delay? Because food once considered sacred, but subsequently rendered impure and hence forbidden to man and beast, had to be destroyed completely, and fire was considered the one sure means of completely destroying an object. The burning had to be effected without delay, because meat spoils quickly and the Torah desired to avoid having the sacrificial service associated with the odor of decaying flesh.
Radbaz: He offers two explanations for the law. 1. An animal designated

as a sacrifice to God thereby became sanctified. But if it became ill or defective, it could no longer be used as a sacrifice. Such an animal had to be totally destroyed so that it could not be used for non-sacred purposes. 2. Jewish mystics believe that the soul of an animal chosen to be sacrificed to God must have emanated from some higher source and it was not of an ordinary creature. Hence, when a physical defect occurred in this animal, it could not have affected its soul. Since it cannot be used as a sacrifice, it cannot be defiled or used for ordinary, everyday purposes. The animal must be burned, because burning brings about its complete destruction and will prevent its future misuse.

References:
B. Yevamot 75a; B. Ḥagigah 24a; B. Zevaḥim 34a, 56b; B. Pesaḥim 24a, 62b; B. Makkot 14b; B. Sotah 29a; Yad, Hilkhot Pesulei Mikdashim, Chap. 18, 19; Yad, Hilkhot Korban Pesaḥ, Chap. 4, 5; Yad, Hilkhot Terumah, Chap. 12; Sefer ha-Mitzvot (Aseh) 90, 91, (Lo Ta'aseh) 129; Sefer Mitzvot Gadol (Aseh) 207, 208, (Lav) 339; Sifra, Sidrah *Tzav;* Sefer ha-Ḥinnukh, Mitzvot 145, 146, 167.

PROHIBITION OF EATING FAT (ḤELEV)

You shall eat no fat [ḥelev] of ox, or sheep, or goat (Leviticus 7:23)

1. The Hebrew term *ḥelev* refers only to the abdominal fat; i.e., fatty tissue on the stomach, kidney, and flank of oxen, sheep, or goats. A distinguishing feature of this forbidden fat is that it can be peeled like a skin.

2. The penalty for deliberately eating forbidden fats is *karet.* One who ate it unintentionally was not subject to punishment but was required to bring a sin-offering.

3. Under rabbinic law, one who ate even the veins that were within the forbidden fatty tissue was subject to the punishment of flogging.

COMMENTATORS

Maimonides, Ḥinnukh: Both believe that these fats were forbidden because they are detrimental to human health.
Abrabanel: One will become fat himself and will lose the ability to function physically or mentally.
Recanati: Fats were forbidden as food because they were included in animal sacrifices, and hence were considered sacred.

References:
B. Zevaḥim 70b; B. Ḥullin 117a; B. Yoma 74a; B. Krittot 4a, 4b; Sifra, Sidrah *Tzav;* Guide of the Perplexed, Part 3, Sec. 48; Yad, Hilkhot Ma'akhalot Assurot, Chap. 7; Sefer ha-Mitzvot (Lo Ta'aseh) 185; Sefer Mitzvot Gadol (Lav) 138; Sefer Mitzvot Katan 204; Shulḥan Arukh, Yoreh De'ah, 64, 117; Sefer ha-Ḥinnukh, Mitzvah 147.

PROHIBITION OF EATING BLOOD

And you shall eat no manner of blood (Leviticus 7:26)

1. Before meat can be eaten, all its blood must be removed by soaking and salting, or by broiling. The former method requires that the meat must be soaked for half an hour to remove all surface blood and to soften the meat. The meat is then thoroughly salted and allowed to remain so for one hour, to permit the salt to penetrate the meat and absorb the blood not visible on the outside. After an hour, the meat is thoroughly rinsed to remove the salt and the blood drawn out by the salt. Meat that was permitted to remain unsoaked for three days could not be made kosher by this means because by this time the blood has become so congealed that soaking or salting would not be effective.

2. The liver contains so much blood that soaking and salting would be of no avail. It must be broiled over an open flame to draw out the blood.

3. It is only by rabbinic decree that we are enjoined from eating blood that has separated itself from the human body. A drop of blood that came from the gums of the teeth is not included in this prohibition.

COMMENTATORS

Maimonides: The peoples of pagan antiquity attached special significance to the blood of animals. Thus, the Chaldeans considered blood as an agent of defilement. The Greeks, on the other hand, used blood for the purpose of communing with spirits and also for fortune-telling. Therefore, in order to stress the distinction between Judaism and idol worship, Jewish law forbade the use of blood except for rituals, sacrifice, and purification.

Naḥmanides: He proposes three other explanations for the prohibition to eat blood:

a. Because man is the only creature of God that recognizes his Maker, he was allowed to eat the flesh of another creature; but it was considered savage to eat blood, because blood is tantamount to the very life of the creature.

b. A human being who ate the blood of animals would himself begin to act like an animal. This may well be because of the mixture of his own blood with that of the animal.

c. Blood was the very life of the animal. As such it was used in the sacrificial rites to substitute for the life of the human transgressor who should have paid with his own life for his transgression against God. How, then, could one eat the substance that was employed as a substitute for one's own blood?

References:
B. Ḥullin 64b (see Tosafot); B. Krittot 20b, 21a; J. Yoma, Chap. 8, Halakhah 3; Guide of the Perplexed, Part 3, Sec. 46; Yad, Hilkhot Ma'akhalot Assurot, Chap. 3, 6, 9; Sefer ha-Mitzvot (Lo Ta'aseh) 184; Sefer Mitzvot Gadol (Lav) 137; Sefer Mitzvot Katan 205; Shulḥan Arukh, Yoreh De'ah, 65; Sefer ha-Ḥinnukh, Mitzvah 148.

THE PERSONAL APPEARANCE OF THE PRIESTS

And Moses said to Aaron and Eleazar and to Ithamar, his sons: Let not the hair of your heads go loose (Leviticus 10:6)
Neither rend your garments (Leviticus 10:6)

1. The outer appearance of the Priests was to be in character with their attitude toward their sacred calling. A High Priest was not to be seen anywhere, even outside the Temple, with untrimmed hair or in torn garments. An Ordinary Priest who came to the Temple to perform his priestly functions without having had his hair trimmed was subject to Divine punishment even though the offerings which he brought were not disqualified.

2. "Let not the hair of your heads go loose. . ." was interpreted to mean that a Priest should not permit his hair to grow untrimmed for more than 30 days. Even an ordinary Israelite was considered guilty of disrespect for the sanctity of the Temple if he appeared there with unshorn locks (but not if the fashion of the day was for men to wear their hair long).

COMMENTATORS

Ḥinnukh: Not even a Priest in his period of mourning for a close relative was permitted to appear unshaven or in torn garments, because this would have a depressing effect on the worshipers. One who is obviously in a state of mourning will not serve to put those around him into the proper frame of mind for worship. As a consequence, the Priest in the Temple was forbidden to show any outward signs of mourning; his duty to his people had to take precedence over his personal feelings.

References:

B. Mo'ed Katan 14b, 15a, 19b, 26b; B. Ta'anit 17b; B. Horayot 12b; B. Sanhedrin 22b, 83a; Sifra, Sidrah *Shemini;* Yad, Hilkhot Bi'at Mikdash, Chap. 1, Secs. 8–11 (Note the disagreement between Maimonides, who asserts that the priest was prohibited to have unshorn hair only when he was in sacred grounds, and the Ravad, who claims that this injunction applies to all times.); Sefer ha-Mitzvot (Lo Ta'aseh) 163, 164; Sefer Mitzvot Gadol (Lav) 301, 302; Sefer ha-Ḥinnukh, Mitzvot 149, 150.

THE DEVOTION TO DUTY EXPECTED OF THE PRIESTS

And you shall not go out from the door of the Tent of Meeting lest you die (Leviticus 10:7)

1. A Priest was expected to devote all his thoughts and energies to his functions in the Temple. His religious duties took precedence over his duty—and desire—to mourn the death of a close relative. However, he was not permitted to perform the sacrificial rites while he was an *onen,* i.e., during the period between the actual death of the relative and the funeral.

2. The High Priest, as distinct from Ordinary Priests, was not permitted any period of mourning whatsoever, but was obliged to carry out the functions of his high office no matter what personal grief might have befallen him.

3. A Priest who violated this law was subject to Divine punishment *(mitah bi-ydei shamayim).*

COMMENTATORS

Ḥinnukh: A Priest who has dedicated his life to the service of God, and who has received the honors, gifts, and privileges due to his sacred calling, must justify the trust placed in him by his people. While performing the sacrificial service, the Priest must give all his thought to the act; he must not perform it mechanically. Therefore, he is permitted to leave the Temple on being informed of the death of a close relative because under such circumstances he could hardly be expected to concentrate on the ritual. The High Priest, however, must be so thoroughly committed to the service of God that he will put it before all personal feelings. He must not interrupt his duties in the Temple, not even when he learns of a death in his immediate family.

References:

B. Sanhedrin 18a, 84a; B. Horayot 12b; J. Mo'ed Katan, Chap. 3, Halakhah 5; Yad, Hilkhot Bi'at Mikdash, Chap. 2; Sefer ha-Mitzvot (Lo Ta'aseh) 165; Sifra, Sidrah *Aḥarei Mot;* Sefer ha-Ḥinnukh, Mitzvah 151.

THE OBLIGATION OF THE PRIESTS TO BE SOBER WHEN ON DUTY IN THE TEMPLE

And the Lord spoke to Aaron 'Drink no wine nor strong drink. . . when you go into the Tent of Meeting. . .' (Leviticus 10:9)

1. Any Priest who entered the Temple area and carried out his functions while in a state of intoxication was subject to Divine punishment.

2. The above rule applied only to one who had drunk at least a quarter of a *log* of undiluted wine at one time. One who had partaken of some other strong drink was subject to the penalty of flogging, but his offerings were not disqualified.

3. The ruling that the Priest had to have a clear mind while performing his functions holds true also in the case of Rabbis or Judges of the *Bet Din*. They, too, are required to stay away from strong drink while deliberating on decisions regarding Jewish law.

COMMENTATORS

Ibn Ezra, Ḥinnukh: Intoxicating drink confuses the mind and impedes speech. Since both a clear mind and clear speech were required in the performance of the priestly functions, Priests were forbidden to partake of wine or other strong drink before appearing in the Temple.

Da'at Zekenim: A Priest in a state of intoxication would become the butt of public ridicule. Furthermore, one tradition has it that the tree from whose fruit Adam ate was a vine, and it was as a punishment for this act of disobedience that man was given a limited life-span instead of the eternal life which originally had been intended for him. Thus a Priest who is in a state of intoxication while performing his religious functions may be regarded as one who is leading his people upon the path to death rather than upon the path of life. This consideration is also the origin of our custom to say, *"le-ḥayyim,"* "to life," when we partake of strong drink.

Abrabanel: One might reason that a Priest, being human, and therefore beset with cares, worries, and doubts like any other human being, might feel justified in partaking of strong drink for no other purpose than to put himself into a calmer, more cheerful state of mind, the better to perform his duties in the Temple. Nevertheless, even under those circumstances, the Priest was forbidden to take any intoxicating drink because he must retain an absolutely clear mind to carry out his dual function of serving at the altar and teaching the people assembled in the Temple.

Maimonides: The mere appearance of an inebriated Priest in the Temple was an insult to the sanctity of the Temple, even when the Priest had no duties to perform there.

Naḥmanides: He takes a less stringent view. He holds that the purpose of this law is simply to keep the Priests from making errors while offering the sacrifices. In his opinion, therefore, a Priest who is intoxicated and enters the Temple area is not guilty of a sin so long as he is not actually on duty there.

References:
B. Sanhedrin 17a, 22b, 83b; B. Krittot 13b; B. Zevaḥim 17b, 18a; Sifra, Sidrah *Shemini,* Sidrah *Emor;* Midrash Rabbah, *Shemini,* Chap. 12, Sec. 1; Midrash Tanḥuma, *Shemini,* Chap. 5; Yad, Hilkhot Bi'at Mikdash, Chap. 1; Sefer ha-Mitzvot (Lo Ta'aseh) 73 (Note the basic difference between Maimonides and Naḥmanides. According to the former, the Priest was punished by lashes only if he performed a service while in a state of intoxication. According to the latter, if while on duty he was intoxicated because of wine that he drank, he would receive the death-penalty from God. If this state of drunkenness was due to other intoxicants, he would receive lashes.); Sefer Mitzvot Gadol (Lav) 300; Sefer ha-Ḥinnukh, Mitzvah 152.

PERMITTED FOODS

These are the living things which you may eat (Leviticus 11:2)
These you may eat of all that are in the waters (Leviticus 11:9)
Even these of them you may eat, the locust after its kinds (Leviticus 11:22)
Of all clean birds you may eat (Deuteronomy 14:11)

1. *Kashrut* is one of the fundamentals of Judaism. Our Sages have taught that *Kashrut* is conducive to holiness. As the popular saying goes, "We are what we eat." The observance of the dietary laws in large measure has enabled the Jewish people to survive through the ages in the midst of a hostile world.

2. The Torah is careful to enumerate in detail the physical characteristics of the animals that are permitted as food. As a result, one who wants to eat the flesh of an animal as food must first examine the animal to make sure that it has all the characteristics of a kosher animal. According to the Rabbis, this inspection is a *mitzvah* in itself and should be performed even if one knows that the animal is of a kosher species.

COMMENTATORS

Ḥinnukh: The author cites the dispute between Maimonides and Naḥmanides relative to the significance of the above *mitzvot.* (The verses telling us what animals we are permitted to eat are counted as *mitzvot* in their own right.) According to Maimonides, the observance of any *mitzvah* involving permitted things but also restrictive qualifications requires particular care. For instance, we are told that we are permitted to eat the meat of an animal, fowl, fish, and so on; but there are also restrictions telling us exactly what types of animal, fowl, and fish are permitted. For this reason, Maimonides contends that the above *mitzvot* entail also an obligation to examine every animal, fish, and fowl one wants to prepare as food in order to see whether they meet the necessary requirements.

Naḥmanides disagrees with Maimonides. Supposing, he asks, that one examines the animal, finds everything acceptable, but then decides not to slaughter it for food? According to Maimonides, he receives credit for fulfilling the *mitzvah* of examining the animal, even if he then decides not to use it as food. According to Naḥmanides, however, this *mitzvah* is dependent on whether he actually eats the meat. Since he has decided against slaughtering and eating the animal, the fact that he has examined the animal to see whether it is kosher cannot in itself constitute a *mitzvah*. Indeed, Naḥmanides holds that under certain circumstances this would even be counted as a transgression, because examining the animal, finding it kosher, and then deciding against eating it, he may be considered as having violated a *mitzvah* telling him what he should eat. In the view of Naḥmanides, the violation of such a *mitzvah* may be as punishable as the violation of a *mitzvah* telling us what he should not eat. The *Ḥinnukh* adopts the view of Naḥmanides.

References:
B. Kiddushin 57a; B. Ḥullin 42a, 59a, 66b, 71a, 140a; B. Zevaḥim 34a; Sifra, Sidrah *Shemini;* Midrash Tanḥuma, *Shemini,* Chap. 6; Midrash Rabbah, *Shemini,* Chap. 13, Sec. 2; Yad, Hilkhot Ma'akhalot Assurot, Chap. 1, 2, 3; Sefer ha-Mitzvot (Aseh) 149, 150, 151, 152; Sefer Mitzvot Gadol (Aseh) 59, 60, 61, 62; Shulḥan Arukh, Yoreh De'ah, 80, Sec. 1, 2, 3, 5; Sefer ha-Ḥinnukh, Mitzvot 153, 155, 158, 470.

FORBIDDEN FOODS

You shall not eat of their flesh and their carcasses you shall not touch (Leviticus 11:8)
Whatsoever hath no fins nor scales in the water is a detestable thing to you (Leviticus 11:12)
And these shall be an abomination among the fowls; they shall not be eaten (Leviticus 11:13)
And all the winged swarming things are unclean to you; they shall not be eaten (Deuteronomy 14:19)

1. The classification of creatures into *kasher* and non-*kasher* is sometimes clearly spelled out by the Torah in terms that we can understand. In other cases, we must look to the Oral Tradition for guidance.

2. *Animals:* All animals that have cloven hooves (hooves divided into two parts along their whole length) and chew the cud, may be eaten. If they have only one of these characteristics, they are forbidden. One example of this is the pig, which is cloven-footed but does not chew the cud.

3. *Fish:* All fish having both fins and scales may be eaten. Scales are defined as thin little plates which are attached to the body of the fish but can be scraped off easily with the hand or a knife. Sturgeon and swordfish are forbidden because they have no scales. The mackerel, on the other hand is *kasher* because it has fins and scales while in the water, losing them only when caught and taken out of the water onto dry land.

4. *Fowl:* The Torah enumerates 24 varieties of fowl that are forbidden. While it lists no physical features of these "unclean" birds, the list permits us to draw certain conclusions regarding the characteristics of fowl that may be eaten as opposed to fowl that is forbidden:

a. the bird must not be a bird of prey;
b. it must have one toe larger than the others;
c. it must have a crop;
d. it must have a gizzard of which the inner lining can be easily removed.

These are the standards by which we must judge any fowl not explicitly named in the biblical text as forbidden.

5. *Locusts:* According to the Torah, locusts were permitted, if they had four wings that covered most of the length and breadth of their bodies, four feet, and jointed legs. According to Ashkenazi authorities, however, locusts may not be eaten because we cannot accurately identify the species. Sephardi Jews, however, do not exclude them from their diet.

6. All other insects are forbidden, but the product of an insect which is not part of the insect's body is permissible. One example of this is honey, which bees produce from the nectar of flowers.

COMMENTATORS

Naḥmanides: Why are we forbidden to eat fish that do not have fins and scales? Fish with fins and scales can swim close to the surface of the water so that, occasionally, they can come up for air. This warms their blood and enables them to rid their bodies of excess fluids and other impurities. By contrast, fish that have no fins or scales keep close to the bottom of the sea, and therefore cannot come up for air to purify their bodies. Obviously, then, the latter as food would be harmful to human health.

Abrabanel: He agrees with the view of Naḥmanides. He rejects an unspecified opinion which claims that fish without fins and scales are stationary and are more like earth-bound creatures. Thus they are, therefore, out of their element in water.

Ibn Ezra, Maimonides: These and most of the other classical commentators attribute one or more of the following characteristics to animals, birds, fish, or small creatures which the Torah classes as forbidden foods:

1. They are esthetically repulsive: examples are horsemeat, eels, roaches, ants, etc.
2. They are injurious to human health.
3. Some of these creatures are predators, surviving by their ability to kill other creatures. For this reason they are out of character with the Jewish attitudes of compassion and mercy.

References:

B. Ḥullin 59a, 60b, 61a, 63b, 66b; Midrash Tanḥuma, *Shemini,* Chap. 6, 7, 8; Yad, Hilkhot Ma'akhalot Assurot, Chap. 1, 2, 3; Sefer ha-Mitzvot (Lo Ta'aseh) 172, 174, 175; Sefer Mitzvot Gadol (Lav) 127, 128, 130; Sefer Mitzvot Katan 207, 208, 209; Shulḥan Arukh, Yoreh De'ah, Chap. 79, 80; Sefer ha-Ḥinnukh, Mitzvot 154, 157, 471.

FORBIDDEN INSECTS AND "CREEPING THINGS"

And these are they which are unclean to you among the swarming things that swarm upon the earth (Leviticus 11:29)

And every swarming thing that swarms upon the earth is a detestable thing; it shall not be eaten (Leviticus 11:41)

Even all swarming things that swarm upon the earth, them you shall not eat; for they are a detestable thing (Leviticus 11:42)

You shall not make yourselves abominable with any swarming thing that swarms (Leviticus 11:43)

Neither shall you defile yourselves with any manner of swarming thing that moves upon the earth (Leviticus 11:44)

1. The Torah is very emphatic in its prohibition of "creeping things" as food. There are some living things that are forbidden as food, but there are others that render a person impure by mere contact.

2. The Torah specifically lists eight "creeping things" that are unclean, so that anyone who touches their carcasses becomes ritually unclean himself: the weasel, the mouse, the "great lizard," the gecko, the land crocodile, the lizard, the sand-lizard, and the chameleon.

3. The dead bodies of these "creeping things" are categorized as *av tumah,* or "arch-defilement." Any person or vessel that comes in contact with these creatures becomes unclean. A person who became unclean in this manner could not enter the area of the Temple nor partake of holy food, until he had immersed himself in a *mikveh* and waited until after sundown. An earthenware vessel that came in contact with a dead creature of these species which did not actually touch the vessel, was considered permanently unfit for use and had to be broken, even if the insect had only hung suspended in the hollow of the vessel and never actually touched the vessel. However, contact with the carcass of a "creeping thing" that had decomposed to the point that not even a dog would eat it did not render either a person or a vessel impure.

4. Snakes, scorpions, worms, and similar reptiles were forbidden as food but contact with them did not render a person or vessel unclean.

5. Insects that breed in filth or decay are forbidden.

6. One who ate any of these forbidden creatures was subject to the penalty of flogging.

COMMENTATORS

Ibn Ezra: How can one have a pure, clean conscience with the knowledge that his own flesh is the product of a diet of insects, snakes, and other vermin?

Abrabanel: He disagrees with Naḥmanides' contention that certain foods were forbidden because they were injurious to man's health. He rejects this view on two grounds: First, there are many people who eat these foods and yet are strong and healthy. Second, Abrabanel refuses to consider the Torah and its *mitzvot* as a mere compendium of medical advice. According to Abrabanel, the true explanation for the laws forbidding these foods lies in the fact that Jews basically find such creatures as snakes and worms repulsive. Since the soul is holy and pure, nothing must be permitted to enter the body—the vessel in which the soul is contained—that would be out of character with the sanctity of the soul.

References:
B. Ḥullin 64a–67b, 126b, 127a; B. Bava Metzia 61b; B. Yoma 39a; B. Pesaḥim 23a; B. Niddah 51b; B. Makkot 16b; B. Shabbat 33a, 90b, 145b; B. Menaḥot 29a; B. Krittot 4b, 22a; B. Me'ilah 16b, 17a; B. Nazir 64a; Sifra, Sidrah *Shemini,* Chap. 12; Midrash Rabbah, *Va-Yikrah,* Chap. 13, Sec. 5; Yad, Hilkhot She'ar Avot ha-Tumah, Chap. 1; Yad, Hilkhot Ma'akhalot Assurot, Chap. 1, 2; Sefer ha-Mitzvot (Aseh) 97, (Lo Ta'aseh) 173, 176, 177, 178, 179 (see Shoresh 9 where Naḥmanides decisively rebuts Maimonides); Sefer Mitzvot Gadol (Aseh) 245, (Lav) 129, 131; Sefer Mitzvot Katan 210, 212; Shulḥan Arukh, Yoreh De'ah, 83, 84; Sefer ha-Ḥinnukh, Mitzvot 156, 159, 162, 163, 164, 165.

FOOD DEFILED BY LIQUIDS

All food which may be eaten, on which water comes shall be unclean (Leviticus 11:34)

1. Food cannot become impure and forbidden for consumption because of contact with something unclean, unless it has first come into contact with water, dew, oil, wine, milk, blood, or honey.

2. Fruits or vegetables can become liable to ritual uncleanness by the above liquids only if they are no longer rooted in the ground. Other liquids do not render food liable to uncleanness.

3. Food that has become decomposed to the point where it is unfit for human consumption cannot thus be rendered liable to defilement by contact with liquids.

4. Foods and liquids, except for water, that have been defiled by contact with liquids from unclean vessels, cannot be purified. Water can be restored to a state of ritual purity by mixing it with water from a *mikveh.*

COMMENTATORS

Maimonides: The refuse deposited by rodents sticks to all moistened vegetation. This law serves as a precautionary, hygienic measure against contact of rodents with food.

Ḥinnukh, Rashbam, Abrabanel: When a fruit or vegetable is rooted in the ground, it is not yet halakhically defined as food. Only after the fruit or vegetable has been harvested does it become edible and subject to the scriptural laws of purity. As long as it is still attached to the soil it is considered inedible and not subject to these laws.

Ḥinnukh: The moistening of food must be deliberately done by the owner of the food. If water should come on the produce after it is no longer attached to the ground, the food is declared edible only if the owner knowingly moistened the food with the intent of making it fit for consumption. Should the produce be moistened accidentally, not with the intent of making it edible, it is considered not yet ready to be eaten.

References:

B. Yoma 80a; B. Ḥullin 36a, 121a; Mishnayyot, Uktzin, Chap. 3; Yad, Tumat Okhlin, Chap. 1, 2; Sefer ha-Mitzvot (Aseh) 98; Sefer Mitzvot Gadol (Aseh) 246; Sefer ha-Ḥinnukh, Mitzvah 160.

TOUCHING AN ANIMAL'S CARCASS

He that touches the carcass [of an animal that died] shall be unclean until evening (Leviticus 11:39)

1. Animals which in themselves are *kasher* are nevertheless forbidden if they are either *terefah* (lit. "torn") or *nevelah* ("carcass"). A *terefah* animal is a *kasher* animal which has been slaughtered by *sheḥitah* but which was found to have a physical defect that rendered it unfit for consumption under Jewish law. A *nevelah* is an animal—*kasher* or non-*kasher*—that died of natural causes (in the case of a *kasher* animal, one that was killed by means other than *sheḥitah*).

2. Persons or vessels are rendered unclean by contact with a *nevelah*. A *nevelah* is regarded as an *av tumah* ("arch-defilement"). The person who touched the *nevelah* and thereby became defiled is regarded as a *rishon le-tumah* ("first source of defilement").

3. If a man carries the whole or part of the *nevelah* (carcass), even if his skin does not actually come into contact with it, both he and his clothes become unclean.

4. If a person eats a *kasher* fowl that has become *nevelah*, he is unclean only at the time the meat passes through his esophagus.

5. Any violation of these laws is subject to the penalty of flogging.

COMMENTATORS

Abrabanel: He explains why an animal that has died of natural causes may not be eaten, even if it is *kasher*. Whereas an animal that was killed by *sheḥitah* was healthy and could have survived if it had not been slaughtered, an animal that died of natural causes may have died of an infectious disease; its meat may therefore carry the infection into the human body. In other words, this prohibition is motivated by hygienic and precautionary measures.

Abrabanel disagrees with Levi ben Gershom, who contends that in both instances—death by slaughter or by natural causes—the meat should be forbidden for human consumption. It is only by the grace of God that we are permitted to eat of the ritually slaughtered animal in order to sustain ourselves in physical health.

References:
B. Niddah 56a; B. Zevaḥim 69b; B. Ḥullin 70b, 117b, 126a, 128b; Sifra, Sidrah *Shemini;* Yad, Hilkhot She'ar Avot ha-Tumah, Chap. 1; Sefer ha-Mitzvot (Aseh) 96; Sefer Mitzvot Gadol (Aseh) 244; Sefer ha-Ḥinnukh, Mitzvah 161.

DEFILEMENT DUE TO DISCHARGES FROM THE BODY

A woman who gives birth to a male child shall be unclean seven days (Leviticus 12:2)
When any man has a discharge from his flesh, his discharge is unclean (Leviticus 15:2)
And if a woman has a discharge and her discharge in her flesh is blood, she shall be in her impurity seven days (Leviticus 15:19)
And if a woman has a discharge of her blood many days, not during the time of her impurity, . . .she is unclean (Leviticus 15:25)

1. According to biblical law, any discharge from the sex organs renders a person unclean, and defiles any person or object with whom that person comes in contact. The biblical attitude toward discharges from the sex organs does not readily and easily lend itself to interpretation. Medical science has attempted to study these discharges for toxic properties, but so far has found no conclusive evidence that they are indeed toxic in character, which would explain their "uncleanness" in medical terms.

2. A woman who has given birth becomes unclean because of the afterbirth and other postnatal discharges. After childbirth, she has to count seven "clean" days for a boy (and 14 "clean" days for a girl). She then immerses herself in a *mikveh.* After this, she is considered ritually clean again.

3. A woman becomes a source of defilement during her menstrual period. Any person with whom she comes into contact with during her period becomes unclean. During the days of the Temple, these laws also applied to sacred vessels with which a woman came into contact during her period.

4. A man with a discharge from his sex organs became unclean and rendered others unclean by contact. Jewish law classes men with such discharges into two categories: (1) The *ba'al keri;* i.e., one who had discharged semen, and (2) the *zav;* one who suffered from a chronic discharge. A *ba'al keri* remained unclean until he had immersed himself in the *mikveh.* The law concerning the *zav* was as follows: If he saw the discharge for only one day, he had to follow the procedure of the *ba'al keri.* But if he saw the discharge for two consecutive days, he was obliged to count seven "clean days" after the two unclean days, and then to immerse himself in a *mikveh* to become ritually clean. If he noticed discharge for three consecutive days, he had to count seven "clean days" after the three unclean days, and then to immerse himself in a *mikveh.* In addition, he had to bring a special offering to the Temple. These obligations applied only to one whose discharge was not due to any sickness, accident or overexertion, but solely to natural causes.

5. A woman during her normal menstrual period is unclean during her entire menstrual period (seven full days even if her discharge lasted for only one day). She then must count seven clean days before going to the *mikveh.* If, at any time during the 11 days that follow she notices a vaginal discharge, she becomes a *zavah*—a woman with a discharge not due to menstruation. If there is such a discharge, and it lasts only one day or two days, she needs to count only one "clean" day before going to the *mikveh.* If it lasts for three consecutive days, she must count seven "clean" days after the third day before going to the *mikveh.* During the days of the Temple, she also had to bring an offering. During her unclean days due to such a discharge, she defiled others by contact.

Ḥinnukh: Disabilities of the body are directly related to moral deficiencies. A woman's menstrual period is considered a sickness because it was attributed by medieval medicine to an overabundance of blood in the pelvic organs. Do the menstrual periods benefit the woman or her husband? Yes, for if a man were permitted to have relations with his wife every day in the year, he would soon become tired of her and search for other women. But since he is commanded to stay away from her during her menstrual periods, his desire for her is kindled anew each month.

Baḥya ben Asher, Sforno, Keli Yakar: Woman was given the menstrual period because of the sin committed by Adam and Eve in the Garden of Eden. Each woman must do her share in atoning for the sin of Eve. After her menstrual period has ended, she is asked to count seven "clean" days, which she should spend in meditation and in atonement for her transgressions. Thereafter, she immerses herself in the ritual waters to remove the stigma of the sin committed by the first man and woman.

References:

B. Niddah 21b, 24b, 36b, 37b, 41b, 43a, 44a, 55a, 56a, 57b, 72b, 73a; B. Shabbat 64b; B. Ketubbot 61a (see Tosafot); B. Megillah 8a; Mishnayyot, Kelim, Chap. 1, Zabim, Chap. 5; Midrash Tanḥuma, *Metzorah,* Chap. 6; Yad, Hilkhot Issurei Bi'ah, Chap. 6, 7, 9, 10, 11; Yad, Hilkhot Mishkav u-Moshav, Chap. 1, 2, 5, 6, 7, 8, 9; Yad, Hilkhot Meḥusrei Kapparah, Chap. 1, 2, 3; Sefer ha-Mitzvot (Aseh) 99, 100, 104, 106; Sefer Mitzvot Gadol (Aseh) 240, 241, 242, 243; Shulḥan Arukh, Yoreh De'ah, 183, 194, 196; Sefer Mitzvot Katan 293; Sefer ha-Ḥinnukh, Mitzvot 166, 178, 181, 182.

OFFERINGS REQUIRED OF A WOMAN WHO HAS GIVEN BIRTH

And when the days of her purification are fulfilled, for a son, or for a daughter, she shall bring a lamb of the first year as a burnt-offering (Leviticus 12:6)

1. On the forty-first day after having given birth to a male infant (on the eighty-first day after giving birth to a female infant) the mother was required to bring two offerings to the Temple—a lamb as an offering of thanksgiving, and a young pigeon or turtledove as a sin-offering.

2. Contrary to the usual practice, she first presented the offering of thanksgiving and only thereafter the sin-offering. As long as she had not fulfilled this obligation, she was not permitted to partake of any sanctified food or to enter the Temple area.

COMMENTATORS

Ibn Ezra: Why did the new mother bring first a burnt-offering and then a sin-offering? According to Ibn Ezra, the burnt-offering was also a sin-offering. It was meant to atone for any vow she might have made to herself in her thoughts during her labor not to allow her husband to come near her again so she would never again have to suffer the pains of childbirth. The turtledove was intended to atone for any such vow that she might have made aloud during her sufferings.

Ḥinnukh, Abrabanel: The sin-offering—the turtledove or pigeon—was to atone for any vows she may have made in her pain that intended she would never want to have another child. They interpret the burnt-offering not as a sin-offering but as the mother's offering of thanksgiving for her recovery.

Keli Yakar: The atonement which the new mother seeks to obtain through her sin-offering is not for herself only but also for the sin of Eve, as a result of which all women have to bear their children in pain. (Originally, before Eve had sinned, God had not intended that childbirth should entail pain.)

References:

B. Nazir 64b; B. Krittot 28a; B. Niddah 31b; Mishnayyot, Kinim; Yad, Hilkhot Meḥusrei Kapparah, Chap. 1; Sefer ha-Mitzvot (Aseh) 77; Sefer ha-Ḥinnukh, Mitzvah 168.

LEPROSY: ITS CAUSES AND CONSEQUENCES

When a man shall have in the skin of his flesh a rising, or a scab or a bright spot (Leviticus 13:2)
But the scaly affliction he shall not shave (Leviticus 13:33)
[The leper's] clothes shall be rent and the hair of his head shall go loose and he shall cover his upper lip and shall cry: Unclean, unclean (Leviticus 13:45)
And the garment in which there is a plague of leprosy [shall be shown to the priest] (Leviticus 13:47)
You shall not go up and down as a talebearer among your people (Leviticus 19:16)
Take heed concerning the plague of leprosy (Deuteronomy 24:8)

1. The Torah treats leprosy as an organic disease, but regards it as the result of moral failings. Thus Miriam was stricken with leprosy immediately after she had slandered her brother Moses, and the Rabbis commented that leprosy came as a punishment for the sin of slander. Because of these moral and spiritual implications of the disease, only a Priest was considered qualified to determine whether or not a person was indeed a leper, and to establish when the leper had been cured.

2. Certain changes in the color of the skin aroused suspicions of leprosy. The appearance of white spots in any one of the following shades called for inspection by a Priest: the brightness of snow, the off-white shades of pure wool, the diminished whiteness of the chalk in the stones of the Temple or of an egg-shell.

3. In examining an individual for leprosy, a Priest would look for three signs: the presence of two white hairs on the affected spot; the patch of leprosy; the raw flesh and the degree of its spread.

4. If a person developed a white spot and there were two white hairs and raw flesh in that area, he was classed as *metzora muḥlat* a "confirmed leper." When either one of these two signs was absent, the suspect was isolated for seven days and then examined again by the Priest. If, on reexamination the Priest could note hairs in the affected area, or there was raw flesh, or the white spot had grown larger, he proclaimed the person to be a "confirmed leper." If reexamination still did not reveal any of these signs, the suspected leper was isolated for another seven-day period. If the third examination revealed any of the symptoms of leprosy, the Priest pronounced the person as a "confirmed leper," but if there still were no symptoms, the Priest declared him ritually clean and discharged him.

5. In the meantime, both the *muḥlat* and the *musgar* (suspected isolated victim) were isolated and sent outside the city limits. As *avot tumah* ("arch-defilements") they defiled everything with which they came in contact.

6. Even a High Priest, who was never supposed to be seen in disorderly attire or to look unkempt, had to let his hair grow, rend his clothes, and cover his upper lip if he was pronounced a *metzora muḥlat*. A woman who was declared a confirmed leper was sent outside the city limits but did not have to rend her clothes, let her hair grow, or cover her upper lip. Both male and female lepers were required to go about shouting, "Unclean, unclean," so that others would be careful to avoid contact with them.

7. There was, also, leprosy of the scalp and beard. A "confirmed leper" suffering from leprosy of the scalp and beard was one whose hair in the affected area had turned white, or who had two strands of golden hair on the affected part of skin. Suspicion was aroused when the hair in these areas fell out with its roots. In these cases, too, the suspected leper had to pass two seven-day periods of isolation at the end of each of which the Priest carefully examined him for signs of leprosy. A suspected leper who during his isolation period shaved off the two golden hairs was subject to the penalty of flogging for making the Priest's work of decision more difficult.

8. Garments, too, could be tainted with leprosy. In the case of cloth, the Priest looked for three signs: a deep red spot, or a deep green spot, and the spread of such a spot. The suspect garment was isolated for seven days; if, at the end of this period the spot had spread outward, the garment had to be burned. If the spot had become a little duller, the garment was washed and kept in isolation for another seven days. If at the end of this second period, the spot had become even duller, the garment was washed once again and then pronounced clean. These laws applied only to cloth which was made out of wool or flax that had been dyed, and which was at least three fingers' breadths long and three fingers' breadths wide.

For leprosy of a house see below, p. 194.

COMMENTATORS

Rashbam, Da'at Zekenim: They agree that since the plague of leprosy was a punishment for slander, arrogance, and greed, even a king who became leprous had to humble himself and turn to the Priest for guidance on how to repent of his sin and thus cure himself of the illness.

Sforno: Leprosy was mostly caused by sexual intercourse during the woman's menstrual period.

Naḥmanides: The security of his home, the guidance of the Torah, and good health should guard the Jew against sin. If, nevertheless, he sins, God will withhold his favor so that the transgressor will be afflicted with plagues.

How do talebearing and slander begin? When one deliberately delves into the private life of another with the express purpose of unearthing information that can serve as fuel for slander. And the punishment for slander is leprosy.

Or ha-Ḥayyim: The laws concerning leprosy apply only to Jews and not to heathens. Heathens are considered as being leprous through and through at all times because of their belief in idols. By contrast, when a Jew, who has the Torah to guide him, commits a sin, it will only be a superficial, "skin-deep" deviation from the path of righteousness marked out by the Torah.

Keli Yakar: Leprosy is caused by slander, a sin in which the transgressor projects his own shortcomings onto his victim. The purpose of the procedure of purification to be undergone by the leper was to force him to face reality and examine his own shortcomings before slandering another. This explanation is in agreement with Maimonides, who stresses that the purpose of having the leper shout, "Unclean, unclean" wherever he went was to have him admit his guilt in public.

Abrabanel: He makes the following observations on this subject:

1. The relationship between the Priest and the leper was not one of physician and patient but more one between a spiritual counselor and a transgressor who had strayed from the path of righteousness.
2. He rejects the view of Naḥmanides that a house with leprous marks on its walls showed that the people who had lived in that house were also afflicted with leprosy.
3. A garment with leprous marks was shown to the Priest in order to have him determine whether it was actually infected or whether the discoloration was due to some other cause such as perspiration or mothiness.

References:
B. Shabbat 26b, 132b, 133a; B. Pesaḥim 112b; B. Makkot 22a; B. Shevu'ot 6b; B. Megillah 8b; B. Mo'ed Katan 5a, 14b, 15a; B. Ketubbot 46a; B. Sanhedrin 30a, 31a; B. Ḥullin 78a; B. Ta'anit 21b; B. Arakhin 15b; J. Niddah, Chap. 2, Halakhah 6; Mishnayyot, Nega'im; Sifre *Ki Tetze;* B. Sotah 23b; Midrash Tanḥuma, *Tazri'a,* Chap. 8, 9, 11; *Metzorah* Chap. 1; Midrash Rabbah, *Bereshit,* Chap. 98, Sec. 23; *Shofetim,* Chap. 5, Sec. 10; *Ki Tetze,* Chap. 6, Sec. 4; Yad, Hilkhot Tumat Tzara'at, Chap. 8, 9, 12, 13; Yad, Hilkhot De'ot, Chap. 7; Sefer ha-Mitzvot (Lo Ta'aseh) 301, 307, 308, (Aseh) 101, 102, 112; Sefer Mitzvot Gadol (Aseh) 234, 235, 238, (Lav) 9, 362, 363; Sefer Mitzvot Katan 124; Sefer ha-Ḥinnukh, Mitzvot 169, 170, 171, 172, 236.

THE REHABILITATION OF THE LEPER

This shall be the law of the leper in the day of his cleansing (Leviticus 14:2)

And on the seventh day he shall shave off all his hair (Leviticus 14:9)

1. We must preface this *mitzvah* with the premise that a person of faith and religious commitment will intelligently accept what is written in the Torah as truths, although they may be most puzzling to him. To the unobservant and to him who lacks faith, the following instances will appear as pure superstition, redolent of the hoary past.

2. On the day he was declared cured and ritually clean, the leper bought a new pottery basin, into which he poured a quarter of a *log* of pure, fresh water. He then brought this basin and two swallows to the Priest. The Priest slaughtered one of the two birds, allowing blood to drip into the basin of water. The bird was then buried. Next, the Priest took some cedar wood and hyssop and tied them together with a red string. The Priest took this bundle and the living bird, and dipped both into the basin of water which also contained the blood of the dead bird. He then sprinkled the mixture of water and blood seven times on the leper. Thereafter, the bird was allowed to fly away free. Following this ritual the Priest would shave the entire body of the leper, who then washed his clothes and immersed himself in a *mikveh.* Only then was he declared cured and ritually clean. He was, however, not permitted to enter the Holy Temple or partake of sacrificial meat until he had brought the offerings which completed the process of purification.

COMMENTATORS

Abrabanel: Why was the leper required to bring two living birds to the Priest? To indicate that the leper was not a lost soul but that he had reached a point when he must turn his attention to the spiritual requirements of life. Why did the one bird have to be slaughtered over an earthen vessel containing water from a running source? The earthen vessel indicated that man is like a piece of pottery and can be broken by God as easily as one can break a piece of pottery. The water reminded the leper that his woes had come upon him because he had violated the laws of the Torah, which are compared to living waters.

Why was the living bird (along with the cedar wood and hyssop) dipped into the blood of the bird that had been slaughtered? To indicate that, for the Jew, leprosy was not an infectious disease but the consequence of sin against God.

Ibn Ezra: Why were cedarwood and hyssop used? The cedar symbolized arrogance; the hyssop humility. This was to imply that, if a man was arrogant and therefore had been stricken with leprosy, it behooved him to humble himself. Unlike Abrabanel, Ibn Ezra considered leprosy to be an infectious disease. Why, he asks, did the Priest send the living bird far away into the open field? So that the bird would not come into contact with humans whom it could infect with the disease.

Or ha-Ḥayyim: The rules of behavior for the leper, including the ones forbidding him to bathe and to comb and trim his hair, run counter to the customary practice of making a sick man comfortable. What was the reason for these rules? To teach that leprosy is not a physical sickness, but a spiritual affliction from which he was cured the moment he repented.

Alshekh: Usually, when a person wishes to repent, he resolves that he will act righteously in the future. This is not enough. Before he can resolve to do better in the future he must eradicate his entire sinful past. It is this thought which was symbolized in the rites of purification prescribed for lepers. The leper first had to be sprinkled with the blood of his sacrifice, then he had to wash his clothes and cut his hair, and only after all this was permitted to return to his community and participate in its religious life.

Ḥinnukh: Why were birds used as offerings for the leper? Because birds chirp and twitter. This was to recall to the leper his own idle slander that caused his affliction. He had to bathe and cut his hair because these acts symbolized his spiritual rebirth as a new, pure human being.

References:

B. Krittot 9b; B. Arakhin 15b; B. Megillah 21a; B. Yevamot 5a; B. Nazir 40b, 41a; B. Sotah 16b; Mishnayyot, Nega'im, Chap. 14; Sifra *Metzora;* Midrash Tanḥuma, *Metzora;* Yad, Hilkhot Tumat Tzara'at, Chap. 11; Sefer ha-Mitzvot (Aseh) 110, 111; Sefer Mitzvot Gadol (Aseh) 236, 237; Sefer ha-Ḥinnukh, Mitzvot 173, 174.

THE PURIFICATION OF THE LEPER

And he shall bathe his flesh in water and he shall be clean (Leviticus 14:9)

1. In Jewish law "bathing" always means immersion in a *mikveh*. A *mikveh* is a pool of fresh water, such as rain water, which must not be drawn through pipes. A *mikveh* basin must be at least one cubit wide, one cubit long, and three cubits deep. The basin must contain water sufficient to cover the entire body: nothing may stand between the body and the water. Bandages, rings, and similar objects worn on the body must be removed prior to immersion.

2. This was the type of immersion that the leper was obliged to experience before becoming ritually clean.

3. It was important that the leper enter the *mikveh* in the proper frame of mind. He had to remember that the bathing of his body symbolized the cleansing of his soul and his desire to start anew with a clean slate.

COMMENTATORS

Ḥinnukh, Abrabanel: The cleansing of the leper's body after he had been declared pure was not to be construed as an act of physical cleanliness, but rather as an act of spiritual dedication to show that he had become pure not only in body but also in mind.
Alshekh: The immersion of the leper in the waters of the *mikveh* was intended to remind him that, having rid himself of his spiritual impurities, he had to submerge himself in the "living waters" of the Torah.

References:
B. Menaḥot 19a; B. Nedarim 36a; B. Krittot 8b, 9b; B. Arakhin 15b; B. Sotah 16a; B. Mo'ed Katan 15b; B. Yevamot 5a; B. Nazir 41a; J. Kila'im, Chap. 9, Halakhah 1; Mishnayyot, Nega'im, Chap. 14; Midrash Tanḥuma, *Metzora,* Chap. 2, 4; Yad, Hilkhot Tumat Tzara'at, Chap. 11; Sefer ha-Mitzvot (Aseh) 110, 111; Sefer Mitzvot Gadol (Aseh) 236, 237; Sefer ha-Ḥinnukh, Mitzvot 173, 174.

THE OFFERING OF THE LEPER

And on the eighth day he shall take two lambs, without blemish (Leviticus 14:10)

1. After he had completed his rehabilitation and purification, the leper was required to bring three offerings—(1) two male lambs, (2) one ewe lamb of the first year without blemish, (3) three-tenths part of an *ephah* of fine flour for a meal-offering mixed with oil, plus one *log* of oil.

2. If the leper was a poor man and could not afford three lambs, it was sufficient for him to bring one he-lamb as a guilt offering, one-tenth part of an *ephah* of fine flour mixed with oil, plus a *log* of oil, and two turtledoves or young pigeons—one for a sin-offering and one for a burnt-offering.

COMMENTATORS

Ḥinnukh: The leper brought his sacrifice because he had yielded to his baser instincts to sin. It is interesting to note that while, according to the Talmud, only slander was punished with leprosy, the *Ḥinnukh* holds that leprosy could come as a punishment for other sins as well.

References:

B. Krittot 8b; B. Nazir 40b; Sifra *Metzora;* Yad, Hilkhot Mekhusrei Kapparah, Chap. 4, 5; Yad, Hilkhot Shegagot, Chap. 10; Sefer ha-Mitzvot (Aseh) 76; Sefer Mitzvot Gadol (Aseh) 236; Sefer ha-Ḥinnukh, Mitzvah 176.

LEPROSY IN A HOUSE

And when you have come to Canaan and I put the plague of leprosy in a house of the land of your possession (Leviticus 14:34)

1. When one noticed a red or green stain on the walls of his house, he had to report it to a Priest immediately. No matter how familiar the owner of the house might have been with the laws of leprosy, he was not permitted to diagnose the case on his own. The Priest then instructed the owner to empty the house before he himself went to inspect it. After the Priest examined the stains, he put the house under quarantine for seven days. On the seventh day, he made another inspection. If he found the color of the spot lighter, he ordered the area on which the spot was seen to be scraped off and the house was declared ritually pure.

2. If the spot remained unchanged, the Priest quarantined the house for another seven days. He returned to the house on the sixth day, which was the thirteenth day after he had first seen the spot. If the spot had become still lighter in color, he instructed the owner to scrape off the area of the spot and the house was declared ritually pure, after the owner had brought an offering of two birds. On the other hand, if the spot had spread, the owner had to remove the bricks in which the spots had lodged themselves, scrape the surrounding area and replaster the entire house. The Priest then put the house under quarantine for a third week. On the nineteenth day of this three-week period, he made his last visit. If he saw that the leprous spot had reappeared, he ordered the house to be destroyed and the debris was taken to a place beyond the city limits.

3. The ritual of the offering of the two birds is described in Leviticus 14:49–53.

4. The laws of leprosy in a house applied only to Jewish homes in the Jewish Homeland during the days of the Temple. Homes in Jerusalem were always exempt from these laws because of the inherent holiness of that city.

COMMENTATORS

Ibn Ezra: He contends that leprosy in the walls of a house is very rare; when it does occur, it is a supernatural phenomenon revealing the power of God. He asks: Why did these laws of leprosy apply only to homes in the Jewish Homeland? He explains that in view of the sanctity of the land, derived from the Temple, every Jew was required to avoid all the signs of moral and spiritual decay which, according to the Rabbis, were symbolized by leprosy.
Maimonides: He agrees with Ibn Ezra that, normally, only a human being could contract leprosy. If, therefore, this disease appeared on the walls of a house, it had to be a supernatural occurrence. He asks what is so calamitous about slander that it should be punishable with leprosy? He points out that casual slander of a fellow man will lead to slander of the Priests which in turn would lead to slander of the Prophets and finally to a desecration of the Divine Name itself. Thus, what seems to be no more than a little gossip may end in blasphemy.
Naḥmanides: He agrees with Ibn Ezra and Maimonides that leprosy in a wall was not a natural phenomenon but showed the work of the hand of God. In support of this belief he cites the fact that, according to the biblical passages referring to leprosy in a house, one may scrape off and replaster a leprous area and yet the plague will reappear in the same area. This phenomenon cannot be explained in terms of science. According to Naḥmanides, therefore, a leprous spot on the wall of one's home indicated that man had allowed even his behavior in his own home to become so depraved that God deemed it necessary to use supernatural means to admonish the sinner.
Da'at Zekenim: If a man has committed the sin of slander, why should the wood and the bricks of his home be afflicted with leprosy for his sin? The author answers that, when a man sins against God, God first warns him by causing damage to his material possessions. Only if this fails will punishment come to the man himself.
Sforno: Why did the Torah require the Priest to instruct the owner of a leprous house to empty the house before he came to inspect the premises? Sforno holds that this was intended to give the owner of the house an opportunity to repent and pray to God to forgive him for his sin—slander—that had brought the plague upon the house. It was felt that, when a man is required to vacate and dismantle his house, it could move him to contrition, humility, and regret.
Baḥya ben Asher: Slander is not the only sin to cause leprosy. He cites

the fact that the Torah describes as many as ten different types of leprosy. From this he concludes that leprosy may be a punishment for the violation of any one of the Ten Commandments. Since the Ten Commandments are considered as the basis of all the *mitzvot,* leprosy may be the penalty for the violation of any commandment in the Torah.

Keli Yakar: Leprous spots on the walls of a home identified the home as having once been the residence of a heathen. Since heathen residences were consecrated to the deities worshiped by their owner, it was incumbent upon the Children of Israel to destroy them. This rule was to apply even to the Temple; when King Manasseh brought idols into the Temple precincts God decreed that the entire Temple should be destroyed. He then points out that, in view of the fact that leprosy is always the result of sin, the commandment that a leprous house be destroyed should be viewed as a God-given boon. Instead of punishing the owner of the house for his transgression, God inflicted His wrath only upon the man's material possessions.

Ḥinnukh: According to the Midrash, the heathens who dwelt in the land of Canaan, upon hearing that the Children of Israel were approaching their land, hid their treasures of gold in the walls of their homes. God therefore smote these houses with leprosy so that the Israelites should destroy them and, in so doing, discover the treasures of the heathens. The *Ḥinnukh* questions the necessity for destroying these homes when God could have informed the people as to the exact location of the treasures through a prophet. He replies that this is one of the many instances in the Torah where we are shown the invisible hand of God at work and His inexplicable, miraculous ways of dealing with man. Of course, he could have used the services of a prophet, but His ways are unknown to us.

Alshekh: He completely rejects the idea that the houses taken over by the Children of Israel should have been stricken with leprosy so that the new Israelite owners should destroy the houses and find all the treasures which the heathens had left there. He does this for two reasons: first, it is incongruous that the Torah should advise the owner to remove all his possessions to avoid unnecessary loss and then proceed to instruct him to destroy the entire building, which is a major loss. Second, if the sin of slander is involved and the loss of the home is a penalty, it is incredible that the sinner should emerge with a gain of unexpected treasure. Even a righteous man would be willing to have his home demolished to find vast treasure. He postulates that the crux of the entire commandment is the confession of the owner when he reports the incident to the Priest. In other words, the crowning achievement in a man's life is when he has courage to come before his spiritual leader and say: "There is a plague in my house, I have slandered others and I now recognize and acknowledge this transgression and ask for assistance in clearing this moral blot from my house."

References:
Mishnayyot, Nega'im, Chap. 14; B. Yoma 11b, 12a; B. Bava Kamma 82b; B. Gittin 82a; B. Nedarim 56b; B. Arakhin 16b; B. Mo'ed Katan 8a; B. Nazir 8b; B. Shevu'ot 17b; Sifra *Metzora;* Midrash Rabbah, *Metzora,* Chap. 17; Midrash Tanḥuma, *Metzora,* Chap. 4; Yad, Hilkhot Tumat Tzara'at, Chap. 14; Sefer ha-Mitzvot (Aseh) 103; Sefer Mitzvot Gadol (Aseh) 239; Sefer ha-Ḥinnukh, Mitzvah 177.

THE OFFERING OF A SACRIFICE ON RECOVERY FROM A CHRONIC DISCHARGE

And on the eighth day he shall take two turtledoves or two young pigeons and come before the Lord to the door of the Tent of Meeting (Leviticus 15:14)
And on the eighth day she shall take two turtledoves or two young pigeons and bring them to the Priest, to the door of the Tent of Meeting (Leviticus 15:29)

1. There were four instances in which a person could become cleansed again only after the bringing of an offering to the Temple after all the other requirements of his purification had been fulfilled. These offerings, known as *meḥusrei kapparah,* were required of a leper, a man who had recovered from a chronic discharge from his sex organs, a woman who had recovered from a chronic vaginal discharge, and of a woman who gave birth. The leper and the man or woman with the chronic discharge brought their offering on the eighth day, the morrow after the seven days of purity and their immersion in a *mikveh.*

2. These individuals were not permitted to come into direct contact with any holy object before they had brought their offerings on the eighth day.

3. A man or a woman who had recovered from a chronic discharge from their genital organs was expected to bring two doves—one as a sin-offering and the other as a burnt-offering.

COMMENTATORS

Naḥmanides, Ḥinnukh: Along with other medieval commentators, they hold that chronic discharges from the genital organs were caused by impure thoughts. Hence, the purpose of the offerings was to remind them to mend their ways. Naḥmanides points out that of the two doves in the offering, the first one was offered in repentance for the sin of having had impure thoughts; the second was intended as an expression of gratitude for having been cured of the disease.
Abrabanel: If the discharge was caused by sin, why did the transgressor have to offer two doves rather than an animal which, being costlier than birds, would have been a more appropriate penalty? He explains that there was always the possibility that the discharge was not due to sin, but to some organic illness.

References:
B. Nazir 44b; B. Megillah 8a; Mishnayyot Zavim; Yad, Hilkhot Meḥusrei Kapparah, Chap. 1; Sefer ha-Mitzvot (Aseh) 74, 75; Sefer Mitzvot Gadol (Aseh) 218, 219; Sefer ha-Ḥinnukh, Mitzvot 179, 183.

IMPURITY DUE TO AN EJACULATION

And if the flow of seed go out from a man, he shall bathe all his flesh in water, and be unclean until the evening (Leviticus 15:16)

1. During the days of the Temple, any male who had an involuntary emission of semen was considered impure. The seed was considered an *av ha-tumah*, arch-defilement, which rendered impure not only the man but also any vessels that had contact with it.

2. Men and vessels defiled by the emission had to be immersed in a *mikveh*.

COMMENTATORS

Abrabanel, Ibn Ezra: When the semen of a man is in his body, or when it is transferred into the body of a woman during marital intercourse, it is alive and has the potential for creating new life. But when it is ejaculated it begins to die at once. The man thus becomes impure for that day, because he has been in contact with something that was alive and then died.

Ḥinnukh: When a man has an accidental ejaculation, it is an indication that he has had impure thoughts. He is therefore punished by being regarded as impure for a whole day.

References:

B. Niddah 22a, 32b, 35a, 43a; B. Shabbat 86b; Yad, Hilkhot Avot ha-Tumah, Chap. 5; Sefer ha-Mitzvot (Aseh) 105; Sefer Mitzvot Gadol (Aseh) 247; Sefer ha-Ḥinnukh, Mitzvah 180.

PROHIBITION AGAINST ENTERING THE HOLY OF HOLIES UNNECESSARILY

Say to Aaron your brother, that he should not come at all times into the holy place (Leviticus 16:2)

1. In view of the sanctity of the Holy of Holies, no one was permitted to enter that area except the High Priest and even he could do so only at stated periods of time on Yom Kippur.

2. A Priest who entered the Holy of Holies at any time or a High Priest who entered the Holy of Holies on any day other than the

Day of Atonement were subject to the penalty of Divine punishment *(mitah bi-ydei shamayim)*.

3. The High Priest was permitted to enter the Holy of Holies only on the Day of Atonement and then only at four points in the service: to offer his personal sacrifices; to bring the blood of the sacrifice into the Holy of Holies; to bring in the pan with the incense; and when he removed the incense pan from the golden altar. If he entered a fifth time, he violated the law and was liable to *karet*.

4. Today, too, we are forbidden to stand upon the Temple Mount. Although the Temple has been destroyed, the area is still holy. Since, according to the Rabbis, all of us today are regarded as being *teme'ei metim* (defiled by contact with dead bodies), we are ritually unclean and are not privileged to stand on the Temple grounds. (The punishment for an unclean person who entered the Temple grounds was *karet*.)

COMMENTATORS

Ḥinnukh: The reason for this injunction was to insure the sanctity of the holiest places in the Temple. Not only were the masses and the Ordinary Priests forbidden to walk about the Temple without purpose, but even the High Priest was allowed to enter the Holy of Holies only at specified times on the Day of Atonement.

Keli Yakar: Why was the High Priest not allowed to enter the Holy of Holies except on the Day of Atonement? Because throughout the rest of the year, the people of Israel were under the influence of the evil inclination *(yetzer ha-ra)*. It was therefore inconceivable that the High Priest, as the representative of a sinning nation, should be permitted to enter this most holy area. Because the Children of Israel sin all year round and their transgressions reflect unfavorably upon the Priest as their spiritual leader, he was denied the right to enter the Holy of Holies. This applied to all the days of the year that we associate with time and space and during which the evil inclination of man is active. On the Day of Atonement, however, Israel overcomes the evil inclination and rises to the level of the angels, because in this state of being the day defies the usual measurements of time and space. Hence, the High Priest has succeeded in bringing his people back to God. Thus, on this day alone, the High Priest is permitted to enter the Holy of Holies.

References:
B. Menaḥot 27b; B. Yoma 53a; B. Eruvin 105a; J. Yoma, Chap. 1, Halakhah 5; Midrash Rabbah, *Aḥarei Mot,* Chap. 21, Sec. 5; Yad, Hilkhot Bi'at Mikdash, Chap. 2; Sefer ha-Mitzvot (Lo Ta'aseh) 68; Sefer Mitzvot Gadol (Lav) 303; Sefer ha-Ḥinnukh, Mitzvah 184.

THE TEMPLE RITUALS FOR THE DAY OF ATONEMENT

With this shall Aaron come into the holy place, with a young bullock for a sin-offering and a ram for a burnt-offering (Leviticus 16:3)

1. During the worship service in the Temple on the Day of Atonement, 15 sacrifices were brought. The rituals and ceremonies associated with these sacrifices were performed by the High Priest, who had to be a married man.

2. These sacrifices included regular offerings, among them the *korban tamid* that was brought every morning and every evening, the daily offering of the High Priest, and, in the event Yom Kippur fell on a Sabbath, the *korban musaf* of the day.

3. There were also the special offerings designated for Yom Kippur known as the *seder ha-yom* (as described in Leviticus 16). These included the High Priest's bullock, which he brought as an atonement for his own transgressions and those of members of his own family, the goat that was brought as a sin-offering for the transgressions of the entire people, and the *sa'ir le-azazel,* the scapegoat that was sent out into the wilderness.

4. While he offered the regular sacrifices the High Priest was dressed in eight splendid, gold-threaded garments. When he performed the Yom Kippur ritual, however, he wore only four made of plain white linen to show his humility and contrition. When one stands before God and in quest of forgiveness, he should stand with broken-heartedness and humility as exemplified by the simple white linen garments. When in the role of a penitent imploring for mercy, one does not appear arrogantly in rich, gold-braided clothes.

5. The High Priest had to change his garments five times during the Day of Atonement. Before each change of garments, he had to immerse himself in a *mikveh*. Before and after each immersion, he washed his hands and feet in a golden basin set aside for that purpose (Exodus 30:17–21).

6. In the course of Yom Kippur, the High Priest made three separate confessions. One was made to beg forgiveness for his own sins and those of his household; the second, to beg forgiveness for himself, his household, and the other Priests. Both these confessions were made during the sacrifice of his personal sin-offering. The third, a plea for forgiveness made on behalf of the entire people of Israel, was made just before the "scapegoat" was sent out into the wilderness. The entire congregation would prostrate itself whenever the ineffable name of God was mentioned and would proclaim "Blessed be His majestic name forever and ever" *(Barukh shem kevod malkhuto le-olam va-ed)*.

COMMENTATORS

Ḥinnukh: It was necessary for God to designate one day each year when the Jew could seek atonement for his sins. If there would be a Day of Atonement only once every two or three years, the accumulated evil would be too great for the world to survive. Therefore God, in His grace, established this "day of forgiveness." He endowed this day with a sanctity that grants pardon because of its intrinsic holiness. In other words, the character of the day itself has endowed it with the power to forgive some of the sins of man.

Keli Yakar: For his personal inspiration, no matter how pious a man may be, or how holy his environment, he must seek spiritual strengthening from time to time. It is in order to obtain spiritual rejuvenation and to demonstrate his faith, and the faith of his entire people, in the

Lord, that he is bidden to enter the Sanctuary on the Day of Atonement.

Naḥmanides: During the service on the Day of Atonement, the High Priest took two goats, of the same size and appearance. One was designated as an offering to God, while the other was sent out into the wilderness to die. Was not Azazel a pagan concept alien to Judaism? To avoid any misunderstanding of the purpose of the goat relegated to Azazel, both of these goats were first brought into the Temple and placed before the altar. The inference was that it was God's instructions, not Israel's pagan proclivities, that resulted in the ritual of sending the goat to Azazel.

Why did God institute this ritual? Naḥmanides quotes *Pirkei de-Rabbi Eliezer* that when the angel Samael complained to God that he had been given control over all nations except Israel, God told him that he would have power over Israel on Yom Kippur if they sinned. The second goat was meant as an offering to Samael, and was sent out into the wilderness, to underscore the idea that it is the wastefulness and destructiveness of the evil thinking of the nations of the world that result in sin and transgression, and eventually in a holocaust.

Abrabanel: This pair of identical goats was intended to remind the Jew of Jacob and Esau, who were identical twins. The goat that was dedicated to God was meant to recall Jacob who lived a life of godliness. The other goat, which was sent out into the wilderness, represented Esau, who lived far away from his people. The casting of lots to decide which of the two goats was to be offered up to God and which allowed to go off into the desert was to remind the Jew of his opportunity to make his own choice between the two opposing ways of life represented by the two animals.

References:

B. Shevu'ot 7b, 8a; B. Yoma 2a, 3a, 4a, 23a, 31b, 32a, 35a, 36b, 37a, 40b, 44a, 45b, 47b, 48a, 51b, 55a, 58b, 59a, 60b, 62a, 62b, 65a, 66a, 67b, 70b; Yad, Hilkhot Avodat Yom Kippurim; Sefer ha-Mitzvot (Aseh) 49; Sefer Mitzvot Gadol (Aseh) 209; Sefer ha-Ḥinnukh, Mitzvah 185.

THE LIMITATION OF THE OFFERING OF SACRIFICES TO THE TEMPLE ONLY

If a man. . .kills an ox, or lamb, or goat. . .and has not brought it unto the door of the Tent of Meeting (Leviticus 17:3–4)
Take heed to yourself that you do not offer your burnt-offerings in every place that you see; only in the place which the Lord will choose (Deuteronomy 12:13–14)
And go unto the place which the Lord shall choose (Deuteronomy 12:26)

1. All sacrifices had to be slaughtered and offered up on the altar in the Temple grounds. If a Priest offered the animal on the altar in the Temple but had slaughtered the animal outside the Temple in full awareness that he had done so, he was punished with *karet*. The Torah went so far as to equate such a violation of the law with the shedding of human blood.

2. This strict law applied only to an offering that was suitable for a Temple ritual. If an unacceptable offering, such as a beast that had a blemish, was slaughtered outside of the Temple, the violation would not be punishable.

3. A Priest was exonerated if he was in the process of preparing the offering. Thus, if a Priest took the flour and the oil of a meal-offering and mixed them outside the Temple grounds but returned to finish the process in its appropriate place, he did not violate the law.

COMMENTATORS

Or ha-Ḥayyim: It was forbidden to set up "branch" Temples anywhere in the land. There could be one Temple only—in Jerusalem.
Naḥmanides: A sacrifice was acceptable only if it was brought in the Temple which God Himself had established as the place where men could attain atonement for their sins. If the Priest offered a sacrifice outside the Temple area, the sacrifice was disqualified. In such a case it was considered that the blood of the animal had been shed in vain and the Priest was guilty of a great sin.

Baḥya ben Asher: Prior to the Flood, man was permitted to eat only fruits and vegetables. After the Flood, he was also permitted to eat meat. During the time of their journey through the wilderness, the Children of Israel were allowed to eat only the flesh of animals that had been offered up as sacrifices. If a Jew ate the flesh of an animal that had been offered up outside the Sanctuary, in violation of the law according to which animal sacrifices could be offered only in the Sanctuary, he was considered to have sinned by having partaken of the meat. The reasoning was as follows: By choosing to ignore the Sanctuary, he had placed himself on the primitive level of Adam, and of the generations that lived before the Flood, and they had not been permitted to eat meat. Therefore meat had been forbidden to him also.

Ḥizzekuni: The Torah was so explicit in its prohibition against offering sacrifices outside the Temple in order to stress the distinction between pagan sacrifices and sacrifices made to the One true God. The pagans offered their sacrifices wherever they chose, but the Children of Israel could bring their offerings to their God only within the Temple so that they would remember to Whom it was that they were offering their sacrifices. To bring an offering to God outside the Temple was an assault on the sublime spiritual relationship between God and the Jew. Symbolically this was equated with bloodshed.

Ḥinnukh: The Temple was the only place where a Jew, free of outside distractions, could commit himself wholly to God. It was therefore the only place where he could properly bring the sacrifices intended as atonements for his transgressions. If he brought such a sacrifice outside the Temple, in the midst of all manner of distracting influences, his sacrifice was in vain and he was considered as if he had killed an animal in violation of the law of God and to no avail.

References:

B. Zevaḥim 107a, 107b, 108b, 112a, 113b, 115a, 118a; B. Kiddushin 43a, 57b; Sifre *Re'eh;* Sifra *Aḥarei Mot;* Midrash Rabbah, *Aḥarei Mot,* Chap. 22, Sec. 4, 6; Yad, Hilkhot Ma'asei ha-Korbanot, Chap. 18, 19; Sefer ha-Mitzvot (Lo Ta'aseh) 89, 90, (Aseh) 84; Sefer Mitzvot Gadol (Lav) 332, 333, (Aseh) 188; Sefer ha-Ḥinnukh, Mitzvot 186, 439, 440.

THE DUTY OF RESPECT FOR ANIMAL LIFE

Whoever takes in hunting any beast or fowl that may be eaten he shall pour out its blood and cover it with dust (Leviticus 17:13)

1. Even though we are permitted to take the life of an animal in order to make a sacrifice to God or to satisfy our need for food, we owe respect to the animal as a creature of God. Since blood represents the very life of any creature, we are bidden to show our respect for life itself by covering the blood of the animals we kill for our needs. This however applies only to *ḥayyot* (wild beasts) and fowl, but not to domesticated animals.

2. The blood had to be poured on a layer of soil which in turn had to be covered with another layer.

3. If the wind swept soil over the blood before the slaughterer was able to do so, and then the blood became uncovered again, it was incumbent upon anyone seeing the blood to cover it. If, however, the blood was covered by someone and was then uncovered by the wind, there was no need to cover it.

COMMENTATORS

Ibn Ezra: Strangers who see blood spilled at some distance away from the sacrificial altar may suspect that the blood was from an animal that that was sacrificed to a heathen deity. To prevent this mistake, we are commanded to cover this blood with dust as a distinguishing sign that this was an offering to God.

Or ha-Ḥayyim: Since blood is the life-stream of the animal it should be accorded the same respect as the body of a human being who has died. We therefore literally "bury" it by covering with earth.

Recanati: The obligation to cover the blood of a dead animal applied only to birds and wild beasts but not to domestic animals. Recanati attempts to explain the distinction by suggesting a basic difference between birds and wild beasts, on the one hand, and domestic animals on the other. Birds and wild beasts live by the laws that God designed for them, independently of the needs or wishes of the human species. Domestic animals, by contrast, live mostly as servants of man. Recanati's view is that animals that are closely identified with nature should be accorded greater respect than those which have been made subservient to human masters. This, according to Recanati, is the reason why the law to cover the blood of a dead animal does not apply to domestic animals.

References:
B. Ḥullin 83b, 84a, 85a, 86b, 87a, 88a, 88b; B. Sotah 16a; Midrash Tanḥuma, *Bereshit,* Chap. 10; Midrash Rabbah, *Bereshit,* Chap. 22, Sec. 18; Yad, Hilkhot Sheḥitah, Chap. 14; Sefer ha-Mitzvot (Aseh) 147; Sefer Mitzvot Gadol (Aseh) 164; Sefer Mitzvot Katan 156; Shulḥan Arukh, Yoreh De'ah, Chap. 28; Sefer ha-Ḥinnukh, Mitzvah 187.

FORBIDDEN MARRIAGES AND SEXUAL RELATIONSHIPS

None of you shall approach to any that is near of kin to him, to uncover their nakedness...I am the Lord (Leviticus 18:6)
The nakedness of your father, and the nakedness of your mother... you shall not uncover (Leviticus 18:7)
You shall not uncover the nakedness of the wife of your father (Leviticus 18:8)
You shall not uncover the nakedness of your sister, the daughter of your father, or the daughter of your mother, whether born at home, or born abroad (Leviticus 18:9)
You shall not uncover the nakedness of the daughter of your son or of the daughter of your daughter (Leviticus 18:10)
You shall not uncover the nakedness of the daughter of your father's wife, begotten of your father: she is your sister, you shall not uncover her nakedness (Leviticus 18:11)
You shall not uncover the nakedness of the sister of your father (Leviticus 18:12)
You shall not uncover the nakedness of the sister of your mother (Leviticus 18:13)

You shall not uncover the nakedness of your father's brother, you shall not approach his wife (Leviticus 18:14)
You shall not uncover the nakedness of your daughter-in-law (Leviticus 18:15)
You shall not uncover the nakedness of your brother's wife (Leviticus 18:16)
You shall not uncover the nakedness of a woman and her daughter (Leviticus 18:17)
You shall not take a woman to her sister, to be a rival to her, to uncover her nakedness beside the other in her lifetime (Leviticus 18:18)

1. A woman is the gift of God to man; she must therefore be treated with respect and reverence. If it is God's design that a man should love a woman, his passions must be kept within the framework of reverence and higher thoughts. To approach the sexual relationship in a selfish manner and like an animal would not be in keeping with this spirit.

2. In this spirit, Judaism tolerates neither extramarital relationships nor marriages that are at variance with the ethical, sociological, and moral standards of an enlightened society.

3. Biblical law forbids the following sexual relationships:

a. Between mother and son, even if the son was not her legitimate child.

b. Between stepmother and stepson, even if the stepmother is no longer married to her stepson's father.

c. Between brother and sister, or half-brother and half-sister. However, a man is permitted to marry his step-sister, i.e., the daughter of either step-parent by a previous marriage.

d. Between a father and daughter, even if she is his illegitimate child, or grandfather (paternal or maternal) and granddaughter.

e. With the sister of either parent, even if that sister is not a legitimate child of his grandparents.

f. With the wife of one's father's brother, i.e., of his father's brother from the same grandfather.

g. With one's daughter-in-law, even if she is no longer married to his son.
h. With the wife of one's brother or half-brother.
i. With a woman and her daughter.
j. With a woman and her son's daughter.
k. With a woman and her daughter's daughter.
l. With one's wife's sister while the wife is still living.

COMMENTATORS

Ibn Ezra: He considers the sex act as being basically offensive in the eyes of God. It is for this reason, he holds, that God asked the people to sanctify themselves by separating themselves from their wives before they received the Ten Commandments. In the view of Ibn Ezra, Adam had first been created without a mate because God's original intention had been for man to reproduce without sexual relationships. However, man was created with a sex drive and so it would have been unreasonable to expect him to stay away from women. Nevertheless, it was felt that some restrictions should be placed upon his sexual relations. He was therefore forbidden to have sexual relations with close relatives, who were likely to be readily accessible to him. Instead, he was forced to "go outside" his immediate family to search for a mate.

Maimonides: He does not take the extreme view of Ibn Ezra, but argues that sexual relations should be kept at a minimum. This is why men are forbidden to have intercourse with close blood relations who live in the immediate environment and for whom they naturally care. Another reason for the prohibition of sex relations or marriage with blood relatives is the simple motive of shame. It is shameful that the trunk (i.e., the father) should copulate with the branch (i.e., his daughter).

Naḥmanides: He does not agree with the idea that sexual relations with blood relatives were forbidden in order to restrict men in their sexual activity. If sex is repulsive and therefore should be minimized, why, he asks, did the Torah permit a man to marry even a thousand women as long as they were not his close relatives. He also points out that, seen from the viewpoint of logic, the best partners in marriage would be close blood-relations who have natural feelings of love and loyalty for one another. Hence he holds that it would be futile to attempt to explain the prohibition of such relations in terms of human logic. God, as a partner in procreation, simply has not revealed the reason for forbidding marriages between close relatives. If we try to rationalize, we might say that it is not medically advisable for close blood-relatives to marry each other.

Sforno: Before the Torah was given, there were instances in Jewish history where close relations married and were, in fact, blessed with extraordinary children. For instance, Amram married Jocheved who was his aunt, and this union produced Aaron, Moses, and Miriam. In this instance, however, the motive behind their marriage was to do the bidding of God. Most people, however, do not choose a mate in order to comply with God's will but in order to have sexual relations. This is the reason why the Torah forbids marriages with blood relatives who would likely be more accessible than women outside the family.

Keli Yakar: In regard to the commandment "None of you shall approach..." (Leviticus 18:6), this author disagrees with those who would construe "approach" to mean actual sex relations. He holds that the term should be construed literally: it is forbidden even to approach a woman whom one cannot marry, because approaching a woman, i.e., seeking her company, must lead to sexual relations.

Recanati: When God created trees, he intended that the branches and twigs that came forth from the trunk should make their own individual contribution to the growth of that tree. If the branches were allowed to bend and twist back into the trunk, the tree would soon wither and decay. Thus will it be with man when he begins to mate with his close relations.

References:

B. Sanhedrin 28b, 38a, 54a, 57b, 58b, 75a, 76a; B. Avodah Zarah 20b; B. Yevamot 3b, 8b, 13a, 13b, 21b, 22b, 23a, 54a, 54b, 55a, 57a; B. Sotah 44a; B. Kiddushin 50b, 80b; B. Makkot 5b; B. Krittot 15a; B. Shabbat 13a, 33a; B. Eruvin 100b; B. Niddah 13b; Midrash Rabbah, *Lekh Lekha,* Chap. 41, Sec. 9, Chap. 70, Sec. 12; *Va-Yikra, Aḥarei Mot,* Chap. 23, Sec. 10, Chap. 24, Sec. 6; Sifra, *Aḥarei Mot;* Yad, Hilkhot Issurei Bi'ah, Chap. 1, 2; Yad, Hilkhot Shegagot, Chap. 1; Yad, Hilkhot Ishut, Chap. 1; Sefer ha-Mitzvot (Lo Ta'aseh) 331–345, 351, 352; Sefer Mitzvot Gadol (Lav) 91, 93, 98–110, 126; Sefer Mitzvot Katan 299, 300, 301, 305, 306, 307, 308, 309, 310, 313, 314; Shulḥan Arukh, Even ha-Ezer, Chap. 15, 16, 21, 22, 33, 34; Sefer ha-Ḥinnukh, Mitzvot 188–206.

SEXUAL ABSTINENCE DURING THE MENSTRUAL PERIOD

And you shall not approach a woman to uncover her nakedness, as long as she is impure by her uncleanliness (Leviticus 18:19)

1. The laws of menstruation are most fundamental to the structure of Judaism. In fact, the violation of these laws warrants Divine punishment.

2. Experience has shown that observance of the laws of *niddah* (sexual abstinence during the menstrual period) makes for happy marriages. It requires the husband to be considerate of his wife during the periods when her bodily chemistry undergoes a change. At the same time, it teaches the wife to regard her intimate relations with her husband not as a way of gratifying her physical desires but rather as a fulfillment of God's plan.

3. A woman learns to establish the dates at which she can expect her monthly period by timing three consecutive periods. Depending on the time of day her periods start, the husband must abstain from relations with her beginning with the night, or the day, before her period begins. According to Jewish law, she remains in a state of *niddah* (isolation) for seven days after her period has stopped. Because of the many complexities of *niddah* laws, rabbinic dicta established that after any staining a woman must "count" seven clean days. On each of these seven "clean" days (which she may begin counting no earlier than at the end of five days following the onset of her period, even if the period lasts less than five days) she must examine her clothes and bedlinen for staining. At the end of her seven "clean" days she immerses herself in a *mikveh*. Thereafter she is permitted to resume sex relations with her husband. Without immersion *(tevilah)* in a proper *mikveh* she may not have relations with her husband, no matter how much time has elapsed since her period.

4. A child conceived during the period of *niddah* (when the couple is forbidden to have intercourse) is considered a *pegam*—a child that is spiritually defective.

COMMENTATORS

Maimonides: The prohibition to have relations with a woman during her menstrual period was one of the restrictions intended to curb man's sexual lust, for if man were allowed to give free rein to his passions he would be in the company of women all day and all night long.

Naḥmanides: According to the Torah, the purpose of sex is reproduction. As a consequence, a woman may not have sexual relations while she has her menstrual period, because she is unable to conceive during that time.

References:

B. Makkot 14a; B. Shevu'ot 18b; B. Sanhedrin 37a; B. Berakhot 55b; B. Niddah 13b, 31b, 64b; J. Sanhedrin Chap. 7, Halakhah 7; Avot de-Rabbi Natan Chap. 2; Midrash Rabbah, *Bereshit,* Chap. 17, Sec. 13; *Va-Yikra,* Chap. 15, Sec. 5; Midrash Tanḥuma, *Metzora,* Chap. 5; Yad, Hilkhot Issurei Bi'ah, Chap. 4; Sefer ha-Mitzvot (Lo Ta'aseh) 346; Sefer Mitzvot Gadol (Lav) 104; Sefer Mitzvot Katan, 293, Shulḥan Arukh, Yoreh De'ah, 183; Sefer ha-Ḥinnukh, Mitzvah 207.

THE PROHIBITION OF HUMAN SACRIFICES TO MOLOCH*

And you shall not give any of your seed to set them apart to Moloch (Leviticus 18:21)

1. The barbaric practice of burning children to death as sacrifices to idols was widespread in ancient pagan societies. The Torah therefore is particularly stern in its prohibition of such sacrifices.

2. Anyone who performed such a sacrifice in full knowledge that it was forbidden was to be stoned to death.

* Moloch was an Ammonite deity, but the prohibition applies to any idol.

COMMENTATORS

Naḥmanides: A man who had worshipped an idol in such a barbaric fashion could not be permitted to enter the Temple to bring sacrifices to the One True God.

Maimonides: He asks how it is possible for a parent to sacrifice a child of his to an idol? He contends that the two precious possessions a person is most fearful of losing are his children and his money. If a pagan priest assures him that if he will bring one of his children as a burnt-offering his other children will grow up healthy and strong and he himself will be prosperous, he may agree to sacrifice one of his children for the sake of his other children and of his wealth. But the Jew is bidden not to have faith in such assurances but to have faith in God alone. If he has no faith in God, nothing he does can possibly help his children or bring him prosperity.

Abrabanel: God granted man the pleasure of sex so that he could beget children. The birth of a child legitimizes and sanctifies the sex act. But if during intercourse it occurs to him that the child he may be begetting might be sacrificed to Moloch, his sex act loses its sanctity and he is considered as if he had "spilled his semen on the ground," an act which Judaism regards as an abomination.

References:
B. Sanhedrin 63b, 64b; B. Megillah 25a; Yad, Hilkhot Avodah Zarah, Chap. 6; Sefer ha-Mitzvot (Lo Ta'aseh) 7; Sefer Mitzvot Gadol (Lav) 40; Sefer Mitzvot Katan 65; Guide of the Perplexed, Part 3, Sec. 37; Sefer ha-Ḥinnukh, Mitzvah 208.

PROHIBITION OF PERVERSE SEXUAL RELATIONS

You shall not lie with a male as one lies with a woman
(Leviticus 18:22)
You shall not lie with any animal to defile yourself thereby
(Leviticus 18:23)
Neither shall any woman stand before an animal to lie down with it
(Leviticus 18:23)

1. The Torah makes it clear that homosexuality is an abomination. Any adult who committed this sin intentionally and with full knowledge of what he was doing was stoned to death. If he had no prior warning, the consequence was excision; if this sin was committed mistakenly, a sin-offering had to be brought.

2. The Torah is no less unequivocal in its prohibition of sexual acts with animals. Any man or woman guilty of such an act with full intent and knowledge of what he or she was doing was stoned to death; the animal had to be put to death in the same manner. If there was no prior warning, he was penalized with excision and the animal was stoned to death. If the act was committed mistakenly, the man brought a sin-offering and the animal was exonerated.

COMMENTATORS

Ibn Ezra: Homosexual relationships are forbidden because they are a perversion of nature and an act of disobedience to the will of God. In sex relationships, God intended man to be the giver, and woman the receiver. He then cites the following statements by other authorities relating to this prohibition: (1) a man must not have sexual relations with a man who has changed his sex and has become a woman; (2) a man must not have sex relations with a hermaphrodite. (Ibn Ezra holds that sex relations between persons of the same sex, or between humans and animals, are forbidden because they cannot produce offspring. These sex relations therefore represent "spilling one's seed in vain.")

Naḥmanides: Homosexual relations are forbidden because they are repulsive and because they cannot result in offspring.

References:

B. Nedarim 51a; B. Sanhedrin 54a, 54b, 55a, 60a; B. Yevamot 83b; B. Gittin 85a; Yad, Hilkhot Issurei Bi'ah, Chap. 1; Yad, Hilkhot Shegagot, Chap. 4; Sefer ha-Mitzvot (Lo Ta'aseh) 348, 349, 350; Sefer Mitzvot Gadol (Lav) 94, 95, 96; Shulḥan Arukh, Even ha-Ezer, Chap. 24; Sefer ha-Ḥinnukh, Mitzvot 209, 210, 211.

THOUGHTS ABOUT FALSE GODS

Do not turn to the idols (Leviticus 19:4)
And that you do not go about after your own heart, and your own eyes (Numbers 15:39)

1. Of the 613 *mitzvot* most (365) are prohibitions. Almost all facets of life are affected by these injunctions. The Torah issues decisive directives, relative to these negative commandments, to cover the source of man's proclivity to transgress. If we are to accept the premise that *Sof ma'aseh be-maḥshavah teḥillah*—an act starts with premeditation—we can understand why the Torah dealt with restrictions against perverted thoughts.

2. We are forbidden not only to worship false gods, but even to give thought to the possibility that they exist at all. It was even considered a serious sin to study the ways in which idols were worshiped.

3. The law forbidding us even to think about idols is construed as applying also to thoughts about other acts forbidden by the Torah.

4. While the mere contemplation of idolatry or sin is not subject to punishment, the Torah wants man to know that it is wrong because it may lead to actual wrongdoing.

COMMENTATORS

Ibn Ezra: A person must not consider idols as the legitimate gods of the pagans but rather as nonentities, unworthy of even the slightest notice.
Naḥmanides: If someone should hear an oracle predict an event and this event should subsequently come to pass exactly as it was forecast, what should his reaction be? Although he basically believes in one God, his heart may prompt him to give credence to the supernatural powers supposedly inherent in oracles. But this would be wrong. He must understand that there exists no supernatural power apart from God and that it was God—not the oracle—who brought about the event which the

oracle happened to predict. It is even forbidden to engage in debate about the existence of pagan gods or the sanctity of their priests.

Alshekh: Why does the Torah warn us against pagan gods? After all, is this prohibition not superfluous for a people who already believe that there is only one God? The answer is that a person may feel justified in worshiping the sun and the stars because they were created by God. The truth, however, is that despite their close association with God, they must not be worshiped, because there is only one God and there can be none beside Him.

Ḥinnukh: What if one does not believe in false gods, but merely studies them academically? This, too, is forbidden, because it is a pure waste of time and it is a sin to waste one's time. The *Ḥinnukh* adds that the sinner may be compared to an alcoholic. Once he begins to sin, he becomes addicted to the habit. Like the alcoholic, also, once he succeeds in breaking the habit, he begins to recognize the beauty and sanctity of life.

References:

B. Shabbat 149a; B. Avodah Zarah 50a; B. Berakhot 12b; B. Megillah 13a; J. Avodah Zarah, Chap. 3, Halakhah 1; J. Berakhot, Chap. 8, Halakhah 7; Sifre *Shelaḥ;* Midrash Rabbah, *Shelaḥ,* Chap. 17, Sec. 7; Yad, Hilkhot Avodah Zarah, Chap. 2; Sefer ha-Mitzvot (Lo Ta'aseh) 10, 47; Sefer Mitzvot Gadol (Lav) 14, 15; Sefer Mitzvot Katan 12; Sefer ha-Ḥinnukh, Mitzvot 213, 387.

THE PROHIBITION OF PARTAKING OF AN INVALID SACRIFICE

Everyone that eats it [i.e., an invalid sacrifice] shall bear his iniquity; for he profaned the holy thing of the Lord (Leviticus 19:8)

1. There were offerings that were totally consumed by fire. Others were divided between the Priest and the donor after the appropriate ritual had been performed. The meat of the animal had to be consumed within a certain period following the offering. Whatever was left after that period had passed was classified as *notar* ("left over") and had to be burned.

2. It was forbidden to eat the meat of a *piggul* (an offering that was invalidated because the Priest or the donor, or both, failed to observe all the laws pertaining to the sacrificial ritual or to the handling of the sacrifice).

3. One who deliberately partook of the meat of *notar* or *piggul* was subject to *karet*. One who did it unintentionally had to bring a sin-offering.

4. The meat of a sin-offering or guilt-offering became *notar* when the morning star appeared on the day following the sacrificial rite. The meat of an offering of thanksgiving became *notar* at sunset of the second day after the sacrificial rite.

COMMENTATORS

Sforno: It is extremely doubtful whether a Priest would approach the Temple with an offering while meditating on the worship of a false deity; but it is possible that, while he is performing the sacrificial rite, he may be thinking of forbidden things. In other words, he might worship God and perform the actual ritual meticulously; but should his mind be occupied with any sinful thoughts, the offering is disqualified and the Priest penalized.

Or ha-Ḥayyim: Why is it that a Priest is subject to the severe punishment of *karet* if he merely contemplates eating the meat of a sacrificial animal after the allotted time limit, while he receives no more than a flogging for actually eating the forbidden food? Because the sacrificial animal serves as a medium of communion between God and the Priest. If at the time of the sacrifice the Priest is not in total communion with God because he contemplates disobeying one of the rules connected with the sacrifice, the whole ritual was performed in vain and the animal is disqualified as an offering. Hence the severe punishment in such a case. On the other hand, if a Priest eats ordinary forbidden food, it is also a sin but not a desecration of a public religious act or of an animal singled out for a holy purpose. Hence the punishment in such a case is not so severe.

Recanati: Every day in a man's life brings with it new challenges, adjustments, and fresh attitudes. Since one day cannot be the exact replica of the day before, it stands to reason that, when a Priest conducts the rituals of the sacrificial rites, he does so with the talents and capacities which are his for that day. To carry over the service from one day to the next detracts from the concerted efforts of the Priest's body and mind from the previous day to that of the following one. It becomes apparent that, on the original day of the sacrifice, the Priest was in some manner lacking in his efforts on behalf of the sacrificial service, thus disqualifying his holy ministrations.

References:
B. Krittot 5a; B. Temurah 3a; B. Zevaḥim 28b, 56b; B. Me'ilah 17b; Yad, Hilkhot Pesulei Mikdashim, Chap. 18; Sefer ha-Mitzvot (Lo Ta'aseh) 131; Sefer Mitzvot Gadol (Lav) 336; Sefer ha-Ḥinnukh, Mitzvah 215.

LEAVING PART OF ONE'S HARVEST FOR THE POOR AND THE STRANGER

You shall not wholly reap the corner of your field (Leviticus 19:9)
Neither shall you gather the gleanings of your harvest (Leviticus 19:9)
And you shall not glean your vineyard (Leviticus 19:10)
Neither shall you glean the fallen fruit of your vineyard (Leviticus 19:10)
You shall leave them for the poor and the stranger: I am the Lord your God (Leviticus 19:10)

1. Jewish ethics require the rich to make adequate provision for the constant care of the poor. It is not enough to give a gift to a poor man and then dismiss him.

2. When a man harvested his field, he was obliged to leave one corner *(pe'ah)* for the poor and the stranger. This "corner" had to be in a specified part (i.e., the far side) of the field so that the poor and the stranger would know where their "corner" was without having to ask the owner. There was also a designated time at which the poor could come to glean from the *pe'ah*: at morning, at noon, and in the evening. The Torah did not specify the exact dimensions of the "corner," but the Rabbis set them at one 60th of the size of the field. The Rabbis urged the owners of the fields to take into consideration the number of poor people in their vicinity when they decided how much land to set aside as their *pe'ah*. If a farmer completed his harvest without remembering to set aside a *pe'ah*, he had to give to the poor a part of his harvest equivalent to the amount he would have had in the *pe'ah* of his field.

3. The poor were entitled also to *leket*, i.e., one or two ears of corn that the farmer might drop as he gathered his harvest. However, the poor were not entitled to anything in excess of two ears dropped by the farmer at a time because the aggregate of such leavings from the complete harvest was likely to be far in excess of the amount the farmer was required to give to the poor.

4. In the case of grape harvests, the poor were entitled to *olelot*, i.e., small clusters of grapes that remained on the vine and to *peret*, i.e., one or two grapes that were dropped at a time in the harvest.

COMMENTATORS

Or ha-Ḥayyim: The law reads, "And when you reap the harvest . . . .Thou shalt not wholly reap the corner of thy field." Why does the Torah first employ the second person plural but then shift to the second person singular? In order to show that no individual has the right to say that he will not give because his own small contribution could be insignificant in view of the great needs of the poor. Why were the laws pertaining to gifts for the poor from the harvest of the field placed immediately after a verse (Leviticus 19:8) referring to *karet*, i.e., excommunication? To show that no matter how gravely an individual has sinned in other respects, he is still expected to give charity to the poor and it will be counted for him as a good deed.
Ḥinnukh: When a person brings happiness into the lives of others by giving charity, he himself will become happier. But when he sits idly by while others starve, he himself will become bitter and demoralized.
Ḥizzekuni: We should help the less fortunate because we are eager to do the bidding of God, not merely because we consider it "proper" or expedient to perform a humanitarian act. This is why the group of laws

dealing with the gifts to the poor from the harvest concludes (Leviticus 19:10) with the declaration: "I am the Lord, your God."

Alshekh: When we leave part of our fields and vineyards unharvested so that the poor can come and take what they need, we must not feel that we are giving them a gift from our own property. Our harvest is ours only through the grace of God, who expects us to act as His agents to see to it that the poor get what they need. The laws of *pe'ah, leket, olelot,* and *peret* are intended to help the poor keep their self-respect. It is far less embarrassing for a poor man to enter an orchard, a field, or a vineyard and take from it that part of the harvest which is considered his rightful share without having to ask the owner's permission than it would be for him to receive grain, fruits, or vegetables from our hands as a gift of charity. We must always remember that whatever we possess is not really ours but God's.

References:

B. Ḥullin 131a, 131b, 134b, 135b, 137a; B. Temurah 6a; B. Yoma 35a; B. Shabbat 23a–b; B. Nedarim 6b; B. Bava Kamma 94a; B. Makkot 16b; J. Pe'ah, Chap. 1, Halakhot 3, 4; Chap. 2, Halakhah 5; Chap. 3, Halakhah 7; Chap. 4, Halakhot 1, 5; Chap. 6, Halakhot 1, 4; Yad, Hilkhot Matnat Aniyim, Chap. 1; Sefer ha-Mitzvot (Aseh) 120, 121, 123, 124, (Lo Ta'aseh) 211, 212, 213, 214; Sefer Mitzvot Gadol (Aseh) 156–160, (Lav) 284, 285, 286, 287; Shulḥan Arukh, Yoreh De'ah, 332; Sefer ha-Ḥinnukh, Mitzvot 216, 217, 218, 219, 220, 221, 222, 223.

FALSEHOOD

You shall not steal; neither shall you deal falsely (Leviticus 19:11)
Nor lie to one another (Leviticus 19:11)

1. Man must not only obey the commands of God, but must also deal righteously with his fellow men. Dishonesty toward a fellow man is tantamount to insulting God Himself.

2. One who illegally appropriates the belongings of another either by theft or by retaining an object he has borrowed or found, and fails to return to its owner when called upon to do so, is guilty of a sin. If he swore that he did not have an object when, in fact, he had it in his possession, he was disqualified from serving as a witness in any court of justice.

3. Furthermore, if he took an oath that he did not possess any of the articles in question and it was later disclosed that he had lied, then he had to return the object, add a fifth of its value, and bring a guilt-offering.

COMMENTATORS

Abrabanel: These *mitzvot* follow the dictates of common sense, but we are asked to observe them out of a higher motivation; namely that they were commanded to us by God.
Ḥinnukh: He considers these commandments as self-evident truisms which require no explanation. Most of the other commentaries also find it unnecessary to elaborate on these *mitzvot.*

References:
B. Shevu'ot 31b, 36b, 49b; Sifra *Kedoshim;* Yad, Hilkhot Shevu'ot, Chap. 1; Sefer ha-Mitzvot (Lo Ta'aseh) 248, 249; Sefer Mitzvot Gadol (Lav) 240, 241; Shulḥan Arukh, Ḥoshen Mishpat, 294, 360, 366, 367; Sefer ha-Ḥinnukh, Mitzvot 225, 226.

DISHONEST DEALINGS

You shall not oppress your neighbor (Leviticus 19:13)
Nor rob him (Leviticus 19:13)
Then he shall restore that which he took away by robbery (Leviticus 5:23)

1. One is not permitted to keep money or property owned by another, or to withhold from another goods or money rightfully due him. Any one who has found an object belonging to someone else and intends to return it to its rightful owner, but purposely puts off doing so, is guilty of a sin. One who has an object belonging to another but tells him that he does not have it, or one who with some unjustifiable excuse puts off paying the wages of one who has worked for him, is considered as if he had committed a theft.

2. Theft is a sin, no matter how small or insignificant the stolen object. For this reason one is not permitted to decide for himself that an object or coin which he has stolen has so little value that it would be folly to return it to its rightful owner.

3. If a person stole an object and has disposed of it, he must compensate the rightful owner with goods or cash of equal value.

4. According to Jewish law, one who stole a plank and used it in building a house must tear down the entire house and return the plank. However, in order to eliminate undue hardship to the guilty party, the Rabbis subsequently issued *takkanat ha-shavim,* an "amendment" to the law, whereby it was declared sufficient if the guilty party made adequate financial restitution for the plank.

5. *Takkanat ha-shavim* also provides that in the case of an individual who has stolen an object, and lost it, and then of his own initiative offers to make restitution for it, his offer should not be accepted—his repentance is to be considered sufficient restitution.

6. If the stolen object has been altered—e.g., if someone stole a bolt of cloth and made a suit from it—the guilty party is expected to pay no more than the original value of the cloth.

7. It is forbidden to buy anything from an individual who has the reputation that he is a thief, because by doing so one would strengthen the hand of a transgressor.

8. Many authorites hold that accepting an object from someone who does not give it of his own free will but only in deference to social or other pressures is tantamount to theft.

COMMENTATORS

Ḥinnukh: Delaying the payment of wages due for work or services rendered is not a sin in itself. Nevertheless, Jewish law forbids it because it may tempt one to withhold such payments altogether, and thus make him guilty of a transgression.

References:
B. Sanhedrin 57a, 59a; B. Gittin 55a; B. Bava Metzia 61b, 111a; B. Sukkah 30a; B. Ta'anit 7b; B. Bava Kamma 66a, 67b, 93b, 94a, 98b, 112a; J. Bava Kamma, Chap. 1, Halakhah 4; Yad, Hilkhot Gezelah, Chap. 1; Sefer ha-Mitzvot (Lo Ta'aseh) 245, 247, (Aseh) 194; Sefer Mitzvot Gadol (Lav) 156, 157, (Aseh) 73; Sefer Mitzvot Katan 271; Shulḥan Arukh, Ḥoshen Mishpat, 359, 360; Sefer ha-Ḥinnukh, Mitzvot 228, 229, 230.

TO PAY FOR DAY LABOR ON THAT DAY

The wages of a hired worker shall not remain with you overnight (Leviticus 19:13)
You shall give him his hire on the same day (Deuteronomy 24:15)

1. An honest day's work is worth an honest day's pay. Payment must be made as soon as possible, not at the pleasure of the employer. The employer must see to it particularly that day workers, who live from hand to mouth, are paid no later than the night following that working day. One who works on the night shift must be paid no later than the day following that working night. These laws are applicable in the case of all day laborers, Jewish or Gentile.

2. An employer who withholds the wages of a day laborer thereby violates four precepts: (a) "You shall not oppress your neighbor," (b) "You shall not steal," (c) "You shall not keep the wages of a hired laborer overnight," and (d) "You shall give him his hire on the same day." Each day that he withholds the wages of his worker represents a new transgression of these precepts.

3. On the other hand, the worker is expected to ask for his wages. Thus, if one gives a pair of shoes to a cobbler for repair and the latter does the work and never demands payment, the employer (or customer) is not guilty of a transgression in not paying him.

4. In disputes involving the payment of wages the Rabbis made every effort to protect the worker. If a worker demanded his pay but his employer contended that he had already been given his wages, all that was required of the worker was that he testify under oath that he had not yet received his pay. The worker's memory was considered more reliable than that of the employer, whose mind was occupied with many other concerns.

COMMENTATORS

Naḥmanides: One who feels compelled to hire himself out as a day laborer is usually in dire financial straits. An employer who hires such an individual must keep in mind that by withholding the worker's wages, he, the employer, may actually cause him to starve.

Recanati: God allocates to all His creatures their daily sustenance. Hence, one who withholds the wages of a day laborer is guilty of frustrating the designs of God. If a man who employs day laborers remembers that he himself expects prompt "payment" in the world to come for the good deeds he has performed in his lifetime, he will not be likely to withhold the wages of the man who works for him.

References:

B. Bava Metzia 83b (see Tosafot), 89a, 110b, 111b, 112a; Sifre *Ki Tetze;* Sifra *Kedoshim;* Yad, Hilkhot Sekhirut, Chap. 11; Sefer ha-Mitzvot (Lo Ta'aseh) 238, (Aseh) 200; Sefer Mitzvot Gadol (Aseh) 90, (Lav) 181; Sefer Mitzvot Katan 261; Shulḥan Arukh, Ḥoshen Mishpat, 339; Sefer ha-Ḥinnukh, Mitzvot 230, 588.

MISGUIDING OR TRAPPING THE UNSUSPECTING

Nor put a stumbling block before the blind (Leviticus 19:14)

The Rabbis render "blind" as "unsuspecting" or "uninformed." Thus, the following acts are examples of "putting a stumbling block before the blind":

1. Offering forbidden food to an unsuspecting individual.
2. Suggesting to someone seeking advice a course of action that will be contrary to his best interests.
3. Putting a knife or other deadly weapon into the hands of a madman.

COMMENTATORS

Ibn Ezra: A man who puts obstacles in the path of the blind may someday find himself to be in need of guidance; therefore why place stumbling blocks in the path of others?

Ḥinnukh: There are three pillars upon which the world is established: truth, mutual confidence, and mutual trust. Without these, society could not survive.

References:

B. Pesaḥim 22b; B. Mo'ed Katan 5a, 17a; B. Kiddushin 32a, 32b; B. Nedarim 62b; B. Bava Metzia 75b; B. Ḥullin 7b; B. Avodah Zarah 14a; B. Pesaḥim 22b; Sifra *Kedoshim;* Yad, Hilkhot Rotze'ah, Chap. 12; Sefer ha-Mitzvot (Lo Ta'aseh) 299; Sefer Mitzvot Gadol (Lav) 168; Sefer Mitzvot Katan 171; Sefer ha-Ḥinnukh, Mitzvah 232.

PERVERSIONS OR MISCARRIAGES OF JUSTICE

You shall do no unrighteousness in judgment (Leviticus 19:15)
In righteousness, shall you judge your neighbor (Leviticus 19:15)
You shall not pervert justice due to the stranger (Deuteronomy 24:17)

1. If at all possible, disputes should be settled by out-of-court arbitration rather than in a court of law. In arbitration there is a possibility that both sides will be satisfied, but if the matter is decided in court one of the two litigants must of necessity be the "loser." If parties in a dispute insist on settling the case in court, the judge should refuse to hear the case. For a judge to attempt to settle a dispute by any means other than arbitration or a court hearing is a perversion of justice.

2. The Rabbis demanded that the judge should be meticulous in ensuring that both parties to a dispute should be equal before the law in every respect, even as regarded the formalities of the court hearing. Thus, neither the plaintiff nor the defendant were to be shown preferential treatment. During the hearing, both of them had to remain standing, or both had to remain seated. It was not permitted that one of the parties should stand while the other was seated. The court also had to insist that both parties should appear in similar clothing because if one of the two parties was to wear more costly garments than the other, the judge might be influenced in his behalf.

3. A judge who had arrived at a decision but purposely delayed handing down his ruling was guilty of a perversion of justice.

4. While it is a grievous sin to pervert justice, there is no penalty of flogging, because it is a *lav she-en bo ma'aseh*—a negative commandment which involves no action. Punishment will come to the judge in another manner.

COMMENTATORS

Or ha-Ḥayyim: The Rabbis teach that on Rosh Ha-Shanah the Almighty allocates for every person the financial means he will need for the coming year. God then expects men to secure these means for themselves through legitimate productivity and the pursuit of justice. Thus, when a judge awards a sum of money to one who is not entitled to it, he is deliberately frustrating God's plans for mankind.

Keli Yakar: If a wealthy man and a poor man appear before a judge to settle a dispute involving money or property, the judge must not rule in favor of the poor man simply in order to spare him the indignity of having to accept charity as a result of the court's decision. While it is true that the wealthy must provide for the less fortunate, this must not lead to a perversion of justice.

References:

B. Sanhedrin 3a, 7a; B. Shevu'ot 30a, 32b; B. Bava Metzia 115a; Midrash Tehillim, Chap. 82; Sifra *Kedoshim;* Sifre *Ki Tetze;* Yad, Hilkhot Sanhedrin, Chap. 20, 21; Sefer ha-Mitzvot (Aseh) 177, (Lo Ta'aseh) 273, 280; Sefer Mitzvot Gadol (Aseh) 106, (Lav) 205, 206; Sefer Mitzvot Katan 225, 232; Shulḥan Arukh, Ḥoshen Mishpat, 17, 33; Sefer ha-Ḥinnukh, Mitzvot 233, 235, 590.

DEFENDING THE VICTIMS OF CRIME

Neither shall you stand idly by the blood of your neighbor
(Leviticus 19:16)

1. There is a famous rabbinic dictum: "He who saves one soul in Israel is as if he had saved the entire world." There are times when in order to save a life, it is even considered meritorious to take the law into one's own hands and shameful to refrain from doing so. Thus, when one sees another pursuing a third person with the obvious intent of murder or rape, he must save the endangered party, even if it means killing the pursuer.

2. However, if the rescuer can achieve his aim without taking the life of the pursuer, he must not kill him. Indeed, if the rescuer sees that he has another alternative e.g., merely to wound the pursuer, but nevertheless takes the pursuer's life, he is considered guilty of murder.

3. The law in Leviticus 19:16 is interpreted by the Rabbis as justifying the destruction of an embryo in the mother's womb in order to save the life of the mother. In such a case, the embryo is regarded as the pursuer, the mother as the intended victim, and the physician as the rescuer. However, if the child's head had emerged from the womb, it is regarded as alive and it is therefore forbidden to destroy one independent life in order to save another life.

4. Not to "stand idly by the blood of one's neighbor" means also to hasten to the rescue of one who is in danger of drowning and to save the possessions of another from theft. However, one is not permitted to kill a thief in an attempt to stop him, because the soul of a human body is more valuable than earthly possessions. However, if a thief is caught breaking into a home at night, he may be presumed to have hostile intentions; therefore, one who kills him in an attempt to stop him is not considered guilty of murder (see Exodus 22:1: "If a thief is found breaking in and is smitten so that he dies, there shall be no bloodguiltiness for him").

COMMENTATORS

Ibn Ezra, Ḥizzekuni: The first half of the verse from Leviticus forbidding us to "stand idly by the blood of our neighbors" is: "You shall not go up and down as a talebearer among your people." The juxtaposition of these two commandments indicates that slander is considered tantamount to murder and that one is obligated to save a person from slander even as one is duty bound to rescue a fellow man pursued by one who seeks to kill him.

Maimonides: If we are permitted, if necessary, to kill a pursuer intent on murder even before he has actually committed the deed, why are we not permitted to act in the same manner toward one who worships idols and desecrates the Sabbath? Are not these sins similar to murder in that they, too, are subject to the death penalty? The answer is that there is a difference: If a pursuer were allowed to carry out his intent to murder, the crime could never be undone, but one who worships idols or des-

ecrates the Sabbath always has a chance to repent and to mend his ways.
Ḥinnukh: When a man is running in order to escape a murderer, he is praying to God to save him. It then becomes our duty, as fellow men and as agents of God, to help save him.

References:
B. Bava Kamma 26a, 28a; B. Sanhedrin 72b, 73a; J. Bava Kamma, Chap. 8, Halakhah 3; Sifre *Ki Tetze;* Sifra *Kedoshim;* Yad, Hilkhot Rotzeaḥ, Chap. 1; Guide of the Perplexed, Part 3, Sec. 40; Sefer ha-Mitzvot (Lo Ta'aseh) 297, (Aseh) 247; Sefer Mitzvot Gadol (Lav) 164, 165, (Aseh) 77; Sefer Mitzvot Katan 78; Shulḥan Arukh, Ḥoshen Mishpat, 425, 426; Sefer ha-Ḥinnukh, 237, 600, 601.

FORBIDDEN HATRED

You shall not hate your brother in your heart (Leviticus 19:17)

We are forbidden to bear hatred for a fellow man in our hearts. If we feel offended or angered by what another has done, we must openly confront that person and demand an explanation from him. Once we have told him our feelings and he has been given a chance to justify his act or to make an apology, we must remove all hatred for him from our hearts and "forgive and forget." One who bears a grudge against a fellow man in his heart is guilty of a transgression.

COMMENTATORS

Ibn Ezra, Ḥinnukh: Society cannot function properly unless people are completely frank and open in their relations with one another. The most despicable sin a man can commit is to harbor a secret hatred against another and wait for an opportune time to strike him down.
Or ha-Ḥayyim: Is it possible for a human being to be completely free of hatred? This exegete suggests that by referring to our fellow man as

"your brother" the Torah tells us that we are indeed able to rid ourselves of hatred, for how much animosity can one have for his brother? If one considers all other men as his brothers, it will be much easier to destroy the hatred in his heart, replacing it with feelings of kindness and compassion as set forth in the commandment that bids us to "love your neighbor as yourself" (Leviticus 19:18).

Naḥmanides: If your fellow man has wronged you and you point out that fact to him, the chances are that he will acknowledge that he has done wrong and ask your pardon. You will then forgive him.

References:

B. Pesaḥim 113b; B. Arakhin 16b; B. Bava Metzia 32b, 62a; B. Shabbat 31a; B. Yoma 9b; Pirkei Avot, Chap. 2; Yad, Hilkhot De'ot, Chap. 6; Sefer ha-Mitzvot (Lo Ta'aseh) 302; Sefer Mitzvot Gadol (Lav) 5; Sefer Mitzvot Katan 17; Sefer ha-Ḥinnukh, Mitzvah 238.

THE DUTY TO REBUKE YOUR NEIGHBOR

You shall rebuke your neighbor (Leviticus 19:17)

1. No one lives on an island by himself. Everyone's life is interwoven with the lives of those around him. As Judaism sees it, every Jew is responsible for the welfare of one's fellow Jews.

2. Concern for the welfare of one's neighbor includes concern for his moral and spiritual growth. The Torah therefore asks us to "rebuke" our fellow Jew if we see that he is doing wrong, and to keep on rebuking him until he mends his ways or until it becomes obvious that our concern succeeds only in arousing his resentment. If we remonstrate with him, we must do so in a kind and gentle manner, pointing out to him that we have no other interest except to help him.

3. It is a sin to shame a sinner in public without first having remonstrated with him in private. The Rabbis say that he who unnecessarily humiliates another man in public forfeits his own share in the world to come.

COMMENTATORS

Ḥizzekuni, Ibn Ezra: By rebuking him in a friendly manner when he has done wrong, we are giving our fellow man a chance to explain his conduct and, if he is innocent, to show that he has done no wrong. **Ḥinnukh, Rashbam:** When one does wrong and is rebuked gently he is likely to acknowledge his guilt and ask for forgiveness. However, should there be no open and candid discussion of the matter, a growing animosity will usurp the place of peace. There is an urgent necessity in life for honesty and rebuke without malice in order to lead to a cordial relationship between men.

Recanati: One of the things that enabled the Jews to survive through the ages was their deep concern for one another. "All Israelites are surety one for the other," our sages said. When one Jew sins, he becomes a weak link in the chain. It is the duty of every Jew to correct the wrongdoings of his fellow Jews, so that he himself may not eventually fall under the influence of sin. Thus, in addition to bringing a wayward fellow man back to the right path, he also will indirectly keep himself from wrongdoing.

References:
B. Yevamot 65b; B. Bava Metzia 31a, 31b, 58b, 59a; B. Arakhin 16b; B. Berakhot 31b; B. Shabbat 54b, 56b; B. Ketubbot 105b; B. Tamid 28a; Pirkei Avot, Chap. 3, Mishnah 16; Avot de-Rabbi Natan 29; Midrash Rabbah, *Va-Yikra,* Chap. 24, Sec. 3; Yad, Hilkhot De'ot, Chap. 6, 7; Sefer ha-Mitzvot (Aseh) 205, (Lo Ta'aseh) 305; Sefer Mitzvot Gadol (Aseh) 11, (Lav) 6; Sefer Mitzvot Katan 126; Sefer ha-Ḥinnukh, Mitzvot 239, 240.

PROHIBITION OF TAKING REVENGE

You shall not take vengeance (Leviticus 19:18)
Nor bear any grudge against the children of your people (Leviticus 19:18)

Though it may be part of human nature to seek vengeance, the Torah forbids us to bear a grudge or to cherish a desire for revenge.

The Rabbis give the following classic examples of the attitudes to which this prohibition applies.

a. A comes to his friend B to borrow a hatchet, but B refuses to lend it to him. The next day B comes to A to borrow a scythe, but A says: "You refused to lend me the hatchet yesterday, so why should I lend you the scythe today?" This is *nekamah* ("revenge or retaliation").

b. B comes to A to borrow a scythe, and A replies: "You see, I am lending you my scythe today, even though you refused to lend me your hatchet yesterday." This is *netirah* ("harboring a grudge").

Both these attitudes are forbidden because they are conducive to vindictiveness and malice.

COMMENTATORS

Ḥinnukh: When one takes revenge, he is in effect, sitting in judgment on his neighbor, forgetting that his neighbor's actions are not for him to avenge and judge; this is the prerogative of God. Besides, how can an individual take it upon himself to exact vengeance for what his neighbor did to him when it was God Himself who willed his neighbor to do as he did?

Alshekh: We are constantly committing wrongs against God, yet He does not wreak His vengeance upon us immediately. This should teach man, too, not to exact vengeance for a wrong done to him but to hope that the guilty party will eventually make amends. The prohibition of taking vengeance immediately follows the commandment to rebuke our neighbor if he does wrong. This is to point up the contrast between the malice of revenge and the kindness of well-meant moral instruction.

Keli Yakar: The admonition "not to bear any grudge against the children of your people" may imply that one may do so in the case of a non-Jew. Why is this so? Because when a Jew wrongs his fellow-Jew, his main purpose is to cause him physical or financial harm. Although these are acts of malice, they do not warrant vengeance; but when a non-Jew harms a Jew, his intention is often to make life so unpleasant for the Jew that he will be forced to abandon his God and the *mitzvot* of Judaism, as a convenient escape from oppression and hardship. This does call for retaliation and is considered not as simple physical vengeance but as avenging God.

References:
B. Yoma 23a; J. Nedarim, Chap. 9, Halakhah 3; Yad, Hilkhot De'ot, Chap. 6; Sefer ha-Mitzvot (Lo Ta'aseh) 304, 305; Sefer Mitzvot Gadol (Lav) 11, 12; Sefer Mitzvot Katan 130, 131; Sefer ha-Ḥinnukh, Mitzvot 241, 242.

LOVING ONE'S NEIGHBOR

You shall love your neighbor as yourself (Leviticus 19:18)

1. Our sages are almost unanimous in their agreement that the biblical commandment to "Love your neighbor as yourself" is the basic pillar upon which the entire Torah is built.

2. The observance of this law includes such "good deeds" as visiting the sick, arranging for the burial of the dead, comforting the bereaved, providing dowries for poor brides, and protecting the possessions of another as if they were his own.

COMMENTATORS

Maimonides: He adheres to a literal interpretation of the scriptural law. A person must strive to love his fellow man exactly as he loves himself. When he protects the person and the possessions of another, he must think and feel as if he were guarding his own possessions.
Naḥmanides: It is impossible to love any fellow man as much as one loves himself. In support of his argument, he cites Rabbi Akiva's statement to the effect that, if a person comes into a situation where he has a choice of saving his own life or that of his companion, his own life takes priority. Naḥmanides interprets the scriptural law to mean that one should pray that one's fellow man should receive all those blessings that one hopes to receive himself, and that one should not allow oneself to envy another for his good fortune, since envy and jealousy breed hatred.
Ibn Ezra: There should be no difference between what a man wishes for

himself and the good that he wishes for his fellow man, for we were all created by one God.

Sforno, Ḥizzekuni: To love your fellow man means putting yourself in his position. For instance, in thinking of a friend who is ill one must say, "If I were ill myself, what would be the choicest blessing I could seek from God?" and then pray that the other should receive that blessing.

Ba'al ha-Turim: He interprets this commandment to mean that one must always be sensitive to the sensibilities of other people. He offers an example: when one is intimate with his wife one should not think of another woman.

Radbaz: This commandment applies only to one who is bound to you by spiritual kinship. It is not necessary to put ourselves out on behalf of one who has cut himself off from the main body of traditional Judaism. He compares the Jewish community to the body of a person. Just as one would never think of deliberately injuring, or purposely neglecting, any part or limb of one's own body, so, too, every Jew must seek the well-being of all other members of the entity that is the Jewish people. He further explains that since man was created in the image of God, he demonstrates his love for God each time he seeks to advance the welfare of his fellow man.

Alshekh: If everyone would obey the commandment to love his fellow man, all men would obey all the other *mitzvot* of the Torah as well. Good relationships with one's fellow man make for a good relationship also with God.

References:

B. Shabbat 31a; B. Niddah 17a; B. Ketubbot 37b; B. Kiddushin 41a; B. Sanhedrin 45a, 84b; B. Bava Metzia 62a; J. Ḥagigah, Chap. 2, Halakhah 1; Avot de-Rabbi Natan, Chap. 16; Yad, Hilkhot De'ot, Chap. 6; Sefer ha-Mitzvot (Aseh) 206; Sefer Mitzvot Gadol (Aseh) 9; Sefer Mitzvot Katan 8; Sefer ha-Ḥinnukh, Mitzvah 243.

FORBIDDEN MIXTURES

You shall not let your cattle breed with a diverse kind . . . you shall not sow your field with two kinds of seed . . . neither shall there come upon you a garment of two kinds of material mixed together (Leviticus 19:19)

You shall not sow your vineyard with two kinds of seed lest the fullness of the seed which you have sown be forfeited together with the increase of the vineyard (Deuteronomy 22:9)

You shall not plough with an ox and an ass together (Deuteronomy 22:10)

You shall not wear a mingled stuff, wool and linen together (Deuteronomy 22:11)

1. Jewish law forbids man to interfere with what it considers the Divine scheme of creation. At the time of creation, God commanded each species of plant and animal to reproduce according to its kind: hence Jewish law forbids one to mix them.

2. It is forbidden to sow two different kinds of seeds, such as wheat and barley, within the space of three handbreadths of each other. One must not even sow close together the seeds of different vegetables that resemble each other. This prohibition, referred to as *kilei zeraim* (a mixture of seeds) is applicable only to soil in Eretz Israel. *Kilei kerem,* sowing the seeds of other vegetables together with grapes, is forbidden even outside Eretz Israel.

3. *Kilei ilanot,* the crossing of fruit species, such as oranges and apples, is forbidden, and according to biblical law one who is engaged in this practice was punished by flogging. However, it is not forbidden to eat the fruits of such a crossing.

4. It is also forbidden to mate two different species of animal, such as a horse and a donkey. (This prohibition does not apply to two different varieties of the same animal species; e.g., a wild horse and a domesticated horse.) Under biblical law, anyone engaging in this practice was punished by flogging, but it is not forbidden to make use of the offspring of such a mixture.

5. Jewish law furthermore forbids the use of an ox and a donkey together as a "team" for plowing or other work. Since the donkey is an unclean (non-kosher) animal, this ruling is taken to imply that a non-kosher animal may not be put with a kosher animal to make a "team." The Rabbis added the prohibition to form "teams" with any two animals that were not allowed to be mated. Anyone who violated this law was punished by flogging; so was anyone who even so much as sat on a cart drawn by a team of two such animals.

6. It is forbidden to wear garments made of a mixture of wool and linen *(sha'atnez)*; this law also forbids the wearing of a woollen garment sewn with threads of linen. Such garments must not be sold or manufactured for sale.

COMMENTATORS

Naḥmanides: God made each plant and creature on earth with its own distinctive features and attributes. When a male and female of two different species are mated, or two different types of vegetation are crossed, the product is a totally new entity. If a man brings about such cross-breeding, he arrogates to himself the right to produce new creatures, a right which belongs to God alone and never to man. Unlike Rashi, who holds that these commandments are not subject to human inquiry, Naḥmanides propounds the following rationale: The prohibition of plowing a field with a team consisting of an ox and a donkey was designed to prevent the mating between the two species. If one is accustomed to use two different species together for work, he will see no reason why he should not put them into the same stable, and this will eventually lead to their mating.

Ibn Ezra: He agrees that mating different animal species is forbidden because it is contrary to God's original pattern of creation. However, he questions whether this explanation can be applied also to the prohibition of crossing various species and of wearing wool and linen. He holds that these prohibitions, too, are aspects of the Law of God, which is perfect, although men cannot fathom the actual reason for them.

He adds that the proscription of having an ox and a donkey on the same team is motivated by God's compassion for all His creatures. Since the ox is stronger than the donkey, putting the two together on one team imposes undue strain on both animals. Either the ox would be compelled to carry most of the burden or the donkey would be taxed trying to keep up with the ox.

Ḥinnukh: The prohibition of putting an ox and a donkey on the same team was intended to spare each of the two animals the hardship of being yoked to a creature so different from itself as the ox and the donkey are from one another.

Recanati: He associates the prohibition of the wearing of garments from a mixture of wool and linen with the story of Cain and Abel. According to this homily, linen, derived from a plant, represents the "fruit of the ground" offered up by Cain, while wool, which is derived from sheep, represents the "firstlings of the flock" which Abel brought as his offering. God's acceptance of Abel's gift and His rejection of Cain's offering led to the first fratricide in the history of mankind. It would seem, then, that linen and wool symbolize two irreconcilable elements.

Da'at Zekenim: The prohibition of wearing garments from a mixture of wool and linen is based on the fact that the curtain in the Temple was woven from wool and linen, and it was forbidden to duplicate the furnishings of the Temple for non-sacred use.

Maimonides: Jews are forbidden to wear garments from a mixture of wool and linen because such garments were worn by pagan priests during their ritual functions.

Sforno: In pre-biblical days it was customary for the Jew to work and mate two different species and to wear garments of *sha'atnez*. When the Jews received the Torah God wished to elevate them above their nomadic way of life by prohibiting these old customs which savored of paganism and were redolent of idolatry.

References:

B. Niddah 61b; B. Betzah 14b; Mishnayyot Kilayim; B. Yevamot 4b, 5b; B. Mo'ed Katan 2b; B. Kiddushin 39a, 56b; B. Ḥullin 60a, 115a; B. Bava Metzia 91a; B. Bava Kamma 54b, 55a; B. Berakhot 22a; B. Bekhorot 17a; B. Menaḥot 43b; J. Kilayim, Chap. 1, Halakhah 1; Chap. 7, Halakhot 2, 3, 4; Chap. 8, Halakhot 1, 4; J. Berakhot, Chap. 6, Halakhah 1; J. Nedarim, Chap. 3, Halakhah 2; Sifre *Kedoshim;* Sifre *Ki Tetze;* Midrash Tanḥuma, *Bereshit,* Chap. 9; *Shelaḥ*, Chap. 15; Midrash Rabbah, *Va-Yishlaḥ*, Chap. 82, Sec. 17; *Bo,* Chap. 13, Sec. 6; Pirkei de-Rabbi Eliezer, Chap. 21; Guide of the Perplexed,

Part 3, Sec. 26, 27, 37, 49; Yad, Hilkhot Kilayim, Chap. 1, 5, 9; Sefer ha-Mitzvot (Lo Ta'aseh) 42, 193, 215, 216, 217, 218; Sefer Mitzvot Gadol (Lav) 145, 279, 280, 281, 282, 283; Sefer Mitzvot Katan 32, 168, 170, 216; Shulḥan Arukh, Yoreh De'ah, 296, 297, 298; Sefer ha-Ḥinnukh, Mitzvot 244, 245, 548, 549, 550, 551.

THE FIRST FOUR YEARS OF A FRUIT-BEARING TREE

And when you shall come into the land . . . you shall count the fruit thereof as forbidden, three years shall it be forbidden unto you; it shall not be eaten (Leviticus 19:23)
And in the fourth year, all the fruits [of the land] shall be holy, for giving praise to the Lord (Leviticus 19:24)

1. The fruit of any tree within the first three years following its planting is called *orlah,* "closed up fruit," and must not be eaten. All such fruit must be burned; if it is in liquid form, it must be buried. According to biblical law, the laws of *orlah* would have applied only to farmers in Eretz Israel. Oral Tradition, however, extends these laws to outside Eretz Israel also. But in cases of doubt as to whether or not a fruit is *orlah,* one need not be as stringent outside Eretz Israel as one must be in the case of fruit grown in the Land.

2. Fruit appearing in the fourth year after the planting is known as *neta revai,* "the planting of the fourth year." This fruit is considered holy; it was set aside for the Priests and could not be eaten outside the walls of Jerusalem. A farmer for whom it would have been an undue hardship to bring his fruit to Jerusalem could "redeem" it with an amount of money equivalent to the value of the fruit plus one-fifth of its value. Instead of the fruit, he would bring this money to Jerusalem and spend it there on food. Today, the "redemption" of *neta revai* is performed with a special coin which is discarded afterward.

3. If a farmer chose to bring the fruit to Jerusalem he had to bring it in its natural state. The only two exceptions were grapes and olives, which he could bring in the form of wine or olive oil.

4. The fruits of trees that were not planted for the sake of the fruit (e.g., oranges from an orchard planted to serve as a hedge, without regard for the fruit), are not subject to the laws of *orlah* and *neta revai.* But if the fruit itself is used, no matter what the purpose (e.g., *etrogim* for the blessing recited over the *lulav* on Sukkot, or olives for oil for the *menorah*), it is subject to these laws.

COMMENTATORS

Ibn Ezra: The fruit of the first three years of a tree was forbidden because such early fruit was not healthy to eat.

Naḥmanides: All foods prohibited by biblical law, including the fruit of trees within the first three years after their planting, were forbidden because they were considered harmful to health.

Maimonides: Jews were forbidden to eat the fruit of trees within the first three years after their planting because the heathens offered the first fruits of a tree as a gift of thanksgiving to their deities for having responded to their incantations and for having caused the tree to bring forth good fruit at an early date. Jews were to leave such early fruit uneaten so that they might not be suspected of having employed similar incantations to make the fruit appear.

Alshekh: During the first three years after the planting of a tree, nature must be left to do its task. In the fourth year, God puts His stamp of approval upon the tree by causing the fruit to ripen and become edible. As a reward for not eating the ripe fruit of the fourth year but giving it to the Priests, God promises that He will bless the future yield of the tree with goodness and abundance.

Baḥya ben Asher: We do not eat the fruit of our trees for a total of five years after their planting. The fruit of the first three years is forbidden because it is not yet mature and therefore not good to eat. The fruit of the fourth year is the first fruit that is edible and therefore also the earliest fruit that can be offered in the Temple. All fruit grown after we have made the offering to God is ours to eat and enjoy.

Keli Yakar: The author compares the early years of a tree to the early days of Creation. Vegetation was created on the third day, but it was not visible until the fourth day, after the creation of the great bearers of light, the sun, the moon and the stars. To recall the order of Creation, the fruit of the first three years is forbidden; that of the fourth year is brought to the Temple, and that of the fifth year is permitted to all for food and enjoyment.

References:

B. Bava Kamma 101a (see Tosafot); B. Kiddushin 54b; B. Rosh ha-Shanah 9b; B. Berakhot 35a, 36b; B. Ḥullin 121a; B. Pesaḥim 22b; Sifra *Kedoshim;* J. Ma'aser Sheni, Chap. 5; Midrash Tanḥuma, *Kedoshim,* Chap. 14; J. Orlah, Chap. 1, 2; Yad, Hilkhot Ma'akhalot Assurot, Chap. 10; Yad, Hilkhot Ma'aser Sheni, Chap. 9, 10; Sefer ha-Mitzvot (Aseh) 119, (Lo Ta'aseh) 192; Guide of the Perplexed, Part 3, Sec. 26; Sefer Mitzvot Gadol (Lav) 146, (Aseh) 137; Sefer Mitzvot Katan 215, 250; Shulḥan Arukh, Yoreh De'ah, 294; Sefer ha-Ḥinnukh, Mitzvah 246, 247.

THE CORRUPT SON

You shall not eat with the blood (Leviticus 19:26)
If a man has a stubborn and rebellious son (Deuteronomy 21:18)

1. The Rabbis construed the prohibition "you shall not eat with the blood" to refer to the following prohibitions:

a. One must not eat the meat of an animal before life has entirely departed from it.

b. One must not eat the meat of an offering before its blood has been sprinkled as prescribed by biblical law.

c. The family of a criminal who has been executed must not, after his funeral, be given the meal customarily offered to mourners on returning from the burial.

d. Every member of a court of justice that has passed a death sentence must fast the entire day on which the sentence is carried out.

e. The prohibition is a warning against gluttony such as that which characterizes the "stubborn and rebellious son" described in Deuteronomy 21:18–21. This last point is used by Maimonides and many other authorities as a basis for establishing a relationship between the two verses quoted at the head of this page.

2. According to biblical law a "stubborn and rebellious son" *(ben sorer u-moreh)* must be brought to court by his parents for punishment.

3. Who is considered a "stubborn and rebellious son"? Any young man three months past *bar mitzvah* age who steals money from his parents and uses it to buy meat and wine, which he then eats and drinks in excess together with bad companions, is considered a "stubborn and rebellious son." Such unbridled appetite for food and drink should be an indication to the boy's parents that this boy is likely to grow up to become a criminal.

4. The first such offense reported by the parents made the boy subject to the penalty of flogging; if he repeated the offense and was again brought to court by his parents he received the death penalty—execution by stoning.

5. At least 23 members of the Sanhedrin had to be present when such an offender was tried. If one of his parents was lame, blind, or deaf, or if one of his parents was unwilling to have him brought to court, the offender was exempt from the death penalty. This meant, in effect, that the death penalty for a "stubborn and rebellious son" was very rarely carried out.

COMMENTATORS

Maimonides, Ḥinnukh: How does a son become "stubborn and rebellious"? Through the fault of parents who are too permissive and permit him to lead a life of irresponsibility. The prohibition "You shall not eat with the blood" means that you must not permit your children to lead a life which will lead them to crime and thus to their death by execution.

Alshekh: He explains why the Torah insists that parents personally bring their "stubborn and rebellious son" to the court of justice. In this manner, he says, the parents acknowledge that they are to blame for the way in which their son has turned out. No child becomes intractable from one day to the next. The process begins when the child is at a very early age when many parents, unfortunately, tend to view such behavior as "just a phase." This is a mistaken notion, and the parents are now asked to face the fact that they failed their child when he was in the greatest need of their guidance.

Ibn Ezra: He is not prepared to place the burden of responsibility entirely on the child. The son can be justifiably tried and punished for his behavior only if the conduct of his parents themselves has been beyond reproach. If they did not provide a good example for him to emulate, they have no right to bring him to court for "stubborn and rebellious" conduct.

He does not associate the prohibition "You shall not eat with the blood" with the "stubborn and rebellious son" but interprets it as a separate prohibition referring to pagan rituals centering around blood.

Abrabanel: He points out the importance of family background in the development of the child. When one of his parents comes from an inferior background, the child is more vulnerable to bad influences than a child of better stock. It was for this reason that the priesthood was given to the descendants of Aaron instead of the descendants of his brother Moses. The wife of Aaron came from better stock than the wife of Moses, who was a Midianite, her father being Jethro, the priest of Midian.

Abrabanel holds that the "stubborn and rebellious" son not only challenges the mores of his parents, but also defies the sovereignty of God. Furthermore, instead of allowing himself to be taught by his elders, he feels a compulsion to teach them. Such defiance of authority and disrespect for his elders is bound to lead him into a life of crime and make him a threat to society. Consequently, lest he jeopardize the lives of others, the parents are duty bound to turn him over to the court of justice.

References:

B. Sanhedrin 63a, 68a, 68b, 69a, 70a, 71a, 71b, 88b, 107a; B. Makkot 10b; Sifre *Ki Tetze;* J. Sanhedrin, Chap. 8, Halakhah 2; Yad, Hilkhot Mamrim, Chap. 7; Sefer ha-Mitzvot (Lo Ta'aseh) 195; Sefer Mitzvot Gadol (Lav) 220; Sefer ha-Ḥinnukh, Mitzvah 248.

PROHIBITION OF SUPERSTITION

Neither shall you practice divination . . . nor soothsaying (Leviticus 19:26)
Do not turn to hosts nor to familiar spirits (Leviticus 19:31)
There shall not be found among you anyone that makes his son or his daughter pass through fire . . . one who uses divination . . . a soothsayer . . . or an enchanter . . . or a sorcerer (Deuteronomy 18:10)
Or a charmer . . . or one who consults a ghost or a familiar spirit . . . or a necromancer (Deuteronomy 18:11)

Superstition is contrary to Jewish law. The following beliefs and practices are expressly forbidden by biblical laws because they tend to lead one away from faith in God:

a. "Divination"—discovering omens in ordinary occurrences. It is forbidden to say: "The fact that this bread fell from my mouth is an omen that I should not go to the place where I intended to go."

b. "Soothsaying"—making one's plans dependent on the position of the stars.

c. Turning to "ghosts and familiar spirits"—making movements or uttering sounds to pretend that one is in communication with the spirits of the dead: e.g., one is forbidden to put into his mouth the bone of an animal called *yido'a* which is supposed to give a message, or to speak in a deep voice as though from the armpit, making believe that the dead are answering his questions. Anyone who continued to engage in such practices after having received a warning was subject, under biblical law, to the death penalty—execution by stoning.

d. "Witchcraft"—claiming to be able to foretell the future by looking at an object on the ground and then going into a trance. Under biblical law, an individual engaging in this practice was subject to the penalty of flogging.

e. "Sorcery"—The Rabbis defined a sorcerer as one who actually could perform acts that seemed supernatural. Such practices were subject to the death penalty—execution by stoning. One who performed sleight-of-hand tricks was subject to the penalty of flogging.

f. "Charmer"—It was forbidden to pronounce magic formulas, to gather snakes or other creatures in one spot, or to practice the art of a snakecharmer. One who performed such acts was subject to the penalty of flogging.

g. "Necromancy"—to stay in a cemetery, sleeping and going without food, in the hope that a certain dead person will appear to one and answer his questions about the past and future. All who performed such acts were subject to the penalty of flogging.

COMMENTATORS

Naḥmanides: If we seek to gain knowledge of the future, we act counter to the will of God. Heathens may feel that they need to look to astrologers and soothsayers for guidance in their lives, but one who believes in God knows that it is God Who guides the stars and that it makes better sense to believe in Him and to act in accordance with His teachings than to turn to the stars and the dead for advice.

Baḥya ben Asher: Only one who is insecure or mentally disturbed will turn to séances, tea-leaf readings, horoscopes, and the like. Such people will be easy prey for practitioners of these arts, who may take advantage of their blind belief and induce them to commit crimes or immoral acts for their own nefarious purposes. One who has faith in God and His Torah will feel no need to turn to black magic for security.

Maimonides: In an era when black magic was almost universally accepted, Maimonides described sorcery in all its forms as pure nonsense.

Alshekh: There are two kinds of persons that may turn to black magic: One who thinks that God does not concern Himself with the personal cases of individuals, and one who feels that although he has been righteous he has had to suffer a great deal. The former should count his blessings and admit to himself that God does care about each individual person. The latter should stop complaining and instead take stock of his deeds; he may find that his sufferings came upon him because, in fact, his conduct made him unworthy of God's beneficence.

Ḥinnukh: The practice of black magic can drive a man away from true religion. One instance in which a prediction comes true or in which a desired event seems to have come about as a result of witchcraft may be sufficient for one who has no faith in God to come to the conclusion that the pattern of human life is not the result of the will of God but stems from a series of accidents, without purpose or direction. But a Jew who truly believes in the Almighty will place his trust in God. **Radbaz:** There is some validity to sorcery. In the netherworld of darkness, spirits can be induced to enter the bodies of those recently deceased who will then be able to reveal messages. This is done by various incantations and incense-burning procedures.

If these practices are forbidden, why did God permit the Witch of Endor to conjure up the body of the Prophet Samuel? Since she could have induced an impure spirit into the body of Samuel, it was far better that God permit the original spirit of Samuel to return to his body. The Jew, however, was bidden never to hearken to the voices of these impure and contaminated spirits, because this is a fundamental precept in pagan worship.

References:
B. Ḥullin 7b, 95b; B. Berakhot 33b; B. Shabbat 75a, 152a; B. Sanhedrin 65a, 65b, 66a, 67a; B. Pesaḥim 113b; B. Nedarim 32a; J. Shabbat, Chap. 6, Halakhah 9; Chap. 7, Halakhah 2; B. Yevamot 4a; Sifre *Shofetim;* Guide of the Perplexed, Part 3, Sec. 37; Sefer ha-Mitzvot (Lo Ta'aseh) 8, 9, 31, 33, 34, 35, 36, 37, 38; Sefer Mitzvot Gadol (Lav) 36, 37, 38, 39, 51, 52, 53, 54; Sefer Mitzvot Katan 136–143; Shulḥan Arukh, Yoreh De'ah 179; Sefer ha-Ḥinnukh, Mitzvot 249, 250, 255, 256, 510, 511, 512, 513, 514, 515.

NOT SHAVING THE CORNERS OF THE HEAD AND THE BEARD

You shall not round the corners of your heads . . . neither shall you mar the corners of your beard (Leviticus 19:27)

1. It is forbidden for a man to shave the hair from his temples, or to have anyone else do this for him. (According to some authorities, this prohibition applies only to shaving with a hand razor.)

2. It is also forbidden for a man to use a hand razor to shave off his beard. A man who does this, commits five violations: the shaving of hair on the two upper cheekbones, on the two jawbones, and on the chin. A man is permitted to use a hand razor for shaving off his moustache, but the Rabbis caution that this really should not be done.

COMMENTATORS

Maimonides, Ibn Ezra: They explain that shaving one's beard and temples was prohibited because this was a pagan custom.

Baḥya ben Asher: Men were forbidden to shave the corners of their beards because the facial beard was a natural feature that distinguished men from women.

References:

B. Makkot 20b; B. Kiddushin 35b; B. Shabbat 152a; B. Nazir 57b, 59a; Yad, Hilkhot Avodah Zarah, Chap. 12 (see Kesef Mishneh which permits scissors); Sefer ha-Mitzvot (Lo Ta'aseh) 43, 44; Sefer Mitzvot Gadol (Lav) 57, 58; Sefer Mitzvot Katan, 70, 71; Shulḥan Arukh, Yoreh De'ah, 181; Sefer ha-Ḥinnukh, Mitzvot 251, 252.

PROHIBITION OF TATTOOING

You shall not make any cuttings in your flesh for the dead . . . nor imprint any marks upon yourself (Leviticus 19:28)

1. It is forbidden to mutilate one's flesh as a sign of mourning, a custom that was widely practiced by pagans.

2. Tattooing, i.e., making incisions into the skin and inserting colors with indelible dyes or inks, is forbidden. During biblical times individuals who engaged in this practice (i.e., both one who does the tattooing and his "subject" who actively cooperates with him) were subject to the penalty of flogging.

COMMENTATORS

Ḥinnukh: Tattooing was forbidden because of its pagan origin.
Sforno: The only "cutting" of the body permitted by biblical law was circumcision.
Or ha-Ḥayyim: When the Torah speaks about cutting one's flesh, it refers to excessive mourning over the dead. The reference to a tattoo is a general prohibition. Why is this so? Because usually, when a person is deeply grieved over the loss of a dear one, he may be so carried away by his sorrow that he begins to mutilate himself. Though this is unpardonable, it is understandable; but in the case of imprinting marks on one's body this is done deliberately, unattended by any trying circumstances. Hence this is an unreasonable practice.

References:
B. Makkot 21a; B. Kiddushin, 36a; Sifra *Kedoshim,* Chap. 6; Yad, Hilkhot Avodah Zarah, Chap. 12; Sefer ha-Mitzvot (Lo Ta'aseh) 41; Sefer Mitzvot Gadol (Lav) 61; Sefer Mitzvot Katan 72; Shulḥan Arukh, Yoreh De'ah, 180; Sefer ha-Ḥinnukh, Mitzvah 253.

PROPER RESPECT FOR THE SANCTUARY

And reverence My Sanctuary (Leviticus 19:30)

1. Visiting the Temple was not to be a casual activity but a deep emotional experience, for it was only in the Temple that the Jew could attempt to commune with God. Hence, the appropriate mood of a Jew who entered the Temple was to be one of awe and reverence.

2. It was forbidden to enter the Temple Mount wearing shoes, carrying a staff in one's hand, or money in one's pocket. It was also forbidden to expectorate on the floor of the Temple, or to use the Temple grounds as a short-cut to some other destination.

3. One entered the Temple grounds from the right-hand side and departed from the left. One moved toward the exit walking backward, so that one did not turn his back upon the Holy of Holies.

4. The Temple Mount still maintains its original sanctity today and Jews are forbidden to set foot upon it.

5. The Jew should consider the synagogue as a temporary substitute for the ancient Temple and treat it with due awe and reverence.

6. However, there can be no replacement for the vessels and other sacred objects in the Temple. Hence, the *menorah* in a synagogue must not have seven branches like the seven-branched candelabrum of the Sanctuary and of the Temple in Jerusalem.

COMMENTATORS

Maimonides: When a person is moved to awe by the splendor of the Temple, he will become spiritually conditioned to carry out the *mitzvot* of the Torah.

Abrabanel: The *mitzvot* and the Sanctuary are not independent of each other. In one accepts the *mitzvot,* he will then also stand in awe of the Sanctuary wherein rests the Presence of God Who gave the *mitzvot* to us.

References:

B. Yevamot 6b; B. Megillah 28a; B. Berakhot 62b; Sifra *Kedoshim,* Chap. 7; Guide of the Perplexed, Part 3, Sec. 45; Yad, Hilkhot Bet ha-Beḥirah, Chap. 7; Yad, Hilkhot Tefillah, Chap. 11; Sefer ha-Mitzvot (Aseh) 21; Sefer Mitzvot Gadol (Aseh) 164; Sefer Mitzvot Katan 6; Shulḥan Arukh, Oraḥ Ḥayyim, 151; Yoreh De'ah 246; Sefer ha-Ḥinnukh, Mitzvah 254.

RESPECT FOR ELDERS

Then you shall rise up before the hoary head and honor the face of the elder (Leviticus 19:32)

1. The profound respect which the Jew confers upon learned men is evidenced by the interpretation which the Rabbis gave to the biblical verse, "And you shall honor the face of the elder." Not only must we respect one who is older in years, but also one who is our superior in wisdom and learning. Common sense teaches that we must help an old person, Jew or non-Jew, and show him sympathy and consideration in word and deed.

2. How can we show our respect for a wise man? We are not permitted to sit in his seat or contradict his counsel. Even an old man must rise when a sage passes by; but this is not necessary when a gesture of respect is out of place, such as in a bath-house.

3. This is particularly true if the sage is his principal instructor, i.e., the one whom he considers his "master" *(rabbo muvhak)*. He must show him respect and reverence at all times. Should the occasion arise when one has to make a choice between showing respect for one's father or one's teacher, he must show deference to the teacher first, because his father only brought him into this world, but his teacher will bring him to the world to come. When a teacher dies, his disciple must rend his garments in mourning, as he would for a close relative.

COMMENTATORS

Ibn Ezra: If one shows disrespect for the elderly, God will see to it that when he, in turn, becomes old, people will show disrespect for him. "As one sows, so shall he reap."

Alshekh: Young people are prone to think that they get on in the world well enough without the advice of elderly people. The Torah here warns us that, if we take this attitude, God is apt to change circumstances so that we will not be able to cope with difficult situations. By not respecting the counsel of our elders, we deprive ourselves of the sagacious advice that would have helped us out of plights.

Ḥinnukh: Man's purpose in life is to acquire more and more wisdom. It is only through wisdom that he can properly appreciate God and worship Him. An aged man surely acquired a great deal of wisdom from the great number of experiences in his life and is likely to know full well what is right and what is wrong. For this wisdom, he should be respected.

Recanati: The reason why we must revere a sage is that peace in the world can be sustained only by the intelligence of man. This quality is incorporated in the very person of the sage. If the world which God created is to be maintained by the characteristic virtues of the wise man, then, by respecting the sage, we are, indeed, respecting God and His creation.

References:

B. Kiddushin 32b, 33a, 33b; B. Berakhot 28a; B. Shabbat 31b; B. Pesaḥim 113b; B. Yevamot 62b; B. Bava Metzia 33a; B. Makkot 22b; B. Ketubbot 103b; B. Sanhedrin 5a; J. Bikkurim, Chap. 3, Sec. 3; Pirkei Avot, Chap. 6; Zohar, *Kedoshim,* 87b; Yad, Hilkhot Talmud Torah, Chap. 6; Sefer ha-Mitzvot (Aseh) 209; Sefer Mitzvot Gadol (Aseh) 13; Sefer Mitzvot Katan 51; Sefer ha-Ḥinnukh, Mitzvah 257.

JUST WEIGHTS AND MEASURES

You shall do no unrighteousness in judgment, in meteyard, in weight, or in measure (Leviticus 19:35)

Just scales, just weights, a just ephah *and a just* hin, *shall you have. I am the Lord your God who brought you out of the land of Egypt* (Leviticus 19:36)

You shall not have in your bag two kinds of weight (Deuteronomy 25:13)

1. Flagrant thefts of all kinds have already been treated in a previous chapter. The *mitzvot* now under consideration deal with a more subtle kind of deception that not everyone can detect.

2. The Jew is cautioned to be exceedingly careful about the weights he puts on his scales and the yardstick he uses when he measures. Here is an illustration: One who uses a cord for measuring distance should not employ the same one for winter and summer, because the prevailing atmosphere may cause it to shrink or expand. Moreover, in adding up a column of figures one should be meticulous in one's calculations.

3. Weights should be made of materials that cannot rust, because rust adds weight. The buyer will thus receive more than his due.

4. The use of unjust weights is no exception to the general rule that a transgression that can be corrected by restitution does not warrant lashes. Since the deceiver is obligated to make up whatever short weight or measure his customer received, he is exonerated from lashes when he has done so.

5. As a precaution it is forbidden to retain false weights and measures in one's possession, even if they are not to be used.

6. The Rabbis were so critical of a person who used false weights and measures that they insisted that this was more blameworthy than incest and immorality. In view of the fact that God brought the Children of Israel out of Egypt in order to teach the world a lesson in honesty and integrity, it follows that a Jew who uses false weights and measures in dealing with either Jew or Gentile denies the lesson of the Exodus.

COMMENTATORS

Ibn Ezra: It is a known truth that the walls of civilization will remain intact only if true justice prevails; they will crumble when justice is perverted.

Or ha-Ḥayyim: He believes that the principle behind the injustice of false weights applies to all kinds of deceptions.

Ba'al ha-Turim: He who violates the law of just weights is considered

to be in rebellion against the entire body of *mitzvot*. One cannot pretend to serve God and, at the same time, deceive one's fellow man.
Alshekh: According to tradition, on Rosh ha-Shanah God decides how much a man's income will be for the year. By using false weights, a man unfairly increases his income and thus interferes with God's plans.
Abrabanel: When God instructed the children of Israel concerning just weights, he admonished them (Leviticus 19:36) to recall their bondage in Egypt. This was purposely done to underscore the true concept of freedom. Freedom must be equated with law and justice, not with anarchy and injustice. A person cannot be allowed to set his own standards of right and wrong in his dealings with his fellow man.
Recanati: For scales to be accurate, both parts must be perfectly parallel. So must it be with man who must be well-balanced and not go to extremes, but remain on the middle road.

References:
B. Bava Batra 88b, 89b (see Tosafot), 90a; B. Bava Metzia 49b, 61b; Sifre *Ki Tetze;* J. Bava Batra, Chap. 5, Halakhah 11; Yad, Hilkhot Genevah, Chap. 7, 8; Sefer ha-Mitzvot (Aseh) 208, (Lo Ta'aseh) 271, 272; Sefer Mitzvot Gadol (Aseh) 72, (Lav) 151, 152; Sefer Mitzvot Katan 264; Shulḥan Arukh, Ḥoshen Mishpat, 231; Sefer ha-Ḥinnukh, Mitzvot 258, 259, 602.

ADOPTING THE CUSTOMS OF OTHER NATIONS

And you shall not walk in the customs of the nations (Leviticus 20:23)

1. There is a uniqueness and individuality about the Jewish people. This is not only proclaimed by the Jew, but is acclaimed by the non-Jew as well. Jewish concepts and teaching, religion and language, stand in a class by themselves. A man may be a citizen of the world, but his character, mores, and dedication will be easily recognizable as being Jewish. The Torah goes further. It demands of the Jew that he be different also in garb and in appearance. Imitating the non-Jew in demeanor, deportment, and dress is termed *ḥukkat ha-goyim,* an act forbidden and punishable with lashes.

2. It must be clearly understood that the principle of *ḥukkat ha-goyim* cannot be applied to every facet of life. For example: if non-Jews live in apartment houses, it does not preclude a Jew from living in an apartment house. What is implied in *ḥukkat ha-goyim* is that we are not to learn or emulate their practices if such are contrary to the spirit and life of the Jew, i.e., if such practices are connected with their religion or are mere purposeless customs with no rational motive.

COMMENTATORS

Recanati: He offers two reasons for this prohibition:

1. Most of the customs of other nations have religious origins. By emulating them we may automatically introduce alien practices and beliefs into our lives, whereas we were intended to be different from the other nations.
2. In our daily prayers, we affirm *"asher kiddeshanu be-mitzvotav,"* "who made us holy through the institution of *mitzvot*." Our lives are guided by *mitzvot;* by accepting the customs of Gentiles, we negate this article of faith.

Ḥizzekuni: Not only is the Jew restrained from following the religious and national customs of the Gentiles, but he is also asked not to follow the customs of individual Gentiles. This may be based on the premise that many national practices begin on the initiative of an individual.

References:

B. Sanhedrin 52b; B. Ḥullin 41b; B. Sotah 49a–b; J. Avodah Zarah, Chap. 11, Sec. 7; Sefer ha-Mitzvot (Lo Ta'aseh) 30; Sefer Mitzvot Gadol (Lav) 50; Shulḥan Arukh, Yoreh De'ah, 178; Sefer ha-Ḥinnukh, Mitzvah 262.

CIRCUMSTANCES IN WHICH A PRIEST MAY RENDER HIMSELF RITUALLY UNCLEAN

There shall none defile himself for the dead among his people (Leviticus 21:1)
For her may he defile himself (Leviticus 21:3)
Neither shall he go to any dead body . . . neither defile himself for his father or for his mother (Leviticus 21:11)

1. In Jewish law and practice, mourning involves the following stages. On the day of the death and until burial has taken place the mourners are called *onenim.* During this period they are forbidden by biblical law to eat meat, drink wine, or (in the case of males) put on *tefillin.* Immediately after the interment—or, when a mourner is unable to attend it, as soon as he hears that it has been completed—it is necessary to make the *keriah:* this is a rent in the garment, at least one handbreadth long, on the left side when mourning for a parent but on the right for any other relative. Now begins the second phase of mourning, the *shivah,* the seven-day period instituted by rabbinical ordinance, during which mourners are forbidden to wash themselves, to sit on a chair, or to wear leather shoes. If they are mourning the death of a parent, they must make a rent on any change of clothing. The *shivah* is followed by *sheloshim,* which lasts until the thirtieth day after death; throughout this time it is forbidden to shave or have the hair cut. Finally, when mourning for a parent, there is a further period of ten months during which all festive gatherings are avoided and sons recite the *kaddish* at daily prayer.

2. It is obligatory upon everyone to mourn the death of a father, mother, brother, sister, son, daughter, and wife.

3. Although a Priest is enjoined to avoid all contacts with persons or objects that defile, he, too, is obligated to supervise and perform the preparations necessary for the seven close relatives mentioned above who have died, although he knows that by thus coming in contact with them, he will defile himself. Should he wittingly defile himself by a corpse other than these except a *met mitzvah* (see below), he is subject to the penalty of lashes.

4. A High Priest is not permitted to defile himself by touching or by even being under the same roof with the corpse of his mother or father. The sanctity of his office denies him the right to indulge in these sentimental attachments; but there is one exception. This is a *met mitzvah,* an unattended corpse. A High Priest walking along the road by himself who has found a corpse with no one else to attend to the needs for burial, is obliged to make the necessary arrangements, even though he will thus defile himself.

COMMENTATORS

Maimonides: He comments on the obvious question why the Ordinary Priest is allowed to defile himself in the case of the death of a near relative, but not in the case of a stranger. After all, the impurity of any dead body is alike, no matter how near or distantly related the deceased may have been to him. He answers that, although there is a prohibition against defilement, there is also the *mitzvah* of *avelut,* mourning and grieving after the deceased. Since there is an extremely important religious and psychological value to mourning, the Ordinary Priest must not be deprived of the benefit of that *mitzvah* when a near relation passes away.
Naḥmanides: Every Ordinary Priest is a potential High Priest who is absolutely forbidden to make contact with any deceased. To condition himself for this possibility, the Priest was allowed to contaminate himself only when a close relation passed on, but not when a stranger died.
Abrabanel: As soon as the soul leaves the body, the body becomes impure and contaminating. In the case of the death of strangers, there is no need for the Priest to attend to the funeral needs, since the family of the deceased will take care of the matter. In the case of the close relatives of a Priest, however, he is responsible to his family to arrange for the funeral because of his superior knowledge of the rules for burial.
Keli Yakar, Ḥinnukh: Why is the Ordinary Priest allowed to defile himself when the death is in his immediate family while the High Priest is not allowed to become defiled even then? The answer is: because the High Priest represents the highest concentration of holiness on earth. The Ordinary Priest is holier than the layman but is not as holy as the High Priest from whom he received the right to be a Priest. Hence, whereas the Ordinary Priest was more restricted than the Israelite,

he was not restrained, as was the High Priest, from all contact with the dead.

Radbaz: He continues the explanation of Maimonides and elaborates upon the significance of the *shivah*. The *shivah* is intended to create an atmosphere where man will be stirred to think in depth about life and death. What has he to show for himself? What has he achieved in life? In what direction will his deeds lead him? All these questions, which must be answered honestly, will lead him to repentance and contrition. Man is bidden to grieve in order to attain those emotions of repentance. He must never assume the attitude that because death is inevitable grief is unnecessary. It is true that no one can escape death, but one can never be sure that life would not have been prolonged had it not been for his transgressions. Can one be sure that he, the mourner, is not curtailing the years of his life because of his sins? These thoughts and their implications are conducive to repentance, humility, and contrition.

The Priest was also obliged to grieve for his close relatives so that he, too, could cleanse himself of the sins that he may have done. Radbaz continues his analysis of the mourning period by projecting the thought that when one mourns a father, for example, he should not selfishly grieve and be saddened because someone dear to him has passed on. Rather, he mourns and bemoans an individual who had the potential to make further substantial contributions to life but whose life was terminated because God was somehow dissatisfied with something in him. In other words, the period of mourning is not so much for the dead as for the living. It is the latter who must take to heart, when comforting mourners, the lessons which the *shivah* seeks to impart.

References:

B. Sotah 23b; B. Yevamot 60a, 114a; B. Nazir 42b, 43a, 43b; B. Zevaḥim 100a; B. Sanhedrin 4a; B. Mo'ed Katan 14b; Midrash Tanḥuma, *Emor,* Chap. 3; Sifra *Emor,* Chap. 1, Sec. 4, 12; Yad, Hilkhot Evel, Chap. 3, Sec. 7; Sefer ha-Mitzvot (Aseh) 37, (Lo Ta'aseh) 166, 167, 168; Sefer Mitzvot Gadol (Aseh) 58, (Lav) 234, 235, 236, 237; Shulḥan Arukh, Yoreh De'ah, 369–374; Sefer Mitzvot Katan 97; Sefer ha-Ḥinnukh, Mitzvot 263, 264, 270, 271.

PROHIBITION AGAINST THE PRIEST'S PROFANING THE NAME OF GOD

And not profane the Name of their God (Leviticus 21:6)
And that they profane not My Holy Name (Leviticus 22:2)

1. A Priest served in the Temple only by virtue of the fact that he was God's appointee to that office. Any deviation in his ministrations was a defamation of God. The Priest was commanded to follow certain rules and regulations; the violation of these in the course of his duty was deserving of censure and punishment.

2. A Priest became defiled, for example, when he touched a corpse. If he continued to carry out his functions in the Temple, he was to be punished. A defiled Priest who ministered in the Temple grounds, was punished with Divine punishment *(mitah bi-ydei shamayim)* and lashes.

3. Customarily, it was the court that decided and administered the lashes. In this case, however, the defiled Priest may be killed by his fellow Priests; they need not wait for a judicial decree.

4. It was also considered a profanation of God's Name if a Priest who had become defiled, after immersion in the *mikveh* (the first stage in his purification), hastened to perform his duties in the Sanctuary without waiting for sunset, when his purification came into effect. (During this intervening period he was called *tevul yom.*) Such behavior was punished by lashes and was also subject to Divine punishment.

5. If a Priest, unaware of his defilement, performed his duties but later became aware that he was defiled, all offerings he had brought during this period of ignorance were disqualified.

COMMENTATORS

Ḥinnukh: Serving in the Temple while in a defiled state is a profanation of God's Name. God alone knows the reason why the defilement of man lasts only until sunset.

The consensus of opinion among commentators is that the Priest is not so invulnerable that he cannot do any wrong. He does not sit in judgment over his fellow-Jew; his mandate is only to serve as emissary of the people of Israel to their God. In this manner the Priests glorify the Name of God. The Israelite expects the Priest to represent him with all his talents. Under these circumstances, when a Priest in the Temple is defiled, he is not fulfilling the mandate of the people and the Name of God is thus profaned.

References:
B. Sanhedrin 51b, 83b; B. Zevaḥim 17a, 45b; Yad, Hilkhot Bi'at Mikdash, Chap. 4, 9; Sefer ha-Mitzvot (Lo Ta'aseh) 75, 76; Sefer Mitzvot Gadol (Lav) 305, 306; Sefer ha-Ḥinnukh, Mitzvot 265, 278.

WOMEN WHOM A HIGH PRIEST MAY NOT MARRY

A woman that is a harlot, or profaned, they shall not take . . .Neither shall he marry a divorced woman, for he is holy unto his God (Leviticus 21:7)
And he shall take a wife in her virginity (Leviticus 21:13)
He shall not take a widow or one divorced, or a profaned woman or a harlot (Leviticus 21:14)
And he shall not profane his seed among his people (Leviticus 21:15)

1. If a Priest is to admonish and castigate the sinner and be the one to lead the transgressor back to repentance, then he himself must lead an exemplary life, free of all moral taint. His standards must be of the highest, with never a cloud of suspicion suspended over his head.

2. There are three types of women whom the Torah forbids a Priest to marry: *gerushah* (divorcee), *ḥallalah* (a profaned woman), and *zonah* (a harlot). *Gerushah* refers to a woman who was divorced. This includes even the divorced wife of the Priest who wants to take his wife back after having divorced her. The Rabbis added the *ḥalutzah,* a woman who was ritually freed by her husband's childless brother. This law is also applicable in modern times. *Ḥallalah* is the offspring of a Priest and a woman he was not permitted to marry. *Zonah* is a harlot. The concept of harlot here intended is not the common concept of a woman who solicits in the streets. When we speak here of a Priest being forbidden to marry a harlot, we also include a convert, a prostitute, and, according to some authorities, a woman who had relations with a *ḥallal.* All these come under the inclusive definition of "harlot" as it pertains to a Priest.

3. In addition to the women mentioned above, a High Priest was barred from marrying a widow or a woman whose virginity was destroyed in a way other than by having had sexual intercourse.

4. While there is no office of High Priest, the laws appertaining to the Ordinary Priest obtain. They are not permitted to marry divorcees, converts, or *ḥalutzot*. If a Priest enters into any one of these forbidden marriages, he must divorce his wife immediately.

COMMENTATORS

Ba'al ha-Turim: Genealogically speaking, a Priest *(Kohen)* can never change his identity. His father was a Priest and his sons will also be Priests; but if he marries a woman who is forbidden to him by the Torah, he casts a cloud over his suitability for this exalted position. When a Priest does contract a forbidden marriage, we are faced with a situation where the man is genetically a Priest, yet shows every indication of being unsuitable for this position.

Abrabanel: He gives two possible interpretations of the verse "For he is holy unto God":

1. This applies to the Priest. Since he is holy to God, he is forbidden to marry these women.

b. This applies to the husband who divorced the woman whom the Priest wants to marry. Since the husband is a God-fearing and an honorable man, he would not divorce his wife unless he had valid reasons for doing so. Why should a Priest marry a woman who deserved to be divorced?

Ibn Ezra: Even a virgin who is converted to Judaism is not allowed to marry a Priest.

Naḥmanides: A High Priest cannot say that, since he may not marry the woman he desires, he will not marry at all. Just as he is commanded not to marry certain women, so is he commanded to marry a virgin.

Ḥinnukh: The life of the High Priest embodies the pursuit of perfection. He must strive in every way to attain this goal and dare not compromise, or be satisfied with less than the total truth. Even in the private area of sexual relations, he must not become subject to a situation that can have an element of dishonesty or an absence of perfection. Any woman who has had sexual relations previously, such as a widow or a divorcee, cannot confer perfect love on her new husband. She will unavoidably retain memories of the man with whom she had previously lived. Only a virgin can come to her husband with true, perfect love and loyalty.

Recanati: He takes a most pragmatic attitude toward the psychological constitution of the Priest. In fact, there is no difference between the sex urge of a layman and of a Priest. At the most unexpected times, a man will think of his intimate relations with his wife. The Priest may find himself thinking along these lines even during his ministrations in the Temple. Hence, if his wife is not above reproach, as in the case of a divorcee, it will affect the high moral standards that are expected of the Priest during the service. For this same reason, a High Priest was even more restricted in his choice of a wife.

References:

B. Horayot 11b, 12b; B. Kiddushin 77a, 77b, 78a; B. Yevamot 20a, 32b, 52a, 54a, 59a, 59b, 61a, 61b, 69a, 81a, 84a, 92a; J. Horayot, Chap. 3, Halakhah 2; J. Yevamot, Chap. 6, Halakhah 2; Yad, Hilkhot Issurei Bi'ah, Chap. 17, 18, 19; Sefer ha-Mitzvot (Aseh) 38, (Lo Ta'aseh) 158, 159, 160, 161, 162; Sefer Mitzvot Gadol (Aseh) 57, (Lav) 121, 122, 123, 124, 125; Sefer Mitzvot Katan 190, 191; Shulḥan Arukh, Even ha-Ezer, 6; Sefer ha-Ḥinnukh, Mitzvot 266, 267, 268, 272, 273, 274.

THE HOLINESS OF THE PRIEST

You shall therefore, sanctify him (Leviticus 21:8)

1. A Priest must be respectfully elevated to a higher status than that of the Jewish layman. The Priest's dignity and image of superiority demand that we accord him due honor and respect. In an open forum, the Priest should be given the right to speak first. At the reading of the Torah the Priest should be the one to be called to read first. Similarly, if a Priest divides anything with a non-Priest, the Priest is given first choice as a matter of courtesy. Many Rabbis maintained that if the Priest wishes to surrender his prerogatives of his own choice and free will, the layman is not bound to accord him priestly privileges.

COMMENTATORS

Ibn Ezra, Naḥmanides, Ḥinnukh: The Priest is the duly appointed representative of God and is His liaison officer with the masses. Accordingly, it is our duty to honor and respect him in word and deed because through him we are blessed, and by showing respect to him we show respect to God.

Or ha-Ḥayyim: He subscribes to the interpretation that if a Priest behaves in an unbeseeming manner, then "You shall keep him holy." In other words, we must admonish and punish him until he returns to a proper way of life, because the people are always in need of religious functionaries. The question that remains is: How does one force a Priest to be holy, when he does not wish to be so? Actually, we are not asking one who never was religious to take on suddenly the life of religion against his wishes; this would, indeed, be very difficult. But the Priest, who for a long time was happy in his sacerdotal functions but who now has either out of sheer convenience or spite disqualified himself, should be made to feel the wrath of the people. "You shall keep him holy" means that we should compel him to remain sanctified, untouched by sordid and ignoble passions.

References:

B. Gittin 59b; B. Yevamot 88b; B. Nedarim 62a; J. Berakhot, Chap. 8, Halakhah 4; Sifra *Emor;* Yad, Hilkhot Kelei ha-Mikdash, Chap. 4; Sefer ha-Mitzvot (Aseh)

32; Sefer Mitzvot Gadol (Aseh) 171; Shulḥan Arukh, Oraḥ Ḥayyim, 135, 201; Sefer ha-Ḥinnukh, Mitzvah 269.

THE NEED FOR THE PHYSICAL PERFECTION OF THE PRIEST

Whosoever he be of your seed in their generations that has a blemish, let him not approach to offer the bread of his God (Leviticus 21:17)
For whatsoever man he be that has a blemish, he shall not approach (Leviticus 21:18)
Only unto the veil may he not enter, nor come near the altar (Leviticus 21:23)

1. Superficially, one may think that it is unfair to disqualify a Priest, who has had the misfortune to be born with a physical handicap or who has been temporarily incapacitated. Upon clear analysis, however, one must concede that a Priest with a visible blemish cannot serve with the same psychological fervor and physical agility as one who is free from any defect.

2. The Talmud enumerates 142 imperfections that disqualify a Priest. Fifty of these are prevalent both in man and in animal. If a Priest possessed any one of them, the offering at which he officiated would be rendered invalid and the Priest was given lashes. Ninety of these defects prevail in man, but not in animals. If a Priest performed his service while afflicted with such a defect, the offering was acceptable but the Priest was punished with lashes. There were two blemishes—eyelashes that had fallen off and that of being toothless—that did not disqualify either the offering or the Priest; but the Priest possessing these two defects should not in the first instance undertake to officiate at a sacrifice.

3. Permanent disqualifications included broken limbs; temporary defects were superficial ones such as a scab. The latter debarred the Priest from carrying out his functions as long as they persisted. An internal defect, such as the absence of a kidney, did not disqualify the Priest from serving. A Priest afflicted with any defect, permanent or temporary, was not only disqualified from taking any part in the sacrificial service but was also precluded from entering certain parts of the Temple which were invested with a special degree of sanctity, i.e., the *heikhal* and the area between the altar and the *ulam*. This last rule is, according to Maimonides, a biblical prohibition; Naḥmanides describes it as a rabbinic ordinance.

COMMENTATORS

Abrabanel: The only place where we may hope for perfection is in the House of God—the symbol of perfection. Everything and everyone involved in the service of the Temple should be commensurately perfect. A Priest who has a physical defect is not perfect and represents a clash with the perfection in the Temple. The Priest cannot say that he is entitled to function as Priest because of his parentage alone. Personal appearance and physical wholeness are important and determine whether or not he is entitled to function as a Priest.
Ḥinnukh: The author also considers the psychological implications of a physically handicapped Priest. The ordinary person tends to lose confidence in a leader who is physically imperfect and requires assistance. When one loses this confidence in the Priest, the whole concept of perfection in the Temple is demolished.
Keli Yakar, Radbaz: They agree with Maimonides that a person's physical actions reflects his spiritual stance. When a Priest is physically defective, it is indicative that he is also spiritually defective. Such a Priest has no place in a Temple which represents spiritual perfection.

References:
B. Bekhorot 38a, 41a, 43a, 43b, 44a, 44b, 45a; B. Ḥullin 24b; B. Eruvin 105a; B. Kiddushin 66b; B. Zevaḥim 98b; Sifra *Emor;* Yad, Hilkhot Bi'at Mikdash, Chap. 6; Sefer ha-Mitzvot (Lo Ta'aseh) 69, 70, 71; Sefer Mitzvot Gadol (Lav) 307, 308; Sefer ha-Ḥinnukh, Mitzvot 275, 276, 277.

THOSE PERMITTED TO EAT OF THE TITHES

Of the hallowed things shall he not eat, until he be clean (Leviticus 22:4)
One who is not a Priest shall not eat of the holy thing (Leviticus 22:10)
A tenant of a Priest, or a hired servant, shall not eat of the holy thing (Leviticus 22:10)
But if a Priest's daughter be married unto a common man, she shall not eat of that which is set apart from the holy things (Leviticus 22:12)

1. The Priests permitted to partake of the tithes and offerings brought to the Temple were those who were ritually clean, physically sound, and mentally alert. Only those possessing these qualifications were granted the rights concomitant with the holy food; others who lacked even one of these qualities were disqualified.

2. In the *mitzvot* under consideration the Torah distinguishes those who may from those who may not partake of *terumah*. (The Bible does not specify any minimum quantity, but the Rabbis mention one-fortieth of the produce as the contribution of a generous man, one-fiftieth from the average man, and one-sixtieth as the amount given by a parsimonious person.) A ritually unclean Priest was forbidden to eat *terumah*.

3. It goes without saying that one who had no association with the priesthood whatsoever was debarred from partaking of *terumah*. Even the hired servant of a Priest was forbidden to share in the *terumah* of his master. A Canaanite slave was permitted to eat of the *terumah,* the reason being that the Priest owned the body of the slave and accepted him as part of the household whereas a hireling did not become a chattel, since he was, in a certain measure, independent. A stranger who partook of the *terumah* was subject to the death penalty by the hand of God.

4. An uncircumcised Priest was forbidden to partake of the *terumah*. While this may appear an unlikely contingency, yet it is possible, because, according to Jewish law, one whose older brothers had died as a result of circumcision was exempt from being circumcised. Such violation on the part of the uncircumcised Priest resulted in the penalty of lashes.

5. The whole of the priestly clan was allowed to partake of *terumah*; but a woman belonging to it who had illicit sex relations and had become a harlot and a *ḥallalah* was barred from *terumah*. If she legitimately married an Israelite, she was prohibited from sharing those portions of an offering donated to the Priest. If she became divorced from her husband, or was widowed and left without living issue, she was permitted to eat of the *terumah*, but of no other holy food.

COMMENTATORS

Ḥinnukh: While these laws relate primarily to the Priest, they apply to all Jews. One must approach the Sanctuary with the utmost awe, respect, and serenity and not with callous indifference. Hence the Priest may not feed a hired stranger from the tithes he receives because this servant is a total stranger who happens to be working for him and is not a recognized member of his household. Furthermore, a Priest who for any valid or even invalid reason cannot measure up to the physical and spiritual requirements of his office is not entitled to eat of the holy things.

References:

B. Yevamot 68a, 68b, 70a, 70b, 74a; B. Sanhedrin 51a, 83b, 84a; J. Bikkurim, Chap. 2, Halakhah 1; Mishnayyot, Terumot, Chap. 7, Ḥallah, Chap. 1, Bikkurim, Chap. 2; B. Sotah 48a; Sifra *Emor;* Yad, Hilkhot Terumot; Sefer ha-Mitzvot (Lo Ta'aseh) 133, 134, 135; Sefer Mitzvot Gadol (Lav) 254, 255, 256, 257, 258; Shulḥan Arukh, Yoreh De'ah, 331; Sefer ha-Ḥinnukh, Mitzvot 279, 280, 281, 282.

THE PROFANATION OF SANCTIFIED THINGS

And they shall not profane the hallowed things of the Children of Israel (Leviticus 22:15)

1. To review the order of the tithes: every year the Jew was expected to give *terumah gedolah*—approximately two percent of his produce—to the Priest. From what remained, he presented a tenth to the Levite. This was called *ma'aser rishon*. Simultaneously, he assigned one tenth *(ma'aser sheni)* which he took to Jerusalem. This was observed on the first, second, fourth and fifth years of the seven-year cycle. In the third and sixth years, he replaced *ma'aser sheni* with *ma'aser ani,* tithes for the poor. The Levite donated to the Priest *terumat ma'aser*—one tenth of the *ma'aser rishon.*

2. Produce from which the Levite's and the Priest's portions had not yet been separated was called *tevel.* If a layman, or even a Levite, ate any food which was still in the state of *tevel*, he was subject to Divine punishment.

COMMENTATORS

Abrabanel: How can sanctified produce be profaned? Profanation occurs when the Priest consigns the untithed produce due to him to strangers not qualified to partake of and benefit from tithes. One might argue: Since the produce is his, why shouldn't he be allowed to do what he wishes with it? The answer is that, when an Israelite presents the Priest with a tithe, he does so out of respect and reverence and in a spirit of holiness, with sentiments prompted by devotion. It would be a disappointment to him to find the Priest failing to treat this sanctified produce with the reverence with which it was given to him.

References:

B. Sanhedrin 83a; B. Yevamot 86a; B. Niddah 32a; B. Zevaḥim 46b; B. Ḥullin 130b; B. Makkot 13a, 17a; B. Sotah 48a; J. Demai, Chap. 6, Halakhah 2; Yad, Hilkhot Ma'akhalot Assurot, Chap. 10; Sefer ha-Mitzvot (Lo Ta'aseh) 153; Sefer Mitzvot Gadol (Lav) 147; Shulḥan Arukh, Yoreh De'ah, 331; Sefer ha-Ḥinnukh, Mitzvah 284; Midrash Rabbah, *Ḥayyei Sarah,* Chap. 60, Sec. 10.

THE UNBLEMISHED SACRIFICE

Everything that has a blemish, shall you not bring near (Leviticus 22:20)
It shall be perfect to be accepted (Leviticus 22:21)
No blemish shall there be therein (Leviticus 22:21)
An offering by fire shall you not bring of them (Leviticus 22:22)
You shall not offer unto the Lord (Leviticus 22:24)
Neither from the hand of a foreigner shall you offer the bread of your God of any of these (Leviticus 22:25)
You shall not sacrifice unto the Lord your God an ox or a sheep wherein is a blemish (Deuteronomy 17:1)

1. The effort to find an animal perfect in appearance, coupled with the knowledge that something perfect was being brought to the Temple; the anticipation that he, the sinner, would emerge from the Temple cleansed and purified—all these were integral parts of the general experience both of the layman and of the Priest at the altar.

2. The offering had first to be chosen. Then it had to be designated as an offering; finally, it had to be sacrificed. Only the choicest and most perfect animals were considered as fit for sacrifices.

3. He who sacrificed a blemished animal received lashes. If he merely designated a defective animal as an offering, prior to actually offering it on the altar, he would receive lashes; but the animal was considered sanctified. Since he could not sacrifice an imperfect animal, he was obliged to redeem the designated offering with money. With the proceeds, he had to buy a perfect animal.

4. The laws of perfection were followed right through to the sprinkling of the blood and the burning of the entrails. In other words, if one designated, sacrificed, spilled of the blood, and burned the entrails of a defective animal, he received 39 lashes, four times. Some question the giving of lashes for merely designating an animal improperly for sacrifice, since it does not amount to an action. The Torah does not prescribe punishment of lashes for a mere thought or intention.

5. In Jewish law, an animal had to go through the processes of *sheḥitah* and *bedikah* before it was ready for consumption. *Sheḥitah* refers to the proper ritual slaughtering by severing the gullet and windpipe. *Bedikah* means the internal examination of the animal. If the animal was found perfect in every aspect after the process of *sheḥitah* but was discovered to be *terefah* owing to an internal defect, the offering was disqualified and the animal burned.

6. All the laws pertaining to the perfection of animals also apply to the ancillary offerings such as wines, oils, flour, wood, and incense that were involved with the principal offering; hence, moldy flour was disqualified.

7. Basing his premise on these laws, Maimonides exhorts the Jew to present his best efforts in any phase of philanthropic action. If one feeds a hungry person he should give him the best food; if he clothes the naked, the clothes should be the finest of his own wardrobe. Finally, if he intends to build a house of worship, it should not be less impressive than his own home, even rivalling and excelling it in spaciousness and elegance.

COMMENTATORS

Naḥmanides: The perfection of this sacrifice must be not only in the robust, physical health of the animal, but also in the thoughts of those present at the sacrifice. Perfection is an all-inclusive term. If at the time of the actual sacrifice the donor has some mental reservations, intending to partake of the meat in an area forbidden because of its being beyond the confines of the Temple, the sacrifice is disqualified as not being perfect in all the necessary details.

Sforno, Ba'al ha-Turim: If the animal is castrated, even though this imperfection is not visibly manifest, the fact that the animal has lost the ability to procreate constitutes an imperfection.

Ḥinnukh: A blemished sacrifice reflects the imperfect motivation of the donor in his act of worship. A person who compromises with his conscience and brings an imperfect animal approaches God with motives less than perfect.

Abrabanel: The worship of God through sacrifices can be performed only by Jews who possess true Jewish, religious concepts. A foreigner is suspect of a lack of the true ideology in regard to sacrifices; he is, therefore, not allowed to offer them.

Or ha-Ḥayyim: He questions the use of the future tense in Deuteronomy 17:1. He claims that the verse speaks of a blemish destined to appear in the future; the blemish may be a passing one, not apparent at the time of the inspection. Or there might be some internal disorder that would necessitate surgery, which would then cause a blemish in the future. The text warns that even a blemish that does not exist but is bound to appear sooner or later disqualifies the animal as a sacrificial offering.

References:

B. Temurah 6b, 7a, 8a, 8b; B. Bekhorot 33b, 38a, 39a, 40a, 41a; B. Menaḥot 56b, 64a; B. Yoma 63b; Sifra *Emor;* Sifre *Shoftim;* Yad, Issurei Mizbe'aḥ, Chap. 1, 2, 3; Sefer ha-Mitzvot (Aseh) 61, (Lo Ta'aseh) 91, 92, 93, 94, 95, 96, 97; Sefer Mitzvot Gadol (Aseh) 176, (Lav) 310, 311, 312, 313, 314, 315; Sefer Mitzvot Katan 254; Sefer ha-Ḥinnukh, Mitzvot 285, 286, 287, 288, 289, 292.

PROHIBITION OF CASTRATION

Neither shall you do thus in your land (Leviticus 22:24)

1. The reason why the practice of euthanasia is not allowed and why we are forbidden to employ contraceptives or resort to unwarranted abortions is because these usurp the prerogatives of God. This applies also to castration. It is God's choice to grant or to deny offspring to his creatures; it is not within the province of man to make so momentous a decision.

2. It is forbidden to emasculate either a human being or an animal. He who commits this sin, is subject to the penalty of lashes.

3. Since the Torah warns against destroying the birth potential, the Rabbis interpret this prohibition to include any medical prophylactic that would achieve the same result. In view of the fact that the commandment "to be fruitful" applies only to the male of the human species, a woman may drink a "cup of *ikarin*" which would prevent her from conceiving.

COMMENTATORS

Ḥinnukh, Abrabanel, Ibn Ezra: The purpose of the sexual act, both in man and among the lower animals is, according to the Divine plan, the perpetuation of the species. Man therefore has no right to allow himself to be castrated or to castrate animals; for by so doing, he is interfering with God's design. Ibn Ezra adds that man must not change any of the physical features with which God has endowed His creatures.

Recanati: When a person permits himself to be castrated or sterilized, he knows that he can never again beget children. If he, nonetheless, undergoes this operation, it becomes apparent that he must be so dissatisfied with the world that he does not care if it ceases to continue. The truth is, however, that there is so much good and beauty in the world for man to enjoy that it would be a disaster if it did terminate. God meant man to enjoy the world; by becoming castrated or sterilized, man demonstrates that he does not enjoy or appreciate what God has given him.

References:
B. Sanhedrin, 70a; B. Kiddushin 25b; B. Shabbat 110b, 111a; B. Ḥagigah 14b; B. Bava Metzia 90b; Yad, Hilkhot Issurei Bi'ah, Chap. 16; Sefer ha-Mitzvot (Lo Ta'aseh) 361; Sefer Mitzvot Gadol (Lav) 120; Sefer Mitzvot Katan 166; Shulḥan Arukh, Even ha-Ezer, 5; Sefer ha-Ḥinnukh, Mitzvah 291.

A SACRIFICIAL ANIMAL MUST BE AT LEAST EIGHT DAYS OLD

But from the eighth day and thenceforth, it may be accepted for an offering made by fire unto the Lord (Leviticus 22:27)

1. In keeping with the central theme of perfection in matters pertaining to the Temple worship, the Torah forbids a calf less than eight days old to be brought as a sacrifice, because it takes that period of time to determine whether the young animal would have been sufficiently strong and healthy to survive the initial stages of life.

2. If a person brings an offering of a calf younger than eight days as a sacrifice, the offering is unacceptable.

3. Parenthetically, the law states that a calf born of a Caesarean section *(yotze dofen)* and a *ben pikuaḥ* (a calf extracted after its mother was slaughtered) are both regarded as unacceptable offerings.

COMMENTATORS

Ḥinnukh: Just as one who has undertaken a deed must execute it to completion, so must the preparatory phases to that deed also have the characteristics of completeness. Hence, when a person brings a sacrifice to God, the offering itself must be of a complete nature. Until an animal has lived eight days, it has not yet met the requirements of completeness. No one can present it as a gift, or use it for barter.

Maimonides: Any animal which is offered as a sacrifice must have a substantial value. An animal less than eight days old, being weak and helpless, has no appreciable value. Its survival is not yet regarded as certain.

Ba'al ha-Turim: He details the reasons given by the Talmud why an animal in the first week of life is unacceptable as a sacrifice. If offered on the first day it might be regarded as symbolic of the creation of Heaven and Earth; on the second it might be considered as representing the firmament, which was created on the second day; on the third it might be intended as an offering to the oceans and the dry land; on the fourth day it could represent a tribute to the sun and the moon; on the fifth day it might be dedicated to the animals which God created on the fifth day; on the sixth day it might commemorate the creation of man. Hence it was necessary to allow these six days and the day of rest (the Sabbath) to elapse before offering the newly-born animal to God.

Ḥizzekuni: Anyone in a state of impurity or defilement, e.g., a leper or one who had been in contact with a corpse, had to wait seven days before entering the Sanctuary. The newly-born animal, likewise, having emerged from a state of impurity, could be brought to the Temple only after a like period had expired.

Abrabanel: An animal that is newly-born is not certain to survive and requires its mother's warmth and care in order to sustain it. It acquires an independent existence within the first eight days of its life.

Keli Yakar: The author takes the opposite view from that advanced by Abrabanel. The moment an animal is born, it possesses the full faculties that the adult of the species has and there is no further development, except in size. If this is so, why must one wait eight days before being permitted to use it as an offering? The answer: because while it is true that seven is a key number in the Jewish religion (Sabbath, *Shemittah,* Jubilee) there is another favored number—eight. Circumcision takes place on the eighth day. Moses chose the eighth day of the initiation of the Tabernacle to proclaim officially to the masses the priestly status of Aaron and his sons. Similarly, the young animal could be offered as a sacrifice only after it had completed its first eight days of existence.

References:

B. Ḥullin 38b; B. Bava Kamma 65b; B. Zevaḥim 12a; B. Bekhorot 57b; B. Shabbat 135b; B. Yoma 63b; Midrash Tanḥuma, *Emor,* Chap. 12; Yad, Hilkhot Issurei Mizbe'aḥ, Chap. 3; Sefer ha-Mitzvot (Aseh) 60; Sefer Mitzvot Gadol (Aseh) 178; Sefer ha-Ḥinnukh, Mitzvah 293.

PROHIBITION AGAINST KILLING AN ANIMAL AND ITS YOUNG ON THE SAME DAY

And a cow or an ewe, it and its young shall you not slaughter on one day (Leviticus 22:28)

You shall not take the mother bird with the young (Deuteronomy 22:6)

You shall let the mother bird go (Deuteronomy 22:7)

1. It was forbidden to slaughter an animal together with its calf within a 24-hour period. If this violation was committed, the penalty was lashes, although the meat was permissible for food.

It was the one who slaughtered last, whether he slaughtered the parent animal or the calf, who was penalized. For example: if one man slaughtered the mother and another person later slaughtered the offspring, the former was exonerated of any punishment, while the latter was subject to the penalty. This law applied only to a permitted domesticated animal *(behemah)*.

2. Similarly it was forbidden to take a mother-bird and its young together. One had to make sure first that he drove the mother-bird away, even if several attempts had to be made. This law, too, applied only to a permitted bird; if one took the mother-bird and its young he was punished with lashes.

3. One would naturally be led to believe that the sole, or at least primary, moral lesson involved in these *mitzvot* is the quality of mercy; but there may be other factors, not brought to light by analysis and rationalization, which should be taken into consideration. There may be therein an element of *gezerat ha-katuv*—a biblical decree not subject to rationalization. How explain, otherwise, the interpretation of some talmudic sages *(tannaim)* that one must avoid slaughtering in one day not only a cow and its calf but also the bull, if it is ascertained beyond question that he sired this calf? In this instance, one cannot say truthfully that the bull has instinctive sentiments concerning the calf.

Furthermore, the law states that only if the mother-bird is sitting on its eggs or was in direct contact with the newly-hatched chick is it forbidden to seize them both at one and the same time. According to rabbinic interpretation, however, if the mother-bird is hovering near the nest without actually touching it, it is permitted to take away the young. Also, one need not send away the mother if the nest is in the house, such as is the case with ducks and geese. Surely, if it is a question of mercy only, this differentiation does not have to be made.

COMMENTATORS

Baḥya ben Asher, Maimonides, Naḥmanides, Ibn Ezra, Abrabanel, Ḥinnukh: They all agree that, essentially, the same purpose lies behind all these *mitzvot*. God looks after the interests of both man and animal. Man, on the highest rung of the animal kingdom, must refrain from using his superior powers savagely toward animals. Even the lower forms of animals have emotions toward their offspring and these emotions should be respected.

Maimonides subscribes to the view that man must consider the feelings of lower animals, but Naḥmanides disagrees on the grounds that had God wanted to pity the lower animals, he would not have allowed man to slaughter them for food.

Naḥmanides suggests that the purpose of these *mitzvot* is directed not toward the animal, but toward man. These *mitzvot* should purge man of callousness, cruelty, and savagery. In other words, whereas man is allowed to slaughter animals for food, it is part of his program of education to learn to temper self-discipline with mercy.

Abrabanel leans toward the premise of Maimonides, though he is not prepared to refute Naḥmanides entirely. In an effort to reconcile both viewpoints, he joins other commentators in introducing a new line of thought. If it is necessary to slaughter an animal for food, at least the cow and calf should not be killed together, in order to demonstrate that man is not intent on destroying the genus of that animal. Therefore, he retains one to procreate its species as a compensation for the loss of the other. Along similar lines, Baḥya advances the theory that if mankind would practice mercy and charity, as taught by the *mitzvah* of the "nest", there could never be genocide.

Keli Yakar: The *mitzvah* of the "nest" and that of honoring parents carry the same reward: "That it may be well with you and enable you to prolong your days." His explanation for this is:

1. If children observe their parents being tender to a mother-bird and its offspring, they will think to themselves: "How much more important is it for children to care tenderly for their parents?" Hence God's promise for fulfilling these *mitzvot* is "that it may be well with you."
2. There is a reason for the existence of everything in the universe. All causes in nature were created by God, the Primary Cause. Parents bring about the birth of a child, but it is God who caused their creation in the first place. Since God gave procreative powers to man and woman, male and female are the causes that stem from the Primary Cause. Through the *mitzvot* of the "nest" and of "honoring one's parents," we acknowledge the Primary Cause and are promised long life as a reward.

Recanati: The popular rationalization for the *mitzvah* of sending the mother-bird away from the nest is that of mercy. Recanati takes an opposing view. He contends that when one sends away the mother-bird, this is a most uncharitable act, because the mother is forcibly removed from her young. It is through this procedure, however, that we say to God, as it were: "Just as we regret doing this unfair act, so we hope that you will regret having forcibly removed the *Shekhinah* (Divine Presence) from our midst, its rightful abode."

References:

B. Berakhot 33b; B. Ḥullin 78a, 78b, 79b, 81b, 82a, 83a, 83b, 85a, 138b, 139a, 139b, 140a, 140b, 141a, 141b, 142b; Sifra *Emor;* Midrash Rabbah, *Devarim,* Chap. 6, Sec. 3; Midrash Tanḥuma, *Emor,* 13; *Ki Tetze,* 2; Guide of the Perplexed, Part 3, Sec, 48; Yad, Hilkhot Sheḥitah, Chap. 12, 13; Sefer ha-Mitzvot (Lo Ta'aseh) 101, (Aseh) 148; Sefer Mitzvot Gadol (Lav) 149, 150, (Aseh) 65; Sefer Mitzvot Katan 167, 275; Sefer ha-Ḥinnukh, Mitzvot 294, 544, 545.

DEDICATION TO GOD

And you shall not profane My Holy Name (Leviticus 22:32)
But I will be hallowed among the Children of Israel (Leviticus 22:32)

1. The two strongest guide-lines for the behavior of the Jew are *Kiddush Ha-Shem*—the sanctification of God's Name—and *Ḥillul Ha-Shem*—the profanation of God's Name. In the daily routine of his life, whatever he does and says and wherever he goes, the Jew must ask himself whether his deed will bring honor and add luster to the Name of God, or be profaning God's Name? This does not refer to prayers or worship, but to everyday activities. To a certain degree, the absence of one is the confirmation of the other. By not desecrating God's Name, one indeed sanctifies Him.

2. To put it succinctly, one sanctifies God's Name when, after he performs a deed, both Jew and non-Jew will comment: "This is the wonderful, Jewish way of life." Such is *Kiddush Ha-Shem*.

3. Maimonides classifies the concept of profaning God's Name under three categories:

a. When force is being used to make a Jew violate a law with the alternative of being put to death, he should choose transgression rather than death. The *mitzvot* were meant to increase life, not to cause death. There are exceptions to the rule when the transgression involves idol-worship, unchastity, or murder. In these instances, the Jew is expected to sanctify God's Name by submitting to death, rather than commit these sins. If a Jew is forced to commit any transgression for the sole purpose of thus indicating his denial of God, he must submit to death rather than commit the sin. The violation of this law is called *Ḥillul Ha-Shem.*

b. If a Jew is not being compelled forcefully to sin, but does so out of sheer spite; that is, in an attempt to proclaim his denial and defiance of God, it is considered a profanation of God's Name, a *Ḥillul Ha-Shem.*

c. If a highly moral person of impeccable character commits a wrong, even of a minor nature, he is profaning the Name of God. For example: One who is famous for his wisdom and piety who buys something for which he can pay, but nevertheless callously defers payment until a later date, thereby brings God and His Torah into disrepute. A man of his position should meticulously avoid a *Ḥillul Ha-Shem;* he should pay his debt without delay.

COMMENTATORS

Sforno: We have witnessed the perfection of God's actions in this world and we should ourselves reciprocate by acting with perfection. To achieve this we must follow the precepts of Judaism and not profane the Name of God.

Saadiah: Desecration of God's Name applies to a person who has doubts about religion and faith in Him. Such a person not only desecrates God's Name, but may cause others to do the same.

Ḥinnukh: We were born to be the servants of the Lord. No servant is a true servant unless he is dedicated to his master with entire body and soul.

Recanati: There was a time when Jews were in bondage in Egypt and did not know what it was to live as human beings. God then brought them out of Egypt and transformed them into "a kingdom of Priests and a holy nation." It was through the wondrous acts of God that they were able to sense the difference between existence as a lowly animal and the life of a dignified person. It behoves us to offer up our lives to defend our God in those matters that imply the absence of God's presence, such as pagan worship, murder, and the like. Only in this manner can we display our dedication to Him who has done so much for us.

References:
B. Yoma 86a; B. Berakhot 21b; B. Megillah 23b; B. Sanhedrin 74b; B. Avodah Zarah 18a; B. Kiddushin 40a (see Tosafot); J. Berakhot, Chap. 7, Halakhah 3; J. Shevi'it, Chap. 4, Halakhah 3; Midrash Tanḥuma, *Metzora,* Chap. 2; Sifra *Emor,* Chap. 9; Yad, Hilkhot Yesodei Torah, Chap. 5; Sefer ha-Mitzvot (Aseh) 9, (Lo Ta'aseh) 63; Sefer Mitzvot Gadol (Aseh) 5, (Lav) 2; Sefer Mitzvot Katan 44, 85; Shulḥan Arukh, Yoreh De'ah, 157; Sefer ha-Ḥinnukh, Mitzvot 295, 296.

CESSATION OF WORK ON FESTIVALS

On the first day, you shall have a holy convocation . . .you shall do no manner of servile work (Leviticus 23:7)
On the seventh day is a holy convocation . . .you shall do no manner of servile work (Leviticus 23:8)

1. These *mitzvot* are laws pertaining to work on the Passover festival, but they also apply to the other two major festivals, Sukkot and Shavuot. To avoid repetition, we will now treat these laws in so far as they relate to Passover, observed in Israel for only seven days. There are three divisions to this festival: the first day, the five intervening days *(ḥol ha-moed)*, and the last day. In the Diaspora, the laws apply to the first two days, the four intermediate days, and the seventh and eighth days.

2. From biblical sources, the Rabbis deduce that the first and seventh day of each festival must be dedicated half to God and half to man. There are restrictions to be observed as well as a festive, joyous spirit to be maintained.

3. All work is prohibited on the first and seventh days, with the exception of cooking and baking for the needs of that day of the festival. Carrying in a public thoroughfare, forbidden on the Sabbath, is permitted on these days. Not all forms of work *(melakhot)* are permitted, however. Types of work usually done as preparation for many days in advance, e.g., hunting, are prohibited. This is, however, a rabbinic prohibition (according to most commentators).

4. An *eruv tavshilin* was instituted by the Rabbis for the purpose of permitting cooking and baking on a festival which falls on a Friday, and the food is to be eaten on the Sabbath which follows. This *eruv* consists of bread and some cooked food which is prepared on Thursday, *erev yom tov* (eve of the festival) or in the Diaspora on Wednesday. The reasoning behind this ritual is that, in truth, the food for the Sabbath was already prepared on Thursday, and this serves as a reminder that we should not consume everything on the festival so that some food should be left for the Sabbath. According to another talmudic view, the prohibition against preparing food for the Sabbath without an *eruv tavshilin* was established to educate the people concerning the stringency of the prohibition of work on the holiday, so that they never prepare on a festival for the subsequent weekdays.

5. There is no difference in the second day *yom tov* observed in the Diaspora, although it was established by rabbinic decree while the first day is of biblical origin. Each one of the two days is equally holy; the only exception made is in the case of burying the dead. On the first of the two days, only non-Jews are permitted to perform the burial; on the second of the two days, even a fellow-Jew is allowed to busy himself with the burial. During *ḥol ha-moed,* he is certainly permitted to do so, but the period of *shivah* begins at the termination of the festival.

6. *Ḥol ha-moed,* as the name implies, is the intermediate period during which some of the restrictions are relaxed, so as to make it appear like ordinary weekdays, but it retains some of the features of the festival. We are only allowed to occupy ourselves with such work as will cause us pecuniary loss if left unattended. Also, work for the communal good or for the necessities of the holiday is permitted. Work of a non-skilled nature or for the purpose of earning one's sustenance for the day is also permitted. Other kinds of work are forbidden.

COMMENTATORS

Ḥinnukh: Although he does not pose the question forthrightly, he is apparently endeavoring to clarify the following difficulty: Why should even unstrenuous work, with the exception of preparing food, be forbidden on a *yom tov* which does not fall on the Sabbath? The leniency of festivals in respect to performing work should not be equated with the stringency of the Sabbath. He offers two answers:

1. The true significance of God's hand in the history and destiny of the Jew can best be impressed upon the minds of children by their parents. It is the parent who can sit down with his child and relate with pride the miracles and wondrous acts performed by God on behalf of their ancestors in Egypt, in the desert, and on Mount Sinai. Hence the educational value inherent in the relating of the wonders and miracles of the festival is of the utmost importance. If we were to give a man the right to work on these days, even if it were light and undemanding work, he might turn his attention to his labor and neglect his important duty as father and educator of his children.
2. In the cessation of work on the festivals, there is an educational potential for adults, as well as for children. With nothing serious to attend to to occupy our time, we have an opportunity to further our own spiritual and cultural progress.

References:

B. Shabbat 106b, 142b; B. Sukkah 27b, 45b; B. Betzah 8b, 28a; B. Makkot 21b; J. Sukkah, Chap. 3, Halakhah 13; B. Ḥagigah 18a; Midrash Rabbah, *Pineḥas,* Chap. 21, Sec. 21, 22; Midrash Tanḥuma, *Re'eh,* Chap. 18; Yad, Hilkhot Shevitat Yom Tov, Chap. 1; Sefer ha-Mitzvot (Aseh) 159, 160, (Lo Ta'aseh) 323, 324; Sefer Mitzvot Gadol (Aseh) 33, 34, (Lav) 70, 71; Sefer Mitzvot Katan 194 (see the thorough analysis of the subject); Shulḥan Arukh, Oraḥ Ḥayyim, 495; Sefer ha-Ḥinnukh, Mitzvot 297, 298, 300, 301.

BRINGING THE FIRST OF THE HARVEST TO THE PRIEST

And you shall bring an offering made by fire unto the Lord seven days (Leviticus 23:8)
Then you shall bring the sheaf of the first fruits of your harvest unto the Priest (Leviticus 23:10)
Neither bread, nor parched corn, nor fresh ears shall you eat (Leviticus 23:14)

1. In Temple days, on each day of the Passover, a *Korban Musaf*—an additional offering in honor of the day—was presented, besides the usual daily offering. Today, we substitute the *Musaf* prayers for the *Korban Musaf*. On the second day of Passover, in addition to the *Korban Musaf*, a free-will offering was brought which consisted of a lamb and of the *Omer*, as a heave-offering.

2. The *Omer* consisted of a specific measure of barley cut from the soil, immediately on the night following the first day of Passover. No new grains were allowed to be eaten before the bringing of the *Omer*; no new cereal could be cut before the cutting of the *Omer*.

3. In Temple days, the new grains were permitted for food immediately after the offering of the *Omer*. Today, since there is no Temple and because of the keeping of two days in the Diaspora which precede *ḥol ha-moed*, we are not permitted to eat of the new grain until after the 17th day of Nisan.

COMMENTATORS

Ḥinnukh: Since the basic component in man's diet is grain, it behooves the Jew not to partake of his grain produce before he first brings some of it as an offering to God as a token of his gratitude for the fruits of the earth. The purpose of this enactment was to train us to be humble before God and to acknowledge the Lord's beneficence in providing us with our means of sustenance. This preparatory act, which was done before we ourselves could enjoy God's gifts, had an important religious value.

References:
B. Kiddushin 36b; B. Rosh ha-Shanah 13a, 16a; B. Menaḥot 68b, 70b, 71a, 72a, 83b, 84a; B. Pesaḥim 23a; B. Krittot 5a; J. Megillah, Chap. 2, Halakhah 7; Mishnayyot, Orlah, Chap. 3, Mishnah 9; Midrash Rabbah, *Emor*, Chap. 28; Yad, Hilkhot Temidim u-Musafim, Chap. 7; Yad Ma'akhalot Assurot, Chap. 10; Sefer ha-Mitzvot (Aseh) 44, (Lo Ta'aseh) 189, 190, 191; Sefer Mitzvot Gadol (Lav) 142, 143, 144, (Aseh) 199; Sefer Mitzvot Katan 217; Shulḥan Arukh, Oraḥ Ḥayyim, Chap. 489, Yoreh De'ah, Chap. 293; Sefer ha-Ḥinnukh, Mitzvot 302, 303, 304, 305.

COUNTING THE DAYS BETWEEN PASSOVER AND SHAVUOT

And you shall count unto you from the morrow after the Sabbath (Leviticus 23:15)

In order to appreciate to the full an overwhelming and momentous experience in life, a person must prepare his mood and direct his perspectives so as to receive its full impact. It was seven weeks after Passover that the most awe-inspiring event in the history of the world took place—the day that the Jews accepted the Torah at Mount Sinai. There must surely have been some prelude to that world-shaking event. This was manifested when the Jew was required to count 49 days after the first day of Passover. It was not to be a casual, unsentimental exercise in the counting of days. On the contrary, he was expected to count with awe and respect each passing day, beginning with the previous evening. Not only was he to proclaim the accumulation of the days, but also to enumerate the number of weeks that had elapsed. This law is in effect to this very day and is referred to as the *sefirat ha-Omer*, "the counting of the days of the *Omer*."

COMMENTATORS

Ḥizzekuni: Why was it so important that the Jew count the days and weeks between Passover and Shavuot? Ḥizzekuni treats this question from a religious-economic aspect. Since two major events took place during these seven weeks, namely, the first cutting of the barley on Passover and the first cutting of the wheat on Shavuot, a sequence of events began to develop: The Jew had to think of the seventh year of the *Shemittah* cycle, when he would be compelled to allow his field to lie fallow for a year, and of the Jubilee year when the field would lie fallow for a period of two years. The importance of counting seven weeks from Passover to Shavuot was to remind man that he had to observe similar periods of seven when, instead of counting days and weeks, he would be counting years—to the Jubilee year.

Ḥinnukh: He deals with the above question and answers that, to a Jew, the greatest event in his history was the presentation of the Torah to him by God on Mount Sinai. The next greatest event, his Exodus from Egypt, was but a prelude to the event at Mount Sinai. Without the Torah, there could be no Jewish nationhood. So precious is this incident of Mount Sinai to the Jew, that from Passover, the anniversary of the Exodus, until Shavuot, the commemorative celebration of the Torah, he counts each day almost impatiently and with great anticipation.

Recanati: Why did a period of seven weeks have to elapse before the Torah was given to the Jews? During their stay in Egypt the Jews were in a state of impurity similar to that of a menstruating woman. Just as she is required to wait until she is once again pure, so a period of cleanliness and sanctification had to pass before Israel's master, God, could join them in spiritual union by the covenant of the Torah.

Alshekh: Why does the Torah instruct the Jew to count 50 days between Passover and Shavuot when, in truth, seven weeks total 49 days? Since the Torah specifies that seven complete weeks must be counted, the last day, the 50th, may not be considered in the same light as the last day of other occasions when counting is necessary. To illustrate this point: One must mourn for seven days for a relative who has died; but if he mourns on only part of the last day, he has already fulfilled his duty. This is not so with the counting of these 49 days; for here, he must wait until this day has been fully completed and the next one, the 50th, has actually begun.

References:
B. Menaḥot 45b, 65b, 66a; B. Ḥagigah 17b; Yad, Hilkhot Temidim u-Musafim, Chap. 7; Sefer ha-Mitzvot (Aseh) 161; Sefer Mitzvot Gadol (Aseh) 200; Sefer Mitzvot Katan 145; Shulḥan Arukh, Oraḥ Ḥayyim, 489; Sefer ha-Ḥinnukh, Mitzvah 306.

SHAVUOT

A holy convocation shall it be unto you . . .you shall do no manner of servile work (Leviticus 23:21)

1. We have already noted that the forty-nine days between Passover and Shavuot were for the Jew a period during which he prepared himself psychologically and conditioned himself emotionally for the great event that was about to take place—the giving to his ancestors of the Torah at Mount Sinai. This festival is known as Shavuot, the festival of "weeks." The giving of the Torah was no ordinary event. It was destined to have the greatest impact on the history of mankind; that is, not only upon the Jew in particular, but upon civilization in general.

2. The laws of working on this festival are identical with those which apply to Passover.

COMMENTATORS

Maimonides: The purpose of counting 49 days between Passover and Shavuot was to emphasize the importance of having received the Torah. The Jew was asked to count the days with loving impatience and eager anticipation in order to await the advent of the day when he, through his ancestors, received the Torah. But why is Passover celebrated a whole week, while Shavuot only for one day (two days in the Diaspora)? Because the full impact of the receiving of the Torah took place in one day. When we celebrate this one day, there can be no mistake as to its motive. The case of the *matzot* is different; for one may eat *matzot* for one day, or even for two or three days, without the feeling that this is anything unusual or of special significance. When, however, he eats only *matzot* and no leavened bread for a whole week, it becomes evident that he does so in commemoration of an important event in the history of his nation.

Keli Yakar: Why did the Torah not clearly identify Shavuot with the day of receiving the Torah? In the same vein, why was not Rosh Ha-Shanah identified, in the Torah, specifically as a day of reckoning before God? The answer to both these questions is that one must not single out one day a year as the only day in which to do some specific and positive action. We must celebrate the receiving of the Torah every day. Each day we should give an account of our actions. Every time the Jew studies the Torah anew, he discovers new truths. To the Torah student, each day is a fresh experience. Celebrating the glory of the Torah cannot be limited only to one day. It is an occasion for joy and ecstasy every day of the year.

Abrabanel: Why did the Torah stress the significance of Shavuot as the celebration of the cutting of the first wheat and completely ignore its significance as the anniversary of receiving the Torah on Mount Sinai? Because the Torah needs no special day to bring to the fore the latter's importance. The Torah itself is sufficient testimony as to its true glory and splendor; but when man sees the first wheat emerge from the earth and becomes aware that he will have an abundance of food, then he must be reminded that it is his duty to rejoice and thank God.

References:

B. Ḥagigah 17b; B. Menaḥot 65b; B. Makkot 21b; B. Shabbat 88a, 88b, 89a, 89b; Midrash Rabbah, Song of Songs, Chap. 2; *Yitro,* Chap. 28, 29; Midrash Tanḥuma, *Yitro;* Guide of the Perplexed, Part 3, Sec. 43; Yad, Hilkhot Yom Tov, Chap. 1; Sefer ha-Mitzvot (Aseh) 162, (Lo Ta'aseh) 325; Sefer Mitzvot Gadol (Aseh) 35, (Lav) 72; Shulḥan Arukh, Oraḥ Ḥayyim 495; Sefer ha-Ḥinnukh, Mitzvot 308, 309.

ROSH HA-SHANAH

A holy convocation (Leviticus 23:24)
You shall do no manner of servile work (Leviticus 23:25)

1. Tishri is the beginning of the year although it is counted as the seventh month in the Jewish calendar.

2. The Torah does not refer to the first of Tishri as a New Year. It calls that holy day "the day of the sounding of the *shofar*." Later, the Rabbis attributed to the first of Tishri the New Year characteristics to which we are accustomed today. This is the day on which God created Adam.

3. In the Diaspora, but not in Eretz Israel, the major festivals—Passover, Shavuot, and Sukkot—have an added day at the beginning and at the end. These added days are called *yom tov sheni shel galuyyot* (second festival day of the Diaspora). Each is a separate day possessing equal sanctity with the preceding day. Rosh Ha-Shanah is observed for two days, both in Israel and in the Diaspora, for both days are considered a *yoma arikhta*—one extended day of 48 hours. This was due to the fact that in the early part of the tannaitic period it was decreed by the Rabbis that a two-day Rosh Ha-Shanah had to be instituted in view of the fact that it depended upon the appearance of witnesses. The first of Tishri is really *Rosh Ḥodesh*—the new month, which was proclaimed after the testimony of two witnesses who saw the new moon. On one occasion the witnesses tarried and this brought about complications in the normal procedure of the Temple. The Rabbis therefore declared that the testimony was not to be accepted after a certain time of the day, so that the following days would automatically be considered as Rosh Ha-Shanah. In order to maintain the holiday discipline for the remainder of the first day, the Rabbis considered all 48 hours as one day.

4. The features of the day are the sounding of the *shofar,* in commemoration of the sacrifice of Isaac, accompanied by the three significant prayers of *malkhuyyot, zikhronot,* and *shofarot.* In these three prayers, the Jew enthrones God as his king and implores Him to remember him for life by virtue of his dedication to Him, as is manifested by the sounding of the *shofar*.

5. The laws of working on Rosh Ha-Shanah are identical with those of Passover and Shavuot.

COMMENTATORS

Ḥinnukh: Why is there a joyous atmosphere on Rosh ha-Shanah? After all, is it not a solemn day of reckoning before God? The answer is that actually it is most fortunate that the Lord asks us to pay our debts to him once a year, for difficult as that may be we do manage, somehow or other, to do so. Were God to wait a long time to demand the payment of our accumulated debts, the effect would be crushing. We rejoice, therefore, on this day, because of God's grace.

Abrabanel: On Rosh Ha-Shanah mankind as a whole must give an account of itself, although its conduct is predestined (known in Judaism as *hashgaḥah kelalit,* "universal providence"). From this aspect, the individual is helplessly enmeshed in the labyrinth of the laws of cause and effect. He cannot alter the cosmos and must often suffer for the deeds of the world as a whole. However the Jew also believes in *hashgaḥah peratit*, "individual providence"; he himself is responsible for his own deeds on account of the power of free will granted to each of us. God demands an account of these deeds, but man has a good chancc of avoiding severe punishment because he is able to counterbalance the punishment for his sins by the reward for the good deeds he has performed. It is for this reason that he rejoices on Rosh Ha-Shanah.

Alshekh: Often when a sovereign imposes fear on his people, this fear serves as an end in itself. It hangs continuously over the people as a warning to keep in line with righteousness, or else suffer death as a consequence. With God, the compassionate Father, the situation is different. The man who has fear of God is automatically in a state of repentance which, in the case of a merciful God, must lead to forgiveness. Thus, we are joyous on Rosh Ha-Shanah because fear of God is already considered an act of repentance. When there is repentance, there is also forgiveness.

References:

B. Rosh ha-Shanah 16a, 32a, 32b, 33b, 34a; B. Makkot 21b; Midrash Rabbah,

Emor, Chap. 29; Yad, Hilkhot Yom Tov, Chap. 1; Sefer ha-Mitzvot (Aseh) 163, (Lo Ta'aseh) 326; Sefer Mitzvot Gadol (Aseh) 36, (Lav) 73; Shulḥan Arukh, Oraḥ Ḥayyim, 495; Sefer ha-Ḥinnukh, Mitzvot 310, 311.

THE DAY OF ATONEMENT (YOM KIPPUR)

You shall afflict your souls (Leviticus 23:27)
And no manner of work shall you do (Leviticus 23:28)
For whatsoever soul it be that shall not be afflicted (Leviticus 23:29)
It shall be unto you a Sabbath of solemn rest (Leviticus 23:32)

1. No man possesses such spiritual and religious strength that he never sins. Judaism believes that sin has its roots in the lusts of the flesh. It is for this reason that on the Day of Atonement, when a Jew makes a valiant effort to commune with his God, he must divest himself of those physical needs which have proved vehicles and agents for his sinning.

2. One who on this day ate food the size of a date, or drank a mouthful of liquid was subject to the penalty of excision. If the violation was unintentional, he was obliged to bring a sin-offering. The Rabbis of the Talmud extended this biblical abnegation of pleasure and comfort to include the washing of the hands and face, wearing shoes made of leather, and indulging in conjugal relations. They made exceptions in the case of those seriously ill who would endanger their lives by fasting. They were compelled to eat on this day, for life takes precedence. Dispensation was also given to a pregnant woman who feels desperately the urge for food. A bride, like a king, was exempt from the prohibition of washing her face on Yom Kippur.

3. With regard to work, Yom Kippur is equated with the Sabbath; but there is one vital difference. In the case of the Sabbath, the penalty was stoning; in the case of the Day of Atonement, it was excision.

COMMENTATORS

Ibn Ezra: The Day of Atonement is not a rest-day for the cessation of work for the physical and cultural benefit of the Jew, as is the Sabbath. It is the day when we must refrain from work in order to devote ourselves entirely to atonement for our sins.

Naḥmanides: He stresses the words of Leviticus 23:28: "In that self-same day," to mean that the essential character of the day is in itself a forgiveness. In other words, besides the rituals and sacrifices that were brought on the Day of Atonement, the very nature of the day is in itself also a source of forgiveness.

Sforno: Why is there a difference in the penalty inflicted for the violation of special physical restrictions on the Day of Atonement, such as eating and bathing, and that for the violation of that day perpetrated by physical work? Why is the penalty for the former *karet* (death by divine visitation), while the penalty for the latter is excision? The reason for this discrepancy is because in the case of the former, one transgresses the restrictions because he is, by nature, unable to overcome his physical urges. In the case of performing work on the Day of Atonement, however, one cannot be acting on account of natural impulses because there is no natural drive to perform work. He who works on Yom Kippur does so out of willful defiance and must therefore be punished severely.

Alshekh: How can the Jew today, without the Temple and its ritual, hope for atonement with the same confidence as in those days when he not only fasted and prayed but also had sacrifices brought on his behalf? Since the Rabbis equate the day before the Day of Atonement with the Day of Atonement itself, that is, preparing oneself for the fast being regarded as important as the fasting itself, this ordained day of preparation takes the place of the sacrifices that we no longer have today.

Abrabanel: There are four reasons why it was the tenth day of Tishri that was chosen by God as the day for repentance and atonement:

a. The creation of the world took place on the first of Tishri and there is a tradition that Adam repented and was purified of his sin on the tenth of that month. This day thus became appropriate for atonement for all future generations.

b. Tradition relates that Abraham circumcised himself on the tenth of Tishri. Since this was the establishment of his covenant with God, it is a suitable day for Abraham's descendants to seek pardon for their sin.

c. Moses ascended Mount Sinai for the second time on the first of Elul. Forty days later, on the tenth of Tishri, he descended with the

Second Tablets. The presentation of the Second Tablets indicated God's pardon for the sin of the Golden Calf. What other day, then, could have been chosen as more appropriate for the expiation of sins? d. Tradition also records that on the tenth of Tishri Moses crouched in a crevice of the mountain and saw God's transcendence pass by. At that moment, God taught him how to gain forgiveness through the Thirteen Attributes of Mercy. In short, Yom Kippur has become the most appropriate day on which to seek atonement by reciting these Thirteen Attributes of Mercy, characteristic of God.

Ḥinnukh: On a day when man exerts all his capacities to be at one with his Maker, there is no place for yielding to physical urges of the body. For this reason, eating, drinking, sexual relations, and other physical activities are forbidden on this day.

Recanati: Why is abstention from food, drink, sex, and other activities looked upon as a means of securing atonement? Because man is constituted of flesh and blood and cannot escape sin. If this be the case, on what grounds has he the right to ask forgiveness for his sins? Only angels do not sin and thus deserve God's mercy. Man, however, by abstaining from these basic human indulgences, plays the role of the angel who has no physical needs and who cannot, as a consequence, sin.

References:

B. Shevu'ot 13a; B. Yoma 80a, 80b, 81a, 82a; B. Rosh ha-Shanah, 20b, 30a, 30b; B. Berakhot 8b; B. Ta'anit 26b; B. Megillah 7b; B. Shabbat 114b (see Tosafot); Sifra *Emor,* Chap. 29; Midrash Rabbah, *Bereshit,* Chap. 2, Sec. 4; *Va-Yikra,* Chap. 3; Guide of the Perplexed, Part 3, Sec. 43; Yad, Hilkhot Shevitat Assor, Chap. 1; Sefer ha-Mitzvot (Aseh) 48, 49, (Lav) 327; Sefer Mitzvot Katan 221; Shulḥan Arukh, Oraḥ Ḥayyim, 604–624; Sefer ha-Ḥinnukh, Mitzvot, 313, 315, 316, 317.

THE FEAST OF TABERNACLES

On the first day shall be a holy convocation (Leviticus 23:35)
You shall do no manner of servile work (Leviticus 23:35)
On the eighth day shall be a holy convocation (Leviticus 23:36)
You shall do no manner of servile work (Leviticus 23:36)

1. While it is true that the Torah applied the name of *Sukkot* ("Tabernacles") to this festival, it is also referred to as *Ḥag ha-Asif*—the "festival of the ingathering" of the produce. It is logical to believe that the latter was the more popular name in the days of the Temple, when agriculture was the mainstay of the people. From talmudic as well as other sources we learn that the festival of Sukkot was a more joyous occasion than that of Passover or Shavuot.

2. The greatest gaiety was displayed on the first night after the festival began. It was the occasion for *Simḥat Bet ha-Sho'evah*—the ritual of the pouring of the water on the altar. The Torah makes no mention of this ritual, but it seems to have been of ancient origin. This was intended as an act of supplication to God to grant the farmers sufficient water for the crops. According to tradition, one who has not seen the celebration of *Simḥat Bet ha-Sho'evah* has never witnessed a truly joyous occasion.

3. As is the case with the other major festival of Passover, Sukkot lasted seven days. Following this celebration came *Shemini Atzeret*—the "Eighth Day of Solemn Assembly," regarded as a festival in its own right.

The Rabbis described *Shemini Atzeret* as an occasion for an intimate gathering of God and His children. In view of the fact that during the seven days of Sukkot the children of Israel brought 70 bullocks as offerings for the 70 nations of the world, God besought them to observe an eighth day because *kasheh alai pridatkhem*—He found their departure difficult without an extra day in their company.

4. The Diaspora *Shemini Atzeret* is celebrated for two days, the second being known as *Simḥat Torah* ("The Rejoicing of the Law," when the annual cycle of reading the Pentateuch is concluded and recommenced). In Israel, *Shemini Atzeret* and *Simḥat Torah* are celebrated on the same day.

5. All work prohibited on the festival days of Passover and Shavuot is also forbidden on the first day of Sukkot and *Shemini Atzeret.*

COMMENTATORS

Abrabanel, Sforno: How could Jews in Jerusalem celebrate eight days of the Feast of Tabernacles and be absent from their homes and fields for so long? They could allow themselves this luxury, since this was the time of the year when the crops were already gathered and stored for the winter and the tensions of survival were accordingly relaxed. The Jew was invited to enjoy the luxury of another day of spiritual inspiration and dedication. We can now understand why Passover was not given an eighth day. At that time of year, the spring, there was preoccupation and deep concern as to whether the next few months would provide the food necessary for survival. The sooner they returned to their homes, the better they could ensure a successful crop. Man must be happy, not worried, during his festive celebration.

References:
B. Ḥagigah 17a, 17b, 18a; B. Sukkah 55b; B. Yoma 21b; B. Makkot 21b; Yad, Hilkhot Yom Tov, Chap. 1; Sefer ha-Mitzvot (Aseh) 166, 167, (Lo Ta'aseh) 328, 329; Sefer Mitzvot Gadol (Aseh) 37, 38, (Lav) 74, 75; Shulḥan Arukh, Oraḥ Ḥayyim, 495; Sefer ha-Ḥinnukh, Mitzvot 318, 319, 321, 322.

THE FOUR SPECIES

And you shall take for yourselves on the first day the fruit of goodly trees, branches of palm trees and boughs of thick trees, and willows of the brook, and you shall rejoice before your God seven days (Leviticus 23:40)

1. According to tradition, the Four Species specified in the Torah consist of the *etrog*—a member of the citrus family; the *lulav*—a shoot of the palm tree; *hadassim*—three twigs of the myrtle tree; and the *aravot*—two twigs of the willow tree.

2. The *lulav* must be at least four handbreadths long; the *hadassim* and the *aravot* must be at least three handbreadths long; and the *etrog* must be no smaller than a normal egg.

3. According to rabbinic prescription, we must bind together the *lulav, hadassim* and *aravot,* and hold them in our right hand, while the *etrog* is grasped in our left hand. Holding both hands together, we are obliged to wave the Four Species in all four directions, as well as upward and downward.

4. Individuals were instructed to perform this ritual only on the first day of Sukkot. In the Temple, the Four Species were taken on each of the seven days of Sukkot. After the Temple was destroyed, Rabban Johanan ben Zakkai decreed that throughout the Jewish world the ritual of the Four Species was to be practiced during all the days of Sukkot in remembrance of the Temple.

5. Originally, also, the Sabbath day did not deter the Jew from fulfilling his obligations concerning the Four Species, when the first day of Sukkot fell on the Sabbath. If the Sabbath came out on any of the other days of Sukkot, the Four Species were not taken into the Temple because of rabbinic ordinance. The original ordinance did not apply to the first day, because of its importance; on the first day the *mitzvah* was of universal application. However, when the second day of the holiday was introduced *(yom tov sheni shel galuyyot)* due to the uncertainty of the calendar, it became imperative to abrogate the ritual of the Four Species on the Sabbath since it was doubtful when the first day actually fell. This custom has remained until today although we now have a fixed calendar.

COMMENTATORS

Ḥinnukh: Since the festive spirit of the people who came to the Temple to celebrate the harvesting of the crops could easily become an orgiastic event, as was the case in pagan harvest celebrations, it was necessary to take every precaution in order to prevent such an occurrence. The Torah, accordingly, instructed the Jew to dance and sing and make merry while clasping these Four Species. This was intended to remind the Jew that in all his revelry there should be a feeling of ecstasy and reverence for God's beneficence to him.

Ḥizzekuni: Why were these four particular kinds of plant-life chosen? Because some bear fruit, such as the *etrog* and the *lulav*-tree, while some do not, such as the myrtle and the willow. Righteous people are compared to fruit-bearing trees, while the unrighteous are compared to trees that do not bear fruit. The implication is that, by holding the Four Species together, we are advocating that both righteous and unrighteous form one unit and resolve together to carry out the Will of God.

Baḥya ben Asher: He quotes most of the rabbinic interpretations of the symbolism inherent in the Four Species and elaborates upon several of them.

1. The *etrog* is compared to Abraham because it is a beautiful fruit; Abraham's old age was beautiful and fruitful. Isaac is compared to the *lulav* by a play upon the word *kappot,* which means "branches," as well as stemming from a root which means "to bind." (The *lulav* has branches and Isaac was bound and ready to be offered as a sacrifice.) Jacob is compared to the myrtle, which is thick with leaves. Similarly, Jacob was blessed with many offspring. Joseph is compared to the willow which dries up quickly, because he died before all his brothers. The Four Species are held together, so that we may seek God's beneficence by virtue of our ancestors: Abraham, Issac, Jacob, and Joseph.
2. The Four Species represent the four parts of the body: the *etrog* is likened to the heart; the *lulav* to the spine; the myrtle to the eyes; and the willow to the lips. These four organs of man's body constitute the four major causes of man's sins. We are given the opportunity to seek atonement for these transgressions by celebrating the festival of the Four Species that remind us of the four agents of sin.

3. The *etrog* tastes good and has a pleasant fragrance; the *lulav*-tree has good fruit but has no fragrance; the myrtle has a pleasant odor but has no fruit; the willow has neither fruit nor odor. Is it not so with people? There are the righteous, who both have scholarship and also perform good deeds; there are those who possess scholarship but have no good deeds to their credit. There are others who have good deeds but no scholarship; while there are others still who have neither good deeds, nor scholarship. God wants us all to join together and work for a common cause, with love toward all and malice toward none.

4. The Four Species remind us of the four great kingdoms from whom Jews suffered and with whom they had to contend: Babylonia, Persia, Greece, and Rome. Just as we survived these great forces, so shall we survive others, with the help of God.

5. The Four Species contain moisture and freshness all the year round. When we take these Four Species into our hands, we pray, sing, and dance with them to indicate that the Torah, which commanded us to observe these laws, should be vibrant and dynamically alive within us all the year round.

6. The *etrog* and the *lulav* produce fruit, symbolic of the fruit that man both enjoys in this world and will enjoy in the world to come. The myrtle is bitter, while the willow droops. All four imply that, if we wish to enjoy the benefits of this world and that to come, we must be prepared, at some times, to experience some bitterness in life, and at all times to be humble in the eyes of God and men.

7. Why are these Four Species taken on the Feast of the Tabernacles? Because these Four Species require a great deal of water. On the Feast of the Tabernacles, with the approach of the winter months, we pray for rain. When holding these Four Species, we ask for an abundance of rain that will give these, and other vegetation, the necessary moisture to flourish.

References:

B. Sukkah 29b, 32a, 32b, 33b, 34a, 34b, 35a, 37b, 38a, 41b, 43a, 45b; B. Megillah 20b; B. Pesaḥim 5a; B. Berakhot 57a; B. Rosh ha-Shanah 16a; J. Sukkah, Chap. 3, Halakhah 1; B. Ta'anit 2b; B. Menaḥot 27a; Midrash Rabbah, *Va-Yikra,* Chap. 10, 13, 30; *Lekh Lekha,* Chap. 40; Midrash Tanḥuma, *Emor,* Chap. 20; Yad, Hilkhot Lulav, Chap. 7, 8; Sefer ha-Mitzvot (Aseh) 169; Sefer Mitzvot Gadol (Aseh) 44; Sefer Mitzvot Katan 193; Shulḥan Arukh, Oraḥ Ḥayyim, 651; Sefer ha-Ḥinnukh, Mitzvah 324.

THE SUKKAH

In booths shall you dwell seven days (Leviticus 23:42)

1. The *sukkah* (booth) had to be made of at least three walls; but it was not the tabernacle itself that was most important. The outstanding feature was the *sekhakh*—the roof-covering that designated it as an acceptable form of a *sukkah*. This *sekhakh* was to comprise anything that grew from the soil and had to be detached from the ground. A *sukkah* that was built under the branches of a tree was disqualified. The *sekhakh* had to be of something that could not become ritually unclean. Furthermore, it could not consist of things that could dry up and decay quickly, such as vegetables, etc.

2. The arrangement of this *sekhakh* was to be done in such a manner that *tziltah merubbah me-ḥamtah*—that there should be more shade than sunshine in the interior of the *sukkah*.

3. Every Jew must eat bread the size of an olive at least on the first night of Sukkot in the *sukkah*. No matter how inclement the weather may be, this aspect of the *mitzvah* must be fulfilled. The basic precept of dwelling in the *sukkah* entails eating, drinking, and sleeping in the *sukkah* both day and night. A meal may not be eaten outside of the *sukkah*, but it is permissible to eat fruit and drink water. Nowadays most people do not sleep in the *sukkah* because of cold weather, and the fulfillment of the precept is through living in the *sukkah* as one normally does in the house.

COMMENTATORS

Ibn Ezra: There are two schools of thought in the Talmud as to the meaning of the word *"sukkot,"* "tabernacles." It could mean either actual "booths" or "huts" or else God's "Clouds of Glory." Ibn Ezra defines "tabernacles" as meaning "booths." Like many other *mitzvot* which are observed in commemoration of the Exodus, the *sukkot* commemorate the tabernacles in which the children of Israel lived when they left Egypt. Why, since Israel left Egypt in the spring, is the festival celebrated in the autumn? Because it was in the autumn that the Israelites built the "booths" in order to protect themselves from the cold.

Rashbam: He, too, considers "tabernacles" to be "booths" and he also asks: Why should Sukkot be observed at the time of the ingathering of the crops? His reply is that the Jew may experience the contrast in the standards of living in a booth with those of living comfortably and securely in his own home, after the harvest has been gathered. It is precisely at harvest-time that the Jew is ordered out of his comfortable house and made to dwell in a temporary hut. The moral is inescapable; by spending some time in a temporary booth when he could live amid plenty, man acknowledges how precarious life is and how much he is indebted to God, who makes things grow and allows him to live comfortably. It is not man's ingenuity alone that brings him opulence but Divine help, lovingly bestowed.

Recanati: His reasoning is based on the definition of "tabernacles" betokening "Clouds of Glory." Why, he asks, is the celebration so soon after the Day of Atonement? Because just as God took the Israelites under His wings as soon as they showed that they had purified themselves from the impurities of Egypt, so were their descendants required to dwell in tabernacles, the symbol of God's protective "Clouds of Glory," soon after they had sanctified themselves on the Day of Atonement and had received pardon for sins committed during the previous year.

Ba'al ha-Turim: He defines "tabernacles" as "booths" and agrees with Saadiah that this *mitzvah* needs no rationalization and must be carried out simply because God asked us to do so. He asks: Is there a logical reason why we celebrate Sukkot at the beginning of the winter? Yes, there is a reason; for if it were celebrated in the spring or summer, one might imagine the booths to be merely shelters from the heat of the sun, such as were common at that time of the year. A booth at the beginning of the winter, however, was an uncommon thing and would thus command special attention.

Naḥmanides: He attempts to clarify as well as validate both interpretations. According to the first definition of tabernacles as "booths," they were to remind the Jew that, although his life was so unsettled that he had to live in a booth, God denied him nothing and he enjoyed life to the full. According to the other interpretation, we are never to forget the miraculous protection God afforded us for 40 years in the desert, when He served as a "Cloud of Glory" that shielded us from extreme heat and other dangers of a climatic nature.

Abrabanel: He also discusses both definitions. According to the first, the moral to be learned is that we must not be carried away from faith in the Almighty, as man is wont to do when he experiences a period of wealth and comfort. According to the second explanation, the lesson to be learned is that God's fatherly love for man is such that every single person and every individual nation is precious to Him to the extent that He sends His personal "Clouds of Glory" to watch over and protect them.

Maimonides: He endorses the first definition. The Jew must realize that if he can willingly and enthusiastically move from his beautiful and permanent home to a small, frail, and haphazardly-built hut, it is because of the greatness of his faith and from the steadfastness shown by his ancestors, even as far back as Abraham, Isaac, and Jacob.

References:
B. Sukkah 2a, 6b, 9b, 27a, 27b, 28b, 36a, 43b; B. Avodah Zarah 3a; B. Shabbat 133b; Yad, Hilkhot Sukkah, Chap. 6; Sefer ha-Mitzvot (Aseh) 168; Sefer Mitzvot Gadol (Aseh) 43; Sefer Mitzvot Katan 93; Shulḥan Arukh, Oraḥ Ḥayyim, 628, 630, 634; Sefer ha-Ḥinnukh, Mitzvah 325.

THE JUBILEE YEAR

And you shall count seven sabbaths of years (Leviticus 25:8)
And you shall hallow the fiftieth year (Leviticus 25:10)
Then you shall make proclamation with the blast of the horn (Leviticus 25:9)
You shall not sow . . . neither reap that which grows of itself in it (Leviticus 25:11)
And the land shall not be sold in perpetuity (Leviticus 25:23)
You shall grant a redemption for the land (Leviticus 25:24)
And if a man sell a dwelling-house in a walled city (Leviticus 25:29)

1. We can best understand the essence of the Jubilee year if we consider the many statements in the Talmud that it is as important to find favor in the eyes of our fellow man, as in the eyes of God.

We can best pay homage to God by first being compassionate to our fellow man.

2. We have already noted the laws of *Shemittah*—the Sabbatical year (see above, p. 108). The Jubilee year was celebrated at the conclusion of seven such Sabbatical years. In other words, when the children of Israel lived in their homeland, they counted seven Sabbatical cycles. On Rosh Ha-Shanah of the 50th year the Sanhedrin proclaimed the Jubilee year. All Jewish slaves immediately ceased their servile work. Ten days later, on Yom Kippur, the *shofar* was sounded—the same *shofar* was used and the same number of blasts sounded as was customary on Rosh Ha-Shanah. Not only did the court sound the *shofar,* but every individual Jew had to do the same. This was a signal for all slaves to return to their homes and all plots of land were to revert back to their original owners, even if they had been resold several times since the first purchase was transacted.

3. The Jubilee year was similar to the Sabbatical year with regard to the crops. The land had to lie fallow both during the 49th year, which was a *Shemittah* year, and the 50th year, which was the Jubilee year. This was indeed an exercise in faith and trust that God would provide sustenance during a two-year period when no sowing, reaping, or harvesting was permitted.

4. The Torah forbids the soil that was fought for in the conquest of the Land of Canaan and then divided and subdivided into areas and parcelled out among the tribes, families, and individuals, to be ever again sold in perpetuity. Thus, even if one contracted to sell his land forever it nevertheless returned to the original owner in the Jubilee year, but if the contract involved a specific sale of 60 years, it did not revert back to its original owner in the Jubilee year. There was an aspect to these laws that was favorable to the buyer; for the seller who desired to repurchase his land and not wait for its return in the Jubilee year could do so only after the purchaser had held on to it for at least two years. The underlying purpose may have been that it is only equitable that a farmer who purchased some land, and by the "sweat of his brow" began to till the soil, plant, and sow, should be granted the right to benefit from the crops for at least two years.

5. The Torah makes a distinction between the sale of a home in cities that were walled from the time of the conquest by Joshua and of those homes that were in unwalled locations. In a walled city the vendor had the right to repurchase his homestead within 12 months after the sale. After that, if unredeemed, the property remained forever with the purchaser and was not affected by the laws of the Jubilee year. The reason for this may well have been that if one was so indifferent and callous to the sentiments usually attached to an old home which had come down through centuries or generations, it would mean very little to him if that home changed ownership again and again. Another reason for this was that the security of the country necessitated that there should be a minimum change in the population of these walled and fortified cities.

COMMENTATORS

Ibn Ezra: Giving the servant his full freedom in the Jubilee year is compared to freeing a bird which has long been in captivity. The bird will sing lustily only when it is free once again and able to soar heavenward. In captivity, it pines and dies. Is it not so with man? He can tolerate only a certain amount of servitude, but must eventually have his independence if he is to survive. The handing of the land back to its owners derives from the concept of eternity. In the case of man, the generations come and go. The term "eternity" may be applied only to God. Only He can possess eternally: man cannot possess land, even though he has purchased it and owned it as long as fifty years.

Sforno: In keeping with the basic premise that the Jubilee year suggests the negation of perpetual ownership, the land that reverts back to its original owners cannot be used by them for their own advantage during that year. Even they must comply with the laws of not sowing and reaping during that period.

Naḥmanides: According to Rashi, "Jubilee" stems from the Hebrew word *yovel,* meaning "horn," because on the day that the Jubilee was proclaimed, a horn was sounded. According to Ibn Ezra, who also mentions the "horn," the emphasis is not on the horn merely because it was sounded, but because when it was sounded the slaves were set free. Naḥmanides stresses that when the "horn" was sounded *deror,* "freedom," was proclaimed. He equates the word *deror* with the word *la-dur* which means to dwell. In other words, the Jubilee signalled the right of the slave to leave his old master and dwell anywhere his feet would carry him in freedom from want and fear.

A home is redeemable for only one year after the sale, whereas land is redeemable on the 50th year. Why is this so? Because man has a vitally close relationship with the land from which he derives his sustenance; while in the case of a home, if after a year he has adjusted himself to the new abode, he does not want to pack up his possessions once more and move. Besides, he probably does not miss his old home any more.

Maimonides: All the laws of the *Shemittah* and Jubilee year were intended to train the Jew in compassion, charity, and justice.

References:

B. Rosh ha-Shanah 8b, 9a, 9b, 16a, 21b, 26a, 27b, 30a, 33a, 33b, 34a, 34b; B. Mo'ed Katan 2b, 3a; B. Arakhin 18b, 31a, 31b, 32b, 33b; B. Ketubbot 84a; B. Sukkah 3b; B. Gittin 36a (see Tosafot), 47a; B. Bava Metzia 79a; B. Kiddushin 21a; J. Rosh ha-Shanah, Chap. 1, Halakhah 2; Sifra *Behar,* Chap. 4; Midrash Tanḥuma, *Behar,* Chap. 1; Guide of the Perplexed, Part 3, Sec. 39; Yad, Hilkhot Shemittah ve-Yovel, Chap. 1, 4, 10; Sefer ha-Mitzvot (Aseh) 136, 137, 140, (Lo Ta'aseh) 220, 221, 222, 223, 224, 225, 226; Sefer Mitzvot Gadol (Aseh) 150, 151, 152, 153, (Lav) 266, 267, 268, 269, 272, 273, 274; Sefer ha-Ḥinnukh, Mitzvot 330, 331, 332, 333, 334, 335, 339, 340, 341.

WRONGING ONE'S NEIGHBOR (EXTORTION)

And if you sell ought to your neighbor . . . you shall not wrong one another (Leviticus 25:14)
And you shall not wrong one another (Leviticus 25:17)

1. The Torah regards an exorbitant profit, whether on the part of the buyer or the seller, as extortion and lays down one-sixth of the market value of the article as the maximum profit which may be made. Any greater profit renders the sale legally invalid, to the extent that the buyer or seller affected is permitted to annul the transaction.

2. Under ideal conditions complete trust and confidence should prevail between the parties to the transaction, and a man's word should be his bond. This situation is however regarded as almost Utopian, and as a result the Torah takes up a pragmatic attitude and cautions against the practice of relying on one's word in consummating a deal, because it leaves the door open to wrong-doing. The Rabbis, interpreting the intent of the biblical law, introduced legal forms of acquisition in addition to those of the Torah, which obviated all guesswork and ambiguity. There were to be specific processes to be followed in order to remove any doubt of the validity of an acquisition.

a. Land can be acquired by *kesef* (money), *shetar* (deed), and *ḥazakah* (possession). There is to be a cash payment made and a deed is to be signed by the purchaser.

b. Ownership of movable objects can pass in several ways:

(i) By *hagbahah*—the buyer lifts up the object in token of purchase.

(ii) By *meshikhah*—the buyer removes the purchased article from the vendor's premises to his own. The Rabbis devised this method in order to protect the purchaser in a case where, after payment *(kesef)*, the object was left temporarily in the vendor's possession and, in case of fire, the latter might not make any effort to save what was no longer his property.

(iii) By *ḥalifin*—bartering one object for the other. When one acquires one object the other automatically becomes the owner of the bartered object.

(iv) By *mesirah*—handing over the reins of an animal or part of an object which is too heavy for *meshikhah*.

COMMENTATORS

Baḥya ben Asher: A person who is verbally insulted is very deeply hurt and his prayer to God for relief is, accordingly, very intense. This kind of supplication is quickly answered by God and the transgressor is readily punished.

Alshekh: All men have a part of God incorporated in them and they possess a soul which stems from Him. Whoever harasses his fellow man, by word or deed, should know that he is inveighing not merely against an ordinary man, but also against God.

Ḥinnukh: Peacefulness leads to blessings and insults prepare the way for spiritual decay. One should avoid provoking insults by countering them with similar abuse; but if these insults persist, he should answer back. This is no different from the case of the thief who comes by stealth in the night, when the Torah permits us to put the intruder to death, in order to protect our possessions. So it is with invectives. A time comes when a person should reply sharply to the offender, no matter how painful this is to him.

Another cause of decay in civilization is fraud. Fraudulent dealing is the result of a person's being dissatisfied with what God has given him and so lusting for more, even if thereby he has to wrong his fellow-man in order to obtain the objects of his desire.

References:

B. Bava Metzia 51a, 56b, 58b, 59a; B. Kiddushin 20a, 26a, 32b; B. Bekhorot 13a; B. Bava Batra 90a; B. Yoma 86a; J. Yevamot, Chap. 8, Halakhah 1; Sifra *Behar,* Chap. 6; Yad, Hilkhot Mekhirah; Sefer ha-Mitzvot (Aseh) 245, (Lo Ta'aseh) 250, 251; Sefer Mitzvot Gadol (Aseh) 82, (Lav) 170, 171; Sefer Mitzvot Katan 272; Shulḥan Arukh, Ḥoshen Mishpat, 189–240; Sefer ha-Ḥinnukh, Mitzvot 336, 337, 338.

PROPERTY RIGHTS OF THE LEVITES

But the fields of the open land about their cities may not be sold (Leviticus 25:34)

And open land round about the cities shall you give unto the Levites (Numbers 35:2)

All the tribe of Levi shall have no portion nor inheritance with Israel (Deuteronomy 18:1)

That they give to the Levites from the inheritance of their possesion (Deuteronomy 18:2)

1. The Priests and Levites, both descendants of the tribe of Levi, were not only sanctified to minister in the Temple, but also by their sanctity epitomized the sublimest ideals in Judaism. Their interests did not consist in war and commerce and other mundane matters, but in inspiring the people with a love for God and peace with all men. It is for this reason that after the conquest of Canaan and the division of the land no territorial section was allocated to the tribe of Levi. Wars and their resultant spoils were not to be the portion or possession of the tribe of Levi.

2. In place of allotting land as the spoils of war, the Torah instructed the remaining tribes to present to the Priests and Levites as a gift 48 cities, of which six were designated as Cities of Refuge, to serve as a haven for the unintentional murderer.

3. Beyond the city-limits the Priests and Levites were given two additional areas. The first was an open space of one-thousand cubits around the city and, beyond that, one of two-thousand cubits for fields for planting.

4. It was contrary to Jewish law to change the character of this development. The Priests and Levites were prohibited from incorporating the planted area into the open area, or the open area into the city limits. The aesthetic features of this planning were intended to reflect the image of eminence and dignity which the Priest and Levite enjoyed in the community. Anyone violating these laws was subject to lashes.

COMMENTATORS

Ḥinnukh: The author makes the following observations on this subject:

a. The reason why the tribe of Levi was not given a portion of the land like the other tribes was that the Priests and Levites, who together constituted the tribe of Levi, might be free from the chores of an agricultural society. The tribe of Levi was designated to concentrate all its talents and efforts on the service of God. It was not even asked to serve as soldiers in time of war.

b. If all their needs were to be supplied by the masses, what need was there for the people to allocate cities for the Levites to live in? The answer given is: because the possession of their own cities was intended to confer stability and dignity on the living standards of the Priests and Levites. While it is true that their needs were taken care of by the tithes given by the people, it was still necessary that they, too, should have comfortable homes for themselves and their families.

c. Why were the cities of refuge incorporated into the cities of the tribe of Levi? There are two possible reasons. Firstly, it is only logical that cities which are inhabited by pious people and whose environment is a sanctified one should be the appropriate place for refuge and atonement for the unintentional murderer. Furthermore, in a city in which the temperament of the people is one of mercy and peace, forgiveness and sympathy, the refugee will be more readily accepted than in an ordinary community more prone to violence and vengeance.

d. The Levites did not purchase their holdings; they were donated to them by Divine decree. While it is true that the Levites lived on these land grants, it was actually the concern of the entire people to keep the land beautiful, as befitted the Levites. Since, in a certain sense, this was a national project, no single person could change the character or design of these land-holdings.

Keli Yakar: Why was the number of cities given to the Levites set at forty-two in addition to the six specific cities of refuge? Because, during their journey in the desert, the Jews made forty-two stops and at each one they were strangers to the place. The cities of the Levites were also designated as places of refuge because, in a certain degree, the Levites were strangers to those land-holdings; hence no one could criticize the fugitive for being a stranger in those cities.

References:

B. Arakhin 28a, 33a; B. Bava Batra 122a; Sifre *Shofetim;* Yad, Hilkhot Shemittah, Chap. 13; Sefer ha-Mitzvot (Lo Ta'aseh) 169, 170, 228, (Aseh) 183; Sefer

Mitzvot Gadol (Aseh) 155, (Lav) 276, 277, 278; Sefer ha-Ḥinnukh, Mitzvot 342, 408, 504, 505.

RELATIONSHIP BETWEEN MASTER AND CANAANITE SLAVE

Of them may you take your bondsmen for me (Leviticus 25:46)
You shall not deliver a slave unto his master (Deuteronomy 23:16)
You shall not wrong him (Deuteronomy 23:17)

1. A Canaanite slave, that is, a non-Jewish slave, could only gain his freedom if someone paid for his redemption, or if his master gave him a document of freedom. This latter case was actually forbidden. Were the master deliberately to cause him the loss of any of his "24 extremities of the body," he was freed from servitude. Otherwise, the slave was destined to serve his master forever. In fact it was forbidden to free him under ordinary circumstances. Furthermore, a woman might not, in the first instance, buy a male slave; this prohibition was based on moral grounds; if she did so, she was forbidden to release him.

2. The Torah restrained society from extraditing any slave who escaped from another land and came to Eretz Israel. The moment the slave stepped on the soil of the Holy Land, he was free. A master who sold a slave to another outside of Eretz Israel automatically granted him his freedom from serving any master; the new master was obligated to give him his document of freedom, albeit he might incur a loss.

3. The word "slavery" today has the most unfavorable connotations. In former times slavery was a common practice and one that was socially acceptable, and the Rabbis opposed any abuse and humiliation of a slave. One was expected to treat one's slaves compassionately and humanely.

COMMENTATORS

Naḥmanides: The Torah refers to a slave who escaped from his Gentile master and with whose nation the Jew is at war. While the slave is in the Jewish camp, he will worship the Jewish God. The bonds of religion are sufficient to warrant his protection by his new Jewish master.

Saadiah: He interprets these verses as referring to the slave's escape from another religion to Judaism. Such a religious defector must be granted complete asylum by the Jew.

Baḥya ben Asher: He believes that the Torah is referring to the Jewish slave of a non-Jewish master who escaped in order to live in Eretz Israel. The bond of the national homeland, which exists between the escaped slave and the people to whose land he has escaped, is sufficient to warrant his protection and to prevent his being extradited.

Alshekh: The slave one possesses should see that one lives an exemplary life; for should he discern any corruption, he will return to his former corrupt life since he sees that his master is no better. By his depraved actions, the master has returned him to his former "master"—pagan worship—which is forbidden.

Abrabanel: When one grants the slave refuge, one must be very careful to see that he becomes integrated properly into the new society. Otherwise this new member is a potential "fifth-columnist" and dangerous to you.

Ḥinnukh: Why should the Jew never free the heathen slave? Because the Jew is dedicated to the worship of the true God and should be constantly occupied in serving Him. This being so, he probably requires servants to perform for him necessary as well as mundane duties and for this he must turn to the heathen slave. If he were to buy a Jewish slave, he would be keeping back a fellow-Jew from spending his time in the worship required by God.

References:

B. Gittin 38b, 45a; B. Niddah 47a; B. Kiddushin 22b; B. Ketubbot 110b; B. Berakhot 47b; Sifre *Ki Tetze;* Yad, Hilkhot Avadim, Chap. 5, 8, 9; Sefer ha-Mitzvot (Aseh) 235, (Lo Ta'aseh) 254, 255; Sefer Mitzvot Gadol (Aseh) 87, (Lav) 180; Shulḥan Arukh, Yoreh De'ah, 267; Ḥoshen Mishpat, 196; Sefer ha-Ḥinnukh, Mitzvot 347, 568, 569.

PROHIBITION AGAINST PROSTRATING ONESELF ON A PATTERNED FLOOR

Neither shall you set up any image of stone to prostrate yourselves (Leviticus 26:1)

1. The Jew was forbidden to prostrate himself on a stone floor which was patterned with designs and figures. There was one exception to this rule: he was permitted to prostrate himself on the floor of the Temple.

2. Today, when the Jew is required to prostrate himself on Yom Kippur, it is mandatory that the floor, if of stone, be covered, so as to act as a separation between him and the floor itself.

COMMENTATORS

Maimonides, Baḥya ben Asher: Prostrating oneself on a mosaic or figured stone floor was a pagan custom and, as a result, forbidden to the Jew.
Ḥinnukh: The author takes issue with the premise of Maimonides on the following grounds; if the similarity to pagan worship was the sole reason for the prohibition, then why was prostrating oneself on the patterned floors of the Temple permitted? Surely every effort should have been made to remove from the Temple every semblance and reminder of paganism? He suggests that the danger lies not only in the fact that this was a pagan custom, but in that the figures and designs on the stones may themselves be worshiped as gods. In the Temple itself, however, there was no such danger, because it was evident to all that it was God, and not the patterned floors or other stone objects, that was to be worshiped.

References:
B. Megillah 22b; B. Avodah Zarah 51a; J. Avodah Zarah, Chap. 4, Halakhah 1; Yad, Hilkhot Avodah Zarah, Chap. 6; Shulḥan Arukh, Oraḥ Ḥayyim, 131 (see Magen Abraham); Sefer ha-Mitzvot (Lo Ta'aseh) 12; Sefer Mitzvot Gadol (Lav) 43; Sefer ha-Ḥinnukh, Mitzvah 349.

DEDICATING THE VALUE OF A PERSON TO THE TEMPLE

When a man shall clearly utter a vow of persons unto the Lord according to your valuation (Leviticus 27:2)

1. Man's utterances should be taken seriously and he should be held accountable for his words. When someone says: "I promise to give the Temple the estimated value of myself, or the value of another person," it is a vow which he must fulfill. We assess an individual's "value" by estimating the price he would fetch if he were sold as a slave. The value of individuals differ. This is the law only if he obligated himself to donate his, or another's value *(damim)*.

2. There is an entirely different set of fixed values that the Torah placed upon different age groups, men and women, if the one who uttered the vow used the term *erekh* (assessment). In this case the Torah is specific as to the amount of payment. If the one to be estimated is of the age from one month to five years, the person making the vow pays five *shekalim* for a male and three *shekalim* for a female. From the age of five to twenty, the "estimated" value *(erekh)* was 20 *shekalim* for a male and ten *shekalim* for a female. If the estimated person was between the ages of twenty and sixty, the value was assessed at 50 *shekalim* for a male and thirty for a female. After the age of sixty, the estimation was 15 *shekalim* for a male and ten for a female. There was no difference whether the subject of estimated value was healthy or was suffering from some illness.

3. All the moneys that came from a person's vows or estimates went for the repairs of the Temple.

COMMENTATORS

Abrabanel: An individual is allowed to make as a vow-offering to God the value of a person, but the Torah does not want one human being to take upon himself the evaluation of another, for this would be not only difficult but also most embarrassing. For this reason, the Torah has set down specific evaluations.

a. If one vows to give the value of an infant under the age of 30 days, he pays nothing because it has yet to be established whether the infant will be viable.

b. If his vow pertains to a child from the age of 30 days to five years old, he pays five *shekalim* for the male because the male child has only attained one-tenth of his maximum potential; since the payment of a vow for a person having reached his maximum potential is 50 *shekalim*, one-tenth of this amount is five *shekalim*. For a female, he pays three *shekalim*, because she has lived 60 months and three *shekalim* are equal to 60 *gerah*.

c. If the vow he makes is for a person between the ages of 20 to 50, the years when man reaches his fullest physical and mental capacities, the evaluation is set at 50 *shekalim*. Whereas in the other evaluations a vow for the worth of a female was exactly half that of the male's, in this category, the evaluation for a female is 30 *shekalim*, instead of 25, because of her added value during her child-bearing years.

d. From the age of 60 and above, one pays ten *shekalim* for the value of a female and 15 *shekalim* for the value of a male. The woman is valued at ten *shekalim* and not, as might have been expected, seven-and-one-half *shekalim*—that is half the value of a man—because a woman of that age is more useful around the house than a man of the same age.

Alshekh: 1. Between the age of one day and 30 days, one pays nothing, for the reason stated by Abrabanel above.

2. Between the age of 30 days and five years, he pays five *shekalim*, because the father derived five benefits from his male child during that period:

a. He witnessed his son emerging from the dangerous 30-day period.
b. He performed the ritual of circumcision.
c. He performed the ritual of the redemption of the first-born.
d. He partially fulfilled his duty of procreation.
e. He fulfilled the *mitzvah* of kindness by supporting the child.

In the case of a female child, seeing that there is no *mitzvah* of circumcision or redemption of the first-born, there remain only three *mitzvot*. This is why he pays only three *shekalim*.

3. Between the ages of five and 20, the individual years themselves are not so much landmarks as are the decades. In other words, there is very little difference between a boy of five and a boy of six, but there is a difference between a boy of five and a boy of 13. Two great events took

place in the boy's life during this period; he was initiated into Torah study at five, and be became responsible for his *mitzvot* at 13; hence the vow calls for a payment of 20 *shekalim.* A female, who is charged with fewer *mitzvot,* is valued at ten *shekalim.*

4. Between the ages of 20 and 50, a male is surrounded with the duties of worship and the study of Torah, Mishnah, Talmud and many *mitzvot,* from which a female is exempt. Hence the vow to dedicate the value of a male means the payment of 50 *shekalim,* while the value of a female involves payment of 30 *shekalim.*

5. From the age of 60 and above, a man has lost more than a major part of his strength, not only six-tenths but at least seven-tenths; hence the remainder of payment is 15 *shekalim* out of a maximum of 50. For a female the payment is ten *shekalim,* because she has not lost proportionately as much strength as the male has during the foregoing period.

References:

B. Arakhin 2a, 4b, 5b, 7b, 18a, 20a, 24a; B. Temurah 2b; B. Bava Metzia 114a; Midrash Tanḥuma, *Be-Ḥukkotai,* Chap. 6; Sifra *Be-Ḥukkotai;* Yad, Hilkhot Arakhin, Chap.1; Sefer ha-Mitzvot (Aseh) 114; Sefer Mitzvot Gadol (Aseh) 128; Sefer ha-Ḥinnukh, Mitzvah 350.

CHANGING THE STATUS OF A DESIGNATED ANIMAL

He shall not change it or alter it . . . then both it and the exchange thereof shall be holy (Leviticus 27:10)

Only the firstling among beasts, which is born as a firstling to the Lord, no man shall sanctify it (Leviticus 27:26)

1. We have already referred to the rules governing the bringing of an offering to the Temple. This was considered a serious and sacred act. For the sincere Jew, such an offering could not be treated with the levity accorded to other merchandise. The animal designated as an offering immediately assumed a measure of sanctity.

2. A person who had designated one animal as an offering and then proceeded to designate another in its place, was punished with lashes and both animals became sanctified. Even if his motivation was pure, he was restrained from changing the sanctity of one animal for that of another. Thus, if he designated five other animals in the place of the one originally designated, thereby improving the status of the offering, all six animals were sanctified.

3. There is a law that no punishment of lashes is meted out to one who violates a negative commandment which does not involve action. There are, however, exceptions to the rule. These are: (a) the person who changes the sanctity of one designated animal for the other through a mere verbal declaration; (b) he who swears falsely in the name of the Lord; and (c) he who curses someone with the name of God. These sins are so grievous that the mere utterance of words is sufficient to bring down a penalty upon the sinner.

4. The animal exchanged for a burnt-offering is sacrificed as a burnt-offering; one exchanged for a sin-offering is isolated until it dies; one exchanged for a guilt-offering must be left to graze until it becomes defective, and then sold and the money used for *olat nedavah*—a communal burnt-offering.

COMMENTATORS

Rashbam: A person who designated an animal to be offered as a sacrifice did so of his own volition; there was no coercion which forced him to make this designation. It is, therefore, obligatory that he honor his resolution implicitly.

Maimonides: A person who makes a liberal pledge to a sacred cause might afterwards use subterfuges and equivocations in an attempt either to evade his vow or to redeem his pledge with a payment much less than he had originally indicated. This evasion may even be attempted under the pretext of a desire to do better than his initial promise. The Torah is emphatic in its declaration that that which was designated as a pledge to God retains its absolute sanctity at all times and must not be changed and profaned by any subterfuge.

Ḥinnukh: The purpose of this rule is to instill a sense of profound respect and reverence for the sacred. The holiness of something that has been so characterized must not be tampered with.

References:

B. Temurah 2a, 2b, 3a, 7b, 9a, 11b, 13a, 17a, 28a, 32b; B. Zevaḥim 9a; B. Bekhorot 14b; B. Bava Metzia 47a; Sifra *Be-Ḥukkotai;* Yad, Hilkhot Temurah; Sefer ha-Mitzvot (Aseh) 87, (Lo Ta'aseh) 106, 107; Sefer Mitzvot Gadol (Aseh) 222, (Lav) 345, 346; Shulḥan Arukh, Yoreh De'ah, 251, 252, 259; Sefer ha-Ḥinnukh, Mitzvot 351, 352, 356.

THE PROCEDURE FOR REDEEMING A DESIGNATED ANIMAL, HOUSE OR FIELD

Then shall he set the animal before the Priest (Leviticus 27:11) *And when a man shall sanctify his house to be holy unto the Lord* (Leviticus 27:14)

1. We have already seen that it is forbidden, *ab initio,* to designate a maimed animal as an offering; also that it was unacceptable to change one designated animal for another. According to the Rabbis, the above-mentioned laws, however, relate to an animal which was designated as an offering but developed a defect before it was offered. In that case, the animal was brought before a Priest who calculated its value. It was then redeemed, and if the redeemer was the one who sanctified the animal, an extra one-fifth of the price was added to the original value. The fifth added was an "outside fifth" which is an "inside quarter." For example, if the animal was worth 100 dollars and 25 dollars were added, the sum-total could then be 125 dollars. Thus 25 becomes one-fifth of 125; but if we were to take an inside fifth, it would mean that we reach the sum of 20 dollars, with the total of 120.

2. If a person designated a house to the Temple and then regretted his action and wanted to redeem it, the Priest had to evaluate the house and the owner had to compensate the Temple treasury with the sum, plus the addition of an outside fifth of its value. If the house chanced to be in a walled city, it could be redeemed by the owner within one year. If the Temple treasury put this house up for sale, the courts could then compel the owner to make the first bid. If someone else bought the house, there was no added fifth and the house belonged to the purchaser forever. If the house was not in a walled city, then it was returned to the original owner at the Jubilee year. The money from the sale of the house was used for Temple maintenance—*(bedek ha-bayit)*.

3. If someone pledged his field to the Temple and then wanted to redeem it, the consequences would vary according to the kind of a field. If it was a *sedeh aḥuzah* (ancestral land), the proprietors were themselves urged to redeem it. The Torah fixed the amount at 50 *shekalim* for every plot in which an *omer* of barley could be planted *(omer* = *Kor* = 30 *se'ah)*. In the Jubilee cycle, it would mean a *shekel* plus one *pundyon* (there are 49 *pundyonot* in a *shekel*) per year. For example: If there were ten years until the Jubilee year and the field had the above dimensions, the redeemer paid ten *shekalim* plus ten *pundyonot*. If the owners refused to redeem the land and a stranger did so, the land returned to the Temple treasury in the Jubilee year. Should no one redeem the land, the priesthood paid its value to the Temple treasury and it became their property.

On the other hand, if it was a *sedeh mikneh* (land acquired by purchase), it could be redeemed by anyone without the penalty of an added fifth; in the Jubilee year it reverted to its original owners. It is evident that a person will normally retain some degree of sentiment concerning an old homestead. Property which has come down to a person through centuries is something that every preceding generation has irrigated with its toil and sweat and should, accordingly, be treasured.

COMMENTATORS

Ḥinnukh: When a man redeems that which he has once designated as holy, he must add 20 percent of the value to the price he pays. Why is this so? This fine was instituted in order to discourage people from redeeming what they had already designated as holy.

Abrabanel, Maimonides: The law demanded an additional 20 percent for a different reason. A person usually values the possessions which are his inheritance and when he does make the vow to sanctify a possession and later wishes to redeem it, he may collude with the Priest who was to evaluate the object for redemption in order to set it at a low price. Twenty percent is added to the price in order to make up for a possible undervaluation through chicanery, as a fine for dishonesty of purpose.

References:

B. Temurah 32b, 33a; B. Menaḥot 100b; B. Bava Kamma 68b, 69b; B. Bekhorot 53a; B. Arakhin 14a, 14b; J. Shekalim, Chap. 4, Halakhah 5; Sifra *Be-Ḥukkotai;* Yad, Hilkhot Arakhin, Chap. 4, 5; Sefer ha-Mitzvot (Aseh) 115, 116, 117; Sefer Mitzvot Gadol (Aseh) 129, 130, 131; Sefer ha-Ḥinnukh, Mitzvot 353, 354, 355.

CONSECRATING POSSESSIONS TO THE TEMPLE OR TO PRIESTS

Notwithstanding, no devoted thing, that a man may devote unto the Lord . . . shall be sold and not be redeemed (Leviticus 27:28)

1. It is elementary logic that when one dedicated and specified something, e.g. money for the repair of the Temple, or an animal for an offering, he had to be sure that the consecrated object was applied to its designated purpose. This verse, however, refers to *ḥerem,* the banned gift, i.e., an article from the enjoyment of which the owner had banned himself but had not specified the one who should benefit thereby. In the case of such a generalized donation, the sanctified object went to the Priests of the *mishmar*—those on duty in the Temple at that time.

2. In the case of these *ḥerem* gifts, nothing could be redeemed from the hands of the Priests, even by payment of a penalty. Nor did a *ḥerem* field revert to its original owners at the Jubilee year.

3. Once a *ḥerem* gift came into possession of the Priest, it no longer retained its character of sanctity and the Priest could do whatever he desired with it.

4. A person can consecrate that which is his own. He can even consecrate his children, his Jewish slaves, or land which he purchased, since they do not belong to him although he does own the benefits of them. Furthermore, if he consecrated the following year's crop, his vow is not binding, since the subject of his vow, did not exist at the time of the vow.

COMMENTATORS

Ḥinnukh: God gives man certain possessions in order that he may enjoy them. Man does not own these things, but merely serves as a guardian for these possessions which actually belong to God. Thus, when a man devotes something to the welfare of the Temple, speaking of this dedication in terms implying irreversible and irrevocable dedication instead of designating it simply as holy, we do his bidding and make this transfer. Unlike other specific designations, this exchanged object can never be redeemed. The reason for this is that the person making the vow should have realized from the outset that the object is not really his and that he had no right to abandon it with such finality, as if he were its uncontestable owner.

Radak: Why may the vower never redeem it? Because the word *"ḥerem"* which he has employed in his vow means "destroyed" or "ceased." As far as the donor is concerned, the donation is nonexistent once it is donated, because of the use of the term *"ḥerem"*. How can one redeem something that does not exist?

Abrabanel: He considers the term *ḥerem* to mean one of two things: either destruction, as used of a city to be destroyed, or total dedication. According to the latter explanation, the most exalted type of donation is when one uses the term *"ḥerem."* This donation has no implied conditions, such as the possibility of redemption, attached to it. The man sincerely intends the object to be dedicated to a holy purpose and there is no mental reservation to the contrary; hence there exists no basis whatsoever for redeeming it.

References:

B. Arakhin 28a, 28b, 29a; B. Gittin 38b; B. Temurah 5b; J. Nedarim, Chap. 1, Halakhah 1; Sifra *Be-Ḥukkotai;* Guide of the Perplexed, Part 3, Sec. 39; Yad, Hilkhot Arakhin, Chap. 6, 7, 8; Sefer ha-Mitzvot (Aseh) 145, (Lo Ta'aseh) 110, 111; Sefer Mitzvot Gadol (Aseh) 132, (Lav) 251, 252; Sefer ha-Ḥinnukh, Mitzvot 357, 358, 359.

TITHING OF ANIMALS AND BRINGING TITHES TO JERUSALEM

The tenth shall be holy unto the Lord (Leviticus 27:32)
It shall be redeemed (Leviticus 27:33)
You may not eat within your gates the tithe of your corn, or of your wine, or of your oil (Deuteronomy 12:17)

1. To summarize what we have already written about the system of tithes: every Jew had to give *terumah gedolah* to the Priest and *ma'aser rishon* to the Levite. In the seven-year *Shemittah* cycle, he also was obliged to set aside *ma'aser sheni* in the first, second, fourth and fifth years. This he brought to Jerusalem, where it was obligatory for him to consume it. In the third and sixth year, he designated a *ma'aser ani*—a tithe for the poor, instead of taking the tithe to Jerusalem.

2. In selecting a tenth of his flock, he had to adhere to a specific ritual. Three times a year were established for one to tithe his flock—15 days before Passover, Shavuot and Sukkot. The owner was not permitted to sell or slaughter any animal without first giving tithe of his flock. He would then gather all his ritually clean animals into a pen separating the cattle from the sheep. To make their exit, the animals would have to pass through an opening which would permit only one to pass through at a time. As each animal came out, he would count one, two, three, etc. until he reached the tenth, which he struck with a stick, painted red, continuing in the same manner until all had passed through.

3. In Jerusalem, he brought the animal into the *azarah* (the Temple court) where it was slaughtered, the fat burned, and the blood sprinkled on the base of the altar. The owner was then permitted to invite his friends to partake of the meat in any part of Jerusalem. The Priest had no gain at all from this animal.

4. The *ma'aser sheni* from grain, oil, and wine also had to be brought to Jerusalem and consumed there. Divergence of opinion exists among early codifiers concerning the penalty for consuming *ma'aser sheni* outside Jerusalem. According to Maimonides, he who did so was punished with lashes for the violation of three different commandments. Naḥmanides maintains that the violation of all three commandments only called for one penalty of stripes.

COMMENTATORS

Ḥinnukh, Radbaz: It would be an ideal situation if the Jew could spend his whole life in the proximity of the great academies of learning, where he could continually develop his spiritual and intellectual potential; but this, unfortunately, is not always possible. A person must usually live where his livelihood dictates. In an agricultural society, such as in ancient Israel, it meant living far away from Jerusalem, the center of all religious and intellectual activity. The ignorance that might prevail in faraway communities could be tragic. The Torah, as a remedy to this, devised that the tithe of the herd or the flock and the second tithe and fourth-year fruits of a new tree should be brought to Jerusalem, so that the remote farmer or some member of his family could spend some time in Jerusalem in intensive study, and thus be enabled on his return to give his community the benefit of his newly acquired knowledge. This does not imply that none of the communities had its own scholars; but there is no substitute for having, at least, one scholar in each family. This would be a more effective means of disseminating knowledge of Torah, besides conferring greater prestige on the family.

References:

B. Bekhorot 53b, 54b, 56a, 57a, 58b, 60b; B. Temurah 5b; B. Me'illah 13a; B. Makkot 16b, 18a, 19b; B. Ḥullin 68b; B. Rosh ha-Shanah, 2a; Sifra *Be-*

Ḥukkotai; Yad, Hilkhot Bekhorot, Chap. 6; Yad, Hilkhot Ma'aser Sheni, Chap. 2; Sefer ha-Mitzvot (Lo Ta'aseh) 109, 141, 142, 143, (Aseh) 78; Sefer Mitzvot Gadol (Aseh) 212, (Lav) 344; Sefer ha-Ḥinnukh, Mitzvot 360, 361, 442, 443.

NUMBERS

THE SANCTITY OF THE TEMPLE AND OF JERUSALEM

Send away from the camp (Numbers 5:2)
And they shall not defile their camp (Numbers 5:3)
He shall not come within the camp (Deuteronomy 23:11)

1. It is self-evident that if the Temple was the very essence of holiness and purity, then there was no place within its confines for the ritually unclean. The Jew had to enter the Temple grounds physically and spiritually perfect, because this holy spot itself exemplified perfection.

2. There were three camps, or perhaps it would be more appropriate to define them as delineated areas. At the time when the Jews were wandering in the desert, the *maḥaneh Israel*—the Israelite camp—was the area where the masses of the tribes of Israel encamped. Inside this area was the *maḥaneh Leviyah*—the Levite camp. This station surrounded the Tabernacle. The third camp, the *maḥaneh Shekhinah,* comprised everything within the curtains of the "Tent of Meeting"—*ohel moed.*

3. When the Temple existed, the *maḥaneh Israel* was bounded by the entrance to Jerusalem to the Temple Mount. The *maḥaneh Leviyah* extended from the entrance to the Temple Mount to the Temple court. The *maḥaneh Shekhinah* stretched from the courtyard entrance to, and including, the Holy of Holies, where the ark rested.

4. A leper was expelled from all three camps and was restricted to houses outside the Jerusalem city limits. This was also true of other "walled cities." The leper was not permitted to reside within them. Those who were afflicted with a running issue from the body *(zivah)*, were sent out of the *maḥaneh Shekhinah* and the *maḥaneh Leviyah,* but could reside in the city of Jerusalem. A person who was a *tame met,* was defiled because he was in contact with a corpse. In such a contingency, he could not enter the *maḥaneh Shekhinah* but was permitted to enter the *maḥaneh Leviyah* and the *maḥaneh Israel.*

5. An unclean person who entered the *maḥaneh Shekhinah* was subject to *karet*. If one who was prohibited from entering *maḥaneh Leviyah* did so, he transgressed a *lo ta'aseh*—a negative prohibition. If a leper entered Jerusalem, he was given lashes.

6. Since the destruction of the Temple, we are regarded as ritually unclean and are forbidden to stand on the Temple Mount—the *Har ha-Bayit*.

COMMENTATORS

Or ha-Ḥayyim, Alshekh: The reason why these verses are placed near to those dealing with the sanctity of the Levite is to show that the Israelites' camp also possessed sanctity, although not to the same degree as the other camps. The Israelites had to display sufficient sensitivity and pride as to expel the leper and other impure persons from the boundaries of their camp, just as the Priests and the Levites banished those disqualified from remaining in their camps.

Ḥinnukh: Impurity is an agent that deters man from combining his natural impulses with godly motivations. To be in a state of impurity is to signal that something has gone wrong with one's drive toward spiritual elevation. The leper was transferred from the camp to symbolize that impurity and sanctity could not exist side-by-side. They must be separated and kept apart until man is ready once again to start his spiritual climb to a nobler life in a state of purity and holiness.

References:

B. Pesaḥim 3a, 66b, 67a, 68a; B. Zevaḥim 117a; B. Eruvin 104b; B. Niddah 28b; B. Sotah 5a; B. Makkot 14b, 15a; Sifre *Ki Tetse, Nasso;* Yad, Hilkhot Bi'at

Mikdash, Chap. 3; Yad, Hilkhot Bet ha-Beḥirah, Chap. 7; Sefer ha-Mitzvot (Aseh) 31, (Lo Ta'aseh) 77, 78; Sefer Mitzvot Gadol (Aseh) 174, (Lav) 304; Sefer ha-Ḥinnukh, Mitzvot 362, 363.

THE NECESSITY FOR CONFESSION

Then they shall confess their sin which they have committed (Numbers 5:7)

1. It is the lure of man's senses and his weakness in failing to resist them that causes him to sin. He becomes spiritually impotent, unable to make the right choice, and does evil. There is a redeeming feature, which is the salvation of man. He possesses a sense of guilt and when he sins something within him disturbs his peace of mind. He wants to redeem himself. He is anxious to correct his ways and mend his life, so that his guilt feeling will be set at peace and he will not be tortured by the ever-present thought that he has erred and is doomed. This he can achieve by repentance. During the days of the Temple, repentance took the form of sacrifice. Later, prayer and charity achieved a similar purpose.

The Torah suspected that these might be grounds for subterfuge and chicanery. A person might merely casually bring an offering to the altar, might perfunctorily say a prayer or make a token gift to charities and then be led to assume that all is well between him and God. This, of course, is no genuine repentance. In fact, it is meaningless. The Torah expected the sinner verbally to confess his sin. He was to say: "O Lord, I have sinned before Thee; I have been obstinate before Thee; I was guilty before Thee," and he had to specify the sin he committed.

The Jew does not subscribe to the aphorism that "confession is good for the soul." In Jewish theology, man's conscience and soul must also confess. It was mandatory that when one brought an offering, or at the approach of Yom Kippur—occasions when he sought forgiveness for his transgressions—he not only had to articulate his confession but was also expected to clear his conscience and purify his soul. This means that if a person stole something, it was not sufficient to bring a sacrifice or to confess his sin. It was also expected of him to return the stolen article. The criterion of sincere repentance is the true change of heart that one has, when faced with the same temptation to commit a sin to which he had previously succumbed.

COMMENTATORS

Maimonides: Through confession, a person recognizes and pinpoints his transgression and resolves to avoid repeating his mistake. He is then assured of forgiveness and salvation. Without this opportunity to confess, there would be less hope for atonement. A man might then feel that he might as well abandon himself to sinning for the rest of his life. Hence, the commandment to confess is really a gift from God and was given for man's benefit.

Ḥinnukh: He proposes two reasons for confession:

1. Through confession a person publicly concedes that he believes in God's existence and in His powers of seeing all that happens in the world, including one's hidden sins.
2. Furthermore, it is likely that a person who has heroically and outspokenly confessed to a specific sin, and also truly regrets it, will not repeat it.

References:

B. Sanhedrin 43b; B. Berakhot 7a, 10a; B. Shabbat 32a, 153a; B. Yoma 36b, 86b, 87a; B. Kiddushin 40b; Midrash Rabbah, *Tetzaveh,* Chap. 38, Sec. 4; Yad, Hilkhot Teshuvah; Guide of the Perplexed, Part 3, Sec. 36; Sefer ha-Mitzvot (Aseh) 73; Sefer Mitzvot Gadol (Aseh) 16; Sefer Mitzvot Katan 53; Shulḥan Arukh, Oraḥ Ḥayyim, 607; Sefer ha-Ḥinnukh, Mitzvah 364.

THE WIFE SUSPECTED OF INFIDELITY

If any man's wife goes astray and acts unfaithfully against him . . . nor put frankincense thereon (Numbers 5:12)

1. Throughout many centuries, Jewish family life has been universally acclaimed and extolled for its purity, beauty, and stability. The marriage was based upon love, trust, and mutual respect. Children were witnesses to these virtues and were inspired by them. As might be expected when dealing with the frailities of human nature, an occasion could arise when a man was confronted with the suspicion that his wife was a *sotah* (unfaithful to him).

2. A *sotah* was a woman whose husband became suspicious of her fidelity and had warned her in the presence of two witnesses against any clandestine meetings with a particular man. This is called *kinnui.* Were she to ignore this warning and meet with this man secretly (i.e., *setirah*), then the only way she could clear herself was to consent to drink of the "bitter waters." She could not be forced to do this; but if she refused, she was to be divorced from her husband and receive no *ketubbah* (financial settlement). The Talmud mentions a difference of opinion whether it is incumbent upon the husband to demand of his suspected wife that she refrain from meeting with the suspected man. According to some, it is obligatory for a suspicious husband to do so. In the opinion of others, should the husband wish to overlook his wife's indiscretion, he may do so.

3. The ritual of the drinking of the "bitter waters" was as follows: After ascertaining that his wife had ignored his warning, the husband brought her before the members of the local court, who listened to the accusations. If *kinnui* and *setirah* had taken place, they assigned two sages to accompany the couple to Jerusalem, where their case was brought before the *Bet Din ha-Gadol*—the highest court comprised of 71 judges. The reason for the company of the two sages was to ensure that during the journey, the husband would have no sex relations with his wife. Were this to happen, the "bitter waters" would not be effective, and he would have to divorce his wife.

In Jerusalem, the court urged the wife to confess her sin. If she still insisted on her innocence, a Priest administered to her an oath that she had not been unfaithful. When she took this oath and still persisted in her innocence, the Priest took a piece of parchment and wrote the vow which she took upon it, including the name of God (Tetragrammaton). A measure of water was poured into a new vessel made of earthenware; a handful of dust from the Temple ground was sprinkled into it and a bitter herb was mixed therein. The Priest also placed into the water a parchment with the vow and the Tetragrammaton written upon it. This parchment remained in the waters until the letters were eradicated. After being humiliated publicly, she drank of this concoction which was called the "bitter waters." Immediately after her drinking the water, the husband brought a meal-offering *(minḥah)* of barley but without the customary oil and frankincense. If her hips began to fall away and her belly to swell, it was a sign that she had actually had a clandestine liaison with another man. If there was no physical change in her, she was declared innocent.

4. If the husband himself, before or after marriage, had indulged in extramarital relations, he had no right to demand that his suspected wife undergo the debasing ritual of the "bitter waters."

5. If the wife was deaf, dumb, blind, or had an arm missing, then she could not be asked to prove her innocence by drinking the "bitter waters."

6. If the woman was found innocent, the Torah promised that God would reward her for having undergone this humiliation. She would conceive and give birth to a beautiful male child.

COMMENTATORS

Maimonides: The procedure which a wife suspected of committing adultery was compelled to undergo was intended to deter married women from engaging in extramarital sex relations. A married woman must not give even the slightest cause for suspicion. Although she can later clear her reputation if she is innocent, the severity of the inquiry and the accompanying shame is a horrible experience.

Naḥmanides: The laws about testing an unfaithful wife are the only instance in the Torah where a *mitzvah* is dependent upon a miracle for its effectiveness. This was purposely designed by God, so that a Jewish wife would never allow herself to bear illegitimate children. Illegitimacy may be countenanced by other nations, but it can never be tolerated by the Jewish people. Why was there no oil in this meal-offering? Because oil is associated with light and this wife was unfaithful with her lover in the dark. Why was there no frankincense? Because the hallowed mothers in Judaism are compared to the sweet aroma of frankincense and this suspected wife has deviated from the pure way of life. Why was an earthen vessel used? Because, just as pottery can never be repaired when broken, so will this woman, if found guilty, be totally destroyed.

Abrabanel: God's name was written on the scroll with the curses and was erased together with them by the water. What was the purpose of this? The purpose of this procedure was to demonstrate that, through her shameful deed, this errant wife brought shame and disgrace upon her people and religion and, so to speak, dishonored the name of God.

Ḥizzekuni: If his wife committed the sin, why does the Torah tell us that the husband had to bring the offering to the Priest? Why did not the wife bring it herself? Because the husband must share part of the guilt for his wife's unfaithfulness. He must have observed that she showed tendencies toward unfaithfulness and yet he chose to ignore her behavior and did not protest and admonish her.

Ḥinnukh: The procedure of testing was necessary because the Jewish people are different from other peoples. In ancient times, the life of a wife suspected of being unfaithful could be terminated abruptly without investigation. Judaism requires that a very thorough investigation be made before any action may be taken. In other words, it intended rather to safeguard the woman's good name than mercilessly to prosecute her.

References:

B. Berakhot 63a; B. Me'illah 18a; B. Yevamot 11a; B. Ketubbot 51b; B. Menaḥot 4a; B. Sotah 2a, 2b, 3a, 4a, 6a, 7a, 8b, 9a, 20a, 24a, 26a, 26b, 27a, 28a, 31a, 47b; J. Sotah, Chap. 1, Halakhah 2; Chap. 2, Halakhah 5; Chap. 4, Halakhot 1, 4; Chap. 6, Halakhah 2; Sifre *Nasso;* Midrash Tanḥuma, *Nasso,* Chap. 1–7; Yad, Hilkhot Sotah; Sefer ha-Mitzvot (Aseh) 223, (Lo Ta'aseh) 104, 105; Sefer Mitzvot Gadol (Aseh) 56, (Lav) 87, 88; Shulḥan Arukh, Even ha-Ezer, Chap. 11, 178; Sefer ha-Ḥinnukh, Mitzvot 365, 366, 367.

RULES CONCERNING THE NAZIRITE

He shall abstain from wine and strong drink . . . and fresh and dried grapes he shall not eat (Numbers 6:3)
From the pressed grapes even to the grapestone (Numbers 6:4)
No razor shall come upon his head . . . the hair of his head shall he allow to grow long (Numbers 6:5)
He shall not come near a dead body (Numbers 6:6)
For his father, his mother, his brother or sister, when they die, he shall not make himself unclean (Numbers 6:7)
Then he shall shave his head on the day of his purification (Numbers 6:9)

1. A person who said: "I take it upon myself to be a nazirite *(nazir)*," was to remain in that state for a period of 30 days. If he specified the length of time, he was obliged to obey the laws of the nazirite during all that time.

2. A nazirite was forbidden to drink or eat grapes and grape-products which included wine, fresh grapes, raisins, vinegar, grape-husks, and grape-kernels. If he ate bread dipped in wine, he violated the law. If he drank a mouthful of wine or ate grapes the size of an olive, he not only received lashes on that score but also an additional penalty of lashes for profaning his vow.

3. In addition to being restrained from drinking wine, the nazirite was also forbidden to cut his hair.

4. The Torah applies both a negative and a positive commandment to the life of a nazirite. The negative commandment forbids him to use a razor or any other mechanical device that will cut the hair to the roots. He is similarly forbidden to tear the hair by the roots. The positive commandment obliges him to insure the continuous growth of the hair. Should a nazirite use a depilatory, he did not violate the negative commandment but he disobeyed the positive commandment.

5. As a general rule, one should not vow to become a nazirite in modern times, because when the period of his vow was concluded the nazirite had to bring an offering. This is now impossible, since we have no Temple where sacrifices can be brought. Maimonides, therefore, contends that if one takes the vow of a nazirite in the Diaspora, he must come to Eretz Israel and remain in that status for the rest of his life, or until the Holy Temple is built and he can bring the requisite offerings.

6. The last of the restraints imposed upon the nazirite was the law forbidding him to come into contact with a dead body. If a nazirite intentionally entered a house in which there was a corpse, he was subject to the penalty of lashes on four distinct counts; for the deed itself, for becoming defiled, for breaking his vow, and for postponing its fulfillment. In such a case he was required to begin his period as a nazirite anew.

7. By rabbinic enactment the term "contact with a dead body" included proximity with the 12 parts of the human body, such as bones, blood, amputated limbs, foetus, etc.

8. If a nazirite became defiled, he was in a state of impurity for seven days. On the third and seventh of these days, he was sprinkled with well-water *(mayyim ḥayyim)* mixed with ashes from the *parah adumah* (the Red Heifer) and had his hair shorn and immersed himself in the *mikveh.* On the eighth day, he brought two doves—one for a burnt-offering, the other for a sin-offering. He also brought a lamb as a guilt-offering and started as a nazirite all over again.

9. We thus see that, all in all, the nazirite was restricted in three things: drinking wine, cutting his hair, and coming in contact with the dead. If he unexpectedly came across a dead person who is a *met mitzvah* (an unattended corpse), the nazirite had to occupy himself with the burial.

10. If after taking upon himself the vows of a nazirite he became a leper and was cured of his leprosy during the period of his vows, he was obliged to cut his hair according to the laws of the leper and incurred no penalty by so doing.

11. Finally when the period of his vow was over, the nazirite had his hair cut and had to offer up a female lamb as a sin-offering, a male lamb as a burnt-offering, and a ram as a peace-offering, with the allocated amount of oil and flour. The shorn hair was burned in the fire in which the peace-offering was cooked. After the Priest had performed these rituals, the nazirite returned to his normal way of life.

COMMENTATORS

Sforno, Abrabanel: Like most exegetes, these two also look upon this restriction of intoxicating liquor to the nazirite not as a form of self-punishment but as a modus vivendi. In other words, if a Jew wishes to be a nazirite and lead a sanctified life, he must first separate himself from wine and other intoxicating liquors capable of arousing in him uncontrollable and undesirable passions.

Sforno: The long, wild hair that the nazirite was commanded to grow was intended to help banish all thoughts of vanity from his mind and permit him to concentrate on his life of consecration.

Abrabanel: The three features of the nazirite—abstinence from wine, not cutting his hair, and avoiding the presence of the dead—are intended to place a crown of holiness on his head. How can he soak himself with wine when the crown of holiness rests upon his head? If the nazirite is holy from head to foot, how can he discard his hair which is also holy? Lastly, since his complete dedication to God is an association with the source of Life Eternal, how can he involve himself with dead bodies which represent departure from life?

Alshekh: He asks two pertinent questions:

1. What was the function of the laws of the nazirite? As we know, only the tribe of Levi, consisting of the Priests and Levites, was ordered to lead a sanctified life in the service of the Temple. The ordinary Jew might feel that he is left out and cheated because of these hereditary positions. The Torah now teaches us that sanctity is not a monopoly of the tribe of Levi, but that any Jew willing to adhere to the laws of the nazirite has the potential of leading the same holy life led by the Priests and the Levites.
2. If the wine is so harmful, why then was it not forbidden to everyone and not only to the nazirite? In fact, quite the contrary seems true. For are we not told to recite the *Kiddush* (Sabbath and festival benediction) over wine? The answer is that, in the first place, the Torah

does not disapprove of intoxicating drinks when taken in moderation. Secondly, one of the fundamental principles of a nazirite is that this resolution must not be the result of some unpleasant experience from which he seeks to escape. One must not take the vows of a nazirite in a sudden fit of anger or despair. On the contrary, one must adopt this holy way of life only after sober meditation.

Alshekh asserts that for the ordinary person, long wild hair is detestable. In the case of the nazirite, every day that his hair grows longer is a progressive manifestation of his successful attempt to overcome the desire for vanity and to lead, instead, a life dedicated to the pursuit of holiness.

Recanati: The word *nazir* stems from the word *"nezer"* which means a crown. In other words, a nazirite has a regal, spiritual eminence. A person completely invested in spirituality cannot be treated in a sacrilegious manner even regarding the hair on his head. The hair may not be cut off and desecrated because it is holy by virtue of its being an organic part of him. It is for this reason that, when his vows are concluded and his hair is cut, it must be burned.

Ba'al ha-Turim: When people notice a nazirite, the very personification of what is spiritual and holy, occupying himself with the dead, they may mistake this for necromancy. This prohibition is meant to avoid such an error.

Ḥinnukh: The author explores the concept of the nazirite as follows: Man was born with great spiritual and intellectual potentials which have been housed in a physical and sensual body. Were it not for the passions and drives of his body, he could be on the level of angels. Hence he must strive to harness these urges of the body and use his intellect to rise to the loftiest heights of holiness. This must not be achieved by destroying the physical "home"—his body and its needs. By placing the spirit and the intellect in a body of flesh and bones, God showed that He wished man to care for his body. To abuse it would be sinful. We can now better understand the virtue of the nazirite. By abstaining from intoxicating liquor, even in moderation, and by not cutting his hair, the nazirite has succeeded in striking a happy balance. He has broken down his vanity and has started his climb to holiness, without completely denying all his corporeal requirements.

The talmudic Rabbis looked upon the nazirite as a sinner (*Nedarim* 10a) who had to bring a sin-offering at the conclusion of his vows. In that case, why do we extol him? Why should he be considered a sinner in the eyes of commentators who even praise him? The *Ḥinnukh* proposes that it is possible that, in a state of zealous motivation, the nazirite may have tipped the balance in favor of the soul at too great expense to the body. Since this is most likely to happen, and it is a sin to abuse one's body, the nazirite must bring a sin-offering to atone for this sin.

The *Ḥinnukh* also explains why an Ordinary Priest, also a holy man, is permitted to come in contact with the dead if the deceased are close relatives, while a nazirite is not allowed to do so. A Priest took no initiative in attaining his status; he was simply born a Priest. The nazirite, however, achieved his holiness by the strength of his own resolution; hence the Torah admonishes him to be firm in his resolve and not be weak in any aspect of his behavior.

Ibn Ezra: Playing on the word *"nazir"*, which has the same origin as the word for "crown," he proposes that the true sovereign is the one who governs his desires and his emotions. It is natural for a man to be interested in tonsorial effects. It is also normal to come in contact with the dead when one takes leave of a departed parent. The nazirite, however, was expected to be in full control over his sentimental behavior and spontaneous emotions and not come in contact with a dead body, even if it was that of a close relative. His status of sanctity should override everything else.

References: PROHIBITION OF WINES:

B. Sotah 2a, 10a; B. Niddah 46a; B. Nedarim 3a; B. Nazir 3b, 4a, 4b, 5a, 9a, 14b, 15a, 34b, 35b, 37a, 38b, 39a; J. Nazir, Chap. 6, Halakhot 1, 2; Midrash Rabbah, *Nasso,* Chap. 20–25; *Va-Yeḥi,* Chap. 98, Sec. 25; *Bo,* Chap. 16, Sec. 2; Yad, Hilkhot Nezirut, Chap. 5; Sefer ha-Mitzvot (Lo Ta'aseh) 202, 203, 204, 205, 206; Sefer Mitzvot Gadol (Lav) 243, 244, 245, 246, 247; Sefer ha-Ḥinnukh, Mitzvot 368, 369, 370, 371, 372.

PROHIBITION AGAINST CUTTING HAIR:

B. Pesaḥim 23a; B. Sotah 16a; B. Ta'anit 11a; B. Kiddushin 57b; B. Nedarim 9b; J. Nazir, Chap. 1, Halakhah 3; Chap. 6, Halakhah 3; Sifre *Nasso;* Midrash Rabbah, *Nasso,* Chap. 10, Sec. 26; Yad, Hilkhot Nezirut, Chap. 1, 5; Sefer ha-Mitzvot (Lo Ta'aseh) 209, (Aseh) 92; Sefer Mitzvot Gadol (Lav) 250, (Aseh) 126; Sefer ha-Ḥinnukh, Mitzvot 373, 374.

PROHIBITION AGAINST COMING IN CONTACT WITH DEAD:

B. Krittot 9a; B. Nazir 18a, 42a, 48a, 48b, 61b, 63a; J. Nazir, Chap. 6, Halakhah 3; Chap. 9, Halakhah 1; Sifre *Nasso;* Midrash Rabbah, *Nasso,* Chap. 10, Sec. 28; Yad, Hilkhot Nezirut, Chap. 5, 7, 8; Sefer ha-Mitzvot (Lo Ta'aseh) 207, 208, (Aseh) 93; Sefer Mitzvot Gadol (Lav) 247, 248, (Aseh) 237; Sefer ha-Ḥinnukh, Mitzvot 375, 376, 377.

THE PRIESTLY BENEDICTION

Thus shall you bless the children of Israel (Numbers 6:23)

1. One of the most moving moments in the synagogue service takes place when the *Kohanim* (Priests) ascend the platform to bless the congregation. In this connection an emphatic warning is necessary that this may lead to misunderstanding. In fact, the nomenclature that is commonly used—Priestly Blessing—is totally misleading. It is not the Priest who blesses, but God. The Priest is merely delegated to utter God's blessings. None should be amazed that an ignoramus who happens to be a Priest serves as an agent for God's blessings upon a congregation of sages. Every Priest is duty bound to perform this function, unless he is disqualified for any one of the following six reasons: a speech defect; a physical defect; he has committed murder or worshiped idols; he is too young to have a fully grown beard; he is intoxicated; he has not washed his hands. With regard to the last disqualification, it is customary that before the Priests ascend the platform, the Levites wash their hands. The Priest who refuses to perform these duties of blessing the people violates the law on three counts.

2. The blessing consists of three parts: "The Lord bless you and keep you; the Lord make His face shine upon you and be gracious unto you; the Lord lift up His countenance unto you and give you peace." The first sentence in the original Hebrew consists of three words; the second of five words; the third of seven words. The pattern is one of gradual crescendo toward the final word of "peace" *(shalom)*.

3. In Temple days, the Priests fulfilled their obligations of benedictions every morning, immediately after the *korban tamid* was offered. Outside of the Temple, the benedictions are recited during the repetition of the *amidah* (portion comprising the Eighteen Benedictions) of every prayer except for the *minḥah* (afternoon) prayers. During festivals or Rosh Ḥodesh the benedictions are said during *musaf* (additional prayers). On Yom Kippur they are said also at *ne'ilah* (closing prayers). This is practised only in Eretz Israel, however. Outside of Eretz Israel the priestly benedictions are recited only on Rosh Ha-Shanah, Yom Kippur, and the three Pilgrim Festivals (Passover, Shavuot, and Sukkot).

4. This is how the Priests performed this rite in the Temple. They would ascend a platform, raise their hands over their heads and spread out their fingers in a prescribed, traditional manner. The High Priest did not raise his hands above his forehead where he wore the *tzitz*, the miter which had the name of God on it. A non-Priest would call out each word of the blessing which was in turn repeated by the Priests. At the conclusion of the entire benediction, which had to be recited without any interruption, the people replied: "Blessed art Thou O Lord, God of Israel, who liveth forever and forever." In the Temple, the Tetragrammaton, (the four-letter word) which comprises God's name *(Yod, Heh, Vav, Heh)* was employed in the Priestly Blessing, that is, the Name was pronounced as it was written. Outside the Temple it is forbidden to pronounce the name of God in this manner. The name is pronounced as "Adonai."

COMMENTATORS

Rashbam: We learn from this biblical commandment to the Priests and from the text of their benediction that when a person invokes a blessing upon another, he must not do so in his own name but in the name of God. Thus one must not say: "I hope you have a complete recovery," but rather: "I hope God grants you a complete recovery."
Ḥinnukh: Who is blessing whom? If it is the Priests who are blessing the people, then why do they say: "May the Lord bless you"? If it is God who is blessing, what need is there for the middleman—the Priest? The answer is that in truth it is God who blesses. We know, however, that man merits God's beneficence according to his good deeds and man must be spiritually prepared and deserving to receive these blessings. By turning to the Priests, holy and sanctified by God, we obtain additional aid in obtaining these desired blessings from Him.
Alshekh: He seems to follow the reasoning of the *Ḥinnukh*. He adds that the benediction of the Priests was intended to set the proper religious atmosphere and to attune the heart of the Jew to seek and receive God's beneficence.

Keli Yakar: The person who is officiating in the synagogue proclaims the words of the Priestly Blessing and the Priest repeats them. What is the reason for this procedure? The Priest is compared to an empty receptacle; hence, he cannot pass on to others something that he himself does not possess. The officiant merely invokes God's blessing upon the Priests. Now that the Priests have been abundantly blessed by God and are "full receptacles," they have plenty to give to those who are in need of blessings. They can now turn to the people and say: "May the Lord bless you."

References:
B. Tamid 27b; B. Ta'anit 27b; B. Ketubbot 24b; B. Berakhot 20b; B. Rosh ha-Shanah 17b, 28b; B. Megillah 18a, 24b, 25a; B. Niddah 70b; B. Ḥullin 49a; B. Shabbat 118b (see Tosafot); B. Sotah 33a, 38a, 38b, 39a; B. Menaḥot 18a; J. Gittin, Chap. 5, Halakhah 9; J. Megillah, Chap. 4, Halakhah 11; B. Kiddushin 71a; Sifre *Nasso;* Midrash Rabbah, *Nasso,* Chap. 11; Midrash Tanḥuma, *Nasso,* Chap. 9, 10; Yad, Hilkhot Tefillah, Chap. 14; Sefer ha-Mitzvot (Aseh) 26; Sefer Mitzvot Gadol (Aseh) 20; Sefer Mitzvot Katan 113; Shulḥan Arukh, Oraḥ Ḥayyim, 128; Sefer ha-Ḥinnukh, Mitzvah 378.

CARRYING THE ARK

Because the service of the holy things belonged to them, they bore them upon their shoulders (Numbers 7:9)
They shall not be removed from it (Exodus 25:15)

1. During the 40-year trek in the desert spanning the Exodus from Egypt and the entry into the Promised Land, the Israelites stopped at various stations for rest and refreshment. The Ark with the Tablets of the Commandments had to be carried by the Levites from station to station, and the staves of the Ark were not to be removed even for a moment.

2. In Temple days, this duty was performed by the Priests themselves, whenever it was necessary to move the Ark from one place to another.

3. In certain communities even today, the *Sefer Torah* (Scroll of the Law) is paraded before a visiting member of the royal family or a high-ranking government official. Some rabbinic sources contend that while this function of the priesthood, namely, the carrying of the Ark, has been officially suspended, it is yet more appropriate that those who claim to be descendants of the tribe of Levi should perform such duties as this when the occasion arises.

COMMENTATORS

Maimonides: This *mitzvah* is actually incumbent upon Priests only. The fact that the Ark was borne by the Levites during the journey in the desert was due to the fact that there were not sufficient Priests for all the duties with which they were charged.

Naḥmanides: He disagrees with Maimonides and contends that Levites as well as Priests were permitted to carry the Ark. He cites passages from the books of Joshua, Samuel, and Kings to prove that, in fact, the Levites did carry the Ark even after the journey in the desert.

Ḥinnukh: The author sides with Sforno and Naḥmanides. He explains the reason for this *mitzvah.* Since the most glorious facet of the Jew is his Torah, it behooves the most honored of Jewry, the Priests and the Levites, to carry this most honored treasure of the Jews—the Ark with the Torah inside.

Da'at Zekenim: Why were the staves fixed permanently to the Ark? Because when the Ark would be moved, there would not be any unnecessary lingering until the staves could be found, put in place, and thus made secure.

Ḥinnukh: He explains that the staves were fixed permanently to the Ark as a safety precaution. A situation could arise when an emergency call would be sounded for the Ark to start on the march. The staves might then hastily be put in place, without paying due attention to their soundness. It was then likely that, on the way, the staves would fall off or break and the Ark would fall to the ground. By fixing the staves to the Ark permanently, this danger was avoided.

References:

B. Yoma 72a; B. Sotah 35a; B. Shabbat 92a; B. Arakhin 11a; B. Menaḥot 98a; Midrash Rabbah, *Nasso,* Chap. 12, Sec. 25; Midrash Tanḥuma, *Va-Yakhel,*

Chap. 7, 8; Yad, Hilkhot Kelei ha-Mikdash, Chap. 2, Halakhot 12, 13; Sefer ha-Mitzvot (Aseh) 24, (Lo Ta'aseh) 86; Sefer Mitzvot Gadol (Aseh) 168, (Lav) 296; Sefer ha-Ḥinnukh, Mitzvot 96, 379.

A SECOND PASSOVER

Yet he shall keep the Passover unto the Lord (Numbers 9:10)

1. Occasions arose when certain Jews could not bring the Paschal lamb offering—*korban pesaḥ*—at its appointed time—the 14th day of the month of Nisan. For example, there were those who were far from Jerusalem when Passover came and could not reach the city at the time when the offering was brought. The Torah, therefore, instituted a Second Passover a month later, on the 14th day of the month of Iyyar, for those prevented from observing the festival in Nisan. The Second Passover offering had the same rules and regulations as the First.

2. There were also those who were personally defiled during the First Passover, such as lepers and those who had a running-issue from their bodies *(zavim)*. There may have also been some who became defiled by contact with a corpse. In all these cases, the celebration was postponed until the Second Passover. Should one find himself in a position during the First Passover where he was not permitted to celebrate and he intentionally failed to offer his Paschal lamb during the Second Passover, he was punished with *karet*.

3. If most of the community found themselves disqualified to offer the Paschal lamb during the First Passover because of being *teme'ei metim*—ritually unclean because of defilement from corpses—they were obliged to proceed with the festivities and sacrifices even in their state of contamination. The reason for this is that such impurity becomes impotent when confronted by a majority of the community in a state of defilement.

4. A non-Jew who was converted immediately after the First Passover, or a boy who reached his *Bar-Mitzvah* after the First Passover, was obliged to bring a *korban pesaḥ* on the 14th of Iyyar.

COMMENTATORS

Ḥinnukh: The world-shaking character of all the events connected with the Exodus suspended the laws of nature and could only have been accomplished through the personal intervention of God. Water turned to blood; frogs and lice came and went at His command; the sea divided itself in half and food rained down from heaven. All these supernatural phenomena were observed even by the lowliest Jew. It is for this reason that the Jew celebrates the festival of Passover with such spirit and emotion. For this reason, also, no Jew should be denied the privilege of this significant celebration. It is God's will that if, for some reason or other, an individual cannot bring the Passover-offering on the fixed date, the 14th of Nisan, he brings the offering a month later.

References:

B. Pesaḥim 66b, 90b, 92a, 92b, 93a, 93b, 115a, 120a; B. Zevaḥim 22b; B. Ḥullin 29a; B. Bekhorot 33a; J. Pesaḥim, Chap. 9, Halakhah 1; Sifre *Be-Ha'alotkha;* Yad, Hilkhot Korban Pesaḥ, Chap. 5, 6; Sefer ha-Mitzvot (Aseh) 57; Sefer Mitzvot Gadol (Aseh) 224; Sefer ha-Ḥinnukh, Mitzvah 380.

BLOWING THE TRUMPETS

You shall blow with the trumpets (Numbers 10:10)

1. Separate and distinct from the *shofar* (the ram's horn) were the silver trumpets which were sounded in the Temple on all festivals, including Rosh Ḥodesh, while the sacrifices were being offered. According to the author of the *Ḥinnukh,* the trumpets were sounded every day. These trumpets were molded from one lump of silver.

2. The Rabbis of the talmudic period interpreted Num. 10:9: "And when you go to war in your land against the adversary that oppresses you, then you shall sound an alarm with the trumpets" to mean that the trumpets were to be sounded not only on festive occasions and on the call to arms, but at any time when the people were faced with a crisis.

3. The sounding of the trumpets took place only in the days of the Temple's existence. Today, on occasions when an entire community is faced with a crisis, the *shofar* is sounded and special prayers recited. (Many explain that the custom of using the *shofar* rather than trumpets is due to the non-availability of trumpets.)

COMMENTATORS

Ḥinnukh: When a person came before God with an offering to seek atonement for sins; when he put on armor and was ready to engage in a battle of life and death; or when he arrived at the Temple to celebrate God's beneficence to His people—on all these occasions, the trumpet was sounded and a heroic effort made to concentrate on the true significance of the occasion. Man's nature is to avoid any tension or distress. The above imminent confrontations are extreme crises when a man will want to pray for success. The Torah's ordinance that trumpets be sounded has the effect of stirring and arousing a man's emotions to the point where he does not stand idly by while something dramatic in his life is happening. Instead, he is physically and spiritually involved and subjectively committed. If he becomes fully aware then of the importance of the impending, momentous occasion because he is aroused by the trumpet, he will exert greater effort and his prayers for Divine aid will be offered with increased earnestness and intensity.

References:

B. Sukkah 55a; B. Rosh ha-Shanah 26b, 27a; B. Ta'anit 15b; B. Avodah Zarah 47a; Sifre *Be-Ha'alotkha,* Chap. 15, Sec. 12; Yad, Hilkhot Ta'anit, Chap. 1; Yad, Hilkhot Kelei ha-Mikdash, Chap. 3; Sefer ha-Mitzvot (Aseh) 59; Sefer Mitzvot Gadol (Aseh) 170; Shulḥan Arukh, Oraḥ Ḥayyim, 576; Sefer ha-Ḥinnukh, Mitzvah 384.

THE SEPARATION OF THE DOUGH (ḤALLAH)

Of the first of your dough you shall set apart a cake for a gift (Numbers 15:20)

1. We have already spoken about *terumah*—the 50th part of his produce that the average Jew was obliged to donate to the Priest. There was another donation that was known as *ḥallah.*

2. Whenever a Jew mixed the ingredients for his bread from wheat, barley, buckwheat, oats, or rye—and the amount was the equivalent of at least forty-three and one-fifth eggs—he was obliged to designate a part of that dough as *ḥallah* for the Priest.

3. The Torah does not specify how much of his dough the Jew had to present to the Priest. The Rabbis, however, fixed the minimum quantity as one twenty-fourth part of the dough of an individual and one forty-eighth part of the dough of a baker.

4. The Torah speaks about *ḥallah* as a duty only in Eretz Israel and only when all the children of Israel will live there. Hence, today we should be exempt from this *mitzvah* because not all Jews live in Eretz Israel. The Rabbis, however, instituted the *mitzvah* of *ḥallah* outside of Eretz Israel so that the laws of *ḥallah* might not be forgotten. It is therefore customary to separate the size of an olive for *ḥallah* and to burn it, since no Priest who is ritually clean is available to eat it. Some are accustomed to give the *ḥallah* to a young Priest, or even an adult, who has ritually immersed himself albeit he may be a *tame met* (ritually unclean because of contact with a corpse). If this custom is followed, then a twenty-fourth of the dough is separated as *ḥallah.*

COMMENTATORS

Ḥinnukh: He makes two interesting comments on this law:

1. Bread is the basic food of man, which he eats daily all his life. In that case, this was an easy way of incorporating a *mitzvah* that would be to man's credit every day of his life—the giving of the first

of the dough to the Priest. Man thus sustains body and soul at the same time.

2. This *mitzvah* also facilitated matters for the Priest who was constantly occupied with the service of the Temple. If the Priest were given the grain, he would have to sift it, grind it into flour, and finally knead the dough before putting it into the oven to bake. Now, however, most of the work had been done for him and all he had to do was to take the gift of dough and bake it.

References:

B. Pesaḥim 37b, 38a; B. Menaḥot 67a, 70b; B. Eruvin 83b; B. Ḥullin 135b; B. Me'illah 15b; B. Kiddushin 53a; B. Shabbat 31b, 32b; J. Ḥallah, Chap. 1, Halakhot 3, 5, 6; Chap. 2, Halakhah 1; Midrash Rabbah, *Bereshit,* Chap. 1, Sec. 6, Chap. 17, Sec. 13; *Ḥayyei Sarah,* Chap. 60, Sec. 15; *Tazria,* Chap. 15, Sec. 6; Yad, Hilkhot Bikkurim, Chap. 5; Sefer ha-Mitzvot (Aseh) 133; Sefer Mitzvot Gadol (Aseh) 141; Sefer Mitzvot Katan 246; Sefer ha-Ḥinnukh, Mitzvah 385.

FOUR-CORNERED FRINGED GARMENTS (TZITZIT)

That they make fringes in the corners of their garments throughout their generations (Numbers 15:38)

1. Any four-cornered garment that a man wears during the day is required to have fringes. The garment must be sufficiently large to cover most of the body of a child old enough to walk alone in the street.

2. When the Torah alludes to a garment, it normally implies one made of wool or flax. Some of the Rabbis, however, decreed that garments made of any cloth are included in the *mitzvah* of *tzitzit.* According to others, all garments of woven material need *tzitziyyot* (fringes). There is a distinction between wool or flax and other material. *Tzitziyyot* made from wool or flax can be used for any material; other than these only the same material as the garment may be used as *tzitzit.*

3. The Torah also speaks about a "blue thread" which was included in these fringes. This thread was dyed blue with the blood of a mollusc called *ḥillazon*. This creature has not been seen or known for centuries; hence, the fringes today are all white. About one hundred years ago, the Rabbi of Radzin in Poland, claimed that he had found this *ḥillazon* and proceeded to dye his fringes with its blood. To this very day, his disciples are the only ones who put a blue thread into their *tzitzit*.

4. The *mitzvah* of *tzitzit* is in effect only during the day, because the Torah employs the words "You shall see it." Some interpret this verse as referring to the type of garment, not the time of day. That is to say that only a garment normally worn by day needs *tzitziyyot,* not bed-covering for use at night, such as a blanket. On the strength of this law, women are exempt from this *mitzvah,* because there is a time element involved. Women are exempt from the fulfillment of most precepts the performance of which depends upon a fixed time.

5. The *mitzvah* of *tzitzit* is considered one of the most important of all the *mitzvot*. The Rabbis equate this one *mitzvah* with the rest of the 613. First, the Torah itself hints at its importance when it says, "When you shall see it, you shall remember all the *mitzvot*." Then the Rabbis, playing on the numerical value of letters, arrive at the conclusion that the five letters of the Hebrew word *tzitzit,* amount to 600, which with the eight threads and the five knots, make a total of 613. One who avoids putting *tzitziyyot* on a garment that requires fringes acts in violation of a positive commandment. The Rabbis taught that God punishes those who avoid wearing garments that require fringes to escape the obligation. It is therefore customary to wear a garment with *tzitziyyot* continually.

COMMENTATORS

Ibn Ezra, Naḥmanides, Keli Yakar: They base their interpretations on the talmudic analogy of the blue thread on this garment to the blue of the sea. The blue of the sea, in turn, reminds us of the blue sky and the blue sky reminds us of the heavens and of God. The purpose of this garment, then, is to serve as a reminder of our Heavenly Father.

Keli Yakar is of the opinion that the blue threads remind one of the ocean and the moral lesson we can learn from it. The ocean must stay within certain, defined bounds. If it overruns these bounds, the result may be catastrophic. The Jew, too, must live within the defined scope of the Torah. To leave these limits would result in tragedy.

Ibn Ezra claims that it is less important for a man to wear this garment during prayer than to wear it at all other times. He needs this reminder all day and not so much when he is praying and is unlikely to commit a sin.

Naḥmanides: The Jew must remember that the word *"tekhelet,"* which means "blue," incorporates the word *"kol,"* which means "all." The Jew is to be reminded that God is his guiding light in all aspects of his life.

Or ha-Ḥayyim: The purpose of this four-cornered garment is to remind the Jew that God is ruler over the four corners of the earth.

Ḥizzekuni: He reasons that when one looks at the fringes of this garment, which remind him of God's *mitzvot,* he will bear in mind that he is God's servant and that his heart and eyes must not be led astray.

Alshekh: The fringes are compared to tying a string around one's finger. When one mindlessly ties a string around one's finger for no special reason, it is meaningless. If one does it to serve as a reminder, the string has significance. So it is with the fringes of one's garment. One must begin with the thought that they are worn for a special purpose: that is, to remind the Jew of the *mitzvot.* Only then can they fulfill their intended purpose.

Abrabanel: Man requires a constant reminder that he is expected to observe the *mitzvot.* Through the ever-present fringes of this garment, it is hoped that the time will come when he will be thinking of the *mitzvot* all the time. The purpose of the reminder is to help the wearer to lead a holy life and this conduct should eventually become natural to him.

References:

B. Menaḥot 39a, 39b, 41b, 42a, 43a, 43b, 44a; B. Kiddushin 33b; B. Sukkah 9a; B. Ḥullin 136a; B. Yevamot 4b; B. Shabbat 23b, 32b, 118b; B. Nedarim 25a; B. Sotah 17a; J. Berakhot, Chap. 1, Halakhah 5; Midrash Rabbah, *Shelaḥ,* Chap. 17, Sec. 7; Midrash Tanḥuma, *Shelaḥ,* Chap. 15; Sifre *Shelaḥ;* Midrash Tehillim, Chap. 90; Yad, Hilkhot Tzitzit; Sefer ha-Mitzvot (Aseh) 14; Sefer

Mitzvot Gadol (Aseh) 26; Sefer Mitzvot Katan 31; Shulḥan Arukh, Oraḥ Ḥayyim, Chap. 8; Sefer ha-Ḥinnukh, Mitzvah 386.

DISTINCTION BETWEEN THE DUTIES OF PRIESTS AND LEVITES

Only to the vessels of the Sanctuary and to the altar they [i.e., the Levites] are not to come near (Numbers 18:3)
But the Levites alone shall do the service of the Tent of Meeting (Numbers 18:6).

1. When a Levite reached the age of 13 he was permitted to sweep the floors of the *azarah* (Temple court) or to shut the doors. At the age of 25 he began his training in *shirah*—the instrumental and vocal music which accompanied the sacrificial service and was the Levites' principal function. One condition was laid down: He must agree to carry out all the duties for which a Levite was eligible and might not refuse or delegate any of them.

2. The apprenticeship of the Levite lasted for a period of five years. After concluding it he underwent a trial and was either approved by the favorable appraisal of his superiors or else rejected on account of his inadequate performance.

3. The active life of the Levite was from 30 to 50 years, throughout which time he took part in the music of the Sanctuary; he also carried some part of the structure or of its equipment during the wandering in the wilderness. Above the age of 50 he was no longer eligible for the latter of these duties, but he might continue to sing, to load up the wagons, and to assist his brethren by acting as doorman as long as his strength lasted.

4. For the sake of efficiency and to avoid duplication or the overlapping of duties, the functions of the various groups of Levites were clearly distinguished. It followed that not only were they debarred from encroaching on the preserves of the Priests, but each Levite was strictly forbidden to perform any duties which had been assigned to another. A Levite who overstepped the bounds of his office was liable to Divine punishment *(mitah bi-ydei shamayim)*. A Priest who performed the duty of a Levite, or of another Priest, was also punished—in the former case with lashes, in the latter by Divine punishment.

COMMENTATORS

Ḥinnukh: These laws were promulgated for two reasons:

1. The positions of the Priests and of the Levites are comparable with those of royal courtiers, each of whom has his particular function. They must, at all times, maintain their proper image and dignity and not change their duties at random.
2. These laws also encouraged efficiency. When everyone does anything at any time, the result will be needless duplication and overlapping of work; but when everyone knows his exact place and precise duty and does it, the result will be maximum efficiency.

References:

B. Arakhin 11a, 11b; B. Sukkah 51a; B. Bekhorot 30b; B. Ḥullin 24a, 24b; Sifre *Koraḥ;* Yad, Hilkhot Kelei ha-Mikdash, Chap. 3; Sefer ha-Mitzvot (Lo Ta'aseh) 72, (Aseh) 23 (See dispute between Maimonides and Naḥmanides in the third Shoresh, whether the duty of the Levites to carry loads on their shoulders applied only to the Sanctuary in the desert, or at all times. Maimonides' position is that this law applied to the Levites in the desert only.) ; Sefer Mitzvot Gadol (Lav) 297, (Aseh) 169; Sefer ha-Ḥinnukh, Mitzvot 389, 394.

THE TEMPLE GUARDS

They shall keep your charge and the charge of all the tent (Numbers 18:3)
But a common man shall not draw near to you (Numbers 18:4)
And you shall keep the charge of the holy things (Numbers 18:5)

1. Among the many and sundry duties that the Priests and Levites performed in the Temple precincts, they were also charged with the responsibility of keeping watch at night.

2. There were three inner stations manned by Priests and there were twenty-one outer stations guarded by Levites. During the night-watch, a foreman, known as *ish Har ha-Bayit*—the man of the Temple Mount—made the rounds of all the stations to ascertain whether the watchmen were alert or sleepy.

3. A stranger who presumed to carry out the rituals of an offering was punished with Divine punishment—*mitah bi-ydei shamayim.* This could be only by one of four *avodot* (types of service): the sprinkling of the blood *(zerikah)* lighting the fire *(haktarah)*, pouring of wine or water *(nisukh ha-yayin, nisukh ha-mayim)*. If a non-Priest did any *avodah* other than the above, he received lashes. There were duties not included in this prohibition, such as the slaughtering of the animals, bringing wood to the altar, or lighting the candelabra.

COMMENTATORS

Maimonides: The purpose of the tribe of Levi's serving as guards outside the Temple was to lend an aura of dignity and awe to the precincts of the Temple.
Ḥinnukh: Since the most important aspect of a visit to the Temple was to communicate with God, the sense of awe induced by the presence of the guards helped to put the worshiper in a frame of mind that would appropriately humble him.

References:
B. Zevaḥim 16a; B. Tamid 26a, 26b; B. Yoma 24a; Sifre *Koraḥ;* Yad, Hilkhot Bet ha-Beḥirah, Chap. 8; Yad, Hilkhot Bi'at ha-Mikdash, Chap. 9; Guide of the Perplexed, Part 3, Sec. 45; Sefer ha-Mitzvot (Lo Ta'aseh) 67, 74, (Aseh) 22; Sefer Mitzvot Gadol (Lav) 309, (Aseh) 165; Sefer ha-Ḥinnukh, Mitzvot 388, 390, 391.

THE TITHE FOR THE LEVITES

For the tithe of the children of Israel, which they set aside as a gift unto the Lord, I have given to the Levites for an inheritance (Numbers 18:24)

1. It has already been noted that after the Jew had designated *terumah gedolah* for the Priest, he was obliged to set aside *ma'aser rishon*—the first tithe of ten percent of his produce—for the Levite. It follows that if a Jew had 100 bushels of corn, he presented two bushels to the Priest, which left him 98 bushels. Of these, he gave the Levite ten percent, i.e., nine and eight-tenths bushels. According to some, the amount given to the Levite was ten bushels. The two percent given to the Priest was not deducted from the original amount for computing tithes since Torah law did not specify any minimum for the Priest. The Rabbis who established this minimum did not want the Levite to lose from the amount he would normally receive.

2. The first tithe was given only from humanly edible produce, which grew from the earth, had specific owners, and was tended and guarded during its growth and harvesting. One could tithe one batch from another batch, providing both batches were of equal quality.

3. There was no sanctity attached to the first tithe. The Levite who received it could feed with it anyone he wished. This is in contrast to the second tithe which was in a state of holiness until it was brought to Jerusalem. Furthermore, the first tithe could be eaten even by one who was ritually unclean.

4. *Tevel*—produce which was ripe for tithing but had not yet been tithed—was forbidden to be eaten. This was applicable not only to an Israelite but also to the Levite and the Priest. In other words, the Priest who grew his own produce was obliged to perform the ritual of separating *terumah* and tithing, and was prohibited from eating from that produce until this was done, although he did not donate his *terumah* to another Priest.

5. According to the Torah, the laws of tithing were in effect only when the children of Israel were settled in their own Land. The Rabbis, however, extended its application to all time and all places. Here again, we have a dispute between Maimonides and Naḥmanides. According to the latter, the designation of the tithe and its presentation to the Levite are two distinct *mitzvot*. According to the former, they are counted as one.

COMMENTATORS

Ḥinnukh: Royal princes are not expected to do manual labor. They should spend all their time in the service of their king. In the religious life, God's princes are the Priests and the Levites. They, too, must not labor for their daily sustenance and the people should provide for them. This is the essential reason for the various tithes given to the tribe of Levi. Since there were twelve tribes, why then was the tithe one-tenth of an individual's wealth and not one-twelfth, which would have been a more equitable contribution to the Levites? The answer is that a tribe of princes must not be put on the same plane as the masses. They should be accorded extra privileges; therefore the tithes were not merely a national project of which they received one-twelfth, but an individual's gift of one-tenth.
Abrabanel: In providing for the tribe of Levi, the Israelites not only made it possible for the Priests and the Levites to be perfectly free to serve God without any drawbacks, but the Israelites themselves, knowing that what they did was right and proper, could feel that they might also worship God without feeling that they had neglected a religious duty.

References:

B. Yevamot 86a; B. Shabbat 119a; B. Pesaḥim 113a; B. Ta'anit 9a (see Tosafot); Midrash Rabbah, *Ekev,* Chap. 3, Sec. 5; Yad, Hilkhot Ma'aser, Chap. 1; Sefer ha-Mitzvot (Aseh) 127 (See Naḥmanides in Shoresh 12. He counts the designation of the tithe and the presentation to the Levite as two separate *mitzvot*); Sefer Mitzvot Gadol (Aseh) 135; Shulḥan Arukh, Yoreh De'ah, 331; Sefer ha-Ḥinnukh, Mitzvah 395

TITHES

Even a tithe of the tithe (Numbers 18:26)

1. After the Levite had received from the Israelite his tithe, which was ten percent of his produce, he himself was obliged to give a tithe to the Priest.

2. Under all circumstances, the tithes to the Priest had to be given. Even if the tithe became ritually defiled, the Priest was to receive it and he could use it for fuel. What was of paramount importance was the necessity that tithing should be done in the most dignified and respectful manner. For example: The Priests were not to go down to the fields and help the farmers in order to be sure that they secure their tithes. The Priests were also not permitted to partake of the tithes until they were formally and reverently presented to them.

3. According to the Bible all the laws of tithing were in effect only for Eretz Israel. The Prophets and Rabbis later added areas very close to the Holy Land and obliged their inhabitants to observe the laws of tithing. When we speak about Eretz Israel, we refer to the territory that was conquered by a king in Israel with the approval of the people. Additional territories conquered by a single tribe or by an individual were not subject to the biblical laws of tithing. Maimonides was forthright in his opinion that the land conquered by Joshua was initially sanctified. It was only when the children of Israel were exiled that the land lost its sanctity. When they returned, the land was resanctified and maintains its holiness until this very day. Nowadays, since not all Jews are in Eretz Israel, tithing is obligatory not by biblical decree but by rabbinic ordinance. Others maintain, however, that the laws of *terumah* and tithing are in force even at present, although not all Jews reside in Eretz Israel. There is a third view, that resanctification of the land did not remain effective after the second expulsion.

COMMENTATORS

Ḥinnukh: Man often takes his sustenance for granted, forgetting that it is a gift from God. In order to show gratitude for His beneficence, man should first set aside something for the servants of God, the Priests, so as to be reminded that it is through God's grace that he has food. If this tithe serves merely as a reminder, why then did the Rabbis set the amount of the tithe at two percent and not at a smaller sum? The answer is that people have a habit of ignoring and forgetting very small and insignificant sums but will remember to pay up more substantial amounts. The Priest, to whom the Israelite pays reverent homage, must realize that his exalted position is due to his service to God in the Temple. In addition to food, the Priest also needs clothing and this is why the first of the fleece belongs to him. The Levite receives his separate tithes from the Israelite, because he assists the Priest. The Levite, however, must also pay tithes to the Priest. All this reminds us to pay homage to God, the Sovereign of Priests, Levites, and Israelites alike.

References:

B. Bekhorot 11b; B. Beẓah 13b; B. Gittin 30b; B. Menaḥot 54b; B. Kiddushin 53a; B. Sanhedrin 90b; B. Ḥullin 135b, 136a, 136b, 137a; J. Ma'aser Sheni, Chap. 5, Halakhah 3; J. Terumot, Chap. 1, Halakhot 1, 4, 5; Chap. 3, Halakhah 3; Tosefta, Ḥullin, Chap. 10; Sifre *Shofetim, Koraḥ;* Midrash Rabbah, *Tetzaveh,* Chap. 38, Sec. 3, *Nasso,* Chap. 8, Sec. 4, 10; Yad, Hilkhot Terumot, Chap. 3, 5; Yad, Hilkhot Bikkurim, Chap. 10; Sefer ha-Mitzvot (Aseh) 126, 129, 144; Sefer Mitzvot Gadol (Aseh) 133, 134, 143; Shulḥan Arukh, Yoreh De'ah, 332, 333; Sefer ha-Ḥinnukh, Mitzvot 396, 507, 508.

THE RED HEIFER

That they bring a red heifer, which has no blemish (Numbers 19:2)
And the clean person shall sprinkle upon the unclean (Numbers 19:19)

1. In Temple days the Priests sought a red heifer, a search which could very well have taken them all over the country, for the requirements were that it should be totally and completely red and should never have borne a yoke on its neck, or been a beast of burden. It should be three or four years old, although being older did not disqualify it. From the days of Moses, until the final destruction of the Second Temple, there were only nine occasions when the red heifer was prepared.

2. A Priest, clothed in his official garments, slaughtered the animal and sprinkled some of its blood seven times in the direction of the *heikhal.* He then ignited a pyre and threw into the fire a piece of cedarwood and hyssop, tied together with a red string. When it was completely burned, the ashes were divided into three parts. One part was set aside for the mixing with ashes of future red heifers; another, for the purification of those who came in contact with the dead; the last part was set aside in the area outside of the *azarah,* for safekeeping *(mishmeret).*

3. Those Priests who either slaughtered or burned the heifer, or were active in its preparation, became ritually unclean and were obliged to immerse themselves and their clothes in the *mikveh,* after which they awaited sunset before resuming their duties or entering the Sanctuary.

4. If the ritual of the red heifer defiled the Priest, it also purified the unclean. By the term "unclean" we refer to those who had come in contact with a corpse.

5. The process of purifying the impure was as follows: A ritually clean person filled an earthenware pot with water drawn from a fresh spring and sprinkled into it the ashes of the red heifer. This mixture was called *mei niddah* or *mei ḥattat.* A ritually clean person sprinkled water from the *mei ḥattat* on the defiled person on the third and seventh day of his impurity. This was done at sunrise. The defiled person would then immerse himself in the *mikveh,* await the setting of the sun, and after the seventh day, become ritually pure.

COMMENTATORS

Ḥinnukh: He professes that he never hesitated to rationalize the *mitzvot* because he felt that youth was eager to ask questions which must be answered appropriately with valid reasons. However, in the case of the red heifer, he admits to the total absence of human logic and makes no comment. These are the sentiments of most of the great classic exegetes who also offer no rationalization for this *mitzvah.*

Abrabanel: Man stands on the highest rung of the ladder of the animal kingdom. His body is purer and his intelligence is superior to that of any other creature. When he dies, he decomposes more rapidly than any other animal. He lives and dies in a distinct class by himself. By coming in contact with corpses, thereby rendering himself unclean, he mars his superior image by not showing appreciation for the superiority which God granted him. The Torah instructed that the person who touched a corpse should be sprinkled with the ashes of a red heifer in order to emphasize that such a person commits a heinous sin and should have been destroyed as the red heifer was. He was guilty of not living up to the high standard expected of him.

In this ritual a cedar and a hyssop are included because great Jews are compared to tall cedars and ordinary Jews to the lowly hyssop. The entire ritual is aimed at both of these categories in equal measure.

References:
B. Yoma 2a, 14a, 42b, 43a, 43b; B. Sotah 46a; B. Niddah 9a; B. Nazir 61b; B. Megillah 20a; B. Kiddushin 25a, 31a, 62a; Mishnayyot, Parah; J. Megillah, Chap. 3, Halakhah 6; Sifre *Ḥukkat;* Midrash Tanḥuma, *Ḥukkat,* Chap. 7, 8; Midrash Rabbah, *Ḥukkat,* Chap. 19, Sec. 3; Yad, Hilkhot Parah Adumah, Chap. 1–5, 11, 15; Sefer ha-Mitzvot (Aseh) 108, 113; Sefer Mitzvot Gadol (Aseh) 232, 233; Sefer ha-Ḥinnukh, Mitzvot 397, 399.

IMPURITY CONVEYED BY A CORPSE

When a man dies in a tent, everyone who comes into the tent and all that is in the tent shall be unclean for seven days (Numbers 19:14)

1. A person who touches or carries, even without touching, or is under one roof with, a corpse, becomes defiled for seven days. The bones and blood of a dead body also have the same effect.

2. Utensils, with the exception of pottery, have the same laws as a human being who comes in contact with the dead. The only way that an earthenware vessel can be defiled is through the inside of the vessel. Therefore, if the vessel is under the same roof with a corpse, it becomes defiled only if its opening is not sealed. Utensils made of stone can never be defiled.

3. A Jew who touches or carries the corpse of a non-Jew becomes defiled. According to some authorities, he remains ritually clean if he merely finds himself under one roof with that corpse. Only a human being can become defiled by coming in contact with the dead.

COMMENTATORS

Ḥinnukh: Man's only claim to sanctity, while alive, is in the possession of a soul. Without the soul, the body is mere waste matter. When this organic matter becomes a vehicle for sin, it pollutes not only the body but also the soul. At death, when the soul departs, the body sinks to the lowest degree of impurity.

Sforno: Why does this ruling of defiling when under one roof apply only to a Jewish corpse and not to that of a non-Jew? Because in life, the body of the Jew was driven by the soul to attain greater heights of spirituality than any other people were capable of attaining. Because of this heightened spirituality, the sins it committed are magnified and considered to be of greater seriousness. It follows then that, proportionately, a body whose sins are regarded as great must be considered more impure than any other body.

References:
B. Shabbat 28a, 83b; B. Berakhot 63b; B. Yevamot 61a; B. Bava Metzia 114b; B. Sukkah 21a; B. Bekhorot 45a; Sifre *Ḥukkat;* Mishnayyot, *Oholot;* Yad, Hilkhot Tumat ha-Met; Sefer ha-Mitzvot (Aseh) 107; Sefer Mitzvot Gadol (Aseh) 231; Sefer ha-Ḥinnukh, Mitzvah 398.

LAWS OF INHERITANCE

Then you shall cause his inheritance to pass to his daughter (Numbers 27:8)

1. The Torah lays down several basic premises on the subject of inheritance. A father may not make a will in which he denies succession to those who are in line to inherit him. He may, however, specify that only one of these should inherit him, and not the others.

2. The order of heirs is as follows: first, sons and their descendants; second, daughters and their descendants. Next comes the father of the deceased, followed by his brothers and their descendants. Should there not be any inheritors from the families enumerated above, the sisters and their descendants benefited. Following them were the father's father, the father's brothers and their descendants, the father's sisters and their descendants, and finally the great-grandfather of the deceased, ad infinitum, up to the twelve tribes and their descendants. Since God assured Israel that there will always remain twelve tribes, there will always be a member of the tribe who is present to inherit.

3. A woman does not inherit from her son nor from her husband. Only by rabbinic decree could a husband inherit from a wife.

4. A first-born son inherits a double share of his father's, but not his mother's, possessions; he cannot, however, claim the same rights in a "future inheritance," i.e., from anything due to accrue to the estate after his father's demise, as, for example, from a loan due for later repayment or a ship which had not yet reached port.

5. Even when these laws were in full effect, the daughters were not completely neglected. Although the sons and their descendants were the first to inherit, the Rabbis were quick to decree that they, the brothers, were obliged to care fully for the needs of their sisters and to provide them with all their necessities, even if they were reduced to abject poverty themselves.

COMMENTATORS

Ḥinnukh: Because of Adam's sin, man is doomed to die. While he was alive, God bestowed upon him material gifts as his own. Ownership implies perpetuity and it is God's wish that this ownership should be everlasting. If this man dies, how does this ownership continue? It continues through his child who is his own flesh. What happens if this man is childless? In this case, his possessions go to his father, brother, uncle, or other relatives, because these possessions have been given to him by God not only for his own merits but also for those of some close or distant relative. On the other hand, if these possessions must be perpetuated and may also have been given to him not on the basis of his own merits, then why may they be passed over to others at all? Why not compel everyone to set apart a portion of his holdings specifically designated as an inheritance? The answer is: God blesses a man with material possessions for his own benefit and enjoyment and he is therefore at liberty to use them solely and completely to that end. It is not permissible for a man to sign over the inheritance to a stranger because, in so doing, he is severing the family-chain of continuity, which was part of God's original design.

References:

B. Bava Batra 106b, 109a, 110a, 115a, 116a, 120a; J. Bava Batra, Chap. 8, Halakhah 1; J. Shabbat, Chap. 2, Halakhah 4; Midrash Tanḥuma, *Pinḥas,* Chap. 9; Sifre *Pinḥas;* Midrash Rabbah, *Pinḥas,* Chap. 21, Sec. 11, 12, 13; Yad, Hilkhot Naḥalot; Sefer ha-Mitzvot (Aseh) 248; Sefer Mitzvot Gadol (Aseh) 96; Shulḥan Arukh, Ḥoshen Mishpat, 276; Sefer ha-Ḥinnukh, Mitzvah 400.

THE LAMB-OFFERING IN THE MORNING AND IN THE EVENING (KORBAN TAMID)

The one lamb shall you offer in the morning and the other lamb shall you offer at dusk (Numbers 28:4)

1. The Priests brought a burnt-offering in the morning and a burnt-offering in the evening. This was called a *korban tamid.* These sacrifices were lambs, one year old and unblemished. Once again, we have a dispute between Maimonides and Naḥmanides on the counting of this *mitzvah.* Maimonides contends that the *korban tamid* of the morning and the one of the evening constitute one *mitzvah.* Naḥmanides contends that the two offerings are to be considered two separate and distinct *mitzvot,* since they are distinct obligations coming at different times.

2. Thirteen Priests busied themselves with the morning offerings. Two additional Priests were necessary for the offering brought at dusk; each one carrying a log for the altar *(shenei gezirei etzim).* The one in the morning was offered at the moment when the first light appeared in the east. This was a signal that all those who wished could begin to bring their individual sacrifices.

3. The *korban tamid* of the evening was offered when the shadows began to fall and dusk to lengthen. After this *korban tamid* was brought no other offerings were sacrificed; however, the fat portions from the animals which were brought by day were brought to the altar to smolder all night. The Rabbis maintain that our morning and afternoon prayers were instituted in commemoration of these morning and afternoon burnt-offerings.

COMMENTATORS

Ḥinnukh: The ritual of offering one lamb in the morning and one lamb at dusk was intended to teach the Jew a most important lesson. Just as it is necessary for him to supply his body with food in the morning and in the evening, so is it important that he realize that he must worship and serve God both in the morning and in the evening. In other words, every day in the year when he brings the lamb as the first offering of the day and another lamb as the last offering of the day, he should remind himself that both by day and night his thoughts should be directed to God.

Abrabanel: He proposes two alternative lines of thinking on this subject:

1. In the national history of the Jew, two great events took place. First, he was liberated from bondage in Egypt and was given the dignity of a freeman. Secondly, and even more important still, he was presented with the Torah, through which he was able to achieve the completeness of a human being. One offering was brought in the morning in honor of the Torah which was presented during the day, and the other offering was brought at dusk in honor of the celebration of freedom which took place at night in the form of the partaking of the Paschal lamb. These two outstanding events actually complement one another and must never be forgotten.
2. A man should be grateful to God for what he considers basic natural phenomena, but which are really the finest gifts that God can bestow on him. First, there is the gift of life; secondly, there is the gift of sustenance. The offering in the morning is an expression of gratitude to God for returning man's soul to him after having had it in His keeping all night. The second offering expresses gratitude for his food and livelihood which God has granted him during the daytime.

References:

B. Tamid 31b; B. Megillah 28a; B. Zevaḥim 11b; B. Pesaḥim 58a, 59a; B. Yoma 25a, 28b; B. Berakhot 17a, 26b; J. Berakhot, Chap. 4, Halakhah 1; Sifre *Pinḥas;* Midrash Tanḥuma, *Pinḥas,* Chap. 13; Yad, Hilkhot Temidim u-Musafim, Chap. 1; Sefer ha-Mitzvot (Aseh) 39. (Note that Naḥmanides considers this ritual as two separate *mitzvot*—the designation of the lamb is one *mitzvah,* and the offering of the lamb is a second *mitzvah.*); Sefer Mitzvot Gadol (Aseh) 190; Sefer ha-Ḥinnukh, Mitzvah 401.

ADDITIONAL OFFERINGS

And on the Sabbath day, two he lambs (Numbers 28:9)
And in your new moon you shall bring a burnt-offering (Numbers 28:11)
And you shall bring an offering made by fire unto the Lord (Leviticus 23:25)
And you shall bring an offering made by fire unto the Lord (Leviticus 23:27)
Seven days shall you bring an offering made by fire unto the Lord (Leviticus 23:36)

1. On every Sabbath and festival an additional offering was brought, to signify the uniqueness of the day. This sacrifice was called a *korban musaf*.

2. The occasions for the *korban musaf* were as follows:

a. On the Sabbath, those Priests who attended to the *korban tamid* of the morning also officiated at the *korban musaf* later in the service.

b. On Rosh Ḥodesh, the same procedure was followed as on the Sabbath.

c. On Passover, a *korban musaf* was offered on each of the seven days of the festival. On the second day, in addition to the *korban tamid* and the *korban musaf,* a burnt-offering was brought in connection with the *omer*.

d. On Shavuot, besides the *korban tamid* and the *korban musaf,* the Priests brought the prescribed number of animals as an auxiliary to the new meal-offerings—"the two breads" *(shtei ha-leḥem)* that characterized that day.

e. On Rosh Ha-Shanah, the day started with the *korban tamid* of the morning, followed by the *musaf* of Rosh Ḥodesh and then by the *korban musaf* of Rosh Ha-Shanah. We apply the well-known rabbinic dictum that *tadir ve-she-eino tadir, tadir kodem,* i.e., that we give precedence to an obligation which is more frequent over a less frequent one, in the event that Rosh Ha-Shanah fell on the Sabbath. The order of the offerings would then be: *korban tamid,* the *musaf* of Sabbath, the *musaf* of Rosh Ḥodesh, and the *musaf* of Rosh Ha-Shanah.

f. On Yom Kippur, three sacrifices were offered: the *korban tamid,* the *korban musaf,* and the prescribed sacrifices which were peculiar to this day.

g. On Sukkot and Shemini Atzeret, only the *korban tamid* and the prescribed *korban musaf* were offered.

3. Today, in the absence of the Temple and the sacrifices, we substitute the *musaf* services and prayers, as it is written, "And let our lips compensate for the sacrifice of bulls" (Hosea 14:3).

COMMENTATORS

Ḥinnukh: Those days in the Jewish calendar that signify an historical event such as Passover, or a purely religious occasion, such as the Sabbath, warrant an extra offering to God as a token of our gratitude. If this is the reason for an additional offering, then what does the first of the month represent and why does it warrant an additional offering? The answer is that the New Moon brings with it radical changes in its effect on man, animals, vegetation, and even on the tides of the sea. The renewal of the moon is connected with the renewal and changes in many phenomena in the world. This process of renewal demands special recognition and is, therefore, accorded an additional offering.

Ḥizzekuni: The Feast of Tabernacles warranted an additional offering for two reasons: 1. The additional joy of the ingathering of the fruits. 2. The many additional features of the festival, such as the *etrog* (citron), the branch of the palm tree, the myrtle, and the willow.

Baḥya ben Asher: The universal character of the Feast of Tabernacles is sufficient reason for offering an additional sacrifice. The Jew has contributed greatly to the welfare of the rest of the nations of the world. On the Feast of Tabernacles, the Jew also brought offerings on behalf of the other nations. This was done in order to rally all nations to join in one common goal in order not so much to bring down Heaven on earth, but even better still, to raise earth to Heaven.

References:
B. Yoma 62b; B. Menaḥot 45b; B. Sanhedrin 36a; B. Ḥullin 60b; B. Rosh ha-Shanah 8b (see Tosafot); B. Zevaḥim 90b (see Tosafot); Midrash Rabbah, *Noaḥ,* Chap. 34, Sec. 9, *Ba-Midbar, Nasso,* Chap. 13, Sec. 13; Sifre *Pinḥas;* Yad, Hilkhot Temidim u-Musafim, Chap. 4, 7, 8, 10; Sefer Mitzvot Gadol (Aseh) 195, 197, 198, 201, 203, 205; Sefer ha-Ḥinnukh, Mitzvot 299, 312, 314, 320, 402, 403, 404.

THE SHAVUOT OFFERINGS

Also on the day of the first fruits . . . you shall bring a new meal-offering unto the Lord (Numbers 28:26)
And you shall present a new meal-offering unto the Lord (Leviticus 23:16)

1. The outstanding ritual of the day was the *minḥah ḥadashah,* the bringing of the "new meal-offering" which was composed of two loaves of bread *(ḥallot)* made from the new wheat. The measurements of these oblong *ḥallot* were seven handbreadths long, four handbreadths wide, and four fingers high. The High Priest had the right to take one loaf, leaving the other for all the other Priests. After this offering, all the new wheat could now be brought by the people as *minḥah* sacrifices.

2. In addition to the *korban musaf,* other offerings were brought in addition to the two loaves. They were seven sheep, a young bullock, and two rams as burnt-offerings; a he-goat for a sin-offering, and two sheep as a peace-offering.

3. The kneading and preparation of the two *ḥallot* took place outside the Temple precincts. The baking, however, was done in the Temple itself.

COMMENTATORS

Abrabanel, Baḥya ben Asher: What was the significance of the "new" meal-offering which was brought to the Temple on Shavuot? Why is it considered new? The answer is that it was on Shavuot that the children of Israel received the Torah. Whereas until then their lives were lived mostly by simple animal instincts alone, they were now a people blessed with intelligence. It is for this reason that the Torah calls the offering on Shavuot a "new" offering. They were a "new" people which had acquired a "new" power of intelligence and they brought their offerings with these "new" attitudes in mind.

Keli Yakar: The fact that the Torah was received by Israel on Shavuot is emphasized by the nomenclature of the offering of the day, *"minḥah ḥadashah."* This document of divine law, the Torah, was to be treated each day in future generations as something new and valuable. Why does not the Torah refer to the holiday of Shavuot as the day of receiving the Torah? Similarly, why does not the Torah specifically refer to Rosh Ha-Shanah as a day of reckoning and repentance? The same answer applies to both questions. A Jew is expected to look upon every day of the year, in every generation, as a day of repentance. He is also expected to look upon the Torah with new enthusiasm and new eager anticipation every day, just as if he had received it that very day.

References:

B. Menaḥot 68a, 68b, 83b, 84b; B. Rosh ha-Shanah 6b; Sifra *Emor, Pinḥas;* Yad, Hilkhot Temidim u-Musafim, Chap. 8; Sefer ha-Mitzvot (Aseh) 45, 46; Sefer Mitzvot Gadol (Aseh) 201, 202; Sefer ha-Ḥinnukh, Mitzvah 307.

SOUNDING THE SHOFAR ON ROSH HA-SHANAH

It is a day of blowing the horn unto you (Numbers 29:1)

1. It is basic to the observance of Rosh Ha-Shanah that the outstanding feature of the day is to hear the sounding of the *shofar*. This is an obligation imposed on every Jewish male. Women are exempt because of the time-element involved, for the *shofar* is sounded only on Rosh Ha-Shanah, and a woman is not obliged to fulfill a *mitzvah* the performance of which is conditioned by a specified time. However, it has become customary for women to listen to the sounding of the *shofar* on Rosh Ha-Shanah.

2. In Temple days, two trumpets were blown in addition to the *shofar*. The trumpets gave forth short notes, while the *shofar* emitted long notes. Today, only the *shofar* is employed.

3. The *shofar* must be made from the hollow horn of a kosher animal, such as a ram or a goat. It should be curved, so as to symbolize our efforts to bend our will to that of God.

4. The sound of the *shofar*, irrespective of its key, must be natural. It is for this reason that if a perforated *shofar* is filled in with a foreign substance it becomes disqualified. For the same reason, if one inserted one *shofar* into another and the sound of the outer *shofar* emerged, the ritual of *teki'at shofar* (blowing of the *shofar*) was unacceptable. Furthermore, if one stood outside a cave or a pit and blew into these areas, the ritual was disqualified because the sound heard was not that of the *shofar*, but an echo.

5. According to Jewish law, every Jew must listen to at least nine sounds during *teki'at shofar*. The sounds themselves were divided into two types; the *teki'ah* had to be an extended note. There were two traditions concerning the sound of *teru'ah*. Some maintained that the *teru'ah* had the sound of a groan; others that it was like a whimper. To satisfy both traditions, the Rabbis included both the *shevarim*, which sounds like three distinct groans and the *teru'ah*, which sounds like nine short whimpers.

6. Today it is customary for the congregation to stand during the sounding of the *shofar*, both before and during the *amidah*. However, the sounding before the *amidah* is known in the Talmud as the "blowings when seated."

7. It is generally understood that the use of the ram's horn was in commemoration of the ram that was caught by its horns in the thicket at the *Akedat Yitzḥak*—the episode when Abraham was about to offer up Isaac as a sacrifice.

8. Although *teki'at shofar* is the special *mitzvah* of Rosh Ha-Shanah, nevertheless if one of its two days falls on the Sabbath we are forbidden to sound the *shofar;* this is a rabbinic decree lest we carry the *shofar* in a public thoroughfare, an act prohibited on the Sabbath.

COMMENTATORS

Saadiah: He offers ten reasons for the sounding of the *shofar* on Rosh Ha-Shanah. In this list, he has the general agreement of other exegetes.

1. God created the heavens and the earth and established his right to its sovereignty. In acknowledgment, we herald our King with the *shofar*.
2. On Rosh Ha-Shanah we begin the Ten Days of Repentance. The *shofar* summons us to repent and thus receive God's blessing.
3. We must remember the momentous occasion when we stood at the foot of Mount Sinai and received the Torah. Then, too, was the *shofar* sounded.
4. It is important that we keep in mind that we must believe in the prophets and their exhortations which are compared to the blasts of a *shofar*.
5. The broken blasts *(shevarim)* of the *shofar* should remind us of the shattered Temple. We must pray for its rededication and reestablishment.
6. We must remember that Abraham obeyed God and was willing to sacrifice his son Isaac. It was a ram that was substituted for Isaac hence the use of a ram's horn.
7. When we hear the broken sounds of the *shofar,* we must also address our prayers to God with broken hearts and full of humility
8. The most important aspect is to recognize the seriousness of the day and to be awed by its sanctity.
9. We must remember, pray, and yearn for the ingathering of all Jews into the Land of Israel, an event which will be heralded by the blasts of the *shofar*.
10. We must remind ourselves to believe implicitly in the resurrection of the dead, which is also to be heralded by the *shofar* sounds in the Messianic age.

References:
B. Shabbat 131b; B. Megillah 20b; B. Rosh ha-Shanah 16a, 26b, 27a, 29b, 30a, 32a, 32b, 33b, 34a; J. Rosh ha-Shanah, Chap. 4, Halakhah 8; J. Sukkah, Chap. 3, Halakhah 1; Midrash Rabbah, *Bereshit,* Chap. 56, Sec. 13, *Emor,* Chap. 29, Sec. 3, 5; Yad, Hilkhot Shofar, Chap. 1, 3; Sefer ha-Mitzvot (Aseh) 170; Sefer Mitzvot Gadol (Aseh) 42; Sefer Mitzvot Katan 92; Shulḥan Arukh, Oraḥ Ḥayyim, 585, 588; Sefer ha-Ḥinnukh, Mitzvah 405.

MAKING AND ANNULLING VOWS

If a man vows a vow unto the Lord . . . he shall not break his word (Numbers 30:3)

What your lips have uttered, that must you keep (Deuteronomy 23:24)

1. Man, with his superior intelligence, should recognize the importance of not making statements indiscreetly or rashly. He should weigh his words and, once uttered, he should abide by them. This includes making a vow and fulfilling it.

2. There are occasions, however, when vows are invalid *ab initio.* Among these is the *neder zerizim*—an oath taken for purposes of convenience but never taken seriously. This we find in business dealings. Another is the *neder havai*, an exaggerated oath; for example, a vow to do something if one saw a million people or a flying camel. An invalid vow could also be a *neder shegagah*—a vow made unintentionally. One thinks that he ate yesterday and takes an oath on that condition when, in truth, he did not eat then. Finally, there is the *neder onesim*—when illness prohibited the fulfillment of a vow, where we assume that the vow would not have been made under such circumstances.

3. There is a difference between a *neder* and a *shevu'ah.* A *neder*—a vow—refers to someone who states, for example, that he will abstain from oranges as from an offering. Even if he doesn't say "like an offering" these words are understood; it means like any other thing which becomes prohibited to a person. A *shevu'ah*—an oath—refers to one who places himself in a special relationship to something; for example, "I swear that I will not eat oranges." In the *neder,* it is the article that is banned; in the *shevu'ah* it is the person himself who is the object of the oath.

4. Exceptions are *nidrei mitzvah* or *nidrei hekdesh,* where the person obligates himself (without using the prescribed language for a *shevu'ah*) to perform a *mitzvah;* for example, he will donate to charity. This is called *neder* although the person obligates himself. Similarly, if a person takes upon himself a *neder* that he will bring an offering, it is incumbent upon him to do so, although the person is involved insofar as he is the subject of the *neder.*

5. If one equates something that is permissible with something that is forbidden by the Torah, this *neder* is invalid. For example, one cannot vow, "This orange shall be forbidden to me as is the flesh of a pig." He can only equate the permissible things with something which becomes forbidden due to speech, i.e., a sacrifice, an object already forbidden through a *neder,* etc.

6. A *shevu'ah,* also can be an oath that one takes to deny himself something that is not forbidden by the Bible, but not to accept something that is forbidden by the Bible. For example: A Jew may not take an oath that he will not put on his *tefillin* (phylacteries), or that he will eat swine's flesh.

7. The Torah, by implication, and the Rabbis in explicit terms, denounce those who resort to vows and oaths. A person should be able to act correctly without taking such extreme measures. Many people regret making a vow soon after uttering it. In that case, if the vow is formally cancelled, it becomes invalid retroactively. This is an annulment. The Torah allowed a way out through *hattarat nedarim*—a release from vows and oaths. In this procedure, a learned sage or three ordinary people can absolve a person from his vow by asking him whether he would still have made it had he known beforehand what the consequences of the vow would have been. A husband can abrogate the vows of his wife and a father can do the same for a daughter during the years before her maturity. Any person who makes a vow or takes an oath, and does not keep it, is subject to the penalty of lashes.

COMMENTATORS

Maimonides, Naḥmanides: Both agree that to take a self-denying vow, e.g., to abstain from drinking wine, is a praiseworthy act and the vow must be observed. While Naḥmanides offers no rationalization of this law, Maimonides holds that vows are useful in helping a man to curb his appetites. These two authorities differ, however, on the question whether the provision in the Torah for cancelling vows is to be included among the *mitzvot.*

Maimonides answers this question in the affirmative. He argues that, since it is a human tendency to undertake obligations which are later regretted or found to be impracticable, the Torah commands us to terminate them in the prescribed way and in no other. The life of a family could become intolerable if each member of the household were inescapably bound by a vow, often taken without due consideration: if each one vowed, for instance, to abstain from a different kind of food. This could clearly cause domestic chaos. The Torah therefore empowers the father to declare invalid vows made by his wife or children. Vows made by an adult male can, in turn, be cancelled by a *Bet Din.*

Keli Yakar: Why does the Torah allow a person to have his vows annulled? Why should he not be compelled to keep them under all circumstances? A person takes a vow either in a moment of anger or after serious meditation. The Rabbis of the Talmud condemned the taking of vows because he who vows exhibits a certain measure of arrogance. If everyone is allowed to eat meat and drink wine, why should he show that he is superior and able to do without these luxuries? A person who took a vow in anger might regret this step the moment his wrath subsided. He is truly penitent and the Torah, therefore, provides a way whereby this man can come to the *Bet Din* to have his vow rendered void; but he who takes a vow with studied meditation will not ask to have it annulled. In such a case, it would be an act of presumption and arrogance.

When a wife or child takes a vow, it is done with the understanding that the master of the house approves; if he does not approve, he may render the vow void.

References:
B. Nedarim 2b, 3b, 8a, 12a, 13a, 13b, 15a, 15b, 16b, 66a, 77a, 77b, 81b, 90a; B. Gittin 35b, 36a; B. Ketubbot 108a; B. Zevaḥim 2b; B. Temurah 2b, 6a; B. Ta'anit 12a; B. Ḥagigah 10a; B. Shevuot 10b, 21a, 26b, 29a; B. Makkot 16a; B. Nazir 38b, 62b; B. Rosh ha-Shanah 6a; B. Menaḥot 103a; B. Shabbat 32b; B. Yevamot 109a, 109b; Pirkei Avot, Chap. 3; J. Rosh ha-Shanah, Chap. 1, Halakhah 1; J. Nedarim, Chap. 1, Halakhot 1, 2; Chap. 2, Halakhah 4; Chap. 6, Halakhot 8, 9; Sifre *Mattot;* Midrash Tanḥuma, *Va-Yishlaḥ,* Chap. 8, *Mattot,* Chap. 1; Midrash Rabbah, *Va-Yetze,* Chap. 70, Sec. 1, 2, *Va-Yishlaḥ,* Chap. 81, Sec. 2; Guide of the Perplexed, Part 3, Sec. 48; Yad, Hilkhot Shevuot, Chap. 6, Halakhah 11; Yad, Hilkhot Nedarim, Chap. 1, Halakhah 11, 12; Sefer ha-Mitzvot (Aseh) 94, 95, (Lo Ta'aseh) 157; Sefer Mitzvot Gadol (Aseh) 124, 125, (Lav) 242; Sefer Mitzvot Katan 81; Shulḥan Arukh, Even ha-Ezer, 74, Yoreh De'ah 203–239; Sefer ha-Ḥinnukh, Mitzvot 406, 407, 475.

CITIES OF REFUGE (AREI MIKLAT)

The manslayer may return unto the land of his possessions (Numbers 35:28)
And you shall accept no ransom for him that fled to his city of refuge (Numbers 35:32)
Three cities shall you separate to you (Deuteronomy 19:2)

1. A remarkable innovation in criminology instituted by the Torah was the concept of "cities of refuge" *(arei miklat),* to which anyone who had killed without premeditation could flee to escape the wrath of the bereaved family.

2. Six cities were designated as places of refuge. In addition, the remaining 42 Levitical cities were also to serve as places of refuge. The difference between those six designated cities and the Levitical cities was that, in the former, there need not have been any cognizance that the city was a place of refuge, and no rent had to be paid by the killer. In the latter, the manslayer had to know that the Levitical city was considered a place of refuge and he had to pay rent for his stay therein.

3. The roads to the cities of refuge were direct and specially marked, to facilitate the escape of the homicide.

4. He was forced to remain in one of these cities of refuge until the death of the High Priest who officiated at that time.

5. At the outset every presumptive murderer fled to these cities of refuge. The court would have them brought before it, where testimony and arguments were heard. The court then made its decision whether the killing was premeditated or not. If it was found to have been intentional, the murderer was executed; if unintentional, the court assigned two sages to accompany the killer to the cities of refuge so that no one would lay a hand upon him. He was to remain in one of these places of refuge until the death of the High Priest and no reason was valid enough to permit him to leave before that time.

6. In addition to the cities of refuge, the altar in the Temple also served as a refuge. If a Priest was in the midst of sacrificing an offering on the altar, he was safe. The court assigned guards to escort him from the altar to the cities of refuge.

7. Anyone who killed a murderer while he was in the protected area was brought to court and executed.

COMMENTATORS

Maimonides, Abrabanel: It is in the nature of man that his own tragedy becomes dimmed in the face of the more serious tragedies of others. A man whose relative was accidentally slain is angry with the slayer and is even prepared to kill him in revenge. When the High Priest dies, this constitutes such a great loss to the whole nation that the anger of the potential avenger subsides. His reflections and meditations on the demise of the High Priest help to calm his emotions. It is now considered safe for the unintentional murderer to leave the city of refuge and return to his own town.

Sforno: Even in cases of accidental killing, some accidents have a greater or lesser degree of deliberateness in them. God knows which are more and which are less deliberate and He arranges the death of the High

Priest so that not every murderer stays in the cities of refuge for the same duration. Some murderers might even die before the High Priest and thus spend all the rest of their lives confined in these cities.

Baḥya ben Asher: Why is an unintentional murderer not penalized with capital punishment? Because there was no unity of action between his heart and his body. His heart told him not to kill and his hands did kill. The moral of this is that man should strive to coordinate his body to follow the dictates of his heart and to direct his life to do God's bidding.

Ḥinnukh: He proposes some reasons for the necessity of the cities of refuge:

1. Killers must not be permitted to remain at large. Although it can happen that a man kills without malice, the fact remains that he has killed someone. While he should not be penalized with capital punishment, he should be penalized with the loneliness of life which the city of refuge imposes upon him.
2. Furthermore, what is gained by taking the life of an unintentional murderer? After all, he did not kill deliberately.
3. The cities of refuge were necessary to keep the killer from mixing in society. Were the accidental murderer to be allowed to mix freely in society, then he would always find himself in the presence of the family of the deceased. This would provoke them and could jeopardize his life.

References:

B. Rosh ha-Shanah 26a; B. Sanhedrin 18b; B. Ketubbot 37b; B. Makkot 7a, 9b, 11a, 11b, 12a, 12b; J. Yoma, Chap. 7, Halakhah 5; Mekhilta, *Mishpatim;* Sifre, *Massei;* Midrash Tanḥuma, *Massei;* Guide of the Perplexed, Part 3, Sec. 40; Yad, Hilkhot Rotze'aḥ u-Shemirat ha-Nefesh, Chap. 1, 5, 8; Sefer ha-Mitzvot (Aseh) 182, 225, (Lo Ta'aseh) 295; Sefer Mitzvot Gadol (Aseh) 75, 76, (Lav) 161; Sefer ha-Ḥinnukh, Mitzvot 408, 409, 410, 413, 520.

THE REQUIREMENT OF TWO WITNESSES

A single witness shall not testify against a person to make him liable to the death penalty (Numbers 35:30)
The testimony of one witness shall not prevail against a man (Deuteronomy 19:15)

1. The extreme zeal of the Jew concerning the due process of the law is evidenced by some of the rules appertaining to the testimony of witnesses. Nothing in any fashion or manner can be introduced before a court that will, even in the slightest, tend to pervert justice.

2. Where a death-sentence is involved, a witness who had testified in favor of the accused could not afterwards say: "I have evidence that will incriminate this man." He was only to state the testimony and remain silent thereafter.

3. In civil cases, however, he could voice his opinion, but he was prevented from becoming a member of the court after serving as a witness. This was true only in cases where the Torah demanded that there be witnesses and judges. When the Rabbis required testimony, it was different. For example: The Rabbis required a messenger who came from a different country to bring a document of divorce from the husband to the wife to testify that he personally had witnessed the writing of the divorce and the required signatures. In that case, he and two others could join to constitute a *Bet Din* and deliver the divorce to the woman.

4. There are times when the testimony of one witness is accepted.
a. If a witness was present when a married woman was intimate with a stranger against whom her husband had made *kinnui* (warning not to meet him clandestinely), then the drinking of the bitter waters was not applied (see above, p. 322).
b. If a person was found dead and there was one witness who saw him being murdered, there was no need to establish which was the nearest city that would be responsible for performing the ritual of *eglah arufah*—the breaking of the heifer's neck.
c. One witness is sufficient to establish that a woman's hus-

band is dead and thus release her from being an *agunah* (an "anchored" wife who could never remarry, because her husband's death had not been established).

COMMENTATORS

Naḥmanides: He offers no rationalization for the *mitzvah* that there must be more than one witness to condemn a person. According to him, it is simply a decree of the Torah.

Abrabanel: His reasoning is that since one man is on trial, it follows, logically, that more than one man is required to prove his guilt—otherwise it is one word against another.

Ḥinnukh: Man's natural propensities, in general, are bad. Of course, he does endeavor to overcome them; but there comes a time in everyone's life, even in the life of the most righteous, when vindictiveness and malice gain the upper hand. One who has an ill feeling towards another will make every effort to bring his enemy down. He will even distort his testimony in order to hurt the other; but it is unlikely that two righteous witnesses will collude to perjure themselves. For this reason, the law requires two witnesses for conviction.

References:

B. Sanhedrin 33b, 34a, 84b; B. Pesaḥim 113b; B. Sotah 2b; B. Ketubbot 21a, 21b, 87a; B. Gittin 71a; B. Makkot 5a, 6a, 6b; B. Yevamot 31b (see Tosafot), 117a; B. Kiddushin 65b, 66a, 74a; B. Bava Batra 160b; B. Bava Kamma 70b, 90b; B. Shevuot 40a; J. Sanhedrin, Chap. 5, Halakhah 4; J. Yoma, Chap. 6, Halakhah 1; Sifre *Shofetim;* Yad, Hilkhot Edut, Chap. 5; Sefer ha-Mitzvot (Lo Ta'aseh) 288, 291; Sefer Mitzvot Gadol (Lav) 213; Sefer ha-Ḥinnukh, Mitzvot 411, 523.

THE APPOINTMENT OF JUDGES

You shall recognize no face in judgment (Deuteronomy 1:17)
Judges and executive officers shall you appoint (Deuteronomy 16:18)

1. When Israel was an autonomous people dwelling on its own land and all its religious activities were centered around the Temple, judges were not elected but rather selected and those who were commissioned to make the appointments were forbidden to show any favoritism whatsoever. The candidates had to meet certain qualifications of the highest level.

2. The highest court was the *Sanhedrin Gedolah,* the major Sanhedrin composed of 71 judges. The head of this body of jurists was called *nasi.* In view of the fact that Moses was the first *nasi,* every succeeding *nasi* was to be considered in the same light as was Moses in his day. To the right of the *nasi,* sat the *av bet din,* "the father of the court." The remaining members were seated in a semi-circle, so that each member could observe his fellow, and the *nasi* and *av bet din* could see them. The *Sanhedrin Gedolah* held court in the Temple, in a room adjacent to the *azarah.*

A *Sanhedrin Ketanah* (lower court) composed of 23 sages, was appointed for every community that had more than than 120 inhabitants. The *Sanhedrin Ketanah* was also headed by a sage; the others sat in a semi-circle facing him. There was also a *Bet Din* comprising three wise men who adjudicated in monetary disputes. A city which did not meet the numerical requirements for which a *Sanhedrin Ketanah* was appointed nevertheless had a *Bet Din* of three.

The *Sanhedrin Ketanah* dealt with death sentences while the highest court judged matters which were of importance to the whole nation, such as the appointment of a king, the establishment of *Sanhedriyot Ketanot* in all sizeable cities, the judgment of an entire tribe which had committed idolatry, and the like.

3. In order to qualify to be a member of the Sanhedrin the judge was to be very erudite in Torah and possess some knowledge of the sciences. His character and family background had to be impeccable. If he was very old, he was disqualified. A eunuch could not serve in the Sanhedrin, nor could one who was childless. In the lower courts consisting of three judges, however, the requirements were not so stringent. Nevertheless, as a minimum, a judge had to be God-fearing and well-versed in Jewish law. It was also necessary that some of the members of the Sanhedrin should be linguists.

Unless he had received special permission from his colleagues, a judge was not to sit as a court of one. God is the only one who may sit by Himself and judge.

4. A member of the Sanhedrin had to possess *semikhah,* the traditional ordination. This was a ritual that started with Moses laying his hands upon the head of Joshua, thus ordaining him as his successor. This chain of ordination continued until the end of the days of the talmudic period. Today, Rabbis are not ordained in the traditional manner. They receive the *hattarat hora'ah*—the license to instruct.

5. Maimonides is of the opinion that, if all the wise men in the Holy Land convened and decided to revive the Sanhedrin in the traditional fashion, they could do so.

COMMENTATORS

Naḥmanides, Ibn Ezra: Both question the need for all small communities to be burdened with lower courts, when the supreme court (the Sanhedrin) sat in Jerusalem continually and everyone went to Jerusalem three times a year. Ibn Ezra replies that one court in Jerusalem would not suffice for the needs of the whole country and that it was therefore necessary that each community also have its own judiciary. Naḥmanides replies that justice is best served when suits are resolved immediately; also, procrastination tends to arouse feelings of animosity in the litigants.
Or ha-Ḥayyim: Why are the judges selected by the people or their representatives? Does this not introduce the danger of the judge being beholden to his benefactors? The answer is that this is the test of a

strong and stable society. Such a society is able to invoke its power to appoint a judge and then to waive its superior position, humbly submitting itself to the judge's authority, prudence, and acknowledged wisdom. **Recanati:** Judges are appointed not only for the purpose of issuing decisions on the basis of strict law but also for the purpose of mediation and compromise.

References:

B. Sanhedrin 2b, 3a, 3b, 6b, 7a, 7b, 8a, 16a, 17b; B. Ketubbot 84a; B. Makkot 7a; B. Shabbat 10a, 139a; J. Sanhedrin Chap. 1, Halakhah 1; Sifre *Devarim, Shofetim;* Midrash Tehillim, Chap, 72; Midrash Tanḥuma, *Be-Shalaḥ,* Chap. 10, *Mishpatim,* Chap. 1–6, *Shofetim,* Chap. 1–6; Midrash Rabbah, *Mishpatim,* Chap. 30, Sec. 1–22; Yad, Hilkhot Sanhedrin, Chap. 1, 3; Sefer ha-Mitzvot (Lo Ta'aseh) 284, (Aseh) 176; Sefer Mitzvot Gadol (Lav) 194, (Aseh) 97; Shulḥan Arukh, Ḥoshen Mishpat, Chap. 1, 5; Sefer ha-Ḥinnukh, Mitzvot 414, 491.

SHEMA: THE ONENESS OF GOD

Hear, O Israel, the Lord our God, the Lord is One (Deuteronomy 6:4)
And you shall love your God, with all your heart (Deuteronomy 6:5)
You shall fear the Lord, your God (Deuteronomy 10:20)

1. If we were, symbolically, to erect a skyscraper composed of the 613 *mitzvot* and if we were to remove one small section known as the Oneness of God, we would not merely leave a small area exposed but the entire edifice would topple and crumble. The concept of *eḥad* ("One") is the foundation of Judaism. The belief in One God must be total and absolute.

2. The Torah then proceeds to instruct us how we are to worship God. We can achieve this through love and fear which come about by standing in wondrous and enraptured awe at the inexplicable manifestations of God's works. It is also demanded of man that he make a supreme effort to emulate the qualities of God.

Every attribute that is godly—such as goodness, compassion, kindness, forgiveness, tolerance, and mercy—should be the goal of every human being. Man's desire for God must be so strong, that he should yearn for it.

Once man becomes captivated, fascinated, and spellbound by the omnipotence of God and feels the urge to understand His ways, a certain measure of fear begins to pervade him. He recognizes his own insignificance and unimportance. Hence, when man is about to commit a sin, he should immediately sense that an Omniscient Power is aware of his movements and thoughts and that they may displease Him. This fear of the "Ever-present Eye" will result in the fear of Heavenly punishment. According to the *Sifre,* the Torah instructs man how to attain love of God. The verse following that which commands man to love God reads: "And these words which I am commanding you today shall be on your heart"; this means that through incessant study of Torah man's heart becomes attached to God.

3. A Jew who is ordered to violate the law of the belief in the oneness of God by committing idolatry or accepting a different belief, must be ready to sacrifice his life rather than consent to do so.

COMMENTATORS

Naḥmanides: The first commandments in the Decalogue concerning the unity of God were pronouncements of fact. The Oneness of God, as expressed in the *Shema,* is to convey the message of religious commitment. He who does not subscribe to the concept of the Oneness of God nullifies all other religious commitments. To love God, one must do so both with the physical love and desire one feels for something beautiful, as well as with the intellectual love and appreciation of serving an Omnipotent Power.

Rashbam: The belief in the unity of God excludes faith in anything that is given the status of a quasi-god, such as the hidden powers involved in sorcery and black magic.

Ba'al ha-Turim: The oneness of God signifies that, although He may sometimes appear to us as a strict judge and at other times as a compassionate father, He is really one and the same God.

Or ha-Ḥayyim: We must love God because He is "the Lord your God"; that is, He has chosen us to be His people and He will be our God.
Ḥinnukh: All civilized people must intellectually acknowledge the oneness of God. Furthermore, the only motive that can effectively prompt us to His bidding is our love for Him.
Recanati: Love is identifiable with *"ḥesed"*, which means kindliness and sympathy. By loving God, it becomes easy for us to love and be kindly to our fellow-men.
Radbaz: No human being can be so saintly as never to sin. A human being, with all his frailties, is prone to do wrong and commit sins. What is expected of him, however, is that he recognize his mistakes and repent by resolving not to repeat the same error. According to Radbaz, the one who sins and arrogantly dismisses from his mind any intention of repenting, violates the *mitzvah* "You shall fear the Lord your God." Apparently, his reasoning is that the sinner recognizes no wrong in his deed and flaunts his misbehavior by displaying that he defies the ever-watchful "eye" of God.

References:
B. Berakhot 6a, 13a, 13b, 15a, 16a, 33b, 34a, 54a, 61a, 61b; B. Sanhedrin 74a; B. Sotah 32b; B. Pesaḥim 56a; B. Rosh ha-Shanah 32b; B. Yoma 86a; B. Ḥullin 91b; B. Shabbat 31a, 31b; J. Berakhot, Chap. 1, Halakhot 5, 8, Chap. 3, Halakhah 5; J. Sanhedrin, Chap. 10, Halakhah 1; J. Sotah, Chap. 5, Halakhah 7; Sifre *Va-Etḥanan;* Midrash Rabbah, *Va-Etḥanan,* Chap. 2, Sec. 22–26; Yad, Hilkhot Teshuvah, Chap. 10, Sec. 5, 6; Yad, Yesodei Torah, Chap. 1, 2; Sefer ha-Mitzvot (Aseh) 2, 3; Sefer Mitzvot Gadol (Aseh) 2, 3; Sefer Mitzvot Katan 2, 3 (Note that there are two possible aspects to this *mitzvah;* the belief in God, per se, and the belief in the Oneness of God. According to Maimonides, the *mitzvah* to believe in God stems from the first of the Ten Commandments: while the belief in the Oneness of God stems from the *Shema*. According to Naḥmanides, however, both the belief and the unity of God stem from the first of the Ten Commandments. Naḥmanides' reasoning is that one is inseparable from the other.); Shulḥan Arukh, Oraḥ Ḥayyim, Chap. 61; Sefer ha-Ḥinnukh, Mitzvot 417, 418.

THE DUTY OF TRANSMITTING THE TEACHING OF THE TORAH

And you shall teach them diligently to your children (Deuteronomy 6:7)

1. To the Jew, Torah education is not a privilege, nor yet a measure of prudence by which he can advance to an economically or intellectually privileged position. It is primarily a religious duty imposed by a biblical commandment. In Jewish eyes no human endeavor deserves greater respect than *talmud Torah*—the study of the Torah in its widest sense. Rabbinical tradition stresses this view to the point of asserting that a learned *mamzer* (offspring of an incestuous or adulterous union, normally regarded as the lowest on the social scale) has precedence over an ignorant High Priest (apex of the Jewish hierarchy). The Jew learns Torah in order to know how to do God's will; thereby he also becomes attached to God and longs to imitate His ways.

2. Whereas almost every advanced society provides for schools and some degree of compulsory education, the Torah places the onus of teaching on the father.

3. When a child begins to speak, he should immediately be taught thc verse: "The Torah that Moses commanded us is an heritage of the Congregation of Israel." Another opinion is that the verse to be taught should be from Proverbs: "My son be attentive to the tradition of your father and do not forsake the teachings of your mother."

4. A Jew is obligated to study at all times and under all circumstances. Some of the greatest minds in Jewish history were those of men who were occupied with menial work, hard labor, and exhausting tasks. Yet, they designated a certain period each day for the study of Torah. The oft-repeated axiom that has come down to us through the ages is: "Forsake the Torah for one day and it will abandon you for two days."

5. Women are exempt from the intensive study of the Torah. They should, however, be taught the various laws pertaining to women, which include almost all negative *mitzvot* and many positive ones. The Jewish woman was traditionally well-versed in the laws of the Sabbath, *kashrut,* family purity, blessings, and, in ancient times, the laws of purity *(taharah)* and impurity *(tumah)*.

COMMENTATORS

Naḥmanides: If the Torah is to remain a permanent possession of Israel, the only way to insure this is for one generation to teach it to the succeeding generation exactly as it was received.

Sforno, Ibn Ezra, Rashbam, Baḥya ben Asher: The teacher must clarify the principles of the Torah with sharp decisiveness and not allow the listener to remain in doubt or perplexity.

Saadiah: The best way to teach Torah is in an attractive manner, even in a story-telling fashion if necessary.

Abrabanel: The Hebrew word, meaning "to teach," has its root in the word *"shenayim,"* which means "two." The reasoning is that the Torah can be understood only if it is taught not merely once, but over and over again.

Alshekh: The verse above is preceded by the command: "And these words . . . shall be upon your heart." This is to impart to us that before we can teach the Torah to our children, we ourselves must be convinced in our own heart that it constitutes our own way of life.

Recanati: It is not enough that man recognizes God philosophically. God must also be seen through His works. In order to do this, we need a "blueprint" of His plans, designs, and requirements. The Torah is this "blueprint." Hence we are to teach our children to understand this Torah, so that they can build for themselves a life-structure that will have moral purpose and religious meaning.

References:
B. Kiddushin 29b, 30a, 82a; B. Sanhedrin 7b, 24a; B. Bava Metzia 85a; B. Bava Batra 21a; B. Sukkah 42a; B. Shabbat 119b; B. Sotah 21a; B. Nedarim 36b; Guide of the Perplexed, Part 1, Sec. 1; Yad, Hilkhot Talmud Torah, Chap. 1; Sefer ha-Mitzvot (Aseh) 11; Sefer Mitzvot Gadol (Aseh) 12; Sefer Mitzvot Katan 105, 106; Shulḥan Arukh, Yoreh De'ah, 246; Sefer ha-Ḥinnukh, Mitzvah 419.

READING OF THE SHEMA

And you shall speak of them when you lie down, and when you rise up (Deuteronomy 6:7)

1. The *Shema,* the basic declaration of faith, comprises three biblical passages beginning with, "Hear O Israel, the Lord is One" (Deuteronomy 6:4–9); "It shall come to pass" (Deuteronomy 11:13–21); "The Lord spoke to Moses" (Numbers 15:37–41). The last of these three extracts deals with the *mitzvot* of *tzitzit.* The reason this section is included is that it speaks also about the Exodus from Egypt. The Jew must acknowledge God's involvement at all times in his destiny. It is incumbent upon the Jew to recite the *Shema* twice a day, in the morning and in the evening.

2. *Keri'at Shema*—the recitation of the morning *Shema*—is permissible from the time of dawn until the third hour of day. It is preferable, however, that it be concluded as the first rays of the sunshine herald the dawn of a new day.

3. The evening *Shema* may be recited from the beginning of evening throughout the night. It is preferable that one should not delay reciting it until midnight, lest he forget to recite it altogether.

4. Concerning this *mitzvah,* there is a dispute between Maimonides and Naḥmanides. In the view of the former, the evening *Shema* and the morning *Shema* constitute one *mitzvah;* according to the latter, they are two separate commandments because they are performed at two separate times.

6. Women are exempted from the *keri'at Shema* because there is a time-element involved.

COMMENTATORS

Ibn Ezra: Coupled with the previous *mitzvah*, "You shall teach," we now have the Jew dedicating himself to his God both by actual speech and also by the meditations of his heart.

Ḥinnukh: God knows the weaknesses of man and how easily he falls into the pitfalls of sin. Man was instructed, therefore, to recite this declaration of faith in God and in His divine commandments by day and night to help him to walk in the path of righteousness by remembering all day long that an omnipresent God is watching every move he makes during every moment of his life.

References:
B. Ḥullin 89a; B. Yoma 19b; B. Berakhot 2a, 2b, 4b, 5a, 9a, 9b, 10b, 13a, 13b, 16a, 20b, 47b, 63b; B. Megillah 3a; B. Sukkah 42a; B. Shabbat 119b; B. Sotah 32a; J. Berakhot, Chap. 1, Halakhah 5, Chap. 2, Halakhah 1; Sifre *Va-Etḥanan;* Yad, Hilkhot Keriat Shema, Chap. 1; Sefer ha-Mitzvot (Aseh) 10 (Note that Maimonides considers the *Shema* of the morning, and that of the evening as one *mitzvah.* Naḥmanides disputes this and contends that, since the *Shema* is recited at different times of the day, these recitations are to be considered as two distinct *mitzvot.);* Sefer Mitzvot Gadol (Aseh) 18; Sefer Mitzvot Katan 104; Shulḥan Arukh, Oraḥ Ḥayyim 61; Sefer ha-Ḥinnukh, Mitzvah 420.

TEFILLIN (PHYLACTERIES)

And you shall bind them for a sign upon your hand. . . And they shall be for frontlets between your eyes (Deuteronomy 6:8)

1. There are certain rituals in Judaism which are referred to in the Torah as an *"Ot"*—a sign of the binding relationship between the Jew and God. The Sabbath is called an *"Ot";* circumcision is described as an *"Ot";* the *mitzvah* of *tefillin* joins the group of *"Otot."*

2. There are two *tefillin,* one placed on the arm *(shel yad)* and the other on the head *(shel rosh)*. They are two four-cornered boxes. A piece of parchment made from the hide of a kosher animal is placed into the *tefillah shel yad,* on which are inscribed four extracts from the Pentateuch. These sections are: Exodus 13:1–10, 11–16; Deuteronomy 6:4–9, 11:13–21. Into the *tefillah shel rosh,* which has four sections, are placed four separate pieces of parchment, each containing one of the same four passages.

3. The *tefillah shel yad* is tied with *retzuot,* leather-straps, to the muscle of the left arm (if the wearer is right-handed) and facing the heart. The *tefillah shel rosh* is placed on the head, not behind the fontanel nor below the hairline.

4. These are considered two separate *mitzvot.* Thus if one has an arm missing, he is yet obligated to wear the *tefillah shel rosh.*

5. On the Sabbath we do not don *tefillin* because Sabbath itself is an *"Ot";* there is no need for two *"Otot"* on the same day.

6. Originally, Jews wore their *tefillin* all day and removed them only at night. Due to the circumstances prevailing in the Diaspora, the *mitzvah* of *tefillin* is now normally carried out in the morning only. The least one can do is to wear *tefillin* during the recitation of the *Shema* and the silent prayer of the *Amidah.* Because there are eight chapters of the Bible inscribed in both *tefillin,* four in the *tefillah shel rosh* and four in the *tefillah shel yad,* one who fails to put on his *tefillin* is regarded as having violated eight positive commandments.

7. *Tefillin* are worn only during the day. Since there is a time-element involved, it is not incumbent upon the woman to fulfill this *mitzvah.*

COMMENTATORS

Ḥinnukh: Man is composed of flesh and blood and, as such, he is subject to many sensual lusts; but he also possesses an opposing force—his soul. The soul deters him from engaging solely in the pursuit of the pleasures of the flesh. The soul, emanating from heaven, is operating far from its base when it is dealing with earthly lusts. Hence it sometimes becomes weak and ineffective and the lusts of the body overcome the prudence of the soul, with the result that the soul requires assistance. One of the guardians of the soul in its battle with the body is the *mitzvah* of *tefillin.* By wearing *tefillin* we help to tip the scale in favor of the soul.

Abrabanel, Alshekh: By wearing the *tefillin* on the arm and the head, indicating that the work of our hands and the thoughts of our brains must be dedicated to God, we have a constant reminder not to follow the dictates of evil inclinations.

Recanati: Because God shows pride in His one and only chosen people, so must we, too, exhibit our pride in the One and Only God. In the *tefillin,* we insert the prayer of the *Shema;* our acknowledgment of the oneness of God serves to remind us of this.

References:

B. Menaḥot 35b, 36a, 36b, 37a, 42b, 43a; B. Berakhot 6a, 15a, 20b, 30b, 47b, 57a; B. Shabbat 49a, 118b, 130a; B. Rosh ha-Shanah 17a; B. Kiddushin 34b, 35a; B. Eruvin 95b; Yad, Hilkhot Tefillin, Chap. 1; Sefer ha-Mitzvot (Aseh) 12, 13; Sefer Mitzvot Gadol (Aseh) 21, 22; Sefer Mitzvot Katan 153; Shulḥan Arukh, Oraḥ Ḥayyim, Chap. 25–45; Sefer ha-Ḥinnukh, Mitzvot 421, 422.

THE MEZUZAH

And you shall write them on the doorposts of your house and upon your gates (Deuteronomy 6:9)

1. The Torah readily acknowledges the fact that man can easily be influenced by his environment. The keenness of his intelligence is blunted, his perspicacity impaired, his powers of analysis and selectivity dulled. He is guided by the forces which surround him. He needs constant reminders that the powers of his reasoning should serve as the basis of his motivations and actions. One of these reminders is the *mezuzah.* In fact, the Rabbis taught us that he who wears *tefillin,* is clothed in a garment with *tzitzit,* and affixes a *mezuzah* to his doorpost—constant reminders of God's ever-watchful eye—will never be entrapped in sin.

2. The *mezuzah* consists of a piece of parchment on which is inscribed by hand and in the script used for the Torah, the two biblical paragraphs: "Hear O Israel" and "It shall come to pass." This parchment is first encased and then nailed to the doorpost of the entrance to a home, as well as to every room therein.

The word *Shaddai,* one of God's names is written on the other side of the parchment and placed in such a manner that it is visible.

3. A *mezuzah* is necessary only in those rooms that are at least 16 cubits square in dimension. Some maintain that this area is a requisite only if four cubits by four cubits can be inscribed into the area. The rooms must have two doorposts with a threshold and a lintel. There is a halakhic authority for the view that if there is no door to the room, no *mezuzah* is required. The prevailing custom is to fix a *mezuzah,* nevertheless. It should be a permanent and respectable human domicile. This, of course, excludes toilets and bathrooms. It also exempts synagogues, because they are already identified with sanctity and thus need no other manifestation of God's presence.

4. The *mezuzah* should be fixed slanted on the doorpost, with the top tilted toward the inside of the room. Except in Eretz Israel, where the ritual must be performed immediately, the occupant of a new house has 30 days to affix his *mezuzah.*

COMMENTATORS

Ḥinnukh, Naḥmanides: The same reasoning that is behind the *mitzvah* of *tefillin,* also applies to the *mitzvah* of the *mezuzah.* That is, the *mezuzah* serves as a reminder of God's Omnipresence and the obligation of every Jew to have faith in Him.

Abrabanel: There are gates and doorposts that belong to an individual; these are parts of his home. There are also gates and doorposts that belong to a nation; these are of its national Homeland. The *mezuzah* is to remind us of the gift of Eretz Izrael, the Jewish national homeland.

Alshekh: What need is there to affix the *mezuzah* to the doorposts of rooms within rooms? This is necessary, so that no one should think that only in public must he avoid doing wrong. The *mezuzah* is a reminder that even in the innermost rooms where he imagines that he is isolated and all by himself, man must refrain from sin.

Recanati: The *mezuzah* affixed to the doorpost of a home serves as a protection against the messengers of evil. When confronted by the name of God, which is on the exterior of the *mezuzah,* these messengers of harm realize that God is watching over this domicile and they will refrain from entering. The word *mezuzot* is a combination of the words *"zaz"* and *"mavet"* which mean literally: "Death: Remove thyself."

References:
B. Sukkah 3b; B. Shabbat 32b, 103b; B. Berakhot 15b; B. Sanhedrin 113a; B. Avodah Zarah 11a; B. Menaḥot 32b, 33a, 33b, 34a, 44a; B. Yoma 10b, 11a, 11b; J. Berakhot, Chap. 1, Halakhah 5; J. Megillah, end of Chap. 4; Mekhilta *Be-Shalaḥ;* Midrash Rabbah, *Ki Tetze,* Chap. 6, Sec. 3; Yad, Hilkhot Mezuzah, Chap. 5; Sefer ha-Mitzvot (Aseh) 15; Sefer Mitzvot Gadol (Aseh) 23; Sefer Mitzvot Katan 154; Shulḥan Arukh, Yoreh De'ah, 285; Sefer ha-Ḥinnukh, Mitzvah 423.

PUTTING GOD AND THE PROPHET TO THE TEST

You shall not try the Lord, your God (Deuteronomy 6:16)

1. Fear and anxiety can weaken man's power to believe and sometimes result in a desire for concrete evidence on which to base his faith. This is a form of arrogance and is severely condemned by the Torah. Many people, while aware of the folly of demanding external proof for the existence of God, may yet seek evidence that His promises to Israel, made through the prophets, will ultimately be fulfilled.

2. Once a prophet has been so designated, we are forbidden to ask him for continuous signs and miracles to validate his prophetic utterances. Even though one may acknowledge unhesitatingly the existence of God, he may not address himself to Him and demand that His promises in the Torah and through His prophets should be brought to fruition forthwith or even in the foreseeable future.

3. There is one exception. Basing their premise on the verse in Malachi 3:10, the Rabbis acquiesced in the legitimacy of man's expectations that God fulfill His promises. There the prophet says: "Bring all the tithes unto the storehouse, and prove Me now by this, says the Lord of Hosts: If I will not open you the window of Heaven and pour you out a blessing." In other words, if the Jew sincerely and honestly brings his tithes, he has a right to expect the Lord to shower down His blessings upon him.

COMMENTATORS

Naḥmanides: One does not need to test God's Omnipotence by questioning the validity and efficacy of the Torah and *mitzvot,* for He has already established beyond any shadow of doubt the binding worth of His word in the incidents of Egypt and the desert. Whatever emanates from God is obviously perfect.

Saadiah: It is forbidden to question whether God can accomplish specific deeds; but it is permissible for man to ask God for signs indicating whether he is doing right in the eyes of the Lord and thus worthy of His blessings.

Baḥya ben Asher: Do not test God by being good and righteous and then expecting your reward to shower down from heaven. No one knows what will ultimately prove to be a blessing for him. The present good may harbor future evils.

Ḥinnukh: Do not ask of God's prophets to show you heavenly signs and miracles at your every whim and fancy. It is God's own decision when He will show miracles and not the prerogative of the prophet. If this were in the power of the prophet, he would be open to ridicule when he could not perform miracles at every call and behest.

Radbaz: Once it is established that a man has fulfilled the requirements of being a prophet of God and a sage, we have no right to test him or question him, just as we have no right to test God Himself.

References:

B. Shabbat 53b; Pirkei Avot, Chap. 1, Mishnah 3; B. Ta'anit 9a; B. Nedarim 62a; B. Arakhin 15a; Yad, Hilkhot Yesodei Torah, Chap. 10; Sefer ha-Mitzvot (Lo Ta'aseh) 64; Sefer Mitzvot Gadol (Lav) 4; Sefer Mitzvot Katan 18 (Note that the last two commentaries interpret this injunction to mean that one must not test God in regard to reward for performing *mitzvot,* except in the case of tithes.); Sefer ha-Ḥinnukh, Mitzvah 424.

PROHIBITION AGAINST INTERMARRIAGE

Neither shall you make marriages with them (Deuteronomy 7:3)

1. Judaism has always discouraged intermarriage. The union of two persons of different religious backgrounds can lead to formidable problems. Often the only solution they can find is spiritual dissolution—the one partner has to abandon his religious heritage and embrace the faith of the other. Judaism is opposed to such a solution.

2. A Jew who marries a non-Jewess violates the law of the Torah. One who cohabits with a non-Jewess without going through any form of marriage is not, according to biblical ordinance, liable to the penalty of 39 lashes, but the Rabbis decreed that such a man would receive lashes for his defiance of authority. This punishment was called *makkat mardut;* the number of stripes was fixed according to the direction of the Court.

3. Our Sages also inferred from Scripture that anyone who broke this law and managed to evade corporal punishment would be subject to the Divine penalty of *karet* (excision).

4. The marriage is permitted when the Gentile partner shows a deep and genuine commitment to Judaism and as a result becomes a proselyte. This then does not, of course, constitute intermarriage.

COMMENTATORS

Maimonides, Baḥya ben Asher: There is a difference of opinion between these two exegetes. Baḥya contends that this prohibition applies to intermarriage with the seven original nations of ancient Palestine, whereas Maimonides asserts that it applies to all Gentiles.

Ḥinnukh: He proposes two reasons for this prohibition:

1. A person can easily be misled by his continual relationship with a Gentile mate.
2. The children of such a union will be brought up without any deep-rooted convictions in religious matters.

Abrabanel: In intermarriage, the major attraction between the Jew and non-Jew can only be sexual. A marriage that is based only on sex can easily lead to the abandonment of Torah discipline.

References:
B. Kiddushin 68b; B. Avodah Zarah 36b; B. Yevamot 76a; B. Sanhedrin 82a; B. Shabbat 56b; J. Avodah Zarah, Chap. 1, Halakhah 9; Yad, Hilkhot Issurei Biah, Chap. 12; Sefer Ha-Mitzvot (Lo Ta'aseh) 52; Sefer Mitzvot Gadol (Lav) 112; Sefer Mitzvot Katan 290; Shulḥan Arukh, Even ha-Ezer, 16; Sefer ha-Ḥinnukh, Mitzvah 427.

PROHIBITION AGAINST ANY CONTACT WITH IDOLS

Do not lust after the silver and gold that is on them (Deuteronomy 7:25)

And you shall not bring an abomination into your house (Deuteronomy 7:26)

1. Those who worship idols and images are accustomed to encrust them with precious stones and gems. One may begin to rationalize and question whether these ornaments are to be considered as part of the idols or not. The Torah, therefore, admonishes the Jew to consider these adornments as part of the idol. We are forbidden to reap any benefits from them whatsoever.

2. There are objects of worship by pagans that the Jew does not place in the category of an idol. We are not forbidden to benefit from a pagan god that was not made by the hands of man. For example: We are permitted to enjoy the benefits of a mountain, a brook, or a fruit-bearing tree, although these may have been designated by pagans as objects of worship.

COMMENTATORS

Ḥinnukh: Though most Jews would never contemplate idol worship itself, some might be greedy for the precious adornments attached to the idols; that is, to the external, glittering prizes. Little do these ignorant people realize that, after removing the silver and gold, they will come face to face with the idol itself and may not possess the spiritual strength to cast it aside.

Maimonides: Consider the following case: A Jew brings an idol into his home and has no intention whatsoever of paying religious homage to it. On the contrary, he intends to destroy it eventually. Suddenly, he meets with some stroke of good fortune. Let us say that he had been encumbered with some property that no one was willing to buy from him and, unexpectedly, this property is in great demand and the proprietor is, naturally, amazed. The first explanation that he can offer for this sudden turn of events is that the idol that he brought into his home was the cause of his sudden good fortune. The thought will not enter his mind that it was God who had blessed him with this unexpected prosperity. This coincidence may bring about his eventual worship of the idol and the abandonment of God.

References:

B. Temurah 28b, 30b; B. Makkot 22a; B. Sotah 4b; B. Avodah Zarah 21a, 45a, 51b, 52a, 54b; J. Avodah Zarah, Chap. 4, Sec. 7, 8; Yad, Hilkhot Avodah Zarah, Chap. 7, 8; Sefer ha-Mitzvot (Lo Ta'aseh) 22, 25; Sefer Mitzvot Gadol (Lav) 45, 46; Sefer Mitzvot Katan 66; Shulḥan Arukh, Yoreh De'ah, 145; Sefer ha-Ḥinnukh, Mitzvot 428, 429.

BLESSING GOD FOR OUR FOOD

And you shall eat and be satisfied and bless the Lord your God (Deuteronomy 8:10)

1. *Birkat ha-mazon,* Grace after Meals, comprises four individual blessings which the Jew recites after eating bread made of the five species of wheat that the Torah specifies. The first three are mandatory by the Torah, the fourth being rabbinic.

2. According to tradition, the text of the first benediction, *ha-zan,* was instituted by Moses; the second, *birkat ha-aretz,* was introduced by Joshua; the third, *boneh Yerushalayim,* was added by David and Solomon; the last, *ha-tov ve-ha-metiv,* was added later by the Rabbis.

3. Although the Torah indicates that Grace after Meals must be recited only after one has enjoyed a full meal and has become satisfied, the Rabbis made this commandment apply even if one has merely eaten a piece of bread the size of an olive.

4. There are other benedictions made after eating, such as *al ha-miḥyah* for cake; *al-ha-gefen* for wine; *al ha-etz* for grapes, olives, dates, and figs. For food that does not grow from the ground, such as water, meat, cheese, etc., the appropriate benediction is *bore nefashot rabbot.*

5. The Rabbis also instituted appropriate blessings before one partakes of any food: *ha-motzi* for bread, *ha-gefen* for wine, *mezonot* for cake, *ha-etz* for fruit from trees, *ha-adamah* for produce from the soil, *she-hakol* for everything not in the above categories.

COMMENTATORS

Naḥmanides: Blessing God for the food He has given us is a very easy *mitzvah* to perform, if we remember the lean and hungry years we may have experienced in the past.

Ba'al ha-Turim: Not only should one bless the Lord when one has eaten and is satisfied, but one should eat and be satisfied because one has blessed God. That is, *"u-verakhta"* ("and you shall bless") should be felt before beginning to eat. What validity is there for this prior blessing? This food really belongs to God; hence what right has man to eat it? In essence, when a person offers a prayer prior to eating, he is thanking God for transferring the food from His possession into man's legitimate possession. The blessing is an expression of gratitude for this transference of title.

Ḥinnukh: Is it not presumptuous for us to offer benedictions to God who is Himself the source of all blessings? What does God gain from our saying "grace" when He is the one who dispenses all benefactions? He answers that it is an undisputed fact that a complete human being is not one who only thinks of himself, but one who is anxious to help to uplift the welfare of his fellow human beings. So it is with God. The completeness of His Divine providence can be felt because He is anxious to bestow beneficence upon man if he will but be deserving of it. The praises of God that we recite after a meal do not constitute a benediction but an act of acknowledgment that in God repose all blessings and that it is to Him that we must turn for the gifts of life. This acknowledgment is all that God asks from us. He is anxious to shower down His blessings upon us because such action is part of the kindly nature of God.

References:
B. Berakhot 20b, 21a, 35b, 36a, 48b, 49b; B. Ḥullin 87a; B. Yevamot 64a; B. Arakhin 4a; B. Sotah 33a; B. Bava Metzia 114a; J. Berakhot, Chap. 3, Halakhah 3, Chap. 7, Halakhah 1; Yad, Hilkhot Berakhot, Chap. 1–5; Sefer ha-Mitzvot (Aseh) 19; Sefer Mitzvot Gadol (Aseh) 27; Sefer Mitzvot Katan 109; Shulḥan Arukh, Oraḥ Ḥayyim, 184; Sefer ha-Ḥinnukh, Mitzvah 430.

LOVING THE PROSELYTE

Love you, therefore, the stranger (Deuteronomy 10:19)

Man has a dislike for the unlike, especially if a stranger suddenly appears who, to the citizen's mind, may become a threat to his socioeconomic security. How much more could a Jew become suspicious of, and hostile to, a convert who is neither a member of his family nor one of his people? The Torah, therefore, warns the Jew against this arrogant and chauvinistic reaction to the stranger who may come into the Jewish fold. Never must his past be recalled and never must he be reminded of his origin. The Jew must extend a warm hand of cordiality and friendship to the convert and inspire him with the feeling that he is wanted and welcome.

COMMENTATORS

Ḥinnukh: Anyone who leaves his people, family, and friends in order to enter the Jewish faith deserves our wholehearted love and esteem. **Keli Yakar:** He challenges the thesis of Maimonides on the relationship between the Jew and the convert to Judaism. Maimonides maintains that if God loved Israel more than any other people, it is because this people is superior to all others. Yet the Jew must love the convert to Judaism, even though he stems from an inferior source. *Keli Yakar* will not accept this premise. He contends that the heavens and the earth and all that is therein were created to serve all of mankind. The fact that one is born a Jew is meaningless unless his deeds merit the love of God. Thus, one should love the convert because he merits the love of God, just as any observant Jew merits this love.

References:
B. Bava Metzia 59b; B. Gittin 57a; B. Shabbat 31a; Midrash Rabbah, *Lekh Lekha,* Chap. 39, Sec. 21; Midrash Ruth, Chap. 2; Tanna de-Vei Eliyahu, Chap. 29; Yad, Hilkhot De'ot, Chap. 6; Sefer ha-Mitzvot (Aseh) 207; Sefer Mitzvot Gadol (Aseh) 10; Sefer ha-Ḥinnukh, Mitzvah 431.

SWEARING IN GOD'S NAME

And by his Name shall you swear (Deuteronomy 10:20)

1. According to Maimonides, a Jew, when swearing, must do so in the name of God; if he does not, he is transgressing the above *mitzvah.* Naḥmanides disagrees, considering it to be a prohibition against swearing in the name of an idol.

2. Since it is conceivable that, if the oath-taking became too frequent an occurrence, the name of God would be used frivolously, the Ravad mentions a *takkanah* (supplementary regulation) of the *Geonim* (post-talmudic scholars) whereby the practice of swearing by God's name before a *bet din* was abolished and another form of oath substituted.

3. Anyone wishing to take an oath in order to confirm the truth of a statement may not combine in it any other name together with the Name of God.

4. It is permitted, and even commendable, to take an oath to serve as a strong motivation in the performance of a *mitzvah.*

COMMENTATORS

Baḥya ben Asher: It is not proper to swear by God's name at the slightest provocation, but, as in the case of the prophet Elijah and the sage Ḥoni ha-Me'aggel, when national crises of major importance arise, it may be necessary to employ the name of God since there must not remain any shadow of doubt as to the purposeful intention of the oath.
Ḥinnukh: When man speaks out on a major issue, he should use the name of God because in this manner he indicates that with his word he considers himself accountable to God. The *Ḥinnukh* then proceeds to expound the famous dispute between Maimonides and Naḥmanides over the implications of this *mitzvah.* According to Maimonides, it is a duty for everyone to use God's name when taking an oath because this adds to the weight and sanctity of his words and becomes a declaration of faith. According to Naḥmanides, however, it is optional and should actually be avoided whenever possible. His reasoning is that very few people have attained the supreme degree of piety needed in order to invoke God's name with proper, deep-seated reverence and sanctification.

References:
B. Temurah 3a; B. Nedarim 10b; B. Shevu'ot 38b, 39a; B. Sanhedrin 63a, 63b (see Tosafot); Midrash Tanḥuma, *Va-Yikra,* Chap. 7; Yad, Hilkhot Shevu'ot, Chap. 11; Sefer ha-Mitzvot (Aseh) 7 (Note that there is a three-way dispute regarding this *mitzvah.* Maimonides declares it to be imperative that an oath be taken in God's name. Naḥmanides maintains that this is a matter of choice. Ravad contends that because of the irresponsibility of people taking an oath in God's name, it is forbidden.); Sefer Mitzvot Gadol (Aseh) 123; Sefer Mitzvot Katan 108; Shulḥan Arukh, Yoreh De'ah, 237; Sefer ha-Ḥinnukh, Mitzvah 435.

PRAYER

You shall fear the Lord, your God. . . Him shall you serve (Deuteronomy 10:20)

1. From the earliest period of Jewish history, we discover that the Jew endeavored to communicate with his God through prayer. Abraham pleaded with God on behalf of Sodom and Gomorrah; Isaac prayed with his wife for the blessing of a child; Jacob implored God to save him from the hands of Esau. These were individuals entreating God as the occasion arose. Also, at an early date in its history, we find the Jewish people, as a whole, supplicating God to relieve them of the burdens of bondage in Egypt. The *Anshei Knesset ha-Gedolah,* in the period after Ezra, composed the *shemoneh esreh,* or as it is more accurately called the *amidah,* as well as the *kiddush,* the *havdalah,* and many other benedictions. The Rabbis added additional prayers as the time went on, and the process continued until the *Siddur* (prayerbook) as we know it today was completed.

2. Referring to the verse in Deuteronomy 11:13: "To love the Lord your God, and to serve him with all your heart," many Rabbis concluded that the meaning of the verse under consideration refers to prayer, because this is the way a Jew serves his God with his heart. The Torah does not specify that prayer must be recited at a certain time or with a certain text. It was only by rabbinic decree that the text and frequency of prayer were decided. It is generally accepted that the three daily prayers correspond to the *korban tamid* (daily sacrifice) of the morning, the *korban tamid* of the afternoon, and the smoldering during the nighttime of the fats and limbs that were left over. On Sabbath and Holidays, the additional prayers of *musaf* commemorated the *korban musaf* in the days of the Temple.

3. To the Jew, prayer is not a casual exercise with expressive words. It must rather be a valiant and heroic effort of man to communicate with God. Before a Jew launches his prayers heavenward, he should sit in meditation as a preparatory step to his attempted rise to great spiritual heights. He must first wash his hands, see that he is decently dressed and in a state of profound concentration.

COMMENTATORS

Ḥinnukh: He makes the following three observations on the necessity and rationale of prayer:

a. Every human being, as one of God's creatures, will be the recipient of certain blessings from Him; but the quality and quantity of these benefactions depend on man's personal efforts. Prayer is one major field of effort toward that goal.

b. Another reason for prayer is not only that prayer serves as a means toward acquiring those things in life that we desire, but that it is also a manifestation of our acknowledgment that there is only One Source Who can grant us the blessings we seek and to Whom we must turn in order to obtain them.

c. He cites the celebrated dispute between Maimonides and Naḥmanides on the basic origin of prayer. According to Maimonides, prayer is a positive directive to be found in the Torah. In other words, prayer is a daily necessity. According to Naḥmanides, the necessity for prayer is found nowhere in the Torah, for prayer is essentially a rabbinic injunction. *Ḥinnukh* attempts to bring these two divergent views closer together and contends that, when Maimonides classes prayer among the biblical commandments, he does not imply that either the type or the time of prayer is prescribed by biblical ordinance. What Maimonides is trying to say, according to *Ḥinnukh,* is that man must recognize the simple and agreed fact that he must implore God for His blessings. Since it is inconceivable that a day passes without man's need for God's benefactions, it follows automatically that he will pray to God every day.

Recanati: He offers two lines of thought:

a. Man must not love or fear God simply because these emotional sensibilities are an integral part of his psychological make-up. Rather, he must detach himself from these personal sensitivities and either love or fear God because of his belief in God's omnipotence and because of his realization that God can either punish or reward him.

b. Although Maimonides contends that the love of God is on a higher plane than the fear of God, he claims that there is an occasion when the fear of God stands higher than the love of God. This occurs when love is the basis of fear. In other words, when man reaches the pinnacle of commitment to God and his love knows no bounds or limitations, then will he rise to fear Him. Fear of God is not just an end in itself, it leads to the full consummation, the final step that follows love.

References:
B. Pesaḥim 22b; B. Sanhedrin 56a; B. Shabbat 31a, 31b; B. Ta'anit 2a; B. Eruvin 65a; B. Bava Kamma 92b; J. Berakhot Chap. 3, 4, 5; Yad, Hilkhot Tefillah, Chap. 1; Yad, Hilkhot Yesodei ha-Torah, Chap. 2; Sefer ha-Mitzvot (Aseh) 4, 5; Sefer Mitzvot Katan 4 (Naḥmanides and Sefer Mitzvot Katan oppose Maimonides, and contend that prayer is not of biblical origin, but is rabbinic in origin, except in times of crisis.); Shulḥan Arukh, Oraḥ Ḥayyim, 89; Sefer ha-Ḥinnukh, Mitzvot 432, 433.

CLINGING TO GOD

To him shall you cleave (Deuteronomy 10:20)

Since God has no corporeal substance, the only way man can cling to God is by emulating, as far as humanly possible, the attributes of God. This can be achieved by close association with those who know and preach God's word. Man's philosophy of life is often guided, molded, and fashioned by those whom he chooses to follow as an apt disciple. It is, therefore, most important that he select as his spiritual master one who is steeped in Torah and revered for his saintliness. It is in this light that the Rabbis of the Mishnah exhort us to "sit in the dust at the feet of the learned." To put it succinctly, we are to honor and revere those who are learned in Torah.

COMMENTATORS

Ibn Ezra: One must cling to God, not only in deed but also in creed.
Maimonides: A human being cannot "cling" to God who is non-

corporeal. What is meant is that one should seek out and cling to those who preach godliness, such as Rabbis, sages, and judges.
Naḥmanides: He disagrees with Maimonides and contends that the significance of this *mitzvah* is that a person should be so passionately motivated to perform the *mitzvot*—a form of clinging to God—that he should be prepared to swear by God's Name that he will fulfill his determination and resolution.
Alshekh: Many people who have sinned run away from God to escape from their guilty conscience. The most effective antidote to this is to cling to God and to have some of His virtues become a part of themselves.
Recanati: Many contend that this *mitzvah* also refers to close associations with the sages and the pious. The Torah specifies that "to Him shall you cleave." How do we reconcile this injunction with the concept of an incorporeal being? By clinging to the sage who lives by God's Torah, we come as close as possible to clinging to God. We cling if not directly to him, then to His way of life. Furthermore, by close contact with the pious and the sages, one learns how to live in the way God wanted us to live; that is, to be kind, merciful, and charitable in the same manner that God conducts Himself toward man.

References:
B. Ketubbot 111b; B. Pesaḥim 49a; B. Sanhedrin 92a–92b; B. Berakhot 7b; Pirkei Avot, Chap. 1; Yad, Hilkhot De'ot, Chap. 6; Sefer ha-Mitzvot (Aseh) 6; Sefer Mitzvot Gadol (Aseh) 8; Sefer Mitzvot Katan 45; Sefer ha-Ḥinnukh Mitzvah 434.

DESTROYING ALL PLACES OF PAGAN WORSHIP

You shall completely destroy all the places wherein the nations whom you are to dispossess served their gods (Deuteronomy 12:2)

1. The Torah instructed the Jew to destroy every vestige of idols in their homeland by grinding them to dust or burning them to ashes and scattering them to the winds.

2. The precept of destroying idols is valid everywhere. The only difference between the Land of Israel and elsewhere is that in the former place one is commanded to ferret out traces of idol-worship and destroy them, while elsewhere the obligation to demolish idols applies only when one confronts them.

COMMENTATORS

Ḥinnukh: The intent of this *mitzvah* is to destroy every single vestige of pagan worship in Israel, to the extent that it will be completely and absolutely obliterated. The coexistence of the worship of the Almighty God and the worship of pagan deities could not be tolerated in the Promised Land.

Abrabanel: Even the buildings where pagan worship took place must be completely destroyed and not remodelled into Jewish places of worship. People might want to remodel these places and say that they are not worshiping in a pagan temple but that they are performing a good deed by transforming a beautiful pagan temple into a Jewish house of worship. Abrabanel contends that, as long as the original edifice stands, it serves as a constant reminder and a visible symbol of pagan worship and is, therefore, undesirable. The Torah instructed the Jew to destroy completely every trace of idolatry.

References:

B. Avodah Zarah 45b, 46a, 51b, 53b; J. Avodah Zarah, Chap. 4, Halakhah 4; Mekhilta, *Yitro,* Chap. 10; Sifre *Re'eh;* Yad, Hilkhot Avodah Zarah, Chap. 7; Sefer ha-Mitzvot (Aseh) 185; Sefer Mitzvot Gadol (Aseh) 14; Sefer Mitzvot Katan 37 (Note that he contends that, in destroying places of pagan worship, one fulfills seven distinct *mitzvot.*); Shulḥan Arukh, Yoreh De'ah, 146; Sefer ha-Ḥinnukh, Mitzvah 436.

THE PROHIBITION OF DESTROYING SACRED OBJECTS

So shall you not do unto the Lord your God (Deuteronomy 12:4)

1. No person was permitted to mar or deface something that was identified and designated as sacred even though, originally, he was the one who fashioned it. For example: It was the Jew who built the Temple. He placed stone upon stone, but once the stone became part of the Temple, it was sanctified and no one was allowed to deface it.

2. God is known by seven names: the Tetragrammaton, *Elo'ah, Shaddai, El, Adonai, Elohim,* and *Tzeva'ot.* Anyone effacing any of these names was punished with lashes.

3. Holy Writ may not be erased or destroyed. Until this very day, we have preserved the custom of burying in a cemetery sacred objects such as used Scrolls of the Law, prayerbooks, Bibles, etc.

COMMENTATORS

Ḥinnukh: He believes that this injunction refers to the physical destruction or irreverent treatment of a sacred object, such as the Torah or the Temple. When one approaches anything holy, one should do so with awe and trepidation. Only thus can one serve God with appropriate fear and respect.

Keli Yakar: "So shall you not do unto the Lord, your God." Do what? Why? He answers that other nations decide where the domicile of their deities shall be. It is the locale which lends sanctity to the deity, such as a mountain or a tree. The Jew, however, is not to do this because God has chosen His own site and it is God who sanctifies the locale.

Alshekh: He poses the same question as the *Keli Yakar,* and answers that one might want to emulate other religions by erecting many places of worship all over the land. Why must we be satisfied with only one Temple and not a temple in the territory of each of the twelve tribes? We must not do this because we run the risk of fragmenting our religion by having twelve temples with twelve distinct allegiances. The same Temple for all Jews can and should be a factor for unity, not for segmentation. But will not some people go astray and not trouble to come to the Temple at all if it is so far away? No! The richness, splendor, and inspiration of the Temple worship will more than offset this inconvenience. No one will leave Judaism because of the inconvenience of the geographical distance to the Temple.

References:
B. Makkot 22a; B. Shabbat 116b, 117a; B. Shevuot 35b; Yad, Hilkhot Yesodei ha-Torah, Chap. 6; Sefer ha-Mitzvot (Lo Ta'aseh) 65; Shulḥan Arukh, Yoreh De'ah, 276; Sefer ha-Ḥinnukh, Mitzvah 437.

NOT TO DEFER PAYMENT OF A PROMISE

And thither shall you bring your burnt-offerings (Deuteronomy 12:6)
Do not defer to pay it (Deuteronomy 23:22)

1. The Torah demands of the Jew that he redeem his promises within a reasonable time after they were made. The reasonable time was defined by the Torah as the first major holiday when the Jew was obligated to go up to Jerusalem to celebrate. At that time, he had to bring all his free-will offerings, sacrifices, and tithes, and if he was lax and did not do so, he violated a positive precept. If, for one reason or another, he could not or did not pay his vows on that occasion, they had to be paid before the next two major holidays had passed. If he did not fulfill his obligations by that time, he clearly violated a negative commandment.

2. One who specifies an amount of money for relief of the poor must pay at once, because there are always poverty-stricken people whose needs are immediate. Even if there are no recipients, the money should be set aside so that when the occasion arises, aid will be available at once.

COMMENTATORS

Sforno: It is not sufficient for one to make a promise to give charity. It is far more important that he pay it immediately, provided he is able to do so. If one does not fulfill his promise readily and punctually, God in His own way will exact that promise from him.

Keli Yakar: During the period between the actual vow and its fulfillment, a man may find himself endeavoring to extricate himself from his obligation by seeking reasons and excuses for not paying this pledge. In order to avoid this, he should fulfill the vow without delay.

Ḥinnukh: Delaying the payment of a promise is merely a sign of indifference and laziness which is deplorable under any circumstances. When the civil authorities demand payment of debts, we respond immediately. Why not at least be as responsive when God demands payment for pledges made to Him?

References:
B. Makkot 23b; B. Berakhot 46a; B. Ḥullin 135b; B. Rosh ha-Shanah 4b, 5b, 6a, 6b; B. Arakhin 6a; J. Rosh ha-Shanah, Chap. 1, Halakhah 1; Sifre *Re'eh, Ki Tetze;* Yad, Hilkhot Ma'asei ha-Korbanot, Chap. 14; Yad, Hilkhot Matnat 'Aniyim, Chap. 8; Sefer ha-Mitzvot (Aseh) 83, (Lo Ta'aseh) 155; Sefer Mitzvot Gadol (Aseh) 187, (Lav) 331; Shulḥan Arukh, Yoreh De'ah, 257; Sefer ha-Ḥinnukh, Mitzvot 438, 574.

EATING THE MEAT OF A REDEEMED ANIMAL

Nevertheless, whatsoever your soul desires, you may slaughter and eat the flesh (Deuteronomy 12:15)

1. What happened to the animal which was designated as an offering and, after becoming sanctified, developed a physical defect which disqualified it? The Torah instructed the Jew to redeem that animal with money and buy another as a substitute. The redeemed offering became de-consecrated and, except for certain reservations, could be used for almost any purpose the owner desired. Shearing of the wool was prohibited and, in a case where the animal died by means other than ritual slaughter, it had to be buried, for it was forbidden to feed it to dogs as was done with other *nevelot*.

2. There were two exceptions to this rule: the first-born which was presented to the Priest and the tithed animal which was given to the Levite. These could not be redeemed, but they could be eaten, although defective.

COMMENTATORS

Ḥinnukh: Once an animal was designated as a sacrifice, it should remain in a state of sanctity whether it was without blemish and thus suitable for an offering, or whether it was maimed and thereby disqualified. God saw fit to grant this grace and thus released the blemished animal to its owner for his own consumption after he had redeemed it by substituting another animal. One may say that although he is permitted to eat of the meat he would rather not do so because the animal at one time was sanctified, and he has strong feelings of reverence in this matter. To this the Torah replies that one must not deprive oneself of what God allows. God instructs us to redeem this animal and use it for our own enjoyment; these instructions must be followed.

References:

B. Bekhorot 15a, 15b, 32a; B. Temurah 21a, 31a; B. Makkot 22a; B. Ḥullin 81a (see Tosafot); Sifre *Re'eh;* Yad, Hilkhot Sheḥitah, Chap. 1; Sefer ha-Mitzvot (Aseh) 86; Sefer Mitzvot Gadol (Aseh) 177; Sefer ha-Ḥinnukh, Mitzvah 441.

RITUAL SLAUGHTER (SHEḤITAH)

Then shall you slaughter of your herd and of your flock (Deuteronomy 12:21)

1. The rules for kosher slaughtering *(sheḥitah),* the Jewish way of killing an animal for the purpose of preparing it as food, are not specified in the written Torah. In the Pentateuch, reference is only made to "You shall slaughter of your herd." The correct procedure of slaughtering was handed down by God to Moses, who in turn transmitted it orally to all the people.

2. While the Jews were journeying in the desert, they were permitted to eat only of the meat of the sacrifices that were brought into the Tabernacle. When they entered the Promised Land and settled throughout the length and breadth of the country, they were allowed to eat meat of kosher animals that were properly slaughtered at any place and at any time.

3. There are many basic requirements in the kosher slaughtering of an animal. The *shoḥet,* or slaughterer, must be thoroughly acquainted with the laws appertaining to the procedure; he must also be technically apt and proficient. In an animal, the major part of the trachea and esophagus must be cleanly cut; in a fowl, at least the major part of one of these must be severed.

4. Before the ritual slaughter begins, the knife used *(ḥalef)* must be examined to ensure that the edge of its blade is perfectly smooth and without the slightest irregularity. Any nick in the blade would cause the animal needless pain, which is contrary to one of the basic principles of *sheḥitah.*

5. A *mumar,* one who is rebellious against Jewish laws, is disqualified from serving as a *shoḥet.* Should he slaughter an animal, the meat is disqualified even though the *sheḥitah* may have been properly conducted according to traditional law.

6. There are five technical deviations in slaughtering an animal that render the meat unacceptable for Jewish consumption: *shehiyah*—the slightest delay in the motion of the hand of the *shoḥet* while passing the knife over the neck of the animal; *derasah*—when the knife, instead of being moved with a backward and forward motion, is pressed down heavily upon the throat of the animal; *haladah*—when the point of the knife is inserted beneath the food-pipe and wind-pipe, i.e., it is hidden. The fourth deviation is called *hagramah*—cutting the neck partly in the prescribed place but mostly outside of that area. Lastly, *ikkur* means the tearing away of the two pipes and dislodging them from their normal positions before severing them.

COMMENTATORS

Maimonides: The natural diet of man is a vegetarian one. Since he discovered meat to be palatable, man is allowed to slaughter an animal in order to eat its meat, but provided he does so in a compassionate manner.

Ḥinnukh: He cites Maimonides' explanation and adds that the Torah did not specify where the incision should be made. What, then, is the reason (apart from reasons of tradition) for making the incision where we do? He answers that severing the wind-pipe and the food-pipe in the neck ensures that the blood spurts out instead of only trickling out. This is an especially efficient method for the Jew, because in addition to being humane, it rids the animal's body of all the blood which the Jew is forbidden to eat.

Recanati: He quotes Naḥmanides who clarifies the question of the right of one creature to take the life of another. His answer is that an ordinary animal functions through its automatic intuitions; it walks, eats, drinks, and sleeps intuitively. Man, however, functions through the strength of his intellect. Man, therefore, was allowed to kill an animal for food, provided he does so humanely.

Keli Yakar: What was the necessity for the entire procedure of ritual slaughter? For the sake of self-discipline, it is far more appropriate for man not to eat meat; only if one has a strong desire for meat does the Torah permit it, and even this only after the trouble and inconvenience necessary in order to satisfy his desire. Perhaps because of the bother and annoyance of the whole procedure he will be restrained from such a strong and uncontrollable desire for meat.

References:
B. Ḥullin 9a, 10b, 27a, 28a, 31a, 84a; B. Menaḥot 29a; Sifre *Re'eh,* 78; Midrash Rabbah, *Lekh Lekha,* Chap. 44, Sec. 9; Chap. 84, Sec. 7; Midrash Tanḥuma, *Re'eh,* Chap. 6; Yad, Hilkhot Sheḥitah, Chap. 1; Sefer ha-Mitzvot (Aseh) 146; Sefer Mitzvot Gadol (Aseh) 63; Sefer Mitzvot Katan 197; Shulḥan Arukh, Yoreh De'ah, Chap. 1; Sefer ha-Ḥinnukh, Mitzvah 451.

PROHIBITION AGAINST EATING THE LIMB OF A LIVE ANIMAL

And you shall not eat the life with the flesh (Deuteronomy 12:23)

1. There are seven statutes known as the Noahide laws, which should act as guidelines for all mankind. One of these is the commandment concerning a limb torn from a living animal. No human being is allowed to eat of the meat of that limb. The cruelty involved in such an act is quite evident.

2. There are distinctions between this prohibition as it pertains to a Jew and as it relates to a non-Jew. A Jew's prohibition is only concerned with kosher animals, while for a Gentile it applies to all animals.

3. One who cuts off a piece of flesh, or tears a limb off a living animal and eats thereof, is punishable with lashes.

COMMENTATORS

All commentaries are unanimous in their explanation. The purpose of this prohibition against eating the limb of an animal while the animal is still alive—a *mitzvah* which is applicable to the Noahide as well as to the Jew—is for man to refrain from an act of unspeakable cruelty and inhumanity. Maimonides adds another reason to that given above. This was a heathen practice and should, therefore, not be imitated by the Jew.

References:

B. Avodah Zarah 6b; B. Pesaḥim 22b; B. Ḥullin 102a, 102b, 128b; J. Nazir, Chap. 6, Halakhah 1; Guide of the Perplexed, Part 3, Sec. 48; Sefer ha-Mitzvot (Lo Ta'aseh) 182; Sefer Mitzvot Gadol (Lav) 136; Sefer Mitzvot Katan 200; Shulḥan Arukh, Yoreh De'ah, 62; Sefer ha-Ḥinnukh, Mitzvah 452.

PROHIBITION AGAINST ADDING TO OR SUBTRACTING FROM THE TORAH

You may not add thereto. . . nor diminish from it (Deuteronomy 13:1)

Since the *mitzvot* of the Torah are divine and unalterable, what is the purpose of the many decrees instituted by our Rabbis? Do they not appear to contravene the above prohibition? In order to answer this question one must explain that such decrees were enacted for one of two reasons. Certain observances were ordained in order that the Jewish people might express its gratitude to God for His acts of deliverance from mortal danger which dated from the post-biblical period; hence, for example, the institution of the festivals of Ḥanukkah and Purim. Other decrees had the function of a "fence," i.e., their purpose was to guard against the possible infringement of biblical laws. The Torah itself empowered Jewish religious leaders to issue such rules (Deuteronomy 17:9–11) and expressly mentions that they are enforceable by sanctions. Nevertheless, the Rabbis did not claim for their edicts the same status as that of the original Torah laws, and there are provisions for modifying them or cancelling them in certain circumstances.

COMMENTATORS

Da'at Zekenim: When a *mitzvah* is performed with a superfluous addition, this accretion disqualifies the entire *mitzvah.* Thus if a man ties on five fringes to the ends of his garment instead of the required four, he not only adds a superfluous fringe and one which is totally uncalled for, but he also disqualifies the existing four fringes that are required. Hence he does not fulfill the *mitzvah*.

Sforno, Ibn Ezra: There is the constant danger that one may add some innovation which constitutes a form of worship that is foreign to the spirit of Judaism. This is why we are forbidden to add to the *mitzvot*.

Ḥinnukh: God is synonymous with perfection and everything that emanates from God is perfect. The Torah, which is God-given, is perfect. Hence the person who adds to or subtracts from the Torah, is in effect challenging the perfection of God.

Naḥmanides: In the light of these *mitzvot,* how do we look upon the teaching of the sages of the Talmud who did change the image of the *mitzvot*? For example: the Torah forbids incest with one's mother. To this, the Rabbis added the prohibition of relations with one's mother's mother. Naḥmanides replies that what the Rabbis did should not be considered an addition to the *mitzvot* but was meant to be a safeguard and a fence around the existing *mitzvot,* as is commanded in Deuteronomy 4:2.

Abrabanel: Is it not possible for us to add to Judaism something that is not necessarily un-Jewish in content? In his reply, he agrees with Maimonides and defends him against his critics. Maimonides maintains forcefully that God wished us to believe in the Torah and in its *mitzvot* as an eternal document. If man is allowed to add to or subtract from the Torah at his own discretion, then he denies the permanent validity of the Torah.

Radbaz: He takes a somewhat different line, being concerned with the possible alterations to the text of the written Torah. If additions and omissions were permitted, it is conceivable that the Torah would become an object for debate and controversy in all times. This cannot be tolerated if the Torah is to constitute the only supreme authority by which the Jew must live. Furthermore, if liberties were to be taken with the text and contents of the Torah, the first thing that people would do would be to expunge those sections of the Torah that do little honor to the Jew as, for example, the worship of the Golden Calf in the desert.

References:

B. Sanhedrin 88b; B. Rosh ha-Shanah 28a, 28b; B. Megillah 14a; Sifre *Re'eh;* Yad, Hilkhot Mamrim, Chap. 2; Sefer ha-Mitzvot (Lo Ta'aseh) 313, 314; Sefer Mitzvot Gadol (Lav) 364, 365; Sefer Mitzvot Katan 177, 178; Shulḥan Arukh, Oraḥ Ḥayyim, 128; Sefer ha-Ḥinnukh, Mitzvot 454, 455.

FALSE PROPHETS

You shall not hearken unto the voice of that prophet (Deuteronomy 13:4)

Often, pure motives in the fulfillment of a *mitzvah* are not in themselves sufficient. Even an innocent approach to something that is forbidden is deplored by the Torah. This comes to light when one listens to an exhortation or to the promulgation of an idea in the name of a strange god. Although the preacher may be pronouncing correct principles, such as the Torah approves, the Jew is forbidden to demand of him that he show some sign or miracle to prove himself as a prophet of God. In other words, the moment he hears someone introducing a strange deity, the Jew is forbidden to listen any longer. Furthermore, the Jew is forbidden even to entertain the thought that there is perhaps some validity in the false prophet and his preachings.

COMMENTATORS

Naḥmanides, Ḥinnukh, Sforno: It is insufficient to say that one does not believe in the false prophets who attempt to mislead him with signs and wonders while he listens at the same time to their speeches on the plea that he wishes to test their dreams and signs. Even to debate the subject with the false prophet is forbidden. A Jew must be on such a spiritual and intellectual level that he finds a sign, wonder, or dream of a self-appointed prophet totally intolerable and deserving of no credence whatsoever, even if only for a moment.

References:
B. Sanhedrin 63b; Yad, Hilkhot Avodah Zarah, Chap. 5; Sefer ha-Mitzvot (Lo Ta'aseh) 14, 28 (Note the difference of opinion between Maimonides, who asserts that the injunction is against merely listening to a false prophet, and Naḥmanides, who contends that this applies only to following the false prophet.); Sefer Mitzvot Gadol (Lav) 33; Sefer Mitzvot Katan 27; Shulḥan Arukh, Yoreh De'ah, Chap. 147; Sefer ha-Ḥinnukh, Mitzvot 86, 456.

PUNISHMENT OF ONE WHO ENTICES TO WORSHIP IDOLS

Do not consent to him. . . nor hearken unto him,. . . and have no considerate eye for him. Do not pity him. . . nor conceal him (Deuteronomy 13:9)

And never again do any such wickedness as this (Deuteronomy 13:12)

1. The sensitivity of Judaism is so utterly opposed to the sin of idol worship that the Rabbis expounding biblical law go to the uttermost extremes in the condemnation and punishment of anyone who compromised with idolatry. Pagan worship is the only sin where the Rabbis condone hatred of the offender and allow a conviction even when the evidence had been obtained by questionable means.

2. The mere incitement of a fellow-Jew to indulge in idol worship is sufficient to warrant the penalty of stoning. Even if the enticer and his victim do not resort to actual worship of an idol, the sin is yet considered extremely severe because through these incitements one may have been led to commit this grave error.

3. The inciter must be despised and destroyed. Hatred of this criminal is a necessity, death, an unavoidable consequence.

4. In Jewish law, the testimony of witnesses who were planted without the knowledge of the victim and were unseen by him, is unacceptable. Normally it is required that the witness must have warned the criminal of the heinousness of his crime and its possible consequences. In the case of an enticer to idol worship, however, it is permitted for two witnesses to remain hidden from sight while the sinner makes his insidious preachments. They can then proceed directly to the court and charge the one who tried to sway others to commit the sin.

COMMENTATORS

Ibn Ezra, Naḥmanides, Sforno: They all agree that "Do not consent" implies that one should not even lend credence to the thoughts and preachings of one who tries to induce a fellow-Jew to worship idols. They disagree, however, on the interpretation of "Nor hearken unto him."

Ibn Ezra: He says that "hearkening" refers to committing the actual sin with prior deliberation.

Naḥmanides: He interprets "hearkening" as agreeing in word to worship other gods, even though one does not actually indulge in the act of worship. He notes also that in this instance the Torah does not call for a prior inquiry into the facts of the case. So serious is the offense that a loyal Jew, as soon as he senses that he is being enticed to worship strange gods, must react immediately and even cast the first stone with which to kill the offender.

Sforno: If one does not permit the thought of idolatry to enter one's mind, one will never reach the point of committing the sin. Should a man begin to deliberate on the pros and cons of the suggestion to worship strange gods, he becomes liable to perform the actual deed.

Or ha-Ḥayyim: He is puzzled how a person can be persuaded to change his belief in the true God and transfer it to a false god. How can one be swayed from so personal a commitment? He offers two explanations:

1. A person is approached with the suggestion that his worship of God is old-fashioned and outmoded. All the imposed restrictions of Judaism should be abandoned because its founders had no idea of the spectacular progress of modern times.
2. A person is approached with the temptation to make his life easier. What need is there for the Jew to continue to live in fear? Let him assimilate with the dominant religious power and thus remove a major source of discrimination.

References:

B. Sanhedrin 29a, 33b, 61b, 85b, 89a; B. Ḥullin 4b; Sifre *Re'eh;* Yad, Hilkhot Avodah Zarah, Chap. 5; Sefer ha-Mitzvot (Lo Ta'aseh) 16, 17, 18, 19, 20, 21; Sefer Mitzvot Gadol (Lav) 26, 27, 28, 29, 30, 31; Sefer Mitzvot Katan 116, 117, 118; Sefer ha-Ḥinnukh, Mitzvot 457, 458, 459, 460, 461, 462.

A CONDEMNED CITY (IR HA-NIDAḤAT)

You shall burn with fire the city. . . it shall be a heap of ruins forever; it shall not be built again. And nothing of that which is doomed shall cleave to your hand (Deuteronomy 13:17–18)

1. Once again we observe the utter, uncompromising antagonism of Judaism to any form of idol worship. All manifestations of such worship had to be ruthlessly annihilated; there could be no question of coexistence with it.

2. The process of corruption started when two or more persons in the same city began to incite the inhabitants to worship a particular idol and their advice was followed.

3. When word reached the Sanhedrin in Jerusalem that this community had gone astray, they immediately dispatched two sages who met with people and warned them against this practice. If the community corrected its ways, the city did not become an *ir ha–nidaḥat.* If it persisted, the city was besieged and invaded. There and then, courts of *Sanhedrin Ketanah* comprising 23 members each, were established, and testimony taken concerning those who were accused of idol worship. If it was found that most members of the community had been guilty of this sin, the *Sanhedrin Gedolah,* the highest court in Jerusalem, had to judge the city. If they condemned it as an *ir ha-nidaḥat,* the idol-worshipers and their families were destroyed by the sword. The belongings of the entire community, including those who were innocent, were brought out into the public thoroughfare and burned in a great conflagration. The city itself was leveled to the ground and was never rebuilt.

4. If the guilty were found to be a minority of the population, they were judged and punished as individuals and the penalty of *ir ha-nidaḥat* did not apply.

5. If it appeared that the city as a whole was guilty of apostasy, proceedings against it could be taken only by the full Sanhedrin of 71 judges sitting in Jerusalem.

6. A city situated in a border district facing enemy territory could not be declared an *ir ha–nidaḥat,* since the demolition of such a border city could have facilitated invasion by the enemy.

COMMENTATORS

Da'at Zekenim: Everything in the condemned city had to be burned publicly, so that there might be no suspicion that the city was conquered and idol-worshiping Jews destroyed in order that those who had condemned it might enjoy the spoils.

Naḥmanides: He disagrees with the opinion of those who contend that children were included in the destruction of the city's inhabitants.

Ba'al ha-Turim: The thought might arise that, in the community of nations, the Jewish nation is very small in numbers. If so, why destroy a whole city of Jewish people? Hence God promises in the very next verse that, if we carry out His wishes, "I will then have compassion on you and multiply you."

Ḥinnukh: When an entire city permits itself to be misled into leaving God and resorting to idol worship, it deserves this severe punishment of having its name completely eradicated.

References:

B. Bava Kamma 82a; B. Bava Metzia 31b; B. Avodah Zarah 34b, 48b; B. Makkot 22a; B. Sanhedrin 15b, 16b, 40a, 71a, 89a, 111b, 112a, 112b, 113b; J. Avodah Zarah, Chap. 4, Halakhah 6, Chap. 5, Halakhah 12; Tosefta, Sanhedrin, Chap. 14; Sifre *Re'eh;* Yad, Hilkhot Avodah Zarah, Chap. 4; Guide of the Perplexed, Part 3, Sec. 41; Sefer ha-Mitzvot (Aseh) 186, (Lo Ta'aseh) 23, 24; Sefer Mitzvot Gadol (Aseh) 15, (Lav) 24, 25; Sefer ha-Ḥinnukh, Mitzvot 464, 465, 466.

PROHIBITION OF EXCESSIVE MOURNING

You shall not cut yourselves . . . nor make a baldness between your eyes for the dead (Deuteronomy 14:1)

1. When it becomes evident that the life of a dear one is extinct, there is a likelihood that the surviving relatives may, in the first transports of grief, react in an extreme manner, perhaps even maiming themselves.

2. This prohibition against inflicting incisions on oneself also applies to an act of homage to an idol. In other words, not only in grief is one restrained from cutting himself but also as a sign of fealty to an idol.

3. A person who cuts his flesh or tears his hair in grief at some other calamity, e.g., when his house collapses or he hears that his ship has been lost at sea, does not actually infringe this prohibition of the Torah; his behavior is, however, condemned.

4. Such acts, if performed in mourning for the dead or in idolatrous worship, are punishable by lashes.

COMMENTATORS

Naḥmanides, Ibn Ezra, Or ha-Ḥayyim, Ḥinnukh, Alshekh, Da'at Zekenim: They all stress the same truth: Man is better off dead than alive. The one who is dead, has met his Maker and has found his peace in a world much better than ours. There is reason for a normal amount of grief by the survivors of the deceased, such as weeping; but there is no room for excessive grief such as is demonstrated in the two laws above. Even when a young child dies, when it is hard to think in terms of his having found his eternal peace, we must nevertheless recognize the fact that, in God's own way, this tragedy may have been a blessing in disguise. In any event, to the Jew, it is the life of eternal peace in the World to Come, not life in this world, that is of cardinal importance. When God, who is totally concerned with man's welfare, brings death, one must not display excessive grief like those to whom death means the final end.

References:
B. Yevamot 13b, 14a; B. Kiddushin 35b, 36a; B. Menaḥot 37b; B. Mo'ed Katan 27b; B. Makkot 20b, 21a; B. Sanhedrin 68a; J. Kiddushin, Chap. 1, Halakhah 7; Sifre *Re'eh;* Zohar, *Shelaḥ,* 159b; Yad, Hilkhot Avodah Zarah, Chap. 12; Sefer ha-Mitzvot (Lo Ta'aseh) 45, 171; Sefer Mitzvot Gadol (Lav) 62, 63; Sefer Mitzvot Katan 73, 74, 75; Shulḥan Arukh, Yoreh De'ah, 180; Sefer ha-Ḥinnukh, Mitzvot 467, 468.

PROHIBITION OF EATING ANY NEVELAH*

You shall not eat of any carrion (Deuteronomy 14:21)

1. Many Jewish theologians argue that any physical enjoyment the body derives from things which are not religiously and reverently prepared can affect the spiritual wellbeing of that person.

2. An animal or fowl that would be acceptable for consumption if it were slaughtered properly becomes *nevelah* if it died a natural death or was slaughtered not by a valid *sheḥitah.* If one partakes of a piece of its carcass, even if no more than the size of an olive, one is rendered liable to lashes. An animal which is forbidden for Jewish consumption, even if it is ritually slaughtered, is not subject to this law. In the first instance, lashes were administered because of eating *nevelah;* in the second instance, the penalty is due to eating unclean food *(basar teme'ah).*

COMMENTATORS

Abrabanel: He cites the reasoning of Naḥmanides to which he takes exception. According to Naḥmanides, the rationalization behind this *mitzvah* is not that the meat of this animal is unpalatable, but that it is

**Nevelah.* The flesh of an animal which has died otherwise than by correct ritual slaughter *(sheḥitah).*

harmful to the human being. Abrabanel rejects this view, suggesting instead that the real reason why this meat is disqualified is not that it is abominable to man but that it is reprehensible to God in view of the fact that it was a pagan custom to eat of this particular kind of meat.

References:

B. Ḥullin 114b, 115a, 115b; B. Krittot 21a; B. Pesaḥim 22b; B. Avodah Zarah 67b; B. Zevaḥim 69a, 69b; Yad, Hilkhot Ma'akhalot Assurot, Chap. 4; Sefer ha-Mitzvot (Lo Ta'aseh) 180; Sefer Mitzvot Gadol (Lav) 133; Sefer Mitzvot Katan 202; Shulḥan Arukh, Yoreh De'ah, 15, 16; Sefer ha-Ḥinnukh, Mitzvah 472.

BRINGING THE TITHES TO JERUSALEM

You shall tithe all the increase of your seed (Deuteronomy 14:22)

1. A person may feel justified in his belief that praying at home is quite adequate. There is, however, a very pronounced difference between the loneliness of house-prayer and the warmth, inspiration, and fervor of prayer in a synagogue. Equally, one may feel that any gesture of gratitude for the many blessings that God showered down upon him can also be adequately expressed at home. Here again there is a marked difference between the home atmosphere and the bringing of the tithe to Jerusalem as a sign of thankfulness for God's beneficence. In the precincts of the Temple, there was a spirit of reverence and an aura of sanctity that moved a person to show gratitude to his Maker. This was the purpose of the commandment that in the first, second, fourth, and fifth years of the seven-year cycle, the Jew was required to take one-tenth of his produce after having separated *terumah* and *ma'aser rishon,* and bring it to Jerusalem where he could joyously consume it.

2. The Torah speaks only of this tithe, *ma'aser sheni,* in terms of corn, wine, and oil. The Rabbis extended it to include other foods which are the produce of the soil or animals as well.

3. Should the transport of this produce be too cumbersome, the Jew was given the alternative of exchanging the value of the food for money and adding "an outside fifth" (which was equal to a fourth of the original value) which he took to Jerusalem to buy foodstuffs which were to be eaten there.

COMMENTATORS

Ḥinnukh, Naḥmanides: The same reasoning that was used in the tithing of animals (Leviticus 27:32) applies also to the tithe of the fruits of the earth. Moreover, the social nature of the occasion in Jerusalem, when the people came there to bring their various tithes, served to strengthen the bonds of love and friendship among them.

Alshekh: How can we expect a person who arrives in Jerusalem to learn to fear God by eating, drinking, and making merry? When the Jew brought his tithe to Jerusalem, he was bringing testimony that it was not only by his own strength and ingenuity that the produce was brought forth from the earth, but rather that it was God's beneficence. When he came to Jerusalem, it was equivalent to bearing gifts to the Lord. He was overjoyed in the presence of God Who, he acknowledged, gave him plentifully. All this constituted fear of and respect for God.

Abrabanel: It is one thing simply to take food to Jerusalem for the purpose of making merry; it is quite another matter when one does it as an act of obedience to God's wishes. Acting in obedience to God is one way of learning to fear Him.

References:

B. Ta'anit 9a; B. Rosh ha-Shanah 8a, 12b; B. Berakhot 45a, 47b; B. Nedarim 59b; B. Bava Metzia 88a, 88b; J. Ma'asrot, Chap. 1, Halakhot 1, 2; J. Orlah, Chap. 1, Halakhah 1; Yad, Hilkhot Ma'aser Sheni; Sefer ha-Mitzvot (Aseh) 128; Sefer Mitzvot Gadol (Aseh) 136; Shulḥan Arukh, Yoreh De'ah, 331; Sefer ha-Ḥinnukh, Mitzvah 473.

REMISSION OF DEBTS IN THE YEAR OF RELEASE

Every creditor shall remit that which he has lent unto his neighbor. He shall not exact payment of his neighbor and his brother (Deuteronomy 15:2)
Take heed to yourself that there be no unworthy thought in your heart (Deuteronomy 15:9)

1. The provisions of the *Shemittah* year include *shemittat kesafim,* the cancellation of debts outstanding at the end of the sixth year of the seven-year cycle (i.e., at the beginning of the *Shemittah* year).

2. Under this law the debtor was free of all obligation to repay the loan, while the creditor was forbidden to accept repayment, in case it was offered to him, unless he first informed the debtor that his indebtedness was cancelled and that any repayment he might make was purely voluntary.

3. When a person borrowed money during the *Shemittah* year, he could, according to some opinions, be sued for payment during the year itself; others hold that, while under an obligation to pay, he could not be sued by his creditor.

4. During the period of the Mishnah it was found that, on the approach of the *Shemittah* year, the rich would often refuse to grant loans for fear that repayment would be delayed until the end of the sixth year and that their capital would thus be irretrievably lost. This situation bore hardly upon the poor, who might be in urgent need of a loan. In order to help them, Hillel I (1st cent. C.E.) devised the legal arrangement known as *prosbul.* This was a formal transfer of the debt to the *Bet Din,* which could claim repayment even during or after the *Shemittah* year and hand over the sum to the original lender.

5. It is essential for the economic structure of Jewish society that every Jew feel duty bound to alleviate the financial burdens of his poor coreligionists. While the *mitzvah* of almsgiving *(tzedakah)* is important, many hold that it is even more important to grant a loan *(gemilut ḥesed)* to one who is in temporary straits. The Torah is quite emphatic in its condemnation of one who withholds a loan merely because of fear of non-payment during the *Shemittah* year. It is for this reason that Hillel was moved to establish the *prosbul.*

COMMENTATORS

Ḥinnukh: The purpose of these laws of cancelling debts in the seventh year of release is twofold:

1. One purpose is to demand of us a maximum effort of faith in view of the fact that there is a great temptation not to grant a loan close to the year of release for fear of its cancellation.
2. Another purpose is to import a lesson in religious ethics. In the year of release, we are expected to forget the loans made by us and not to desire money once ours which we have since lent to someone else. Still less should we consider coveting someone else's money or possessions, since they never belonged to us at all. As David said: "For we have given unto You what came from Your hand."

Naḥmanides: The suspension of debt-collecting in the seventh year of release is compared to the cessation of work on the Sabbath—the seventh day of the week. It is not enough that we stop work; even the very thought of work must not enter our minds. Similarly, it is not enough merely to release a debt. Even the very thought of its collection must not occur in our thoughts.

Abrabanel: Why is the Torah more emphatic in exhorting us to cancel debts than it is in other cases of philanthropy? Because we are dealing here with human psychology. It is one thing when a person decides to make a charitable donation; it is quite another matter when a loan is made in good faith and the borrower waits until the year of release so that he need not repay the loan. Hence does the Torah plead with us to forget the payment because, after all, it is really God's money and He has the right to tell us—the temporary bankers—what is best to do with it.

References:

B. Arakhin 28b, 33a; B. Gittin 36a, 37b; B. Makkot 3b; B. Kiddushin 38b; B. Ketubbot 68a; B. Shevuot 45a, 49a; B. Mo'ed Katan 2b; J. Rosh ha-Shanah, Chap. 1, Halakhah 2, Chap. 3, Halakhah 5; Tosefta Shevi'it, Chap. 8; Pe'ah,

Chap. 4; Sifre *Re'eh;* Yad, Hilkhot Shemittah ve-Yovel, Chap. 9; Sefer ha-Mitzvot (Aseh) 141, (Lo Ta'aseh) 230, 231; Sefer Mitzvot Katan 258, 259; Shulḥan Arukh, Ḥoshen Mishpat, 67; Sefer ha-Ḥinnukh, Mitzvot 475, 477, 480.

GIVING CHARITY KINDLY AND GENEROUSLY

You shall not harden your heart (Deuteronomy 15:7)
But you shall surely open wide your hand unto him (Deuteronomy 15:8)

1. In an enlightened society, almost everyone agrees that to give charity is a virtue. There are, however, vast differences of opinion as to what constitutes charity and what is a charitable case, as well as to what extent relief must be offered.

2. Charity is not to be reduced to the mere essentials of life. It takes into account the social status of the poor as well. For example: If a person who was accustomed to riding on a horse became impoverished, it is incumbent upon the community to supply him with a horse so that he may retain his image in society. But there are priorities. That is, the poor of one's family takes priority over the poor who are strangers, those of the community, in which he lives have preference over those of other communities.

3. In Judaism, the apex of charitable deeds is the *pidyon shevuyim,* the ransoming of Jews from heathen captivity.

4. On the other hand, we have guidelines as to who should feel free to approach charitable institutions for assistance. For example: If one has sufficient food for two meals (i.e., enough for one day), he should not seek help at the free-kitchens. If he has food for 14 meals (i.e., enough for the complete week), he should not present himself at the charity queue where food for the week was distributed to the needy of the town, although he will thereby lack the additional Sabbath meal.

5. The distinguishing psychological feature of the Jew is his sense of charity. This sign of his Jewishness is stamped into the very essence of his make-up. In Jewish thought it is inconceivable to be a Jew and yet not be charitable. It is for this reason, that the Torah insists very emphatically that charity is not merely a virtue but an inescapable duty.

COMMENTATORS

Ibn Ezra: In assisting the poor one must not do so grudgingly or half-heartedly. In addition to giving financial support, one must also extend a hand of wholehearted encouragement.

Or ha-Ḥayyim: The reward that one receives for giving charity is not only financial in character, for God repays charitable people in many other ways. For our own benefit, let us not harden our heart but open our hand and give generously.

Abrabanel: He proposes three reasons why the Torah dictates that charity should be considered as mandatory and not optional:

1. When a person deposits money in a bank, he expects that institution to carry out all the promissory and financial instructions that he issues. When the bank refuses to do so, he will withdraw his entire account and deposit it elsewhere. Similarly, man is God's bank on earth. If we refuse to fulfill his wishes, He will naturally withdraw His bounty and bestow it elsewhere, thus impoverishing its former owner.
2. Charity is another exercise in faith. Arithmetically, a person may conclude that the more he distributes to others, the less he will have. God promises us the very reverse.
3. Pragmatically, no one possesses the prescience of when the wheel of fortune will stop spinning and who will then be on top. The person who should distribute charity today may well find himself at the other end of the scale, where he will himself need the charity of others.

References:

B. Bava Batra 9b, 10a; B. Ketubbot 67b; B. Bava Metzia 31b; B. Gittin 37a; B. Shabbat 151b; B. Sukkah 29b, 49b; B. Ta'anit 8b; Pirkei Avot, Chap. 5; Midrash Rabbah, *Bereshit,* Chap. 12, Sec. 15; *Mishpatim,* Chap. 31, Sec. 2, 3, 5; *Tetzaveh,* Chap. 36, Sec. 3; *Behar,* Chap. 34, Sec. 1, 2, 6; Midrash Tanḥuma, *Mishpatim,* Chap. 8; Midrash Tehillim, Chap. 17, 50, 52, 118; Yad, Hilkhot Matnat Aniyim, Chap. 7, 8, 9, 10; Sefer ha-Mitzvot (Lo Ta'aseh) 232, (Aseh) 195;

Sefer Mitzvot Gadol (Lav) 289, (Aseh) 93; Sefer Mitzvot Katan 248, 249; Shulḥan Arukh, Yoreh De'ah, 247; Sefer ha-Ḥinnukh, Mitzvot 478, 479.

PROVIDING FOR THE LIBERATED JEWISH SLAVE

You shall not let him go away empty (Deuteronomy 15:13)
You shall furnish him liberally out of your flock (Deuteronomy 15:14)

1. A convicted thief who was unable to restore what he had stolen was sold into slavery by the court, the purchase-price being given to the person from whom he had stolen. An impoverished person who could not support himself and his family might also sell himself as a slave. In neither case could the period of servitude exceed six years (i.e., until the next *Shemittah* year). Furthermore, in order to assure his future and avoid a situation which might lead to his being enslaved again, the Torah required the master, when discharging him from his service, to make him a substantial gift. According to the Rabbis, it was to be no less than 30 *selaim* which, in Temple days, was quite a substantial sum.

2. The type of gifts was to be in the form of self-producing products such as seed or livestock, not money or clothes.

3. If a slave who was judged by the court as having to work for the master for six years suddenly came into money, thus enabling him to make restitution so that he could be freed earlier, then he was not provided by his master when he left his service.

4. According to some opinions this *mitzvah* of *ha'anakah* (bestowing a generous gift) applies even when we discharge a hired worker from our service.

COMMENTATORS

Ibn Ezra: It is not sufficient that the Jewish slave be granted his freedom; it is also necessary that we enable him to obtain an honorable status in society once he is freed. In other words, we must give him financial assistance when he is liberated so that when he enters society once again, he will be able to do so with dignity.

Alshekh: He proposes several reasons why a master is compelled to send away his Jewish slave with liberal provisions:

1. If a person sold himself to you as a slave, then you have acquired him "illegally," because his first master, God, has never relinquished His ownership of him. Hence, when on being emancipated he returns to the service of his original master, you must compensate him for this temporary illegal possession.
2. You have derived greater benefit from the services of the slave than did the slave from his service to you. As a result, you must show your appreciation of his efforts by sending him off to his freedom with liberal financial assistance. Such a compensatory act is due to him.
3. One must not forget that both master and slave are in the same category: both are servants of God. What both possess belongs to their master—God. It is for this reason, that God instructs one slave to assist the other.
4. It is unfortunate that one man is forced to sell himself as a slave to another because of his critical financial condition. The master who buys the slave must realize that, by employing the slave, he can help him to become rehabilitated and reenter society. If upon his release, the master sends him out into the world in the same financial situation he was in when he first engaged him, then the master has not helped the slave to become rehabilitated. On the other hand, when the master sends him out into society with a liberal assistance, it is probable that the former slave will succeed in life and will not have to resort to selling himself again into slavery. The master might then question: Why should he be the one to worry about the slave's welfare? Why should he be responsible for sending him off with financial backing? Is it his fault that the slave went into debt in the first place? The Torah's reply to these questions is that the Jews' ancestors also owed God a great number of debts and God was dissatisfied with their spiritual "payments." Yet He brought them out of Egypt, gave them their freedom, and also gave them a generous supply of material possessions when they left their place of bondage. Surely, the least we can do is to

imitate God's ways when we return freedom to a slave. We too, must provide him with sufficient material possessions so that he will be able to start off with proper direction as a free man.

References:
B. Kiddushin 14b, 15a, 16b, 17a, 17b; J. Kiddushin, Chap. 1, Halakhah 2; Sifre *Re'eh,* 120; Yad, Hilkhot Avadim, Chap. 3; Sefer ha-Mitzvot (Lo Ta'aseh) 233, (Aseh) 196; Sefer Mitzvot Gadol (Lav) 178, (Aseh) 84; Sefer ha-Ḥinnukh, Mitzvot 481, 482.

COMMUNAL CELEBRATION OF THE PASCHAL SACRIFICE

You may not sacrifice the Passover-offering within any of your gates which the Lord your God gave you (Deuteronomy 16:5)

1. There were times in Jewish history when Jews were permitted to have their own private *bamot* (altars). Before the Sanctuary in the desert was erected, as well as during the conquest of the land, communal sacrifices took place in Gilgal, and after the destruction of Shiloh in Nob and Gibeah. Even when sacrifices were permitted at these individual altars, the Passover-sacrifice was not permitted to be offered at the individual altar but had to be brought to the central, public altar.

2. The reasoning is simple. The Exodus from Egypt was such a world-shaking event that it not only affected the destiny of the Jew but, through him, the future of mankind. This called for a celebration that was not to be merely a casual holiday of a private nature, but rather a national expression of happiness and gratitude to God. *Be-rov am, hadrat melekh,* a king's glory is reflected by the multitude of his subjects who pay homage to him.

COMMENTATORS

Ḥinnukh: He offers two reasons why a private celebration of the Passover was prohibited:

1. A celebration among a host of friends and fellow-celebrants is more joyful and inspiring than a private one.
2. Because of the great national significance of the festival of Passover, it behoves the individual Jew to submerge his individuality and join in a communal, festive environment.

Abrabanel: In truth, there is no reason why a person cannot enjoy himself with a small group of friends as much as he does with a large assembly of people. The reason why the Jew was asked to bring his Paschal lamb and to celebrate its offering publicly in the Temple was only that God instructed him so to do and not for any other particular social reason.

References:
B. Zevaḥim 114b; Sefer ha-Ḥinnukh, Mitzvah 487. (See Minḥat Ḥinnukh for an explanation why every commentary, including Maimonides, whom the Ḥinnukh usually meticulously follows, excludes this *mitzvah* from its roll of 613 *mitzvot*. The Ḥinnukh stands alone in incorporating this *mitzvah*.)

THE THREE ANNUAL PILGRIMAGES

Three times a year shall all your males appear. . . and they shall not appear before the Lord with empty hands (Deuteronomy 16:16)
Take heed to yourself that you forsake not the Levite (Deuteronomy 12:19)
And you shall rejoice in your festival (Deuteronomy 16:14)
Three times shall you celebrate unto Me in the year (Exodus 23:17)

1. The Torah required every Jew to appear in Jerusalem on three occasions during the year—Passover, Shavuot, and Sukkot. The Torah also demanded that he should not come empty-handed but should bring with him three animals for three different sacrifices. The first was to be a *korban re'iyah*—"the sacrifice of appearance." This was to be a burnt-offering. The second—

shalmei ḥagigah (a peace-offering) was brought in honor of the celebration of the specific holiday. The third was *shalmei simḥah*—a peace-offering to be eaten to enhance the joy and happiness of the occasion. Women were exempt from participating in the first two offerings but were expected to join in the third.

2. All males were expected to fulfill the *mitzvah* of *re'iyah* and bring a *korban re'iyah* with the exceptions of a minor and one who was deaf, dumb, insane, blind, crippled, uncircumcised, aged, sick, in a delicate state of health, or in a state of ritual uncleanness.

3. While the ritual aspects of these visits were important, the character of the festivities was even more so. It was not sufficient for a head of a family to gather his family and friends around the festive tables of the *shalmei ḥagigah* and the *shalmei simḥah* in order to celebrate the significance of the festivals. What was more important was that he invite the poor and the destitute, and particularly the Levite, to join him and his family in the festivity. The Torah goes out of its way to make mention of the Levite because he received no portions of meat from any of the offerings brought to the Temple. A truly joyous festive celebration is one in which the Jew is not only happy himself, but also brings gladness into the hearts of others.

4. Today, we are also expected to celebrate our festivals with the same fervor and gaiety, with meat and drink and to be joined therein by those less fortunate, just as in Temple days. The only difference is that we have no sacrifices today, because we have no Temple. Donations to charity or to institutions of learning are the present day equivalent of the traditional festive sacrifices.

COMMENTATORS

Ibn Ezra: Why does it say in Exodus 23:14, "Shall you celebrate unto Me"? Because since these three celebrations may coincide with those of the pagans in the temples of their gods and idols, God did not want to confuse those occasions with the three annual Jewish visits to the Temple. For this reason He stressed "unto Me."

Sforno: The festive spirit of the three visits to the Temple was intended to counteract the enthusiasm shown by our ancestors when they danced around the Golden Calf.

Naḥmanides: These three major festivals have economic and agrarian aspects, as well as being historical anniversaries. An agricultural people naturally prays for the joy of reaping and storing the year's produce. The Jew came to the Temple, at different seasons of the year, to offer his gratitude to God for not withholding His beneficence at the different seasons—the dew, rain, and sunshine—as a result of which his sustenance is assured.

Ḥinnukh: The pilgrimages were made so that the Jew could thank God for the miracles He had performed on each of the three festivals. Not that one cannot feel grateful at home; but in the Temple the atmosphere is more solemn, stirring, and impressive. Furthermore, on the Feast of Tabernacles, on the seventh year of the seven-year cycle *(Shemittah),* when it was announced in the Temple that all debts were to be cancelled, the Jew was a convinced witness that total and unquestioned possession belongs to God only. We are reminded not to forget the Levite on this day. Since the Levite has no land, having dedicated his life to ministering to our spiritual needs, it is only fitting that we invite him to join in our festivities.

Abrabanel: There were five reasons for visiting the Temple during the three major holidays:

1. The Jews were given three extraordinary gifts by God; Freedom, Torah, and Land. They visited the Temple on Passover to thank God for their freedom, as symbolized by the Exodus; on Shavuot to thank God for the Torah which was given to them on Mount Sinai on Shavuot; and on the Feast of Tabernacles, to thank God for the Land and its produce, as indicated by the season in which this festival falls when the farmer has harvested the produce of the soil.
2. These visits express the fundamental belief that, if God so wills it, nothing is impossible of fulfillment.
3. The people are inspired by the rich pageantry and the performance of the rituals by the Priests and Levites.
4. The common spiritual interests and joyous conviviality that united the people together during the pilgrimages to the Temple helped to further peace and cordiality among them all the year round.
5. The people, particularly those living in faraway communities,

were thus able to ascertain the opinions of the great sages and of the high courts in order to clarify complicated problems in religious law which had perplexed them and their Rabbis in their own small communities. The great academies of learning and the Sanhedrin were located in Jerusalem.

References:

B. Kiddushin 34a, 34b; B. Rosh ha-Shanah 4b, 6b; B. Mo'ed Katan 8b; B. Ḥagigah 2a, 3a, 4a, 17a; B. Sukkah 49b; B. Pesaḥim 8b, 109a; Sifre *Re'eh;* Yad, Hilkhot Ḥagigah, Chap. 1, 2; Yad, Hilkhot Shevitat Yom Tov, Chap. 6; Sefer ha-Mitzvot (Aseh) 52, 53, 54, (Lo Ta'aseh) 156, 229; Sefer Mitzvot Gadol (Aseh) 227, 228, 229, (Lav) 361; Shulḥan Arukh, Oraḥ Ḥayyim, 529; Sefer ha-Ḥinnukh, Mitzvot 88, 450, 488, 489, 490.

PROHIBITION AGAINST PLANTING AN ASHERAH OR BUILDING A MEMORIAL OF STONE

You shall not plant an Asherah of any kind of tree beside the altar of the Lord your God (Deuteronomy 16:21)
Neither shall you set up a pillar (Deuteronomy 16:22)

1. An Asherah is any type of tree planted near a house of worship. Since this was a pagan custom, the Torah prohibited the planting of any tree in the *Azarah* (courtyard of the Temple where the altar stood).

2. For the same reason it was forbidden to erect, in any place, a stone pillar to mark a place of worship—even worship of the true God.

COMMENTATORS

Alshekh: Since both an Asherah and a pillar are of idolatrous origin, they are forbidden. He raises the following question: Should a person plant a tree at the entrance to the Temple not with the motive of the idol-worshipers, i.e., to serve as a signpost to guide the people to their pagan temples, but in order to beautify the grounds of the Temple of God? Or if one intends to erect a large pillar in the Temple not to sacrifice upon it as the pagans did, but merely for its aesthetic beauty, would he then be acting sinfully? The answer is: Yes; for in both instances, the actions are forbidden because they may eventually lead to pagan worship. The process of drifting from Judaism to paganism begins at first with small, insignificant changes such as a tree or a pillar, which later escalate into more serious deviations until the process ends in complete apostasy. This reasoning, according to Naḥmanides, applies to all Jewish places of worship. They must be free from every foreign religious influence, no matter how harmless they may appear at first.

References:

B. Sanhedrin 7b; B. Zevaḥim 46b, 60a; B. Tamid 28b; B. Avodah Zarah 48a, 52a; Sifre *Shofetim;* J. Avodah Zarah, Chap. 4, Halakhah 4; Yad, Hilkhot Avodah Zarah, Chap. 6; Sefer ha-Mitzvot (Lo Ta'aseh) 11, 13; Sefer Mitzvot Gadol (Lav) 41, 44; Sefer Mitzvot Katan 163; Shulḥan Arukh, Yoreh De'ah, 145; Sefer ha-Ḥinnukh, Mitzvot 492, 493.

AUTHORITY OF THE RABBINATE

According to the Law which they shall teach you, and according to the judgment which they tell you, shall you do; you shall not turn aside from the sentence which they shall declare unto you, to the right hand nor to the left (Deuteronomy 17:11)

1. In the course of Jewish history, there were those who rejected the authority of the Torah—the Written Law; these were branded as *apikorsim* (heretics). Others accepted the Written Law but denied the authority of the *Torah she-be-Al-Peh*—the Oral Law. The *halakhah* (religious legislation) categorized these also as *apikorsim.* A society cannot exist without obedience to the law. There must be a self-imposed discipline on the part of every member of the community to obey the decisions of the highest rabbinical authorities. If we believe in the authority of Moses, it follows that we must also believe in the authority of the succeeding sages. To deny the entire tradition of rabbinic influence on Jewish law or to stultify it by not acknowledging its continuity is tantamount to abrogating the entire legal system. In other words, either we believe that contemporary rabbinic authority is as binding as was that of Moses and the Written Law, or we reject Jewish law in its entirety.

2. The question arises concerning one who desires to be selective in his submission to Jewish law. The Torah, in this *mitzvah*, admonishes us that we may not be discriminatory in our obedience to Jewish law; whatever the Rabbis teach as *halakhah* must be accepted. If this principle were abandoned, the result would be a number of legal systems in Judaism, each pandering to the whims and follies of people, each of whom would select the law that best suited him. This is obviously impossible in a strong, purposeful, and orientated society such as the Jewish community.

COMMENTATORS

Maimonides, Naḥmanides: Here we have the classic difference of opinion between these two giants of *halakhah* as to the source of rabbinical authority. According to Maimonides, the command "You shall not turn aside" implies acceptance by the Jew of (1) the traditional (Masoretic) text of the scriptures, (2) the laws deduced from scripture by the thirteen hermeneutical rules of R. Ishmael *(shelosh-esreh middot she-ha-Torah nidreshet bahem)*, and (3) the decrees *(gezerot)*, ordinances *(takkanot)*, and customs *(minhagim)* instituted by the sages. Naḥmanides regards the first two categories only as included in the biblical injunction. Laws which are of rabbinical origin are not, in his view, enforceable by the same sanctions as those expressly stated in or directly derived from the Torah.

Abrabanel: He deals with the necessity to heed the words of spiritual leaders "even if they call the left hand right and the right hand left," as the Talmud explains the concluding words of the verse. He makes the following observations:

1. This depends upon one's point of view. If one stands before three wise men, his right hand will be on their left. Even so, one must obey them because their side is the just one. If we paraphrase this parable, we see that a petitioner thinks that his opinion is right from his vantage point. The wise men, however, say he is wrong because from their unbiased position they are really right. Their opinion must prevail in all cases of doubt or contention.

2. The wise men will never say that the right side, if it indeed is the right side, is the left one. Truth will prevail at all times, if we listen to them.

3. A rare occasion may arise when the wise men will contend that the right side is the left one; even then, there is not sufficient ground for defying their authority. They are overwhelmingly on the side of truth and their authority must not be compromised because of a rare error.

4. True, the petitioner must be steadfast in his position when he feels that right is right and left is left. He must never compromise and never be ready to accept right as left and left as right; but the Torah here speaks of no ordinary situation. Emergencies and crises may arise. In these circumstances, the wise men may feel impelled to call right left, and left right. In this case, despite the fact that the petitioner may assume that the wise men's decision is wrong, yet "You shall not turn aside from the sentence which they shall declare unto you, to the right hand nor to the left."

References:

B. Shabbat 23a, 23b; B. Horayot 4a; B. Berakhot 19b; B. Rosh ha-Shanah 25a; J. Berakhot, Chap. 1, Halakhah 2; J. Horayot, Chap. 1, Halakhah 1; Yad, Hilkhot Mamrim, Chap. 1, 3; Sefer ha-Mitzvot (Aseh) 174, (Lo Ta'aseh) 312 (See Shoresh 1 for the complete analysis of the position of Naḥmanides who disputes the basic premise of Maimonides.); Sefer Mitzvot Gadol (Aseh) 111, (Lav) 217; Tur, Ḥoshen Mishpat, Chap. 14; Sefer ha-Ḥinnukh, Mitzvot 495, 496.

APPOINTING A KING

One from your brethren shall you set him over you . . . you may not set a foreigner over you (Deuteronomy 17:15)
Only he shall not acquire a multitude of horses for himself (Deuteronomy 17:16)
Neither shall he have a multitude of wives . . . neither shall he greatly multiply silver and gold unto himself (Deuteronomy 17:17)
He shall write him a copy of this law into a book (Deuteronomy 17:18)

1. Upon entering the Promised Land the Children of Israel were admonished on three matters; to choose a king, to destroy the Amalekites, and to build a Temple.

2. A Jewish king could not be the offspring of a convert. He was to be appointed by the *Sanhedrin Gedolah* with the approval of a prophet.

3. The basic ritual of enthroning a king was his anointment. Once he was anointed, the throne became hereditary to the extent that if he died and left a young immature son, the monarchy was kept for the son until he would be able to assume his royal duties as king.

4. The king's conduct must be above reproach, so that the people would sense the awe and majesty of the monarch and render every homage due him. When he passed by, his subjects were expected to rise and bow before him. There was one exception to the rule; namely, the High Priest. He was not obligated to rise or make special efforts of paying homage to the king. Furthermore, one who was preoccupied with the performance of a *mitzvah* was exempt from these obligations.

5. Devotion and respect had to be shown to the king. Any rebellion against, or any abuse of, a king was punishable with death by the sword if the king willed it. The king could then confiscate the criminal's possessions.

6. To launch a war expressly commanded by God *(milḥemet* *mitzvah),* the king needed no approval. These wars included those against the seven nations of the Land of Canaan, the destruction of Amalek, and the wars for survival. For an "optional" war *(milḥemet reshut),* he first needed the approval of the Sanhedrin.

7. A king was not permitted to acquire horses to an abnormal extent. All that the Torah granted him were sufficient horses for his immediate use.

8. A king was not to keep a very large harem. According to tradition, a Jewish king could have not more than 18 wives.

9. A king was not to increase his cash reserves to the point where he kept them in treasuries, so that he could gloat over them. He was only permitted that amount of ready cash necessary for his needs. He was permitted to accumulate wealth to be used for the nation's benefit.

10. The most significant part of a king's life was the fact that he could not make a move without being accompanied by a *Sefer Torah* (Scroll of the Law). The king was required either to write a Scroll of the Law or to commission someone to do it for him. As we will see later, this *mitzvah* of writing a *Sefer Torah* was incumbent upon every Jew. In addition to that *mitzvah,* he was obliged to write an additional *Sefer Torah* in his capacity as a king. It was this second *Sefer Torah* that accompanied him wherever he went and was to be in his sight wherever he stood.

COMMENTATORS

The division of opinion as to the true interpretation of the *mitzvah* of appointing a king, stems from the vagueness of the language of the Torah. If it meant that the appointment of a king was obligatory, then why did the prophet Samuel wax indignant when the people first suggested that a king be appointed? If, on the other hand, royalty was frowned upon, then why did the Torah suggest the concept of the king? The overwhelming preponderance of opinion, including that of Abrabanel and Alshekh, is that the institution of the monarchy was alien to the spirit of Judaism. The Torah, however, anticipated a time when the people would call for a king and therefore legislated for this eventuality.

Keli Yakar: He is almost alone in his thesis that the appointment of a king was a necessity. His reasoning is that a king represented a symbol of authority; without discipline, a nation would fall into chaos.

Ibn Ezra: He comments on verse 16 that, after leaving Egypt, the Israelites were forbidden ever to return. Since in ancient times Egypt was a a major source of horses, this was a reason for warning the king not to acquire an excessive number of them.

Ḥinnukh: The author follows a similar line of reasoning. If the king were allowed to stock his stables without restriction, he would send agents to purchase horses in Egypt, thus setting up an Israelite settlement there.

Ibn Ezra: Commenting on the acquisition of wealth, he states that a king will tend to become greedy and acquire wealth by overtaxing the people. Alshekh continues that if this does happen, the king will be dethroned by the people who will revolt against this rank injustice.

Ibn Ezra, Naḥmanides, Alshekh: On the subject of a king's obligation to write for himself a *Sefer Torah,* they agree that the purpose is twofold:

1. The presence of the Torah at all times within the King's reach will instill in him a fear of God.
2. By reading and studying the Torah, he will learn how to apply righteous leadership to his people.

Ḥinnukh: The power of a king inspires awe. He can destroy or build, enrich or impoverish, kill or let live. Some restraining power was required to keep him in check. The presence of the Torah before him at every moment of his life served that purpose. He was ever reminded that the Torah demanded of him compassion and justice.

References:

B. Sanhedrin 20b, 21b, 22a, 22b; B. Ketubbot 17a; B. Bava Batra 91b; B. Sotah 41a, 41b (see Tosafot); B. Horayot 11b; B. Kiddushin 32b, 76b; B. Bava Kamma 88a; B. Berakhot 9b; B. Yevamot 45b, 102a; J. Sanhedrin, Chap. 2, Halakhah 6; J. Sotah, Chap. 8, Halakhah 3; J. Kiddushin, Chap. 4, Halakhah 5; Sifre *Shofetim;* Midrash Rabbah, *Shofetim,* Chap. 5; Yad, Hilkhot Melakhim, Chap. 1, Sec. 11; Chap. 3; Yad, Hilkhot Sefer Torah, Chap. 7; Sefer ha-Mitzvot (Aseh) 17, 173, (Lo Ta'aseh) 362, 363, 364, 365; Sefer Mitzvot Gadol (Aseh) 25, 114, (Lav) 221, 222, 223, 224; Sefer ha-Ḥinnukh, Mitzvot 497, 498, 499, 501, 502, 503.

NOT RETURNING TO EGYPT

You shall henceforth return no more that way (Deuteronomy 17:16)

1. A country which was so degenerate as to attempt genocide of the Jews or impose unspeakable hardships and oppressions upon them is no place for a Jew to reside in.

2. We are forbidden by the Torah to take up permanent residence in Egypt lest we be corrupted by the example of immoral living which prevailed there. A temporary stay in the country was, however, ruled to be permissible.

COMMENTATORS

Naḥmanides: The Egyptians were the most degenerate of nations. Not returning to Egypt was a salutary measure to avoid learning their depraved ways of life.

Baḥya ben Asher: He considers this a temporary injunction, effective only in biblical days. It was probably instituted because the Egyptian bondage was still fresh in the minds of the Jews, but the ban was not intended to remain in force forever. There have been Jewish communities in Egypt for thousands of years. (In fact, Maimonides and many other great luminaries lived in Egypt. Those who see the ban as still in effect reason that, in view of the fact that Maimonides was a court physician, his residence there was involuntary.)

Radbaz: How did a Jewish community develop and flourish in Egypt, seeing that there was a biblical injunction against Jews returning there? Some authorities argue that the prohibition affected only those who leave Israel to settle in Egypt; but those who immigrated to Egypt from other countries were not affected by this injunction. He finds this view difficult to accept. He suggests, instead, that Jews may have gone to Egypt not for the purpose of settling there but for business reasons. While they were there, they discovered that discriminatory steps had been taken against Jews in their native countries and that it would be imprudent to return to their domiciles. As a result, they remained in

Egypt as a matter of survival and not from premeditated choice. On the other hand, he is curious to know why such luminaries as Maimonides and others lived in Egypt, contrary to the wishes of the Torah. He defends Maimonides by contending that he was in jeopardy because he was summoned by the king to serve as his personal physician. Had this request been rejected, it might have cost him his life. Realizing that the same question would be directed at himself, Radbaz confesses that although he lived in Egypt for several years and founded an academy there, he felt compelled to leave Egypt and return to Jerusalem.

References:

B. Sukkah 51b; J. Sukkah, Chap. 5, Halakhah 1; J. Sanhedrin, Chap. 10, Halakhah 4; Yad, Hilkhot Melakhim, Chap. 5; Sefer ha-Mitzvot (Lo Ta'aseh) 46; Sefer Mitzvot Gadol (Lav) 227; Sefer ha-Ḥinnukh, Mitzvah 500; Mekhilta *Be-Shalaḥ*.

THE PARTS OF THE ANIMAL THAT BELONG TO THE PRIEST

That they shall give unto the Priest, the shoulder and the two cheeks and the maw (Deuteronomy 18:3)

1. Whenever a Jew slaughtered a clean animal to eat, the Torah enjoined that the Priest was to be presented with *matnot kehunnah* (priestly donations)—the right shoulder, the two jaws, and the maw. These three parts possessed no special character of holiness. They were simply gifts for services rendered by the Priests for the nation.

2. The Priest could either eat these parts in any place he so desired or he could assign them to a non-priestly friend, or even sell them in the marketplace for cash. A daughter of a Priest, married to a non-Priest, could also partake of these parts and even feed her husband therefrom. A *ḥallalah* (the daughter of a Priest born of a woman forbidden to him) could not share in these parts of the animal.

COMMENTATORS

Ibn Ezra: Why are these three particular parts given to the Priest? The shoulder is given because of the Priest's arm which slaughters the peace-offerings; the cheeks are given because the Priest's mouth offered the benediction; and the stomach is given because the Priest had to examine the inwards of the animal. Another reason is that these parts are the best cuts of meat.

Maimonides: He gives a different answer to the same question. The shoulder is the foremost limb of an animal; the cheeks (or jaws) are the foremost parts of the body; the stomach is the foremost of the inner organs. Hence they come under the category of "first-fruits" and belong to the Priest.

Ralbag: These parts belonged to the Priest because he is the strong spiritual arm of Jewry; the shoulder, because he prays to God on their behalf; the jaws and stomach because it is due to the prayers of the Priest that God grants the Jew his sustenance.

Abrabanel: There are three types of sins for which a person must seek atonement. There are sins committed by word of mouth, as symbolized by the jaws; those committed by actual deed, as symbolized by the shoulder; those committed by thought only as symbolized by the inwards.

Baḥya ben Asher: He offers yet another symbolic interpretation. These gifts were bestowed upon the Priest because of the zeal of Pinḥas in the incident of the Midianite woman. He took a spear (shoulder), and prayed for guidance (jaws), and thrust the spear through their stomachs (inwards). Since Pinḥas was a Priest, his descendants were granted these parts.

References:

B. Ḥullin 130b, 132a, 132b, 133b, 134b, 135a, 136b; Sifre *Shofetim* 165, *Koraḥ* 117; Yad, Hilkhot Bikkurim, Chap. 9; Guide of the Perplexed, Part 3, Sec. 39; Sefer ha-Mitzvot (Aseh) 143; Sefer Mitzvot Gadol (Aseh) 142; Shulḥan Arukh, Yoreh De'ah, 61; Sefer ha-Ḥinnukh, Mitzvah 506.

DIVISION OF PRIESTLY DUTIES

And if a Levite, out of one of your gates where he sojourns, comes out of all Israel (Deuteronomy 18:6)

1. When sacrifices were first instituted and the Priests' duties became excessively onerous, Moses arranged for eighty priestly watches to be in charge of the ministrations in the Tabernacle in the desert. These consisted of eight groups of Priests who were assigned to perform their duties on specific days. These were known as *mishmarot*. Later, this roster was expanded to 24 watches. The purpose of this division of priestly duties was to bring order, efficiency, and decorum into the activities in the Temple. At the head of each rota was a *Rosh ha-Mishmar,* whose duty it was to see that every Priest under his jurisdiction was given an equal opportunity to serve.

2. There was a change of guard every Sabbath morning, when a new *mishmar* (watch) would present itself and relieve the outgoing *mishmar*.

3. During the three major festivals, when the throngs would come to Jerusalem with their sacrifices, the system of *mishmarot* was suspended and any accredited Priest who happened to be standing nearby could be requested to officiate at the service of offerings. This applied only to offerings brought for the specific festivals; other sacrifices, brought in payment of vows and promises, had to be offered by a Priest of the current *mishmar*.

4. Later the early Prophets instituted the roster of what is known as *Anshei Ma'amad*—consisting of pious laymen who were present as representatives of the people at the offerings brought in the name of the people. There were 24 *ma'amadot,* which, like the *mishmarot,* changed every Sabbath.

COMMENTATORS

Maimonides, Ḥinnukh: They conclude that the division of duty in the Temple service among 24 sets of priestly functionaries was established so as to bring more order, efficiency, and decorum into the activities of the Priest. It would prevent chaos and occasions for dispute among the Priests.

Maimonides: He characterizes the division of the Priests into watches to officiate at fixed times as a positive *mitzvah* enacted for the sake of preserving order and decorum in the service of the Sanctuary. He notes, however, that the Torah expressly lays down that no properly qualified Priest, irrespective of his *mishmar,* may be debarred from officiating on a festival. Naḥmanides disagrees with this view. He holds that, while the Torah permits the division of the Priests into groups (which we are taught to believe is a part of the Oral Law—*Halakhah le-Moshe mi-Sinai*), it allows any Priest to serve at any time, even on ordinary weekdays, unless the division into *mishmarot* has already been made.

Baḥya ben Asher: Why could not the Priests come and go as they chose? Why is it necessary to fix certain periods for service in the Temple? In Jewish theology, the Temple on earth and the service therein were intended to parallel the worship and the service of the angels in heaven before God. According to the Kabbalah, the angels were subdivided into 24 sections so that each group could worship and praise the Lord in its own way. Just as there is no jealousy among the angels, so should there be no jealousy among the Priests.

References:

B. Bava Kamma 109b; B. Sukkah 55b, 56a; B. Berakhot 12a; B. Arakhin 11a; B. Ta'anit 27a; B. Yoma 23a; B. Menaḥot 107b; Sifre *Shofetim* 168; Midrash Rabbah, *Va-Yishlaḥ,* Chap. 78, Sec. 1; Yad, Hilkhot Kelei ha-Midrash; Sefer ha-Mitzvot (Aseh) 36; Sefer Mitzvot Gadol (Aseh) 172; Sefer ha-Ḥinnukh, Mitzvah 509.

LISTENING TO THE PROPHET

Unto him shall you hearken (Deuteronomy 18:15)

1. Once a man has gained recognition as a genuine prophet and proceeds to exhort the people to obey the dictates of the Torah, it is incumbent upon every Jew to respect and obey him. Whoever fails to do so is subject to Divine punishment.

2. Even if such a prophet declares that a particular *mitzvah* is suspended, while making it clear that this is a one-time measure taken in face of a quite exceptional emergency, the Jew must still obey him—unless he incites the people to idolatry. Such a case occurred when Elijah offered up sacrifices on Mount Carmel in order to prove the falsity of the prophets of Baal. His act implied a temporary suspension of the law according to which offerings could be brought only in Jerusalem.

3. On the other hand, if the prophet seeks to root out a *mitzvah* in its entirety, this indicates that he is a false prophet and he must be executed by strangulation.

4. By the same token, a prophet who is inspired of God but who refuses to follow God's instructions to go out among the people, also acts in violation of this law and is liable to be visited with Divine punishment.

COMMENTATORS

Ḥinnukh: The apex of man's spiritual achievement is the attainment of prophecy. Every intellectual proposition can be questioned, challenged, and doubted. Prophecy cannot undergo critical analysis because it stems from the source of perfection. Very seldom do we find a person able to scale the highest rung of this ladder of intellectual pursuit, one which extends from the face of earth below to the heavens above. Very few men have accomplished this and very few generations were privileged to witness this phenomenon. Thus, when a man arises who satisfies the qualifications of a prophet, we should listen to him.

References:
B. Makkot 24a; B. Yevamot 90b; B. Sanhedrin 89b, 90a; Sifre *Shofetim;* Yad, Hilkhot Yesodei ha-Torah, Chap. 7, 8, 9; Sefer ha-Mitzvot (Aseh) 172; Sefer Mitzvot Gadol (Aseh) 6; Sefer Mitzvot Katan 25; Sefer ha-Ḥinnukh, Mitzvah 516.

SPEAKING FALSELY IN GOD'S NAME

Which I have not commanded him to speak (Deuteronomy 18:20)
You shall not be afraid of him (Deuteronomy 18:22)

1. Even in prophecy, instances of perjury may be expected. A false prophet is one who issued pronouncements that were never transmitted to him by God in a vision but were the figments of his own imagination. Similarly, one who plagiarized a prophecy from another was speaking falsely in God's name. For example: Hananiah, son of Azur, prophesied that God had broken the yoke of the King of Babylon. He had never received that message from God but had merely deduced it from a similar prophecy made by Jeremiah.

2. In both cases, the Sanhedrin was convened, charges were brought against the false prophet, and he was executed by strangulation.

3. Men who had the audacity to speak falsely in the name of God were usually people of important stature and influence. The Torah admonishes society not to be intimidated by these individuals, however great their prestige, but to insist that their death-sentence be carried out.

COMMENTATORS

Ḥinnukh: Prophecy is one of the most important lines of communication between God and man. When a man dares to speak falsely in God's name, he deprives the people of a sacred and genuine source whereby to learn God's will and promises. The loftiness of the concept of prophecy is degraded and cheapened by this imitator.

Maimonides: He cites an earlier author who states that reverence for God must be so strong that a person is forbidden to speak lightly of Divine inspiration. For example, one may not frivolously say: "God told me so."

References:
B. Sanhedrin 16a, 89a; Sifre *Shofetim;* Yad, Hilkhot Avodah Zarah, Chap. 5; Sefer ha-Mitzvot (Lo Ta'aseh) 27, 29; Sefer Mitzvot Gadol (Lav) 34, 35; Sefer Mitzvot Katan 13, 115; Sefer ha-Ḥinnukh, Mitzvot 517, 519.

SPEAKING IN THE NAME OF OTHER GODS

Or that shall speak in the name of other gods (Deuteronomy 18:20)

1. How could a Jewish prophet speak before Jews in the name of gods other than their own? Can we imagine that such a prophet would find an audience? Yet this might happen if the prophet delivered a message which agreed at all points with the Torah but he attributed it to some strange deity.

COMMENTATORS

Naḥmanides: He draws a clear distinction between two cases; that of a man who states that in a dream some heathen deity *(Pe'or)* appeared to him and instructed him to advise his people to observe one of the prescribed *mitzvot.* In this case, there is no penalty since it is not with such a case that this restriction deals. The other case is that of a man who says that he has been in contact with *Pe'or* and is convinced that *Pe'or* is god and has instructed him to advise the people to observe some of the prescribed *mitzvot* of the Torah. Under these circumstances, he deserves the prescribed death penalty.

References:
B. Sanhedrin 16a, 63b, 89a; Sifre *Shofetim* 177, 178; Yad, Hilkhot Avodah Zarah, Chap. 5; Sefer ha-Mitzvot (Lo Ta'aseh) 26; Sefer Mitzvot Gadol (Lav) 32; Sefer Mitzvot Katan 114; Sefer ha-Hinnukh, Mitzvah 518.

ENCROACHING ON THE PROPERTY OF ANOTHER

You shall not remove your neighbor's landmark (Deuteronomy 19:14)

In a free economy, it is not only conceivable but it is also a daily occurrence that the financially strong can devise ways of encroaching on the rights and property of the weak. The inescapable result is that the rich become richer and the poor become poorer. The Torah warns us against *hassagat gevul*—enroaching on another's property. Technically, this commandment deals with land-ownership that is seized unscrupulously, by changing the boundary lines. Such action amounts, of course, to robbery and, as such, is already forbidden by the Torah. The effect of this further prohibition is to make the offender doubly guilty if the encroachment takes place on the sacred soil of Israel.

COMMENTATORS

Baḥya ben Asher, Abrabanel: The man who encroaches on the property of another casts doubt upon God's creation of the world and His design for its apportionment among its inhabitants. Applying this originally to the division of the land among the twelve tribes, the Rabbis later extended the principle to individual holdings. In other words, it was apparently God's express wish that each man have the piece of land that is in his possession. This land is a gift from God. By infringing on the property rights of another one defies God's intent and purpose. **Alshekh:** If God so wishes, He will broaden the boundaries of one's property; but when one tries to diminish his neighbor's boundaries and someone else does the same to him, this may become an accepted pattern among men. It constitutes interference with God's plans.

References:
B. Shabbat 85a; Sifre *Shofetim* 188; Yad, Hilkhot Genevah, Chap. 7; Sefer ha-Mitzvot (Lo Ta'aseh) 246; Sefer Mitzvot Gadol (Lav) 153; Shulḥan Arukh, Ḥoshen Mishpat, 156, 237, 268; Sefer ha-Ḥinnukh, Mitzvah 522.

EXEMPTIONS FROM ARMY SERVICE

The Priest shall approach and speak unto the people (Deuteronomy 20:2)
Fear not, nor be alarmed (Deuteronomy 20:3)
He shall not go to war, neither shall he be charged with any business . . . he shall be free for his house one year (Deuteronomy 24:5)

1. Both in a *milḥemet mitzvah* (war commanded by God) and in a *milḥemet reshut* (optional war), one of the first steps taken was to anoint a *meshu'aḥ milḥamah,* a Priest appointed to the army anointed with the appropriate holy oils for that purpose. He addressed the troops when they approached the enemy and, a second time, when they were about to engage in actual battle. In his first address, he specified the conditions under which a soldier should leave the battlefield; namely, one who built a home and had not yet lived in it; one who had planted a vineyard and had not yet tasted of its fruit; and one who had betrothed a maiden and had not yet married her. In his second speech, the Priest urged the troops not to be timid of heart in battle; to be convinced of the justice of the cause in which they were fighting, and to put their faith in God who would come to their aid. These words of encouragement were repeated by a subordinate official. Next the *meshu'aḥ milḥamah* repeated the list of exempt categories, and this time his words were relayed by a *shoter*—a sort of military constable—in a voice audible to all. The *shoter* added one more category, the fainthearted, interpreted by the Rabbis to include anyone troubled by a guilty conscience who feared that he might lose his life in battle as a punishment for some secret sin. Finally this whole proclamation was repeated by a second *shoter*.

2. Those who qualified for these exemptions from military service were obliged to build roads and supply their fellow soldiers with food and drink.

3. The Torah provides exemptions for those who recently built a house and had just begun to live in it, or had planted a vineyard and had just started to eat of its fruits, or for one who had married recently. In these instances, during the first year, the soldier was exempt from military service and from many other duties attached to the war effort.

4. Exemptions from military service applied only in the case of a *milḥemet reshut*. In a *milḥemet mitzvah* no one was freed from military duty.

5. If good order and military discipline are to be maintained, there must be no faint hearts among the troops. Morale can be weakened and the chance of victory lost through the bad example of a few cowards. The Torah warned the Jewish soldier that in battle he must forget about his wife, children, and his prized possessions and concentrate all his capacities and talents on destroying the enemy. If he shows timidity, it will affect the morale of those with whom he serves in battle. The Torah condemns the weak-hearted soldier as if he were a murderer.

COMMENTATORS

Ibn Ezra: He makes two observations:

1. We believe that a man's span of life is predestined and that he will die at the specified time, whether he is on the battlefield or at home enjoying peaceful domestic life. If this is so, what good does military exemption serve? Ibn Ezra answers that a person who is not free from sin is vulnerable to the Angel of Death in times of danger such as in war, more than at any other time in his life.
2. The officers ask: "Who is fearful and alarmed in war?" Ibn Ezra comments that there are certain people who cannot hurt anyone, even an enemy, in war. The Priest referred to these people because they could demoralize others.

Or ha-Ḥayyim: Returning safely from war is a miracle and God will not perform a miracle for one who is rendered undeserving by having committed a grave sin.

Ḥinnukh: Why should marriage be sufficient grounds for a year's exemption from military duty? Because a soldier's life during a war may become sexually promiscuous; but if a young man who has just married is permitted to spend a year with his wife and thus enter upon family life, he learns to build a relationship with a woman which is based only on love, honor, and decency. These elements are absent in promiscuous relationships. It is God's wish that man should live according to rules of decency and not sink into depravity.

Naḥmanides: Even an honest man, who has no great sins on his conscience, should return home if he feels afraid. A person who is in such a state will not defend himself properly in the battle and, barring a miracle, is doomed to be killed. Since God prefers that the world continue according to the laws of nature and not by depending upon miracles—unless these be absolutely necessary—this man should not be mobilized for war.

Abrabanel: The reason that one is exempt from military service if he has just betrothed a woman, acquired a new home, or planted a new vineyard, is that he would suffer anguish in not fulfilling the *mitzvot* associated with these three eventful experiences in life. We are dealing with God-fearing soldiers, not those who are afraid of being killed because of sins they have committed. They are sent home for an entirely different reason. These soldiers, being pious men, would experience real distress if they were to build a new home and not carry out the *mitzvah* of erecting a parapet on the roof. The same holds good if they were to plant a vineyard and not bring the fourth-year fruit to the Temple as is prescribed in the Torah; or if one betrothes a woman and does not marry her, since he is deprived of the *mitzvah* of begetting children.

References:

B. Sotah 42a, 42b, 43a, 43b, 44a, 44b; B. Kiddushin 13b; B. Sukkah 3b; J. Sotah, Chap. 8, Halakhot 4, 8; Yad, Hilkhot Melakhim, Chap. 6, 7; Sefer ha-Mitzvot (Lo Ta'aseh) 58, 311, (Aseh) 191, 214 (Note the difference between Maimonides and Naḥmanides on the verse "You shall not panic." Maimonides contends that this is a command. If God is with you in battle, then you have no reason to panic. Naḥmanides argues that this is a promise: If you will consider God as being with you, then there is no need to panic.); Sefer Mitzvot Gadol (Aseh) 120, 121, (Lav) 230, 231; Sefer ha-Ḥinnukh, Mitzvot 526, 581, 582.

PEACE TERMS

You shall offer peace to it (Deuteronomy 20:10)

1. The Torah instructs the Jew to issue a call for peace before engaging in war with the enemy. Sharp debate broke out among early classical commentators as to whether the call for peace applied only to an optional war, or also to mandatory wars, such as those with the seven Canaanite nations and the Amalekites. According to Maimonides the obligation to offer peace to the enemy applied to all wars. Rashi disagrees and holds that only optional wars *(milḥamot reshut)* required that a call for peace should precede hostilities; in a mandatory war *(milḥemet mitzvah)* no such preliminaries were required.

2. Be that as it may, Maimonides is quite decisive, however, in interpreting the meaning of the call for peace. According to him, peace meant three things: subservience to the Jewish people, serving the king in all ways, and accepting the Noahide Laws.

3. Should the enemy accept these terms, all war efforts were immediately to be abandoned. On their rejection, it would depend on the nation that refused to cooperate. If it was one of the Canaanite nations, everyone had to be destroyed—men, women, and children. If it was another nation, only the men were killed.

COMMENTATORS

Baḥya ben Asher: In the dispute over whether the call for peace is applicable only to optional wars or also to wars of duty, such as those waged by Joshua against the seven Canaanite nations, he agrees with the majority opinion that it is applicable to all wars. He feels that the preservation of peace is of the highest importance. Everyone agrees that if the call for peace is not accepted, then at the successful conclusion of the last battle in a war of choice, mere submission, shown by payment of tribute and the acceptance of the Laws of Israel, is sufficient. On the other hand, in a mandatory war, man, woman, and child must be destroyed. The reasoning behind this differentiation is that in the case of an optional war the Israelites were intent only on subduing the opposing nation so that it would pose no threat to their security. The moment that this was accomplished, the purpose of the war was achieved; whereas in the case of the mandatory war, where God instructed the Israelites to go out and destroy the seven nations, it was a war against the ideologies of paganism which were deeply ingrained in these peoples. The land could not tolerate, at one and the same time, both the religion of the Jew and the religion of the pagan. One of these had to be destroyed. It was God's wish that pagan-worship be destroyed. Hence if it be His decree that these pagans perish, the Israelite must carry out what was ordained.

A question arises: Why were the Canaanite children doomed? The answer he gives is that if paganism was to be eradicated, then all those involved in pagan worship, including the children, had also to be destroyed. The natural question that follows this is: Why could not the children be saved and brought up in isolation from heathenism? Baḥya replies that there is no explicit reason except that if God, Who is merciful, saw fit to issue this decree, it is apparent that He saw in these children no possibility of reform whatsoever.

Baḥya then proceeds to ask: Even if we do allow that these children were so indoctrinated that they would not change, what harm could they do at this tender age? He answers by comparing these children to one who has a gangrenous limb and permits that limb to be amputated in order to save the whole body. There does exist the possibility of these children growing up and infecting all mankind with their disease; here it is preferable to take no chances and destroy them.

This total destruction can come about only when the pagans do not accept the basic laws of civilized religion. They are, however, spared if they undertake to accept the seven Noahide laws.

References:

B. Sotah 32a, 35b (see Tosafot); J. Shevi'it, Chap. 6, Halakhah 1; Sifre *Shofetim;* Yad, Hilkhot Melakhim, Chap. 6; Sefer ha-Mitzvot (Aseh) 190; Sefer Mitzvot Gadol (Aseh) 118; Sefer ha-Ḥinnukh, Mitzvah 527.

PROHIBITION AGAINST DESTROYING TREES

You shall not destroy the trees thereof (Deuteronomy 20:19)

1. The injunction of *bal tashḥit* (you shall not destroy) was originally related to the commandment not to destroy fruit-bearing trees. The wanton destruction of trees in war is a sign of unbridled barbarism. The Rabbis extended the concept of *bal tashḥit* to include any act of unprincipled waste or destruction of things that can be of benefit to man. Reckless demolition is an effrontery against God, since everything is His creation.

2. Only if a tree is barren in fruit-bearing or is infecting the surrounding foliage may it be cut down.

COMMENTATORS

Saadiah, Baḥya ben Asher: One must not tear and cut down trees indiscriminately during a war, because it is foolish to consider a tree as an enemy. It is senseless to give vent to one's hostility on trees, since they have not done anything antagonistic by growing on enemy territory.
Ibn Ezra: Trees supply man with many vital benefits; it is accordingly wrong to abuse them by felling them indiscriminately. Trees are too valuable for our welfare.
Naḥmanides: During a war, the troops can often become so insanely destructive as to destroy vegetation needlessly. This mad destruction is indicative of the attitude that there may be no tomorrow. This is an attitude especially prevalent on the battlefield, where death appears to be the only certainty. God has pledged to the Jew that there will be a tomorrow for them; they must accordingly trust in Him.
Hinnukh: To the righteous person, no man is so unimportant that one may ignore his loss and not try to save him. In the same light no living thing, not even a mustard seed, is so insignificant that it may be destroyed without reasonable cause.

References:
B. Ta'anit 7a; B. Bava Kamma 91b; B. Kiddushin 32a; B. Shabbat 67b, 129a; B. Makkot 22a; Pirkei de-Rabbi Eliezer, Chap. 34; Yad, Hilkhot Melakhim, Chap. 7; Sefer ha-Mitzvot (Lo Ta'aseh) 57; Sefer Mitzvot Gadol (Lav) 229; Sefer Mitzvot Katan 175; Sefer ha-Ḥinnukh, Mitzvah 529.

A CITY'S RESPONSIBILITY FOR A MURDER COMMITTED IN ITS VICINITY

Which may neither be plowed nor sown . . . and there in the valley they shall break the heifer's neck (Deuteronomy 21:4)

1. If a corpse was found on the road, the cause of the death being unknown, the Sanhedrin was to be notified immediately. It then dispatched five of its elders to measure the distance between the corpse and the nearest community, upon whose shoulders was placed the guilt for this tragedy. Should there be a village with a small population nearer than a larger city with a greater population, the guilt was attached to the latter city although it was a little further away. The reasoning apparently was that the chances of foul play were more apt to originate in a city with a large population than in a town with a few people. The law applied to all cities in Eretz Israel except for Jerusalem.

2. After it was determined which city was to be indicted, the court of that city would be charged with burying the dead person and bringing a heifer less than two years old to an untilled valley where the ritual of expiation took place. The heifer had to be one which had never borne a yoke on its neck. The court then chopped off its neck with an ax, washed their hands, and proclaimed: "Our hands did not shed this blood . . ." (Deuteronomy 21:7–8).

3. The valley could never be tilled or sown again. The reason for this procedure was, according to the Rabbis: "Let the heifer which has never produced fruit be killed in a spot which has never produced fruit, to atone for the death of a man who was denied the opportunity of producing fruit [i.e., of procreating]."

4. The Rabbis also clarify the pronouncement of the city's elders, "Our hands did not shed this blood," to mean that their community did not permit this stranger to enter its gates without offering food or accompanying him on his way out of the city.

5. It is interesting to note that *met mitzvah koneh mekomo*—the corpse was to be buried at the place where he was found. Also the heifer whose neck was broken was to be buried in the valley where the ritual took place. If a witness to the crime appeared, the ritual did not take place, since in this case evidence was available.

COMMENTATORS

Ibn Ezra: Had not the city been corrupt, it would have been inconceivable that a murderer should have originated from it.

Avi Ezer: He clarifies Ibn Ezra's point of view. It is the duty of society to be concerned not only with the physical welfare of its members but also with their moral and spiritual health. If the community fulfills this duty, murder will not take place in its midst. When a community fails in this obligation, it must bear the burden of responsibility for the murder and seek atonement through this procedure.

Sforno: The attitude of a community must be that not only will it not tolerate known criminals within its own confines, but that it will help to root out crime from all over the land. A community that refuses to take this attitude bears the guilt for a murder which is committed in its vicinity, whether or not the criminal hailed from it.

Alshekh: The procedure of measuring the distance from the corpse to the nearest city was not performed in order to ascertain where the criminal was most likely to have come from. In fact, this question may never be solved. The purpose was to pinpoint the city that had probably failed in its responsibilities to its inhabitants or to its visitors.

Maimonides: The procedure of measuring the distance between the corpse and the nearest city, as well as the declaration of innocence on the part of the elders and the breaking of the heifer's neck, all tend to create an atmosphere of crisis in a city. Consequently, the investigations will eventually lead to the discovery of the criminal. Furthermore, the owner of the land where the corpse was found will intensify his search for the criminal, because as long as the crime remains unsolved his land may not be plowed. This entails a financial loss to the owner.

Naḥmanides: He rejects the rationalization of Maimonides and suggests that the entire subject be considered as pure dogma and not as a means used in detecting the criminal.

Abrabanel: Why was the heifer's neck broken? Because breaking the neck avoids a face-to-face confrontation with the animal. This reflects the nature of this crime. The victim was not openly confronted with evidence to justify his being killed. He was killed stealthily, from the back of the neck as it were.

References:
B. Makkot 10b, 22a; B. Ḥullin 11a, 24a; B. Krittot 6a, 26a; B. Pesaḥim 26a; B. Sotah 44b, 47b; B. Avodah Zarah 29b; B. Zevaḥim 70b; B. Ketubbot 37b; B. Bava Batra 23b (see Tosafot); J. Sotah, Chap. 9; Sifre *Shofetim;* Yad, Hilkhot Rotze'aḥ, Chap. 9, 10; Yad, Hilkhot Me'elah, Chap. 8; Guide of the Perplexed, Part 3, Sec. 40; Sefer ha-Mitzvot (Aseh) 181, (Lo Ta'aseh) 309; Sefer Mitzvot Gadol (Aseh) 78, (Lav) 166; Sefer ha-Ḥinnukh, Mitzvot 530, 531.

CAPTIVE WOMEN

And you see among those in captivity a woman of beauty and you have a desire for her (Deuteronomy 21:11)
You may not sell her for money . . . if you have no delight in her (Deuteronomy 21:14)

1. It is unrealistic to demand of a soldier, in the heat of battle, to stop and ask himself whether what he is about to do is moral, or if the food he is about to eat is kosher, or the drink he is about to imbibe acceptable. He is liable to eat and drink anything he desires because his mood is such that he has no time or patience to ponder the issue. Similarly, a soldier who captures a beautiful woman will not stop to rationalize but will give way to his lust for her. The Torah is very decisive, however, in its demands of this soldier after his unbridled passions have been satisfied and have subsided.

2. After this personal encounter with his beautiful prize of war, he is forbidden to marry her unless she is willing to become a convert to Judaism. According to some commentaries he is forbidden to have relations with her until he has brought her to his home and she has undergone the prescribed rituals. Others maintain that he may have sexual relations once before bringing her home. She is to remain in his home for 30 days to grieve over the loss of her family and her religion. She is to shave her head and let her nails grow, so that she will become repulsive to him. After this month of grief he waits two more months before marrying her. Some commentaries maintain that if she rejects this proposal, he must try to convince her during a twelve-month period, and if she persists she merely has to accept the Noahide Laws and is then sent out free. These commentaries maintain that under no circumstances can he compel her to accept conversion and marriage. There is however, another view according to which the preliminary waiting period is necessary only if she is not willing to become a convert. If she consents, he can marry her immediately. After the waiting period he is permitted to coerce her into conversion and live with her. This is the only instance where forced conversion was valid to the extent that there was no prohibition against cohabitation with a non-Jewess. The offspring of such a union were not considered Jewish.

3. When she had spent several months in his household and he then decided against marrying her, he was obliged to give her her freedom. He could not sell her into slavery nor could he oblige her to serve him as a slave.

4. A Priest who went through the same initial experience could not marry the beautiful captive woman because a prerequisite to marriage would be conversion and a convert was forbidden to marry a Priest. However, those authorities that permit intercourse once before bringing her home, permit this to a Priest as well as a non-Priest.

COMMENTATORS

Maimonides: The question of the length of the period of mourning by the captured gentile woman over her family is one of prime interest to most commentators. Maimonides believes that weeping has a therapeutic value. The woman captured is, most likely, depressed and dejected. For her, tears are a relief and an outlet for anguish.

Ibn Ezra: Having been separated from her family, who may have perished during the war, this woman should be given the opportunity to mourn for her loved ones as anyone else is entitled to do in such circumstances.

Naḥmanides: The captive woman, in her dire straits of being separated from her family and torn from her social and religious environment, will cry to her pagan idols to save her from her fate. Only when she sees that this fails will she be amenable to change over to a more acceptable religion and, by forgetting her past associations, most likely wish to marry a Jew.

Naḥmanides seems to lean toward the view of Rabbi Johanan in the Jerusalem Talmud, who disagreed with the sages of the Babylonian Talmud regarding the act of seduction. According to the sages, a soldier in the heat, strain, and violence of a battle has not the necessary mental balance to realize that the seduction he is committing is wrong. In order that he may have sexual relations with this woman, she must first go through the procedure which the Torah prescribes. Rabbi Johanan forbids even the first sexual act with her until this prescribed procedure is fulfilled.

Keli Yakar: How was it that a soldier captured a woman in the battle area? What was she doing there? She was a camp-follower, a prostitute, placed by the enemy near the Jewish camp in order to demoralize the soldiers.

Ḥinnukh: He acknowledges the unusual state of mind of a soldier during the stress of battle. The Torah ordains a procedure whereby, in order to blunt the soldier's sexual appetite, the woman is made to follow a plan that would make her repulsive to him, i.e., cutting off her hair and nails and mourning for a month. Had the Torah not allowed him to marry this woman in certain circumstances, he would be likely to keep her as his mistress because of his sexual desire for her. Furthermore, elements of compassion and respect must enter the picture. If after his first sensual encounter with her he is no longer attracted to her, then he has no right to debase her further by selling her or by compelling her to become his slave or servant.

References:

B. Kiddushin 21b, 22a, 68b; B. Sotah 35b; B. Sanhedrin 21a; B. Yevamot 47a; Sifre *Ki Tetze;* Midrash Tahḥuma, *Ki Tetze,* Chap. 1; Yad, Hilkhot Melakhim, Chap. 8; Sefer ha-Mitzvot (Aseh) 221, (Lo Ta'aseh) 263, 264; Sefer Mitzvot Gadol (Aseh) 122, (Lav) 232, 233; Sefer ha-Ḥinnukh, Mitzvot 532, 533, 534.

LAWS PERTAINING TO HANGING

And you hang him on a tree (Deuteronomy 21:22)
You shall not allow his body to hang on the tree all night . . . you shall bury him on the same day (Deuteronomy 21:23)

1. According to most rabbinical opinions, all malefactors whose offense carried the death-penalty by stoning were afterwards hanged; this was done in order to deter anyone who might have contemplated committing similar offenses. Some hold, however, that this procedure was followed only in the case of the blasphemer and idol-worshiper. There was to be no exhibition of the body, because a few moments after the criminal was hanged he was to be cut down and buried with dignity due to him as one formed in the Divine Image.

2. A woman condemned to die by stoning was never hanged, for reasons of modesty.

3. The Rabbis interpreted the concept of immediate burial of those hanged to include all who were dead. In other words, even if a person died from natural causes, it is a transgression of the law to delay the burial until the next day. However, if the delay is in honor of the deceased, it is permitted.

COMMENTATORS

Ḥinnukh: The necessity for hanging an offender is in order to display to public gaze the man who has blasphemed the name of God and thus frighten those who witness this sight.

Naḥmanides: The most wretched thing that can happen to a man is not simply to be put to death but to be hung on a tree in a public thoroughfare. Hanging a person just long enough to bring home this message is not frowned upon. Prolonged exposure of the body, however, was inappropriate in the Holy Land. He clarifies the reasoning of Ibn Ezra who also believes that the Holy Land must not be made profane by hanging men. What Ibn Ezra meant is that there is a separate injunction against the profanation of the Land.

Sforno: The essence of man is his soul, which emanates from God and which forms the basis of the concept of the creation of man in the Image of God. To keep a man hanging unnecessarily dishonors this Godly Image.

Rashbam: He gives two reasons for not allowing a body to remain hanging overnight:

1. People might be prone to curse the judges who gave the sentence, without realizing that they were only doing their elementary duty.
2. It is even more probable that people would touch the dead person and thereby themselves become ritually unclean.

Abrabanel: He offers two lines of reasoning:

1. Though God demanded death by hanging as a penalty, He did not indicate a prolonged period of exposure on the gallows. Society has no right to be more zealous than God has indicated as necessary.
2. It is unhygienic to keep a decomposing corpse out in the open and not to bury it before it begins to emit a noisome stench.

Alshekh: When a man has sinned to the degree where he is sentenced to die by stoning, he has not only violated the law but he has also deliberately scarred his soul which must give an account of itself before God when his life on earth has terminated. Through death, the soul is purified and is given a clean slate. Hanging this blasphemous sinner on a tree demonstrates that he has been cleansed and purified and has returned to the Tree of Eternal Life. The motivation behind the hanging is brought to the fore thereby and there is no need for a protracted hanging.

References:

B. Yevamot 79a; B. Sanhedrin 38b, 45b, 46b, 47a; B. Bava Kamma 82b; B. Shabbat 30b; J. Kiddushin, Chap. 4, Halakhah 1; J. Nazir, Chap. 7, Halakhah 1; Sifre *Ki Tetze;* Yad, Hilkhot Sanhedrin, Chap. 15; Yad, Hilkhot Avel, Chap. 14; Sefer ha-Mitzvot (Aseh) 230, 231, (Lo Ta'aseh) 66; Sefer Mitzvot Gadol (Aseh) 103, 104, (Lav) 197; Shulḥan Arukh, Yoreh De'ah, 357; Sefer ha-Ḥinnukh, Mitzvot 535, 536, 537.

RETURNING LOST POSSESSIONS

You shall restore them unto your brother (Deuteronomy 22:1)

1. The true test of a person's character lies in those border areas of human behavior in which either of two opposed lines of action is defensible. The reaction of one who finds lost property belonging to another is a case in point. The finder can easily feel tempted to seek an excuse for retaining the lost article without any sense of guilt, even though such a course of action may amount to robbing his fellow man.

2. The Torah considers the return of a lost object to its owner as a positive *mitzvah*. A Jew must protect the object found and wait for its identification by its rightful owner.

3. Where it is certain that the lost article had been abandoned by its owner, having despaired of ever retrieving it, the finder may keep the article. Thus, if the article found was unidentifiable, the finder may rest assured that the loser had abandoned all hope of ever retrieving this loss, and therefore retain it.

4. Such objects as can be easily identified, such as an animal with a specific brand or a monogrammed shirt and similar lost objects, must be announced publicly and returned to the owner, provided he properly and adequately identifies the article. If after the public proclamation no one comes forward to claim it, the object remains with the finder who becomes a *shomer sakhar* (a paid keeper), in view of the fact that the *mitzvah* of looking after this article may exempt him from fulfilling another *mitzvah* which might entail financial loss, on the principle that one who is engaged in one *mitzvah* is exempt from performing another at the same time.

5. A Priest sees a lost article lying in a cemetery. While the *mitzvah* of returning lost property applies, of course, to him as to every Jew, he is yet not allowed to defile himself by approaching within four cubits of a grave. This places him in a dilemma. The law in such a case is that he must leave the *mitzvah* of restoring the lost article to a non-Priest.

6. Caring for the possessions of another is not limited to "finding and returning." This commandment includes the obligation of everyone to care for the possessions of others in every respect. An example: One who sees that an onrushing river is about to demolish the home of another must work feverishly to put up a dam or dike, in order to prevent a disaster. In a sense, he is returning a lost object to its rightful owner.

COMMENTATORS

Baḥya ben Asher: He associates the law of returning a stray animal with "You shall love your neighbor as yourself." A violation of the former amounts to a breach of the latter. There is also a metaphysical aspect to these laws. When a person dies, he loses his soul and God regains possession of it. Just as this person will want his soul returned to him when the dead will rise again, so should he be careful in his lifetime to return material losses to their legitimate owners.

Alshekh: The preceding section of the Torah deals with the marriage of a captured maiden during war. This is followed by the laws of returning losses to their legitimate owners. There is a lesson to be learned from this sequence. A man may reason that his capturing of a heathen girl constitutes the performance of a good deed; namely, to bring a non-believer into the Jewish fold. He may consider that he has actually saved a life and has returned it to its rightful place. Yet it seems that the Torah frowns upon this action by castigating him and asking him to refrain from such imprudence. If we follow this through to its logical conclusion, it would seem that the Torah does not expect one to go out of his way in returning a "lost" animal to the rightful owner. Alshekh answers that this is not true, since the heathen girl never belonged to the sphere of godliness. When she is captured, she cannot be considered as having been lost. In the case of the lost animal, however, it did belong to someone; hence we are requested to return that which legally belongs to someone else.

Abrabanel: The motive behind these edicts is to awaken a feeling of compassion and mutual consideration, even to the extent of not delaying the return of the lost article once the rightful owner has been ascertained.

Keli Yakar: If someone finds something valuable, he may try to find all sorts of ways and excuses in order not to return it, even though its original owner has convincingly identified it as his own. The finder may be able to camouflage the facts for himself and for others, but he cannot hide the truth from God.

Ḥinnukh: Society can exist only when there is cooperation. Everyone should be able to feel that in the absence of his own personal attention to his possessions, there will always be someone to give them necessary care.

Recanati: Man often values his possessions as much as his very life; so when one loses something that had a specific identification, he will feel the hurt and the pain of its absence as if it were his own life that was lost. The person who finds this lost object and does not return it to its rightful owner is contributing to the owner's extreme distress and mental anguish.

References:

B. Bava Metzia 23b, 25a, 26a, 27a, 28b, 30a, 30b, 31a, 31b, 33a; B. Sanhedrin 73a; B. Bava Kamma 54b, 113b; B. Avodah Zarah 26b; J. Bava Metzia, Chap. 1, Halakhah 1; Sifre, *Ki Tetze;* Mekhilta, *Mishpatim;* Yad, Hilkhot Gezelah, Chap. 11; Sefer ha-Mitzvot (Aseh) 204, (Lo Ta'aseh) 269; Sefer Mitzvot Gadol (Aseh) 74, (Lav) 159; Sefer Mitzvot Katan 252; Shulḥan Arukh, Ḥoshen Mishpat, 259, 263; Sefer ha-Ḥinnukh, Mitzvot 538, 539.

DRESSING IN THE CLOTHING OF THE OPPOSITE SEX

A woman shall not wear that which pertains to a man. . . neither shall a man put on a woman's garment (Deuteronomy 22:5)

1. The Torah teaches us that the distinction between the sexes was part of the Divine plan of creation, when the bodies of man and woman were given certain visibly distinguishable characteristics. Any attempt to conceal these differences amounts to a virtual defiance or denial of God's purpose.

2. A man is forbidden to dress in a woman's garb. He is restrained from shaving his face when it is done for the purpose of appearing feminine, or to bedeck himself with jewelry worn by women.

3. A woman, too, should not dress herself in men's clothing or in military armor, or employ any other means of appearing masculine.

4. The Rabbis included in this injunction the prohibition of a man pulling out grey hairs from his head in order to appear more youthful. Even if a man dyes his hair so as to retain his youthful appearance, he is violating this law. In all instances, such a violation calls for a penalty of lashes.

COMMENTATORS

Naḥmanides, Rashbam: A woman who dresses in armor like a man going into battle will be led into a life of lewdness. A man who dresses like a woman employs this ruse in order to be able to mix freely with women in order to seduce them. This same principle also applies to a woman who dresses in man's clothing.

Abrabanel: The wearing of a woman's clothes by a man or a man's clothes by a woman will lead to homosexuality.

Ḥinnukh: Anything that symbolizes lewdness, such as a man dressing as a woman and a woman dressing as a man, falls under the general category of sexual immorality and is forbidden.

Radbaz: In the sociological relationship between husband and wife, it was intended both by nature and temperament that the wife should be somewhat subservient to the husband. If this is so, it is understandable why a man should not dress like a woman, because this would indicate a degradation. But why should a woman dressing as a man be condemned? Is she not attempting to upgrade herself? He answers that when two souls are lowered upon earth, one of a woman and the other of a man, God intended them to remain distinctive in their physical make-up and external appearance. Any change in this pattern would be counteracting God's design and is therefore forbidden, irrespective of whether it is upgrading or downgrading.

References:

B. Nazir 59a; B. Shabbat 94b; B. Avodah Zarah 29a (see Tosafot); J. Shabbat, Chap. 6, Halakhah 1; Yalkut Shimoni, *Ki Tetze,* Chap. 930; Guide of the

Perplexed, Part 3, Sec. 37; Yad, Hilkhot Avodah Zarah, Chap. 12; Sefer ha-Mitzvot (Lo Ta'aseh) 39, 40; Sefer Mitzvot Gadol (Lav) 59, 60; Sefer Mitzvot Katan 33; Shulḥan Arukh, Yoreh De'ah, 156, 182; Sefer ha-Ḥinnukh, Mitzvot 542, 543.

MAKING A PARAPET FOR THE ROOF

You shall make a parapet for your roof . . . that you bring not blood upon your house; if any man fall from there (Deuteronomy 22:8)

1. To what extent may a person live by faith alone and in violation of the natural law? May he say to himself: "I will lean over a precipice and if I fall to my death, then it must have been the will of God"? May he dig a deep pit and leave it uncovered and say to himself: "If anyone falls into it and dies, it must be that God willed it so"? The answer is obvious! Faith may and should direct our lives, but we cannot defy the natural law. If he leans over a precipice, then he must realize that he will fall to his death and that only a miracle will save him. Since the Torah guides us in every aspect of our lives, it also deals with commandments that pertain to the dangers that are man-made.

2. The basic law pertaining to the perils that man creates for himself deals with the erection of a parapet around the roof of a home. It was customary for people to go up to the roofs. Without a railing to protect them from falling off, people's lives were in jeopardy. The Rabbis added that any form of peril created by man, such as digging a well and leaving it uncovered, is a violation of this law.

3. The parapet must be so high and strong that it will definitely prevent an accident that will lead to tragedy.

4. The Rabbis went even further than that, making it a violation of the law if one drank from a polluted stream or put coins into one's mouth, because of the probability that germs are usually found on the coins. In keeping with the central theme of avoiding all hazards, the Rabbis forbade the Jew to put himself into any dangerous place.

COMMENTATORS

Baḥya ben Asher, Keli Yakar, Abrabanel: These exegetes, in their analyses of the requirement of a railing on the roof, rely heavily on the talmudic view (*Shabbat* 32): granted that the man who thus falls to his death was predestined to die because of his own sins, why should his death occur in your house, perhaps partly due to your negligence?

Alshekh: His reasoning is similar to that above. He asks: Why did the sinner fall to his death just in this house and not in any other house that he may have visited? He replies that a man may not have been unalterably sentenced to death by God. He may be on the brink of such a sentence but as yet not have been condemned. The fact that he is sinning again by consorting with another sinner, one who had not placed a railing on his roof, is enough to tip the scales and confirm his death-sentence.

Ḥinnukh: There were men who, because of the heights of godliness that they scaled, were able to overcome laws of nature, such as pain and death by burning. This was true in the cases of Abraham, Daniel, and others. In our own day, nobody has yet reached those spiritual heights. One must, therefore, take every precaution to protect one's life. Whoever goes to war should arm himself adequately and not rely on miracles. Similarly, if one has an unrailed roof or an uncovered ditch, one must take measures to protect his fellow man from all harm that these areas of danger can cause.

References:

B. Shabbat 32a; B. Ḥagigah 14b; B. Sukkah 3b; B. Ḥullin 136a; B. Ketubbot 41b; B. Bava Kamma 15b, 51a; B. Mo'ed Katan 11a; Sifre *Ki Tetze;* Yad, Hilkhot Rotze'aḥ, Chap. 11; Sefer ha-Mitzvot (Aseh) 184, (Lo Ta'aseh) 298; Sefer Mitzvot Gadol (Aseh) 79, (Lav) 167; Sefer Mitzvot Katan 152; Shulḥan Arukh, Ḥoshen Mishpat, 427; Sefer ha-Ḥinnukh, Mitzvot 546, 547.

THE RITUAL OF MARRIAGE

If a man take a wife and go in unto her and hate her (Deuteronomy 22:13)

There shall be no harlot of the daughters of Israel (Deuteronomy 23:18)

1. There are no overt differences between a wife, an unmarried woman, and even a harlot. The relations between a man and any of these women are fundamentally the same, with the exception that he is joined to his wife by a ritual which is absent in the other two cases. Judaism demands that this union between man and wife should be a partnership that is hallowed and carries mutual obligations. Love, mutual respect, decency, and understanding must permeate the two lives which are being united. This is the meaning of the laws of *ḥuppah* and *kiddushin*.

2. In ancient times the procedure of marriage was as follows: A man could consecrate a woman as his wife *(kiddushin)*, in any of three ways. He must, in the presence of two witnesses (1) make her a gift of appreciable monetary value *(kesef)*, (2) present her with a document *(shetar)* formally ratifying the marriage, or (3) have sexual intercourse *(bi'ah)* with her with the express purpose of making her his wife. The last method, though legally valid was discouraged, since it involved a breach of decency; any man who practiced it was punished by lashes. Whichever method was adopted, the bride's consent was an essential condition. Upon the completion of this stage, the girl became *arusah* (betrothed). She was considered a wife in nearly every respect. If any other man cohabited with her, he was liable to the death penalty as an adulterer.

3. A time and place were fixed for the wedding *(nissu'in)*. On the appointed day the bride and groom underwent the *ḥuppah* ceremony. According to some authorities this was effected by the act of *yiḥud*, when the couple remained and took some food together in a room alone. Others hold that the essential was the bride's entry into the bridegroom's domain. She thereupon became a married woman *(eshet ish)* with all the rights and obligations attached to this state.

4. A man also obligates himself at the time of marriage by a contract known as *ketubbah,* in which he undertakes to provide for his wife in the manner customary for Jewish husbands and to discharge any additional obligations which may have been negotiated.

5. Many centuries ago it became customary to combine the ceremonies of *erusin (kiddushin)* and *nissu'im.* This was done because of the many cases in which, perhaps as the result of unsettled conditions, the groom disappeared during the intervening period and his bride could not ascertain whether he was alive or dead. In such a case she became *agunah* ("anchored" to him), even before the actual marriage ceremony *(nissu'in)* had been performed, and yet could not marry anyone else. Such a regrettable possibility was avoided when the ceremony of *ḥuppah* followed immediately upon that of *erusin,* as is now invariably the practice.

6. According to Jewish law, a newly married couple must spend the entire first week after the marriage together in order to become properly adjusted to each other. During this time the groom is not even allowed to attend to his business or profession. This is known as the week of *"Sheva Berakhot,"* from the seven benedictions which are recited at every meal when new guests join in the festivities.

COMMENTATORS

Maimonides: The reason why a *minyan* (assembly of ten adult males) is required for the rites of *ḥuppah* and *kiddushin* is that the man publicly invites society, as it were, to take cognizance of the fact that this woman is henceforth his wife. If secret marriages were permitted, a man would be able to legalize a short-term liaison, even with a prostitute, and give her the outward status of a married woman.
Ḥinnukh: A man is expected to prove to a woman that he cares for her

sufficiently to want to make her his wife. With this approach he impresses upon her that he has won and claims her lifelong faithfulness and love. Without some prior token of his honorable intention and high esteem of her worth, his relationship with her would be no different from a liaison with a prostitute. This is the fundamental reason for the presentation of a ring by the bridegroom to his bride, even though the intrinsic value of the ring may be very small.

Recanati: Why indeed must there be a ritual of *kiddushin*? Why should not a man take a woman out of the market-place and live with her without any religious ceremony? The answer is that the ceremony of *kiddushin* stems from the incident between the serpent and Eve. It was the serpent that brought the instinct of lasciviousness into Eve's life, thus making lust a concomitant feature of the procreative act. The rite of *kiddushin* transforms animal lust into a wholesome human need. Lasciviousness is replaced by a sanctified relationship.

Naḥmanides: How do we set about abolishing prostitution and upholding the dignity of marriage? In opposition to the attitude taken by many so-called "enlightened" nations, i.e. that prostitution is the oldest profession, fulfills a natural human need, and is ineradicable, Naḥmanides holds that those responsible for the maintenance of law and order should close all brothels and vigilantly stop all other avenues of such traffic.

References:

B. Kiddushin 2b, 4b, 5a, 7a, 9a, 51a; B. Betzah 36b; B. Mo'ed Katan 18b; B. Bava Batra 48b; B. Ketubbot 73b; B. Yevamot 55b; B. Sanhedrin 54b; Yad, Hilkhot Ishut, Chap. 1, 3; Yad, Hilkhot Na'arah Betulah, Chap. 2; Yad, Hilkhot Issurei Bi'ah, Chap. 18; Guide of the Perplexed, Part 3, Sec. 49; Sefer ha-Mitzvot (Aseh) 213, (Lo Ta'aseh) 355; Sefer Mitzvot Gadol (Aseh) 48; Sefer Mitzvot Katan 183; Shulḥan Arukh, Even ha-Ezer, Chap. 26, 177; Sefer ha-Ḥinnukh, Mitzvot 552, 570.

THE PENALTY FOR FALSELY ACCUSING A WIFE OF HAVING COMMITTED ADULTERY BEFORE NISSU'IN

And she shall be his wife . . . he may not put her away all his days (Deuteronomy 22:19)

1. When a man was convinced that his newly-wedded wife was not chaste, he came before a court of twenty-three—because a death penalty might be involved—and said to them: "In my first conjugal relationship with my wife I discovered that she was not a virgin. I suspect that she was untrue to me during the period of *erusin* and I produce these witnesses to substantiate my suspicion."

2. The court investigated the accusation. If they found it to be true, the wife was stoned to death.

3. Should the court find this to be slander, the husband was flogged and had to pay his wife's father 100 *shekalim* as compensation. Furthermore, he could never divorce her even if her entire body was inflicted with boils or even if she were blind. She was to remain his wife forever.

4. If the father produced witnesses who absolutely contradicted the evidence of the husband's witnesses, the latter were put to death by stoning since they wanted to make the woman liable to the death sentence by their false testimony.

COMMENTATORS

Maimonides: He offers three reasons for the three penalties administered to a man who slanders his wife by wrongly accusing her of having committed adultery:

1. The fine of 100 *shekalim:* There is no doubt that the husband disliked his wife and by slandering her wished to rid himself of her. If so, why did he not give her the 50 *shekalim* as guaranteed by the *ketubbah* and divorce her according to the accepted manner? He wanted, instead, to save the 50 *shekalim* by slandering her and thereby

ridding himself of her at no cost. As a penalty for his scheming act of slander, he is forced to pay 100 *shekalim*.

2. The punishment of lashing: The husband, through his vicious slander, attempted to embarrass and humiliate his wife. The court, as a result, issued a verdict that he be lashed so that he would himself experience the feeling of being shamed and humiliated.

3. He may never divorce her: Sex, and interest in a younger, prettier girl may have been the motives for his slander against his wife. He attempted to get rid of his unattractive wife so that he could marry his new love. When the desires of the flesh and sexual greediness can bring this man falsely to malign his wife, the just penalty is that he never be allowed to divorce her against her will.

Abrabanel: He applies the reasoning of Maimonides regarding the appropriateness of the punishments. Whereas the latter, however, sees in the slander a grave injustice against the wife, Abrabanel suggests that the injustice was committed primarily against the woman's parents, whose suffering when their daughter was maligned must have been immeasurable.

References:

B. Makkot 15a; B. Arakhin 15a; B. Bekhorot 49b; B. Sotah 23b; B. Sanhedrin 8b; B. Ketubbot 22a, 44b, 45b, 46a, 46b; J. Ketubbot, Chap. 3, Halakhah 6, Chap. 4, Halakhah 4; Sifre *Ki Tetze;* Guide of the Perplexed, Part 3, Sec. 49; Yad, Hilkhot Na'arah Betulah, Chap. 3; Yad, Hilkhot Issurei Bi'ah Chap. 1, 3; Sefer ha-Mitzvot (Aseh) 219, (Lo Ta'aseh) 359; Sefer Mitzvot Gadol (Aseh) 55, (Lav) 86; Sefer ha-Ḥinnukh, Mitzvot 553, 554.

THE INNOCENT VICTIM OF A RAPE

But unto the maiden you shall do nothing (Deuteronomy 22:26)

According to Jewish law, there are three cases in which a person must submit to death rather than be forced to sin: if one is bidden to commit murder, worship idols, or perform an act of gross immorality. In all these cases the principle is *yehareg ve-al ya'avor* (one should allow oneself to be killed rather than sin). There are, however, different opinions on the question whether this principle applies to a married woman who is forced to submit to sexual intercourse. It is agreed that such a woman is not punishable as an adulteress, nor, for that matter, is any penalty inflicted by the courts on a person who commits an unlawful act under threat of death.

COMMENTATORS

Ḥinnukh: In stating that the victim of rape is not liable to punishment, the Torah means to convey a general principle which applies over a much wider field. No person who is coerced into committing an offense is to suffer a penalty.

References:
B. Bava Kamma 28b; B. Avodah Zarah 54a; B. Ketubbot 51b; B. Kiddushin 10a; B. Nedarim 27a; B. Sanhedrin 73a, 74a; J. Ketubbot, Chap. 3, Halakhah 9; Sifre *Ki Tetze;* Yad, Hilkhot Sanhedrin, Chap. 20; Sefer ha-Mitzvot (Lo Ta'-aseh) 294; Sefer Mitzvot Gadol (Lav) 201; Sefer ha-Ḥinnukh, Mitzvah 556.

PENALTY FOR RAPING A VIRGIN

Then the man that lay with her shall give to the young woman's father 50 shekalim *of silver, and she shall be his wife. . . he may not put her away all his days* (Deuteronomy 22:29)

1. If a man forcibly seduces a virgin from the age of three to six months after attaining the age of puberty, he must take her as a wife and may never divorce her, no matter how repulsive she may be to him. There are four penalties to which he is subjected; he must pay the father of the girl 50 silver *shekalim;* he must pay compensation for the disgrace caused to the family; he must pay for the depreciation of the girl's value; and finally he must pay for the pain inflicted on the girl during the rape. All these remunerations are paid to the father of the victim.

2. If he divorced his wife surreptitiously, he is compelled to remarry her; if he was a Priest, the divorce was valid and as a member of the priesthood he may not marry a divorcee—but he received the punishment of lashes.

3. In those areas of the world today where Jews are still under the jurisdiction of Jewish law, a Jewish court cannot impose penalties *(kenasim)*—since there are no judges who have ritual ordination *(semikhah)*. In the case of rape, the criminal would not pay the 50 *shekalim,* but he could be compelled to marry the victim and keep her as his wife for the rest of his life, since this is not considered a *kenas,* but a *mitzvah.*

COMMENTATORS

Ḥinnukh: He proposes two reasons why a man who raped a virgin is so severely punished:

1. Were a man who rapes a virgin lightly dealt with, it would encourage him to continue this dastardly practice without the fear of consequences which he would later regret. But if he realizes beforehand that he will be compelled to marry and sustain her, pay her father damages, and never be permitted to divorce her no matter how much he may come to dislike her, then this may act as a deterrent to his wicked lusts.
2. From the girl's angle, it will serve to restore to her some measure of social position and self-respect. Otherwise, she would be subjected to painful, psychological anguish, abuse, shame, and disgrace in society.

Abrabanel: On the subject of the severity of the punishment for raping a virgin, he reasons as follows: There is a difference between seduction and rape. Usually, a young man of a respectable family will not seduce a girl of equal social position. All he has to do is to ask her for her hand in marriage. There is no need for a criminal act in such a case. He will, however, turn his attentions to the underprivileged. If she will share his bed with him, he promises either to marry her eventually—a tempting prospect for a girl who dreams of bettering herself in life—or else he will promise her a gift of money which, too, is seductive when she anticipates what she can do with it. The girl is thus given some basis of hope. In the case of rape, however, the man's wickedness and barbarism do not move him to any promises. He neither promised her marriage nor offered her any gain of money. It was sheer brutality on his part. Because of this, the Torah sentences him to pay her father damages for causing him grief. Furthermore, because he did not plight his troth unto her he is punished by being compelled to marry her and keep her forever as his wife.

References:
B. Ketubbot 29b, 38a, 38b, 39a, 39b, 40b, 41a; J. Ketubbot Chap. 3, Halakhah 1; Chap. 4, Halakhah 1; Sifre *Ki Tetze;* B. Makkot 15a; Yad, Hilkhot Na'arah Betulah, Chap. 1; Sefer ha-Mitzvot (Aseh) 218, (Lo Ta'aseh) 358; Sefer Mitzvot Gadol (Aseh) 54, (Lav) 84; Sefer Mitzvot Katan 182, 187; Shulḥan Arukh, Even ha-Ezer, Chap. 177; Sefer ha-Ḥinnukh, Mitzvot 557, 558.

SEXUAL MUTILATION

He who is crushed or marred in his privy organs shall not enter into the assembly of the Lord (Deuteronomy 23:2)

1. A man whose sex organs are mutilated may not marry into Jewish society; if he does, he is subject to the penalty of lashes. He is, however, allowed to marry a proselyte; this applies even to Priests, who are normally forbidden to marry anyone who is not born a Jewess.

2. Should the injury to his genitals be inherited or the result of illness—either case being considered an act of God—this prohibition does not apply and the man may marry anyone he chooses. This means that, whereas one who voluntarily allowed himself to be castrated or sterilized is subjected to the penalty for having shown that he had no wish or intention of begetting children, one who was impotent or sterile through no fault of his own might hope to be cured of his disability sooner or later and is therefore allowed to marry a Jewess.

COMMENTATORS

Abrabanel, Maimonides: They give two reasons for this prohibition:

1. Since this man is unable to procreate, marriage for him is devoid of real purpose and reason.
2. Furthermore, such a man must know that his undisclosed impotence will drive his wife to illicit relations with other men; he will, therefore, be a contributing factor to her immorality.

Ḥinnukh: Why this general law? After all, there are circumstances when such a man is permitted to marry. *Ḥinnukh* answers that this law was made in order to discourage men from undergoing any sort of castration or sterilization in order to derive financial or other gains from this condition. An example of this would be a eunuch who takes pride in the fact that he lives in the splendor of a palace.

References:

B. Yevamot 20b, 70a, 75a, 75b, 76a; B. Ḥullin 45b; Sifre *Ki Tetze;* Yad, Hilkhot Issurei Bi'ah, Chap. 16; Guide of the Perplexed, Part 3, Sec. 49; Sefer ha-Mitzvot (Lo Ta'aseh) 360; Sefer Mitzvot Gadol (Lav) 118, 119; Sefer Mitzvot Katan 297, 298; Shulḥan Arukh, Even ha-Ezer, Chap. 5; Sefer ha-Ḥinnukh, Mitzvah 559.

PROHIBITION AGAINST A MARRIAGE TO A MAMZER

A mamzer *shall not enter into the assembly of the Lord* (Deuteronomy 23:3)

1. A *mamzer* is the offspring of the union of a man and woman in the following categories:

a. A child born as a result of incest, i.e., where the union is prohibited with the punishment of *karet* (excision). There can be no valid *kiddushin* in this case because under no circumstances could the parents have married in Jewish law.

b. A child born to a married woman by some man other than her lawful husband, i.e., the offspring of an adulterous union. This category is extended to include a *shetuki* (a child whose mother is known but whose father is unidentified) and an *asufi* (an abandoned child found in a public place), both of whose parents are known.

c. The child of a woman who, acting on the assumption that her husband had died, remarried and had a child from the second husband. Her first husband, however, was proved to be alive. In this case the child from the second husband is a *mamzer*.

2. In these instances, the offspring is a *mamzer* and prohibited from marrying anyone except another *mamzer* or a proselyte.

3. If an unmarried woman gave birth to a child, the court would try to ascertain who the father was. On being assured by the mother that the father was a Jew, they would declare the child legitimate. If the father could not be identified, the child became a *shetuki* and suffered the disabilities of a *mamzer*.

It should be clearly understood that the Jewish law does not penalize a child merely for being born out of wedlock. The concept of *mamzerut* applies only to cases in which the marriage would be invalid in Jewish law. For this reason the English word "bastard," with its very different connotation, is not a correct equivalent of *mamzer*. In a decently ordered society, even though there may be irregular unions, there will be no *mamzerim*.

COMMENTATORS

Naḥmanides: The Jew attaches great importance to the strength of the family unit. It is inconceivable to him that an element which might reduce the strength of this valuable asset be admitted into the family. No chances must be taken because too much is at stake. It is on the strength of this reasoning that Naḥmanides interprets the word *mamzer* to mean one whose lineage is not fully known and whose origin cannot be accurately determined. This person may, or may not, have the best credentials; but so long as the records of his background are not open for examination, he must be excluded from the Jewish community insofar as marriage is concerned.

Ḥinnukh: The concept of marriage to the Jew is one that closely relates to holiness. A *mamzer* was conceived in a state of unholiness (being the result of forbidden relations between a man and a woman). Just as we are concerned with protecting our community from various other noxious elements, so is the marriage of a Jewish girl to a *mamzer* one which must be avoided at all costs.

Maimonides: Why is a bastard penalized because of the immoral action of his parents? This was meant to be a deterrent against immoral behavior. In other words, the man and woman who have illicit relations should realize that because of their immorality their children will be penalized by society and severely limited in their choice of a mate.

References:

B. Yevamot 76a, 76b, 77b, 78b; B. Kiddushin 67a, 69a, 73a, 75a; B. Horayot 13a; J. Kiddushin, Chap. 3, Halakhah 14; Midrash Rabbah *Nasso,* Chap. 9, Sec. 4; Yad, Hilkhot Issurei Bi'ah, Chap. 15; Sefer ha-Mitzvot (Lo Ta'aseh) 354; Sefer Mitzvot Gadol (Lav) 117; Sefer Mitzvot Katan, 295; Shulḥan Arukh, Even ha-Ezer, Chap. 4; Sefer ha-Ḥinnukh, Mitzvah 560.

RELATIONS BETWEEN JEWS, AMMONITES, MOABITES, EDOMITES, AND EGYPTIANS

An Ammonite or a Moabite shall not enter into the assembly of God (Deutoronomy 23:4)

You shall not seek their peace nor their well-being (Deuteronomy 23:7)

You shall not abhor an Edomite . . . you shall not abhor an Egyptian (Deuteronomy 23:8)

1. According to Torah tradition, any gentile who sincerely accepted Judaism was welcomed as a convert. He became a Jew immediately, entitled to all the privileges of a Jew. In the case of a male Ammonite and Moabite, conversion was permitted, but marriage to a Jewish girl was prohibited forever. On the other hand, an Ammonite or Moabite girl could be converted and marry into Jewish society immediately. There was another difference between other nations and between Ammon and Moab. Before engaging in war against an enemy, the Torah exhorted the Jew to call for peace. This was not the case with the Ammonites and the Moabites.

2. With regard to Egyptians and Edomites, the injunction against marriage with Jews was in effect for only three generations. In other words, the great-grandchild of an Egyptian or Edomite who had been converted to Judaism might marry into Jewish society.

3. These laws were in effect only during the early biblical period and the First Commonwealth. Since the days of Sennacherib, King of Assyria, most of the nations have lost their genealogical identities. Accordingly, since we do not know exactly who the Ammonites and Edomites really are, we permit the conversion of any gentile and extend to him immediately the rights and privileges of a Jew.

COMMENTATORS

Maimonides: The Torah gives a reason for excluding each of these four nations from marrying Jews. The Ammonites offered no food to the Jews in the desert. The Moabites engaged a sorcerer to curse them. The Edomites and Egyptians are excluded to a lesser degree, since although the Egyptians enslaved the Jews, they showed them kindness at the beginning. Similarly, although the Edomites warred against the Jews, they are considered their brothers by virtue of being descendants of Esau who was Jacob's brother. Even though one fights with his brother, and may suffer wrong at his hands, he is still a brother.
Naḥmanides: Ammon and Moab were more severely ostracized than the others because they were descendants of Lot. Knowing what Abraham

did for Lot, they should have shown gratitude to the Jews and should have been more appreciative.

Keli Yakar: The real reason why Ammon and Moab were banished from fellowship with the Jew was not because of the mere refusal to offer the Jews food in the desert, but rather because of the subtle motive behind their refusal. They hoped that if the Jews were compelled to continue marching while hungry, it would not take too long before they would come back to these nations begging for food and promising them anything in return. The Jews would then be an easy prey to be led into the way of life of the heathen.

Abrabanel: He asks two questions. Firstly, did we not read in Deuteronomy 2:28 that the Moabites sold food to the Jews? Then why does the Torah say, "because they did not meet you with bread and water"? Secondly, since Edom also did not offer food to the tired and hungry Israelites, why was not their punishment equated to that of the Moabites? His answer is that the Moabites did not offer food as an act of sympathy; they merely sold it for profit. This necessitated long, financial negotiations. The strategy was one of delay, so that the Jews would meanwhile perish in the desert and never reach their destination. In answer to the second question, he says that Edom, whose ancestor was Esau, had a logical, albeit untenable, grievance against the Israelites whose ancestor was Jacob. According to them, Jacob stole the birthright from Esau; but the Ammonites and the Moabites had no such excuse for their behavior whatsoever.

Ḥinnukh: When an exhausted people seeks help urgently and depends on this help for survival and another nation which is in a position to help them refuses to offer that assistance, the latter nation is solely bent on genocide. That the Jews could not tolerate the Ammonites and Moabites at any time is only a natural consequence of the barbaric behavior toward them during their period of helplessness.

References:

B. Sanhedrin 103b; B. Bava Kamma 38b, 92b; B. Berakhot 28a, 63b; B. Yevamot 68a, 69a, 76b, 77a, 77b, 78a; B. Kiddushin 74a, 74b, 75a; J. Yevamot, Chap. 8, Halakhah 3; Sifre *Ki Tetze;* Midrash Tanḥuma, *Pinḥas,* Chap. 3; Midrash Rabbah, *Bereshit, Va-Yetze,* Chap. 74, Sec. 13; Song of Songs, Chap. 2, Sec. 16; Midrash Tehillim, Chap. 60, Sec. 1; Guide of the Perplexed, Part 3, Sec. 42; Yad, Hilkhot Issurei Bi'ah, Chap. 12; Sefer ha-Mitzvot (Lo Ta'aseh) 53, 54, 55, 56; Sefer Mitzvot Gadol (Lav) 113, 114, 115, 116; Shulḥan Arukh, Even ha-Ezer, Chap. 4; Sefer ha-Ḥinnukh, Mitzvot 561, 562, 563, 564.

SANITARY CONDITIONS IN THE CAMPS

You shall have a place also outside the camp (Deuteronomy 23:13)
And a paddle shall you have among your weapons (Deuteronomy 23:14)

1. The saying is that "Cleanliness is next to Godliness." In Judaism, cleanliness is intrinsically associated with Godliness.

2. A military camp was to be considered a locale where God's Presence *(Shekhinah)* should be felt and experienced. This could not be achieved if dirt and filth marred the beauty, hygienic requirements, and religious activities of the camp.

3. It was for this reason that the Torah insisted that an area be designated outside the camp-confines for the purpose of providing relief for bodily needs. Among the equipment issued to each soldier, there was to be a spade or paddle with which to dig a hole for the disposal of excrement.

COMMENTATORS

Ibn Ezra: Covering the excrement was necessary, because anything that is disgusting or offensive to the sight leaves an evil effect on the soul and can turn the mind to impure thoughts.

Naḥmanides, Ḥinnukh, Abrabanel: The type of warrior in a camp that will soon face the enemy is a righteous, God-fearing man. A military camp manned by such a religious element may justifiably be called a holy spot. Such a locale must not present the revolting sight nor foul odor of human excrement.

Ḥinnukh: The author adds one other factor—that of national pride. It is a source of pride when non-Jewish dignitaries visit a Jewish military camp and find it clean and hygienic.

Maimonides: When soldiers note that their camp is not an animals' den but rather a place of purity and sanctity, they become aware that God's spirit pervades there, keeping a watchful eye over them. This serves as a tremendous morale and spiritual stimulus for the army, lending power to its physical prowess and solid determination to triumph over its foes.

References:
B. Yoma 75b; B. Ketubbot 5a; B. Berakhot 25b; B. Shabbat 150a; Sifre *Ki Tetze;* Guide of the Perplexed, Part 3, Sec. 41; Yad, Hilkhot Melakhim, Chap. 6; Sefer ha-Mitzvot (Aseh) 192, 193; Sefer Mitzvot Gadol (Aseh) 119; Sefer ha-Ḥinnukh, Mitzvot 566, 567.

UNACCEPTABLE OFFERINGS TO THE TEMPLE

You shall not bring the hire of a harlot nor the price of a dog into the House of the Lord your God (Deuteronomy 23:19)

1. When one brings an offering to the Temple, he must bring it with pure thoughts and ethically-clean hands. When one brings as an offering the exchange of a dog or the price paid for the service of a harlot, it is disqualified and its donor flogged.

2. The "price of a harlot" means that an offering was brought of an animal which had been given to a harlot for her services. The "price of a dog" means an animal that had been exchanged for a dog.

3. The "price of a harlot" applies only to a woman who would be forbidden to marry the man who associated with her. In any other case the animal paid as reward for her favors was permissible as an offering in the Temple.

4. In either case, the ban is upon the offering itself. Should the animal be exchanged for some other article presented to the Temple, it was accepted. For example: If the disqualified offering was sold for cash and another animal was bought with that money, or the money was used to buy wheat which was then ground into flour, the newly-acquired objects would be acceptable as offerings.

5. Difference of opinion exists between Maimonides and other authorities over the number of lashes that one receives if, at one and the same time, one brings as offerings the hire of a harlot and the price of a dog. Maimonides contends that he receives 39 lashes, but according to the other authorities he is subject to double flogging.

COMMENTATORS

Ibn Ezra: It would obviously be a disgrace for the Temple to accept gifts from such tainted sources.

Ḥinnukh: Why should an animal which came from the payment for a harlot's favors be disqualified from being brought to the Temple? Because it is likely that, at the moment of the offering, the origin and source of the animal may enter the mind of the offerer, thus profaning his thought and distracting his solemn meditations. Under these conditions, the offering is disqualified. This line of reasoning is also true in the case of the gift of the value of a dog to the Temple. A sacrifice was intended to make a man humble. If during the offering he thinks of the vicious dog and its unbridled stubborness, it may cause him to be in a state of aggressiveness, instead of being swayed by prayerful contrition.

Naḥmanides: If the sinner were to bring this particular sacrifice as a meaningful symbol of repentance for his sin, we would view this gift from a different aspect. The truth is, however, that in the case of a harlot, for example, she will continue to sin. All that she means by her gift to the Temple is that she wants to do something temporarily to ease her conscience and assuage the feelings of guilt which assail her. The same is true of those who use dogs to attack people. Because of their insincerity and the subtle deceit involved, the offering itself is classified as if it had a physical defect. Hence it is disqualified as unworthy of being placed on the altar in God's holy Temple.

References:

B. Temurah 29a, 29b, 30a, 30b; B. Avodah Zarah 17a, 62b; B. Yevamot 59b; Sifre *Ki Tetze;* Yad, Hilkhot Issurei Mizbe'aḥ, Chap. 4; Sefer ha-Mitzvot (Lo Ta'aseh) 100; Sefer Mitzvot Gadol (Lav) 316, 317; Shulḥan Arukh, Oraḥ Ḥayyim, 153, Sec. 21; Sefer ha-Ḥinnukh, Mitzvah 571.

WORKERS AND DOMESTIC ANIMALS MUST BE ALLOWED TO EAT OF THE CROP WHILE HARVESTING

When you go into your neighbor's vineyard, you may eat grapes to your fill as you desire. . . but you may not put anything in your own vessel (Deuteronomy 23:25)

But you may not put a sickle to your neighbor's standing corn (Deuteronomy 23:26)

You shall not muzzle an ox when he is treading out the corn (Deuteronomy 25:4)

1. The Talmud makes this law apply only to laborers. There is a distinctively Jewish morality in the socioeconomic relationship between management and labor. The Torah demands of the laborer "a fair day's work for a fair day's pay"; but it also requires of the employer understanding and compassion.

2. Workers in the orchards and vineyards may not be restrained by the owner from partaking of the fruit they are harvesting. They may eat as much as they wish without deduction from their wages and without being reprimanded. This rule applies only to those who are gathering the produce of the soil. A cowman may not drink any of the milk while milking nor a cheesemaker eat any of the cheese. A worker who is handling produce of the soil which has been detached from the earth *(talush)* may eat from it until his part of the work is finished; if he is engaged to harvest the crop from the soil, he may eat only from the basket he has just filled.

3. The laborer may not interrupt his work in order to partake of the crop. When harvesting the vineyard, he may eat only while he is actually working, while turning at the end of a row or while on his way from the winepress to refill his basket. He may not transfer this right to his wife or children. But, so long as he does not steal any of his employer's time, he may eat as much of the crop as he wishes.

4. The master is not only urged to show compassion for the laborer; he must also treat his animal with kindness and consideration. He is not allowed to muzzle it while plowing. It must be allowed to eat as much of the crop as it could. To scare the animal by shouting at it is also forbidden.

5. Anyone violating these laws was liable to the penalty of lashes.

COMMENTATORS

Baḥya ben Asher: Why should a laborer be permitted to satiate himself with the fruits which he is reaping for the owner? Why this special privilege? Because the Torah takes a realistic line. It is natural for a laborer who is in the vineyard to taste of the grapes. So strong is this urge that even if this were considered a sin, he would probably still yield to it. Since the Torah takes man's nature into consideration and does not demand the impossible of him, it allows the laborer to eat his fill without violating the law.

Ḥinnukh: Basically, the purpose of these laws is to instill in us a goodness of heart and a sensitive concern for our fellow man and for the domestic animal; but there is more to these laws than simply being exercises in religious ethics. A man who gives of his labor and strength to till the soil and prays anxiously for its produce, as well as the ox that labors to till the soil—though they are not the actual owners of the crop—should not be denied enjoyment, and the fruits of their labor.

References:

B. Me'illah 13a; B. Bava Kamma 54b; B. Bava Metzia 87b, 88b, 90b, 92a, 92b; J. Ma'asrot, Chap. 2, Halakhah 4; J. Bava Metzia, Chap. 7, Halakhah 2; Sifre *Ki Tetze;* Yad, Hilkhot Sekhirut, Chap. 12, 13; Sefer ha-Mitzvot (Aseh) 201, (Lo Ta'aseh) 219, 267, 268; Sefer Mitzvot Gadol (Aseh) 91, (Lav) 182, 183, 184; Sefer Mitzvot Katan 273, 274; Shulḥan Arukh, Ḥoshen Mishpat, 331, 336, 337; Sefer ha-Ḥinnukh, Mitzvot 576, 577, 578, 596.

DIVORCE

And write her a bill of divorcement (Deuteronomy 24:3)
Her former husband, who sent her away may not take her again to be his wife (Deuteronomy 24:4)

1. Judaism sees marriage not only as a mere legal bond, but as a sanctification of the relationship between man and woman. According to Jewish tradition, 40 days before the birth of a child a proclamation is made in heaven who is to be its mate. Nevertheless, it can happen that a marriage contracted on earth becomes untenable because of the incompatibility of the partners. In such a case it can be terminated by divorce.

2. In biblical times, if a man found fault with his wife on social, economic, or religious grounds, the Torah instructed him merely to issue a "bill of divorcement." This instrument was called *sefer keritut*—"a bill of severance." In the Talmud it is called a *get*.

3. The Torah speaks succinctly when dealing with the *sefer keritut,* but the sages derived from the scriptural text the following provisions relating to divorce:

(a) The husband must issue the divorce of his own volition and may not be coerced into doing so. There are indeed cases in which the courts may bring pressure upon him to divorce his wife, but even so, he must express his acquiescence.

(b) The divorce must be exclusively by means of a written document.

(c) The content of the *get* must be that she is completely freed from him, severing them entirely from one another.

(d) The *get* must be written for a particular woman. The husband may not tell a scribe "I have several wives named Sarah; write a *get* in the name of Sarah so that I can use it to divorce whichever one I please."

(e) When the writing of the *get* is completed, it must be ready for presentation to the wife; if it is attached to the ground so that it must first be severed from it, it is invalid.

(f) Witnesses must be present when the *get* is delivered to the wife.

(g) She, or her appointed agent, must receive the *get*. No unauthorized person may accept it on her behalf.

(h) The *get* must be given by the husband as an instrument of divorce and for no other purpose.

(i) Only the husband or his agent may deliver the *get*. No unauthorized person may perform this mission for him.

4. If a divorced woman marries another man who later dies or divorces her, she may not remarry her first husband.

5. About the year 1000 C.E. Rabbi Gershom of Mainz, whose authority on *halakhah* was accepted throughout Europe, issued an edict whereby a man might not divorce his wife except with her consent. This edict remains valid today.

6. A woman who is divorced or widowed may not remarry before 90 days have elapsed. The purpose of this rule is to determine whether she may have become pregnant by her former husband and thus avoid any doubt about paternity.

COMMENTATORS

Maimonides: In contrast to other nations, where a man who wishes to divorce a wife merely orders her to leave his house, the Jew must go to a *Bet Din* and secure a document of divorce. This is tantamount to a public announcement that this man divorced this woman. Such a public announcement is essential because otherwise this woman could masquerade as a widow or a married woman and thus create complicated social problems.

Abrabanel: A man is charged with the duty of providing for his family. This often necessitates his going out into the world of business, one which is extremely competitive and which can also be cruel and crushing. When he chooses a wife, he expects help and compatibility at home in the form of peace, quiet, and love. If, for some reason or other, there is no compatibility, he may divorce her.

He cites Ralbag, who suggests that the reason the Torah forbade a man to remarry his wife if she has in the interim been married and divorced by another man, is to preclude the possibility that a man collude with his wife to leave him, marry another man, and make life so miserable for him that he will willingly make a cash settlement and divorce her, so that she can return to her first husband with this gain.

Ḥinnukh: The Jewish approach to divorce is more reasonable than that of other religions which forbid divorce under any circumstances. It is far more prudent to dissolve the marriage when incompatibility exists than to continue under strain and friction.

References:

B. Sotah 5b, 16a; B. Bava Batra 168a; B. Yevamot 11b, 26b, 37b, 63b, 113b; B. Ketubbot 46b, 47a, 74a; B. Pesaḥim 112a, 113b; B. Sanhedrin 22a; B. Niddah 70a; B. Kiddushin 5a, 6a, 9b, 13b, 14b, 41a, 67b, 78a; B. Gittin 10a, 20a, 20b, 21b, 24b, 77a, 78a, 78b, 82b, 85a, 87a, 90a, 90b; J. Gittin, Chap. 2, Halakhah 3, Chap. 6, Halakhah 1, Chap. 8, Halakhot 1, 3, Chap. 9, Halakhot 1, 10; J. Yevamot, Chap. 10, Halakhah 4, Chap. 14, Halakhah 1; Sifre *Ki Tetze;* Yad, Hilkhot Gerushin, Chap. 1–11; Sefer ha-Mitzvot (Aseh) 222, (Lo Ta'aseh) 356; Sefer Mitzvot Gadol (Aseh) 50, (Lav) 82; Sefer Mitzvot Katan 184, 189; Shulḥan Arukh, Even ha-Ezer, Chap. 10, 115, 178; Sefer ha-Ḥinnukh, Mitzvot 579, 580.

TAKING SECURITY FOR A LOAN

One shall not take a mill or an upper mill-stone as a pledge (Deuteronomy 24:6)
You shall not enter his house to fetch his pledge (Deuteronomy 24:10)
You shall not sleep with his pledge (Deuteronomy 24:12)
You shall restore the pledge (Deuteronomy 24:13)
Nor take the widow's garment as a pledge (Deuteronomy 24:17)

1. "Justice tempered with mercy" is not sufficient for the Jew. Compassion and understanding must be the guidelines for the relationship between man and man.

2. A person lends money to another for which he demands security. He has every right to do so. This is justice. He may not, however, enter the home of the borrower and take the pledged object. He must wait until the borrower delivers it to him or until an agent of the *Bet Din* brings it to him. Furthermore, he may not demand an object that the borrower needs for his daily sustenance, such as the millstones of a miller or the tools of a craftsman. If the lender did this he was flogged. If the object comprised two parts, such as a mill and an upper millstone, he is subject to a double penalty of lashes.

3. Both the lender and the agent of a court must wait outside until the borrower brings forth the pledge from his home. There is a difference, however, namely that while the court attendant may take the pledge from the borrower by force, the lender may not do so.

4. Should the object be an article needed by the lender during a specific time of the day, it must be returned to the owner for that period. For example: If the lender received a blanket as a pledge, he must return it to the borrower for the duration of the night. If he received a plow, he must return it for the duration of the day.

5. A person could not demand security from a widow who became indebted to him. When the due date arrived and she admitted to the loan, she paid and discharged her debt.

6. There are some exceptions to the rule. As an illustration: If a person owed his employee the wages for a day's labor, the laborer is permitted to forcibly enter the home of the employer and take any security he desires for his wages.

COMMENTATORS

Most commentators refer to Exodus 22:25–26, which deals with the taking of a pledge from the borrower as a security. The verses end with: "When he cries unto me, then will I hear; for I am gracious." In the interpretation of this last verse, there is a divergence of opinion.

Ibn Ezra: He cites Saadiah, who sees in the possession of the pledge during the day a safeguard for the lender. If the pledge were permitted to remain with the borrower all the time, he could use the same object as a pledge for another concurrent debt.

Da'at Zekenim: He offers two different interpretations for the verse, "When he cries unto me":

1. The borrower will cry to God, pleading that he is no different than the lender. Why should the lender enjoy a comfortable night's sleep while he, the borrower, does not because his bed-garment was taken from him as a security? "Where is the justice in this?" he will cry.
2. On the other hand, the borrower may cry to God and ask for blessings for the lender who, although he had a just claim to the pledge, nevertheless left it with the borrower. God will grant his wish and the lender will be blessed for his deed.

Naḥmanides: When God warns us that He will listen to the cries of the maltreated debtor, it will make no difference who the petitioner is. Everyone has feelings, whether he is righteous or wicked, and God listens to the prayers of all men.

Sforno: God reasons that it is an act of grace for the lender to have some compassion for the debtor. It the lender is too severe with the debtor, the debtor will cry out to God in agony and He will answer by taking some of the lender's wealth and giving it to the debtor in order to alleviate his dire financial straits.

Keli Yakar: He comments on the words: "You shall restore to him the pledge when the sun goes down." If a person holding a pledge dies, he obviously cannot return the pledge to the owner and his children might not be inclined to do so. Hence until the sun goes down, that is until the sun sets on his life, he must instruct his children to return the pledge to the lender and so avoid eventual difficulties and complications.

Alshekh: If the lender is severely exacting of the borrower, the latter will be compelled to give pledge upon pledge until the lender has him completely under his control. He will then cry out to Me and I will surely listen.

Ḥinnukh: The author does not see in these *mitzvot* any basis for either berating the borrower or glorifying the lender. The latter is doing no more than his duty, while the former is the victim of circumstances. These *mitzvot,* which combine justice with mercy, are necessary for the law and order of a country and the welfare of society.

References:

B. Bava Metzia 31b, 113a, 113b, 114a, 114b, 115a, 115b, 116a; J. Nazir, Chap.

6, Halakhah 2; Sifre *Ki Tetze;* Yad, Hilkhot Malveh ve-Loveh, Chap. 3; Sefer ha-Mitzvot (Lo Ta'aseh) 239, 240, 242, (Aseh) 199; Sefer Mitzvot Gadol (Lav) 187, 188, 189, 190, (Aseh) 94; Sefer Mitzvot Katan 266, 267, 268, 269, 270; Shulḥan Arukh, Ḥoshen Mishpat, Chap. 6, 97; Sefer ha-Ḥinnukh, Mitzvot 583, 585, 586, 587, 591.

LEAVING WHAT WAS LEFT IN THE FIELDS FOR THE POOR

You shall not go back to fetch it. . . it shall be for the stranger, for the fatherless, and for the widow (Deuteronomy 24:19)

1. A farmer and his employees, who were binding and gathering up the sheaves of corn and chanced to overlook one, may not return to collect the forgotten sheaf, for this belongs to the poor and destitute. Should the laborer, but not the owner, overlook the sheaf or vice versa, the owner but not the laborer, the law of the forgotten sheaf does not apply.

2. From what we have learned concerning gifts to the poor, we arrive at the following facts:

The Vineyard—the poor are entitled to the single grapes found on the ground *(peret)*, young grapes *(olelot)*, the forgotten clusters *(shikḥah)*, and the corner of the vineyard *(pe'ah)*.

The Corn-Field—the poor may lay claim to the gleanings *(leket)*, the forgotten sheaves, and the corner of the field.

Fruit-Trees—the poor may take from the forgotten fruit and from the corner of the orchard.

3. When the Torah speaks about the *ger* (the stranger) who is deserving of the gifts to the poor, it has in mind the convert to Judaism.

4. One who violated this law must make restitution to the poor. Even if he had already changed the character of the wheat and had turned it into bread, he need not hand over these particular loaves but compensation must be made to the poor.

COMMENTATORS

Ḥinnukh: One can recognize the person who is truly happy and grateful to God when he is concerned with making others contented as well. But if a person selfishly and avariciously gathers in all his produce and has no interest in those less fortunate, it is a sign that he is unhappy and bitter. God expects us to enjoy life and to go on being grateful and contented. This is the reason for these *mitzvot.*

Abrabanel: It betokens a spiritually and physically emancipated person that he provides extensive social welfare for the poor. These laws were given to the Jew so that the world may see how emancipated this nation is, since it has no economic fears when observing these *mitzvot.*

Baḥya ben Asher: Customarily, when one makes a donation to charity, one is pleased when it is widely announced and the donor receives publicity thereby. By means of the *mitzvah* to leave forgotten sheaves for the poor, a lesson is given in true philanthropy; that is, in giving charity without the full blare of public fanfares.

Keli Yakar: He offers two reasons for the laws pertaining to the prohibition against returning to pick up produce, once it has been left behind:

1. It is important for man always to look ahead and not backward. We should take note of what happened to Lot's wife when she looked back because of her anxiety for the possessions she had left behind. Similarly, the farmer does not know whether or not he will find anything by retracing his steps in the field.
2. A person must not ask what will be left for himself and his children by giving away tithes, first fruits, the corner of his field, and so forth. When the Children of Israel left Egypt, they came out lacking a great deal; nevertheless, God blessed them with a rich and plentiful land. So will it be with one who gives what is required of him to give. One might think that he has not as much as he would like to have and that, by giving charity, he will lack even more. God therefore promises to provide enough for all.

References:

Mishnayot, Pe'ah, Chap. 6; B. Bava Metzia 11a; B. Sotah 45a; J. Pe'ah, Chap. 4, Halakhot 3, 5, Chap. 5, Halakhot 6, 7, Chap. 6, Halakhot 3, 5, 6, 8; Tosefta, Pe'ah, Chap. 3; Sifre *Ki Tetze;* Sifra *Kedoshim;* Yad, Hilkhot Matnat Aniyim, Chap. 5; Sefer ha-Mitzvot (Lo Ta'aseh) 214, (Aseh) 122; Sefer Mitzvot Gadol (Lav) 288, (Aseh) 156; Shulḥan Arukh, Yoreh De'ah 331; Sefer ha-Ḥinnukh, Mitzvot 592, 593.

THIRTY-NINE LASHES

The judge shall cause him to lie down and to be beaten in his presence (Deuteronomy 25:2)
He shall not exceed forty strokes (Deuteronomy 25:3)

1. Anyone who transgressed a negative commandment of the Torah *("lo ta'aseh")* was subject to the penalty of lashes if:

(a) The sin consisted in an action, not a mere failure to act *(yesh bo ma'aseh)*;

(b) the Torah did not prescribe a positive commandment *(aseh)* or a payment *(tashlumin)* by which the transgression could afterward be rectified *(lav ha-nittak le-aseh, le-tashlumin)*;

(c) the negative commandment must not be one for which the offender is liable to a more severe penalty, i.e., capital punishment *(nittan le-azharat mitat Bet Din)*.

2. When the court decided on the penalty of lashes, an expert was called in to establish whether the offender could take the full number of 39 lashes. This was the maximum number which could be administered at any one time. If the offender was physically weak, the expert would decide how many lashes he could bear. The number had to be divisible by three, thus, if the expert recommended 20, only 18 were actually given. If the expert had found the offender fit to receive the full number but the latter showed signs of weakness while the penalty was being carried out, it was stopped and he was remitted the remainder of the lashes.

3. If the condemned man received even one lash beyond his power of endurance and died as a result, the officer who had administered the punishment was banished to one of the *arei miklat* (cities of refuge; see above, p. 364).

4. The concept of forbidding unnecessarily severe punishment was extended by the Rabbis to include an unprovoked slap by anyone on the person of another. Whoever acted in this manner was flogged if the damage was assessed at less than a *perutah;* if it equalled or exceeded a *perutah,* he paid compensation and was not flogged.

COMMENTATORS

Maimonides: According to Scripture, the number of lashes given is 40. The Rabbis, however, reduced the number of lashes by one, so that in the event of an error of one, the person would not be flogged more than his due.

Naḥmanides: He concurs with the midrashic explanation why the Torah specified the number of 40 lashes (although by traditional exegesis the true number is only 39). The reason for this is that the sinner violated the Torah which was given in 40 days. Furthermore, he brought this calamity upon his body that begins to form 40 days after conception.

Baḥya ben Asher: He suggests two reasons for the 39 lashes:

1. When a man sins against God, he deserves the death sentence. His religious spirit can be considered as good as dead. The numerical value of the Hebrew letters *tet* and *lamed* is 39 and these two letters spell *tal* which means "dew." The inference is that the dew of atonement of the 39 lashes should serve to resurrect the dead, religious spirit of the one who has sinned against his God.
2. A person may be held responsible for his sins and be punished accordingly, when he reaches the age of 13. When the court decides that one should be given a lighter sentence, the number of lashes is three, and since the age when penalties may first be administered is 13, these two numbers (three and 13), when multiplied by each other, equal 39—the traditional number of lashes.

Abrabanel: Why are 39 lashes considered legal, whereas just one additional lash is considered a severe punishment and is strictly forbidden? The answer is: When a man receives his punishment according to the law, that is 39 lashes, he has fully paid his debt to God and society and is considered innocent. Each extra lash would be considered as punishing an innocent man.

References:

B. Sanhedrin 10a, 10b, 33b, 84b, 85a, 86b; B. Megillah 7b; B. Shabbat 89b, 73a; B. Shevuot 36a; B. Bava Metzia 115a; B. Ketubbot 32a, 32b, 33a, 33b, 35b; B. Makkot 2b, 4b, 5a, 22a, 22b, 23a; J. Sanhedrin, Chap. 11, Halakhah 1; J. Terumot, Chap. 7, Halakhah 1; Sifre *Ki Tetze;* Midrash Tanḥuma, *Ba-Midbar,* Chap. 23; Yad, Hilkhot Sanhedrin, Chap. 16; Yad, Hilkhot Ḥovel u-Mazik, Chap. 5; Sefer ha-Mitzvot (Aseh) 224, (Lo Ta'aseh) 300; Sefer Mitzvot Gadol (Aseh) 105, (Lav) 199; Sefer Mitzvot Katan 84; Shulḥan Arukh, Ḥoshen Mishpat, Chap. 420; Sefer ha-Ḥinnukh, Mitzvot 594, 595.

MARRYING OR FREEING THE WIDOW OF A CHILD-LESS DECEASED BROTHER

The wife of the dead shall not marry outside to one not of his kin. . . her husband's brother shall go into her (Deuteronomy 25:5)
And loose his shoe from off his foot (Deuteronomy 25:9)

1. If a married man dies without leaving children, the Torah obliges his brother to marry the widow and beget children and thus perpetuate the name of the deceased. This is called *yibbum*—a levirate marriage. This law does not operate if the widow, or any other woman had given birth to a child by the deceased who lived after the father's demise, even if but a minute. The law applies only to brothers who had the same father as the deceased.

2. Should the brother refuse to marry her, the alternative was *ḥalitzah*—the unbinding of the shoe. This ritual called upon the widow to untie the laces of the shoe on the foot of her brother-in-law, as a sign of severance from the attachment the Torah imposed upon them. She then spat on the ground before him, to indicate her contempt for the man who refused to perpetuate the name of his deceased brother. Should either of the two parties involved be sterile, it is obvious that no *ḥalitzah* or marriage would be required because the underlying theme of the entire commandment is to beget children. This object could not be attained, under the circumstances.

3. In the early history of the Jewish religion, all that was required in a levirate marriage was for the brother to cohabit with the widow. However, it was decreed by the early Sages—the *Soferim*—that a levirate marriage must take the same form as the normally accepted ritual of marriage and must be preceded by a *ma'amar* (a declaration) which is the counterpart of *kiddushin.*

4. A *yavam* (the brother of the deceased) may not marry or release the *yevamah* (the childless widow) until 91 days have elapsed from the death of her husband. This was intended so as to ascertain whether she was pregnant or not from her deceased partner in marriage.

5. The oldest brother is the one first called upon to meet the requirements of this commandment. If he refuses to comply, the court endeavors to persuade the other brothers. If they also reject the proposal, the eldest brother is again approached and is compelled to take action in giving her *yibbum* or *ḥalitzah*.

6. Some Oriental Jews practice both *yibbum* and *ḥalitzah*. Ashkenazi Jews, however, generally practice only *ḥalitzah*. In the State of Israel the Chief Rabbinate has forbidden *yibbum* completely.

COMMENTATORS

Naḥmanides: This is not a simple ritual and hence does not lend itself to simple rationalization. Since the first such incident recorded is attributed to Judah and his daughter-in-law Tamar, it is possible that the Torah was recording a custom which was already a tradition in pre-biblical days. In any event, whether it was such a custom or not, the Torah considers it a shameless act on the part of the deceased's brother if he does not obey the law which asks him to marry his brother's childless widow. This is the only situation where the Torah permits him to marry his brother's wife; under any other circumstances, she is forbidden to him.

Ba'al ha-Turim: The reason that the widow spits in the brother-in-law's presence if he refuses to marry her is because phlegm looks like sperm. She symbolically rebukes her brother-in-law by spitting and implies that she does this because he has refused to give his seed and so honor and perpetuate the name of his dead brother.

Abrabanel: He propounds two thoughts on the obligation of a man to marry his widowed and childless sister-in-law:

1. Man seeks physical and spiritual perpetuity. While his soul is deposited in various non-corporeal domiciles, his physical perpetuity is attained only through his children. When a man dies childless, the soul which was part of the team of body and soul sinks into despair. It can be remedied if something be done to bring into the world a child which may be identified as the son of the deceased. This can be achieved only if the brother and the wife of the deceased, who according to tradition was part of his body (that is, his rib), will join together to

beget a child. This is the nearest approximation possible to the physical perpetuation of the departed.

2. In this ritual of *yibbum,* there are benefits both for the deceased and the widow. Man works and struggles all his life to leave an inheritance for his family. He also leaves traditions for his children to follow. It is a tragedy when a person goes to his grave knowing that there is no child to inherit him. There is a certain measure of comfort in the knowledge that, even after he is gone, two close relations—his wife and his brother—will produce a child who will bear his name and receive his inheritance.

The wife benefits because, through the child she bears by her late husband's brother, she remains part of the family and enjoys the security of family life. Without a child, she might be asked by the family to leave, since there would be no bonds tying her to them.

Abrabanel offers another explanation for the wife's spitting. She was prepared to serve as his wife for the sake of his dead brother, but he repudiated her. Accordingly, he deserves to be spat upon and humiliated.

References:

B. Niddah 44a; B. Bava Batra 12b, 109a, 115a; B. Bekhorot 52a, 52b; B. Yoma 13b; B. Sanhedrin 31b; B. Mo'ed Katan 21a; B. Sotah 32a; B. Kiddushin 13b, 14a; B. Yevamot 3b, 4a, 7b, 8a, 8b, 13a, 13b, 17b, 19b, 20a, 22b, 24a, 24b, 29b, 30a, 30b, 31b, 35b, 39a, 40a, 41b, 44a, 54a, 54b, 79b, 92b, 101a, 102a, 102b, 103b, 104a, 104b, 105a, 105b, 106b, 111b, 117b; Sefer ha-Ḥinnukh, Mitzvot 597, 598, 599; J. Yevamot, Chap. 1, Halakhah 1, Chap. 4, Halakhah 1; Chap. 5, Halakhah 1, Chap. 6, Halakhah 1, Chap. 12, Halakhah 6; J. Kiddushin, Chap. 1, Halakhah 1; J. Nedarim, Chap. 3, Halakhah 2; Sifre *Ki Tetze;* Midrash Tanḥuma, *Mishpatim,* Chap. 7; Midrash Rabbah, *Lekh Lekha,* Chap. 43, Sec. 13; *Va-Yeshev,* Chap. 85, Sec. 6; Zohar, *Pinḥas,* 215; *Ki Tetze,* 281; Yad, Hilkhot Yibbum ve-Ḥalitzah; Sefer ha-Mitzvot (Lo Ta'aseh) 357, (Aseh) 216, 217; Sefer Mitzvot Gadol (Lav) 83, (Aseh) 51, 52; Sefer Mitzvot Katan 185, 188; Shulḥan Arukh, Even ha-Ezer, 159, 165, 166.

REMEMBERING TO ERASE THE MEMORY OF AMALEK

Remember what Amalek did unto you (Deuteronomy 25:17)
You shall blot out the rememberance of Amalek. . . do not forget (Deuteronomy 25:19)

1. The first adversaries faced by the Children of Israel after the Exodus, were the Amalekites. The latter sensed an "easy kill" in the helpless and defenseless Israelites and were tempted to attack them. It is for this reason that the Torah admonishes the Jew never to forget—neither in word nor in thought—what the Amalekites were intent on doing to them at the dawn of their history.

2. Some authorities maintain that the obligation of this *mitzvah* is not incumbent upon the Jewess. The clash that the Children of Israel had with Amalek was on the battlefield. The daughters of Israel were never permitted at the war front. Hence, the danger of extermination was not directed at the Jewish woman but at the menfolk.

COMMENTATORS

Ibn Ezra, Abrabanel: Why this most severe punishment for the Amalekites? Because all the other nations, upon hearing of God's interest in the Israelites and the great miracles He performed for them during the Exodus, avoided war with the Jews for fear of God's punishment; Amalek however, was convinced that it was not God that caused these events but that it was simply superior intelligence and ability that brought the Jews their success. Amalek was the only nation that belittled God's influence in the destiny of the Jews and attempted to destroy them. It is because of the Amalekites' effrontery against God that they were so severely punished.

Naḥmanides: The Jews, descendants of Jacob, were relatives of the Amalekites, descendants of Esau. Whereas the Jews had no animosity toward the Amalekites, the latter came from far-off distances with one purpose in mind—to destroy Israel. This behavior is hardly to be expected of a relative. Furthermore, war is strange to the Jewish way of life and is considered a pernicious evil. It was Amalek who first forced the Jews to engage in warfare in self-defense.

Ḥinnukh: Amalek was the first to demonstrate to the other nations of the world how not to be afraid of the Jews and their God by seeking to destroy them. From the time of the Exodus to our present day, Jews have been plagued with an unbroken chain of nations who, like Amalek, have attempted to exterminate them.

References:

B. Megillah 18a, 30a; B. Bava Batra 21b; B. Sanhedrin 20b; Mekhilta, *Be-Shalaḥ;* Sifre *Ki Tetze,* 296; Midrash Rabbah, *Be-Shalaḥ,* Chap. 26, Sec. 2, 3, 4; Midrash Tanḥuma, *Ki Tetze,* Chap. 4–11; Pirkei de-Rabbi Eliezer, Chap. 44; Zohar, *Be-Shalaḥ,* 66a; Yad, Hilkhot Melakhim, Chap. 5; Sefer ha-Mitzvot (Aseh) 188, 189, (Lo Ta'aseh) 59; Sefer Mitzvot Gadol (Aseh) 114, 115, (Lav) 226; Sefer Mitzvot Katan 147; Shulḥan Arukh, Oraḥ Ḥayyim, 685; Sefer ha-Ḥinnukh, Mitzvot 603, 604, 605 (Note that Ḥinnukh exempts women from this *mitzvah* on the grounds that it is part of the conquest of Canaan and women are not required to participate in the conquest.).

CONFESSION RECITED CONCERNING TITHES

I have removed the hallowed things out of my house (Deuteronomy 26:13)

I have not eaten of it in my mourning . . . I have removed thereof being unclean. . . nor have I given of it for the dead (Deuteronomy 26:14)

1. To recapitulate the *mitzvah* of the tithes: Throughout the seven-year cycle, the Jew gave the annual *terumah* to the Priest. In the first and second years, he gave ten percent of his produce to the Levite *(ma'aser rishon)* and he took ten percent *(ma'aser sheni)* to Jerusalem, where he consumed the food. In the third and sixth years, instead of proceeding to Jerusalem, he presented the tithe to the poor *(ma'aser ani)*. On the afternoon of the last day of Passover of the fourth and seventh years, he came into the Temple and made his oral confession that during the previous three years he had discharged his duties and obligations concerning all offerings, tithes, and donations that were imposed upon him.

2. He also asserted that he had not partaken of *ma'aser sheni* while in a state of *aninut*—the day of demise and burial of one of the seven closest relatives whom it is incumbent to mourn. He declared furthermore that he was not ritually defiled while eating of the *ma'aser sheni,* nor did he partake of the food when it was *tame* (impure), although he was ritually pure.

3. He affirmed that all of his obligations were carried out according to the prescribed formula and that he had only derived such personal benefit from the tithe as eating, drinking, and anointing himself. Secondary benefits were not permitted. If he wished to sell *ma'aser sheni,* he could not use the money to buy a coffin or shrouds for a *met mitzvah,* or even clothing for himself. The money had to be redeemed for food in Jerusalem, where it was eaten.

COMMENTATORS

Ibn Ezra: When making this confession, the Israelite wished God to witness that he had done his duty conscientiously and punctiliously. He asks that God may also fulfill his request by blessing his labors and soil with fruitfulness.

Abrabanel: Men were eager to bring donations to the Temple because of the publicity and the enhancement of their image in the presence of those who thronged to the Temple precincts. In the case of the tithe for the poor, however, which was distributed at the gates where the poor people gathered, one might be reluctant and uncharitable in one's heart when distributing these alms. The Jew is therefore commanded to confess aloud that he has given with all the purity of motivation at his command, in order that this confession may lead him to adopt this attitude toward charity.

Abrabanel derives three implications from the three elements in the confession, in which the donor says that he has not performed any forbidden action with the produce:

1. *Oni,* "grief"—Playing upon the words *oni* with an *aleph* which means "grief" and *oni* with an *ayin* which means "poverty," he contends that the intent of this confession was as follows: "Although there were times when I myself needed charity, I nevertheless gave a tithe of the little that I had then to others even less fortunate, and did not retain any of it for myself."

2. *Tame,* "impure"—In this instance, the man states: "What I gave was honest and pure. I did not give just a little wheat, mixed with a lot of chaff."

3. *Met,* that is, non-existent. Some people, when asked if they have given charity to the poor, reply in the affirmative and name some poor family of whom no one has ever heard. It is later ascertained that this family is non-existent. The Israelite is asked to state that he has been honest in his gifts to the poor and did not pretend to give to persons who, in truth, were never alive.

Ḥinnukh: He suggests a reason why the Torah forbids the eating of *ma'aser sheni* by one who is in a state of *aninut.* It would not be fitting for a person who was grief-stricken or depressed to present himself before royalty. Similarly, one who had just suffered a bereavement could not be expected to concentrate his thoughts properly, as was required when eating consecrated foods. It is clear that the eating of holy food was in itself tantamount to the bringing of a sacrifice, since the eating of sacrificial meat by the Priests procured the atonement of the Israelite who brought the offering.

References:

Mishnayyot, Ma'aser Sheni, Chap. 5; B. Bava Metzia 88a; B. Yevamot 73b, 74a; B. Megillah 20b; B. Sotah 32b, 47b, 48a; B. Makkot 19b; B. Zevaḥim 99a, 99b; B. Pesaḥim 36b, 91b; J. Bikkurim, Chap. 2, Halakhah 2; J. Ta'anit, Chap. 1, Halakhah 4; Pirkei Avot, Chap. 5; J. Ma'aser Sheni, Chap. 2, Halakhah 8, Chap. 5, Halakhah 1; Sifre *Ki Tavo;* Mekhilta, *Mishpatim,* Chap. 19; Yad, Hilkhot Ma'aser Sheni, Chap. 3, 11; Sefer ha-Mitzvot (Aseh) 131, (Lo Ta'aseh) 150, 151, 152; Sefer Mitzvot Gadol (Aseh) 138 (Naḥmanides and Sefer Mitzvot Gadol argue that the negative injunctions of this *mitzvah* are not derived from these biblical verses but from others.); Sefer ha-Ḥinnukh, Mitzvot 607, 608, 609, 610.

WALKING IN GOD'S WAYS

And walk in His ways (Deuteronomy 28:9)

1. *Imitatio Dei* (Imitation of God) is a slogan used by the early Church Fathers and popularized in the Middle Ages. To the Jew, this concept of trying to acquire the attributes of God dates back to the Torah which exhorted him "And walk in his ways." How can man, with all his deficiencies, weaknesses, and limitations, reach out toward the vast expanse of godliness? Where does he get the means of ascending to these unparalleled, spiritual heights? The Talmud explains the apparent incongruity. Man can be compassionate and considerate as God is. He can do everything with righteousness, which is God's way. Maimonides interprets the precept of "walking in God's way" as an invitation to follow the "golden mean," i.e., to avoid extremes. He should avoid anger, yet not be apathetic to what is happening; he should not desire anything except necessities; he should be neither miserly nor a spendthrift.

2. The reason that the Prophets described God's attributes (merciful, holy, kind, righteous, etc.) was that man might strive after those attributes. *Imitatio Dei* asks of man to free himself of his animal tendencies and follow the path toward spirituality.

COMMENTATORS

Ibn Ezra: Walking is action; hence, "to walk in God's ways" means putting His ways into action. Faith alone is not sufficient, for God requires our active participation in His ordering of the world.

Abrabanel: If we were literally to "walk" in His ways, then we would abstain from food, drink, sex, and all other functions of the body; but this would be the wrong approach. What God meant was that these activities can become a source of blessing, if they are performed with "walking in His ways" in mind, instead of being inspired by animal instincts.

References:
B. Sotah 14a; B. Shabbat 133b; Sifre *Ekev;* Yad, Hilkhot De'ot; Sefer ha-Mitzvot (Aseh) 8; Sefer Mitzvot Gadol (Aseh) 7; Sefer Mitzvot Katan 46, 47; Sefer ha-Ḥinnukh, Mitzvah 611.

ASSEMBLING ON THE FEAST OF TABERNACLES EVERY SEVENTH YEAR

Gather all the people together, the men and the women and the little ones, and your sojourner (Deuteronomy 31:12)

On the first of the intermediate days of Sukkot, when the last year of the seven-year cycle had ended and a new year had started, trumpets were sounded to proclaim to all Jews who had come to celebrate the festival in Jerusalem that they should assemble in the center of the women's court. A platform was erected and there the king sat, surrounded by the masses. A Torah was brought in by a beadle, who handed it to the head of the community who, in turn, passed it on to the deputy High Priest. It was then given to the High Priest, who presented it to the king. The monarch unfolded the Scroll at the Book of Deuteronomy and pronounced the appropriate prayer before reading from the Torah. He then read from the beginning of Chapter 1 to Chapter 6, verse 10, and continued with Chapter 11, verse 13, up to verse 22. He concluded his recitation with Chapter 14, verse 22, until the end of Chapter 28. The king would then roll the Scroll together and recite the closing prayer, customarily pronounced after the Reading of the Torah, and he would add seven more benedictions. This ceremony is known as the *mitzvah* of *hakhel* ("gather together").

COMMENTATORS

Ibn Ezra: Why were the strangers gathered together? Because when they hear the principles of the Torah, they may perhaps be won over to Judaism.

Naḥmanides: Why were the young children, who could not even understand the proceedings, gathered together? Because it is advisable to begin a child's religious training at a tender age. He will ask questions and receive inspiring answers. This will affect his behavior and attitudes in the future.

Keli Yakar: Why was this *mitzvah* so important that it necessitated the assembling of all the people? Why did this assembly take place on the feast of Tabernacles? Why, particularly, did this assembly take place at the beginning of the eighth year of the agricultural Sabbatical cycle?

There are mistakes which the individual makes for which he repents and seeks forgiveness on Rosh Ha-Shanah and the Day of Atonement. In this manner, he makes peace with his conscience, with God, as well as with his fellow man; but there are also sins which a nation commits. It permits, for example, the economic exploitation of the poor by the wealthy to pass unnoticed. In such cases, the entire nation must resolve publicly to mend its ways. This national resolve could only have its full impact at a nation-wide gathering, especially on a day that features the *"agudah,"* the joining of the four species—the *etrog,* the *lulav,* the *hadassim,* and the *aravot*—all of which symbolize the importance of national unity and interest in the social welfare and the economic security of all constituents. This gathering was held after the agricultural Sabbatical year when all financial pursuits ended, in order to stress the fact that the ills and crises that a nation faces are often due to the arrogance and greed of the select rich, who show no consideration for the poor.

Ḥinnukh: The Torah is the crowning glory of the Jew. When a huge gathering assembles, people tend to inquire why the crowd has gathered. The answer will be that it is to hear the special reading of the Torah. Since people like to "follow the crowd," they will take an avid and personal interest in the *mitzvot* because of the unique setting.

References:

B. Sotah 41a; B. Rosh ha-Shanah 12b; B. Arakhin 28b; B. Ḥagigah 3a; J. Ḥagigah, Chap. 1, Halakhah 1; Avot de-Rabbi Natan, Chap. 18; Yad, Hilkhot Ḥagigah, Chap. 3; Sefer ha-Mitzvot (Aseh) 16; Sefer Mitzvot Gadol (Aseh) 230; Sefer ha-Ḥinnukh, Mitzvah 612.

WRITING A SEFER TORAH

Now therefore, write you this song for me (Deuteronomy 31:19)

1. The last *mitzvah* of the Torah, namely the duty of every Jew to write himself, or have written for him, a *Sefer Torah* (Scroll of the Law) is very significant. It is not sufficient to be related to the Torah in a detached and objective way. What is required of the Jew is to involve himself personally and subjectively—body and soul—in the commandments of the Torah. The influence of the commandments on the life of the Jew is valueless unless he is enveloped and submerged in the Divine guidance which the *mitzvot* indicate. It is for this reason that we are exhorted to write a *Sefer Torah*. Even if we have Scrolls as family heirlooms, it is still incumbent upon us to fulfill this *mitzvah* for ourselves.

2. The writing of a *Sefer Torah* must be done in accordance with all the traditional regulations. Thus it must be written by hand on parchment made from the skin of a clean (i.e., not forbidden) animal; the scribe must have the intention to write the Scroll for the express purpose of its being a *Sefer Torah;* the various sheets comprising the Scroll must be sewn together with the sinews of a clean animal, etc.

3. We are forbidden to sell a *Sefer Torah* (unless originally purchased for this reason) except for raising money to get married, to study Torah, or for ransoming captives.

4. A *Sefer Torah* disqualified because of irregularities in the script or because decay has set in is buried next to the graves of pious sages.

5. We must rise and remain standing when someone approaches or passes by bearing a *Sefer Torah*. It is the holiest object in the Jewish ritual and the profoundest respect must therefore be shown to it.

COMMENTATORS

Ibn Ezra: When a Jew is bitterly complaining about his ill-fortune and vexing problems, there should be a Torah available immediately for his guidance. In the Torah, he will find solutions to his problems.

Ḥinnukh: He makes three observations:

1. Everyone seeks the most comfortable and convenient way of life. Instead of having the trouble of going to a neighbor and borrowing a Torah to study and then being obliged to return it, it is best that each person have his own *Sefer Torah* ready at hand.
2. This *mitzvah* applies even to one who has inherited a *Sefer Torah.* If he writes or orders his own *Sefer Torah,* more Scrolls of the Law will be written and be available to those who neither can write one themselves nor possess the means to buy one. Furthermore, there is a certain element of excitement and added interest when one studies from a newly-written *Sefer Torah.*
3. This *mitzvah* does not limit itself to a *Sefer Torah.* It also includes the purchase of other religious books. The advice of *Ḥinnukh* is that a religious library should be a feature of every Jewish home.

References:

B. Sanhedrin 21b; B. Eruvin 21b, 54b, 64a; B. Shabbat 104a; B. Ketubbot 50a; B. Bava Metzia 85b; B. Bava Batra 13b, 14a; B. Menaḥot 30a, 30b; Tosefta, Sanhedrin, Chap. 4; Midrash Rabbah, *Nasso,* Chap. 14, Sec. 6; Yad, Hilkhot Sefer Torah, Chap. 7, 10; Sefer ha-Mitzvot (Aseh) 18; Sefer Mitzvot Gadol (Aseh) 24; Sefer Mitzvot Katan 155; Shulḥan Arukh, Yoreh De'ah, Chap. 270; Sefer ha-Ḥinnukh, Mitzvah 613.

Index

*Bold numbers indicate major references.

—unacceptable offerings, **472–473**
—*see also:* Sanctuary
Temple Mount, 200, **247–248**, **318–319**, 343
Ten Commandments, 30, 62, 196, 209, 372, 373
Ten Days of Penitence, 360
Tent of Meeting, 318
Terefah, **92–93**, **181–182**, 268
Terumah, *see* Tithes
Testimony, duty to give, **150–151**
Testing God and His prophets, **381–382**
Tetragrammaton, 323, 331, 395
Theft, 35, 36, **47–49**, 53, 54, 56, 78ff, 90, 100, 151, 154, **220–222**, 223, **228**, 241, 250, 302, 321, 417, 438, 452, 470, 474
Tithes, 11, 23, **90–91**, 111, 114, 125, **264–266**, 304, **316–318**, **337–338**, **344–347**, 382, 396, 398, **411–412**, 482, 489ff
—affirmations concerning, **489–491**
—profanation of, 266
Torah
—adding or subtracting, **402–403**
—reading of, 261, 291, 493, 494
—receiving of, xiv, **281–284**, 358, 360 422
Torah scribe, 495
Torah scroll, *see Sefer Torah*
Torah study, 38, 284, 310, 317, 372, **374–375**, 392, 429, 495, 496
Trees
—sacred to pagans, *see* Asherah
—wanton destruction of, 444
Trumpets, sounding of, **335–336**, 359, 493
Two-witness rule, **367–368**, 458
Tzedakah, 413
—*see also:* Charity; *Gemilut Ḥasadim*; Philanthropy
Tzitzit, **338–341**, 376, 379, 403

Unclaimed property, *see Hefker*
Unintentional sins, **149–150**
Unleavened bread, *see Matzah*
Usury, **98–100**

Vegetarianism, 400
Vengefulness, **231–233**, 304, 365, 368
Vestments, priestly, **122–124**, 156, 201–202, 348
Vows, 162, 163, 185, **308–310**, 314, 315, 323, **325ff**, **361–364**, **396–397**, 433
—annulment of, **362–363**

Wages, *see* Employees, treatment of
War, 303ff, 336, 428, **439–443**, 444, 447, 449, 453, 457, 469, **488–489**
—peace terms, **442–443**
Washing, *see* Purification rituals
Wasteful destruction, ban on, **444**
Wedding ring, 460
Wedding rites, *see* Marriage, ceremonial laws
Weights, just, **250–252**
Widows, **84–85**, 259, 260, 265, 367–368, 477, 479, **485–487**
Wife, suspected, *see Sotah*
Willow twigs, *see Aravot*
Wine, 26, 37, 39, **134–135**, 141, 146, 239, 268, 317, **325ff**, 343, 363, 386, 411
Wisdom acquiring, 250, 317
Witchcraft, 68, **83**, **243**, **245**
Witnesses, 34, 45, 47, **50–52**, 79, 86, **95–96**, 98, **102–104**, **150–151**, 285, 322, **367–368**, 405, 446, 458, 461, 476
—disqualified, 103–104, 221
—*see also:* Two-witness rule
Women, 3, 4, 6, 9, 22, 24ff, 42–44, 47, 54, 55–56, 61, 62, **63–66**, **81–82**, 103, 112, 129, 152, 166, **182–185**, 187, 197–198, **207–210**, **211–212**, **228**, 246, **258–260**, 265, 287, 305, 308–310, **322–324**, 339, **351–352**, **358–359**, 362–363, 367–368, **374–375**, 376, 378, 421, 428, 431, 440–441, **447–450**, 453, **454–455**, **458–460**, **461–465**, **466–469**, 472–473, **476–478**, **485–487**, 488
Work, categories forbidden on Sabbath, *see Avot Melakhah*; *Melakhah*, concept of
Work, forbidden on festivals, **278–279**, 283, 286, 291